Avotaynu Monograph Series

WOWW Companion

A Guide to the Communities Surrounding Central & Eastern European Towns

compiled by Gary Mokotoff

Avotaynu, Inc.
Teaneck, NJ 07666

Requests for permission to make copies of any part of this publication should be addressed to:

Avotaynu, Inc.
P.O. Box 900
Teaneck, NJ 07666

Printed in the United States of America

99 98 97 96 95   5 4 3 2 1

Library of Congress Cataloging-in-Publication Data
Mokotoff, Gary
        WOWW companion: a guide to the communities surrounding Central and Eastern European towns / compiled by Gary Mokotoff.
        p.   cm. — (Avotaynu monograph series)
ISBN 0-9626373-6-X
        1. Europe, Eastern—Gazetteers. 2. Europe, Central—Gazetteers. 3. Jews—Europe, Eastern—Directories. 4. Jews—Europe, Central—Directories. I. Mokotoff, Gary. Where once we walked. II. Title. III. Series.
DJK6.M65 1995   914.7'0003—dc20   95-1210
                                                                    CIP

How to Use This Book

The gazetteer *Where Once We Walked* provides information on more than 21,000 localities in Central and Eastern Europe where Jews lived before the Holocaust, including the latitude and longitude of the towns. Many users of *Where Once We Walked (WOWW)* have found it useful to know which localities are situated near a particular town. The *WOWW Companion* enables the reader both to identify these neighboring towns and, if desired, to create a rough map of the area.

In the *WOWW Companion*, the entire region of Central and Eastern Europe documented in *Where Once We Walked* is represented by a grid, each section of which represents 10 minutes of latitude by 10 minutes of longitude (a minute equals 1/60th of a degree). In that region, a minute is roughly equivalent to 16 kilometers or 10 miles. Perform the steps indicated below to determine in which grid section your town is located and which other towns are nearby. The town of Warka, Poland, and its neighboring localities are used to illustrate the process.

Steps	Notes
1. Using *Where Once We Walked*, determine the latitude and longitude of the desired town.[1]	In *Where Once We Walked*, look up the name of the town and find the latitude and longitude. Warka is located at 51°47' latitude and 21°12' longitude (noted in *WOWW* on page 384 as 51°47'/21°12'). Write these coordinates on a piece of paper, deleting the symbols for degrees (°) and minutes ('): 5147 2112.
2. Derive the six-digit, two-part numerical code for latitude and longitude.	This code uses the first three numbers of the latitude and the first three numbers of the longitude. For Warka, the first part of the code is 514 and the second part is 211. Write the six-digit code on your paper: 514 211.

[1]Other sources may be used, but be aware that gazetteers do not necessarily agree on the exact latitude/longitude of a town, especially those of larger cities.

Steps	Notes
3. Using the code you have derived, find the entry for the town of Warka in the *WOWW Companion*.	The entries in the *WOWW Companion* are arranged in two columns. For each town, the following information is listed (see Table 1): • Six-digit, two-part code representing the latitude and longitude (e.g., 514 211). • The actual latitude/longitude of the town (symbols omitted) (e.g., 5147/2112). • Town name (e.g., Warka). You determined in Step 2 that the code for Warka is 514 211. a. Search the entries for the first part of the code for Warka: 514. Entries are arranged in sequence by first part of the code. The first entry for code 514 appears on page 156. b. Starting on page 156, search among the 514 entries for the second part of the code for Warka: 211. Note that within the section for code 514, entries are arranged in sequence by the second part of the code. The complete code, 514 211, appears on page 158. For code 514 211, the third entry is for Warka as shown in Table 1.
4. Determine the names of other towns within the same grid section.	The towns that share a grid code are among the towns closest in proximity to the town of interest. Several towns share the same grid code as Warka, 514 211. These include Budy Augustowskie, Boska Wola and Rozniszew. Procedures for plotting the towns on a grid map are given in Step 7 below. **Note:** If the town of interest is nearer to the border of a grid section than to its center, the closest towns may be located in one or more adjacent grid sections. See Steps 5 and 6 below to determine the codes for adjacent grid sections.

Table 1. Sample entry in *WOWW Companion*
(from page 158).

```
514 210  5148/2106  Brzezinki
514 210  5149/2105  Nowa Wies (Grojec)
514 211  5141/2112  Budy Augustowskie
514 211  5143/2110  Boska Wola
514 211  5147/2112  Warka
514 211  5148/2118  Rozniszew
514 212  5140/2129  Swierze Gorne
514 212  5141/2126  Ryczywol
```

515/210	515/211	515/212
514/210	Warka 514/211	514/212
513/210	513/211	513/212

Figure 1. Grids including and surrounding Warka.

Steps	Notes
5. Determine the codes for adjacent grid sections.	Examine the pattern of the grid sections in Figure 1. As you move up (north), the latitude codes increase by 1; as you move down (south), the latitude codes decrease by 1. As you move to the right (east), the longitude codes increase by 1; as you move to the left (west), the longitude codes decrease by 1. Choose the grid sections of interest to you and note their code numbers on a copy of the grid (see Figure 2). **Important note:** When adding or subtracting 1 from each part of a grid section code, be aware that each degree of latitude or longitude is comprised of 60 minutes. When you add 1 minute of latitude to 55°59', the result is not 55°60', but rather 56°00'. Consequently, when adding 1 to latitude code 555, the next higher coordinate is not 556, but **560**. Similarly, subtracting 1 from latitude code 550 does not yield 549, but rather **545**. This pattern may become clearer with a quick perusal of the codes in the text.
6. Find the codes in the *WOWW Companion* for towns in adjacent grid sections.	Repeat Steps 3 and 4 for each grid section of interest. List the town names and their respective grid code(s), and their latitude and longitude coordinates on your paper. Procedures for plotting the towns on a grid map are given in Step 7 below.

Steps	Notes
7. Plot the towns on a grid map.	If you wish to plot the coordinates of each town to create a map of the area, use a copy of the template in Figure 2. Each grid boundary line is divided into 10 segments, each of which represents 1 minute. As noted in Step 3, the latitude and longitude coordinates are listed in the *WOWW Companion* for each town entry.
	Refer to Figure 3 as you complete the following procedures.
	a. First, plot the location of the town of interest. Warka's coordinates are 5147/2112. For plotting purposes, the most important numbers are the final digits in the coordinates for latitude (i.e., 7) and longitude (i.e., 2).
	• Label the grid section in which you will plot Warka: 514 211. (This section represents the latitudes between 51°40' and 51°49', and the longitudes between 21°10' and 21°19'.)
	• Label the intersecting lines with their appropriate latitude and longitude coordinates: e.g., 51°40', 51°50', 21°10', 21°20', etc.
	• From the horizontal line labeled 5140, count upward 7 marks to find Warka's latitude: 51°47'.
	• From there, count 2 marks to the right to find Warka's longitude: 21°12'. Mark that point and note the town name.
	b. In the same manner, plot the remaining towns with the same grid section code.
8. Plot the neighboring towns on the grid map.	Repeat Step 7 for each town in the selected grid sections. Refer to Figure 3.

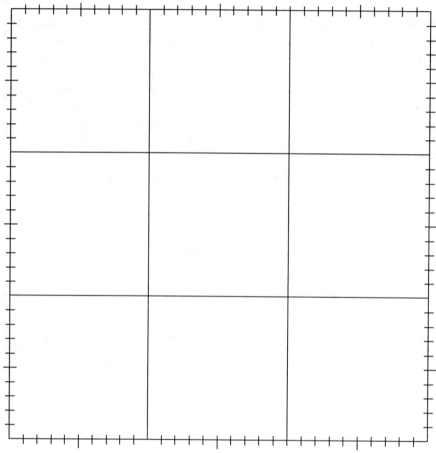

Figure 2. Grid template

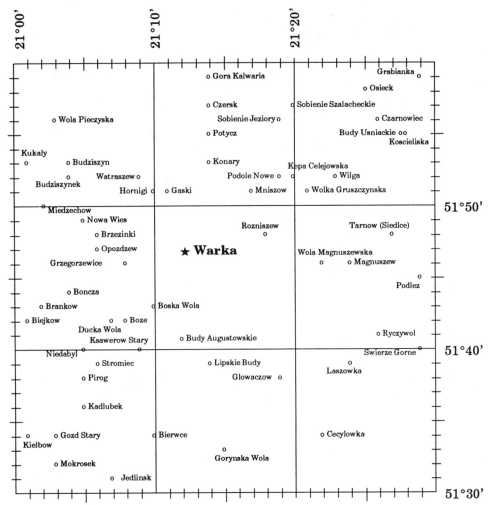

Figure 3. Map created from data in *WOWW Companion* showing towns in the grid sections surrounding Warka, Poland.

352	242	3523/2428	Rethimnon
353	240	3531/2401	Canea
362	281	3625/2810	Rhodes
365	271	3653/2719	Kos
370	220	3702/2207	Kalami
371	365	3712/3658	Karla Marksa
373	224	3738/2243	Argos
374	205	3747/2054	Zakinthos
374	232	3745/2326	Aiyina
375	212	3751/2123	Cavala
375	233	3757/2338	Piraeus
380	234	3800/2344	Athens
381	214	3814/2144	Patrai
381	231	3819/2319	Thebes
382	233	3828/2336	Khalkis
382	260	3823/2607	Khios
383	212	3838/2125	Agrinion
385	204	3858/2045	Preveza
391	205	3910/2059	Arta
392	215	3922/2155	Karditsa
392	225	3922/2257	Volos
393	214	3933/2146	Trikkala
393	220	3930/2200	Thessaly
393	222	3938/2225	Larissa
394	195	3940/1950	Kerkira
394	205	3940/2051	Ioannina
395	221	3953/2210	Elasson
401	223	4015/2230	Katerini
401	255	4015/2553	Alexandroupolis
402	353	4027/3532	Samothraki
403	211	4033/2115	Kastoria
403	221	4032/2211	Veroia
403	225	4038/2258	Thessaloniki
404	212	4048/2126	Florina
404	230	4045/2304	Langadas
405	242	4056/2425	Kavalla
410	204	4107/2048	Ohrid
410	212	4102/2120	Bitola
410	233	4103/2333	Serrai
410	245	4107/2456	Xanthi
410	252	4106/2525	Comotini
410	252	4106/2525	Komotini
411	241	4110/2411	Drama (Greece)
411	261	4112/2618	Souflion
412	220	4121/2201	Kosani
412	222	4121/2227	Udovo
412	223	4126/2239	Strumica
412	245	4128/2452	Ribnitsa
412	262	4122/2626	Dhidhimotikon
412	263	4121/2630	Didymotihou
413	205	4132/2056	Osoj
413	222	4138/2228	Radovis
413	234	4134/2344	Gotse Delchev
413	234	4139/2341	Kornitsa
413	235	4136/2351	Debren
413	245	4136/2459	Kupen
413	252	4139/2522	Kurdzhali
413	263	4130/2631	Orestias
414	210	4141/2109	Kovac
414	214	4142/2148	Titov Veles
414	221	4144/2212	Stip
414	222	4142/2221	Kosevo
414	225	4143/2251	Berovo
414	245	4140/2458	Davidkovo
414	261	4146/2612	Svilengrad
414	262	4149/2622	Shtit
415	205	4152/2053	Toplica
415	213	4158/2137	Kadino
415	223	4153/2230	Vinica
415	224	4158/2247	Delcevo
415	253	4156/2533	Khaskovo
420	212	4200/2129	Skopje
420	230	4201/2306	Blagoevgrad
420	244	4209/2445	Plovdiv
420	245	4201/2452	Asenovgrad
420	251	4205/2512	Debur
421	185	4217/1851	Budva
421	204	4213/2045	Prizren
421	213	4219/2139	Presevo
421	222	4212/2221	Kriva Palanka
421	223	4218/2239	Lozno
421	224	4217/2241	Kyustendil
421	230	4216/2307	Stanke Dimitrov
421	242	4212/2420	Pazardzhik
421	252	4212/2520	Chirpan
421	262	4214/2626	Drama (Bulgaria)
422	184	4229/1843	Perast
422	185	4224/1855	Cetinje
422	211	4222/2110	Urosevac
422	223	4229/2231	Belut
422	233	4220/2333	Samokov
422	253	4225/2538	Stara Zagora
422	260	4229/2601	Nova Zagora
422	263	4229/2630	Yambol
423	180	4239/1807	Dubrovnik
423	210	4232/2108	Lipljan
423	252	4237/2524	Kazanluk
423	265	4239/2659	Polyanovgrad
423	272	4230/2728	Burgas
424	165	4246/1655	Lastovo
424	185	4246/1858	Niksic
424	205	4244/2050	Staro Poljance
424	210	4240/2102	Ade
424	210	4241/2105	Obilic
424	210	4248/2102	Ropica
424	211	4240/2110	Pristina
424	231	4241/2319	Sofiya
424	233	4246/2334	Bukhovo

424	261	4240/2619	Slivno
425	170	4258/1708	Korcula
425	182	4253/1826	Bileca
425	202	4259/2020	Tutin
425	205	4253/2052	Kosovska Mitrovica
425	215	4259/2157	Leskovac
425	251	4252/2519	Gabrovo
425	262	4253/2627	Kotel
425	264	4250/2647	Esen
430	203	4308/2031	Novi Pazar
430	223	4309/2236	Pirot
430	241	4300/2412	Asen
431	162	4311/1627	Hvar
431	170	4318/1702	Makarska
431	180	4316/1807	Nevesinje
431	182	4316/1828	Jugovici
431	190	4313/1901	Crna Gora
431	200	4316/2000	Sjenica
431	215	4319/2154	Nis
431	230	4314/2307	Berkovitsa
431	233	4312/2333	Vratsa
431	265	4316/2655	Kolarovgrad
431	272	4311/2726	Provadiya
431	275	4313/2755	Varna (Bulgaria)
432	174	4321/1749	Mostar
432	184	4327/1842	Zakmur
432	231	4325/2313	Mikhaylovgrad
432	243	4325/2437	Pleven
433	162	4331/1626	Split
433	163	4333/1630	Solin
433	175	4339/1758	Konjic
433	183	4330/1837	Jelec
433	192	4336/1923	Sjeverin
433	193	4333/1936	Banja
433	205	4337/2053	Vrnjci
433	214	4332/2143	Aleksinac
433	232	4332/2323	Vladimirovo
433	263	4332/2631	Razgrad
433	275	4334/2750	Tolbukhin
433	433	4331/4338	Nalchik
434	155	4344/1553	Sibenik
434	181	4344/1817	Gracanica
434	190	4348/1901	Rogatica
434	191	4348/1917	Visegrad
434	195	4343/1950	Rozanstvo
434	231	4349/2314	Lom
434	242	4342/2429	Gigen
434	243	4347/2430	Corabia
434	245	4342/2454	Nikopol (Bulgaria)
434	265	4344/2653	Kitanchevo
434	265	4349/2657	Tarkan
435	160	4352/1609	Drnis
435	170	4350/1701	Livno
435	181	4352/1819	Rajlovac
435	181	4359/1811	Visoko
435	182	4350/1825	Sarajevo
435	195	4352/1951	Titovo Uzice
435	200	4351/2002	Pozega
435	202	4354/2021	Cacak
435	211	4359/2115	Svetozarevo
435	212	4352/2125	Paracin
435	221	4354/2217	Zajecar
435	225	4359/2256	Calafat
435	225	4359/2252	Vidin
435	233	4358/2337	Birca
435	252	4359/2520	Alexandria
435	255	4350/2557	Ruse
435	255	4356/2559	Remus
435	424	4356/4244	Kislovodsk
440	151	4407/1515	Zadar
440	152	4407/1523	Donji Zemunik
440	155	4403/1551	Bjelina
440	172	4403/1727	Bugojno
440	172	4408/1724	Donji Vakuf
440	180	4408/1808	Zgosca
440	181	4401/1816	Breza
440	183	4407/1835	Olovo
440	185	4405/1857	Han Pijesak
440	191	4406/1918	Srebrenica
440	202	4402/2027	Gornji Milanovac
440	205	4401/2055	Kragujevac
440	220	4406/2206	Bor (Yugoslavia)
440	242	4407/2421	Caracal
440	245	4407/2459	Rosiori De Vede
440	255	4400/2559	Daia
440	263	4405/2638	Oltenita
440	271	4407/2716	Silistra
441	171	4416/1717	Vinac
441	173	4415/1735	Turbe
441	174	4414/1740	Travnik
441	175	4413/1755	Zenica
441	180	4411/1809	Ivnica
441	184	4414/1842	Kladanj
441	185	4411/1857	Vlasenica
441	190	4417/1909	Drinjaca
441	195	4413/1955	Dracic
441	195	4416/1953	Valjevo
441	203	4418/2035	Arandelovac
441	204	4416/2042	Topola
441	210	4411/2106	Lapovo
441	211	4414/2111	Svilajnac
441	223	4418/2235	Prahovo
441	283	4411/2839	Constanta
442	154	4426/1542	Vranik
442	163	4422/1631	Szoboticza
442	171	4421/1717	Jajce
442	172	4420/1723	Bucici
442	172	4429/1724	Borak

442	180	4425/1803	Orahovica
442	180	4426/1803	Zepce
442	180	4427/1809	Zavidovici
442	190	4423/1907	Zvornik
442	212	4422/2125	Petrovac
442	220	4428/2207	Donji Milanovac
442	230	4427/2306	Petra
442	241	4427/2414	Gradistea
442	260	4420/2605	Jilava
442	280	4426/2807	Dunarea
442	340	4425/3401	Simeiz
443	152	4433/1523	Gospic
443	162	4434/1621	Bosanski Petrovac
443	175	4437/1752	Teslic
443	180	4437/1800	Tesanj
443	184	4433/1841	Tuzla
443	191	4430/1911	Banja Koviljaca
443	194	4437/1947	Vladimirci
443	201	4433/2015	Konatice
443	203	4438/2032	Ripanj
443	205	4439/2056	Smederevo
443	211	4437/2112	Pozarevac
443	215	4439/2157	Berzasca
443	222	4438/2226	Petrovo Selo
443	223	4437/2237	Kladovo
443	224	4438/2240	Turnu Severin
443	243	4434/2436	Negreni
443	270	4432/2708	Albesti
443	273	4434/2731	Marculesti
443	284	4438/2845	Sinioe
443	333	4436/3332	Sevastopol
443	341	4430/3410	Yalta
443	341	4433/3417	Gurzuf
444	155	4449/1552	Bihac
444	162	4445/1625	Lusci Palanka
444	164	4443/1642	Tomina
444	164	4446/1640	Sanski Most
444	171	4446/1710	Banja Luka
444	180	4444/1805	Doboj
444	183	4449/1837	Dubrave
444	191	4445/1913	Bijeljina
444	194	4445/1943	Sabac
444	201	4441/2019	Umka
444	201	4443/2014	Boljevci
444	202	4444/2029	Jajinci
444	205	4445/2059	Kovin
444	213	4446/2132	Veliko Gradiste
444	222	4442/2225	Orsova
444	251	4441/2518	Palade
444	251	4443/2519	Gaesti
444	262	4442/2627	Dridu Movila
444	334	4443/3349	Tole
444	335	4445/3352	Bakhchisaray
444	342	4440/3425	Alushta
445	151	4452/1514	Otocac
445	153	4453/1537	Plitvicka Jezera
445	155	4454/1550	Vrsta
445	155	4458/1557	Cazin
445	161	4453/1610	Bosanska Krupa
445	164	4459/1642	Prijedor
445	175	4459/1755	Derventa
445	182	4453/1826	Gradacac
445	182	4454/1822	Donji Skugric
445	184	4452/1849	Brcko
445	184	4452/1841	Pula
445	184	4456/1847	Rajevo Selo
445	185	4452/1858	Racinovci
445	185	4453/1852	Gunja
445	185	4457/1859	Soljani
445	185	4459/1856	Vrbanja
445	193	4458/1937	Sremska Mitrovica
445	194	4453/1946	Hrtkovci
445	195	4451/1950	Nikinci
445	200	4459/2004	Golubinci
445	201	4450/2013	Dobanovci
445	201	4456/2014	Nova Pazova
445	201	4459/2010	Stara Pazova
445	201	4459/2017	Stari Banovci
445	202	4450/2024	Zemun
445	203	4450/2030	Beograd
445	203	4452/2039	Pancevo
445	211	4456/2117	Dupljaja
445	212	4454/2126	Byala Cherkova
445	220	4456/2200	Bozovici
445	221	4456/2211	Putna
445	244	4450/2443	Samara
445	245	4451/2452	Pitesti
445	252	4451/2529	Vacaresti
445	252	4458/2524	Teis
445	253	4459/2539	Moreni
445	260	4457/2601	Ploesti
445	284	4454/2843	Babadag
445	340	4457/3406	Simferopol
445	345	4451/3458	Sudak
450	133	4505/1338	Rovinj
450	150	4509/1506	Partizanska Dreznica
450	162	4503/1622	Bosanski Novi
450	171	4509/1715	Bosanska Gradiska
450	173	4507/1731	Davor
450	180	4506/1808	Klakar
450	180	4508/1801	Bosanski Brod
450	180	4509/1802	Slavonski Brod
450	181	4507/1818	Svilaj
450	182	4502/1825	Zasavica
450	182	4504/1828	Bosanski Samac
450	182	4504/1829	Samac Slavonski
450	182	4509/1826	Beravci
450	183	4507/1832	Babina Greda

450	184	4504/1842	Zupanja
450	185	4509/1857	Komletinci
450	190	4509/1902	Nijemci
450	191	4500/1913	Morovic
450	191	4506/1911	Vasica
450	191	4508/1914	Sid
450	192	4507/1925	Erdevik
450	193	4500/1934	Lacarak
450	193	4505/1930	Calma
450	193	4506/1939	Grgurevci
450	194	4501/1949	Ruma
450	194	4508/1947	Vrdnik
450	195	4506/1952	Irig
450	200	4503/2005	Indija
450	200	4506/2000	Maradik
450	200	4507/2004	Beska
450	202	4507/2023	Centa
450	203	4501/2039	Crepaja
450	203	4504/2036	Debeljaca
450	203	4506/2038	Kovacica
450	204	4507/2044	Padina
450	205	4504/2058	Alibunar
450	210	4504/2102	Banatski Karlovac
450	211	4507/2118	Vrsac
450	213	4505/2132	Varadia
450	213	4507/2135	Cacova
450	214	4502/2142	Oravita
450	225	4502/2256	Ombod
450	231	4503/2317	Tirgu Jiu
450	233	4506/2331	Ciucuresti
450	235	4509/2353	Calinesti
450	240	4501/2402	Bodhaza
450	254	4509/2543	Cimpinita
450	255	4504/2559	Plopeni
450	255	4505/2556	Goruna
450	263	4504/2639	Ulmeni
450	265	4509/2650	Buzau
450	272	4508/2722	Bagdad
450	281	4508/2811	Iglita
450	294	4509/2940	Sulina
450	333	4508/3336	Saki
450	343	4503/3436	Belogorsk
450	350	4502/3506	Staryy Krym
450	352	4502/3523	Feodosiya
450	390	4502/3900	Krasnodar
450	414	4503/4149	Stavropol
451	134	4518/1347	Vrani
451	140	4515/1402	Gologorica
451	143	4516/1434	Kraljevica
451	143	4518/1432	Bakar
451	144	4511/1442	Crikvenica
451	151	4516/1514	Ogulin
451	154	4511/1549	Velika Kladusa
451	155	4518/1559	Topusko
451	163	4513/1633	Kostajnica
451	165	4516/1654	Jasenovac
451	171	4515/1718	Dragalic
451	172	4515/1726	Resetari
451	172	4516/1723	Nova Gradiska
451	173	4512/1739	Nova Kapela
451	174	4517/1748	Pleternica
451	180	4510/1800	Brodski Varos
451	181	4511/1813	Sapci
451	181	4512/1812	Garcin
451	182	4510/1824	Velika Kopanica
451	182	4519/1825	Akovo
451	183	4514/1839	Retkovci
451	183	4517/1833	Stari Mikanovci
451	183	4517/1837	Vodinci
451	184	4513/1844	Andrijasevci
451	184	4517/1849	Vinkovci
451	185	4513/1857	Slakovci
451	190	4510/1909	Tovarnik
451	190	4515/1904	Cakovci
451	190	4517/1900	Negoslavci
451	191	4514/1917	Sarengrad
451	191	4518/1916	Mladenovo
451	192	4513/1923	Ilok
451	192	4515/1922	Backa Palanka
451	193	4513/1932	Susek
451	194	4512/1944	Beocin
451	194	4513/1940	Cerevic
451	195	4512/1956	Sremski Karlovci
451	195	4515/1950	Novi Sad
451	195	4515/1953	Petrovaradin
451	195	4518/1958	Kac
451	200	4517/2000	Budisava
451	201	4513/2018	Titel
451	201	4515/2010	Vilovo
451	201	4518/2011	Mosorin
451	202	4512/2023	Perlez
451	202	4519/2028	Ecka
451	204	4516/2046	Jarkovac
451	210	4514/2108	Plandiste
451	215	4518/2155	Resita
451	221	4517/2215	Golet
451	275	4516/2759	Braila
451	280	4515/2809	Macin
451	282	4516/2828	Isaccea
451	284	4510/2848	Tulcea
451	332	4512/3322	Yevpatoriya
451	340	4517/3403	Leninskoye
451	354	4518/3547	Lenino
451	370	4517/3700	Sennaya
452	135	4527/1351	Gradin
452	141	4520/1419	Opatija
452	141	4523/1416	Kriva (Yugoslavia)
452	142	4520/1426	Susak

452	142	4521/1424	Rijeka
452	142	4522/1421	Kastav
452	142	4523/1428	Jelenje
452	145	4529/1453	Vas
452	150	4520/1508	Gomirje
452	150	4522/1505	Vrbovsko
452	150	4526/1502	Srpske Moravice
452	153	4520/1536	Krnjak
452	153	4527/1530	Duga Resa
452	153	4529/1533	Karlovac
452	160	4529/1600	Pokupsko
452	161	4520/1618	Kraljevcani
452	162	4527/1621	Moscenica
452	162	4529/1622	Sisak
452	163	4521/1633	Sunja
452	163	4524/1638	Kratecko
452	164	4529/1647	Kutina
452	165	4520/1659	Novska
452	165	4526/1654	Banova Jaruga
452	170	4523/1709	Donji Caglic
452	170	4527/1706	Kukunjevac
452	170	4529/1700	Antunovac
452	171	4525/1710	Lipik
452	171	4526/1712	Pakrac
452	173	4520/1736	Brestovac Pozeski
452	174	4520/1741	Slavonska Pozega
452	175	4524/1756	Bektez
452	175	4525/1753	Kutjevo
452	182	4528/1820	Budimci
452	183	4526/1836	Hrastin
452	183	4527/1832	Semeljci
452	184	4522/1842	Markusica
452	184	4523/1845	Antin
452	184	4525/1842	Laslovo
452	184	4527/1840	Ernestinovo
452	185	4520/1851	Nustar
452	185	4525/1854	Trpinja
452	185	4529/1859	Dalj
452	190	4521/1900	Vukovar
452	191	4523/1914	Bac
452	192	4527/1921	Ratkovo
452	193	4522/1936	Backi Petrovac
452	194	4521/1944	Kisac
452	195	4525/1953	Temerin
452	200	4523/2004	Zabalj
452	200	4524/2000	Gospodinci
452	200	4528/2004	Curug
452	201	4523/2019	Aradac
452	202	4523/2023	Zrenjanin
452	203	4529/2033	Zitiste
452	205	4521/2050	Boka
452	205	4527/2059	Fodorhaz
452	205	4527/2052	Jasa Tomic
452	211	4524/2114	Deta
452	221	4525/2213	Caransebes
452	223	4524/2233	Poiana Marului
452	231	4521/2314	Lupeni
452	231	4523/2316	Vulcan
452	232	4525/2322	Petroseni
452	232	4527/2325	Petrila
452	253	4521/2533	Sinaia
452	261	4525/2618	Nehoiu
452	270	4523/2703	Rimnicu Sarat
452	274	4520/2748	Muchea
452	274	4523/2749	Cotu Lung
452	275	4527/2759	Filesti
452	280	4527/2803	Galati
452	281	4527/2817	Reni
452	282	4526/2827	Nagornoye (Bessarabia)
452	284	4521/2842	Novaya Nekrasovka
452	285	4521/2850	Izmail
452	290	4525/2902	Kislitsa
452	291	4527/2916	Kiliya
452	293	4524/2935	Vilkovo
452	333	4526/3336	Novoselovskoye
452	335	4529/3356	Sverdlovsk
452	362	4521/3628	Kerch
453	133	4532/1334	Piran
453	134	4532/1340	Izola
453	134	4533/1344	Koper
453	144	4538/1440	Draga
453	151	4534/1512	Crnomelj
453	152	4537/1529	Ozalj
453	153	4539/1531	Krasic
453	155	4535/1552	Pisarovina
453	155	4537/1558	Dubranec
453	160	4535/1603	Kravarsko
453	161	4536/1612	Lekenik
453	161	4538/1617	Susa
453	163	4534/1637	Popovaca
453	165	4535/1656	Garesnica
453	170	4532/1701	Uljanik
453	170	4535/1706	Dezanovac
453	170	4539/1701	Hercegovac
453	171	4531/1712	Badljevina
453	171	4535/1714	Daruvar
453	173	4537/1732	Vocin
453	174	4533/1743	Slatinski Drenovac
453	174	4537/1748	Mikleus
453	175	4532/1759	Fericanci
453	175	4536/1753	Cacinci
453	175	4537/1757	Obradovci
453	180	4530/1806	Nasice
453	180	4533/1803	Urdenovac
453	180	4534/1807	Klokocevci
453	181	4539/1814	Sljivosevci
453	182	4532/1827	Brodanci
453	182	4535/1828	Bizovac

453	182	4537/1827	Ladimirevci
453	182	4539/1825	Valpovo
453	183	4532/1834	Cepin
453	183	4534/1839	Retfala
453	183	4537/1832	Petrijevci
453	184	4533/1842	Osijek
453	184	4534/1843	Donji Grad
453	184	4538/1842	Darda
453	185	4532/1857	Aljmas
453	190	4532/1908	Bogojevo
453	190	4536/1906	Sonta
453	191	4530/1912	Karavukovo
453	191	4537/1912	Doroslovo
453	192	4534/1925	Ruski Krstur
453	192	4539/1928	Crvenka
453	193	4534/1939	Vrbas
453	193	4537/1932	Kula
453	194	4533/1948	Srbobran
453	194	4535/1940	Novi Vrbas
453	195	4531/1956	Nadalj
453	200	4532/2002	Backo Gradiste
453	200	4536/2008	Novi Becej
453	200	4537/2003	Becej
453	200	4537/2003	Obesce
453	202	4539/2025	Basaid
453	204	4534/2043	Srpski Itebej
453	205	4533/2059	Giulvaz
453	205	4539/2054	Uivar
453	210	4531/2108	Ciacova
453	211	4539/2110	Sag
453	213	4539/2136	Buzias
453	230	4532/2301	Rusor
453	241	4539/2416	Lazaret
453	252	4538/2525	Vulcan (Brasov)
453	253	4530/2534	Predeal
453	253	4538/2535	Brasov
453	283	4530/2834	Kotlovina
453	283	4534/2836	Vladychen
453	284	4535/2847	Maryanovka
453	285	4538/2850	Vasilyevka (Bessarabia)
453	290	4531/2908	Kamyshevka
453	292	4533/2920	Shevchenkovo (Bessarabia)
453	292	4537/2924	Trudovoye
453	293	4534/2932	Desantnoye
453	333	4537/3331	Munus
453	343	4536/3434	Mayskoye (Crimea)
453	344	4534/3447	Pshenichnoye
454	141	4540/1413	Piuski
454	141	4547/1414	Postojna
454	151	4548/1510	Novo Mesto
454	153	4540/1539	Jastrebarsko
454	153	4543/1536	Gorica Svetojanska
454	160	4542/1607	Novo Cice
454	160	4544/1604	Velika Gorica
454	160	4548/1600	Zagreb
454	161	4548/1615	Dugo Selo
454	162	4544/1625	Klostar Ivanic
454	162	4544/1622	Tarno
454	163	4545/1637	Cazma
454	164	4547/1649	Ivanska
454	165	4548/1657	Nova Raca
454	170	4546/1704	Veliki Grdevac
454	171	4540/1715	Ivanovo Selo
454	171	4542/1710	Grubisno Polje
454	172	4540/1726	Miokovicevo
454	172	4543/1729	Pivnica
454	173	4545/1735	Cabuna
454	173	4548/1730	Suhopolje
454	174	4542/1742	Podravska Slatina
454	174	4546/1740	Gornji Miholjac
454	174	4548/1745	Sopje
454	174	4549/1749	Dravasztara
454	174	4549/1747	Revfalu
454	175	4547/1759	Moslavina Podravska
454	175	4549/1757	Pisko
454	175	4549/1753	Zalata
454	180	4545/1804	Viljevo
454	180	4549/1804	Cun
454	180	4549/1800	Hirics
454	180	4549/1807	Tesenfa
454	181	4540/1818	Marjanci
454	181	4544/1817	Podgajci Podravski
454	181	4545/1810	Donji Miholjac
454	181	4548/1813	Dravaszabolcs
454	181	4549/1810	Dravacsehi
454	182	4541/1825	Belisce
454	182	4544/1828	Novi Bezdan
454	182	4547/1826	Beremend
454	182	4549/1823	Kistapolca
454	182	4549/1822	Siklosnagyfalu
454	183	4546/1837	Beli Manastir
454	183	4547/1832	Luc
454	183	4548/1837	Branjin Vrh
454	183	4548/1832	Illocska
454	184	4545/1841	Karanac
454	184	4545/1845	Knezevi Vinogradi
454	184	4547/1847	Suza
454	184	4548/1848	Zmajevac
454	185	4540/1859	Apatin
454	185	4548/1856	Backi Monostor
454	190	4541/1905	Prigrevica
454	190	4544/1901	Kupusina
454	190	4546/1907	Sombor
454	191	4549/1915	Conoplja
454	192	4542/1923	Sivac
454	193	4549/1939	Backa Topola
454	194	4540/1942	Feketic

454	194	4543/1940	Mali Idos
454	200	4542/2005	Backo Petrovo Selo
454	200	4546/2008	Mol
454	200	4548/2008	Ada
454	201	4543/2018	Novo Milosevo
454	203	4540/2037	Nova Crnja
454	211	4545/2113	Timisoara
454	212	4544/2129	Bazos
454	214	4543/2148	Jabar
454	225	4545/2254	Hunedoara
454	225	4549/2257	Cristur
454	230	4546/2300	Batiz
454	230	4548/2301	Bacia
454	240	4548/2409	Sibiu
454	242	4543/2428	Porumbacu De Sus
454	245	4544/2456	Telechi Recea
454	245	4548/2457	Hurez
454	250	4544/2505	Bucium
454	253	4543/2538	Sinpetru
454	253	4546/2539	Bod
454	255	4547/2559	Valea Mica
454	255	4548/2551	Ozun
454	260	4547/2602	Dobolii De Sus
454	260	4547/2608	Papauti
454	260	4549/2600	Borosneu Mare
454	261	4546/2616	Comandau
454	264	4546/2647	Sipotele
454	265	4546/2658	Arva
454	270	4546/2703	Odobesti
454	271	4542/2711	Focsani
454	271	4549/2717	Doaga
454	273	4541/2731	Ivesti
454	280	4541/2800	Mogos
454	280	4545/2803	Foltesti
454	282	4541/2824	Vulkaneshty
454	282	4546/2823	Gavanosy
454	283	4541/2837	Bolgrad
454	284	4544/2849	Kalchevaya
454	284	4547/2844	Chervonoarmeyskoye
454	290	4548/2900	Vinogradnoye
454	291	4541/2916	Novoselovka
454	291	4549/2915	Kamenskoye
			(Bessarabia)
454	292	4543/2927	Strumok
454	293	4540/2931	Nerushay
454	294	4541/2945	Liman
454	294	4548/2942	Trapovka
454	294	4548/2947	Vishnevoye
454	295	4546/2951	Balabanka
454	295	4548/2953	Kochkovatoye
454	335	4543/3357	Krestyanovka
454	335	4546/3355	Novaya Derevnya
454	342	4543/3424	Dzhankoy
455	133	4557/1339	Nova Gorica

455	152	4559/1529	Brestanica
455	153	4554/1535	Brezice
455	154	4552/1546	Brdovec
455	155	4559/1558	Donja Stubica
455	160	4555/1600	Kasina
455	160	4558/1602	Gornja Stubica
455	161	4558/1616	Zelina
455	163	4557/1636	Zabno (Yugoslavia)
455	164	4553/1647	Gudovac
455	165	4554/1651	Bjelovar
455	171	4552/1718	Spisicbukovica
455	171	4557/1714	Pitomaca
455	172	4550/1723	Virovitica
455	172	4558/1728	Barcs
455	172	4558/1729	Paylova
455	173	4554/1739	Totujfalu
455	173	4557/1737	Kastelyosdombo
455	173	4559/1735	Darany
455	174	4550/1746	Dravakeresztur
455	174	4551/1742	Felsoszentmarton
455	174	4553/1748	Bogdasa
455	174	4553/1746	Dravafok
455	174	4554/1742	Lakocsa
455	174	4559/1742	Gyongyosmellek
455	175	4550/1752	Sosvertike
455	175	4551/1759	Vajszlo
455	175	4552/1751	Sellye
455	175	4553/1755	Oszro
455	175	4554/1752	Kakics
455	175	4555/1753	Okorag
455	175	4557/1758	Magyarmecske
455	175	4558/1755	Sumony
455	180	4550/1806	Dravapiski
455	180	4550/1806	Kemes
455	180	4551/1804	Adorjas
455	180	4555/1807	Siklosbodony
455	180	4556/1801	Ozdfalu
455	180	4557/1805	Baksa
455	180	4558/1808	Gorcsony
455	180	4559/1802	Gerde
455	181	4551/1814	Harkany
455	181	4551/1818	Siklos
455	181	4552/1810	Diosviszlo
455	181	4552/1813	Terehegy
455	181	4554/1819	Kistotfalu
455	181	4554/1811	Szava
455	181	4557/1813	Bosta
455	181	4557/1815	Nemeti
455	181	4557/1814	Szalanta
455	181	4558/1810	Regenye
455	181	4559/1818	Egerag
455	182	4550/1824	Nagyharsany
455	182	4552/1827	Villany
455	182	4553/1826	Villanykovesd

455	182	4553/1829	Viragos
455	182	4554/1825	Ivanbattyan
455	182	4554/1828	Pocsa
455	182	4554/1820	Vokany
455	182	4555/1827	Kisbudmer
455	182	4556/1827	Nagybudmer
455	182	4558/1826	Belvardgyula
455	182	4558/1822	Peterd
455	183	4550/1836	Ivandarda
455	183	4550/1830	Magyarboly
455	183	4551/1837	Sarok
455	183	4552/1834	Lippo
455	183	4552/1831	Marok
455	183	4554/1836	Majs
455	183	4558/1831	Boly
455	183	4559/1832	Szajk
455	183	4559/1831	Versend
455	184	4553/1842	Dubosevica
455	184	4557/1843	Kolked
455	184	4559/1848	Homorud
455	184	4559/1842	Mohacs
455	184	4559/1845	Saros
455	185	4551/1856	Bezdan
455	185	4553/1857	Kolut
455	185	4557/1856	Hercegszanto
455	190	4559/1906	Ridica
455	191	4556/1910	Stanisic
455	192	4552/1928	Stara Moravica
455	192	4554/1927	Pacir
455	192	4558/1926	Bajmok
455	194	4555/1946	Cantavir
455	200	4556/2009	Coka
455	200	4556/2005	Senta
455	200	4558/2006	Sanad
455	201	4550/2019	Idos
455	201	4550/2010	Padej
455	201	4551/2016	Sajan
455	201	4553/2014	Jazovo
455	201	4553/2010	Ostojicevo
455	202	4550/2029	Kikinda
455	202	4556/2025	Mokrin
455	215	4554/2153	Bara
455	221	4551/2211	Faget
455	222	4552/2229	Grind
455	225	4556/2251	Mintia
455	230	4559/2308	Mada
455	231	4550/2312	Orastie
455	231	4555/2312	Geoagiu
455	232	4556/2325	Tartaria
455	233	4558/2334	Sebes
455	234	4556/2340	Cut
455	240	4553/2403	Ocna Sibiului
455	241	4558/2417	Buia
455	245	4551/2458	Fagaras
455	253	4553/2534	Racosul De Jos
455	254	4554/2546	Arcus
455	254	4557/2549	Zalan
455	255	4551/2556	Reci
455	255	4553/2553	Anghelus
455	260	4550/2604	Brates
455	260	4551/2601	Let
455	260	4552/2602	Telechia
455	260	4553/2605	Surcea
455	260	4555/2606	Martineni
455	260	4556/2608	Hatuica
455	261	4551/2611	Covasna
455	261	4553/2611	Pava
455	261	4554/2611	Zabala
455	261	4557/2614	Ghelinta
455	261	4557/2610	Imeni
455	261	4559/2615	Ojdula
455	270	4554/2705	Panciu
455	271	4553/2714	Marasesti
455	271	4556/2717	Nicoresti
455	272	4552/2725	Tecuci
455	275	4552/2754	Bujor
455	281	4554/2811	Kagul
455	281	4556/2815	Kotyugany
455	282	4558/2828	Verkhnyaya Albota
455	284	4551/2842	Kopchak
455	284	4554/2840	Taraclia Cahul
455	285	4553/2851	Ogorodnoye
455	290	4550/2906	Zadunayevka
455	290	4555/2905	Novaya Ivanovka
455	290	4559/2903	Volnoye
455	291	4553/2918	Pryamobalka
455	292	4550/2929	Dmitriyevka
455	292	4550/2923	Vinogradovka
455	292	4558/2926	Chervono Glinskoye
455	292	4559/2925	Artsiz
455	293	4551/2937	Tatarbunary
455	293	4558/2930	Pavlovka
455	294	4559/2942	Zarya
455	295	4552/2956	Zheltyy Yar
455	295	4557/2958	Diviziya
455	300	4552/3005	Tuzly
455	300	4558/3005	Shirokoye
455	301	4558/3017	Primorskoye
		(Bessarabia I)	
460	143	4602/1430	Ljubljana
460	143	4609/1438	Dob
460	145	4603/1450	Litija
460	151	4609/1514	Lasko
460	154	4601/1542	Bizeljsko
460	154	4604/1545	Klanjec
460	155	4600/1556	Oroslavje
460	155	4602/1555	Zabok
460	155	4605/1555	Zacretje

460	161	4607/1612	Budinscina
460	161	4607/1617	Hum Breznicki
460	162	4609/1620	Novi Marof
460	163	4602/1632	Krizevci
460	163	4605/1636	Vojakovac
460	164	4600/1640	Cvrstec
460	170	4602/1704	Urdevac
460	171	4602/1718	Bolho
460	171	4603/1712	Ferdinandovac
460	171	4603/1717	Heresznye
460	171	4605/1714	Vizvar
460	171	4607/1713	Belavar
460	172	4601/1722	Peterhida
460	172	4602/1722	Babocsa
460	172	4605/1727	Csokonyavisonta
460	172	4606/1720	Haromfa
460	172	4609/1726	Gorgeteg
460	172	4609/1724	Rinyaszentkiraly
460	173	4601/1738	Istvandi
460	173	4603/1733	Szulok
460	173	4607/1735	Homokszentgyorgy
460	173	4608/1739	Nemetlad
460	174	4601/1746	Hobol
460	174	4601/1743	Nemeske
460	174	4603/1748	Szigetvar
460	174	4605/1745	Somogyapati
460	174	4607/1743	Somogyhatvan
460	174	4608/1740	Patosfa
460	174	4608/1748	Szuliman
460	175	4600/1750	Dencshaza
460	175	4600/1752	Katadfa
460	175	4601/1753	Rozsafa
460	175	4603/1759	Szentlorinc
460	175	4605/1757	Dinnyeberki
460	175	4605/1759	Helesfa
460	175	4606/1759	Bukkosd
460	175	4609/1750	Szentlaszlo
460	180	4601/1805	Nagybicserd
460	181	4600/1811	Gyod
460	181	4601/1817	Pecsudvard
460	181	4602/1818	Kozarmisleny
460	181	4604/1810	Mecsekalja
460	181	4605/1814	Pecs
460	181	4607/1816	Mecsekszabolcs
460	181	4607/1819	Somogy
460	182	4600/1821	Lothard
460	182	4600/1827	Nyomja
460	182	4600/1828	Szederkeny
460	182	4602/1828	Mariakemend
460	182	4603/1823	Ellend
460	182	4604/1825	Berkesd
460	182	4604/1827	Katoly
460	182	4604/1828	Szello
460	182	4605/1820	Bogad
460	182	4605/1821	Romonya
460	182	4606/1821	Hird
460	182	4606/1823	Pereked
460	182	4609/1821	Hosszuheteny
460	182	4609/1827	Nagypall
460	182	4609/1825	Pecsvarad
460	183	4600/1833	Babarc
460	183	4603/1831	Liptod
460	183	4604/1831	Maraza
460	183	4605/1834	Himeshaza
460	183	4606/1831	Puspoklak
460	183	4608/1839	Palotabozsok
460	183	4608/1836	Szebeny
460	183	4609/1837	Vemend
460	184	4602/1844	Kanda
460	184	4605/1846	Dunaszekcso
460	184	4605/1840	Somberek
460	185	4600/1855	Davod
460	185	4602/1857	Csatalja
460	185	4603/1854	Nagybaracska
460	185	4606/1856	Batmonostor
460	185	4607/1859	Vaskut
460	185	4609/1853	Szeremle
460	190	4602/1903	Gara
460	191	4603/1916	Madaras
460	191	4607/1910	Bacsbokod
460	192	4605/1925	Kunbaja
460	192	4608/1920	Bacsalmas
460	194	4606/1940	Subotica
460	195	4609/1958	Horgos
460	200	4603/2006	Novi Knezevac
460	200	4604/2003	Kanjiza
460	200	4607/2003	Martonos
460	200	4608/2006	Krstur
460	201	4604/2015	Banatsko Arandelovo
460	201	4609/2017	Kubekhaza
460	203	4604/2037	Ujfala
460	204	4604/2044	Saravale
460	205	4603/2052	Periam
460	205	4607/2055	Szemlak
460	214	4606/2141	Radna
460	222	4600/2227	Zam
460	222	4602/2223	Seliste
460	222	4605/2226	Almasel
460	224	4600/2247	Gialacuta
460	224	4608/2247	Brad
460	224	4608/2247	Frunza
460	232	4600/2329	Poieni
460	232	4600/2328	Vintu De Jos
460	233	4604/2335	Alba Iulia
460	233	4608/2332	Sard
460	233	4609/2331	Ighiu
460	234	4601/2345	Vingard
460	240	4605/2407	Micasasa

460	243	4607/2436	Noul Sasesc
460	251	4603/2516	Homorod
460	253	4605/2536	Baraolt
460	253	4607/2535	Doboseni
460	253	4609/2537	Filia
460	254	4605/2541	Batanii Mari
460	254	4605/2540	Bodos
460	255	4601/2550	Malnas
460	255	4603/2550	Micfalau
460	255	4606/2552	Bicsad
460	260	4600/2608	Tirgu Secuesc
460	260	4602/2603	Turia
460	260	4604/2609	Poian
460	261	4603/2618	Bretcu
460	261	4606/2612	Valea Scurta
460	262	4609/2627	Poiana Sarata
460	271	4608/2711	Adjudu Vechi
460	273	4603/2735	Bucuresti
460	273	4609/2732	Pogonesti
460	275	4605/2756	Slivna
460	281	4606/2817	Badyku Moldavskoye
460	281	4609/2810	Goteshty
460	282	4603/2825	Aleksandreshty
460	282	4609/2824	Kisseliya
460	283	4603/2832	Biruintsa
460	284	4600/2840	Kazakliya
460	284	4601/2844	Kiryutnya
460	284	4603/2849	Tirashpol
460	284	4606/2841	Baurchi
460	285	4602/2856	Valya Perzhiy Noue
460	285	4603/2850	Chadyr Lunga
460	285	4607/2852	Besh Gioz
460	285	4609/2858	Tvarditsa
460	290	4603/2906	Yarovoye
460	290	4605/2900	Maloyaroslavets Pervyy
460	290	4609/2905	Maloyaroslavets Vtordy
460	291	4601/2910	Rovnoye
460	291	4603/2912	Luzhanka
460	291	4603/2917	Veselyy Kut
460	293	4605/2935	Svetlodolinskoye
460	294	4601/2940	Sarata
460	294	4606/2943	Plakhteyevka
460	295	4600/2957	Sergeyevka
460	295	4602/2956	Kolesnoye
460	295	4605/2953	Yaroslavka
460	295	4608/2954	Nikolayevka Novorossiyskaya
460	300	4606/3003	Marazleyevka
460	300	4607/3004	Alekseyevka
460	302	4608/3023	Saba
460	302	4608/3023	Saba Targ
460	302	4608/3023	Shabo
460	323	4607/3238	Novorossiysk
460	325	4607/3255	Skadovsk
460	331	4605/3318	Khorly
460	334	4606/3342	Armyansk
461	142	4614/1422	Kranj
461	144	4613/1444	Buc
461	150	4610/1503	Trbovlje
461	150	4617/1504	Polzela
461	151	4614/1516	Celje
461	154	4610/1545	Pregrada
461	155	4610/1553	Krapina
461	155	4610/1555	Radoboj
461	160	4613/1607	Ivanec
461	162	4610/1623	Ljubescica
461	162	4613/1626	Varazdinske Toplice
461	162	4615/1629	Jalzabet
461	162	4618/1626	Bartolovec
461	162	4618/1620	Varazdin
461	163	4615/1637	Ludbreg
461	163	4617/1633	Martijanec
461	164	4611/1643	Rasinja
461	164	4618/1644	Mali Bukovec
461	164	4619/1649	Donja Dubrava
461	165	4610/1650	Koprivnica
461	165	4611/1654	Peteranec
461	165	4613/1655	Drnje
461	165	4617/1656	Ortilos
461	165	4617/1657	Zakany
461	165	4618/1652	Legrad
461	170	4610/1709	Zdala
461	170	4612/1709	Berzence
461	170	4614/1707	Alsok
461	170	4616/1706	Csurgo
461	170	4617/1703	Porrogszentkiraly
461	170	4618/1705	Csurgonagymarton
461	170	4619/1701	Patro
461	171	4610/1712	Somogyudvarhely
461	171	4611/1718	Tarany
461	171	4615/1711	Szenta
461	171	4618/1718	Somogyszob
461	172	4612/1727	Labod
461	172	4613/1722	Nagyatad
461	172	4614/1723	Henesz
461	172	4616/1728	Nagykorpad
461	172	4617/1722	Otvoskonyi
461	173	4614/1738	Kadarkut
461	173	4618/1733	Csokoly
461	173	4618/1737	Gige
461	173	4618/1730	Kisbajom
461	174	4610/1747	Somogyharsagy
461	174	4611/1740	Hedrehely
461	174	4611/1744	Vasarosbec
461	174	4616/1744	Zselickisfalud
461	174	4617/1744	Szilvasszentmarton
461	174	4619/1745	Kaposszerdahely
461	175	4611/1756	Csebeny

461	175	4615/1754	Galosfa
461	175	4617/1759	Godre
461	175	4617/1755	Hajmas
461	175	4617/1750	Simonfa
461	180	4610/1803	Szentkatalin
461	180	4613/1800	Bakoca
461	180	4613/1804	Felsomindszent
461	180	4613/1808	Oroszlo
461	180	4614/1801	Baranyaszentgyorgy
461	180	4615/1807	Sasd
461	180	4618/1809	Vasarosdombo
461	180	4619/1805	Jagonak
461	181	4610/1815	Szentimre
461	181	4612/1816	Komlo
461	181	4612/1812	Magyarszek
461	181	4615/1819	Magyaregregy
461	181	4616/1819	Karasz
461	181	4617/1813	Kisvaszar
461	181	4618/1811	Gerenyes
461	181	4618/1818	Kobleny
461	182	4613/1828	Mecseknadasd
461	182	4613/1825	Obanya
461	182	4616/1824	Maza
461	182	4616/1823	Szaszvar
461	182	4617/1828	Nagymanyok
461	182	4618/1824	Gyore
461	183	4613/1836	Bataapati
461	183	4613/1839	Moragy
461	183	4616/1830	Hidas
461	183	4617/1838	Szalka
461	183	4618/1832	Bonyhad
461	184	4611/1844	Bataszek
461	184	4612/1844	Alsonyek
461	184	4612/1842	Kovesd
461	184	4615/1845	Sarpilis
461	184	4617/1846	Decs
461	184	4619/1846	Ocseny
461	185	4611/1858	Baja
461	185	4615/1859	Ersekcsanad
461	190	4611/1909	Csavoly
461	190	4615/1909	Rem
461	190	4617/1900	Sukosd
461	191	4610/1917	Matetelke
461	191	4611/1918	Tatahaza
461	191	4616/1914	Borota
461	192	4613/1923	Melykut
461	192	4618/1920	Janoshalma
461	193	4612/1937	Kelebia
461	193	4617/1930	Kisszallas
461	200	4612/2007	Gyalaret
461	200	4617/2004	Kiskundorozsma
461	201	4613/2015	Deszk
461	201	4613/2012	Szoreg
461	201	4615/2010	Szeged
461	201	4616/2013	Tape
461	202	4610/2028	Ladany
461	202	4611/2026	Kiszombor
461	202	4613/2029	Mako
461	203	4610/2035	Apatfalva
461	203	4610/2037	Magyarcsanad
461	203	4618/2036	Rakos
461	203	4619/2030	Foldeak
461	204	4610/2045	Nadlac
461	204	4615/2044	Csanadpalota
461	204	4619/2049	Mezohegyes
461	204	4619/2044	Pitvaros
461	210	4610/2104	Rovine
461	210	4617/2101	Battonya
461	211	4611/2119	Arad
461	220	4617/2206	Chisindia
461	220	4619/2207	Buteni
461	222	4616/2221	Gurahont
461	223	4619/2237	Luncsoara
461	225	4617/2254	Cris
461	230	4616/2304	Abrud
461	230	4617/2304	Abrud Sat
461	231	4617/2319	Barbesti
461	234	4612/2341	Teius
461	234	4617/2345	Sincrai
461	234	4618/2343	Aiud
461	235	4611/2355	Blaj
461	241	4612/2417	Bazna
461	241	4613/2419	Blajel
461	241	4618/2414	Adamus
461	241	4618/2413	Kiralyfala
461	242	4610/2421	Medias
461	244	4613/2448	Sighisoara
461	250	4616/2506	Porumbenii Mici
461	250	4616/2508	Porumbenii Mari
461	250	4619/2501	Cechesti
461	251	4615/2511	Lutita
461	251	4615/2513	Mugeni
461	251	4615/2515	Oteni
461	251	4617/2511	Dobeni
461	251	4617/2514	Hoghia
461	251	4618/2514	Forteni
461	251	4618/2518	Odorhei
461	252	4610/2521	Oraseni
461	252	4611/2526	Craciunel
461	252	4611/2523	Sinpaul
461	252	4614/2523	Martinis
461	252	4614/2527	Meresti
461	252	4615/2526	Aldea
461	252	4616/2524	Ghipes
461	252	4616/2529	Lueta
461	255	4616/2556	Sinmartin
461	260	4613/2606	Plaesii De Jos
461	260	4614/2606	Plaesii De Sus

461 263 4617/2637 Tirgu Ocna
461 265 4611/2656 Caiuti Tirg
461 270 4611/2704 Sascut Sat
461 271 4610/2714 Lespezi
461 272 4612/2723 Podu Turcului
461 274 4614/2740 Birlad
461 280 4618/2808 Falciu
461 281 4617/2814 Kaniya
461 282 4611/2824 Baymakliya
461 283 4610/2839 Beshalma
461 283 4614/2839 Kirsova
461 283 4616/2831 Sadyk
461 283 4618/2839 Komrat
461 284 4618/2847 Bashkaliya
461 285 4611/2852 Dzholtay
461 285 4613/2857 Kiriyet Lunga
461 285 4615/2850 Avdarma
461 290 4612/2909 Tarutino
461 290 4615/2903 Podgornoye
461 290 4618/2901 Serpnevoye
461 291 4614/2912 Berezina
461 291 4618/2915 Borodino
461 292 4614/2920 Veselaya Dolina
461 292 4616/2925 Krasnyanka
461 292 4619/2921 Nadezhdovka
461 293 4610/2939 Mirnopolye
461 293 4612/2939 Negrovo
461 294 4617/2947 Roylyanka
461 295 4617/2952 Staraya Tsarichanka
461 300 4610/3004 Monashi
461 302 4612/3021 Belgorod Dnestrovskiy
461 302 4616/3026 Ovidiopol
461 344 4611/3446 Genichesk
461 410 4614/4108 Smidovicha
462 134 4629/1347 Kranjska Gora
462 140 4622/1408 Bled
462 141 4621/1411 Radovljica
462 143 4629/1435 Eisenkappel
462 144 4629/1446 Topla
462 150 4625/1500 Topolsica
462 154 4627/1540 Race
462 155 4625/1552 Ptuj
462 161 4621/1613 Petrijanec
462 162 4623/1626 Cakovec
462 163 4620/1637 Prelog
462 163 4628/1638 Felsoszemenye
462 164 4620/1647 Donji Vidovec
462 164 4622/1649 Kotoriba
462 164 4623/1641 Gorican
462 164 4624/1648 Totszerdahely
462 164 4625/1645 Egyeduta
462 164 4625/1649 Totszentmarton
462 164 4626/1644 Letenye
462 164 4627/1641 Muraratka

462 165 4620/1657 Belezna
462 165 4622/1652 Murakeresztur
462 165 4623/1650 Molnari
462 165 4626/1654 Szepetnek
462 165 4627/1659 Nagykanizsa
462 165 4628/1653 Eszteregnye
462 165 4628/1652 Rigyac
462 170 4622/1707 Iharosbereny
462 170 4623/1704 Poganyszentpeter
462 170 4626/1702 Bagolasanc
462 170 4627/1708 Mihald
462 170 4629/1708 Zalaszentjakab
462 171 4624/1712 Inke
462 171 4625/1718 Vese
462 171 4626/1715 Nemesded
462 171 4629/1719 Nagyszakacsi
462 171 4629/1713 Somogysimonyi
462 172 4620/1721 Alsosegesd
462 172 4621/1721 Felsosegesd
462 172 4628/1720 Tapsony
462 173 4620/1738 Kisasszond
462 173 4621/1737 Kiskorpad
462 173 4623/1731 Nagybajom
462 173 4625/1736 Somogysard
462 173 4626/1739 Mezocsokonya
462 173 4626/1735 Ujvarfalva
462 174 4620/1741 Bardudvarnok
462 174 4620/1742 Kaposszentbenedek
462 174 4622/1740 Kaposfo
462 174 4622/1743 Kaposmero
462 174 4622/1744 Kaposujlak
462 174 4622/1748 Kaposvar
462 174 4625/1742 Hetes
462 174 4625/1747 Kaposfured
462 174 4627/1749 Somogyaszalo
462 174 4627/1744 Varda
462 175 4620/1758 Kaposkeresztur
462 175 4622/1755 Taszar
462 175 4623/1750 Toponar
462 175 4624/1752 Orci
462 175 4625/1759 Kisgyalan
462 175 4625/1755 Zimany
462 175 4628/1758 Bussu
462 175 4628/1754 Magyaratad
462 175 4629/1758 Kazsok
462 180 4620/1808 Kaposszekcso
462 180 4620/1804 Kercseliget
462 180 4621/1801 Kisberki
462 180 4622/1801 Nagyberki
462 180 4623/1804 Attala
462 180 4623/1807 Dombovar
462 180 4623/1806 Kapospula
462 180 4623/1809 Ujdombovar
462 180 4626/1801 Golle

462 180	4629/1804	Nak	
462 181	4621/1814	Magocs	
462 181	4625/1815	Dobrokoz	
462 181	4627/1819	Kurd	
462 182	4623/1823	Cel	
462 182	4623/1825	Kisvejke	
462 182	4625/1827	Tevel	
462 182	4628/1821	Csibrak	
462 182	4629/1825	Hogyesz	
462 183	4621/1836	Kakasd	
462 183	4624/1838	Harc	
462 183	4624/1839	Sioagard	
462 183	4624/1834	Zomba	
462 183	4628/1832	Felsonana	
462 184	4621/1843	Szekszard	
462 184	4626/1847	Tolna	
462 184	4629/1841	Szedres	
462 185	4623/1850	Bogyiszlo	
462 185	4623/1858	Dusnok	
462 185	4625/1855	Fajsz	
462 185	4628/1850	Fadd	
462 185	4629/1857	Batya	
462 190	4620/1903	Nemesnadudvar	
462 190	4624/1907	Hajos	
462 190	4627/1902	Miske	
462 190	4629/1905	Homokmegy	
462 191	4625/1911	Csaszartoltes	
462 193	4626/1930	Kiskunhalas	
462 194	4620/1941	Pusztamerges	
462 194	4629/1945	Kiskunmajsa	
462 195	4628/1959	Kistelek	
462 200	4622/2006	Sandorfalva	
462 200	4629/2005	Sovenyhaza	
462 201	4620/2013	Algyo	
462 202	4625/2020	Hodmezovasarhely	
462 203	4625/2038	Bekessamson	
462 204	4621/2044	Ambrozfalva	
462 204	4625/2044	Totkomlos	
462 205	4623/2052	Vegegyhaza	
462 205	4624/2055	Mezokovacshaza	
462 205	4625/2054	Reformatuskovacshaza	
462 205	4627/2058	Magyarbanhegyes	
462 205	4627/2054	Totbanhegyes	
462 205	4628/2054	Nagybanhegyes	
462 210	4620/2108	Dombegyhaz	
462 210	4623/2104	Magyardombegyhaz	
462 210	4625/2107	Dombiratos	
462 210	4626/2103	Kunagota	
462 211	4621/2118	Curtici	
462 211	4625/2111	Kevermes	
462 214	4620/2142	Pincota	
462 214	4623/2143	Seleus	
462 214	4628/2147	Gurba	
462 215	4626/2151	Ineu	
462 215	4629/2159	Beliu	
462 220	4622/2207	Sebis	
462 222	4628/2228	Vascau	
462 225	4622/2255	Lunca De Jos	
462 225	4622/2253	Nemes	
462 230	4621/2302	Bazesti	
462 230	4622/2303	Mihoesti	
462 230	4622/2303	Topanfalva	
462 230	4625/2302	Certege	
462 233	4627/2334	Toroczko	
462 235	4623/2353	Uioara De Sus	
462 235	4625/2357	Vajdaszeg	
462 240	4627/2404	Bogata	
462 240	4628/2409	Cuci	
462 240	4629/2406	Ludus	
462 241	4621/2414	Bobohalma	
462 241	4624/2416	Cucerdea	
462 241	4626/2419	Ogra	
462 241	4627/2414	Sfintu Gheorghe	
462 242	4621/2423	Abus	
462 242	4622/2429	Bahnea	
462 242	4628/2423	Chirileu	
462 242	4629/2428	Nyaradto	
462 243	4624/2434	Vames Odriheiu	
462 243	4626/2435	Corbesti	
462 243	4627/2437	Gruisor	
462 243	4627/2439	Oaia	
462 243	4627/2433	Tirimioara	
462 243	4629/2438	Acatari	
462 243	4629/2436	Foi	
462 244	4621/2447	Vetca	
462 244	4622/2446	Salasuri	
462 244	4623/2444	Chendu Mare	
462 244	4623/2448	Cibu	
462 244	4624/2441	Balauseri	
462 244	4624/2447	Bordosiu	
462 244	4624/2443	Chendu Mic	
462 244	4624/2445	Dumitreni	
462 244	4625/2444	Calimanesti	
462 244	4626/2448	Viforoasa	
462 244	4628/2441	Roteni	
462 244	4629/2448	Adrianu Mare	
462 244	4629/2442	Pasareni	
462 245	4624/2455	Bezid	
462 245	4625/2454	Bezidu Nov	
462 245	4626/2450	Armenis	
462 245	4626/2450	Singeorgiu De Padure	
462 245	4629/2450	Neaua	
462 245	4629/2459	Solocma	
462 250	4621/2509	Cobatesti	
462 250	4622/2501	Goagiu	
462 250	4622/2508	Tarcesti	
462 250	4623/2506	Turdeni	
462 250	4624/2508	Cehetel	

462 250	4625/2509	Firtusu
462 250	4627/2503	Atid
462 250	4628/2503	Cusmed
462 250	4629/2508	Atia
462 251	4621/2517	Ulcani
462 252	4623/2522	Zetea
462 254	4621/2548	Miercurea Ciuc
462 254	4622/2548	Toplita Ciuc
462 254	4625/2547	Ciceu
462 254	4625/2545	Siculeni
462 255	4623/2550	Sumuleu
462 262	4625/2626	Comanesti
462 262	4628/2629	Moinesti
462 263	4627/2635	Secatura
462 264	4625/2645	Orasa
462 265	4620/2659	Racaciuni
462 265	4623/2656	Valea Rea
462 270	4620/2705	Pancesti
462 270	4629/2706	Parincea Tirg
462 272	4625/2729	Puesti Sat
462 273	4624/2736	Ibanesti (Bucovina)
462 281	4628/2815	Leovo
462 282	4620/2827	Vishnevka
462 282	4621/2820	Ganaseny De Pedure
462 282	4621/2821	Plesheny
462 282	4622/2825	Kochuliya
462 282	4624/2823	Tigech
462 282	4625/2828	Misheny
462 282	4626/2827	Yargora
462 282	4628/2829	Bayush
462 283	4622/2831	Borogany
462 283	4626/2837	Dezginzhe
462 283	4628/2838	Chenak
462 284	4622/2849	Chok Maydan
462 284	4626/2845	Chekur Menzhir
462 285	4620/2858	Bessarabka
462 285	4623/2855	Iordanovka
462 285	4624/2855	Karabetovka
462 285	4627/2853	Sadakliya
462 285	4628/2850	Staraya Bogdanovka
462 285	4629/2857	Novaya Iserliya
462 290	4622/2906	Nadrechnoye
462 290	4628/2907	Tarutino Nou
462 290	4629/2903	Vysochanskoye
462 291	4622/2918	Yuryevka
462 291	4623/2913	Yevgenyevka
462 291	4624/2917	Yelizavetovka
462 291	4626/2917	Sturzeni Tighina
462 292	4620/2928	Staroselye
462 292	4627/2928	Alexandreni
462 292	4628/2921	Lesnoye
462 293	4626/2937	Volontirovka
462 294	4622/2946	Russko Ivanovka
462 294	4626/2946	Chistovodnoye

462 294	4628/2949	Karagasany
462 295	4620/2959	Starokazachye
462 295	4623/2952	Kaplany
462 295	4627/2959	Krokmazy
462 300	4621/3003	Kazatskoye
462 300	4623/3003	Udobnoye
462 303	4628/3034	Dalnik
462 304	4628/3044	Odessa
462 403	4622/4034	Shaumyana
463 132	4637/1322	Hermagor
463 134	4633/1343	Arnoldstein
463 135	4636/1350	Villach
463 141	4634/1417	Firnitz
463 141	4638/1418	Klagenfurt
463 143	4639/1438	Volkermarkt
463 145	4631/1452	Mezica
463 145	4633/1458	Ravne Na Koroskem
463 150	4635/1501	Dravograd
463 150	4635/1503	Otiski Vrh
463 151	4637/1513	Radlje Ob Dravi
463 153	4631/1531	Loka
463 153	4633/1539	Maribor
463 160	4638/1607	Murski Crnci
463 160	4639/1606	Tropovci
463 161	4631/1612	Ljutomer
463 161	4635/1618	Crensovci
463 161	4636/1615	Beltinci
463 162	4634/1627	Lendava
463 162	4637/1625	Genterovci
463 162	4639/1621	Dobrovnik
463 163	4630/1638	Csornyefold
463 163	4634/1636	Szecsisziget
463 163	4635/1635	Kerkatotfalu
463 163	4636/1637	Iklodbordoce
463 163	4637/1639	Csomoder
463 163	4637/1633	Lenti
463 163	4637/1630	Redics
463 163	4638/1634	Mumor
463 164	4632/1644	Bazakerettye
463 164	4632/1642	Lispeszentadorjan
463 164	4633/1647	Banokszentgyorgy
463 164	4634/1641	Kanyavar
463 164	4635/1640	Domefolde
463 164	4639/1644	Gutorfolde
463 164	4639/1648	Pusztaederics
463 165	4630/1655	Homokkomarom
463 165	4630/1659	Palin
463 165	4631/1657	Fuzvolgy
463 165	4633/1655	Bocska
463 165	4633/1656	Magyarszerdahely
463 165	4634/1658	Kacorlak
463 165	4635/1650	Szentliszlo
463 165	4635/1655	Zalaszentbalazs
463 165	4636/1657	Poloskefo

463	165	4636/1650	Pusztamagyarod
463	165	4638/1656	Hahot
463	170	4630/1704	Kisrecse
463	170	4631/1708	Galambok
463	170	4632/1706	Csapi
463	170	4633/1703	Nagybakonak
463	170	4633/1705	Zalaujlak
463	170	4634/1706	Zalamerenye
463	170	4635/1708	Garabonc
463	170	4636/1700	Gelse
463	170	4637/1703	Kerecseny
463	170	4637/1707	Nagyrada
463	170	4638/1700	Kiliman
463	170	4638/1704	Orosztony
463	170	4639/1700	Alsorajk
463	170	4639/1707	Zalaszabar
463	171	4630/1716	Nemesvid
463	171	4632/1717	Csakany
463	171	4632/1711	Komarvaros
463	171	4633/1711	Kiskomarom
463	171	4634/1718	Somogyfeheregyhaz
463	171	4635/1716	Savoly
463	171	4635/1718	Somogysamson
463	171	4636/1711	Balatonmagyarod
463	171	4638/1716	Fonyed
463	171	4638/1719	Hollad
463	172	4630/1726	Mesztegnyo
463	172	4631/1724	Gadany
463	172	4631/1725	Keleviz
463	172	4635/1727	Boronka
463	172	4635/1721	Horvatkut
463	172	4635/1725	Marcali
463	172	4639/1724	Kethely
463	172	4639/1729	Somogyszentpal
463	173	4631/1732	Libickozma
463	173	4631/1734	Somogyfajsz
463	173	4632/1735	Pusztakovacsi
463	173	4634/1730	Csomend
463	173	4635/1731	Nikla
463	173	4636/1737	Oreglak
463	173	4637/1732	Taska
463	173	4639/1735	Buzsak
463	174	4630/1742	Somogyjad
463	174	4631/1740	Osztopan
463	174	4634/1741	Somogyvamos
463	174	4635/1740	Somogyvar
463	174	4637/1746	Gamas
463	175	4630/1750	Mernye
463	175	4630/1753	Szentgalosker
463	175	4631/1755	Raksi
463	175	4632/1757	Igal
463	175	4633/1751	Ecseny
463	175	4635/1754	Bonnya
463	175	4635/1750	Felsomocsolad
463	175	4635/1757	Somogyacsa
463	175	4636/1752	Kisbarapati
463	175	4639/1756	Andocs
463	180	4631/1800	Somogyszil
463	180	4633/1807	Szakcs
463	180	4636/1807	Koppanyszanto
463	180	4636/1803	Torokkoppany
463	180	4637/1808	Erteny
463	180	4639/1805	Csaba
463	181	4630/1818	Gyulaj
463	181	4632/1811	Kocsola
463	181	4635/1812	Nagykonyi
463	181	4635/1816	Pari
463	181	4638/1817	Tamasi
463	181	4638/1817	Tusko
463	182	4632/1823	Szakaly
463	182	4633/1829	Gyonk
463	182	4634/1826	Szarazd
463	182	4635/1825	Regoly
463	182	4637/1826	Keszohidegkut
463	182	4638/1829	Miszla
463	182	4639/1825	Belecska
463	183	4630/1834	Kistormas
463	183	4631/1835	Kolesd
463	183	4632/1831	Varsad
463	183	4634/1838	Kajdacs
463	183	4636/1831	Udvari
463	184	4638/1842	Gyorkony
463	184	4638/1840	Nagydorog
463	185	4630/1854	Gerjen
463	185	4631/1855	Fokto
463	185	4632/1850	Dunaszentgyorgy
463	185	4634/1855	Uszod
463	185	4636/1854	Dunaszentbenedek
463	185	4637/1855	Gederlak
463	185	4638/1852	Paks
463	190	4631/1903	Halom
463	190	4631/1907	Oregcserto
463	190	4632/1900	Kalocsa
463	190	4634/1904	Szakmar
463	190	4638/1900	Dunapataj
463	191	4632/1916	Kecel
463	191	4637/1918	Kiskoros
463	192	4635/1923	Soltvadkert
463	194	4634/1946	Jaszszentlaszlo
463	195	4638/1957	Palmonostora
463	200	4636/2007	Csanytelek
463	200	4637/2002	Tomorkeny
463	201	4632/2012	Mindszent
463	201	4635/2014	Szegvar
463	201	4639/2016	Szentes
463	202	4631/2024	Raros
463	202	4635/2022	Derekegyhaz
463	203	4635/2030	Nagymagocs

463 203	4635/2038	Szentetornya
463 204	4632/2048	Pusztafoldvar
463 204	4634/2040	Oroshaza
463 205	4633/2053	Csanadapaca
463 205	4638/2050	Csorvas
463 210	4630/2102	Medgyesegyhaza
463 210	4634/2107	Apati
463 210	4635/2102	Ujkigyos
463 211	4632/2115	Elek
463 211	4632/2111	Ketegyhaza
463 211	4636/2114	Szentbenedek
463 211	4639/2117	Gyula
463 212	4639/2120	Gyulavari
463 213	4632/2131	Chisineu Cris
463 213	4637/2131	Zerind
463 213	4638/2130	Iermata Neagra
463 213	4638/2133	Tamasda
463 214	4636/2145	Pancoja
463 214	4638/2142	Satu Nou Na Saud
463 214	4638/2140	Vadasz
463 215	4635/2158	Craiova
463 220	4630/2205	Hasmas
463 222	4631/2228	Luh
463 225	4630/2257	Giurgiu
463 234	4631/2342	Cornesti
463 234	4634/2347	Turda
463 234	4635/2343	Szind
463 234	4637/2342	Tureni
463 235	4633/2353	Cimpia Truzii
463 235	4633/2354	Ghiris
463 240	4630/2400	Grindeni
463 240	4634/2405	Taureni
463 240	4636/2408	Zau De Cimpie
463 241	4633/2412	Budiul De Campie
463 241	4633/2419	Capusu De Cimpie
463 241	4635/2411	Sacalul De Campi
463 241	4638/2413	Saulia
463 242	4632/2426	Berghia
463 242	4633/2428	Panet
463 242	4635/2423	Band
463 242	4638/2426	Culpiu
463 242	4639/2423	Sincai
463 243	4631/2431	Mureseni
463 243	4633/2434	Tirgu Mures
463 243	4635/2431	Bardesti
463 243	4636/2435	Chinari
463 243	4636/2439	Ernei
463 243	4637/2432	Voiniceni
463 243	4638/2438	Dumbravioara
463 243	4639/2433	Pacureni
463 244	4631/2445	Galesti
463 244	4631/2443	Maiad
463 244	4632/2448	Miercurea Nirajului
463 244	4634/2448	Iobageni
463 244	4634/2444	Mosuni
463 244	4634/2448	Vargata
463 244	4636/2447	Vadu Mures
463 244	4638/2449	Hodosa
463 244	4638/2445	Ilioara
463 244	4639/2444	Iara De Mures
463 244	4639/2447	Mura Mare
463 245	4631/2455	Abud
463 245	4632/2458	Chibed
463 245	4632/2452	Eremieni
463 245	4633/2452	Bereni
463 245	4633/2453	Torba
463 245	4635/2451	Maia
463 245	4636/2455	Silea Nirajului
463 245	4638/2452	Damieni
463 250	4631/2503	Siclod
463 250	4632/2509	Ocna De Sus
463 250	4632/2508	Ocna De Jos
463 250	4633/2508	Praid
463 250	4633/2507	Sasveres
463 250	4635/2504	Sovata
463 253	4639/2538	Voslobeni
463 254	4635/2547	Sindominic
463 260	4635/2602	Ghimes
463 261	4631/2612	Brusturoasa
463 265	4634/2654	Bacau
463 274	4634/2742	Lipovat
463 274	4638/2744	Vaslui
463 281	4637/2815	Sarata Rezeshty
463 281	4639/2818	Pobeda
463 282	4631/2826	Kazanzhik
463 282	4631/2821	Kupkuy
463 282	4636/2823	Kovyrluy
463 283	4632/2832	Beshtemak
463 283	4633/2837	Zhavgur
463 283	4635/2837	Yalpuzheny
463 283	4636/2832	Saratsika Veke
463 284	4632/2847	Chimishliya
463 284	4635/2845	Yekaterinovka
463 285	4633/2856	Mikhaylovka (Bessarabia)
463 285	4635/2855	Selemet
463 290	4631/2902	Troitskoye
463 290	4634/2907	Tarakliya
463 290	4635/2900	Batyr
463 290	4637/2900	Chufleshty
463 291	4631/2910	Petrovka
463 291	4632/2918	Tokuz
463 291	4634/2915	Salkutsa
463 291	4639/2919	Verkhnyaya Maryanovka
463 292	4630/2924	Saitsy
463 292	4631/2927	Brezoya
463 292	4635/2921	Opachi
463 292	4637/2921	Zaim

463	292	4638/2925	Kaushany
463	293	4632/2934	Feshtelitsa
463	293	4633/2932	Purkary
463	293	4635/2931	Yermokliya
463	293	4636/2932	Popovka
463	294	4630/2945	Slobozia
463	294	4636/2942	Chobruchi
463	294	4636/2947	Raskaytsy
463	294	4638/2940	Talmaz
463	295	4630/2955	Oloneshty
463	302	4637/3025	Vygoda (Transnistria)
463	313	4637/3133	Ochakov
463	323	4631/3231	Golaya Pristan
463	323	4638/3236	Kherson
463	324	4637/3243	Tsyurupinsk
463	341	4631/3418	Gornostayevka
463	344	4637/3441	Chervonyy Prapor
464	122	4645/1225	Sillian
464	133	4648/1330	Spittal an der Drau
464	134	4648/1343	Radenthein
464	140	4644/1405	Waiern
464	145	4647/1455	Goding
464	151	4645/1512	Schwanberg
464	153	4646/1532	Leibnitz
464	154	4641/1545	Sladki Vrh
464	155	4642/1559	Radkersburg
464	160	4643/1601	Cankova
464	160	4644/1607	Bodonci
464	160	4646/1602	Pertoca
464	160	4648/1602	Rogasovci
464	161	4640/1610	Murska Sobota
464	161	4641/1617	Bogojina
464	161	4641/1615	Tesanovci
464	161	4643/1610	Puconci
464	161	4644/1616	Fokovci
464	161	4645/1610	Moscanci
464	161	4646/1612	Kukec
464	161	4647/1618	Domanjsevci
464	161	4649/1612	Gornji Petrovci
464	162	4640/1629	Resznek
464	162	4642/1620	Bukovnica
464	162	4643/1621	Motvarjevci
464	162	4644/1625	Szentgyorgyvolgy
464	162	4644/1623	Velemer
464	162	4645/1629	Alsoszenterzsebet
464	162	4646/1620	Magyarszombatfa
464	162	4647/1625	Magyarfold
464	162	4649/1622	Davidhaza
464	162	4649/1621	Kotormany
464	163	4640/1633	Lentikapolna
464	163	4642/1633	Zalabaksa
464	163	4643/1631	Csesztreg
464	163	4644/1635	Porszombat
464	163	4645/1634	Kalocfa
464	163	4646/1630	Kerkakutas
464	163	4646/1633	Kozmadombja
464	164	4640/1648	Tofej
464	164	4641/1641	Nova
464	164	4642/1646	Zalatarnok
464	164	4646/1647	Gellenhaza
464	164	4647/1641	Kustanszeg
464	164	4647/1646	Nagylengyel
464	164	4648/1643	Csonkahegyhat
464	164	4648/1645	Milej
464	164	4649/1641	Nemetfalu
464	165	4640/1651	Sojtor
464	165	4641/1657	Potrete
464	165	4643/1651	Bak
464	165	4643/1657	Zalaszentmihaly
464	165	4645/1656	Poloske
464	165	4646/1657	Nemesszentandras
464	165	4647/1650	Bocfolde
464	165	4647/1657	Bucsuszentlaszlo
464	165	4647/1653	Csatar
464	165	4647/1657	Nemessandorhaza
464	165	4648/1652	Botfa
464	165	4648/1651	Puszta
464	170	4640/1703	Dioskal
464	170	4641/1700	Felsorajk
464	170	4643/1701	Pacsa
464	170	4644/1707	Zalaapati
464	170	4645/1702	Vorru
464	170	4645/1701	Zalaigrice
464	170	4646/1704	Getye
464	170	4646/1702	Szentpeterur
464	170	4648/1703	Tilaj
464	170	4648/1707	Zalacsany
464	170	4649/1700	Nagykapornak
464	170	4649/1709	Nemesbuk
464	171	4640/1716	Vors
464	171	4640/1710	Zalavar
464	171	4641/1718	Balatonszentgyorgy
464	171	4643/1719	Balatonbereny
464	171	4643/1710	Sarmellek
464	171	4646/1711	Alsopahok
464	171	4646/1717	Gyenesdias
464	171	4646/1715	Keszthely
464	171	4647/1710	Felsopahok
464	171	4647/1711	Heviz
464	172	4640/1723	Balatonujlak
464	172	4642/1723	Balatonkeresztur
464	172	4648/1726	Szigliget
464	172	4649/1729	Badacsonytordemic
464	173	4640/1739	Lengyeltoti
464	173	4644/1733	Fonyod
464	173	4648/1731	Badacsonytomaj
464	174	4641/1741	Gyugy
464	174	4643/1741	Szollosgyorok

464	174	4645/1745	Latrany
464	174	4647/1740	Balatonboglar
464	174	4647/1742	Balatonlelle
464	174	4649/1747	Balatonszemes
464	175	4641/1751	Karad
464	175	4641/1759	Zics
464	175	4644/1758	Kapoly
464	175	4645/1752	Kotcse
464	175	4645/1750	Nagycsepely
464	175	4647/1751	Szolad
464	180	4642/1804	Kanya
464	180	4642/1806	Tengod
464	180	4644/1802	Tab
464	180	4644/1800	Zala
464	180	4645/1807	Babonymegyer
464	180	4648/1807	Nyim
464	180	4648/1809	Som
464	180	4649/1801	Jaba
464	181	4641/1817	Fornad
464	181	4641/1818	Kecsege
464	181	4642/1811	Iregszemcse
464	181	4643/1818	Furged
464	181	4643/1813	Nagyszokoly
464	181	4645/1814	Magyarkeszi
464	181	4647/1818	Felsonyek
464	181	4648/1810	Nagybereny
464	181	4649/1817	Szabadhidveg
464	182	4641/1827	Pincehely
464	182	4643/1829	Tolnanemedi
464	182	4645/1824	Ozora
464	182	4649/1829	Mezoszilas
464	183	4641/1832	Vadkert
464	183	4643/1838	Palfa
464	183	4645/1833	Simontornya
464	183	4646/1839	Cece
464	183	4647/1836	Saregres
464	184	4643/1840	Vajta
464	184	4648/1842	Alap
464	185	4641/1858	Madocsa
464	185	4644/1858	Bolcske
464	185	4645/1855	Szentandras
464	185	4648/1856	Dunafoldvar
464	190	4648/1900	Polya
464	190	4648/1900	Solt
464	191	4642/1912	Akaszto
464	191	4643/1916	Csengod
464	191	4649/1915	Fulopszallas
464	192	4643/1924	Pahi
464	192	4648/1922	Izsak
464	195	4643/1951	Kiskunfelegyhaza
464	200	4642/2009	Csongrad
464	200	4648/2008	Csepa
464	200	4648/2001	Tiszaujfalu
464	200	4649/2000	Alpar
464	200	4649/2005	Tiszasas
464	201	4644/2013	Magyartes
464	201	4648/2012	Szeleveny
464	202	4641/2028	Fabiansebestyen
464	203	4640/2036	Gadoros
464	204	4641/2040	Nagyszenas
464	204	4646/2048	Kondoros
464	210	4641/2106	Bekescsaba
464	210	4643/2104	Mezomegyer
464	210	4646/2108	Bekes
464	210	4649/2102	Mezobereny
464	211	4644/2115	Doboz
464	211	4649/2110	Ludad
464	212	4644/2129	Kotegyan
464	212	4645/2123	Sarkad
464	212	4648/2123	Sarkadkeresztur
464	213	4648/2139	Salonta
464	213	4648/2130	Ujszalonta
464	215	4643/2151	Taut
464	215	4646/2157	Tinca
464	220	4645/2202	Chesa
464	222	4640/2221	Beius
464	222	4642/2226	Pocioveliste
464	225	4646/2259	Ciuleni
464	230	4647/2302	Valcaul Ungureasca
464	230	4648/2301	Calata
464	230	4649/2302	Horlacea
464	232	4641/2325	Finisel
464	232	4641/2327	Savadisla
464	232	4642/2327	Vlaha
464	232	4644/2329	Floresti Cluj
464	232	4644/2326	Luna De Sus
464	232	4645/2323	Gilau
464	233	4641/2332	Salicea
464	233	4646/2336	Cluj
464	233	4647/2339	Szamosfalva
464	234	4646/2343	Dezmir
464	234	4649/2345	Apahida
464	235	4640/2357	Ceanu Mare
464	235	4646/2358	Felsoszovat
464	240	4642/2403	Frata
464	240	4642/2400	Soporu De Cimpie
464	240	4647/2408	Camarasu
464	240	4647/2408	Pusztakmaras
464	240	4648/2402	Mociu
464	241	4641/2418	Pogaceaua
464	241	4641/2412	Velcherul De Campi
464	241	4643/2416	Barlibas
464	241	4643/2416	Sinpetru De Cimpie
464	241	4645/2410	Sarmas
464	241	4645/2411	Sarmasel
464	242	4640/2427	Sabed
464	242	4644/2427	Milasel
464	242	4646/2422	Urmenis

464	242	4648/2421	Sopteriu
464	242	4649/2426	Milas
464	243	4640/2439	Gornesti
464	243	4641/2434	Paingeni
464	243	4642/2435	Toldal
464	243	4644/2435	Onuca
464	243	4646/2431	Faragau
464	243	4647/2433	Tonciu
464	244	4641/2445	Petrilaca De Mures
464	244	4642/2447	Habic
464	244	4644/2449	Beica De Sus
464	244	4644/2448	Beica De Jos
464	244	4644/2443	Petelea
464	244	4645/2442	Apalina
464	244	4646/2443	Iernuteni
464	244	4646/2442	Reghin
464	244	4646/2446	Solovastru
464	244	4647/2448	Jabenita
464	244	4648/2445	Ideciu De Jos
464	245	4643/2452	Serbeni
464	245	4644/2451	Cacuciu
464	245	4644/2454	Chincis
464	245	4644/2454	Comori
464	245	4644/2452	Sinmihaiu De Padure
464	245	4646/2451	Gurghiu
464	245	4646/2455	Hodac
464	245	4646/2456	Ibanesti (Transylvania)
464	245	4647/2452	Casva
464	253	4643/2537	Gheorgheni
464	253	4645/2532	Lazarea
464	253	4649/2531	Ditrau
464	262	4646/2629	Borlesti
464	264	4643/2642	Buhusi
464	265	4644/2659	Damienesti
464	271	4641/2713	Plopana Tirg
464	272	4642/2720	Pungesti
464	273	4640/2734	Risnita
464	280	4641/2804	Husi
464	280	4649/2806	Drinceni
464	281	4642/2818	Semenovka (Bessarabia)
464	281	4646/2813	Danku
464	281	4648/2812	Kalmatsuy
464	282	4640/2824	Chadyr
464	282	4640/2820	Minzhir
464	282	4640/2828	Orak
464	282	4646/2822	Karpineny
464	283	4642/2833	Karakuy
464	283	4644/2831	Sarata Galbena
464	284	4642/2842	Gura Galbena
464	284	4642/2848	Porumbrey
464	284	4645/2842	Ionyaska
464	284	4647/2847	Moleshty
464	285	4640/2851	Sagaydak
464	285	4643/2857	Karbuna
464	285	4645/2850	Chigirleny
464	285	4646/2854	Rezeny
464	285	4649/2859	Budey
464	290	4641/2903	Kaynary
464	290	4644/2901	Gangura
464	290	4649/2908	Dzhamany
464	291	4641/2910	Kashkaliya
464	291	4644/2912	Zolotiyevka
464	292	4643/2925	Tanatary
464	292	4647/2922	Farladyany
464	292	4649/2929	Bendery
464	293	4640/2930	Kirnatseny
464	293	4640/2936	Leontyevo
464	293	4643/2932	Kirkayeshty
464	293	4643/2938	Kopanka
464	293	4647/2936	Kitskany
464	301	4642/3011	Shcherbanka
464	331	4647/3310	Lvovo
464	332	4649/3329	Kakhovka
464	351	4642/3510	Akimovka
464	362	4644/3621	Primorskoye
464	364	4645/3647	Berdyansk
465	124	4650/1247	Lienz
465	133	4656/1336	Leoben
465	140	4652/1405	Bischofsberg
465	145	4650/1450	Wolfsberg
465	153	4659/1530	Hausmannstatten
465	155	4653/1554	Gleichenberg Dorf
465	155	4657/1553	Feldbach
465	160	4656/1601	Fehring
465	160	4656/1608	Jennersdorf
465	161	4650/1612	Sulinci
465	161	4653/1617	Orfalu
465	161	4654/1615	Apatistvanfalva
465	161	4655/1610	Neumarkt an der Raab
465	161	4656/1615	Rabatotfalu
465	161	4657/1617	Szentgotthard
465	161	4659/1617	Rabafuzes
465	162	4650/1628	Nagyrakos
465	162	4654/1624	Kondorfa
465	162	4659/1622	Alsoronok
465	162	4659/1621	Felsoronok
465	163	4651/1634	Felsojanosfa
465	163	4651/1636	Zalalovo
465	163	4652/1633	Hegyhatszentjakab
465	163	4653/1635	Szoce
465	163	4656/1630	Ivanc
465	164	4651/1640	Salomvar
465	164	4652/1648	Andrashida
465	164	4652/1644	Boncodfolde
465	164	4652/1643	Kavas
465	164	4652/1649	Sagod
465	164	4654/1643	Hagyarosborond
465	164	4654/1646	Zalaboldogfa

465	164	4655/1641	Ozmanbuk
465	164	4658/1645	Karatfold
465	164	4659/1642	Doborhegy
465	164	4659/1644	Gerse
465	164	4659/1649	Hegyhatszentpeter
465	165	4650/1651	Zalaegerszeg
465	165	4651/1656	Alsonemesapati
465	165	4651/1650	Kaszahaza
465	165	4652/1657	Nemesapati
465	165	4653/1656	Alibanfa
465	165	4653/1654	Zalaszentivan
465	165	4654/1658	Kemendollar
465	165	4655/1651	Nagypali
465	165	4655/1659	Zalaistvand
465	165	4655/1653	Zalaszentlorinc
465	165	4656/1651	Deneslak
465	165	4656/1652	Egervar
465	165	4657/1653	Vasboldogasszony
465	165	4659/1651	Gyorvar
465	170	4650/1707	Kustany
465	170	4651/1707	Gyulevesz
465	170	4651/1706	Kehida
465	170	4651/1701	Padar
465	170	4652/1701	Bezered
465	170	4653/1705	Zalakoppany
465	170	4653/1707	Zalaszentlaszlo
465	170	4655/1707	Zalaudvarnok
465	170	4656/1705	Kisszentgrot
465	170	4657/1704	Aranyod
465	170	4657/1705	Zalaszentgrot
465	170	4658/1700	Pakod
465	170	4658/1704	Tuskeszentpeter
465	170	4658/1702	Zalaber
465	170	4659/1709	Szalapa
465	170	4659/1706	Turje
465	171	4650/1711	Karmacs
465	171	4651/1713	Rezi
465	171	4651/1711	Vindornyafok
465	171	4653/1712	Vindornyalak
465	171	4653/1714	Zalaszanto
465	171	4654/1710	Vindornyaszollos
465	171	4656/1715	Bazsi
465	171	4656/1710	Kisgorbo
465	171	4659/1717	Sumeg
465	172	4650/1729	Nemesgulacs
465	172	4651/1728	Kisapati
465	172	4651/1722	Lesencetomaj
465	172	4652/1729	Gyulakeszi
465	172	4652/1721	Lesenceistvand
465	172	4653/1726	Tapolca
465	172	4655/1728	Zalahalap
465	173	4650/1738	Revfulop
465	173	4651/1731	Kaptalantoti
465	173	4651/1736	Kovagoors
465	173	4653/1730	Diszel
465	173	4653/1736	Koveskal
465	173	4653/1734	Szentbekkalla
465	173	4653/1734	Velete
465	173	4655/1734	Monostorapati
465	173	4657/1737	Kapolcs
465	173	4658/1738	Vigantpetend
465	173	4659/1734	Taliandorogd
465	174	4653/1745	Balatonakali
465	174	4653/1741	Zanka
465	174	4654/1749	Balatonudvari
465	174	4654/1741	Tagyon
465	174	4655/1743	Felsodorgicse
465	174	4655/1741	Szentantalfa
465	174	4656/1740	Balatoncsicso
465	174	4656/1746	Vaszoly
465	174	4657/1747	Pecsely
465	174	4659/1745	Barnag
465	174	4659/1742	Nagyvazsony
465	174	4659/1741	Nemesleanyfalu
465	175	4650/1759	Balatonendred
465	175	4650/1750	Balatonszarszo
465	175	4650/1754	Koroshegy
465	175	4653/1757	Zamardi
465	175	4655/1754	Tihany
465	175	4657/1753	Balatonfured
465	175	4658/1754	Balatonaracs
465	175	4658/1752	Meleghegy
465	175	4659/1759	Alsoors
465	175	4659/1756	Nadas
465	180	4653/1805	Balatonkiliti
465	180	4653/1808	Balatonszabadi
465	180	4653/1808	Siojut
465	180	4653/1809	Siomaros
465	180	4653/1801	Somogyfok
465	180	4654/1802	Balatonujhely
465	180	4654/1803	Siofok
465	181	4650/1817	Mezokomarom
465	181	4652/1810	Adand
465	181	4656/1815	Enying
465	181	4656/1815	Kenese
465	181	4657/1814	Balatonbozsok
465	182	4651/1821	Lajoskomarom
465	182	4652/1827	Deg
465	182	4657/1829	Kaloz
465	182	4658/1823	Kislang
465	183	4650/1831	Pusztaegres
465	183	4652/1838	Sarszentmiklos
465	183	4653/1838	Sarbogard
465	183	4658/1834	Sarszentagota
465	184	4656/1846	Mezofalva
465	184	4658/1840	Nagylok
465	185	4650/1857	Dunaegyhaza
465	185	4653/1857	Apostag

465	185	4655/1859	Dunavecse
465	185	4659/1856	Sztalinvaros
465	190	4658/1900	Szalkeszentmarton
465	191	4653/1913	Szabadszallas
465	192	4656/1929	Kerekegyhaza
465	193	4655/1935	Hetenyegyhaza
465	194	4654/1942	Kecskemet
465	200	4651/2004	Tiszaug
465	200	4653/2007	Tiszakurt
465	200	4654/2009	Tiszainoka
465	200	4656/2007	Okecske
465	200	4656/2006	Tiszakecske
465	200	4656/2005	Ujkecske
465	201	4650/2017	Kunszentmarton
465	201	4658/2012	Cibakhaza
465	201	4659/2015	Reti
465	201	4659/2015	Tiszafoldvar
465	202	4652/2029	Bekesszentandras
465	202	4654/2024	Ocsod
465	203	4650/2039	Csabacsud
465	203	4652/2033	Szarvas
465	204	4656/2047	Endrod
465	205	4656/2050	Gyoma
465	210	4653/2102	Korostarcsa
465	210	4658/2105	Korosladany
465	211	4655/2116	Veszto
465	212	4654/2121	Okany
465	213	4652/2132	Mezogyan
465	213	4653/2135	Geszt
465	213	4655/2130	Zsadany
465	213	4658/2136	Biharugra
465	214	4655/2144	Cefa
465	214	4655/2148	Gepiu
465	214	4657/2144	Sinnicolau Romin
465	215	4657/2159	Cordau
465	215	4657/2151	Les
465	215	4659/2158	Ciheiu
465	220	4655/2201	Mierlau
465	220	4658/2202	Betfia
465	220	4659/2200	Haieu
465	221	4651/2211	Ceica
465	221	4651/2217	Racas
465	222	4659/2228	Dobricionesti
465	223	4652/2234	Damis
465	223	4655/2239	Lorau
465	223	4656/2236	Balanca Grosi
465	223	4656/2237	Bratca
465	223	4656/2232	Suncuius
465	223	4657/2235	Balnaca
465	223	4657/2238	Beznea
465	223	4657/2238	Valea Neagra De Cris
465	223	4659/2238	Borod
465	223	4659/2238	Cornitel
465	223	4659/2234	Topa De Cris
465	223	4659/2231	Vadu Crisului
465	224	4651/2240	Remeti Bihor
465	224	4653/2240	Ponoara
465	224	4655/2241	Bulz
465	224	4657/2244	Bucea
465	224	4657/2249	Ciucea
465	225	4650/2257	Alunisu
465	225	4651/2250	Tranisu
465	225	4652/2257	Morlaca
465	225	4654/2255	Hodisu
465	225	4655/2254	Poeni
465	225	4655/2253	Valea Draganului
465	230	4650/2301	Domosu
465	230	4651/2309	Nadasu
465	230	4652/2303	Huedin
465	230	4655/2309	Petrinzel
465	230	4657/2308	Almasu
465	231	4650/2318	Macau
465	231	4651/2315	Inucu
465	231	4651/2312	Leghea
465	231	4653/2315	Aghiresu
465	231	4655/2315	Ticu
465	231	4656/2312	Petrindu
465	231	4656/2317	Stoboru
465	231	4657/2311	Tamasa
465	231	4658/2312	Cuzaplac
465	231	4659/2315	Sutoru
465	232	4651/2321	Turea
465	232	4652/2323	Sardu
465	232	4657/2326	Berindu
465	232	4657/2323	Topa Mica
465	232	4658/2328	Cristorel
465	232	4659/2320	Dolu
465	233	4653/2338	Feiurdeni
465	233	4659/2330	Aschileu Mare
465	233	4659/2336	Chidea
465	234	4652/2348	Jucu De Jos
465	234	4655/2348	Bontida
465	234	4655/2346	Rascruci
465	234	4656/2340	Borsa Cluj
465	234	4657/2345	Luna De Jos
465	234	4658/2349	Iclozel
465	234	4659/2348	Iclod
465	234	4659/2343	Lujerdiu
465	235	4650/2357	Vaida Camaras
465	235	4651/2351	Gadalin
465	235	4651/2359	Palatca
465	235	4652/2355	Tauseni
465	235	4652/2352	Visea
465	235	4656/2350	Cojocna
465	235	4656/2353	Sic
465	235	4658/2355	Sacalaia
465	240	4654/2409	Buza
465	240	4654/2401	Puini

465 240	4654/2404	Sucutard
465 240	4657/2404	Ghioli
465 240	4657/2407	Nasal
465 240	4657/2403	Taga
465 240	4658/2406	Diviciorii Mici
465 240	4659/2405	Diviciorii Mari
465 240	4659/2402	Mahal
465 241	4651/2411	Catina
465 241	4652/2415	Budatelec
465 241	4652/2412	Copru
465 241	4652/2419	Micestii De Cimpie
465 241	4659/2411	Chiochis
465 241	4659/2416	Matei
465 241	4659/2412	Strugureni
465 242	4651/2425	Orosfaia
465 242	4656/2429	Iuda
465 242	4658/2426	Dipsa
465 242	4659/2428	Albestii Bistritei
465 242	4659/2424	Galatii Bistritei
465 243	4653/2434	Logig
465 243	4655/2431	Teaca
465 243	4656/2437	Uila
465 243	4657/2432	Pinticu
465 243	4659/2435	Posnas
465 243	4659/2439	Sieut
465 244	4652/2446	Brincovenesti
465 244	4654/2449	Maioresti
465 244	4654/2447	Porcesti
465 244	4655/2446	Ripa De Sus
465 244	4656/2446	Ripa De Jos
465 244	4658/2443	Gledin
465 245	4655/2451	Rusii Munti
465 245	4656/2454	Deda
465 245	4656/2454	Filea
465 250	4650/2500	Ratosnya
465 250	4657/2506	Lunca Bradului
465 250	4659/2502	Rastolita
465 251	4659/2514	Stinceni
465 252	4655/2526	Galautas
465 252	4655/2520	Toplita
465 253	4657/2534	Borsec
465 254	4657/2546	Tulghes
465 254	4659/2542	Corbu
465 262	4655/2620	Piatra Neamt
465 264	4658/2641	Bozienii De Sus
465 265	4651/2650	Secueni
465 265	4655/2655	Roman
465 271	4651/2714	Bacesti
465 272	4650/2726	Negresti
465 272	4659/2720	Tibana
465 274	4652/2745	Codaesti
465 274	4659/2747	Trestiana
465 275	4657/2756	Raducaneni
465 280	4653/2800	Dubarsi
465 280	4655/2807	Nemtseny
465 280	4656/2808	Balaureshty
465 281	4650/2817	Krasnoarmeyskoye
465 281	4655/2811	Katsaleny
465 281	4656/2816	Buzhory
465 281	4659/2812	Sapte Sate
465 281	4659/2812	Shishkany
465 282	4650/2825	Bolchany
465 282	4653/2825	Lapushna
465 282	4657/2820	Bogicheny
465 282	4658/2829	Dakhnovichi
465 282	4659/2827	Dragusheny
465 283	4650/2836	Kotovsk (Bessarabia)
465 283	4653/2837	Fundu Galbena
465 283	4655/2833	Loganeshty
465 283	4656/2839	Novyye Ruseshty
465 284	4652/2846	Kosteshty Lapusna
465 284	4653/2841	Pozhareny
465 284	4654/2840	Bardar
465 284	4654/2849	Malyye Mileshty
465 284	4656/2847	Yaloveny
465 284	4658/2843	Dancheny
465 284	4659/2840	Surucheny
465 285	4650/2850	Zembreny
465 285	4655/2854	Bachoy
465 290	4650/2902	Pugoy
465 290	4654/2909	Tsyntsareny
465 291	4653/2918	Bul'boka
465 291	4656/2913	Novaya Kobuska
465 291	4658/2911	Staraya Kobuska
465 292	4651/2922	Garbovat
465 292	4651/2922	Gyrbovets
465 292	4652/2929	Varnitsa
465 292	4656/2928	Gura Bykuluy
465 300	4651/3005	Razdelnaya
465 320	4658/3200	Nikolayev
465 332	4650/3326	Berislav
465 352	4650/3522	Melitopol
470 094	4709/0949	Bludenz
470 103	4708/1034	Landeck (Austria)
470 130	4707/1308	Badgastein
470 134	4708/1348	Tamsweg
470 141	4706/1410	Murau
470 144	4704/1441	Obdach
470 144	4709/1444	Weisskirchen in Steiermark
470 150	4702/1507	Kowald
470 150	4704/1505	Koflach
470 150	4705/1509	Tregist
470 152	4702/1524	Strassgang
470 152	4704/1527	Graz
470 152	4707/1521	Judendorf
470 152	4708/1521	Gratkorn
470 153	4705/1531	Kainbach

470	160	4705/1606	Deutsch Kaltenbrunn
470	161	4700/1612	Eltendorf
470	161	4706/1617	Deutsch Tschantschendorf
470	161	4708/1614	Rauchwart im Burgenland
470	162	4704/1620	Gussing
470	162	4706/1628	Eberau
470	162	4706/1629	Szentpeterfa
470	162	4707/1621	Punitz
470	162	4708/1628	Oberbildein
470	163	4701/1636	Kormend
470	163	4704/1633	Nagykolked
470	163	4708/1635	Jak
470	163	4709/1639	Kisunyom
470	164	4703/1642	Hidashollos
470	164	4703/1641	Molnaszecsod
470	164	4703/1648	Vasvar
470	164	4704/1645	Rabahidveg
470	164	4706/1648	Puspoktamasi
470	164	4707/1648	Gutahaza
470	164	4707/1645	Szentlerant
470	164	4707/1649	Zsennye
470	164	4708/1643	Domotori
470	164	4708/1644	Sorkifalud
470	164	4708/1642	Sorkikapolna
470	164	4709/1646	Nemeskolta
470	165	4701/1653	Olaszfa
470	165	4703/1654	Csillaghegy
470	165	4704/1657	Csipkerek
470	165	4705/1651	Alsoujlak
470	165	4706/1654	Szemenye
470	165	4707/1655	Egervolgy
470	165	4708/1651	Rum
470	165	4709/1652	Balozsameggyes
470	165	4709/1655	Bejcgyertyanos
470	170	4700/1702	Zalaveg
470	170	4703/1708	Zalaerdod
470	170	4705/1707	Keled
470	170	4706/1701	Hosszupereszteg
470	170	4707/1707	Duka
470	171	4700/1712	Kisvasarhely
470	171	4701/1718	Csabrendek
470	171	4701/1714	Zalagyomoro
470	171	4702/1710	Dabronc
470	171	4703/1713	Ukk
470	171	4704/1712	Megyer
470	171	4704/1713	Rigacs
470	171	4706/1716	Kisberzseny
470	171	4706/1717	Veszprempinkoc
470	171	4706/1716	Zalagalsa
470	171	4707/1718	Apacatorna
470	171	4707/1710	Janoshaza
470	171	4708/1711	Kemenespalfa
470	171	4708/1712	Nagykamond
470	172	4700/1727	Nyirad
470	172	4704/1721	Kaptalanfa
470	172	4704/1722	Nemeshany
470	172	4704/1727	Pusztamiske
470	172	4706/1726	Devecser
470	172	4707/1722	Somlojeno
470	172	4707/1723	Somlovasarhely
470	172	4708/1724	Borszorcsok
470	173	4700/1737	Ocs
470	173	4701/1731	Szoc
470	173	4702/1732	Halimba
470	173	4704/1733	Csekut
470	173	4704/1730	Csota
470	173	4706/1734	Ajka
470	173	4706/1732	Tosokberend
470	173	4708/1734	Ajkarendek
470	173	4709/1737	Kislod
470	173	4709/1739	Varoslod
470	174	4701/1747	Totvazsony
470	174	4707/1744	Szentgal
470	174	4708/1745	Herend
470	174	4708/1742	Remete
470	175	4701/1757	Felsoors
470	175	4703/1753	Nemesvamos
470	175	4706/1755	Veszprem
470	175	4707/1754	Jutas
470	175	4707/1757	Kadarta
470	175	4709/1757	Gyulafiratot
470	180	4702/1801	Balatonalmadi
470	180	4702/1807	Balatonkenese
470	180	4703/1801	Vorosbereny
470	180	4705/1805	Papkeszi
470	180	4707/1808	Berhida
470	180	4707/1807	Peremarton
470	180	4707/1804	Vilonya
470	180	4709/1801	Hajmasker
470	181	4700/1815	Lepseny
470	181	4700/1817	Mezoszentgyorgy
470	181	4701/1810	Akarattya
470	181	4701/1813	Balatonfokajar
470	181	4703/1811	Csajag
470	181	4703/1815	Fule
470	181	4703/1818	Polgardi
470	181	4704/1811	Kungos
470	181	4706/1815	Jeno
470	182	4700/1827	Nagylang
470	182	4701/1827	Soponya
470	182	4702/1825	Csosz
470	182	4705/1824	Tac
470	182	4707/1823	Szabadbattyan
470	182	4709/1820	Sarszentmihaly
470	183	4700/1833	Sarkeresztur
470	183	4702/1831	Aba

470	183	4703/1839	Sarosd
470	183	4706/1835	Seregelyes
470	184	4703/1848	Perkata
470	184	4704/1841	Szabadegyhaza
470	184	4708/1846	Pusztaszabolcs
470	184	4709/1849	Ivancsa
470	185	4701/1857	Racalmas
470	185	4704/1853	Szentmihaly
470	185	4705/1856	Makad
470	185	4707/1852	Adony
470	185	4707/1854	Lorev
470	185	4708/1857	Szigetbecse
470	190	4701/1902	Tass
470	190	4702/1908	Kunszentmiklos
470	190	4705/1900	Domsod
470	192	4702/1927	Ladanybene
470	192	4704/1923	Tatarszentgyorgy
470	192	4708/1926	Orkeny
470	193	4701/1933	Lajosmizse
470	194	4702/1947	Nagykoros
470	195	4700/1955	Kocser
470	195	4707/1956	Tortel
470	200	4703/2004	Jaszkarajeno
470	200	4706/2009	Toszeg
470	201	4702/2013	Vezseny
470	201	4703/2016	Varsany
470	201	4704/2011	Tiszavarkony
470	201	4705/2014	Rakoczifalva
470	203	4700/2038	Mezotur
470	203	4708/2034	Kuncsorba
470	204	4706/2045	Turkeve
470	205	4702/2058	Devavanya
470	205	4702/2058	Kigyos
470	211	4701/2111	Cako
470	211	4702/2118	Csokmo
470	211	4702/2110	Szeghalom
470	211	4706/2113	Fuzesgyarmat
470	212	4706/2121	Darvas
470	212	4706/2124	Vekerd
470	212	4708/2128	Furta
470	212	4708/2126	Zsaka
470	213	4700/2130	Komadi
470	213	4700/2139	Korosnagyharsany
470	213	4701/2130	Csoma
470	213	4701/2130	Kereszter
470	213	4701/2136	Korosszakal
470	213	4701/2133	Magyarhomorog
470	213	4702/2138	Korosszegapati
470	213	4707/2134	Mezosas
470	213	4707/2139	Told
470	214	4704/2141	Berekboszormeny
470	214	4704/2148	Tarian
470	214	4707/2146	Artand
470	214	4707/2149	Bors
470	214	4708/2143	Biharkeresztes
470	215	4704/2156	Oradea
470	215	4704/2150	Palota
470	215	4704/2152	Sintandrei
470	215	4706/2154	Episcopia Bihorului
470	215	4707/2158	Paleu
470	215	4709/2155	Biharea
470	220	4701/2202	Cheriu
470	220	4701/2201	Rontau
470	220	4702/2203	Osorheiu
470	220	4703/2203	Fughiu
470	220	4708/2201	Cetariu
470	220	4709/2205	Sisterea
470	220	4709/2202	Tautelec
470	221	4703/2216	Telechiu
470	221	4703/2219	Tetche
470	221	4704/2212	Tileagd
470	221	4707/2217	Tiganestii De Cris
470	221	4708/2216	Picleu
470	221	4709/2211	Burzuc
470	222	4701/2226	Butani
470	222	4701/2223	Pestere
470	222	4702/2223	Astileu
470	222	4702/2229	Grosi Somes
470	222	4702/2227	Ortiteag
470	222	4703/2222	Chistag
470	222	4703/2226	Tinaud
470	222	4704/2225	Alesd
470	222	4704/2225	Keszter
470	222	4709/2229	Sinteu
470	223	4701/2231	Gheghie
470	223	4702/2230	Auseu
470	223	4709/2238	Aleus
470	223	4709/2237	Halmasd
470	224	4706/2249	Ban
470	224	4707/2244	Valcau De Jos
470	225	4703/2253	Pria
470	225	4704/2253	Cizer
470	225	4705/2254	Plesca
470	225	4705/2255	Stirciu
470	225	4706/2257	Seredeiu
470	225	4707/2253	Peceiu
470	225	4708/2259	Catalu
470	225	4709/2259	Catalusa
470	230	4702/2304	Buciumi Salaj
470	230	4703/2304	Bodia
470	230	4704/2308	Agrij
470	230	4706/2307	Treznea
470	230	4707/2308	Ciomirna
470	231	4700/2316	Zimbor
470	231	4704/2317	Hida
470	231	4708/2312	Chichisa
470	231	4708/2312	Romita
470	232	4700/2322	Ugrutiu

470	232	4701/2324	Dragu
470	232	4709/2326	Girbou
470	233	4702/2334	Panticeu
470	233	4703/2338	Cubles Somesani
470	233	4704/2332	Recea Cristur
470	233	4707/2335	Antas
470	233	4708/2332	Escu
470	233	4708/2333	Jurca
470	233	4708/2339	Olpret
470	233	4709/2334	Ciubanca
470	234	4701/2341	Stoiana
470	234	4702/2343	Pruneni
470	234	4704/2344	Corneni
470	234	4707/2342	Babdiu
470	234	4707/2349	Codor
470	234	4708/2343	Suares
470	234	4709/2342	Razbuneni
470	235	4701/2359	Fizesu Gherlii
470	235	4702/2352	Baita Salaj
470	235	4702/2355	Gherla
470	235	4702/2354	Szamosuovar
470	235	4704/2352	Nima
470	235	4706/2359	Nires
470	235	4706/2356	Salatiu
470	235	4707/2351	Ocna Dejului
470	235	4708/2356	Mica
470	235	4709/2352	Dej
470	240	4700/2408	Tentea
470	240	4702/2409	Vita
470	240	4703/2406	Ceaba
470	240	4704/2404	Batin
470	240	4704/2400	Top
470	240	4705/2407	Valea Ungurasului
470	240	4707/2403	Darot
470	240	4707/2409	Malin (Romania)
470	240	4707/2403	Unguras
470	240	4709/2403	Ciresoaia
470	241	4700/2411	Apatiu
470	241	4700/2419	Vermis
470	241	4701/2416	Corvinesti
470	241	4703/2415	Enciu
470	241	4704/2410	Beudiu
470	241	4705/2418	Chirales
470	241	4705/2415	Feleac
470	241	4706/2412	Nuseni
470	241	4706/2417	Sirioara
470	241	4709/2419	Sieu Odorhei
470	241	4709/2418	Sieu Sfint
470	242	4701/2425	Herina
470	242	4701/2421	Lechinta
470	242	4701/2427	Neteni
470	242	4703/2425	Saratel
470	242	4704/2424	Crainimat
470	242	4704/2428	Monariu
470	242	4704/2420	Tigau
470	242	4705/2421	Arcalia
470	242	4705/2423	Sieu Magherus
470	242	4706/2420	Chintelnic
470	242	4708/2429	Bistrita
470	243	4700/2437	Sieu Nasaud
470	243	4701/2431	Mariselu
470	243	4704/2437	Dumitrita
470	243	4704/2437	Ragla
470	243	4705/2432	Budus
470	243	4708/2434	Ghinda
470	244	4702/2441	Ardan
470	244	4708/2442	Cusma
470	253	4703/2531	Bilbor
470	261	4707/2610	Mitocu Balan
470	270	4702/2703	Bira
470	275	4705/2755	Kostuleny
470	275	4708/2758	Bratuleny
470	280	4700/2805	Grozeshty
470	280	4703/2807	Soltaneshty
470	280	4705/2801	Baksheny
470	280	4708/2804	Boldureshty
470	281	4705/2811	Nisporeny
470	281	4705/2816	Yurcheny
470	281	4707/2812	Varzareshty
470	282	4702/2825	Chuchuleny
470	282	4702/2820	Sekareny
470	282	4703/2829	Gorodka
470	282	4703/2825	Novyye Dragusheny
470	282	4708/2823	Lozovo
470	282	4709/2826	Vornicheny
470	283	4701/2833	Ulma
470	283	4708/2836	Strasheny
470	283	4709/2831	Panasheshty
470	284	4701/2841	Nimoreny
470	284	4704/2840	Trusheny
470	284	4706/2846	Gidigich
470	284	4707/2848	Gulboka
470	284	4708/2843	Sirets
470	284	4709/2846	Draslicheny
470	285	4700/2850	Kishinev
470	285	4702/2858	Kolonitsa (Bessarabia)
470	285	4709/2856	Grushevo
470	290	4701/2908	Chimisheny
470	290	4704/2908	Balabaneshty
470	290	4708/2900	Bashkany
470	290	4709/2905	Onitskany
470	291	4706/2918	Delakeu
470	291	4706/2911	Korzhevo
470	291	4707/2910	Dubossary
470	291	4709/2918	Grigoriopol
470	292	4705/2921	Pugacheny
470	295	4709/2951	Alexandrovka
470	324	4704/3249	Snigirevka

470	325	4706/3257	Bobrovyy Kut
470	325	4707/3259	Kalininskoye
470	331	4702/3319	Ratndorf
470	341	4700/3410	Rubanovka
470	373	4706/3733	Zhdanov
471	093	4714/0936	Feldkirch
471	093	4717/0939	Rankweil
471	101	4715/1011	Warth
471	110	4718/1104	Telfs
471	112	4716/1124	Innsbruck
471	113	4715/1130	Rinn
471	113	4717/1136	Wattens
471	124	4717/1249	Bruck an der Grossglocknerstra
471	144	4710/1440	Judenburg
471	144	4711/1445	Zeltweg
471	144	4712/1441	Fohnsdorf
471	144	4713/1449	Knittelfeld
471	145	4712/1450	Apfelberg
471	151	4716/1519	Frohnleiten
471	152	4712/1521	Peggau
471	153	4713/1537	Weiz
471	154	4719/1541	Koglhof
471	161	4710/1610	Stegersbach
471	161	4712/1617	Rohrbach an der Teich
471	161	4714/1619	Grosspetersdorf
471	161	4715/1615	Rotenturm an der Pinka
471	161	4717/1612	Oberwart
471	161	4719/1617	Stadtschlaining
471	162	4710/1621	Kohfidisch
471	162	4711/1627	Horvatlovo
471	162	4714/1627	Kisnarda
471	162	4718/1627	Rechnitz
471	163	4712/1639	Gyongyosherman
471	163	4712/1634	Narai
471	163	4714/1635	Olad
471	163	4714/1633	Ondod
471	163	4714/1637	Szombathely
471	163	4715/1637	Kamon
471	163	4717/1639	Sopte
471	163	4718/1635	Perenye
471	163	4719/1634	Pose
471	164	4711/1646	Vasszecseny
471	164	4712/1645	Bardos
471	164	4712/1647	Kenez
471	164	4715/1648	Porpac
471	164	4717/1647	Vat
471	164	4719/1644	Acsad
471	165	4710/1652	Rabakovacsi
471	165	4711/1656	Nyoger
471	165	4712/1654	Ikervar
471	165	4715/1656	Sarvar
471	165	4718/1656	Alsopaty
471	165	4718/1650	Alsoszeleste
471	165	4718/1652	Olbo
471	165	4719/1656	Felsopaty
471	170	4710/1707	Egyhazashetye
471	170	4710/1703	Kald
471	170	4712/1704	Vasarosmiske
471	170	4713/1701	Gerce
471	170	4714/1709	Alsosag
471	170	4715/1709	Celldomolk
471	170	4716/1704	Nagysimonyi
471	170	4717/1707	Kemenesmihalyfa
471	170	4719/1703	Ostffyasszonyfa
471	171	4710/1718	Iszkaz
471	171	4710/1717	Kerta
471	171	4711/1711	Alsosack
471	171	4712/1715	Kispirit
471	171	4712/1714	Nagypirit
471	171	4712/1711	Nemeskocs
471	171	4713/1716	Csogle
471	171	4713/1710	Izsakfa
471	171	4717/1713	Mersevat
471	171	4717/1718	Nemesszalok
471	171	4718/1714	Kulsovat
471	171	4719/1716	Marcalgergelyi
471	171	4719/1716	Szergeny
471	171	4719/1717	Vinar
471	171	4719/1710	Vonock
471	172	4710/1722	Somloszollos
471	172	4711/1728	Noszlop
471	172	4714/1721	Nagyalasony
471	172	4716/1728	Norap
471	172	4717/1726	Daka
471	172	4717/1722	Nyarad
471	172	4719/1726	Borsosgyor
471	173	4710/1733	Magyarpolany
471	173	4712/1738	Farkasgyepu
471	173	4713/1736	Bakonyjako
471	173	4717/1731	Tapolcafo
471	173	4718/1733	Adasztevel
471	173	4718/1736	Homokbodoge
471	173	4719/1736	Ugod
471	174	4711/1741	Csehbanya
471	174	4715/1744	Bakonybel
471	175	4716/1752	Zirc
471	175	4717/1758	Bakonynana
471	175	4717/1754	Nagyesztergar
471	175	4718/1750	Borzavar
471	175	4718/1757	Dudar
471	180	4712/1809	Novak
471	180	4712/1808	Varpalota
471	180	4717/1802	Jasd
471	180	4719/1805	Bakonycsernye
471	180	4719/1800	Cseteny
471	180	4719/1802	Szapar
471	181	4712/1816	Csor

471	181	4712/1811	Inota
471	181	4715/1812	Bakonykuti
471	181	4717/1812	Isztimer
471	181	4718/1816	Fehervarcsurgo
471	181	4719/1814	Bodajk
471	182	4712/1825	Szekesfehervar
471	182	4715/1821	Sarkeresztes
471	182	4718/1820	Magyaralmas
471	182	4719/1825	Zamoly
471	183	4711/1837	Agard
471	183	4712/1839	Gardony
471	183	4714/1837	Sukoro
471	183	4717/1830	Patka
471	183	4718/1833	Lovasbereny
471	183	4719/1837	Vereb
471	184	4714/1841	Kapolnasnyek
471	184	4717/1846	Baracska
471	184	4719/1844	Kajaszo
471	184	4719/1847	Martonvasar
471	185	4710/1857	Rackeve
471	185	4715/1854	Ercsi
471	185	4716/1850	Rackeresztur
471	185	4716/1859	Szigetcsep
471	185	4719/1858	Tokol
471	190	4710/1900	Pereg
471	190	4712/1901	Kiskunlachaza
471	190	4713/1909	Bugyi
471	190	4714/1901	Aporka
471	190	4716/1900	Majoshaza
471	191	4711/1919	Dabas
471	191	4713/1917	Sari
471	191	4718/1914	Ocsa
471	191	4719/1910	Alsonemedi
471	192	4710/1920	Gyon
471	192	4713/1923	Ujhartyan
471	192	4715/1922	Kakucs
471	193	4713/1933	Danszentmiklos
471	193	4714/1937	Irsa
471	193	4715/1937	Albertirsa
471	193	4715/1930	Nyaregyhaza
471	193	4717/1933	Pilis
471	194	4710/1948	Cegled
471	194	4713/1941	Cegledbercel
471	194	4719/1946	Lapos
471	195	4718/1951	Tapioszollos
471	200	4711/2000	Abony
471	200	4712/2001	Szek
471	200	4716/2008	Zagyvarekas
471	200	4718/2005	Ujszasz
471	201	4711/2018	Szajol
471	201	4711/2012	Szolnok
471	201	4713/2019	Tiszapuspoki
471	201	4718/2016	Besenyszog
471	202	4711/2025	Torokszentmiklos
471	202	4716/2027	Nagykoru
471	202	4718/2029	Tiszabo
471	203	4712/2035	Ormenyes
471	203	4716/2032	Fegyvernek
471	204	4713/2046	Kisujszallas
471	204	4715/2041	Kenderes
471	205	4714/2052	Dorogma
471	205	4719/2056	Karcag
471	210	4714/2109	Szerep
471	210	4719/2107	Muszaly
471	210	4719/2107	Puspokladany
471	211	4713/2114	Biharnagybajom
471	211	4714/2119	Bihardancshaza
471	211	4714/2112	Sarretudvari
471	211	4718/2114	Barand
471	211	4719/2118	Tetetlen
471	212	4711/2127	Bakonszeg
471	212	4712/2120	Nagyrabe
471	212	4713/2122	Bihartorda
471	212	4715/2122	Sap
471	212	4718/2122	Foldes
471	213	4710/2137	Mezopeterd
471	213	4712/2139	Vancsod
471	213	4713/2133	Berettyoujfalu
471	213	4714/2137	Szentpeterszeg
471	213	4719/2135	Tepe
471	214	4710/2145	Bedo
471	214	4711/2148	Nagykereki
471	214	4712/2144	Bojt
471	214	4714/2140	Gaborjan
471	214	4715/2142	Hencida
471	214	4717/2147	Esztar
471	214	4717/2149	Pocsaj
471	214	4719/2140	Konyar
471	215	4713/2156	Tamaseu
471	215	4714/2153	Niuved
471	215	4714/2152	Parhida
471	215	4715/2150	Kismarja
471	215	4715/2157	Rosiori Satu Mare
471	220	4712/2208	Fegernic
471	220	4712/2209	Sarcau
471	220	4713/2203	Salard
471	220	4715/2209	Cenalos
471	220	4715/2203	Sintimreu
471	220	4718/2200	Diosig
471	221	4712/2218	Derna
471	221	4712/2218	Sacalasau
471	221	4712/2212	Spinus
471	221	4713/2215	Dernisoara
471	221	4714/2216	Tria
471	221	4715/2211	Sarsig
471	221	4717/2214	Chislaz
471	221	4718/2218	Chiraleu
471	221	4719/2215	Abramut

471	221	4719/2212	Cubulcut
471	222	4712/2225	Cuzap
471	222	4712/2228	Varzari
471	222	4713/2229	Borumlaca
471	222	4713/2226	Varviz
471	222	4713/2224	Voivozi
471	222	4715/2225	Spurcani
471	222	4716/2221	Bogeiu
471	222	4716/2223	Ciutelec
471	222	4716/2220	Tauteu
471	222	4718/2227	Ghida
471	222	4718/2225	Margine
471	222	4719/2223	Abram
471	222	4719/2221	Chiribis
471	222	4719/2224	Cohani
471	222	4719/2226	Suiug
471	223	4710/2239	Drighiu
471	223	4713/2234	Marca
471	223	4714/2239	Ip
471	223	4714/2233	Port
471	223	4715/2234	Lesmir
471	223	4715/2232	Suplacu De Barcau
471	223	4717/2232	Balc
471	223	4717/2234	Sumal
471	223	4718/2237	Camar
471	223	4719/2232	Almasu Mare
471	224	4712/2244	Nusfalau
471	224	4714/2243	Bilghez
471	224	4714/2248	Simleu Silvaniei
471	224	4714/2240	Zauan
471	224	4715/2247	Ceheiu
471	224	4716/2243	Cristelec
471	224	4717/2243	Oroszmezo
471	224	4718/2242	Carastelec
471	224	4719/2243	Doh
471	224	4719/2248	Maeriste
471	225	4710/2254	Crasna
471	225	4711/2251	Ratin
471	225	4712/2256	Virsoli
471	225	4714/2253	Periceiu
471	225	4715/2251	Badacin
471	225	4717/2257	Borla
471	225	4717/2259	Guruslau
471	225	4719/2259	Coseiu
471	225	4719/2251	Lompirt
471	230	4712/2309	Moigrad
471	230	4712/2306	Ortelec
471	230	4712/2300	Panic
471	230	4712/2303	Zalau
471	230	4714/2308	Mirsid
471	230	4715/2308	Firminis
471	230	4717/2305	Doba Mare
471	230	4718/2301	Diosod
471	230	4718/2305	Doba Mica
471	230	4719/2306	Verveghiu
471	231	4710/2314	Jac
471	231	4712/2315	Creaca
471	231	4715/2319	Turbuta
471	231	4716/2312	Cuceu
471	231	4716/2315	Jibou
471	231	4717/2318	Husia
471	231	4719/2316	Somes Odorhei
471	232	4712/2326	Cristolt
471	232	4712/2320	Gilgau
471	232	4713/2321	Tihau
471	232	4715/2324	Cristoltel
471	232	4715/2321	Surduc
471	232	4716/2324	Solona
471	232	4717/2321	Ciocmani
471	232	4718/2324	Babeni
471	232	4719/2325	Cuciulat
471	232	4719/2328	Lozna
471	233	4711/2339	Calna
471	233	4711/2334	Ceaca
471	233	4711/2332	Zalha
471	233	4713/2332	Pintak
471	233	4713/2337	Simisna
471	233	4713/2333	Valea Hranei
471	233	4716/2330	Valea Loznei
471	233	4717/2339	Glod Somes
471	233	4719/2336	Ciumeni
471	234	4711/2340	Bogata De Jos
471	234	4712/2343	Bogata De Sus
471	234	4712/2347	Citcau
471	234	4712/2345	Vad Cluj
471	234	4713/2349	Salisca
471	234	4714/2345	Valea Grosilor
471	234	4716/2343	Dobrocina
471	234	4717/2343	Galgau
471	234	4718/2345	Poiana Blenchii
471	235	4710/2355	Cusdrioara
471	235	4710/2357	Manasturel
471	235	4710/2353	Urisor
471	235	4711/2352	Caseiu
471	235	4712/2350	Coplean
471	235	4714/2353	Rugasesti
471	235	4715/2357	Ciceu Corabia
471	235	4717/2359	Canciu
471	235	4718/2353	Chiuesti
471	240	4710/2404	Branistea
471	240	4710/2406	Malut
471	240	4711/2408	Coldau
471	240	4712/2401	Reteag
471	240	4712/2403	Uriu
471	240	4714/2409	Caianu Mic
471	240	4715/2401	Ciceu Giurgesti
471	240	4716/2403	Negrilesti
471	240	4718/2407	Dobricel

471 240	4718/2409	Spermezeu
471 241	4711/2411	Beclean
471 241	4711/2418	Sintereag
471 241	4713/2413	Sasarm
471 241	4714/2415	Chiuza
471 241	4715/2418	Nimigea De Jos
471 241	4716/2418	Mocod
471 241	4717/2419	Mititei
471 241	4717/2419	Nimigea De Sus
471 242	4710/2421	Blajenii De Jos
471 242	4710/2423	Blajenii De Sus
471 242	4714/2426	Cepari
471 242	4714/2422	Mintiu
471 242	4717/2425	Lusca
471 242	4717/2424	Nasaud
471 242	4717/2426	Rebreanu
471 242	4717/2427	Rebrisoara
471 242	4718/2421	Salva
471 243	4710/2431	Altdorf (Romania)
471 243	4711/2438	Dorolea
471 243	4711/2434	Iad
471 243	4713/2433	Slatinita
471 243	4717/2436	Feldru
471 243	4717/2432	Nepos
471 243	4719/2430	Rebra
471 244	4713/2446	Bistrita Birgaului
471 244	4713/2441	Josenii Birgaului
471 244	4713/2440	Mijlocenii Birgaului
471 244	4713/2444	Prundu Birgaului
471 244	4713/2442	Susenii Birgaului
471 244	4714/2446	Tiha Birgaului
471 244	4719/2440	Ilva Mica
471 244	4719/2445	Lesu
471 245	4714/2450	Muresenii Birgaului
471 252	4714/2520	Neagra Sarului
471 252	4716/2523	Panaci
471 254	4713/2545	Madei
471 262	4712/2622	Tirgu Neamt
471 264	4715/2644	Pascani
471 270	4712/2700	Tirgu Frumos
471 271	4713/2716	Podu Iloaie
471 273	4710/2736	Iasi
471 273	4711/2734	Copou
471 274	4712/2748	Ungeny
471 274	4714/2746	Zagorancha
471 275	4713/2755	Chetyreny
471 280	4710/2800	Kyrneshty
471 280	4710/2809	Selishty
471 280	4711/2806	Vyantory
471 280	4712/2805	Gaureny
471 280	4713/2805	Balaneshty
471 280	4713/2803	Mileshty
471 280	4715/2805	Temeleutsy
471 280	4718/2800	Staryye Redeny
471 281	4710/2814	Choreshty
471 281	4712/2814	Pyrzholteny
471 281	4713/2814	Gorodishche (Moldavia)
471 281	4713/2814	Gorodishche (Bessarabia)
471 281	4714/2812	Peticheni
471 281	4715/2818	Novyye Selishty
471 281	4716/2819	Kalarash
471 281	4716/2819	Nishkany
471 281	4716/2811	Sipoteny
471 282	4711/2827	Bykovets
471 282	4711/2821	Sadova
471 282	4714/2825	Pitushka
471 282	4718/2821	Rechula
471 283	4714/2831	Zubreshty
471 283	4715/2832	Kiriyanka
471 283	4717/2835	Kobylka
471 283	4717/2833	Oneshty
471 283	4718/2833	Tsyganeshty
471 284	4710/2845	Mikautsy
471 284	4712/2844	Zamchozhi
471 284	4714/2849	Mikleshty
471 284	4716/2846	Peresechino
471 284	4716/2843	Teleshovo
471 284	4718/2840	Bezeny
471 285	4710/2857	Zagaykany
471 285	4714/2856	Gertop Mare
471 285	4714/2852	Ishnovets
471 285	4717/2851	Ivancha
471 285	4719/2859	Trebuzheny
471 290	4713/2900	Izbeshty
471 290	4713/2902	Kruglik
471 290	4716/2904	Zhevreny
471 290	4717/2900	Mashkautsy
471 290	4719/2905	Golerkany
471 291	4713/2910	Kriulyany
471 303	4710/3036	Kotovskoye
471 305	4712/3055	Berezovka
471 314	4719/3147	Novaya Odessa
471 325	4718/3251	Bereznegovatoye
471 331	4719/3318	Bolschaja Aleksandrovka
471 351	4716/3514	Mikhaylovka
471 354	4714/3544	Tokmak
471 365	4710/3654	Sachki
471 372	4712/3720	Volodarskoye
471 385	4712/3856	Taganrog
471 394	4715/3945	Rostov
472 093	4726/0939	Lustenau
472 094	4722/0941	Hohenems
472 094	4725/0944	Dornbirn
472 101	4724/1017	Oberstdorf
472 104	4725/1047	Bichlbach
472 104	4729/1044	Breitenwang

472	104	4729/1043	Reutte
472	111	4726/1115	Mittenwald
472	130	4720/1309	Sankt Veit im Pongau
472	134	4723/1341	Schladming
472	135	4727/1359	Oblarn
472	144	4725/1445	Kalwang
472	150	4725/1500	Trofaiach
472	151	4726/1518	Kapfenberg
472	155	4723/1557	Kleinschlag
472	160	4722/1607	Pinkafeld
472	161	4721/1613	Jormannsdorf
472	162	4724/1625	Lockenhaus
472	162	4726/1621	Pilgersdorf
472	162	4726/1625	Piringsdorf
472	162	4727/1622	Unterrabnitz
472	162	4729/1621	Oberrabnitz
472	163	4720/1631	Koszegszerdahely
472	163	4720/1635	Nagycsomote
472	163	4721/1633	Koszegdoroszlo
472	163	4723/1633	Koszeg
472	163	4724/1630	Rattersdorf
472	163	4725/1637	Horvatzsidany
472	163	4725/1639	Kiszsidany
472	163	4725/1630	Liebing
472	163	4727/1630	Oberloisdorf
472	163	4728/1632	Unterpullendorf
472	164	4722/1648	Gor
472	164	4722/1641	Tomord
472	164	4724/1643	Csepreg
472	164	4724/1649	Locs
472	164	4726/1643	Szakony
472	164	4727/1649	Felszopor
472	164	4727/1647	Kereszteny
472	164	4727/1641	Repcevis
472	164	4727/1641	Zsira
472	164	4728/1649	Ujker
472	164	4729/1648	Nemesker
472	164	4729/1644	Sopronhorpacs
472	164	4729/1642	Und
472	164	4729/1646	Volcsej
472	165	4720/1658	Jakfa
472	165	4720/1651	Posfa
472	165	4721/1653	Hegyfalu
472	165	4722/1652	Mesterhaza
472	165	4722/1659	Uraiujfalu
472	165	4723/1655	Nagygeresd
472	165	4723/1653	Porladany
472	165	4724/1653	Nemesladony
472	165	4725/1651	Simasag
472	165	4727/1655	Ivan
472	165	4729/1654	Pusztacsalad
472	170	4721/1704	Csonge
472	170	4723/1705	Kenyeri
472	170	4723/1706	Rabakecsked
472	170	4725/1708	Papoc
472	170	4725/1701	Repcelak
472	170	4726/1707	Rabakecol
472	170	4728/1706	Beled
472	170	4728/1702	Cirak
472	171	4720/1713	Kemenesmagasi
472	171	4721/1718	Kemeneshogyesz
472	171	4722/1718	Magyargencs
472	171	4726/1714	Kemenesszentpeter
472	171	4727/1713	Vag
472	171	4728/1718	Szany
472	172	4720/1724	Asszonyfa
472	172	4720/1722	Mezolak
472	172	4720/1728	Papa
472	172	4722/1722	Nagyacsad
472	172	4724/1722	Nemesgorzsony
472	172	4724/1729	Takacsi
472	172	4726/1722	Marcalto
472	172	4727/1720	Rabaszentandras
472	172	4727/1724	Ujmalomsok
472	172	4728/1727	Csikvand
472	172	4729/1723	Sobor
472	173	4722/1737	Csot
472	173	4723/1735	Vanyola
472	173	4724/1731	Vaszar
472	173	4726/1738	Lovaszpatona
472	173	4727/1732	Gecse
472	173	4728/1730	Gyarmat
472	173	4729/1738	Kajar
472	173	4729/1738	Kispec
472	173	4729/1730	Tetszentkut
472	174	4720/1741	Bakonykoppany
472	174	4721/1746	Fenyofo
472	174	4723/1748	Bakonyszentlaszlo
472	174	4723/1742	Papateszer
472	174	4724/1740	Bakonyszentivan
472	174	4725/1748	Bakonygyirot
472	174	4725/1744	Bakonytamasi
472	174	4726/1741	Nagydem
472	174	4727/1748	Romand
472	175	4721/1756	Bakonyoszlop
472	175	4721/1753	Csesznek
472	175	4722/1753	Bakonyszentkiraly
472	175	4722/1759	Csatka
472	175	4723/1752	Keresztur
472	175	4726/1755	Rede
472	175	4726/1751	Sikator
472	175	4726/1750	Veszpremvarsany
472	175	4728/1754	Bakonybank
472	175	4728/1758	Bakonyszombathely
472	175	4728/1750	Lazi
472	180	4722/1807	Nagyveleg
472	180	4722/1802	Sur
472	180	4724/1801	Acsteszer

472	180	4724/1804	Aka
472	180	4726/1807	Felsodobos
472	181	4721/1816	Csokako
472	181	4723/1812	Mor
472	181	4726/1814	Pusztavam
472	181	4729/1819	Oroszlany
472	182	4721/1820	Csakbereny
472	182	4724/1827	Csakvar
472	183	4724/1838	Tabajd
472	183	4726/1836	Alcsut
472	183	4726/1832	Vertesboglar
472	183	4727/1833	Bodmer
472	183	4727/1835	Felcsut
472	183	4729/1838	Bicske
472	183	4729/1831	Szar
472	184	4721/1845	Tordas
472	184	4722/1841	Val
472	184	4723/1844	Gyuro
472	184	4724/1847	Pusztazamor
472	184	4727/1845	Etyek
472	184	4728/1849	Bia
472	184	4728/1849	Torbagy
472	185	4720/1856	Szazhalombatta
472	185	4722/1856	Erd
472	185	4722/1851	Tarnok
472	185	4724/1859	Nagyteteny
472	185	4726/1855	Torokbalint
472	185	4727/1858	Budaors
472	190	4720/1905	Taksony
472	190	4721/1905	Dunaharaszti
472	190	4721/1903	Szigetszentmiklos
472	190	4724/1907	Soroksar
472	190	4725/1901	Budatateny
472	190	4725/1905	Csepel
472	190	4726/1903	Budafok
472	190	4726/1907	Pesterzsebet
472	190	4727/1902	Albertfalva
472	190	4727/1908	Kispest
472	191	4724/1912	Pestimre
472	191	4724/1917	Vecses
472	191	4726/1912	Pestlorinc
472	191	4728/1914	Rakoshegy
472	191	4729/1917	Rakoscsaba
472	191	4729/1915	Rakoskeresztur
472	191	4729/1916	Rakosliget
472	192	4721/1927	Monor
472	192	4723/1925	Peteri
472	192	4723/1921	Ullo
472	192	4725/1924	Gyomro
472	192	4725/1927	Mende
472	192	4727/1920	Ecser
472	192	4727/1922	Maglod
472	192	4729/1921	Pecel
472	193	4721/1933	Benye
472	193	4721/1938	Pand
472	193	4724/1937	Tapiosag
472	193	4725/1932	Uri
472	193	4727/1930	Tapiosap
472	193	4727/1933	Tapiosuly
472	193	4727/1936	Tapioszecso
472	193	4729/1935	Koka
472	194	4720/1945	Tapioszentmarton
472	194	4722/1941	Tapiobicske
472	194	4725/1945	Nagykata
472	194	4727/1942	Szentmartonkata
472	195	4720/1957	Tapiogyorgye
472	195	4720/1953	Tapioszele
472	195	4722/1951	Farmos
472	200	4722/2006	Jaszalsoszentgyorgy
472	200	4723/2004	Janoshida
472	200	4726/2003	Alattyan
472	200	4729/2000	Jasztelek
472	201	4722/2010	Jaszladany
472	201	4727/2013	Jaszkiser
472	202	4720/2027	Kotelek
472	202	4723/2024	Tiszasuly
472	202	4724/2027	Tiszaroff
472	202	4727/2028	Tiszabura
472	202	4729/2029	Kanyar
472	202	4729/2021	Pely
472	203	4722/2038	Kunhegyes
472	203	4729/2039	Tiszaabadszalok
472	204	4726/2048	Kunmadaras
472	204	4729/2044	Tiszaszentimre
472	205	4729/2056	Nagyivan
472	211	4721/2117	Kaba
472	211	4725/2110	Nadudvar
472	212	4723/2129	Hajduszovat
472	212	4727/2124	Hajduszoboszlo
472	213	4721/2134	Derecske
472	213	4724/2138	Sarand
472	213	4727/2138	Mikepercs
472	214	4724/2140	Hajdubagos
472	214	4724/2145	Hosszupalyi
472	214	4724/2147	Monostorpalyi
472	215	4723/2154	Nagyleta
472	215	4723/2152	Vertes
472	215	4724/2157	Kokad
472	215	4725/2159	Almosd
472	215	4728/2153	Ujleta
472	220	4720/2205	Cadea
472	220	4720/2203	Ciocaia
472	220	4721/2206	Sacueni
472	220	4723/2208	Cherechiu
472	220	4726/2207	Chesereu
472	220	4726/2203	Silindru
472	220	4727/2200	Bagamer
472	220	4729/2206	Simian

472	221	4720/2218	Petreu
472	221	4721/2214	Crestur
472	221	4721/2211	Olosig
472	221	4724/2216	Buduslau
472	221	4726/2211	Adoni
472	221	4726/2214	Otomani
472	221	4727/2211	Tarcea
472	221	4728/2219	Salacea
472	221	4729/2213	Galospetreu
472	222	4721/2228	Dijir
472	222	4721/2220	Marghita
472	222	4723/2227	Patal
472	222	4725/2221	Chet
472	222	4728/2222	Pir
472	222	4728/2229	Sauca
472	223	4723/2236	Cehal
472	223	4725/2234	Cehalut
472	223	4727/2231	Cean
472	223	4729/2237	Sarauad
472	223	4729/2235	Tasnad
472	224	4722/2241	Zalnoc
472	224	4723/2246	Bobota
472	224	4723/2248	Dersida
472	224	4726/2248	Giorocuta
472	224	4726/2246	Supuru De Sus
472	224	4728/2241	Chegea
472	224	4728/2248	Supuru De Jos
472	224	4729/2241	Sacaseni
472	225	4721/2257	Samsud
472	225	4721/2250	Sarmasag
472	225	4723/2253	Chiesd
472	225	4723/2258	Ser
472	225	4725/2256	Bogdand
472	225	4728/2256	Babta
472	230	4720/2302	Chilioara
472	230	4721/2301	Archid
472	230	4721/2306	Mineu
472	230	4722/2308	Salatig
472	230	4723/2304	Leleiu
472	230	4724/2302	Hodod
472	230	4726/2308	Motis
472	230	4727/2308	Oarta De Jos
472	230	4728/2302	Bicai
472	230	4728/2304	Oarta De Sus
472	230	4729/2309	Basesti
472	231	4720/2311	Domnin
472	231	4720/2318	Tranis
472	231	4721/2311	Deja
472	231	4722/2319	Napradea
472	231	4722/2313	Notig
472	231	4723/2310	Nadis
472	231	4723/2317	Szamosseplak
472	231	4725/2318	Benesat
472	231	4725/2315	Biusa
472	231	4725/2311	Cehu Silvaniei
472	231	4726/2318	Ticau
472	231	4726/2311	Ulciug
472	231	4727/2316	Arduzel
472	231	4727/2319	Chelinta
472	231	4728/2318	Ulmeni Salj
472	231	4729/2316	Minau
472	232	4720/2327	Letca
472	232	4720/2323	Soimuseni
472	232	4721/2325	Ciula
472	232	4721/2329	Lemniu
472	232	4723/2320	Cheud
472	232	4723/2327	Varaiu
472	232	4724/2324	Fericea
472	232	4725/2328	Durusa
472	232	4727/2326	Stejera
472	232	4728/2329	Buciumi Satu Mare
472	232	4728/2329	Buciumi
472	232	4729/2324	Iadara
472	233	4720/2338	Ileanda
472	233	4720/2336	Rogna
472	233	4721/2334	Perii Vadului
472	233	4722/2332	Rastoci
472	233	4724/2335	Boiu Mare
472	233	4729/2331	Ciolt
472	234	4720/2349	Gostila
472	234	4721/2345	Baba
472	234	4722/2349	Dealu Mare
472	234	4723/2343	Vima Mare
472	234	4724/2343	Vima Mica
472	234	4725/2344	Peteritea
472	234	4725/2340	Salnita
472	234	4727/2347	Razoare
472	234	4729/2348	Cufoaia
472	235	4724/2351	Rohia
472	235	4725/2350	Poiana Porcului
472	235	4727/2355	Damacuseni
472	235	4727/2359	Suciu De Jos
472	235	4727/2352	Tirgu Lapus
472	235	4729/2351	Borcut
472	240	4721/2404	Breaza Somes
472	240	4724/2409	Agries
472	240	4726/2402	Suciu De Sus
472	240	4729/2401	Olahlapos
472	241	4720/2417	Zagra
472	241	4723/2411	Tirlisua
472	242	4722/2424	Cosbuc
472	242	4726/2424	Telciu
472	243	4724/2433	Parva
472	244	4721/2444	Poiana Ilvei
472	244	4722/2441	Singeorz Bai
472	244	4723/2448	Magura Ilvei
472	244	4724/2445	Maieru
472	244	4725/2449	Rodna

472 245	4722/2454	Ilva Mare
472 245	4727/2454	Sant
472 245	4727/2454	Ujradna
472 251	4721/2515	Dorna Cindrenilor
472 251	4726/2519	Iacobeni
472 252	4721/2522	Vatra Dornei
472 254	4725/2549	Negrileasa
472 254	4728/2546	Stulpicani
472 260	4723/2606	Slatioara
472 260	4727/2601	Draceni
472 260	4729/2607	Baisesti
472 260	4729/2601	Miron
472 261	4727/2618	Falticeni
472 262	4724/2625	Mesteceni
472 262	4729/2620	Tarna Mare
472 263	4720/2631	Iorcani
472 264	4721/2640	Heci
472 265	4726/2654	Hirlau
472 272	4720/2728	Tiganasi
472 273	4720/2737	Skulyany
472 273	4725/2735	Unteny
472 273	4727/2736	Lukacheny
472 273	4728/2735	Valya Rusuluy
472 274	4724/2748	Bushila
472 274	4724/2742	Novyye Choropkany
472 274	4724/2743	Staryye Choropkany
472 274	4725/2743	Stolnicheny
472 274	4728/2744	Skumpiya
472 275	4720/2753	Pyrlitsa
472 275	4724/2757	Teshkureny
472 275	4725/2753	Staryye Negureny
472 275	4726/2756	Kosheny
472 275	4727/2754	Tsygira
472 275	4729/2750	Novaya Chelakovka
472 275	4729/2752	Staraya Chelakovka
472 280	4722/2800	Korneshty
472 280	4724/2809	Napadeny
472 280	4724/2803	Sineshty
472 280	4725/2806	Kondrateshty
472 280	4728/2803	Bobletichi
472 281	4720/2819	Gerbovets
472 281	4720/2812	Palanka
472 281	4722/2819	Godzhineshty
472 281	4722/2819	Onishkany
472 281	4723/2815	Derenev
472 281	4724/2811	Kornovo
472 281	4724/2813	Redeny
472 281	4725/2816	Girovo
472 281	4726/2817	Girisheny
472 281	4727/2811	Kuchoya
472 282	4722/2827	Bravicha
472 282	4722/2823	Melesheny
472 282	4722/2822	Tsibirika
472 282	4725/2826	Bogzeshty
472 282	4726/2824	Krasnosheny
472 282	4727/2826	Vasiyeny
472 282	4729/2826	Leusheny
472 283	4721/2837	Vatich
472 283	4722/2836	Dyshkovo
472 283	4722/2832	Getlovo
472 283	4722/2830	Saseni
472 283	4723/2839	Morozeny
472 283	4723/2835	Putsuntei
472 283	4723/2834	Vyprovo
472 283	4725/2839	Bryanovo
472 283	4726/2839	Bravicheny
472 283	4729/2837	Chekolteny
472 283	4729/2831	Korobcheny
472 284	4722/2843	Isakovo
472 284	4722/2849	Orgeyev
472 284	4722/2849	Vascauti Soroca
472 284	4729/2844	Kokorozeny
472 285	4720/2856	Furcheny
472 285	4725/2859	Susleny
472 285	4726/2856	Berezlozhi
472 285	4728/2859	Bulayeshty
472 290	4721/2907	Malovata
472 290	4723/2907	Oksentiya
472 290	4726/2905	Vyshkautsy
472 290	4728/2906	Nizhniye Zhory
472 290	4728/2906	Sredniye Zhory
472 290	4729/2904	Verkhniye Zhory
472 295	4720/2951	Zatishye
472 310	4725/3100	Mostovoye
472 311	4721/3114	Veselinovo
472 311	4726/3111	Sukhaya Balka Pervyy Uchastok
472 321	4724/3219	Plyushchevka
472 350	4724/3501	Zlatopol
472 352	4724/3522	Zelenyy Gay
472 370	4723/3704	Rozovka
473 073	4735/0738	Weil am Rhein
473 073	4738/0736	Eimeldingen
473 073	4738/0735	Markt
473 073	4739/0734	Kirchen
473 074	4733/0740	Grenzach
473 074	4737/0740	Lorrach
473 074	4738/0744	Wehr
473 074	4739/0749	Schopfheim
473 081	4737/0813	Waldshut
473 081	4738/0816	Tiengen
473 092	4739/0929	Friedrichshafen
473 093	4737/0934	Oberdorf
473 094	4730/0946	Bregenz
473 094	4733/0941	Lindau
473 094	4734/0940	Bodolz
473 094	4734/0941	Hoyren
473 095	4735/0951	Scheidegg

473	095	4735/0955	Weiler in Allgau
473	101	4736/1014	Gnadenberg
473	110	4730/1106	Garmisch Partenkirchen
473	110	4736/1104	Oberammergau
473	130	4738/1300	Berchtesgaden
473	131	4734/1319	Unterberg
473	133	4733/1339	Hallstatt
473	134	4733/1341	Obertraun
473	140	4732/1406	Stainach
473	141	4734/1414	Liezen
473	142	4734/1427	Admont
473	142	4735/1423	Frauenberg
473	142	4739/1420	Spital am Pyhrn
473	145	4732/1453	Eisenerz
473	152	4733/1520	Turnau
473	153	4731/1530	Wartberg
473	153	4736/1538	Honigsberg
473	154	4736/1541	Murzzuschlag
473	154	4736/1545	Spital am Semmering
473	154	4738/1549	Semmering
473	160	4733/1605	Aspang Markt
473	160	4739/1608	Scheiblingkirchen
473	161	4731/1611	Krumbach Markt
473	161	4737/1617	Wiesmath
473	161	4739/1617	Hochwolkersdorf
473	162	4731/1624	Drassmarkt
473	162	4731/1628	Stoob
473	162	4731/1622	Weingraben
473	162	4732/1624	Kaisersdorf
473	162	4732/1626	Neutal
473	162	4735/1628	Lackenbach
473	162	4736/1624	Kobersdorf
473	162	4737/1623	Oberpetersdorf
473	163	4730/1631	Oberpullendorf
473	163	4731/1634	Nebersdorf
473	163	4732/1633	Grosswarasdorf
473	163	4732/1635	Kleinwarasdorf
473	163	4732/1638	Kroatisch Minihof
473	163	4734/1630	Unterfrauenhaid
473	163	4735/1633	Horitschon
473	163	4736/1638	Deutschkreutz
473	163	4738/1636	Magyarfalva
473	164	4730/1647	Lovo
473	164	4732/1640	Nikitsch
473	164	4733/1645	Sopronkovesd
473	164	4736/1642	Nagycenk
473	164	4736/1644	Pereszteg
473	164	4736/1645	Sopronszecseny
473	164	4739/1640	Balf
473	165	4731/1655	Csapod
473	165	4733/1650	Rojtokmuzsaj
473	165	4735/1653	Fertoszentmiklos
473	165	4735/1652	Szerdahely
473	165	4735/1659	Vitnyed
473	165	4736/1655	Fertoendred
473	165	4736/1654	Petohaza
473	165	4737/1650	Fertoszeplak
473	170	4730/1701	Gyoro
473	170	4731/1701	Himod
473	170	4734/1705	Babot
473	170	4736/1702	Kapuvar
473	170	4736/1707	Szarfold
473	170	4736/1705	Veszkeny
473	170	4738/1705	Osli
473	171	4730/1714	Szil
473	171	4731/1710	Magyarkeresztur
473	171	4732/1718	Rabacsanak
473	171	4733/1711	Potyond
473	171	4733/1716	Szilsarkany
473	171	4734/1711	Bogyoszlo
473	171	4735/1712	Jobahaza
473	171	4735/1710	Rabatamasi
473	171	4736/1718	Dor
473	171	4736/1712	Farad
473	171	4737/1715	Csorna
473	171	4737/1712	Kovecses
473	172	4731/1721	Egyed
473	172	4731/1725	Morichida
473	172	4734/1720	Rabapordany
473	172	4735/1726	Rabacsecseny
473	172	4738/1722	Kony
473	172	4738/1729	Rabapatona
473	172	4739/1725	Enese
473	173	4730/1734	Gyomore
473	173	4731/1736	Felpec
473	173	4731/1731	Tet
473	173	4733/1734	Gyorszemere
473	173	4736/1737	Kisbarathegy
473	173	4736/1732	Koronco
473	173	4738/1735	Gyirmot
473	174	4730/1748	Gyorasszonyfa
473	174	4731/1745	Ravazd
473	174	4733/1745	Gyorszentmarton
473	174	4734/1745	Gyorsag
473	174	4734/1747	Pazmandfalu
473	174	4734/1746	Pazmandhegy
473	174	4737/1748	Per
473	175	4730/1751	Tapszentmiklos
473	175	4731/1756	Kerekteleki
473	175	4731/1750	Tap
473	175	4734/1753	Mezoors
473	175	4738/1759	Babolna
473	175	4739/1755	Bana
473	175	4739/1752	Bonyretalap
473	180	4730/1809	Csaszar
473	180	4730/1802	Kisber
473	180	4731/1800	Aszar
473	180	4732/1804	Ete

473	180	4735/1804	Csep
473	180	4735/1800	Tarkany
473	180	4738/1805	Nagyigmand
473	180	4739/1806	Kisigmand
473	181	4731/1814	Dad
473	181	4732/1811	Szak
473	181	4733/1816	Komlod
473	181	4733/1810	Szend
473	181	4736/1813	Kocs
473	181	4739/1819	Tata
473	182	4731/1822	Vertessomlo
473	182	4733/1827	Felsogalla
473	182	4733/1820	Kornye
473	182	4734/1824	Alsogalla
473	182	4734/1823	Banhida
473	182	4734/1825	Tatabanya
473	182	4737/1823	Vertesszollos
473	182	4739/1822	Baj
473	182	4739/1820	Tovaros
473	183	4731/1837	Csabdi
473	183	4737/1831	Tarjan
473	183	4739/1836	Bajna
473	183	4739/1831	Hereg
473	184	4733/1843	Zsambek
473	184	4735/1840	Szomor
473	184	4736/1846	Perbal
473	184	4737/1847	Tinnye
473	184	4738/1844	Uny
473	185	4731/1856	Budakeszi
473	185	4731/1850	Paty
473	185	4734/1858	Pesthidegkut
473	185	4735/1853	Nagykovacsi
473	185	4735/1856	Solymar
473	185	4737/1850	Piliscsaba
473	185	4737/1854	Pilisszentivan
473	185	4737/1855	Pilisvorosvar
473	185	4738/1858	Csobanka
473	190	4730/1905	Budapest
473	190	4732/1907	Pestujhely
473	190	4734/1908	Rakospalota
473	190	4734/1905	Ujpest
473	190	4736/1903	Bekasmegyer
473	190	4737/1903	Budakalasz
473	190	4737/1900	Pilisborosjeno
473	190	4738/1909	Alag
473	190	4738/1908	Dunakeszi
473	190	4739/1902	Pomaz
473	191	4731/1914	Cinkota
473	191	4732/1916	Kistarcsa
473	191	4732/1910	Rakosszentmihaly
473	191	4733/1914	Csomor
473	191	4734/1917	Kerepes
473	191	4736/1915	Mogyorod
473	191	4737/1912	Fot
473	191	4738/1919	Szada
473	191	4739/1917	Veresegyhaz
473	192	4732/1924	Isaszeg
473	192	4736/1922	Godollo
473	192	4738/1925	Egerszeg
473	192	4739/1926	Domony
473	193	4731/1933	Dany
473	193	4733/1937	Zsambok
473	193	4734/1931	Valko
473	193	4735/1932	Vacszentlaszlo
473	193	4737/1934	Galgaheviz
473	193	4737/1936	Tura
473	193	4738/1931	Hevizgyork
473	193	4739/1930	Aszod
473	194	4730/1948	Jaszfelsoszentgyorgy
473	194	4731/1945	Szentlorinckata
473	194	4731/1940	Toalmas
473	194	4733/1948	Pusztamonostor
473	194	4734/1943	Jaszfenyszaru
473	194	4736/1942	Boldog
473	195	4730/1955	Jaszbereny
473	195	4738/1959	Jaszarokszallas
473	195	4739/1950	Csany
473	200	4731/2009	Jaszapati
473	200	4731/2000	Jaszjakohalma
473	200	4734/2001	Jaszdozsa
473	200	4736/2003	Tarnaors
473	200	4737/2005	Erk
473	201	4735/2011	Jaszszentandras
473	201	4736/2017	Heves
473	201	4738/2012	Boconad
473	201	4739/2010	Tarnamera
473	202	4732/2023	Tarnaszentmiklos
473	202	4737/2022	Atany
473	202	4739/2021	Tenk
473	203	4730/2030	Kiskore
473	203	4731/2039	Tiszaderzs
473	203	4734/2032	Tiszanana
473	203	4735/2036	Sarud
473	203	4738/2036	Ujlorincfalva
473	204	4732/2048	Tiszaigar
473	204	4734/2044	Tiszaszollos
473	204	4737/2046	Tiszafured
473	204	4739/2040	Poroszlo
473	205	4731/2050	Tiszaors
473	205	4738/2054	Egyek
473	212	4737/2121	Balmazujvaros
473	213	4732/2138	Debrecen
473	213	4735/2130	Macs
473	213	4736/2134	Jozsa
473	214	4731/2145	Fancsika
473	214	4736/2146	Hajdusamson
473	215	4732/2154	Vamospercs
473	215	4735/2154	Nyirmartonfalva

473	215	4736/2159	Nyiracsad
473	220	4731/2209	Valea Lui Mihai
473	220	4732/2200	Budaabrany
473	220	4733/2202	Nyirabrany
473	220	4738/2209	Peneszlek
473	221	4731/2216	Vasad
473	221	4733/2212	Curtuiuseni
473	221	4735/2218	Piscolt
473	221	4736/2219	Resighea
473	222	4730/2227	Chereusa
473	222	4731/2221	Andrid
473	222	4732/2223	Dindesti
473	222	4732/2227	Sudurau
473	222	4733/2224	Irina
473	222	4734/2225	Portita
473	222	4735/2226	Vezendiu
473	222	4738/2220	Sanislau
473	222	4739/2220	Ciumesti
473	222	4739/2224	Marna Noua
473	223	4731/2231	Santau
473	223	4731/2234	Tasnadu Nou
473	223	4732/2238	Cig
473	223	4734/2233	Cauas
473	223	4738/2232	Ghenci
473	224	4732/2247	Acis
473	224	4734/2247	Giungi
473	224	4735/2244	Teghea
473	224	4736/2248	Ghirisa
473	224	4737/2242	Craidorol
473	225	4731/2258	Stina
473	225	4732/2255	Bolda
473	225	4733/2251	Beltiug
473	225	4734/2257	Socond
473	225	4735/2259	Hodisa
473	225	4735/2253	Szakasz
473	225	4736/2256	Gerausa
473	225	4738/2253	Ardud
473	230	4731/2306	Odesti
473	230	4731/2300	Soconzel
473	230	4732/2309	Baita (Satu Mare)
473	230	4732/2300	Cuta
473	230	4736/2300	Medisa
473	230	4736/2303	Solduba
473	231	4730/2314	Arinis
473	231	4732/2318	Salsig
473	231	4733/2319	Girdani
473	231	4736/2313	Birsau De Sus
473	231	4739/2316	Iegheriste
473	232	4730/2320	Miresu Mare
473	232	4731/2328	Somcuta Mare
473	232	4732/2323	Fersig
473	232	4733/2321	Danestii Chioarului
473	232	4734/2322	Pribilesti
473	232	4734/2326	Satulung
473	232	4735/2320	Farcasa
473	232	4735/2325	Hideaga
473	232	4735/2324	Mogosesti
473	232	4736/2326	Pusztahidegkut
473	232	4736/2322	Tamaia
473	232	4737/2324	Coltirea
473	232	4737/2329	Lapusel
473	232	4738/2327	Bozinta Mare
473	232	4739/2322	Ardusat
473	232	4739/2325	Busag
473	233	4730/2332	Berchezoaia
473	233	4731/2330	Berchez
473	233	4731/2339	Copalnic
473	233	4732/2335	Coas
473	233	4732/2333	Remetea Chioarului
473	233	4734/2336	Coruia
473	233	4734/2333	Culcea
473	233	4735/2336	Chechis
473	233	4735/2334	Sacalaseni
473	233	4736/2331	Coltau
473	233	4737/2332	Mocira
473	233	4737/2334	Satu Nou De Jos
473	233	4739/2330	Sasar
473	233	4739/2339	Tautii De Sus
473	234	4730/2341	Copalnic Manastur
473	234	4731/2345	Cernesti
473	234	4732/2344	Laschia
473	234	4733/2341	Berinta
473	234	4733/2348	Ciocotis
473	234	4734/2345	Fauresti
473	234	4735/2346	Plopis
473	234	4736/2345	Cetatele
473	234	4736/2342	Sindresti
473	234	4737/2344	Bontaieni
473	234	4738/2345	Negreia
473	235	4733/2356	Cupseni
473	235	4736/2359	Strimbu Baiut
473	240	4730/2401	Lapus
473	240	4737/2400	Baiut
473	242	4732/2426	Romuli
473	242	4738/2426	Sacel
473	242	4739/2421	Salistea De Sus
473	243	4739/2433	Moiseiu
473	244	4739/2440	Borsa Maramures
473	250	4734/2508	Cirlibaba Noua
473	250	4735/2508	Cirlibaba
473	252	4731/2527	Pojorita
473	252	4732/2524	Fundu Moldovei
473	252	4737/2520	Breaza
473	253	4732/2534	Cimpulung Moldovenesc
473	253	4737/2539	Frumosu
473	253	4739/2534	Vatra Moldovitei
473	254	4732/2548	Frasin
473	254	4733/2549	Bucsitura

473	254	4734/2541	Vama (Bucovina)
473	254	4739/2546	Poiana Miculvi
473	255	4732/2559	Capu Codrului
473	255	4733/2554	Gura Humorului
473	255	4733/2557	Paltinoasa
473	255	4738/2554	Cacica
473	255	4738/2558	Partestii De Jos
473	255	4739/2555	Partestii De Sus
473	260	4730/2605	Braesti
473	260	4730/2600	Capu Cimpului
473	260	4732/2602	Berchisesti
473	260	4733/2605	Dragoesti
473	260	4734/2608	Vorniceni
473	260	4735/2609	Zaharesti
473	260	4736/2603	Ilisesti
473	260	4738/2603	Balaceana
473	261	4737/2618	Tisauti
473	261	4738/2613	Sfintu Ilie
473	261	4738/2615	Suceava
473	262	4734/2621	Plavalar
473	262	4738/2629	Corocaesti
473	263	4732/2632	Liteni
473	272	4730/2727	Solonet
473	272	4732/2726	Bivolari
473	272	4734/2729	Kalineshty
473	272	4737/2727	Viishora
473	272	4739/2720	Tompeshti Vek
473	273	4731/2739	Mustyatsa
473	273	4736/2733	Navyrnets
473	274	4730/2748	Novaya Sarata
473	274	4731/2744	Staraya Sarata
473	274	4732/2740	Novyye Sochi
473	274	4734/2742	Faleshty
473	274	4737/2741	Pynzareny
473	274	4738/2743	Yelenovka
473	275	4736/2753	Glinzheny (Balti)
473	275	4739/2757	Pompa
473	280	4730/2804	Flamynzeny
473	280	4733/2802	Lazo
473	280	4735/2809	Brezheny
473	280	4738/2809	Lazovsk
473	280	4739/2803	Staryye Bilicheny
473	281	4730/2817	Myndreshty
473	281	4732/2812	Zgordeshty
473	281	4737/2814	Kopacheny
473	282	4730/2824	Ineshty
473	282	4730/2822	Teleneshty
473	282	4732/2828	Verezheny
473	282	4734/2823	Baneshty
473	282	4735/2820	Prepelitsa
473	282	4737/2828	Kazaneshty
473	282	4738/2821	Pepeny
473	282	4739/2829	Staryye Brynzeny
473	283	4732/2833	Staryye Sarateny
473	283	4734/2834	Tsyntsareni
473	283	4736/2835	Indarepnish
473	283	4736/2830	Staryye Kitskany
473	283	4738/2839	Skortseny
473	284	4732/2847	Sirota
473	284	4734/2840	Kishtelnitsa
473	284	4735/2848	Bushovka
473	284	4737/2845	Giduleny
473	284	4737/2849	Kuyzovka
473	285	4730/2852	Chegoreny
473	285	4730/2853	Khodorozha
473	285	4731/2852	Biyeshty
473	285	4731/2850	Kipercheny
473	285	4733/2858	Izvory
473	285	4733/2855	Pogrebeny
473	285	4733/2852	Vorotets
473	290	4730/2902	Lopatna
473	290	4733/2901	Stodolna
473	290	4734/2901	Lalovo
473	292	4732/2927	Krasnyye Okny
473	295	4732/2955	Dolinskoye
473	305	4738/3059	Domanevka
473	312	4733/3120	Voznesensk
473	323	4733/3230	Novopoltavka
473	341	4733/3414	Kapulovka
473	342	4734/3424	Kamenka Dneprovskaja
473	342	4734/3424	Nikopol
473	343	4739/3435	Gorodishche (Dnepropetrovsk)
473	363	4737/3634	Krasnoselka
473	364	4730/3646	Gorkiy
473	364	4734/3645	Sladkovodnoye
473	365	4731/3650	Proletarskiy
473	365	4733/3656	Novgorod
473	365	4733/3651	Zelenopolye
473	365	4735/3650	Nadezhnaya
474	073	4740/0734	Efringen
474	073	4748/0738	Mullheim
474	074	4748/0741	Badenweiler
474	074	4749/0745	Bad Sulzburg
474	075	4741/0751	Hausen
474	080	4746/0808	Sankt Blasien
474	081	4740/0810	Waldkirch
474	081	4740/0814	Weilheim
474	082	4744/0826	Stuhlingen
474	084	4740/0847	Elmendshofen
474	084	4742/0845	Gailingen
474	084	4743/0845	Randegg
474	084	4746/0847	Hilzingen
474	085	4741/0854	Schienen
474	085	4744/0858	Radolfzell
474	085	4744/0852	Worblingen
474	085	4746/0850	Singen
474	090	4742/0900	Horn (Germany)

474	091	4740/0911	Konstanz	474	163	4741/1633	Kertvaros
474	091	4742/0916	Meersburg	474	163	4741/1636	Sopron
474	091	4744/0919	Ahausen	474	163	4743/1630	Schattendorf
474	091	4746/0910	Uberlingen	474	164	4745/1648	Illmitz
474	093	4745/0934	Oberzell	474	165	4742/1655	Pamhagen
474	093	4746/0936	Weissenau	474	165	4745/1650	Apetlon
474	093	4747/0937	Ravensburg	474	165	4746/1659	Tadten
474	095	4741/0950	Wangen	474	170	4746/1702	Andau
474	101	4743/1019	Kempten	474	170	4747/1708	Mosonszentjanos
474	105	4749/1054	Schongau	474	170	4747/1709	Mosonszentpeter
474	111	4741/1112	Murnau	474	170	4747/1707	Pusztasomorja
474	111	4742/1118	Polten	474	171	4741/1715	Bosarkany
474	112	4740/1122	Kochel	474	172	4740/1724	Bezi
474	112	4745/1123	Penzberg	474	172	4742/1722	Gyorsovenyhaz
474	113	4746/1134	Bad Tolz	474	172	4744/1723	Lebeny
474	114	4745/1146	Ostin	474	172	4744/1726	Mosonszentmiklos
474	114	4747/1141	Schaftlach	474	172	4744/1729	Otteveny
474	115	4743/1157	Fischbachau	474	172	4749/1722	Horvatkimle
474	120	4740/1201	Bayrischzell	474	173	4741/1738	Gyor
474	120	4746/1209	Neubeuern	474	173	4742/1733	Abda
474	121	4747/1212	Lauberg	474	173	4743/1737	Gyorujfalu
474	123	4746/1239	Ruhpolding	474	173	4744/1735	Gyorzamoly
474	123	4748/1238	Eisenarzt	474	173	4744/1731	Kunsziget
474	125	4744/1253	Bad Reichenhall	474	173	4745/1739	Alsovamos
474	130	4741/1306	Hallein	474	173	4746/1731	Bolganymajor
474	130	4747/1305	Aigen	474	173	4746/1733	Dunaszeg
474	130	4748/1305	Gnigl	474	173	4746/1739	Gyorszabadi
474	130	4748/1302	Maxglan	474	174	4742/1744	Gyorszentivan
474	130	4748/1302	Salzburg	474	174	4743/1740	Bacsa
474	133	4743/1337	Bad Ischl	474	174	4746/1742	Nagybajcs
474	142	4743/1420	Windischgarsten	474	175	4748/1756	Okolicna Na Ostrove
474	155	4740/1557	Enzenreith	474	175	4748/1752	Zemianska Olca
474	155	4740/1556	Gloggnitz	474	180	4742/1801	Acs
474	155	4741/1551	Payerbach	474	180	4744/1807	Komarom
474	155	4742/1550	Reichenau	474	180	4746/1808	Komarno
474	155	4747/1554	Puchberg am Schneeberg	474	181	4740/1811	Mocsa
				474	181	4742/1816	Naszaly
474	160	4741/1608	Seebenstein	474	181	4744/1810	Szony
474	160	4743/1605	Neunkirchen (Austria)	474	181	4747/1817	Kratke Kesy
474	160	4746/1603	Hettmannsdorf	474	182	4740/1827	Tardosbanya
474	161	4743/1611	Pitten	-474	182	4741/1821	Szomod
474	161	4743/1614	Walpersbach	474	182	4744/1820	Dunaalmas
474	161	4744/1614	Lanzenkirchen	474	182	4744/1822	Neszmely
474	161	4747/1617	Neudorfl	474	182	4745/1829	Piszke
474	161	4748/1615	Wiener Neustadt	474	182	4745/1827	Sutto
474	162	4743/1620	Neustift an der Rosalia	474	182	4746/1825	Moca
474	162	4744/1629	Drassburg	474	183	4741/1836	Nagysap
474	162	4744/1624	Mattersburg	474	183	4744/1834	Bajot
474	162	4746/1629	Antau	474	183	4745/1830	Labatlan
474	162	4746/1620	Sauerbrunn	474	183	4746/1833	Nyergesujfalu
474	162	4746/1628	Stottera	474	184	4741/1841	Sarisap
474	162	4747/1623	Sigless	474	184	4742/1843	Csolnok
474	162	4748/1623	Pottsching	474	184	4743/1844	Dorog
474	163	4741/1631	Agfalva	474	184	4743/1848	Kesztolc

474	184	4743/1840	Tokod
474	184	4748/1845	Esztergom
474	184	4748/1844	Nana
474	185	4740/1854	Pilisszanto
474	185	4746/1855	Domos
474	185	4747/1858	Nagymaros
474	185	4747/1853	Pilismarot
474	185	4748/1855	Zebegeny
474	185	4749/1852	Szob
474	190	4740/1905	Szentendre
474	190	4741/1908	Alsogod
474	190	4741/1907	Szigetmonostor
474	190	4742/1909	Felsogod
474	190	4743/1906	Pocsmegyer
474	190	4745/1906	Tahitotfalu
474	190	4747/1908	Vac
474	191	4741/1916	Gyar
474	191	4741/1916	Orszentmiklos
474	191	4742/1918	Vacbottyan
474	191	4743/1912	Szod
474	191	4743/1914	Vacratot
474	191	4744/1918	Kisnemedi
474	191	4744/1919	Puspokszilagy
474	191	4744/1916	Vachartyan
474	191	4745/1913	Vacduka
474	191	4748/1911	Kosd
474	191	4748/1915	Penc
474	192	4740/1927	Iklad
474	192	4742/1923	Galgamacsa
474	192	4742/1921	Vackisujfalu
474	192	4744/1923	Galgagyork
474	192	4746/1928	Erdokurt
474	192	4746/1922	Puspokhatvan
474	192	4748/1923	Acsa
474	192	4749/1920	Csovar
474	193	4742/1938	Hered
474	193	4743/1933	Verseg
474	193	4744/1936	Nagykokenyes
474	193	4745/1930	Kallo
474	193	4746/1933	Erdotarcsa
474	193	4746/1935	Hehalom
474	193	4748/1934	Egyhazasdengeleg
474	193	4748/1936	Palotas
474	193	4749/1935	Kisbagyon
474	193	4749/1939	Szarvasgede
474	194	4740/1941	Hatvan
474	194	4742/1947	Hort
474	194	4744/1947	Ecsed
474	194	4744/1941	Lorinci
474	194	4747/1945	Rozsaszentmarton
474	194	4747/1941	Zagyvaszanto
474	194	4748/1942	Apc
474	194	4749/1948	Gyongyospata
474	195	4741/1956	Vamosgyork
474	195	4742/1959	Adacs
474	195	4743/1954	Atkar
474	195	4744/1956	Gyongyoshalasz
474	195	4746/1951	Nagyrede
474	195	4747/1956	Gyongyos
474	195	4748/1952	Gyongyostarjan
474	200	4741/2007	Nagyfuged
474	200	4744/2002	Karacsond
474	200	4745/2006	Detk
474	200	4746/2003	Gyongyoshalmaj
474	200	4746/2004	Hevesugra
474	200	4747/2002	Visonta
474	201	4740/2010	Tarnazsadany
474	201	4741/2019	Erdotelek
474	201	4744/2016	Kal
474	201	4744/2015	Kompolt
474	201	4746/2015	Kapolna
474	201	4748/2014	Aldebro
474	201	4749/2015	Feldebro
474	202	4742/2026	Besenyotelek
474	202	4743/2025	Dormand
474	202	4743/2029	Mezotarkany
474	202	4745/2025	Fuzesabony
474	202	4746/2029	Szihalom
474	202	4748/2021	Kerecsend
474	202	4748/2025	Maklar
474	203	4743/2038	Egerlovo
474	203	4745/2032	Mezoszemere
474	203	4749/2035	Mezokovesd
474	204	4741/2049	Tiszababolna
474	204	4741/2045	Tiszavalk
474	204	4742/2040	Borsodivanka
474	204	4742/2043	Negyes
474	204	4746/2040	Szentistvan
474	204	4749/2041	Keresztespuspoki
474	204	4749/2044	Mezonagymihaly
474	205	4741/2052	Tiszadorogma
474	205	4744/2057	Arokto
474	205	4749/2055	Mezocsat
474	210	4742/2100	Tiszacsege
474	210	4747/2100	Tiszakeszi
474	210	4748/2108	Folyas
474	213	4740/2131	Hajduboszormeny
474	213	4745/2130	Vidpuszta
474	213	4749/2130	Hajdudorog
474	214	4741/2140	Hajduhadhaz
474	214	4741/2140	Monostor
474	214	4743/2141	Teglas
474	214	4744/2145	Bokony
474	214	4746/2147	Gesztered
474	214	4748/2146	Erpatak
474	214	4748/2141	Ujfeherto
474	215	4741/2155	Nyiradony
474	215	4744/2159	Nyirmihalydi

474	215	4745/2159	Nyirgelse
474	215	4746/2152	Balkany
474	215	4746/2155	Szakoly
474	215	4749/2151	Biri
474	220	4742/2208	Nyirbeltek
474	220	4742/2203	Nyirlugos
474	220	4744/2207	Encsencs
474	220	4746/2209	Piricse
474	220	4748/2204	Nyirbogat
474	221	4747/2211	Nyirpilis
474	221	4749/2211	Nyirvasvari
474	222	4741/2221	Berea
474	222	4741/2228	Carei
474	222	4744/2224	Urziceni
474	222	4745/2228	Berveni
474	222	4746/2223	Vallaj
474	222	4747/2222	Merk
474	223	4741/2236	Moftinu Mic
474	223	4743/2236	Domanesti
474	223	4748/2238	Csengerujfalu
474	223	4749/2237	Ura
474	224	4741/2240	Ghilvaci
474	224	4741/2243	Terebesti
474	224	4744/2243	Doba
474	224	4744/2248	Satmarel
474	224	4748/2246	Vetis
474	224	4749/2245	Dara
474	224	4749/2243	Oar
474	225	4740/2253	Szatmarhegy
474	225	4741/2251	Madaras Satu Mare
474	225	4743/2257	Orosfala
474	225	4745/2255	Amati
474	225	4746/2257	Ambud
474	225	4746/2258	Petin
474	225	4747/2258	Cucu
474	225	4747/2256	Martinesti
474	225	4748/2253	Satu Mare
474	230	4740/2305	Homorodu De Jos
474	230	4741/2300	Tataresti
474	230	4743/2300	Hrip
474	230	4743/2308	Lipau
474	230	4744/2306	Caraseu
474	230	4745/2303	Culciu Mare
474	230	4745/2307	Potau
474	230	4746/2306	Babasesti
474	230	4746/2301	Corod
474	230	4747/2301	Berindan
474	230	4747/2309	Mediesu Aurit
474	230	4748/2300	Odoreu
474	231	4740/2311	Marius
474	231	4741/2315	Crucisor
474	231	4742/2319	Pomi
474	231	4742/2318	Roztoka (Romania)
474	231	4743/2311	Valea Vinului
474	231	4744/2312	Borhid
474	231	4745/2317	Seini
474	231	4745/2312	Someseni
474	231	4746/2312	Apa
474	231	4746/2318	Viile Apei
474	231	4749/2310	Iojib
474	232	4741/2322	Aciua
474	232	4742/2324	Circirlau
474	232	4742/2324	Sikarlo
474	232	4743/2321	Ilba
474	232	4743/2320	Sabisa
474	232	4748/2323	Turvekonya
474	232	4749/2321	Racsa
474	233	4740/2335	Baia Mare
474	233	4741/2338	Ferneziu
474	233	4745/2336	Firiza
474	235	4740/2352	Cavnic
474	235	4744/2357	Budesti Maramures
474	235	4745/2354	Breb
474	235	4745/2350	Cracesti
474	235	4746/2351	Desesti
474	235	4746/2354	Hoteni
474	235	4746/2357	Sirbi
474	235	4747/2353	Harnicesti
474	235	4747/2356	Ocna Sugatag
474	235	4748/2354	Satu Sugatag
474	235	4749/2356	Giulesti
474	240	4740/2409	Botiza
474	240	4742/2407	Poienile Glodului
474	240	4743/2405	Glod Maramures
474	240	4745/2406	Slatioara (Marmaros)
474	240	4747/2408	Strimtura
474	240	4747/2401	Valeni
474	240	4749/2404	Barczanfalva
474	241	4741/2418	Dragomiresti
474	241	4741/2414	Ieud
474	241	4742/2419	Bocicoiel
474	241	4742/2416	Cuhea
474	241	4743/2413	Sieu
474	241	4744/2413	Rozavlea
474	241	4747/2415	Leordina
474	241	4748/2417	Ruscova
474	242	4743/2424	Viseu De Mijloc
474	242	4743/2426	Viseu De Sus
474	242	4744/2422	Viseu De Jos
474	242	4749/2426	Poienile De Sub Munte
474	251	4741/2515	Moldova Sulita
474	251	4748/2510	Shepit
474	252	4746/2528	Argel
474	253	4741/2532	Moldovita
474	254	4747/2543	Sucevita
474	254	4748/2546	Voevodeasa
474	254	4749/2549	Marginea
474	255	4740/2559	Comanesti Suceava

474	255	4741/2557	Botosana
474	255	4742/2558	Cajvana
474	255	4742/2551	Solca
474	255	4744/2556	Arbore
474	255	4746/2558	Iaslovat
474	255	4749/2554	Volovat
474	260	4744/2609	Darmanesti
474	260	4745/2606	Danila
474	260	4745/2608	Maritei
474	260	4745/2604	Slobozia Pruncului
474	260	4746/2605	Iacobesti
474	260	4747/2608	Calinesti Enache
474	260	4747/2600	Milisauti
474	260	4748/2609	Calinesti Cuparencu
474	260	4749/2604	Granicesti
474	260	4749/2609	Serbauti
474	260	4749/2602	Tibeni
474	261	4741/2617	Burdujeni
474	261	4741/2615	Itcani
474	261	4741/2610	Mihoveni
474	261	4743/2612	Patrauti
474	262	4745/2622	Hantesti
474	262	4746/2626	Bucecea
474	264	4743/2645	Stauceni (Bucovina)
474	264	4745/2640	Botosani
474	270	4740/2701	Stanesti
474	271	4746/2719	Kuban
474	271	4748/2715	Braneshty
474	271	4749/2717	Vasileutis
474	272	4740/2729	Chuchulya
474	272	4740/2723	Kukhneshty
474	272	4742/2720	Bolotino
474	272	4743/2727	Kazhba
474	272	4743/2728	Voroshilovo
474	272	4746/2727	Gizhdiyany
474	273	4740/2736	Ustye (Bessarabia)
474	273	4742/2737	Staryye Limbeny
474	273	4747/2731	Glodyany
474	273	4748/2737	Staraya Yablona
474	273	4749/2737	Novaya Yablona
474	274	4741/2740	Staraya Obrezha
474	274	4743/2749	Reutsel
474	274	4745/2743	Staryye Fundury
474	275	4740/2750	Marandeny
474	275	4746/2756	Beltsy
474	275	4747/2755	Slobodzeya Beltsy
474	280	4743/2806	Sangereii Noui
474	280	4747/2804	Novyye Gechi
474	280	4749/2806	Aleksandreny
474	280	4749/2808	Tipilesti
474	281	4740/2814	Nicolaevca
474	281	4743/2815	Dragoneshty
474	281	4744/2810	Radoya
474	281	4747/2817	Sherbeshty
474	282	4744/2825	Shtefaneshty
474	282	4745/2828	Kapreshty
474	282	4746/2824	Chutuleshty
474	282	4747/2823	Kashunka
474	282	4748/2826	Domuluzhany
474	283	4741/2830	Ordashey
474	283	4745/2834	Gauzeny
474	283	4745/2836	Raspopeny
474	283	4747/2835	Dobrusha
474	283	4747/2834	Recheshty
474	283	4748/2833	Zagorna
474	284	4741/2840	Ignatsey
474	284	4741/2849	Trifeshty
474	284	4743/2844	Pecheshtya
474	284	4744/2849	Syrkovo
474	284	4745/2845	Fuzovka
474	284	4745/2849	Piskareshty
474	284	4745/2842	Samashkany
474	284	4748/2843	Olishkany
474	284	4749/2848	Sholdaneshty
474	285	4741/2852	Chinisheutsy
474	285	4741/2858	Sakharna
474	285	4742/2854	Yekimoutsy
474	285	4745/2858	Rezina
474	285	4745/2853	Tsarevka
474	285	4745/2852	Tsekhnauts
474	285	4746/2858	Chorna
474	285	4748/2853	Lipcheny
474	285	4748/2856	Mateutsy
474	285	4749/2853	Glinzheny (Orhei)
474	290	4745/2900	Rybnitsa
474	291	4745/2915	Kruglyak
474	293	4742/2933	Sobolevka
474	293	4745/2932	Kotovsk (Ukraine)
474	295	4743/2958	Ananyev
474	305	4748/3057	Nikolayevka
474	323	4741/3230	Novyy Bug
474	331	4744/3315	Ingulets
474	334	4740/3344	Apostolovo
474	340	4740/3403	Ordzhonikidze
474	351	4749/3511	Zaporozhye
474	363	4740/3634	Novo Zlatopol
474	363	4741/3637	Veselaya Yevreyka
474	363	4745/3638	Roskoshnoye
474	364	4744/3640	Priyutnoye
475	074	4751/0743	Sulzburg
475	074	4753/0744	Staufen
475	081	4754/0813	Neustadt
475	083	4755/0838	Geisingen
475	083	4756/0830	Allmendshofen
475	083	4757/0830	Donaueschingen
475	084	4759/0849	Tuttlingen
475	090	4751/0901	Stockach
475	090	4759/0907	Messkirch

475 093	4759/0935	Musbach	
475 094	4759/0943	Hagnaufurt	
475 094	4759/0941	Laimbach	
475 100	4750/1002	Leutkirch	
475 101	4753/1013	Gronenbach	
475 101	4756/1018	Ottobeuren	
475 101	4759/1010	Memmingen	
475 102	4751/1028	Ebersbach	
475 102	4751/1025	Obergunzburg	
475 102	4756/1024	Engetried	
475 102	4757/1024	Markt Rettenbach	
475 103	4750/1030	Neuenried	
475 103	4753/1037	Kaufbeuren	
475 105	4757/1059	Oberhausen (Augsburg)	
475 110	4757/1106	Diessen	
475 111	4750/1118	Seeshaupt	
475 111	4755/1117	Tutzing	
475 111	4757/1118	Feldafing	
475 112	4755/1125	Wolfratshausen	
475 112	4759/1122	Kempfenhausen	
475 112	4759/1128	Unterschaftlarn	
475 114	4752/1149	Wattersdorf	
475 114	4754/1147	Valley	
475 120	4751/1208	Rosenheim	
475 120	4752/1200	Bad Aibling	
475 121	4754/1212	Prutting	
475 121	4756/1216	Immling	
475 123	4753/1239	Traunstein	
475 125	4751/1259	Freilassing	
475 125	4756/1251	Watzing	
475 125	4757/1256	Waging am See	
475 125	4759/1257	Lamprechtshausen	
475 133	4758/1330	Doging	
475 134	4750/1347	Traunkirchen	
475 134	4755/1348	Gmunden	
475 135	4757/1353	Kottendorf	
475 142	4753/1427	Reichraming	
475 144	4753/1443	Gaflenz	
475 144	4758/1446	Waidhofen an der Ybbs	
475 155	4752/1558	Waidmannsfeld	
475 155	4753/1557	Neusiedl	
475 160	4752/1607	Markt Piesting	
475 160	4752/1602	Waldegg	
475 160	4757/1606	Berndorf	
475 160	4757/1605	Pottenstein	
475 161	4753/1614	Felixdorf	
475 161	4753/1615	Sollenau	
475 161	4755/1611	Hirtenberg	
475 161	4755/1613	Leobersdorf	
475 161	4757/1612	Gainfarn	
475 161	4757/1613	Kottingbrunn	
475 161	4757/1617	Teesdorf	
475 161	4758/1612	Bad Voslau	
475 161	4758/1619	Oberwaltersdorf	
475 162	4750/1625	Stinkenbrunn	
475 162	4751/1622	Neufeld an der Leitha	
475 162	4752/1622	Ebenfurth	
475 162	4759/1628	Mitterndorf an der Fischa	
475 162	4759/1620	Trumau	
475 163	4750/1637	Oslip	
475 163	4751/1631	Eisenstadt	
475 163	4751/1632	Kismarton	
475 163	4751/1630	Oberberg	
475 163	4754/1631	Loretto	
475 163	4758/1636	Mannersdorf am Leithagebirge	
475 163	4759/1639	Sommerein	
475 164	4750/1640	Oggau	
475 165	4750/1655	Frauenkirchen	
475 165	4753/1654	Gols	
475 165	4759/1651	Parndorf	
475 170	4758/1700	Zurndorf	
475 171	4751/1711	Mosonszolnok	
475 171	4752/1719	Mariakalnok	
475 171	4752/1717	Mosonmagyarovar	
475 171	4754/1712	Level	
475 171	4755/1710	Hegyeshalom	
475 171	4758/1713	Bezenye	
475 171	4758/1717	Dunakiliti	
475 172	4750/1728	Hedervar	
475 172	4750/1725	Kumling	
475 172	4750/1722	Magyarkimle	
475 172	4752/1723	Arak	
475 172	4752/1728	Lipot	
475 172	4753/1720	Halaszi	
475 172	4754/1725	Kisbodak	
475 172	4755/1728	Bodiky	
475 172	4756/1723	Cikolasziget	
475 173	4754/1735	Gabcikovo	
475 173	4755/1730	Trstena Na Ostrove	
475 173	4757/1736	Vrakun	
475 173	4759/1737	Dunajska Streda	
475 173	4759/1731	Velka Luc	
475 174	4750/1740	Balon	
475 174	4752/1746	Calovo	
475 174	4756/1743	Hrobonovo	
475 180	4755/1800	Kolarovo	
475 180	4759/1800	Zemne	
475 181	4752/1812	Hurbanovo	
475 181	4753/1812	Bohata	
475 181	4754/1819	Pribeta	
475 181	4756/1819	Svaty Mikulas	
475 181	4759/1816	Dvory nad Zitavou	
475 181	4759/1810	Nove Zamky	
475 182	4750/1825	Vojnice	
475 182	4754/1825	Strekov	
475 182	4757/1825	Dubnik	

475	182	4759/1824	Jasova
475	183	4752/1834	Sarkan
475	183	4755/1839	Bina
475	183	4755/1830	Svodin
475	183	4758/1831	Velke Ludince
475	184	4759/1847	Vamosmikola
475	185	4751/1850	Ipolydamasd
475	185	4752/1853	Marianosztra
475	185	4753/1856	Kospallag
475	185	4754/1859	Kiralyret
475	185	4756/1850	Nagyborzsony
475	190	4750/1902	Nogradveroce
475	190	4751/1907	Szendehely
475	190	4752/1901	Szokolya
475	190	4755/1903	Nograd
475	190	4756/1908	Retsag
475	190	4756/1907	Tolmacs
475	190	4757/1903	Diosjeno
475	190	4758/1907	Borsosbereny
475	191	4750/1915	Keszeg
475	191	4751/1918	Nezsa
475	191	4752/1912	Osagard
475	191	4753/1915	Alsopeteny
475	191	4753/1912	Felsopeteny
475	191	4753/1919	Legend
475	191	4756/1917	Ketbodony
475	191	4756/1919	Kisecset
475	191	4756/1916	Romhany
475	191	4757/1914	Szatok
475	191	4757/1912	Tereske
475	191	4758/1919	Debercseny
475	191	4758/1917	Szente
475	192	4750/1921	Nogradsap
475	192	4750/1927	Vanyarc
475	192	4751/1924	Galgaguta
475	192	4752/1925	Bercel
475	192	4752/1923	Nogradkovesd
475	192	4755/1923	Becske
475	192	4756/1927	Szanda
475	192	4757/1929	Liszkopuszta
475	192	4757/1927	Tereny
475	192	4758/1921	Magyarnandor
475	192	4759/1922	Cserhathalap
475	192	4759/1920	Mohora
475	193	4750/1932	Szirak
475	193	4752/1938	Csecse
475	193	4754/1936	Ecseg
475	193	4756/1933	Bokor
475	193	4756/1935	Cserhatszentivan
475	193	4757/1933	Kutaso
475	193	4758/1937	Felsotold
475	194	4750/1941	Jobbagyi
475	194	4751/1941	Szurdokpuspoki
475	194	4755/1942	Paszto
475	194	4756/1944	Hasznos
475	194	4758/1941	Matraszollos
475	194	4759/1947	Matraverebely
475	194	4759/1944	Samsonhaza
475	195	4750/1954	Gyongyosoroszi
475	195	4758/1956	Matramindszent
475	195	4758/1950	Nagybatony
475	195	4759/1954	Doroghaza
475	195	4759/1950	Maconka
475	195	4759/1955	Szuha
475	200	4750/2007	Domoszlo
475	200	4751/2009	Kisnana
475	200	4755/2002	Parad
475	200	4756/2007	Recsk
475	200	4757/2002	Bodony
475	200	4757/2005	Matraderecske
475	200	4759/2002	Matraballa
475	201	4751/2014	Verpelet
475	201	4753/2012	Tarnaszentmaria
475	201	4756/2012	Sirok
475	201	4759/2016	Bator
475	202	4751/2029	Novaj
475	202	4752/2026	Ostoros
475	202	4754/2023	Eger
475	202	4756/2022	Felnemet
475	202	4756/2029	Noszvaj
475	202	4758/2025	Felsotarkany
475	203	4753/2037	Tard
475	203	4754/2032	Bogacs
475	203	4755/2038	Tibolddaroc
475	203	4756/2032	Cserepfalu
475	203	4757/2037	Kacs
475	203	4758/2030	Bukkzserc
475	204	4750/2047	Gelej
475	204	4750/2042	Mezokeresztes
475	204	4752/2041	Mezonyarad
475	204	4753/2041	Alsoabrany
475	204	4754/2041	Felsoabrany
475	204	4755/2045	Vatta
475	204	4756/2049	Emod
475	204	4757/2042	Borsodgeszt
475	204	4757/2040	Saly
475	204	4758/2045	Harsany
475	204	4759/2047	Bukkaranyos
475	205	4752/2053	Igrici
475	205	4753/2058	Nemesbikk
475	205	4754/2057	Hejobaba
475	205	4754/2055	Hejopapi
475	205	4756/2053	Hejoszalonta
475	205	4757/2055	Szakald
475	205	4758/2059	Girincs
475	205	4758/2053	Hejokeresztur
475	205	4758/2057	Nagycsecs
475	205	4759/2057	Korom

475	205	4759/2056	Muhi
475	205	4759/2050	Nyekladhaza
475	210	4750/2101	Tiszatarjan
475	210	4751/2107	Bogatkozetanya
475	210	4752/2107	Polgar
475	210	4753/2102	Oszlar
475	210	4753/2104	Tiszapalkonya
475	210	4756/2105	Tiszaszederkeny
475	210	4757/2102	Sajooros
475	210	4757/2100	Sajoszoged
475	210	4758/2103	Kesznyeten
475	212	4751/2126	Hajdunanas
475	212	4758/2122	Budszentmihaly
475	212	4758/2121	Tiszavasvari
475	212	4759/2124	Takarostanya
475	214	4753/2148	Feketeszek
475	214	4755/2146	Nyirjes
475	214	4757/2143	Nyiregyhaza
475	214	4757/2148	Oros
475	214	4759/2148	Nyirpazony
475	214	4759/2148	Pazony
475	215	4752/2156	Kallosemjen
475	215	4753/2152	Kiskallo
475	215	4753/2151	Nagykallo
475	215	4756/2159	Magy
475	215	4756/2153	Napkor
475	215	4758/2156	Apagy
475	220	4750/2201	Kisleta
475	220	4750/2208	Nyirbator
475	220	4753/2202	Mariapocs
475	220	4753/2206	Nyirgyulaj
475	220	4753/2200	Pocspetri
475	220	4756/2209	Kantorjanosi
475	220	4756/2203	Ofeherto
475	220	4758/2201	Besenyod
475	220	4758/2200	Levelek
475	221	4752/2211	Nyircsaszari
475	221	4752/2216	Nyirkata
475	221	4754/2210	Nyirderzs
475	221	4755/2213	Hodasz
475	221	4755/2216	Nyirmeggyes
475	221	4758/2215	Jarmi
475	221	4759/2212	Or
475	221	4759/2215	Papos
475	222	4750/2222	Fabianhaza
475	222	4752/2224	Nagyecsed
475	222	4754/2220	Nyircsaholy
475	222	4756/2228	Geberjen
475	222	4756/2226	Gyortelek
475	222	4757/2223	Kocsord
475	222	4757/2220	Mateszalka
475	222	4758/2228	Matolcs
475	222	4758/2228	Tolgyes
475	222	4758/2227	Tunyog
475	223	4751/2233	Tyukod
475	223	4752/2237	Patyod
475	223	4753/2234	Porcsalma
475	223	4754/2238	Hermanszeg
475	223	4754/2237	Szamossalyi
475	223	4755/2234	Rapolt
475	223	4755/2236	Szamosujlak
475	223	4755/2231	Szatmarokorito
475	223	4756/2233	Cegenydanyad
475	223	4756/2230	Fulposdaroc
475	223	4756/2234	Gyugye
475	223	4757/2239	Majtis
475	223	4757/2236	Zsarolyan
475	223	4758/2238	Kisszekeres
475	223	4758/2237	Nagyszekeres
475	223	4759/2231	Fehergyarmat
475	223	4759/2238	Nemesborzova
475	223	4759/2234	Penyige
475	224	4750/2241	Csenger
475	224	4751/2249	Dorolt
475	224	4751/2245	Nagygec
475	224	4752/2247	Atea
475	224	4752/2244	Csengersima
475	224	4752/2240	Szamosangyalos
475	224	4752/2242	Szamosbecs
475	224	4752/2240	Szamostatarfalva
475	224	4753/2249	Peles
475	224	4754/2241	Csegold
475	224	4754/2248	Zajta
475	224	4755/2244	Csaszlo
475	224	4755/2248	Rozsaly
475	224	4756/2246	Gacsaly
475	224	4756/2240	Jank
475	224	4757/2242	Kisnameny
475	224	4757/2248	Tisztaberek
475	224	4758/2246	Turricse
475	224	4759/2244	Csaholc
475	224	4759/2241	Vamosoroszi
475	225	4750/2257	Botiz Satu Mare
475	225	4751/2252	Lazuri
475	225	4754/2257	Micula
475	225	4755/2253	Bercu
475	225	4756/2251	Mehtelek
475	225	4757/2252	Garbolc
475	225	4758/2251	Nagyhodos
475	225	4759/2258	Cidreag
475	225	4759/2259	Porumbesti
475	230	4752/2308	Livada
475	230	4753/2301	Agris
475	230	4756/2305	Turulung
475	230	4758/2305	Babesti
475	230	4758/2301	Forgolany
475	230	4758/2301	Halmeu
475	230	4759/2302	Dobolt

475 231	4750/2317	Orasu Nou	475 255 4754/2553 Fratautii Vechi
475 231	4751/2319	Prilog	475 255 4754/2556 Maneuti
475 231	4756/2314	Gherta Mica	475 255 4757/2551 Fratautii Noi
475 231	4758/2313	Gheria Mare	475 255 4758/2557 Bainet
475 231	4759/2313	Turt	475 255 4758/2553 Belaya Krinitsa
475 232	4750/2324	Vama	475 255 4759/2557 Bagrinovka
475 232	4750/2324	Vama (Satu Mare)	475 260 4750/2601 Satu Mare (Bucovina)
475 232	4752/2326	Luna	475 260 4751/2607 Calafindesti
475 232	4754/2328	Certeze	475 260 4752/2601 Dornesti
475 232	4755/2321	Boinesti	475 260 4756/2605 Negostina
475 232	4756/2324	Bixad	475 260 4757/2604 Siret
475 232	4756/2328	Moiseni	475 260 4758/2609 Mihaileni
475 232	4756/2323	Trip	475 260 4759/2608 Sinautii De Jos
475 232	4757/2321	Tirsolt	475 261 4750/2617 Zvoristea
475 233	4759/2338	Remeti	475 261 4752/2618 Maghera
475 234	4757/2349	Sarasau	475 261 4752/2612 Zamostea
475 234	4758/2342	Sapinta	475 261 4753/2616 Hapai
475 234	4759/2346	Cimpulung La Tisa	475 261 4754/2610 Balinesti
475 235	4750/2357	Feresti	475 261 4756/2610 Rogojesti
475 235	4751/2356	Berbesti	475 261 4757/2610 Piriu Negru
475 235	4751/2359	Oncesti	475 262 4750/2626 Mitoc
475 235	4753/2357	Vad Maramures	475 262 4753/2623 Saucenita
475 235	4753/2359	Valea Porcului	475 262 4753/2625 Vaculesti
475 235	4756/2353	Sighet	475 262 4757/2627 Broscauti
475 235	4757/2355	Bila Cirkev	475 262 4757/2624 Dorohoi
475 235	4757/2354	Solotvina	475 263 4754/2633 Dimacheni
475 235	4757/2358	Virismort	475 263 4756/2633 Corlateni
475 235	4758/2359	Craciunesti	475 264 4753/2647 Plopenii Mari
475 235	4759/2354	Stredni Apsa	475 265 4753/2651 Vicolenii Mari
475 240	4750/2401	Nanesti	475 265 4756/2653 Vlasinesti
475 240	4753/2402	Costiui	475 265 4757/2652 Saveni
475 240	4754/2403	Rona De Sus	475 270 4755/2700 Slobozia Hanesti
475 240	4755/2401	Rona De Jos	475 270 4757/2702 Borolea
475 240	4758/2400	Bocicoiu Mare	475 270 4757/2709 Ripiceni
475 240	4758/2401	Velikiy Bychkov	475 270 4758/2709 Staryye Kukoneshty
475 241	4750/2414	Petrova	(Bessarabia
475 241	4752/2412	Bistra	475 270 4759/2708 Karpach
475 241	4755/2410	Valea Viseului	475 271 4750/2717 Paskautsy
475 241	4756/2411	Delovoye	475 271 4751/2713 Kosteshty
475 242	4750/2424	Repedea	475 271 4751/2719 Petrushany
475 245	4759/2453	Grynyava	475 271 4752/2716 Druitory
475 250	4754/2508	Ploska	475 271 4752/2715 Proskuryany
475 250	4759/2506	Sergii	475 271 4755/2716 Varatik
475 251	4752/2513	Selyatin	475 271 4758/2718 Drutsa
475 252	4753/2525	Brodina	475 271 4758/2718 Pochumbeny
475 253	4754/2535	Gura Putnei	475 272 4750/2722 Kamenka
475 253	4755/2533	Straja	475 272 4752/2720 Galashany
475 254	4753/2546	Voitinel	475 272 4753/2721 Malayeshty
475 254	4754/2544	Vicovu De Jos	475 272 4755/2727 Sturdzeny
475 254	4755/2545	Bilca	475 272 4756/2723 Khiliutsy
475 254	4755/2548	Galanesti	475 272 4758/2726 Pyrzhota
475 254	4756/2541	Vicovu De Sus	475 272 4759/2722 Zaykany
475 255	4751/2555	Radauti	475 273 4750/2730 Danul
475 255	4754/2553	Fratautii Pe Suceava	475 273 4751/2739 Alunish

475	273	4755/2737	Rakariya
475	273	4756/2733	Ivanushka
475	273	4758/2733	Ryshkany
475	273	4759/2737	Ramazany
475	274	4753/2747	Grinautsy
475	274	4754/2741	Recha
475	274	4756/2743	Chepariya
475	274	4758/2742	Nikoreny
475	275	4750/2750	Strymba
475	275	4750/2751	Syngureny
475	275	4752/2750	Peleniya
475	275	4755/2759	Bolshiye Asnashany
475	275	4757/2757	Dominteny
475	275	4757/2757	Petreny
475	275	4757/2752	Sofiya (Bessarabia)
475	275	4759/2759	Novyye Popeshty
475	280	4750/2808	Putineshty
475	280	4753/2802	Kubolta
475	280	4754/2809	Ivaneshti
475	280	4754/2800	Moara De Pyatre
475	280	4756/2809	Sevirovo
475	280	4757/2807	Frumushika
475	280	4757/2808	Trifaneshty
475	281	4751/2812	Prazhilo
475	281	4752/2815	Bagrineshty
475	281	4752/2811	Gura Kaynary
475	281	4753/2817	Floreshty
475	281	4753/2815	Markuleshty
475	281	4753/2819	Varvarovka
475	281	4754/2818	Floresti Sat
475	281	4759/2816	Staryye Radulyany
475	282	4750/2822	Gindeshty
475	282	4753/2821	Bobuleshty
475	282	4753/2828	Gertop
475	282	4753/2821	Gura Kamenka
475	282	4754/2821	Gvozdovo
475	282	4756/2828	Koshernitsa
475	282	4758/2828	Ciornita
475	282	4759/2823	Cherepkovo
475	283	4750/2830	Pogorna
475	283	4751/2833	Kotyuzhany
475	283	4754/2839	Kunicha
475	283	4755/2839	Poyana
475	283	4756/2836	Nizhniye Kugureshty
475	283	4757/2831	Vaskautsy
475	283	4759/2833	Vertyuzhany
475	284	4750/2849	Shipka
475	284	4752/2840	Kobylnya
475	284	4752/2845	Shestachi
475	284	4754/2843	Kushmirka
475	284	4756/2849	Vad Rashkov
475	284	4759/2842	Zhabka
475	285	4752/2853	Alchedary
475	285	4753/2855	Kuratura
475	285	4757/2850	Rashkov
475	291	4758/2912	Krutnoye
475	293	4756/2937	Balta
475	294	4759/2942	Aranyos
475	300	4753/3005	Gvozdovka Vtoraya
475	301	4751/3015	Lyubashevka
475	302	4756/3021	Krivoye Ozero
475	303	4752/3036	Vradiyevka
475	310	4750/3109	Konstantinovka
475	325	4750/3250	Kazanka
475	332	4755/3321	Krivoy Rog
475	334	4752/3341	Emmes
475	334	4755/3346	Izluchistoye
475	335	4758/3354	Novo Vitebsk
475	340	4756/3402	Bazavluchok
475	342	4757/3420	Miropol
475	345	4750/3456	Khortitsa
475	351	4750/3519	Kryukov
480	073	4802/0735	Breisach
480	073	4803/0739	Ihringen
480	074	4805/0744	Eichstetten
480	074	4808/0742	Endingen
480	074	4809/0745	Riegel
480	075	4800/0751	Emmerdingen
480	075	4800/0751	Freiburg im Breisgau
480	075	4808/0751	Emmendingen
480	080	4806/0801	Mittel Biberach
480	081	4803/0812	Furtwangen
480	081	4808/0814	Triberg
480	082	4804/0828	Villingen
480	083	4801/0832	Bad Durrheim
480	083	4804/0832	Schwenningen am Neckar
480	084	4801/0840	Talheim
480	084	4805/0843	Spaichingen
480	091	4804/0917	Scheer
480	091	4805/0913	Sigmaringen
480	092	4800/0925	Friedberg (Baden)
480	092	4803/0920	Mengen
480	092	4806/0925	Planegg
480	092	4809/0928	Riedlingen
480	093	4801/0930	Saulgau
480	093	4804/0937	Buchau
480	094	4806/0948	Biberach an der Riss
480	095	4802/0955	Rottum
480	095	4804/0957	Ochsenhausen
480	100	4802/1009	Heimertingen
480	100	4803/1005	Berkheim
480	100	4805/1009	Fellheim
480	101	4800/1011	Amendingen
480	101	4801/1013	Eisenburg
480	101	4801/1015	Schwaighausen
480	101	4809/1010	Osterberg
480	102	4803/1029	Mindelheim

480	102	4808/1021	Korb
480	103	4801/1036	Bad Worishofen
480	103	4806/1034	Tussenhausen
480	104	4800/1047	Waal
480	104	4802/1044	Buchloe
480	104	4804/1048	Igling
480	105	4803/1052	Landsberg am Lech
480	105	4805/1053	Kaufering
480	111	4804/1116	Oberpfaffenhofen
480	111	4806/1118	Argelsried
480	111	4808/1112	Schongeising
480	112	4800/1121	Starnberg
480	112	4804/1122	Gauting
480	112	4806/1127	Grafelfing
480	112	4806/1124	Krailling
480	112	4809/1127	Pasing
480	113	4802/1136	Oberhaching
480	113	4803/1132	Pullach im Isartal
480	113	4803/1138	Unterhaching
480	113	4804/1131	Solln
480	113	4807/1138	Perlach
480	113	4809/1135	Munchen
480	114	4806/1144	Haar
480	114	4808/1140	Kirchtrudering
480	120	4807/1203	Schutzen
480	121	4804/1214	Wasserburg am Inn
480	123	4802/1233	Trostberg
480	124	4800/1249	Fridolfing
480	124	4804/1246	Tittmoning
480	131	4801/1315	Friedburg
480	133	4805/1334	Ampfelwang
480	134	4801/1343	Attnang
480	134	4803/1347	Rustorf
480	140	4806/1407	Sipbachzell
480	141	4808/1413	Neuhofen an der Krems
480	142	4803/1425	Steyr
480	142	4804/1427	Haidershofen
480	144	4804/1448	Hausmenning
480	144	4805/1448	Mauer Bei Amstetten
480	145	4807/1452	Amstetten
480	150	4803/1508	Purgstall
480	150	4805/1508	Schauboden
480	150	4808/1503	Neumarkt an der Ybbs
480	150	4808/1508	Wieselburg
480	151	4800/1510	Scheibbs
480	151	4803/1513	Oberndorf an der Melk
480	152	4806/1524	Kilb
480	152	4806/1520	Mank
480	152	4807/1528	Bischofstetten
480	153	4801/1538	Lilienfeld
480	153	4805/1537	Kreisbach
480	153	4806/1536	Wilhelmsburg
480	154	4806/1545	Michelbach Markt
480	155	4801/1553	Kaumberg
480	155	4809/1555	Altlengbach
480	160	4803/1605	Alland
480	160	4806/1607	Stangau
480	161	4800/1616	Tribuswinkel
480	161	4801/1614	Baden
480	161	4801/1617	Traiskirchen
480	161	4802/1618	Guntramsdorf
480	161	4803/1617	Gumpoldskirchen
480	161	4805/1614	Hinterbruhl
480	161	4805/1617	Modling
480	161	4806/1617	Brunn am Gebirge
480	161	4807/1611	Kaltenleutgeben
480	161	4807/1616	Perchtoldsdorf
480	161	4807/1618	Siebenhirten Bei Wien
480	161	4808/1619	Erlaa Bei Wien
480	161	4808/1615	Kalksburg
480	161	4808/1616	Rodaun
480	161	4809/1618	Atzgersdorf
480	161	4809/1618	Liesing
480	161	4809/1616	Mauer Bei Wein
480	162	4801/1629	Gramatneusiedl
480	162	4802/1626	Velm
480	162	4804/1621	Laxenburg
480	162	4805/1620	Biedermannsdorf
480	162	4805/1626	Himberg
480	162	4806/1627	Oberlanzendorf
480	162	4806/1627	Unterlanzendorf
480	162	4806/1628	Zwolfaxing
480	162	4807/1628	Altkettenhof
480	162	4807/1620	Vosendorf
480	162	4808/1621	Inzersdorf Bei Wien
480	162	4808/1628	Schwechat
480	163	4802/1631	Ebergassing
480	163	4805/1636	Kleinneusiedl
480	163	4805/1631	Rauchenwarth
480	163	4807/1636	Fischamend Markt
480	164	4801/1647	Bruckneudorf
480	165	4801/1659	Gattendorf
480	165	4801/1656	Neudorf Bei Parndorf
480	165	4802/1656	Potzneusiedl
480	165	4806/1659	Edelstal
480	165	4807/1651	Petronell
480	165	4808/1654	Bad Deutsch Altenburg
480	165	4809/1656	Hainburg an der Donau
480	170	4801/1706	Deutsch Jahrndorf
480	170	4803/1702	Pama
480	170	4803/1709	Rusovce
480	170	4805/1704	Kittsee
480	170	4808/1707	Petrzalka
480	170	4809/1707	Bratislava
480	171	4800/1712	Rajka
480	171	4802/1719	Samorin
480	171	4808/1713	Podunajske Biskupice
480	172	4807/1725	Rastice

480	173	4800/1737	Male Blahovo
480	173	4809/1731	Jelka
480	174	4805/1742	Tomasikovo
480	174	4807/1745	Horne Saliby
480	175	4801/1759	Neded
480	175	4802/1757	Vlcany
480	175	4806/1758	Sok
480	175	4806/1751	Tesedikovo
480	175	4808/1751	Diakovce
480	175	4809/1756	Trnovec nad Vahom
480	180	4803/1804	Palarikovo
480	180	4806/1804	Tvrdosovce
480	181	4803/1816	Besenov
480	181	4805/1811	Surany
480	181	4806/1818	Radava
480	181	4809/1811	Komjatice
480	182	4801/1825	Kolta
480	182	4801/1821	Semerovo
480	182	4807/1823	Pozba
480	182	4807/1820	Svatusa
480	183	4800/1831	Farna
480	183	4806/1832	Tekovske Luzany
480	183	4808/1831	Ondrejovce
480	184	4803/1840	Zeliezovce
480	184	4804/1849	Kubanovo
480	184	4804/1840	Mikula
480	184	4809/1846	Santovka
480	185	4800/1852	Perocseny
480	185	4801/1854	Kemence
480	185	4802/1855	Bernecebarati
480	185	4802/1851	Tesa
480	185	4803/1852	Vyskovce nad Iplom
480	185	4804/1858	Sahy
480	185	4804/1859	Tesmak
480	190	4800/1908	Horpacs
480	190	4800/1906	Nagyoroszi
480	190	4803/1903	Dregelypalank
480	190	4803/1900	Hont
480	190	4804/1904	Ipelske Predmostie
480	190	4805/1908	Blh nad Iplom
480	190	4805/1906	Velka Ves nad Iplom
480	190	4808/1903	Ipelske Ulany
480	191	4800/1912	Ersekvadkert
480	191	4801/1917	Csesztve
480	191	4802/1910	Dejtar
480	191	4803/1914	Ipolyszog
480	191	4805/1918	Balassagyarmat
480	191	4806/1915	Lesenice
480	191	4806/1918	Slovenske Darmoty
480	192	4802/1924	Nogradmarcal
480	192	4802/1920	Szugy
480	192	4803/1926	Csitar
480	192	4804/1921	Patvarc
480	192	4805/1926	Hugyag
480	192	4805/1925	Orhalom
480	193	4802/1935	Nagyloc
480	193	4802/1932	Rimoc
480	193	4804/1938	Nogradmegyer
480	193	4805/1931	Szecseny
480	193	4808/1935	Endrefalva
480	193	4808/1932	Ludany
480	193	4808/1931	Szecsenyhalaszi
480	193	4809/1936	Piliny
480	194	4802/1942	Lucfalva
480	194	4803/1949	Vizslas
480	194	4804/1947	Zagyvapalfalva
480	194	4805/1943	Kishartyan
480	194	4806/1947	Baglyasalja
480	194	4806/1941	Sagujfalu
480	194	4807/1943	Etes
480	194	4807/1940	Karancssag
480	194	4807/1949	Salgotarjan
480	194	4808/1945	Karancsalja
480	194	4809/1944	Karancslapujto
480	195	4801/1950	Kisterenye
480	195	4801/1959	Nadujfalu
480	195	4801/1954	Nemti
480	195	4802/1957	Homokterenye
480	195	4802/1959	Matranovak
480	195	4806/1956	Barna
480	195	4809/1958	Cered
480	200	4801/2006	Petervasara
480	200	4802/2006	Erdokovesd
480	200	4802/2007	Varaszo
480	200	4805/2003	Istenmezeje
480	201	4802/2016	Egerbocs
480	201	4802/2012	Fedemes
480	201	4803/2010	Bukkszenterzsebet
480	201	4803/2017	Egercsehi
480	201	4803/2019	Mikofalva
480	201	4803/2011	Tarnalelesz
480	201	4805/2017	Bekolce
480	201	4806/2019	Balaton
480	201	4807/2015	Borsodnadasd
480	201	4809/2015	Jardanhaza
480	202	4802/2021	Monosbel
480	202	4803/2022	Belapatfalva
480	202	4804/2021	Bukkszentmarton
480	202	4806/2024	Szilvasvarad
480	202	4808/2026	Nagyvisnyo
480	202	4809/2021	Csernely
480	202	4809/2023	Lenarddaroc
480	203	4801/2039	Bekenypuszta
480	203	4806/2039	Hamor
480	203	4809/2030	Malyinka
480	204	4801/2042	Kisgyor
480	204	4803/2047	Goromboly
480	204	4804/2048	Hejocsaba

480	204	4806/2041	Diosgyor
480	204	4806/2047	Miskolc
480	204	4809/2048	Szirmabesenyo
480	205	4800/2051	Malom
480	205	4800/2055	Onod
480	205	4800/2057	Sajohidveg
480	205	4801/2057	Berzek
480	205	4801/2050	Malyi
480	205	4802/2058	Kulsobocs
480	205	4802/2054	Sajopetri
480	205	4803/2058	Bocs
480	205	4803/2051	Kistokaj
480	205	4803/2054	Sajolad
480	205	4804/2053	Alsozsolca
480	205	4804/2059	Hernadnemeti
480	205	4804/2050	Szirma
480	205	4805/2058	Hernadkak
480	205	4806/2052	Felsozsolca
480	205	4806/2058	Gesztely
480	205	4807/2055	Onga
480	205	4808/2052	Arnot
480	210	4802/2105	Tiszaluc
480	210	4805/2108	Taktaharkany
480	210	4808/2105	Harangod
480	210	4808/2101	Ujcsanalos
480	210	4809/2100	Sostofalva
480	211	4801/2110	Tiszadob
480	211	4802/2115	Tiszadada
480	211	4803/2113	Taktakenez
480	211	4805/2115	Prugy
480	211	4807/2111	Taktaszada
480	211	4809/2111	Bekecs
480	211	4809/2116	Mezozombor
480	212	4801/2123	Tiszalok
480	212	4803/2121	Csobaj
480	212	4803/2128	Tiszaeszlar
480	212	4803/2123	Tiszatardos
480	212	4804/2125	Tiszaladany
480	212	4806/2129	Tiszanagyfalu
480	212	4807/2125	Tokaj
480	212	4808/2128	Rakamaz
480	212	4808/2121	Tarcal
480	213	4806/2139	Buj
480	213	4809/2139	Tiszabercel
480	214	4801/2142	Nyirszollos
480	214	4803/2143	Kotaj
480	214	4804/2148	Kemecse
480	214	4804/2146	Maga
480	214	4807/2148	Tiszarad
480	214	4807/2149	Vasmegyer
480	214	4808/2143	Ibrany
480	214	4808/2146	Nagyhalasz
480	214	4809/2141	Paszab
480	215	4800/2153	Senyo

480	215	4801/2158	Nyiribrony
480	215	4801/2156	Nyirtet
480	215	4801/2150	Nyirtura
480	215	4803/2153	Nyirbogdany
480	215	4804/2157	Szekely
480	215	4806/2159	Berkesz
480	215	4807/2155	Demecser
480	215	4807/2153	Kek
480	215	4809/2151	Beszterec
480	215	4809/2157	Gegeny
480	220	4800/2205	Baktaloranthaza
480	220	4801/2203	Nyirkercs
480	220	4802/2205	Nyirjako
480	220	4802/2208	Rohod
480	220	4803/2203	Laskod
480	220	4803/2200	Ramocsahaza
480	220	4804/2205	Petnehaza
480	220	4806/2206	Nyirkarasz
480	220	4807/2202	Nyirtass
480	220	4808/2207	Gyulahaza
480	220	4809/2209	Baka
480	220	4809/2209	Szabolcsbaka
480	221	4800/2219	Opalyi
480	221	4800/2210	Vaja
480	221	4802/2217	Nyirparasznya
480	221	4803/2219	Nagydobos
480	221	4804/2212	Nyirmada
480	221	4804/2214	Pusztadobos
480	221	4806/2219	Vitka
480	221	4807/2214	Ilk
480	221	4808/2212	Gemzse
480	221	4808/2219	Vasarosnameny
480	221	4809/2218	Kisvarsany
480	222	4800/2227	Nabrad
480	222	4801/2225	Kersemjen
480	222	4801/2225	Szamosker
480	222	4803/2224	Panyola
480	222	4803/2222	Szamosszeg
480	222	4805/2228	Gulacs
480	222	4805/2220	Olcsva
480	222	4805/2221	Olcsvaapati
480	222	4807/2229	Hete
480	222	4807/2223	Jand
480	222	4808/2228	Fejercse
480	222	4808/2221	Gergelyiugornya
480	222	4809/2226	Takos
480	223	4800/2237	Mand
480	223	4803/2231	Kisar
480	223	4803/2234	Nagyar
480	223	4803/2239	Turistvandi
480	223	4804/2231	Tivadar
480	223	4805/2238	Szatmarcseke
480	223	4806/2232	Tarpa
480	223	4809/2231	Marokpapi

480 224	4801/2241	Fulesd	
480 224	4802/2248	Botpalad	
480 224	4803/2243	Kolcse	
480 224	4803/2245	Somkad	
480 224	4806/2247	Milota	
480 224	4806/2249	Tiszabecs	
480 224	4806/2245	Tiszacsecse	
480 224	4806/2243	Tiszakorod	
480 224	4808/2243	Vary	
480 225	4801/2250	Kispalad	
480 225	4802/2257	Palad	
480 225	4803/2252	Magosliget	
480 225	4804/2252	Uszka	
480 225	4806/2250	Vilok	
480 230	4801/2300	Nevetlefalu	
480 230	4801/2309	Tamaseni	
480 230	4805/2303	Fekete Ardo	
480 230	4806/2309	Bocicau	
480 230	4807/2306	Tekehaza	
480 230	4809/2308	Korolevo	
480 230	4809/2302	Vinogradov	
480 231	4800/2319	Camarzana	
480 231	4802/2310	Batarci	
480 231	4803/2310	Comlausa	
480 231	4805/2310	Valea Seaca	
480 231	4806/2312	Vagas	
480 231	4806/2319	Velyatin	
480 232	4803/2328	Bushtyna	
480 232	4803/2325	Vishkovo	
480 232	4805/2325	Steblevka	
480 232	4807/2326	Krajnikov	
480 232	4807/2323	Sokirnitsa	
480 232	4808/2327	Htusovo	
480 232	4809/2327	Danilovo	
480 233	4800/2335	Teceu Mic	
480 233	4801/2335	Tyachev	
480 233	4804/2332	Vonigovo	
480 233	4807/2336	Tereblya	
480 233	4808/2331	Sandrovo	
480 233	4809/2335	Dulovo	
480 233	4809/2337	Uglya	
480 234	4801/2340	Bedevlya	
480 234	4803/2344	Belovarec	
480 234	4804/2343	Olnkhovtsy	
480 234	4805/2340	Okrouhla	
480 234	4805/2345	Ternovo	
480 234	4807/2346	Neresnitsa	
480 234	4808/2349	Ganichi	
480 234	4808/2349	Podplesa	
480 235	4800/2350	Nizhna Apsha	
480 235	4800/2358	Verkhneye Vodyanoye	
480 235	4801/2358	Apsilsa	
480 235	4809/2353	Kaliny	
480 240	4800/2406	Kosovskaya Polyana	
480 240	4803/2404	Kobyletskaya Polyana	
480 241	4801/2410	Vilkovtsy	
480 241	4803/2412	Rakhov	
480 241	4803/2419	Volchi	
480 241	4805/2415	Rafajlowa	
480 241	4807/2415	Belin	
480 241	4808/2417	Kvasy	
480 242	4802/2422	Bogdan	
480 242	4804/2426	Lugi	
480 244	4809/2447	Verkhovina	
480 245	4806/2459	Stebni	
480 250	4800/2505	Putila	
480 250	4801/2504	Torichi	
480 250	4803/2502	Dikhtenets	
480 250	4808/2503	Merinitseni	
480 250	4808/2504	Petrashani	
480 252	4805/2529	Banilov (Siret)	
480 252	4809/2522	Migovoye	
480 253	4800/2534	Krasnoilsk	
480 253	4801/2534	Krasnoputna	
480 253	4802/2539	Izhevtsy	
480 253	4803/2537	Mezhirechye	
480 253	4806/2536	Cheresh	
480 253	4807/2535	Davidovka	
480 254	4802/2547	Kupka	
480 254	4805/2549	Karapchu	
480 254	4806/2548	Iordaneshte	
480 254	4806/2546	Ropcha	
480 255	4800/2558	Cherepkovtsy	
480 255	4801/2557	Volchinets (Lapusna)	
480 255	4803/2550	Suchaveni	
480 255	4804/2551	Presekareni	
480 255	4805/2556	Glybokaya	
480 260	4802/2604	Terebleshti	
480 260	4804/2605	Staneshti De Zhos	
480 260	4805/2604	Staneshti De Sus	
480 260	4806/2601	Karapchiv	
480 260	4807/2601	Tarashany	
480 261	4802/2616	Corjauti	
480 261	4808/2619	Baranca	
480 261	4809/2615	Gertsa	
480 262	4806/2623	Cristinesti	
480 262	4806/2628	Lisna	
480 262	4808/2629	Baseu	
480 262	4808/2629	Mlenauti	
480 262	4808/2625	Suharau	
480 263	4801/2631	Cracalia	
480 263	4801/2635	Grivita Noua	
480 263	4803/2631	Arborea	
480 263	4804/2639	Havirna	
480 264	4805/2642	Mileanca	
480 264	4806/2641	Ghitcauti	
480 264	4809/2648	Bivolu Mic	
480 265	4804/2656	Adaseni	

480	265	4806/2652	Nichiteni
480	265	4807/2650	Putureni
480	265	4808/2651	Cotusca
480	265	4809/2658	Crasnaleuca
480	265	4809/2653	Ghireni
480	270	4800/2702	Flondora
480	270	4800/2705	Hriteni
480	270	4802/2706	Serpenita
480	270	4803/2705	Livenii Vechi
480	270	4803/2707	Staryy Badrazh
480	270	4805/2708	Brynzeny
480	270	4808/2707	Burlaneshty
480	270	4809/2704	Lopatnik
480	271	4800/2719	Pochembautsy
480	271	4803/2715	Terebna
480	271	4804/2716	Porchulyanka
480	271	4805/2715	Zabrichen
480	271	4807/2713	Bleshtenautsy
480	272	4803/2721	Stolnichany
480	272	4805/2725	Bratushany
480	272	4806/2723	Kupchino
480	272	4809/2724	Parkova
480	273	4802/2732	Shtubiyeny
480	273	4803/2737	Mikhayleny
480	273	4805/2737	Baraboy
480	273	4807/2739	Bricheva
480	274	4802/2748	Drokiya Ii
480	274	4802/2740	Okyu Alb
480	274	4803/2746	Glavan
480	274	4807/2749	Drokiya I
480	274	4809/2747	Myndyk
480	275	4802/2755	Barancha
480	275	4802/2756	Nadushita
480	275	4805/2754	Ketrosy
480	275	4806/2752	Shury
480	280	4801/2807	Kaynariy Vek
480	280	4804/2805	Bolbochi
480	280	4806/2801	Verkhniye Popeshty
480	280	4808/2801	Zguritsa
480	281	4801/2814	Vodyany
480	281	4803/2814	Dumbraveny
480	281	4806/2818	Volovy
480	281	4808/2811	Khristichi
480	281	4809/2818	Soroki
480	282	4800/2825	Solonets
480	282	4803/2822	Stoykany
480	282	4804/2828	Slobodzeya Voronkovo
480	282	4806/2824	Rakovets
480	283	4801/2835	Napadovo
480	283	4805/2837	Cherlina
480	283	4805/2831	Voronkovo
480	283	4807/2830	Liublin Colonie
480	284	4801/2842	Senatovka
480	290	4806/2907	Kodyma
480	300	4808/3005	Savran
480	302	4804/3025	Triduby
480	304	4800/3048	Konetspol
480	305	4803/3053	Golta
480	305	4803/3052	Pervomaysk
480	321	4803/3212	Bobrinets
480	340	4807/3408	Gulyay Pole
480	361	4809/3615	Chaplino
480	362	4807/3623	Prosyanaya
480	374	4800/3748	Donetsk
480	374	4800/3748	Stalin
480	383	4802/3835	Torez
481	074	4812/0746	Kenzingen
481	074	4815/0749	Ettenheim
481	074	4816/0749	Altdorf
481	074	4816/0744	Rust
481	074	4817/0749	Mahlberg
481	074	4817/0748	Orschweier
481	075	4817/0752	Schmieheim
481	075	4818/0750	Kippenheim
481	080	4811/0804	Elzach
481	080	4817/0805	Haslach
481	082	4814/0823	Schramberg
481	082	4814/0822	Unterdorf
481	083	4810/0837	Rottweil
481	083	4817/0834	Oberndorf
481	084	4811/0845	Schorzingen
481	084	4814/0845	Dautmergen
481	085	4817/0851	Balingen
481	090	4813/0902	Ebingen
481	090	4815/0901	Tailfingen
481	092	4814/0928	Zwiefalten
481	092	4816/0923	Tigerfeld
481	094	4810/0940	Grundsheim
481	094	4817/0944	Ehingen
481	095	4814/0953	Laupheim
481	095	4818/0954	Dellmensingen
481	100	4810/1007	Altenstadt
481	100	4810/1007	Illereichen
481	100	4813/1004	Dietenheim
481	100	4819/1002	Ay
481	101	4814/1011	Obenhausen
481	101	4818/1010	Weissenhorn
481	102	4811/1029	Kirchheim im Schwaben
481	102	4813/1022	Hohenraunau
481	102	4815/1020	Deisenhausen
481	102	4815/1022	Krumbach
481	102	4817/1028	Thannhausen
481	102	4818/1022	Neuburg an der Kammel
481	102	4819/1027	Munsterhausen
481	103	4812/1036	Reichertshofen
481	103	4815/1039	Siegertshofen
481	103	4816/1033	Seifriedsberg

481	103	4818/1032	Ziemetshausen
481	104	4810/1043	Hiltenfingen
481	104	4811/1045	Schwabmunchen
481	104	4817/1040	Fischach
481	105	4810/1051	Lager Lechfeld
481	111	4811/1115	Furstenfeldbruck
481	112	4812/1120	Olching
481	112	4816/1126	Dachau
481	112	4817/1126	Prittlbach
481	113	4813/1132	Feldmoching
481	114	4814/1141	Ismaning
481	115	4818/1156	Erding
481	120	4816/1209	Dorfen
481	120	4816/1203	Thann
481	122	4811/1226	Kraiburg am Inn
481	122	4816/1225	Ampfing
481	123	4815/1230	Altmuhldorf
481	123	4815/1232	Muhldorf
481	124	4814/1242	Neuotting
481	124	4818/1247	Erlbach
481	125	4810/1250	Burghausen
481	133	4813/1330	Ried im Innkreis
481	135	4812/1357	Krenglbach
481	140	4810/1402	Wels
481	141	4815/1412	Pasching
481	141	4818/1418	Linz
481	142	4812/1428	Enns
481	143	4814/1431	Mauthausen
481	143	4816/1435	Schwertberg
481	150	4810/1505	Ybbs an der Donau
481	150	4811/1504	Persenbeug
481	150	4813/1509	Marbach an der Donau
481	150	4817/1503	Isper
481	151	4811/1511	Erlauf
481	151	4813/1517	Weitenegg
481	152	4812/1524	Loosdorf
481	153	4811/1538	Stattersdorf
481	153	4812/1538	Sankt Polten
481	153	4816/1537	Kleinrust
481	153	4817/1535	Obritzberg
481	153	4818/1538	Statzendorf
481	154	4814/1549	Murstetten
481	154	4814/1542	Pottenbrunn
481	154	4815/1544	Jeutendorf
481	154	4815/1545	Kapelln
481	154	4816/1541	Herzogenburg
481	154	4817/1540	Ederding
481	155	4811/1555	Maria Anzbach
481	155	4811/1552	Tausendblum
481	155	4812/1554	Neulengbach
481	155	4814/1555	Asperhofen
481	155	4817/1554	Atzenbrugg
481	155	4817/1556	Michelhausen
481	160	4811/1605	Pressbaum
481	160	4813/1609	Gablitz
481	160	4814/1609	Mauerbach
481	160	4815/1600	Sieghartskirchen
481	160	4817/1605	Chorherrn
481	160	4817/1600	Judenau
481	160	4817/1607	Tulbing
481	160	4818/1600	Langenrohr
481	161	4812/1610	Purkersdorf
481	161	4813/1614	Hadersdorf
481	161	4816/1615	Weidlingbach
481	161	4818/1613	Hintersdorf
481	161	4818/1616	Kierling
481	161	4818/1619	Klosterneuburg
481	162	4812/1622	Wien
481	162	4815/1624	Floridsdorf
481	162	4818/1621	Langenzersdorf
481	163	4810/1636	Probstdorf
481	163	4812/1633	Grossenzersdorf
481	163	4813/1630	Aspern an der Donau
481	163	4815/1630	Breitenlee
481	163	4816/1638	Markgrafneusiedl
481	163	4818/1634	Deutsch Wagram
481	164	4813/1641	Leopoldsdorf im Marchfelde
481	164	4815/1644	Untersiebenbrunn
481	164	4816/1642	Obersiebenbrunn
481	165	4810/1653	Engelhartstetten
481	165	4810/1650	Loimersdorf
481	165	4816/1654	Marchegg
481	165	4819/1659	Zohor
481	170	4813/1709	Raca
481	170	4816/1702	Mast
481	170	4817/1702	Stupava
481	171	4811/1716	Ivanka Pri Dunaji
481	171	4815/1713	Svaty Jur
481	171	4817/1716	Pezinok
481	172	4811/1726	Kostolna Pri Dunaji
481	172	4813/1724	Senec
481	172	4814/1728	Reca
481	173	4810/1735	Velke Ulany
481	173	4812/1739	Sladkovicovo
481	173	4814/1734	Puste Ulany
481	173	4819/1730	Cifer
481	174	4812/1743	Galanta
481	174	4812/1743	Hody
481	174	4817/1744	Sered
481	174	4819/1743	Horny Cepen
481	175	4810/1754	Veca
481	175	4818/1757	Velke Zaluzie
481	180	4810/1804	Polny Kesov
481	180	4813/1809	Branc
481	180	4813/1804	Mojmirovce
481	180	4819/1805	Nitra
481	181	4810/1817	Kmetovo

481	181	4812/1817	Martinova
481	181	4814/1814	Pana
481	181	4815/1819	Vrable
481	181	4818/1817	Male Chyndice
481	182	4814/1822	Telince
481	182	4819/1820	Slepcany
481	183	4813/1836	Levice
481	184	4817/1840	Gondovo
481	185	4810/1854	Merovce
481	192	4815/1920	Modry Kamen
481	193	4811/1932	Nogradszakal
481	193	4813/1936	Litke
481	193	4814/1938	Ipolytarnoc
481	194	4810/1942	Karancskeszi
481	194	4811/1945	Karancsbereny
481	194	4811/1945	Palhaza
481	194	4817/1940	Panicke Dravce
481	195	4810/1952	Somosko
481	195	4810/1950	Somoskoujfalu
481	195	4815/1951	Belina
481	195	4816/1950	Filakovo
481	200	4812/2008	Kissikator
481	200	4815/2003	Gemerske Dechtare
481	200	4816/2007	Simonovce
481	200	4817/2005	Sirkovce
481	200	4818/2005	Jesenske
481	201	4811/2016	Arlo
481	201	4813/2018	Ozd
481	201	4814/2016	Bolyok
481	201	4814/2012	Hangony
481	201	4814/2019	Sajovarkony
481	201	4814/2014	Szentsimon
481	201	4815/2016	Uraj
481	201	4817/2011	Chramec
481	201	4817/2010	Dubovec
481	201	4817/2018	Vlkyna
481	201	4818/2015	Rimavska Sec
481	201	4819/2017	Ciz
481	202	4810/2026	Nekezseny
481	202	4811/2029	Bantapolcsany
481	202	4811/2024	Sata
481	202	4813/2024	Borsodbota
481	202	4813/2026	Uppony
481	202	4815/2022	Center
481	202	4815/2024	Kirald
481	202	4815/2025	Sajomercse
481	202	4816/2023	Sajonemeti
481	202	4816/2028	Sajovelezd
481	202	4817/2023	Het
481	202	4817/2021	Sajopuspoki
481	202	4818/2022	Banreve
481	202	4818/2026	Putnok
481	202	4819/2020	Abovce
481	202	4819/2024	Serenyfalva
481	203	4810/2039	Parasznya
481	203	4810/2032	Tardona
481	203	4811/2030	Dedes
481	203	4812/2039	Kondo
481	203	4813/2039	Alacska
481	203	4813/2031	Banfalva
481	203	4814/2031	Banhorvat
481	203	4815/2038	Kazincbarcika
481	203	4815/2032	Nagybarca
481	203	4816/2038	Barcika
481	203	4816/2035	Sajoivanka
481	203	4816/2034	Vadna
481	203	4817/2030	Dubicsany
481	203	4817/2035	Sajokaza
481	203	4819/2038	Kurityan
481	204	4810/2044	Sajobabony
481	204	4810/2047	Sajokeresztur
481	204	4811/2040	Radostyan
481	204	4811/2041	Sajolaszlofalva
481	204	4812/2047	Sajoecseg
481	204	4812/2042	Sajokapolna
481	204	4813/2048	Boldva
481	204	4813/2043	Sajoszentpeter
481	204	4814/2040	Berente
481	204	4815/2048	Ziliz
481	204	4816/2046	Borsodszirak
481	204	4816/2041	Mucsony
481	204	4817/2045	Finke
481	204	4817/2049	Nyomar
481	204	4817/2040	Szuhakallo
481	204	4818/2040	Disznoshorvat
481	204	4818/2044	Edeleny
481	204	4819/2048	Balajt
481	204	4819/2045	Borsod
481	205	4810/2051	Sajopalfala
481	205	4811/2051	Sajovamos
481	205	4812/2050	Sajosenye
481	205	4812/2056	Szikszo
481	205	4813/2058	Aszalo
481	205	4815/2055	Alsovadasz
481	205	4817/2055	Homrogd
481	205	4817/2059	Leh
481	205	4818/2050	Hangacs
481	205	4818/2057	Monaj
481	205	4819/2050	Damak
481	210	4810/2109	Legyesbenye
481	210	4811/2100	Alsodobsza
481	210	4811/2103	Megyaszo
481	210	4813/2109	Monok
481	210	4814/2102	Nagykinizs
481	210	4815/2100	Halmaj
481	210	4815/2103	Hernadkercs
481	210	4815/2103	Kiskinizs
481	210	4816/2104	Felsodobsza

481	210	4817/2102	Csobad
481	210	4817/2106	Hernadszentandras
481	210	4817/2104	Inancs
481	210	4817/2108	Pere
481	210	4819/2105	Forro
481	210	4819/2107	Fugod
481	210	4819/2100	Rasonysapberencs
481	211	4810/2112	Szerencs
481	211	4811/2113	Ond
481	211	4812/2117	Mad
481	211	4812/2118	Szenttamas
481	211	4813/2114	Ratka
481	211	4814/2112	Golop
481	211	4814/2114	Tallya
481	211	4817/2112	Abaujszanto
481	211	4818/2112	Abaujker
481	211	4818/2118	Sima
481	211	4819/2115	Boldogkoujfalu
481	211	4819/2110	Gibart
481	212	4810/2122	Bodrogkeresztur
481	212	4811/2122	Bodrogkisfalud
481	212	4811/2128	Zalkod
481	212	4812/2123	Szegi
481	212	4813/2124	Szegilong
481	212	4815/2126	Olaszliszka
481	212	4816/2122	Erdobenye
481	212	4816/2128	Vamosujfalu
481	212	4817/2127	Tolcsva
481	212	4819/2126	Erdohorvati
481	213	4810/2136	Gava
481	213	4810/2134	Vencsello
481	213	4811/2133	Balsa
481	213	4811/2130	Szabolcs
481	213	4812/2137	Galszecs
481	213	4812/2132	Kenezlo
481	213	4813/2131	Viss
481	213	4816/2130	Rudnok
481	213	4816/2130	Sarazsadany
481	213	4817/2131	Bodrogolaszi
481	213	4819/2135	Sarospatak
481	214	4812/2140	Fuzes
481	214	4812/2143	Tiszakarad
481	214	4818/2143	Bodroghalom
481	214	4819/2148	Karcsa
481	214	4819/2140	Vajdacska
481	215	4814/2156	Dombrad
481	215	4815/2154	Cigand
481	215	4815/2158	Tiszakanyar
481	220	4810/2200	Patroha
481	220	4811/2204	Ajak
481	220	4811/2207	Anarcs
481	220	4812/2201	Retkozberencs
481	220	4813/2205	Kisvarda
481	220	4813/2209	Pap
481	220	4815/2200	Kekcse
481	220	4816/2205	Doge
481	220	4816/2206	Fenyeslitke
481	220	4818/2207	Komoro
481	220	4818/2201	Szabolcsveresmart
481	220	4819/2203	Revleanyvar
481	221	4810/2217	Nagyvarsany
481	221	4811/2217	Gyure
481	221	4811/2212	Lovopetri
481	221	4811/2219	Tiszaszalka
481	221	4812/2211	Nyirlovo
481	221	4812/2216	Revaranyos
481	221	4812/2218	Tiszavid
481	221	4813/2216	Kopocsapati
481	221	4814/2210	Jeke
481	221	4814/2218	Tiszaadony
481	221	4815/2214	Ujkenez
481	221	4816/2218	Tiszakerecseny
481	221	4816/2211	Tornyospalca
481	221	4817/2217	Matyus
481	221	4817/2213	Mezoladany
481	221	4819/2217	Lonya
481	221	4819/2212	Mandok
481	221	4819/2214	Tiszamogyoros
481	222	4810/2228	Csaroda
481	222	4812/2227	Gelenes
481	222	4812/2225	Vamosatya
481	222	4814/2226	Barabas
481	222	4815/2228	Kosiny
481	223	4810/2233	Beregsurany
481	223	4812/2232	Beregdaroc
481	223	4813/2239	Beregovo
481	224	4810/2247	Beregbene
481	224	4814/2245	Beregi
481	224	4817/2248	Beregujfalu
481	225	4813/2253	Shalanki
481	230	4819/2308	Bilki
481	230	4819/2303	Irshava
481	231	4810/2318	Khust
481	231	4812/2319	Iza
481	231	4813/2311	Rokosov
481	232	4811/2327	Nizhneye Selishche
481	232	4812/2324	Nankovo
481	232	4813/2328	Kopasnovo
481	232	4814/2320	Koshelevo
481	232	4816/2326	Gorinchovo
481	232	4816/2323	Lipsha
481	233	4810/2335	Kolodne
481	233	4811/2334	Krichevo
481	233	4812/2333	Comalovo
481	233	4812/2330	Zlatary
481	233	4814/2333	Dragovo
481	234	4812/2349	Tarasovka
481	235	4810/2353	Dubovoye

481 235	4811/2353	Valendorf
481 235	4813/2356	Krasna
481 235	4814/2356	Taracs Kraszna
481 235	4819/2356	Ustchorna
481 242	4816/2421	Yasinya
481 242	4819/2429	Yablonitsa (Kuty)
481 242	4819/2429	Yablonitsa (Yasinya)
481 243	4817/2434	Vorokhta
481 245	4810/2457	Verkhniy Yasenov
481 245	4811/2454	Krivorovnya
481 245	4815/2455	Szeparowce
481 245	4815/2459	Yavorov (Kossuv)
481 245	4818/2453	Brustury
481 250	4811/2506	Rostoki
481 250	4812/2508	Zakharicheni
481 250	4813/2504	Rozhen Velikiy
481 250	4817/2509	Kuty Stary
481 250	4817/2500	Sokolovka (Stanislawow)
481 250	4818/2503	Gorod
481 250	4818/2506	Moskalyuvka
481 250	4819/2506	Kosov
481 250	4819/2508	Smodna
481 251	4810/2519	Beregomet
481 251	4812/2512	Vizhnichioara Mika
481 251	4815/2515	Matyjowce
481 251	4815/2511	Vizhnitsa
481 251	4816/2511	Kuty
481 251	4817/2517	Ispas
481 252	4810/2523	Babicheva
481 252	4812/2524	Seleshche
481 252	4813/2525	Lukavets
481 253	4810/2539	Panka
481 253	4812/2534	Komarovtsi
481 253	4812/2531	Zhadova
481 253	4816/2539	Kabeshti
481 253	4817/2536	Kostintsy
481 254	4810/2543	Storozhinets
481 254	4815/2540	Bruskovtsy
481 254	4816/2542	Bobovtsy
481 254	4819/2542	Drachinets
481 255	4811/2553	Velikiy Kochurov
481 255	4812/2556	Voloka
481 255	4814/2551	Kamennaya
481 255	4818/2556	Chernovtsy
481 260	4812/2605	Lukovitsa
481 260	4813/2602	Molodiya
481 260	4817/2608	Boyany
481 261	4813/2617	Marshintsy
481 261	4813/2617	Novoseltsy
481 261	4813/2617	Sulitsa Noua
481 262	4810/2628	Alba
481 262	4811/2620	Oroftiana De Sus
481 262	4813/2627	Vanchikovtsy
481 262	4819/2627	Forostna
481 263	4811/2635	Darabani
481 263	4814/2639	Ivancauti
481 263	4815/2636	Mamalyga
481 263	4818/2637	Podvornoye
481 263	4818/2633	Stalnovtsy
481 264	4810/2644	Bivolu Mare
481 264	4814/2648	Radauti Dorohoi
481 264	4815/2640	Criva
481 264	4815/2640	Kriva
481 264	4816/2643	Drepkovtsy
481 264	4816/2648	Lipkany
481 265	4810/2659	Tetskany
481 265	4811/2657	Cotu Miculinti
481 265	4812/2651	Miorcani
481 265	4812/2656	Pereryta
481 265	4815/2658	Balasineshty
481 265	4819/2656	Berlintsy
481 270	4810/2705	Feteshty
481 270	4813/2707	Trinka
481 270	4814/2703	Korzhevtsy
481 270	4816/2705	Karakushany
481 270	4819/2709	Kolikoutsy
481 271	4810/2710	Gordineshty
481 271	4810/2719	Yedintsy
481 271	4814/2716	Glinoya
481 271	4814/2712	Volodeni
481 271	4817/2712	Balkauts De Zhos
481 271	4818/2718	Chepeleutsy
481 271	4819/2712	Balkautsy
481 272	4813/2726	Rusyany
481 272	4815/2726	Paladiya
481 272	4815/2726	Ruzhnitsa
481 272	4816/2725	Barlyadyany
481 272	4817/2720	Ginkautsi
481 272	4817/2723	Grinautsi
481 273	4814/2736	Dondyushany
481 273	4814/2731	Redyu Mare
481 273	4819/2734	Chernolevka
481 273	4819/2737	Klimautsy
481 274	4810/2740	Tyrnovo
481 274	4813/2740	Tarnova Hotin
481 274	4813/2741	Tsaul
481 274	4816/2741	Plopy
481 274	4818/2747	Sudarka
481 275	4810/2757	Kotova
481 275	4814/2759	Derkautsy
481 275	4815/2755	Vysoka
481 275	4816/2751	Krishkautsy
481 280	4813/2804	Badichany
481 280	4815/2805	Livezi
481 281	4810/2812	Rublenitsa
481 281	4813/2818	Kosoutsy
481 281	4814/2810	Kureshnitsa
481 281	4815/2810	Goloshnitsa

481 281	4815/2817	Yampol (Podolia)	
481 282	4817/2823	Dobryanka	
481 285	4812/2853	Peschanka	
481 285	4816/2854	Rudnitsa	
481 291	4810/2911	Britovka	
481 292	4813/2922	Chechelnik	
481 293	4812/2930	Olgopol	
481 302	4810/3027	Goloskovo	
481 304	4815/3047	Iosipovka	
481 313	4819/3132	Novo Ukrainka	
481 325	4813/3258	Bratolyubovka	
481 374	4815/3742	Groznyy	
481 380	4818/3803	Gorlovka	
481 381	4814/3813	Yenakiyevo	
481 391	4810/3910	Kamennoye	
481 392	4812/3920	Spartak	
482 074	4821/0746	Nonnenweier	
482 075	4820/0752	Lahr	
482 075	4821/0750	Dinglingen	
482 075	4822/0753	Friesenheim	
482 075	4824/0756	Diersburg	
482 075	4829/0756	Offenburg	
482 080	4822/0800	Nordrach	
482 080	4824/0801	Gengenbach	
482 082	4826/0825	Freudenstadt	
482 083	4822/0838	Sulz	
482 083	4825/0838	Dettingen	
482 083	4826/0839	Rexingen	
482 084	4822/0848	Haigerloch	
482 084	4822/0847	Weildorf	
482 084	4823/0841	Fischingen	
482 084	4825/0846	Muhringen	
482 084	4826/0841	Horb	
482 084	4826/0842	Nordstetten	
482 085	4821/0859	Hechingen	
482 085	4827/0851	Bieringen	
482 085	4828/0856	Rottenburg	
482 090	4827/0908	Bronnweiler	
482 090	4827/0907	Gomaringen	
482 091	4829/0913	Reutlingen	
482 092	4822/0929	Buttenhausen	
482 093	4825/0930	Munsingen	
482 093	4829/0935	Heuberg	
482 095	4825/0954	Herrlingen	
482 100	4820/1002	Gerlenhofen	
482 100	4823/1006	Neuhausen	
482 100	4824/1001	Neu Ulm	
482 101	4822/1019	Ichenhausen	
482 101	4826/1012	Leipheim	
482 101	4827/1016	Gunzburg	
482 102	4824/1026	Scheppach	
482 102	4826/1024	Burgau	
482 102	4829/1022	Offingen	
482 104	4823/1047	Schlipsheim	
482 104	4823/1049	Westheim	
482 104	4828/1043	Lauterbrunn	
482 105	4820/1052	Goggingen	
482 105	4821/1059	Friedberg an der Ach	
482 105	4821/1050	Leitershofen	
482 105	4821/1054	Pfersee	
482 105	4822/1053	Augsburg	
482 105	4822/1056	Kriegshaber	
482 105	4822/1051	Stadtbergen	
482 110	4828/1108	Aichach	
482 113	4822/1134	Jarzt	
482 114	4824/1140	Auerbach (Schwaben)	
482 114	4824/1144	Freising	
482 115	4823/1156	Berglern	
482 115	4824/1159	Wartenberg	
482 115	4828/1156	Moosburg	
482 122	4827/1221	Vilsbiburg	
482 123	4820/1233	Niedertaufkirchen	
482 123	4822/1230	Neumarkt Sankt Veit	
482 123	4824/1236	Massing	
482 124	4824/1246	Eggenfelden	
482 125	4826/1256	Pfarrkirchen	
482 131	4821/1312	Rotthalmunster	
482 140	4825/1402	Sankt Martin im Muhlkreise	
482 141	4820/1411	Ottensheim	
482 141	4824/1416	Kirchschlag Bei Linz	
482 145	4829/1457	Arbesbach	
482 152	4822/1523	Gut am Steg	
482 153	4820/1537	Meidling	
482 153	4824/1535	Stein an der Donau	
482 153	4825/1536	Krems an der Donau	
482 154	4820/1548	Gemeinlebarn	
482 154	4821/1542	Nussdorf an der Traisen	
482 154	4821/1544	Traismauer	
482 154	4824/1547	Grafenworth	
482 154	4826/1549	Fels am Wagram	
482 154	4827/1541	Gobelsburg	
482 154	4828/1540	Langenlois	
482 155	4827/1555	Oberstockstall	
482 155	4828/1559	Grossweikersdorf	
482 160	4820/1603	Tulln	
482 160	4824/1605	Seitzersdorf Wolfpassing	
482 160	4824/1601	Stetteldorf am Wagram	
482 161	4820/1616	Hadersfeld	
482 161	4820/1618	Kritzendorf	
482 161	4820/1610	Zeiselmauer	
482 161	4823/1613	Stockerau	
482 162	4820/1621	Bisamberg	
482 162	4821/1620	Korneuburg	
482 162	4824/1629	Ulrichskirchen	
482 162	4826/1629	Hautzendorf	
482 162	4826/1629	Unterolberndorf	
482 162	4828/1625	Grossrussbach	

482	162	4828/1628	Niederkreuzstetten
482	163	4821/1632	Pillichsdorf
482	163	4827/1639	Hohenruppersdorf
482	164	4821/1644	Ganserndorf
482	164	4821/1646	Tallesbrunn
482	164	4823/1640	Raggendorf
482	164	4827/1644	Spannberg
482	164	4829/1640	Niedersulz
482	165	4822/1650	Angern
482	165	4823/1650	Mannersdorf an der March
482	165	4828/1656	Gajary
482	165	4829/1651	Durnkrut
482	170	4820/1703	Lozorno
482	170	4826/1701	Malacky
482	171	4820/1719	Modra
482	172	4824/1722	Casta
482	172	4825/1726	Dlha
482	173	4822/1736	Trnava
482	174	4826/1748	Hlohovec
482	175	4822/1757	Aleksince
482	175	4826/1753	Pastuchov
482	175	4829/1759	Nove Sady
482	180	4825/1805	Vycapy Opatovce
482	180	4827/1806	Preselany
482	181	4825/1818	Velcice
482	182	4820/1822	Tesare nad Zitavou
482	182	4823/1824	Zlate Moravce
482	182	4824/1825	Knazice
482	182	4825/1825	Topolcianky
482	183	4821/1834	Svaty Benadik
482	183	4824/1839	Brehy
482	183	4826/1839	Nova Bana
482	184	4829/1844	Zarnovica
482	185	4820/1851	Badan
482	185	4821/1854	Beluj
482	185	4827/1854	Banska Stiavnica
482	190	4821/1904	Krupina
482	191	4826/1912	Neresnica
482	193	4821/1935	Halic
482	194	4820/1947	Bolkovce
482	194	4820/1940	Lucenec
482	194	4824/1943	Kalinovo
482	194	4826/1947	Zelene
482	195	4821/1955	Dolne Zahorany
482	200	4820/2005	Pavlovce
482	200	4821/2004	Rimavske Janovce
482	200	4823/2002	Rimavska Sobota
482	201	4820/2018	Chanava
482	201	4820/2015	Ivanice
482	201	4821/2013	Radnovce
482	201	4823/2011	Batka
482	201	4824/2011	Rokytnik
482	201	4825/2018	Behynce
482	201	4827/2019	Gemer
482	201	4828/2015	Rasice
482	201	4829/2017	Hrkac
482	202	4820/2020	Riecka
482	202	4821/2026	Kelemer
482	202	4822/2024	Neporadza
482	202	4823/2026	Gomorszollos
482	202	4823/2029	Zadorfalva
482	202	4824/2022	Hubovo
482	202	4825/2020	Safarikovo
482	202	4825/2027	Szuhafo
482	202	4826/2020	Starna
482	202	4829/2021	Bretka
482	203	4820/2036	Felsonyarad
482	203	4820/2035	Jakfalva
482	203	4821/2033	Doveny
482	203	4822/2031	Alsoszuha
482	203	4822/2036	Felsokelecseny
482	203	4823/2038	Rudabanya
482	203	4823/2035	Zubogy
482	203	4824/2031	Ragaly
482	203	4825/2033	Imola
482	203	4826/2036	Kano
482	203	4826/2030	Trizs
482	203	4827/2035	Egerszog
482	203	4827/2038	Szollosardo
482	203	4827/2037	Teresztenye
482	203	4828/2031	Aggtelek
482	203	4828/2037	Tornakapolna
482	203	4828/2039	Varboc
482	203	4829/2034	Josvafo
482	203	4829/2038	Szinpetri
482	204	4821/2047	Ladbesenyo
482	204	4821/2045	Szendrolad
482	204	4823/2041	Szuhogy
482	204	4824/2048	Abod
482	204	4824/2044	Szendro
482	204	4825/2040	Alsotelekes
482	204	4825/2047	Galvacs
482	204	4826/2048	Meszes
482	204	4827/2045	Szalonna
482	204	4828/2046	Martonyi
482	204	4828/2042	Perkupa
482	205	4820/2055	Kupa
482	205	4820/2058	Selyeb
482	205	4820/2053	Tomor
482	205	4821/2052	Lak
482	205	4822/2059	Abaujszolnok
482	205	4822/2056	Felsovadasz
482	205	4823/2052	Szakacsi
482	205	4824/2058	Abaujlak
482	205	4824/2056	Gadna
482	205	4824/2053	Irota
482	205	4826/2057	Gagybator

482 205	4826/2059	Gagyvendegi	
482 205	4828/2054	Rakaca	
482 205	4828/2051	Rakacaszend	
482 205	4828/2057	Szaszfa	
482 210	4820/2102	Detek	
482 210	4820/2108	Encs	
482 210	4821/2106	Abaujdevecser	
482 210	4821/2109	Alsomera	
482 210	4821/2102	Beret	
482 210	4822/2102	Bakta	
482 210	4822/2109	Felsomera	
482 210	4823/2102	Szarazkek	
482 210	4824/2102	Alsogagy	
482 210	4826/2103	Csenyete	
482 210	4826/2101	Felsogagy	
482 210	4826/2107	Fulokercs	
482 210	4827/2104	Litka	
482 210	4828/2108	Pusztaradvany	
482 210	4828/2106	Szemere	
482 210	4829/2101	Buttos	
482 210	4829/2109	Radvany	
482 211	4820/2114	Boldogkovaralja	
482 211	4821/2112	Alsocece	
482 211	4821/2115	Arka	
482 211	4822/2112	Felsocece	
482 211	4823/2115	Korlat	
482 211	4823/2113	Vizsoly	
482 211	4824/2118	Fony	
482 211	4824/2111	Novajidrany	
482 211	4825/2111	Garadna	
482 211	4825/2114	Vilmany	
482 211	4826/2117	Hejce	
482 211	4827/2115	Goncruszka	
482 211	4827/2110	Hernadvecse	
482 211	4828/2117	Gonc	
482 211	4829/2110	Hernadpetri	
482 212	4820/2128	Komloska	
482 212	4823/2126	Haromhuta	
482 212	4827/2129	Kishuta	
482 212	4829/2122	Telkibanya	
482 213	4820/2132	Hercegkut	
482 213	4820/2136	Vegardo	
482 213	4821/2131	Makkoshotyka	
482 213	4825/2137	Rudabanyacska	
482 213	4826/2138	Szephalom	
482 213	4827/2132	Kovacsvagas	
482 213	4827/2136	Mikohaza	
482 213	4828/2137	Alsoregmec	
482 213	4829/2132	Fuzerradvany	
482 213	4829/2138	Luhyna	
482 214	4820/2145	Karos	
482 214	4821/2142	Alsoberecki	
482 214	4822/2142	Felsoberecki	
482 214	4822/2146	Streda nad Bodrogom	

482 214	4824/2140	Satoraljaujhely
482 214	4824/2149	Somotor
482 214	4825/2147	Ladmovce
482 214	4826/2149	Zemplin
482 214	4827/2141	Mala Trna
482 214	4828/2146	Cejkov
482 215	4820/2155	Nagyrozvagy
482 215	4820/2150	Pacin
482 215	4820/2158	Ricse
482 215	4821/2157	Kisrozvagy
482 215	4821/2158	Semjen
482 215	4822/2159	Cseke
482 215	4823/2155	Velky Hores
482 215	4824/2157	Maly Hores
482 215	4825/2157	Kiralyhelmec
482 215	4825/2159	Kralovsky Chlmec
482 215	4828/2157	Bol
482 215	4828/2155	Vojka
482 215	4829/2158	Solnicka
482 220	4821/2208	Tuzser
482 220	4821/2205	Zemplenagard
482 220	4822/2202	Damoc
482 220	4822/2200	Laca
482 220	4822/2209	Tiszabezded
482 220	4823/2209	Gyorocske
482 220	4823/2200	Pribenik
482 220	4823/2206	Velke Trakany
482 220	4825/2203	Biel
482 220	4826/2206	Cierna
482 220	4827/2206	Botany
482 220	4828/2202	Leles
482 221	4821/2213	Eperjeske
482 221	4823/2214	Tiszaszentmarton
482 221	4825/2211	Zahony
482 221	4825/2213	Zsurk
482 221	4826/2212	Chop
482 222	4824/2228	Csomonya
482 223	4822/2234	Goronda
482 223	4828/2236	Rakoshino
482 223	4829/2231	Znyatsevo
482 224	4826/2241	Varpalanka
482 224	4827/2243	Mukachevo
482 224	4827/2243	Oroszveg
482 224	4827/2243	Rosvigovo
482 224	4828/2246	Kolchino
482 225	4820/2256	Ardanovo
482 225	4821/2254	Dorogobratovo
482 225	4824/2253	Szala
482 231	4821/2314	Zadneye
482 231	4822/2317	Dolgoye (Ii)
482 231	4825/2316	Bronka
482 231	4827/2315	Kushnitsa
482 231	4829/2313	Keretski
482 231	4829/2316	Lisicovo

482	232	4825/2325	Jelenkowate
482	233	4821/2332	Nizhnyaya Bystraya
482	233	4822/2332	Nizhne Bystraya
482	233	4827/2332	Vuchkovo
482	233	4829/2338	Sinevir
482	234	4826/2341	Kolochava
482	234	4827/2340	Negrovets
482	235	4821/2354	Russkaya Mokraya
482	235	4822/2358	Lopukhov
482	235	4823/2350	Nemetskaya Mokra
482	242	4825/2425	Starunia
482	242	4825/2425	Zuraki
482	243	4820/2434	Kremintsy
482	243	4824/2436	Mikulichin
482	243	4827/2430	Tirimia Mare
482	243	4827/2433	Yaremcha
482	243	4828/2435	Dora
482	244	4823/2448	Tekucha
482	244	4825/2445	Banya Berezov
482	244	4825/2449	Verkhniy Berezov
482	244	4827/2449	Sloboda
482	244	4828/2444	Chernyye Oslavy
482	244	4829/2442	Belyye Oslavy
482	245	4820/2450	Kosmach
482	245	4823/2459	Utoropy
482	245	4824/2451	Berezuv Nizhny
482	245	4824/2454	Lucha
482	245	4824/2457	Yablonov
482	245	4825/2455	Berezow Sredni
482	245	4825/2459	Stopchatuv
482	245	4828/2457	Klyuchev
482	245	4829/2451	Rungury
482	250	4821/2502	Pistyn
482	250	4823/2509	Khimchin
482	250	4827/2500	Myshin
482	251	4820/2513	Kobaki
482	251	4820/2517	Miliye
482	251	4822/2513	Rozhnov
482	251	4824/2519	Dzhuruv
482	251	4825/2514	Trostyanets (Snyatyn)
482	251	4826/2517	Ilintsy (Chernovtsy)
482	251	4827/2514	Troitsa
482	251	4828/2510	Debeslavtse
482	251	4828/2518	Zabolotov
482	251	4829/2512	Semakovtsy (Kolomyya)
482	251	4829/2511	Zamulintse
482	252	4820/2529	Babin (Bucovina)
482	252	4820/2522	Vilyavche
482	252	4821/2525	Zamostye
482	252	4822/2521	Banilov (Ceremus)
482	252	4823/2520	Popiyelniki
482	252	4824/2524	Dragasymuv
482	252	4824/2527	Knyazhe
482	252	4824/2522	Tuchapy
482	252	4826/2520	Rudniki
482	252	4827/2528	Karluv
482	252	4827/2526	Vidinov
482	252	4828/2521	Oleshkuv
482	252	4828/2524	Volchkovtsy
482	253	4821/2538	Zelena (Bucovina)
482	253	4823/2538	Nepolokovtsy
482	253	4823/2531	Vashkovtsy
482	253	4823/2536	Zavale
482	253	4824/2531	Zaluche
482	253	4827/2534	Snyatyn
482	253	4828/2539	Gavrileshte
482	253	4829/2538	Khliveshte
482	254	4820/2542	Glinitsa
482	254	4820/2548	Revna
482	254	4821/2548	Altmamayeshti
482	254	4822/2547	Luzhany
482	254	4822/2540	Revakouts
482	254	4822/2545	Shipintsy
482	254	4824/2548	Vitelyuvka
482	254	4825/2542	Oshekhliby
482	254	4826/2546	Kitsman
482	254	4829/2542	Davideshte
482	254	4829/2545	Klivodin
482	255	4820/2557	Sadgura
482	255	4827/2556	Vaslouts
482	255	4828/2559	Khoroshovtsy
482	255	4828/2554	Malyy Kochurov
482	255	4829/2555	Verbouts
482	255	4829/2555	Verbovtsy (Tarnopol)
482	260	4823/2607	Toporovtsy
482	260	4825/2602	Chernavka
482	260	4825/2608	Kolinkovtsy
482	260	4829/2601	Dobronovtsy
482	261	4820/2618	Dinovtsy
482	261	4825/2610	Grozintsi
482	261	4825/2619	Zarozhan
482	261	4826/2616	Klishkovtsy
482	261	4826/2615	Malintsy
482	261	4827/2611	Shilovtsy
482	262	4821/2629	Belauts
482	262	4825/2626	Dolinen
482	262	4825/2620	Shirovtsy
482	262	4826/2621	Nedoboyevtsy
482	263	4820/2634	Nesfoyya
482	263	4822/2632	Khazhdeu De Sus
482	263	4823/2636	Mikhaylyanka
482	263	4827/2631	Dankovtsy
482	263	4827/2639	Perkovtsy
482	263	4829/2630	Khotin
482	264	4828/2642	Moshanets
482	265	4821/2657	Kotyudzhen
482	265	4823/2652	Larga
482	265	4823/2655	Sankaitsy

482	265	4827/2655	Volchinets (Hotin)
482	265	4828/2650	Kelmentsy
482	270	4822/2706	Brichany
482	270	4823/2706	Grimankautsy
482	270	4825/2708	Vashkovtsy Khotin
482	270	4828/2704	Grubna
482	271	4820/2714	Markeutsy
482	271	4821/2716	Korestautsy
482	271	4821/2711	Trebiskauts
482	271	4824/2716	Mendikauts
482	272	4822/2720	Khodoroutsy
482	272	4823/2726	Oknitsa
482	272	4827/2723	Sekuren
482	272	4827/2725	Sokiryany
482	273	4824/2731	Lipnik (Bessarabia)
482	273	4825/2732	Byrnovo
482	273	4826/2737	Verezhen
482	273	4828/2735	Nashlavcha
482	274	4827/2747	Ataki
482	274	4827/2748	Mogilev Podolskiy
482	275	4821/2753	Rughi
482	275	4823/2751	Arioneshty
482	280	4820/2803	Yaruga
482	282	4822/2820	Dzygovka
482	284	4823/2842	Gorodkovka
482	285	4823/2853	Kryzhopol
482	285	4823/2859	Zhabokrich
482	290	4829/2901	Kitay Gorod
482	291	4823/2911	Tatarovka
482	291	4826/2910	Verkhovka
482	291	4828/2913	Dimidovca
482	293	4822/2931	Bershad
482	293	4825/2932	Voytovka
482	293	4829/2938	Mankovka
482	294	4829/2941	Shumilovo
482	301	4821/3017	Grushka
482	302	4823/3028	Golovanevsk
482	311	4823/3111	Dobrovelichkovka
482	334	4825/3342	Pyatikhatki
482	342	4822/3427	Krinichki
482	345	4827/3459	Dnepropetrovsk
482	351	4828/3512	Igren
482	353	4820/3531	Sinelnikovo
482	362	4827/3626	Petropavlovka
482	370	4820/3705	Grishino
482	384	4822/3843	Adrianopol
482	415	4821/4150	Morozovsk
483	074	4835/0749	Kehl
483	075	4832/0759	Appenweier
483	075	4832/0753	Willstatt
483	075	4836/0752	Bodersweier
483	075	4839/0755	Rheinbischofsheim
483	080	4834/0803	Ulm
483	080	4835/0801	Renchen
483	080	4838/0804	Achern
483	084	4830/0847	Baisingen
483	084	4832/0841	Unterschwandorf
483	084	4833/0843	Nagold
483	085	4831/0850	Bondorf
483	090	4830/0906	Wankheim
483	090	4832/0903	Tubingen
483	090	4836/0906	Dettenhausen
483	091	4832/0916	Metzingen
483	091	4834/0912	Dornach
483	092	4833/0927	Oberlenningen
483	092	4838/0921	Nurtingen
483	093	4835/0934	Neidlingen
483	094	4836/0943	Deggingen
483	100	4838/1002	Gerstetten
483	101	4832/1013	Oberstotzingen
483	101	4833/1017	Sontheim an der Brenz
483	101	4835/1012	Hurben
483	102	4830/1027	Aislingen
483	102	4830/1029	Glott
483	102	4833/1022	Gundelfingen
483	102	4834/1026	Lauingen
483	103	4830/1034	Ellerbach
483	103	4834/1039	Binswangen
483	103	4836/1033	Hochstadt an der Donau
483	104	4830/1040	Emersacker
483	104	4833/1041	Wertingen
483	104	4836/1043	Buttenwiesen
483	104	4837/1048	Allmannshofen
483	104	4838/1040	Gremheim
483	104	4838/1045	Lauterbach (Bavaria)
483	110	4835/1106	Pottmes
483	111	4833/1116	Schrobenhausen
483	111	4838/1115	Berg im Gau
483	113	4832/1131	Pfaffenhofen an der Ilm
483	113	4835/1135	Eschelbach an der Ilm
483	120	4832/1209	Landshut
483	123	4838/1230	Dingolfing
483	124	4832/1247	Jagerndorf
483	131	4832/1319	Furstenzell
483	131	4833/1314	Ortenburg
483	131	4837/1317	Otterskirchen
483	131	4838/1311	Vilshofen
483	132	4835/1329	Passau
483	132	4836/1328	Hals
483	133	4834/1339	Obernzell
483	133	4839/1338	Hauzenberg
483	142	4839/1422	Rozmberk nad Vltavou
483	142	4839/1426	Ujvasar (Bohemia)
483	143	4830/1430	Freistadt
483	144	4831/1448	Liebenau (Austria)
483	150	4832/1505	Marbach am Walde
483	151	4836/1513	Rudmanns

483	153	4839/1539	Horn (Austria)
483	154	4838/1549	Eggenburg
483	155	4831/1555	Ziersdorf
483	155	4833/1551	Ravelsbach
483	155	4836/1553	Niederschleinz
483	160	4830/1604	Breitenwaida
483	160	4833/1605	Hollabrunn
483	160	4838/1601	Obersteinabrunn
483	160	4839/1605	Kalladorf
483	161	4838/1612	Kleinweikersdorf
483	161	4839/1617	Stronsdorf
483	162	4832/1629	Ladendorf
483	162	4833/1624	Niederleis
483	162	4837/1624	Gnadendorf
483	162	4839/1623	Gaubitsch
483	163	4830/1637	Schrick
483	163	4832/1632	Paasdorf
483	163	4833/1639	Kettlasbrunn
483	163	4834/1634	Mistelbach an der Zaya
483	163	4837/1638	Erdberg
483	164	4832/1645	Zistersdorf
483	164	4834/1642	Maustrenk
483	164	4835/1649	Palterndorf
483	164	4838/1648	Altlichtenwarth
483	164	4838/1643	Grosskrut
483	165	4830/1652	Jedenspeigen
483	165	4832/1654	Drosing
483	165	4834/1651	Niederabsdorf
483	165	4837/1655	Hohenau
483	165	4839/1654	Rabensburg
483	170	4830/1700	Velke Levare
483	170	4838/1709	Sastin
483	174	4830/1743	Velke Kostolany
483	174	4831/1748	Drahovce
483	174	4838/1744	Vrbove
483	175	4830/1759	Velke Ripnany
483	175	4832/1754	Ardanovce
483	175	4835/1751	Banka
483	175	4836/1750	Piestany
483	180	4831/1801	Luzany
483	180	4835/1809	Jacovce
483	181	4834/1811	Topolcany
483	181	4836/1818	Nedanovce
483	181	4838/1818	Zabokreky nad Nitrou
483	182	4831/1825	Skycov
483	182	4836/1829	Felfalu
483	182	4838/1828	Oslany
483	185	4835/1853	Ladomer
483	190	4835/1908	Zvolen
483	192	4834/1925	Detva
483	194	4830/1941	Malinec
483	194	4834/1943	Ipel
483	195	4834/1950	Kokava nad Rimavicou
483	195	4836/1954	Klenovec
483	195	4838/1957	Hacava
483	200	4830/2007	Hostisovce
483	200	4835/2002	Poproc
483	200	4835/2006	Ratkova
483	200	4835/2004	Ratkovska Sucha
483	200	4837/2006	Sirk
483	200	4839/2003	Ratkovske Bystre
483	201	4830/2013	Polina
483	201	4833/2014	Drzkovce
483	201	4834/2018	Gicze
483	201	4836/2011	Nandraz
483	201	4838/2014	Jelsava
483	202	4830/2023	Coltovo
483	202	4830/2029	Kecovo
483	202	4831/2023	Bohunovo
483	202	4831/2020	Meliata
483	202	4831/2023	Tiba
483	202	4832/2025	Ardovo
483	202	4833/2024	Plesivec
483	202	4837/2021	Rozlozna
483	203	4833/2032	Silica
483	203	4834/2037	Silicka Jablonica
483	203	4838/2030	Brzotin
483	204	4830/2040	Szin
483	204	4830/2049	Tornabarakony
483	204	4831/2045	Bodvarako
483	204	4831/2041	Szogliget
483	204	4831/2047	Tornaszentandras
483	204	4832/2044	Bodvaszilas
483	204	4833/2049	Bodvalenke
483	204	4833/2046	Komjati
483	204	4834/2047	Tornanadaska
483	204	4836/2045	Hrhov
483	204	4838/2046	Borka
483	205	4830/2057	Keresztete
483	205	4830/2056	Pamleny
483	205	4834/2051	Hidvegardo
483	205	4834/2052	Hostovce nad Bodvou
483	205	4836/2050	Dvorniky
483	205	4836/2053	Turna nad Bodvou
483	205	4837/2050	Zadiel
483	205	4839/2059	Debrad
483	210	4830/2100	Perecse
483	210	4831/2101	Kany
483	210	4832/2104	Buzica
483	210	4833/2103	Resica
483	210	4836/2104	Cecejovce
483	210	4836/2102	Mokrance
483	210	4838/2104	Panovce
483	211	4830/2114	Hidasnemeti
483	211	4830/2117	Zsujta
483	211	4831/2116	Tornyosnemeti
483	211	4832/2119	Abaujvar
483	211	4833/2112	Perin

483	211	4835/2117	Belza
483	211	4837/2115	Haniska
483	211	4839/2118	Buzice
483	212	4830/2127	Nyiri
483	212	4831/2128	Fuzerkomlos
483	212	4832/2122	Panyok
483	212	4833/2125	Hollohaza
483	212	4835/2123	Skaros
483	212	4835/2128	Slanska Huta
483	212	4836/2120	Hernadcsany
483	212	4836/2121	Zdana
483	212	4837/2122	Nizna Mysla
483	212	4838/2129	Slanec
483	212	4838/2123	Vysna Mysla
483	212	4839/2124	Pocskai
483	213	4831/2138	Michalany
483	213	4833/2134	Brezina
483	213	4833/2138	Lastovce
483	213	4835/2134	Kuzmice
483	213	4836/2133	Slivnik
483	213	4839/2134	Kerestur
483	214	4831/2143	Kysta
483	214	4831/2149	Sirnik
483	214	4832/2144	Novosad
483	214	4833/2147	Garany
483	214	4835/2140	Upor
483	214	4838/2143	Trebisov
483	215	4834/2155	Male Raskovce
483	215	4834/2159	Vojany
483	215	4835/2158	Drahnov
483	215	4836/2155	Slavkovce
483	215	4837/2151	Falkusovce
483	215	4838/2156	Budkovce
483	215	4838/2153	Dubravka
483	220	4832/2207	Budince
483	220	4832/2207	Klacany
483	220	4833/2202	Cicarovce
483	220	4833/2205	Velke Kapusany
483	220	4835/2202	Lieskova
483	220	4837/2204	Pavlovce nad Uhom
483	220	4838/2209	Bezovce
483	221	4830/2214	Strumkovka
483	221	4833/2218	Kereknye
483	221	4837/2210	Lekarovce
483	221	4837/2219	Radvanka
483	221	4837/2218	Uzhgorod
483	221	4839/2213	Jenkovce
483	222	4831/2228	Valkaja
483	223	4831/2236	Kalnik
483	223	4832/2230	Seredne
483	223	4832/2230	Seredneye
483	224	4831/2246	Nizhnyaya Viznitse
483	224	4831/2248	Obava
483	225	4832/2254	Pasika
483	225	4833/2259	Svalyava
483	225	4835/2255	Hnyla
483	230	4834/2304	Sasovka
483	230	4835/2305	Butla
483	230	4835/2305	Husne Wyzne
483	230	4835/2305	Matkow
483	230	4835/2305	Wysocko Wyzne
483	230	4835/2305	Zadzielsko
483	230	4838/2303	Gankovitsa
483	231	4835/2315	Hutar
483	231	4835/2315	Plawie
483	231	4835/2315	Tucholka
483	232	4834/2327	Lozansky
483	232	4834/2329	Soyma
483	232	4835/2327	Repinne
483	232	4835/2324	Tuska
483	232	4836/2329	Majdan
483	232	4838/2323	Kelechin
483	232	4839/2326	Holatin
483	232	4839/2323	Izky
483	233	4832/2330	Mezhgorye
483	233	4838/2331	Verkhnyaya Bystra
483	234	4835/2345	Mizun Stary
483	234	4835/2341	Sinevir Polyana
483	235	4835/2355	Witwica
483	241	4831/2416	Maksimets
483	241	4832/2416	Verpole
483	242	4832/2420	Zelenaya
483	242	4834/2426	Pasechna
483	242	4838/2428	Bitkov
483	242	4839/2429	Molodkov
483	243	4831/2439	Zarechye
483	243	4831/2439	Zarechye (Tarnopol)
483	243	4832/2438	Delyatin
483	243	4837/2432	Pnyuv
483	243	4838/2434	Nadvornaya
483	243	4839/2431	Yavoruv
483	244	4831/2449	Mlodyatyn
483	244	4833/2442	Dobrotuv
483	244	4833/2445	Lanchin
483	244	4834/2449	Sadzavka
483	244	4835/2445	Felizienthal
483	244	4835/2442	Krasna (Nadvorna)
483	244	4835/2442	Krasna (Turka)
483	244	4837/2448	Kubayuvka
483	244	4837/2440	Verkhniy Maydan
483	244	4838/2445	Maydan Sredni
483	244	4839/2446	Glinki (Stanislawow)
483	245	4830/2452	Novo Markovka
483	245	4830/2459	Verbionzh Vyzhny
483	245	4831/2454	Pechenezhin
483	245	4831/2459	Sopov
483	245	4832/2458	Kiydantsy
483	245	4833/2456	Knyazhdvur

483	245	4835/2454	Tolmachik
483	245	4836/2457	Rakovchyk
483	245	4837/2457	Lesnaya Slobodka
483	250	4832/2502	Kolomyya
483	250	4833/2500	Dyatkovtsy
483	250	4834/2504	Pyadyki
483	250	4835/2508	Turka
483	250	4836/2501	Malaya Kamenka
483	250	4838/2506	Kamionka Wielka
483	250	4839/2501	Korshev
483	250	4839/2502	Liski (Stanislawow)
483	251	4832/2513	Zagaypol
483	251	4833/2518	Kulachkovtsy
483	251	4834/2518	Khomyakovka
483	251	4834/2516	Malyy Gvozdets
483	251	4834/2510	Podgaychiki (Tarnopol)
483	251	4835/2517	Gvozdets
483	251	4838/2512	Dzurkiv
483	251	4838/2514	Rosokhach
483	252	4832/2525	Gankovtsy
483	252	4832/2529	Krasnostavtsy
483	252	4832/2527	Zadubrovtsy
483	252	4835/2522	Slobodka (Stanislawow)
483	252	4835/2522	Slobodka Polna
483	252	4836/2526	Torgovitsa (Stanislawow)
483	252	4837/2522	Soroki (Stanislawow)
483	252	4837/2523	Verbovtsy
483	252	4839/2527	Chernyatin
483	252	4839/2528	Glushkovskoye
483	253	4831/2532	Rusov
483	253	4831/2534	Stetseva
483	253	4833/2531	Podvysokoye
483	253	4835/2538	Borovtse
483	253	4837/2532	Yasenev Polnyy
483	253	4839/2533	Serafintsy
483	254	4832/2540	Yuzhenitse
483	254	4833/2544	Verenchanka
483	254	4835/2546	Kadobovtsy
483	254	4835/2540	Kiselev
483	254	4836/2549	Chinkeu
483	254	4837/2544	Kreshchatik
483	254	4838/2544	Zaleshchiki
483	254	4839/2543	Kostrizhevka
483	254	4839/2548	Repuzhintsy
483	255	4830/2556	Yurkovtsy
483	255	4831/2551	Zastavna
483	255	4833/2558	Pogorelovka
483	255	4834/2558	Okno
483	255	4834/2552	Tauteny
483	255	4835/2553	Dorosauti
483	255	4835/2555	Zazulintsy
483	255	4836/2550	Vasilou
483	255	4837/2557	Bogdanovka (Tarnopol)
483	255	4837/2558	Brodok
483	255	4837/2552	Grudek
483	255	4838/2552	Kulakovtse
483	260	4831/2605	Rzhavintsy
483	260	4832/2606	Gorosheve
483	260	4834/2603	Onut
483	260	4836/2601	Mittsau
483	260	4836/2604	Samuseni
483	260	4837/2602	Mosoreni
483	260	4838/2601	Kolodrobka
483	260	4838/2605	Pilipche
483	261	4833/2610	Olkhovets
483	261	4835/2619	Panevtsy
483	261	4835/2615	Zvinyachka
483	261	4837/2618	Kudrintsy
483	261	4837/2610	Melnitsa Podolskaya
483	261	4839/2610	Ivane Puste
483	262	4830/2622	Belovtsy
483	262	4830/2624	Rukshin
483	262	4832/2625	Kozachuvka
483	262	4832/2624	Okopy
483	263	4831/2630	Braga
483	263	4833/2630	Zhvanets
483	264	4830/2645	Lenkovtsy
483	264	4833/2649	Grushevtsy
483	264	4833/2641	Voronovitsa (Bessarabia)
483	265	4830/2656	Buzovitsa
483	265	4832/2652	Babin (Bessarabia)
483	270	4830/2703	Ivanovtsy
483	270	4832/2702	Polivanov Yar
483	270	4833/2705	Molodovo (Bessarabia)
483	270	4835/2708	Staraya Ushitsa
483	271	4830/2713	Romankovtsy
483	271	4835/2710	Korman
483	271	4836/2718	Neporotovo
483	271	4838/2719	Kalyus
483	272	4831/2728	Kobalchin
483	273	4832/2738	Yaryshev
483	274	4832/2744	Izrailovka
483	274	4832/2748	Ozarintsy
483	274	4837/2743	Kukavka
483	274	4838/2748	Vendichany
483	275	4836/2757	Sledy
483	275	4839/2756	Tropovo
483	280	4832/2807	Chernevtsy
483	280	4835/2800	Conatcauti
483	283	4832/2837	Komargorod
483	283	4832/2831	Tomashpol
483	283	4838/2837	Goryshkovka
483	284	4832/2846	Vapnyarka
483	290	4832/2902	Kapustyany
483	291	4831/2911	Trostyanets
483	291	4836/2917	Chetvertinovka

483	291	4837/2914	Olyanitsa
483	291	4839/2912	Lukashevka
483	295	4832/2958	Ternovka
483	300	4830/3000	Ladizhnenka
483	301	4833/3015	Ladyzhinka
483	302	4838/3027	Dubovo
483	304	4839/3047	Torgovitsa (Ukraine)
483	321	4830/3218	Kirovograd
483	325	4834/3255	Novaya Praga
483	342	4839/3420	Verkhnedneprovsk
483	343	4830/3437	Dneprodzerzhinsk
483	351	4837/3512	Novomoskovsk
483	355	4831/3552	Pavlograd
483	380	4832/3800	Uzava (Artemovsk)
483	380	4835/3800	Artemovsk
483	383	4838/3836	Pervomaysk (Kommunarsk)
483	384	4830/3847	Kommunarsk
483	392	4834/3920	Voroshilovgrad
484	075	4840/0757	Freistett
484	080	4842/0809	Buhl
484	080	4844/0803	Hildmannsfeld
484	080	4844/0801	Lichtenau
484	080	4846/0803	Stollhofen
484	081	4845/0815	Baden Baden
484	081	4846/0810	Sinzheim
484	081	4847/0812	Oos
484	081	4848/0816	Dolgesheim
484	081	4849/0818	Rotenfels
484	082	4841/0821	Forbach
484	082	4846/0820	Gernsbach
484	082	4847/0821	Horden
484	082	4848/0820	Gaggenau
484	082	4848/0826	Herrenalb
484	083	4845/0833	Wildbad im Schwarzwald
484	084	4843/0844	Calw
484	085	4843/0854	Schafhausen
484	090	4842/0901	Sindelfingen
484	090	4844/0909	Mohringen
484	091	4841/0913	Bernhausen
484	091	4841/0910	Echterdingen
484	091	4842/0913	Plieningen
484	091	4843/0918	Nellingen
484	091	4845/0918	Esslingen
484	091	4846/0911	Stuttgart
484	091	4847/0912	Weil im Dorf
484	091	4848/0917	Fellbach
484	093	4841/0938	Jebenhausen
484	093	4848/0932	Schorndorf
484	094	4841/0946	Sussen
484	094	4842/0940	Goppingen
484	094	4848/0947	Gmund (Baden)
484	094	4848/0947	Schwabisch Gmund
484	095	4842/0954	Weissenstein
484	100	4848/1002	Essingen
484	101	4840/1019	Zoschingen
484	102	4845/1029	Aufhausen
484	102	4848/1029	Hurnheim
484	102	4849/1028	Ederheim
484	103	4842/1037	Unterbissingen
484	103	4843/1037	Bissingen
484	103	4843/1033	Diemantstein
484	103	4845/1030	Bollstadt
484	103	4847/1035	Monchsdeggingen
484	104	4842/1048	Donauworth
484	104	4842/1040	Oppertshofen
484	104	4846/1040	Harburg
484	105	4841/1054	Rain
484	105	4842/1053	Genderkingen
484	105	4845/1054	Graisbach
484	105	4845/1057	Schweinspoint
484	110	4842/1101	Burgheim
484	110	4845/1104	Rennertshofen
484	110	4847/1100	Trugenhofen
484	110	4848/1107	Hutting
484	111	4842/1113	Untermaxfeld
484	111	4844/1111	Neuburg an der Donau
484	112	4846/1126	Ingolstadt
484	113	4841/1137	Geisenfeld
484	113	4846/1137	Vohburg an der Donau
484	115	4840/1158	Pfeffenhausen
484	115	4849/1151	Abensberg
484	121	4841/1212	Ergoldsbach
484	124	4841/1241	Landau an der Isar
484	124	4843/1241	Ganacker
484	125	4847/1252	Plattling
484	130	4847/1303	Hengersberg
484	133	4848/1333	Freyung
484	134	4842/1348	Breitenberg
484	140	4845/1405	Hurka
484	141	4846/1417	Vetrni
484	141	4849/1413	Boletice
484	141	4849/1419	Cesky Krumlov
484	142	4841/1425	Hnevanov
484	142	4844/1429	Kaplice
484	143	4840/1432	Mikoly
484	143	4841/1435	Malonty
484	143	4841/1430	Mladonov
484	145	4842/1453	Weitra
484	145	4846/1458	Ceske Velenice
484	150	4846/1501	Hoheneich
484	151	4849/1517	Waidhofen an der Thaya
484	152	4840/1520	Grosspoppen
484	152	4847/1524	Grosssiegharts
484	153	4842/1534	Poigen
484	153	4843/1531	Messern

484	153	4849/1537	Zissersdorf	484	202	4840/2022	Stitnik
484	154	4841/1545	Sigmundsherberg	484	202	4844/2025	Nizna Slana
484	154	4843/1543	Kainreith	484	202	4846/2025	Gocs
484	154	4847/1540	Geras	484	202	4847/2025	Vlachovo
484	155	4841/1557	Zellerndorf	484	202	4849/2022	Dobsina
484	155	4842/1555	Deinzendorf	484	203	4840/2032	Roznava
484	155	4842/1551	Pulkau	484	204	4844/2045	Smolnik (Slovakia)
484	155	4845/1556	Obernalb	484	204	4845/2047	Smolnicka Huta
484	155	4845/1557	Retz	484	204	4848/2048	Mnisek nad Hnilcom
484	160	4842/1603	Jetzelsdorf	484	205	4841/2059	Jasov
484	160	4842/1609	Obritz	484	210	4841/2107	Semsa
484	160	4846/1600	Unterretzbach	484	210	4845/2108	Vysny Klatov
484	160	4849/1606	Vrbovec	484	210	4845/2101	Zlata Idka
484	161	4840/1611	Mailberg	484	211	4840/2110	Mala Ida
484	161	4842/1611	Grosskadolz	484	211	4841/2116	Barca
484	161	4843/1618	Wulzeshofen	484	211	4842/2115	Kosice
484	161	4845/1614	Jaroslavice	484	212	4840/2125	Blazice
484	161	4846/1616	Hradek	484	212	4841/2126	Ruskov
484	162	4843/1623	Laa an der Thaya	484	212	4844/2128	Svinica
484	163	4840/1638	Poysdorf	484	212	4845/2121	Rozhanovce
484	163	4845/1634	Drasenhofen	484	212	4847/2129	Vysna Kamenica
484	163	4848/1638	Mikulov	484	213	4842/2139	Secovce
484	164	4841/1641	Herrnbaumgarten	484	213	4845/2131	Kosicky Klecenov
484	165	4846/1653	Breclav	484	213	4846/2139	Kravany
484	170	4843/1708	Gbely	484	213	4848/2139	Cabov
484	171	4848/1710	Holic	484	214	4841/2149	Banovce nad Ondavou
484	172	4841/1722	Senica	484	214	4842/2148	Vasarhely
484	172	4843/1724	Sobotiste	484	214	4843/2147	Horovce
484	172	4848/1728	Vrbovce	484	214	4844/2145	Tusice
484	173	4840/1732	Brezova pod Bradlom	484	214	4846/2140	Stankovce
484	173	4845/1734	Myjava	484	214	4847/2142	Secovska Polianka
484	173	4845/1732	Tura Luka	484	214	4849/2142	Sacurov
484	174	4847/1742	Stara Tura	484	215	4840/2150	Lozin
484	174	4849/1748	Moravske Lieskove	484	215	4841/2153	Vrbnica
484	175	4845/1750	Nove Mesto nad Vahom	484	215	4842/2156	Lastomir
484	175	4847/1754	Beckov	484	215	4842/2159	Rebrin
484	181	4843/1816	Banovce nad Bebravou	484	215	4843/2153	Krasnovce
484	183	4843/1833	Novaky	484	215	4844/2159	Cecehov
484	183	4846/1838	Prievidza	484	215	4844/2151	Pozdisovce
484	184	4844/1846	Handlova	484	215	4845/2156	Michalovce
484	184	4846/1846	Raztocno	484	215	4846/2156	Stranany
484	185	4842/1855	Kremnica	484	215	4848/2153	Petrovce nad Laborcom
484	190	4840/1908	Badin	484	215	4849/2151	Nacina Ves
484	190	4843/1908	Radvan	484	215	4849/2154	Zbudza
484	190	4844/1909	Banska Bystrica	484	220	4841/2208	Svatus
484	190	4846/1908	Svaty Jakub	484	220	4842/2202	Inacovce
484	190	4849/1908	Spania Dolina	484	220	4844/2205	Blatne Revistia
484	191	4840/1919	Hrochot	484	220	4844/2206	Vysne Revistia
484	193	4849/1939	Brezno nad Hronom	484	220	4845/2201	Hazin
484	195	4841/1957	Tisovec	484	220	4847/2208	Ubrez
484	200	4841/2007	Nagyrocze	484	220	4849/2200	Kaluza
484	200	4844/2003	Muran	484	220	4849/2204	Kusin
484	201	4847/2019	Vysna Slana	484	221	4840/2215	Krcava
484	202	4840/2026	Sebespatak	484	221	4842/2211	Porostov

484	221	4843/2216	Kolibabovce
484	221	4845/2211	Sobrance
484	221	4845/2214	Tibava
484	221	4846/2212	Horna
484	221	4847/2216	Konus
484	221	4849/2218	Podhorod
484	221	4849/2211	Vysna Rybnica
484	222	4844/2228	Perechin
484	222	4848/2225	Berezny Velky
484	223	4843/2236	Turyanremety
484	224	4840/2245	Poroshkov
484	225	4845/2255	Butelka Nizna
484	225	4845/2255	Butelka Wyzna
484	225	4845/2255	Tureczki Wyzne
484	225	4845/2255	Tureczki Nizne
484	230	4845/2305	Wysocko Nizne
484	230	4846/2306	Nizhniye Veretski
484	231	4840/2318	Podobovets
484	231	4842/2314	Guklivyy
484	231	4842/2318	Rozsoska
484	231	4843/2311	Volovets
484	232	4840/2321	Pilipets
484	232	4842/2325	Lahovec
484	232	4842/2322	Nizhne Studenyy
484	232	4844/2321	Verkhne Studenyy
484	232	4845/2325	Toustobaby
484	232	4847/2320	Oporets
484	232	4847/2326	Volosyanka
484	232	4849/2322	Lavochne
484	233	4840/2334	Torun (Ukraine)
484	233	4844/2339	Vyshkov
484	233	4845/2335	Stynawa Nizna
484	233	4845/2335	Truchanow
484	234	4845/2345	Siemiginow
484	235	4845/2355	Czolhany
484	235	4845/2355	Huziejow Stary
484	235	4845/2355	Solukow
484	240	4848/2401	Sukhodul
484	240	4849/2408	Rypne
484	241	4840/2419	Krichka
484	241	4841/2416	Porogi
484	241	4842/2418	Yablonka
484	241	4844/2415	Lukvitsa
484	241	4845/2410	Jasien (Dolina)
484	241	4846/2412	Slivki
484	241	4849/2413	Nebylov
484	241	4849/2411	Pereginsko
484	242	4840/2428	Babche
484	242	4841/2423	Lubenets
484	242	4842/2425	Solotwina
484	242	4843/2423	Rakovets (Bogorodchany)
484	242	4843/2425	Zazheche
484	242	4845/2426	Dzvinyach
484	242	4845/2422	Kosmach (Bogorodchany)
484	242	4846/2422	Rosilno
484	242	4848/2427	Glebuvka
484	242	4848/2423	Khmelevka
484	242	4849/2425	Glemboke
484	243	4840/2436	Nezavizov
484	243	4841/2432	Gvozd
484	243	4841/2438	Tarnovitsa Lesna
484	243	4842/2436	Fitkuv
484	243	4842/2438	Pererosl
484	243	4844/2439	Tsutsyluv
484	243	4845/2435	Gorokholina
484	243	4845/2437	Grabovets
484	243	4848/2432	Bogorodchany
484	243	4848/2431	Lyakhovitse
484	244	4840/2442	Paryshche
484	244	4841/2443	Gavrilovka
484	244	4842/2449	Strupkuv
484	244	4844/2440	Volosov
484	244	4845/2442	Kamienna
484	244	4845/2446	Vinograd (Tlumach)
484	244	4845/2445	Zalukiew
484	244	4846/2440	Tysmenichany
484	244	4847/2446	Lipovka (Ivano Frankovsk)
484	244	4848/2443	Bratkovtse
484	244	4849/2442	Khomyakuv
484	245	4841/2455	Lesnoy Khlebichin
484	245	4841/2451	Molodyluv
484	245	4842/2452	Goloskuv
484	245	4844/2451	Otynya
484	245	4846/2456	Gostov
484	245	4846/2454	Ostra Mogila
484	245	4847/2456	Ternovitsa
484	250	4842/2506	Zhukov (Stanislawow)
484	250	4843/2501	Bogorodychyn
484	250	4845/2506	Khotimir
484	250	4846/2502	Bortniki (Tlumach)
484	250	4848/2500	Korolyuvka
484	250	4848/2506	Ozeryany (Stanislawow)
484	251	4842/2517	Chortovets
484	251	4842/2510	Obertin
484	251	4845/2518	Voronuv (Stanislawow)
484	251	4846/2514	Garasymuv
484	251	4846/2515	Nezviska
484	251	4847/2518	Semenuva
484	251	4848/2518	Rakovets (Gorodenka)
484	251	4848/2510	Zhivachev
484	251	4849/2513	Isakov
484	252	4840/2522	Okno (Stanislawow)
484	252	4842/2522	Tyshkovtsy
484	252	4844/2522	Oleyeva Kornyuv
484	252	4845/2522	Oleyeva Korolevka

484 252	4845/2525	Petlikowce Stare	
484 252	4847/2529	Daleshova	
484 252	4847/2527	Dubka	
484 252	4848/2520	Kornyuv	
484 252	4848/2523	Olkhovets (Stanislawow)	
484 252	4848/2528	Repuzhyntse	
484 252	4849/2526	Chernelitsa	
484 253	4840/2530	Gorodenka	
484 253	4841/2538	Gorodnitsa (Stanislawow)	
484 253	4843/2538	Ivano Zolot	
484 253	4844/2535	Potochishche	
484 253	4845/2535	Dzuryn	
484 253	4845/2535	Rydoduby	
484 253	4846/2532	Semakovtsy	
484 253	4846/2536	Ustechko	
484 253	4847/2530	Kolyanki	
484 253	4847/2536	Mikhalche	
484 253	4849/2536	Nyrkov	
484 254	4842/2547	Berdykovtse	
484 254	4842/2544	Dzvinyach (Tarnopol)	
484 254	4842/2544	Zvinyach	
484 254	4843/2546	Dupliska	
484 254	4844/2545	Ugrinkovtsy	
484 254	4846/2541	Torskoye	
484 254	4847/2545	Ginkovtse	
484 254	4847/2545	Vezhbova	
484 254	4847/2540	Yakubovka	
484 254	4848/2544	Vorgulintsy	
484 254	4849/2544	Golovchyntse	
484 254	4849/2543	Karolyuvka	
484 254	4849/2549	Shersheniovtse	
484 255	4841/2551	Lesechniki	
484 255	4843/2555	Novoselka Kostyukova	
484 255	4844/2559	Oleyevo Korolevka	
484 255	4845/2555	Hadynkowce	
484 255	4845/2555	Szwajkowce	
484 255	4846/2550	Meshkov	
484 255	4846/2559	Stshalkovtse	
484 255	4847/2553	Bilche Zolotoye	
484 255	4848/2550	Oleksintse	
484 255	4849/2556	Glubochek	
484 260	4841/2603	Babintsy	
484 260	4842/2606	Nizhneye Krivche	
484 260	4842/2602	Shyshkovtse	
484 260	4842/2607	Verkhneye Krivche	
484 260	4844/2602	Skovyatin	
484 260	4846/2605	Volkovtsy	
484 260	4848/2603	Borshchev	
484 260	4848/2603	Borshchuv	
484 260	4848/2606	Slobodka Mushkatovka	
484 260	4849/2600	Veshkhnyakovtse	
484 261	4840/2614	Zalesye (Borshchev)	
484 261	4842/2611	Germakovka	
484 261	4843/2613	Nivra	
484 261	4846/2612	Turilche	
484 261	4849/2610	Ivankov	
484 262	4846/2624	Orinin	
484 263	4840/2634	Kamenets Podolskiy	
484 263	4842/2636	Skala Zbruch	
484 263	4842/2636	Zinkovtsy	
484 264	4846/2648	Bleshchanovka	
484 264	4846/2643	Shatava	
484 264	4848/2647	Mikhalovka	
484 265	4846/2659	Velikiy Zhvanchik	
484 272	4844/2726	Verbovets	
484 273	4844/2731	Murovanyye Kurilovtsy	
484 273	4848/2738	Snitkov	
484 274	4841/2743	Nemerichi	
484 274	4842/2742	Vinozh	
484 274	4843/2748	Luchinchik	
484 274	4847/2749	Khrenovka	
484 275	4843/2750	Luchinets	
484 275	4847/2752	Stepanki	
484 275	4849/2755	Karyshkov	
484 280	4845/2805	Shargorod	
484 281	4841/2818	Dzhurin	
484 282	4846/2821	Derebchin	
484 283	4847/2834	Shpikov	
484 285	4841/2852	Nestervarka	
484 285	4841/2852	Tulchin	
484 291	4840/2915	Ladyzhin	
484 291	4845/2913	Kharpachka	
484 291	4845/2917	Yarmolintsy	
484 292	4848/2923	Gaysin	
484 293	4843/2934	Kublich	
484 294	4840/2944	Teplik	
484 295	4846/2955	Talalayevka	
484 295	4848/2952	Sychevka	
484 300	4847/3000	Oradovka	
484 301	4845/3013	Uman	
484 302	4842/3027	Babanka	
484 313	4847/3139	Novomirgorod	
484 322	4849/3224	Yelizavetgradka	
484 323	4843/3238	Znamenka	
484 323	4849/3230	Tsibulevo	
484 352	4842/3520	Khashchevoye	
484 354	4845/3549	Vyazovka	
484 373	4843/3732	Kramatorsk	
484 383	4846/3837	Nizhneye	
484 443	4845/4430	Volgograd	
485 081	4850/0815	Kuppenheim	
485 081	4850/0813	Niederbuhl	
485 081	4851/0812	Rastatt	
485 081	4852/0817	Muggensturm	
485 082	4853/0820	Malsch	
485 082	4857/0824	Ettlingen	
485 083	4858/0837	Konigsbach	

485	084	4853/0842	Pforzheim
485	085	4856/0858	Vaihingen an der Enz
485	090	4854/0907	Asperg
485	090	4856/0904	Unterriexingen
485	090	4857/0907	Bietigheim
485	091	4850/0918	Waiblingen
485	091	4850/0911	Zuffenhausen
485	091	4852/0915	Aldingen
485	091	4852/0911	Kornwestheim
485	091	4854/0911	Ludwigsburg
485	092	4857/0926	Backnang
485	093	4853/0932	Rudersberg
485	093	4853/0939	Welzheim
485	100	4850/1006	Aalen
485	100	4852/1006	Wasseralfingen
485	100	4857/1008	Ellwangen
485	101	4852/1015	Lauchheim
485	102	4850/1029	Herkheim
485	102	4851/1021	Bopfingen
485	102	4851/1026	Pflaumloch
485	102	4852/1029	Baldingen
485	102	4853/1028	Wallerstein
485	102	4858/1028	Fremdingen
485	103	4851/1037	Alerheim
485	103	4851/1033	Grosselfingen
485	103	4851/1030	Nordlingen
485	103	4853/1032	Lopsingen
485	103	4856/1030	Maihingen
485	103	4856/1039	Megesheim
485	103	4857/1036	Ottingen
485	103	4857/1030	Utzwingen
485	103	4858/1037	Hainsfarth
485	104	4851/1049	Flotzheim
485	104	4852/1043	Wemding
485	104	4853/1048	Otting
485	104	4856/1045	Dockingen
485	104	4856/1043	Polsingen
485	104	4856/1042	Trendel
485	104	4858/1044	Hechlingen
485	104	4858/1041	Hussingen
485	104	4858/1040	Steinhart
485	105	4850/1050	Monheim
485	105	4854/1056	Langenaltheim
485	105	4856/1058	Pappenheim
485	105	4857/1058	Osterdorf
485	105	4857/1055	Treuchtlingen
485	110	4853/1100	Mornsheim
485	111	4851/1110	Ochsenfeld
485	111	4853/1111	Eichstatt
485	112	4853/1125	Schelldorf
485	112	4857/1129	Dorndorf
485	114	4858/1141	Riedenburg
485	115	4855/1152	Kelheim
485	122	4850/1223	Geiselhoring
485	123	4853/1234	Straubing
485	124	4855/1241	Bogen
485	124	4855/1249	Schwarzach
485	125	4850/1258	Deggendorf
485	132	4855/1322	Spiegelau
485	140	4851/1404	Racin
485	142	4850/1428	Velesin
485	142	4856/1429	Roudne
485	142	4859/1428	Ceske Budejovice
485	143	4854/1430	Doudleby
485	145	4851/1455	Halamky
485	145	4853/1457	Rapsach
485	145	4853/1453	Tust
485	145	4855/1455	Klikov
485	150	4852/1507	Heidenreichstein
485	150	4854/1508	Eggern
485	150	4856/1503	Litschau
485	151	4853/1519	Merkengersch
485	151	4855/1514	Kautzen
485	151	4857/1516	Grosstaxen
485	152	4852/1524	Karlstein
485	152	4853/1523	Munchreith an der Thaya
485	152	4859/1521	Slavonice
485	153	4851/1530	Raabs an der Thaya
485	154	4852/1548	Felling
485	154	4852/1544	Safov
485	154	4854/1549	Vranov nad Dyji
485	160	4851/1603	Znojmo
485	161	4857/1619	Miroslav
485	162	4859/1624	Olbramovice
485	163	4859/1631	Pohorelice
485	164	4852/1640	Pavlov
485	164	4856/1644	Hustopece
485	165	4850/1651	Podivin
485	165	4859/1652	Klobouky
485	170	4852/1708	Hodonin
485	171	4851/1714	Skalica
485	171	4854/1719	Straznice
485	171	4859/1716	Bzenec
485	172	4857/1724	Veseli nad Moravou
485	172	4859/1725	Kvacice
485	172	4859/1724	Ostrozske Predmesti
485	172	4859/1723	Uhersky Ostroh
485	173	4859/1732	Hluk
485	174	4858/1745	Ordejov
485	175	4850/1750	Bosaca
485	175	4852/1759	Kostolna
485	180	4851/1801	Trencianska Turna
485	180	4854/1802	Trencin
485	180	4856/1807	Trencianska Tepla
485	180	4858/1807	Nemsova
485	181	4855/1810	Trencianske Teplice
485	181	4858/1811	Dubnica nad Vahom

485	182	4851/1823	Dlhe
485	183	4850/1836	Poruba
485	184	4852/1846	Budis
485	185	4852/1852	Turcianske Teplice
485	185	4853/1853	Raksa
485	185	4858/1853	Valentova
485	185	4859/1853	Rakovo
485	191	4850/1913	Kaliste
485	191	4852/1914	Polianka
485	200	4858/2006	Liptovska Teplicka
485	203	4855/2038	Markusovce
485	203	4857/2034	Spisska Nova Ves
485	204	4857/2048	Spisske Vlachy
485	205	4851/2056	Gelnica
485	205	4855/2052	Krompachy
485	205	4858/2057	Vitaz
485	210	4852/2100	Jaklovce
485	210	4853/2100	Margecany
485	210	4858/2101	Hrabkov
485	210	4858/2106	Zipov
485	211	4851/2113	Kysak
485	211	4851/2116	Lemesany
485	211	4851/2119	Sarisske Bohdanovce
485	211	4859/2116	Solivar
485	213	4852/2138	Vechec
485	213	4856/2136	Sol
485	213	4859/2138	Michalok
485	214	4850/2146	Posa
485	214	4851/2146	Nizny Hrabovec
485	214	4853/2140	Cemerne
485	214	4854/2144	Sedliska
485	214	4854/2141	Vranov nad Toplou
485	214	4855/2146	Tovarne
485	214	4857/2143	Benkovce
485	214	4859/2141	Kvakovce
485	215	4852/2154	Oreske
485	215	4852/2152	Stare
485	215	4852/2150	Strazske
485	215	4856/2155	Humenne
485	215	4857/2156	Kochanovce
485	215	4859/2158	Udavske
485	220	4850/2206	Jovsa
485	220	4850/2209	Poruba pod Vihorlatom
485	220	4859/2209	Snina
485	221	4850/2210	Vysne Remety
485	222	4854/2224	Ubla
485	222	4854/2228	Velikiy Bereznyy
485	222	4857/2220	Klenova
485	222	4858/2226	Ulic
485	223	4857/2236	Kostrina
485	224	4855/2245	Dydiowa
485	224	4856/2249	Tiha
485	225	4855/2258	Libukhora
485	225	4855/2255	Rozlucz
485	225	4855/2255	Rypiany
485	225	4855/2255	Szumiacz
485	230	4855/2305	Topolnica Szlachecka
485	230	4855/2305	Wolosianka Wielka
485	230	4857/2304	Verkhneye Vysotskoye
485	230	4859/2303	Komarniki
485	231	4855/2318	Oryava
485	232	4851/2327	Slavskoye
485	232	4855/2325	Bania Kotowska
485	232	4855/2320	Mochnata
485	232	4855/2328	Tukhlya
485	232	4858/2329	Grebenov
485	233	4855/2335	Dobrohostow
485	233	4855/2335	Orow
485	234	4855/2345	Hurnie
485	235	4854/2355	Veldzizh
485	235	4856/2355	Vygoda
485	235	4857/2355	Novoselitsa (Khodorov)
485	235	4858/2355	Myta
485	240	4851/2407	Sloboda Dubenska
485	240	4853/2404	Spas
485	240	4854/2409	Demnya
485	240	4854/2400	Grabov (Dolina)
485	240	4856/2409	Rozhnyatov
485	240	4858/2401	Dolina
485	241	4851/2417	Krasna (Kalush)
485	241	4853/2410	Tsenyava
485	241	4855/2413	Rovnya
485	241	4855/2414	Topolska
485	241	4856/2419	Landestreu
485	241	4857/2411	Svarichov
485	241	4858/2415	Berlogy
485	241	4859/2412	Broshnev Osada
485	241	4859/2415	Tuzhiluv
485	242	4851/2428	Klusow
485	242	4854/2423	Grabovka
485	242	4855/2422	Ugrynuv Sredni
485	242	4856/2425	Zavoy
485	242	4857/2420	Novitsa
485	242	4858/2426	Yavoruvka
485	243	4851/2439	Radcha
485	243	4852/2436	Lisets
485	243	4853/2438	Drogomirchany
485	243	4857/2436	Rybnoye
485	244	4851/2443	Cherneyev
485	244	4852/2441	Chukaluvka
485	244	4853/2444	Khryplin
485	244	4854/2440	Krekhovtse
485	244	4854/2445	Myketyntse
485	244	4855/2445	Konkolniki
485	244	4855/2446	Ugorniki
485	244	4855/2440	Zagvuzdzh
485	244	4856/2443	Ivano Frankovsk
485	244	4856/2441	Pasechna (Ivano

Frankovsk)

485 244	4857/2445	Volchinets (Stanislowow)
485 244	4858/2446	Kolodeyevka (Ivano Frankovsk)
485 244	4859/2449	Uzin
485 245	4854/2451	Tysmenitsa
485 245	4855/2455	Dytiatyn
485 250	4850/2508	Olesha
485 250	4852/2500	Tlumach
485 250	4852/2502	Ugorniki (Tlumach)
485 250	4854/2507	Kutyska
485 250	4855/2505	Muzylow
485 250	4857/2506	Nizhnev
485 250	4859/2504	Lipa (Stanislawow)
485 250	4859/2500	Petrilov
485 251	4851/2512	Dolina (Ivano Frankovsk)
485 251	4851/2517	Petrov
485 251	4852/2517	Snovidov
485 251	4855/2515	Stinka
485 251	4856/2510	Koropets
485 252	4850/2523	Kopachintsy
485 252	4850/2529	Latach
485 252	4853/2526	Beremyany
485 252	4853/2521	Kostelniki
485 252	4854/2526	Zhnibrody
485 252	4854/2520	Zolotoy Potok
485 252	4855/2525	Bobulince
485 252	4855/2522	Skomorokhy
485 252	4856/2526	Duliby (Pomortsy)
485 252	4856/2520	Sokoluv (Podgaytsy)
485 252	4856/2520	Sokoluv
485 252	4858/2526	Pomortsy
485 252	4859/2523	Leshchantse
485 253	4851/2531	Drogichuvka
485 253	4851/2534	Sadki (Tarnopol)
485 253	4852/2536	Tsapovka
485 253	4855/2535	Buryakovka
485 253	4857/2534	Bazar
485 253	4858/2532	Kshyvoluka
485 253	4858/2534	Palashevka
485 254	4850/2549	Shypovtse
485 254	4850/2544	Tolstoye
485 254	4852/2544	Svidova
485 254	4853/2541	Antonuv
485 254	4854/2543	Mukhavka
485 254	4854/2549	Ulashkovtsy
485 254	4855/2545	Dereniowka
485 254	4855/2545	Kobylowloki
485 254	4855/2545	Krowinka
485 254	4855/2545	Plebanowka
485 254	4856/2544	Naguzhanka (Czortkow)
485 254	4857/2543	Dolina (Tarnopol)
485 254	4857/2548	Rosokhach (Tarnopol)

485 254	4857/2544	Yagelnitsa
485 254	4858/2543	Shulganuvka
485 254	4859/2542	Yagelnitsa Stara
485 255	4851/2556	Konstantsya
485 255	4853/2557	Ozeryany
485 255	4855/2555	Chlopowka
485 255	4855/2555	Kluwince
485 255	4855/2550	Sosolyuvka
485 255	4856/2559	Davidkovtse
485 255	4856/2554	Zalese (Chortkov)
485 255	4858/2557	Kolendzyany
485 255	4858/2557	Novosyulka
485 260	4851/2600	Kozachizna
485 260	4851/2600	Lanovtse (Tarnopol)
485 260	4852/2606	Rudka (Tarnopol)
485 260	4853/2600	Zelenitsa
485 260	4855/2605	Losyach
485 260	4856/2609	Bosyry
485 260	4858/2602	Velikiye Chornokontsy
485 260	4859/2600	Slobodka (Tarnopol)
485 261	4851/2612	Skala Podolskaya
485 261	4851/2612	Volokhi
485 261	4854/2610	Burdyakovtsy
485 261	4857/2610	Kotsyubinchiki
485 262	4854/2623	Zarechanka
485 263	4857/2633	Smotrich
485 264	4852/2641	Balin
485 265	4854/2650	Dunayevtsy
485 270	4851/2706	Minkovtsy
485 271	4850/2717	Novaya Ushitsa
485 272	4852/2722	Zamekhov
485 273	4859/2730	Yaltushkov
485 274	4852/2747	Kopaygorod
485 274	4854/2749	Popovtsy
485 274	4857/2741	Kuzmintsy
485 275	4852/2754	Chervona
485 275	4858/2759	Noskovtsy
485 281	4852/2815	Penkovka
485 282	4854/2825	Krasnoye
485 284	4850/2842	Pechora
485 285	4850/2857	Bratslav
485 285	4854/2856	Bugakov
485 285	4855/2857	Czukow
485 285	4858/2851	Nemirov
485 290	4850/2907	Semenki
485 292	4850/2925	Zarudnyce
485 293	4852/2934	Granov
485 294	4854/2940	Narayevka
485 294	4856/2942	Terlitsa
485 295	4850/2958	Khristinovka
485 304	4853/3042	Talnoye
485 305	4856/3058	Katerinopol
485 342	4857/3429	Tsarichanka
485 362	4853/3623	Lozovaya

485	373	4852/3737	Slavyansk
485	374	4854/3743	Raygorodok
485	382	4855/3826	Lisichansk
490	074	4909/0747	Dahn
490	075	4907/0752	Erlenbach
490	075	4908/0750	Busenberg
490	080	4906/0800	Bergzabern
490	080	4908/0806	Billigheim (Rhineland Pfalz)
490	080	4908/0805	Ingenheim
490	080	4908/0801	Klingenmunster
490	081	4901/0815	Hagenbach
490	082	4900/0829	Durlach
490	082	4901/0824	Karlsruhe
490	082	4908/0821	Leimersheim
490	083	4900/0832	Berghausen
490	083	4900/0830	Grotzingen
490	083	4902/0835	Johlingen
490	083	4903/0832	Weingarten
490	083	4905/0835	Obergrombach
490	083	4905/0833	Untergrombach
490	083	4906/0839	Heidelsheim
490	083	4908/0836	Bruchsal
490	084	4902/0841	Diedelsheim
490	084	4903/0842	Bretten
490	084	4904/0845	Bauerbach
490	084	4904/0840	Gondelsheim
490	084	4906/0848	Flehingen
490	084	4906/0848	Sickingen
490	084	4907/0847	Bahnbrucken
490	084	4907/0843	Munzesheim
490	084	4909/0846	Menzingen
490	084	4909/0841	Oberowisheim
490	085	4904/0856	Zaberfeld
490	085	4908/0854	Eppingen
490	085	4909/0859	Gemmingen
490	085	4909/0858	Stebbach
490	090	4901/0903	Freudenthal
490	090	4909/0908	Grossgartach
490	090	4909/0906	Schluchtern (Baden)
490	091	4904/0913	Schozach
490	091	4907/0910	Horkheim
490	091	4908/0913	Heilbronn
490	091	4908/0919	Lehrensteinsfeld
490	091	4909/0917	Weinsberg
490	092	4908/0923	Affaltrach
490	094	4906/0946	Hessental
490	094	4906/0944	Schwabisch Hall
490	094	4906/0945	Steinbach (Wurttemberg)
490	094	4906/0945	Steinbach Bei Hall
490	094	4907/0945	Unterlimpurg
490	100	4907/1004	Ingersheim
490	100	4909/1005	Crailsheim
490	101	4903/1014	Unterdeufstetten
490	101	4904/1019	Dinkelsbuhl
490	101	4907/1018	Schopfloch
490	102	4901/1022	Monchsroth
490	102	4903/1028	Aufkirchen
490	102	4904/1029	Wittelshofen
490	102	4907/1023	Durrwangen
490	102	4909/1026	Dentlein am Forst
490	103	4902/1037	Schobdach
490	103	4903/1031	Gerolfingen
490	103	4903/1036	Wassertrudingen
490	103	4906/1037	Dennenlohe
490	103	4909/1033	Bechhofen
490	104	4900/1042	Hohentrudingen
490	104	4901/1045	Heidenheim
490	104	4903/1048	Dittenheim
490	104	4903/1043	Samenheim
490	104	4904/1043	Gnotzheim
490	104	4906/1040	Cronheim
490	104	4906/1045	Gunzenhausen
490	104	4907/1044	Unterwurmbach
490	105	4901/1051	Markt Berolzheim
490	105	4902/1059	Weissenburg in Bayern
490	105	4903/1052	Alesheim
490	105	4903/1055	Weimersheim
490	105	4904/1058	Ellingen
490	105	4907/1050	Gundelsheim (Bavaria)
490	105	4907/1056	Ramsberg
490	110	4907/1107	Heideck
490	110	4909/1102	Muhlstetten
490	111	4905/1116	Aue
490	111	4905/1113	Thalmassing
490	111	4907/1119	Obermassing
490	111	4908/1113	Eysolden
490	112	4902/1129	Beilngries
490	112	4903/1121	Greding
490	112	4907/1127	Berching
490	113	4901/1134	Toging
490	114	4903/1147	Hemau
490	115	4904/1151	Wachenhofen
490	115	4906/1159	Wolfsegg
490	120	4901/1206	Regensburg
490	120	4901/1204	Sallern
490	120	4902/1206	Stadtamhof
490	120	4908/1208	Regenstauf
490	122	4901/1223	Wiesent
490	122	4901/1224	Worth an der Donau
490	122	4904/1224	Brennberg
490	122	4909/1227	Geresdorf
490	125	4905/1253	Viechtach
490	130	4904/1306	Bodenmais
490	131	4901/1314	Zwiesel
490	131	4902/1312	Rabenstein
490	131	4908/1314	Zelezna Ruda

490 133	4901/1335	Kvilda	
490 133	4909/1334	Kasperske Hory	
490 133	4909/1331	Rejstejn	
490 134	4903/1347	Vimperk	
490 134	4905/1342	Zdikov	
490 135	4900/1358	Volovice	
490 135	4907/1350	Ckyne	
490 140	4901/1400	Prachatice	
490 140	4907/1405	Bavorov	
490 141	4906/1412	Libejovice	
490 141	4907/1419	Nakri	
490 141	4909/1414	Cicenice	
490 141	4909/1411	Vodnany	
490 142	4902/1426	Bavorovice	
490 142	4903/1426	Hluboka nad Vltavou	
490 142	4909/1421	Driten	
490 143	4906/1435	Sevetin	
490 143	4909/1439	Bosilec	
490 144	4901/1444	Brilice	
490 144	4901/1447	Trebon	
490 150	4901/1506	Nova Bystrice	
490 150	4909/1500	Jindrichuv Hradec	
490 151	4901/1510	Konrac	
490 151	4901/1513	Skalka	
490 151	4907/1512	Kunzak	
490 152	4905/1526	Dacice	
490 153	4902/1534	Jemnice	
490 154	4903/1548	Moravske Budejovice	
490 160	4908/1603	Hrotovice	
490 161	4903/1619	Moravsky Krumlov	
490 162	4904/1628	Dolni Kounice	
490 162	4906/1623	Ivancice	
490 163	4902/1637	Zidlochovice	
490 163	4908/1637	Modrice	
490 165	4902/1655	Damborice	
490 165	4909/1652	Slavkov U Brna	
490 170	4901/1707	Kyjov	
490 170	4904/1702	Zdanice	
490 170	4909/1700	Bucovice	
490 171	4907/1711	Korycany	
490 172	4904/1727	Uherske Hradiste	
490 173	4902/1739	Uhersky Brod	
490 174	4902/1749	Bojkovice	
490 180	4909/1800	Valasske Klobouky	
490 181	4900/1814	Ilava	
490 181	4902/1817	Ladce	
490 181	4902/1813	Pruske	
490 181	4909/1818	Ihriste	
490 182	4903/1825	Dolny Lieskov	
490 182	4904/1820	Belusa	
490 182	4907/1827	Povazska Bystrica	
490 182	4908/1826	Orlove	
490 182	4908/1820	Puchov	
490 183	4905/1838	Rajec	
490 185	4904/1856	Turciansky Svaty Martin
490 185	4906/1856	Priekopa
490 185	4907/1855	Vrutky
490 190	4905/1903	Podhradie
490 190	4906/1900	Sucany
490 191	4905/1919	Ruzomberok
490 191	4907/1911	Hubova
490 192	4903/1929	Lubela
490 192	4906/1925	Liptovska Tepla
490 192	4907/1928	Tvarozna
490 193	4905/1937	Liptovsky Svaty Mikulas
490 194	4902/1944	Liptovsky Hradok
490 200	4904/2005	Strba
490 201	4903/2018	Poprad
490 201	4904/2017	Velka Ida
490 201	4904/2017	Velka Pri Poprade
490 202	4904/2020	Spisska Sobota
490 202	4907/2023	Huncovce
490 202	4907/2027	Lubica
490 202	4907/2022	Velka Lomnica
490 202	4908/2026	Kezmarok
490 203	4902/2036	Levoca
490 204	4900/2045	Spisske Podhradie
490 204	4909/2047	Tichy Potok
490 205	4900/2057	Siroke
490 205	4901/2058	Fricovce
490 205	4906/2051	Nizny Slavkov
490 205	4908/2059	Rozkovany
490 205	4909/2051	Brezovica nad Torysou
490 205	4909/2058	Hethars
490 210	4900/2104	Chminany
490 210	4901/2102	Bertotovce
490 210	4903/2101	Hermanovce
490 210	4903/2104	Jarovnice
490 210	4905/2102	Uzovske Peklany
490 210	4906/2106	Sabinov
490 211	4900/2115	Presov
490 211	4901/2117	Lubotice
490 211	4901/2111	Maly Saris
490 211	4901/2117	Nizna Sebastova
490 211	4901/2116	Sarisske Luky
490 211	4903/2112	Velky Saris
490 211	4906/2119	Demjata
490 211	4907/2114	Terna
490 211	4909/2119	Slovenske Raslavice
490 212	4904/2127	Chmelov
490 212	4905/2122	Chmelovec
490 212	4909/2124	Stulany
490 213	4901/2133	Bystre
490 213	4901/2135	Skrabske
490 213	4902/2130	Hanusovce nad Toplou
490 213	4907/2131	Giraltovce
490 213	4909/2130	Brezov
490 214	4901/2142	Dobra nad Ondavou

490	214	4903/2147	Kosarovce
490	214	4903/2142	Trepec
490	214	4904/2145	Dapalovce
490	214	4909/2142	Brusnica
490	215	4908/2156	Vysna Radvan
490	220	4908/2206	Nizna Jablonka
490	220	4909/2207	Vysna Jablonka
490	221	4900/2214	Stakcin
490	221	4905/2219	Velka Polana
490	221	4908/2214	Zvala
490	222	4901/2223	Kolbasov
490	222	4904/2225	Runina
490	222	4907/2221	Ruske
490	222	4909/2229	Wetlina
490	223	4906/2239	Ustrzyki Gorne
490	223	4909/2234	Berehy Gorne
490	224	4900/2241	Stavnoye
490	224	4901/2246	Bystry
490	224	4904/2242	Wolosate
490	224	4909/2247	Gorishnyy Dzvinyach
490	225	4901/2254	Syanki
490	225	4903/2253	Beniowa
490	225	4906/2252	Sokoliki
490	230	4900/2306	Bukovinka
490	230	4904/2309	Bagnovate
490	230	4904/2300	Borinya
490	230	4906/2306	Ilnik
490	230	4909/2302	Turka (Lwow)
490	232	4901/2325	Korostov
490	232	4906/2329	Krushelnitsa
490	232	4909/2325	Podgorodtsy
490	233	4902/2331	Skole
490	233	4903/2331	Libochora
490	233	4904/2331	Klimiec
490	233	4905/2336	Pobuk
490	233	4906/2332	Korchyn
490	233	4906/2332	Korczyn (Skole)
490	233	4906/2335	Verkhneye Sinevidnoye
490	234	4903/2347	Tysov
490	235	4902/2353	Goshov
490	235	4902/2354	Tyapche
490	235	4904/2352	Bolekhov
490	235	4907/2353	Lisovitse
490	235	4909/2352	Morshin
490	240	4900/2409	Krekhovichi
490	240	4900/2402	Rakhinya
490	240	4904/2401	Trostyanets (Dolina)
490	240	4906/2402	Beleyev
490	240	4908/2404	Bolshaya Turya
490	240	4909/2401	Dzedushitse Male
490	241	4901/2415	Kotyatiche Golyn
490	241	4902/2413	Kadobna
490	241	4906/2411	Bolokhuv
490	241	4906/2415	Zavadka
490	241	4907/2415	Zbora
490	241	4909/2418	Stankova
490	242	4900/2424	Podmikhale
490	242	4901/2422	Kalush
490	242	4904/2420	Mostishche
490	242	4905/2425	Wyspa
490	242	4909/2426	Staryye Tomashevtsy
490	243	4902/2433	Bednarov
490	243	4903/2434	Brin
490	243	4903/2436	Sapaguv
490	243	4903/2438	Viktoruv
490	243	4905/2435	Medina
490	243	4906/2436	Temerovtse
490	243	4907/2438	Bludniki
490	243	4908/2430	Syulko
490	243	4908/2430	Voynilov
490	243	4909/2432	Dorogov
490	244	4901/2449	Ganushovtse
490	244	4902/2444	Selets (Stanislawow)
490	244	4902/2447	Zhovten
490	244	4905/2446	Dubovtsy
490	244	4905/2445	Dubryniow
490	244	4907/2444	Galich
490	244	4909/2449	Medukha
490	245	4900/2454	Rozhnyuv
490	245	4901/2459	Luka (Stanislawow)
490	245	4901/2450	Poberezhye
490	245	4902/2455	Dolgov
490	245	4902/2451	Marinopol
490	245	4902/2458	Ustse Zelene
490	245	4904/2456	Trostsyantse
490	245	4905/2453	Tumizh
490	245	4906/2452	Deleyuv
490	245	4909/2455	Gorozhanka
490	250	4905/2505	Baranow (Monasterzyska)
490	251	4902/2516	Barysh
490	251	4905/2510	Monastyriska
490	251	4909/2513	Dobrovody
490	252	4904/2524	Buchach
490	252	4905/2525	Bohatkowce
490	252	4905/2525	Denysow
490	252	4905/2524	Dzvinogorod
490	252	4907/2522	Pshevloka
490	252	4909/2522	Osovtse
490	253	4900/2534	Polovtse
490	253	4905/2535	Luka Wielka
490	253	4905/2535	Warwarynce
490	253	4909/2534	Laskovtsy
490	254	4901/2548	Chortkov
490	254	4902/2546	Biala (Myslenice)
490	254	4902/2546	Byala (Chortkov)
490	254	4902/2549	Vygnanka
490	254	4903/2540	Belobozhnitsa

490	254	4903/2541	Kalinovshchizna
490	254	4903/2547	Naguzhanka
490	254	4904/2545	Skorodintsy
490	254	4905/2545	Baworow
490	254	4905/2545	Magdalowka
490	254	4905/2545	Suszczyn
490	254	4906/2540	Kosow
490	255	4900/2555	Shmankovtse
490	255	4902/2559	Probezhna
490	255	4905/2555	Hlibow
490	255	4905/2555	Ilawcze
490	255	4906/2556	Kopychintsy
490	255	4908/2552	Sukhostav
490	255	4909/2559	Mazuruvka
490	255	4909/2552	Yablonov (Tarnopol)
490	260	4901/2604	Tolstenkoye
490	260	4905/2604	Vasilkovtsy
490	260	4907/2601	Nizhborg Novyy
490	260	4908/2603	Staryy Nizhborok
490	260	4909/2602	Myshkovtse
490	260	4909/2607	Samoluskovtsy
490	261	4900/2613	Shidlovtsy
490	261	4901/2610	Sidorov
490	261	4904/2613	Gusyatin
490	261	4908/2610	Luchkovtsy
490	261	4909/2610	Tribukhovtsy
490	262	4900/2622	Chemerovtsy
490	263	4906/2635	Kupin
490	264	4901/2647	Ternova
490	264	4906/2645	Kosogorka
490	265	4905/2655	Solobkovtsy
490	270	4905/2704	Zinkov
490	271	4902/2714	Vinkovtsy
490	274	4900/2745	Martinovca
490	274	4904/2741	Balki
490	274	4904/2740	Bar
490	280	4902/2806	Zhmerinka
490	280	4905/2801	Mezhirov
490	281	4906/2810	Brailov
490	282	4903/2820	Voroshilovka
490	282	4906/2820	Gnivan
490	283	4901/2830	Tyvrov
490	284	4906/2841	Voronovitsa
490	290	4904/2905	Zhornishche
490	291	4907/2912	Ilintsy
490	292	4900/2927	Dashev
490	293	4907/2937	Balabanovka
490	300	4902/3009	Sokolovka
490	300	4904/3006	Konela
490	302	4905/3025	Buki
490	304	4906/3043	Ryzhanovka
490	305	4905/3058	Zvenigorodka
490	312	4902/3125	Shpola
490	312	4907/3127	Burty
490	314	4908/3142	Rotmistrovka
490	320	4902/3206	Kamenka (Cherkassy)
490	320	4902/3206	Kamenka Cherkaskyi
490	324	4904/3240	Chigirin
490	331	4905/3315	Svetlovodsk
490	332	4904/3325	Kremenchug
490	341	4909/3412	Kobelyaki
490	344	4909/3444	Nekhvoroshcha
490	352	4901/3522	Pereshchepino
490	355	4908/3553	Sakhnovshchina
490	370	4909/3705	Zavody
491	064	4914/0647	Differten
491	064	4916/0647	Wadgassen
491	064	4917/0648	Bous
491	064	4918/0646	Lisdorf
491	064	4919/0645	Saarlouis
491	070	4914/0700	Saarbrucken
491	070	4917/0707	Sankt Ingbert
491	071	4914/0715	Blieskastel
491	072	4915/0722	Zweibrucken
491	072	4919/0720	Homburg an der Saar
491	073	4912/0736	Pirmasens
491	073	4914/0738	Rodalben
491	073	4916/0734	Thaleischweiler
491	073	4917/0736	Hoheinod
491	073	4918/0733	Herschberg
491	073	4919/0731	Oberhausen
			(Wallhalben)
491	073	4919/0733	Saalstadt
491	073	4919/0732	Wallhalben
491	074	4913/0742	Munchweiler
491	074	4917/0746	Leimen
491	074	4917/0740	Waldfischbach
491	075	4912/0758	Annweiler
491	080	4912/0807	Landau in der Pfalz
491	080	4913/0802	Albersweiler
491	080	4914/0806	Bochingen
491	080	4916/0808	Edesheim
491	080	4917/0809	Edenkoben
491	080	4918/0808	Maikammer
491	081	4910/0818	Rulzheim
491	081	4914/0813	Niederhochstadt
491	081	4915/0817	Niederlustadt
491	081	4915/0816	Oberlustadt
491	081	4916/0819	Schwegenheim
491	081	4917/0816	Gommersheim
491	081	4917/0810	Venningen
491	081	4919/0812	Lachen
491	082	4910/0829	Graben
491	082	4910/0825	Liedolsheim
491	082	4911/0822	Sondernheim
491	082	4913/0822	Germersheim
491	082	4914/0827	Philippsburg
491	082	4915/0821	Lingenfeld

491 082	4918/0821	Harthausen
491 082	4919/0824	Dudenhofen
491 082	4919/0826	Speyer
491 083	4912/0839	Langenbrucken
491 083	4913/0839	Kislau
491 083	4915/0830	Waghausel
491 083	4918/0834	Reilingen
491 083	4919/0833	Hockenheim
491 084	4911/0845	Odenheim
491 084	4913/0843	Ostringen
491 084	4914/0846	Eichtersheim
491 084	4914/0847	Michelfeld
491 084	4914/0840	Mingolsheim
491 084	4915/0841	Malsch Bei Wiesloch
491 084	4918/0842	Wiesloch
491 085	4910/0857	Richen
491 085	4911/0859	Berwangen
491 085	4911/0856	Ittlingen
491 085	4912/0850	Hilsbach
491 085	4914/0855	Steinsfurt
491 085	4915/0850	Duhren
491 085	4915/0859	Ehrstadt
491 085	4915/0853	Sinsheim
491 085	4916/0851	Hoffenheim
491 085	4918/0858	Neckarbischofsheim
491 085	4918/0856	Waibstadt
491 085	4919/0852	Eschelbronn
491 085	4919/0859	Helmstadt
491 085	4919/0853	Neidenstein
491 090	4910/0904	Massenbach
491 090	4911/0903	Massenbachhausen
491 090	4912/0900	Kirchardt
491 090	4913/0906	Bonfeld
491 090	4914/0906	Bad Rappenau
491 090	4914/0908	Bad Wimpfen
491 090	4914/0900	Grombach
491 090	4915/0904	Babstadt
491 090	4915/0902	Obergimpern
491 090	4916/0909	Heinsheim
491 090	4916/0905	Siegelsbach
491 090	4918/0905	Huffenhardt
491 090	4918/0902	Wollenberg
491 090	4919/0906	Hochhausen
491 090	4919/0908	Neckarzimmern
491 091	4911/0914	Neckarsulm
491 091	4914/0913	Bad Friedrichshall
491 091	4914/0915	Odheim
491 091	4915/0910	Offenau
491 091	4916/0918	Stein am Kocher
491 091	4917/0910	Gundelsheim
491 091	4918/0917	Neudenau
491 092	4919/0927	Olnhausen
491 092	4919/0925	Widdern
491 093	4912/0930	Ohringen
491 093	4918/0931	Ernsbach
491 094	4912/0948	Braunsbach
491 094	4917/0941	Kunzelsau
491 094	4918/0941	Nagelsberg
491 095	4913/0953	Dunsbach
491 095	4915/0955	Gerabronn
491 100	4913/1006	Hengstfeld
491 100	4914/1007	Michelbach an der Lucke
491 100	4918/1002	Wiesenbach
491 101	4913/1016	Breitenau
491 101	4919/1019	Hagenau
491 102	4910/1020	Feuchtwangen
491 102	4915/1025	Aurach
491 102	4918/1025	Leutershausen
491 102	4918/1027	Wiedersbach
491 102	4919/1024	Jochsberg
491 102	4919/1026	Oberramstadt
491 103	4910/1039	Ornbau
491 103	4914/1031	Herrieden
491 103	4918/1035	Ansbach
491 103	4918/1039	Sachsen
491 104	4910/1042	Altenmuhr
491 104	4912/1040	Triesdorf
491 104	4914/1044	Wolframs Eschenbach
491 104	4915/1049	Windsbach
491 104	4917/1041	Lichtenau (Bavaria)
491 104	4917/1047	Neuendettelsau
491 110	4911/1101	Friedrichsgmund
491 110	4912/1101	Georgensgmund
491 110	4915/1106	Roth Bei Nurnberg
491 111	4910/1117	Meckenhausen
491 111	4912/1112	Hilpoltstein
491 112	4910/1127	Muhlhausen (Bavaria)
491 112	4917/1128	Neumarkt in der Oberpfalz
491 113	4912/1130	Freystadt
491 113	4919/1130	Pilsach
491 114	4914/1141	Velburg
491 115	4910/1157	Fischbach
491 120	4919/1209	Kronstetten
491 121	4913/1216	Bleich
491 123	4912/1231	Roding
491 124	4913/1240	Cham
491 125	4910/1251	Kotzting
491 125	4918/1251	Furth im Wald
491 130	4918/1309	Nyrsko
491 131	4913/1318	Zejbis
491 131	4916/1318	Cachrov
491 131	4916/1310	Desenice
491 131	4918/1319	Besiny
491 131	4918/1311	Hodousice
491 132	4910/1328	Hartmanice
491 132	4916/1326	Hory Matky Bozi

491 132	4916/1324	Velhartice	
491 132	4918/1326	Kolinec	
491 133	4913/1338	Zihobce	
491 133	4914/1331	Susice	
491 133	4916/1336	Cepice	
491 133	4916/1338	Zichovice	
491 134	4919/1343	Horazdovice	
491 135	4910/1353	Volyne	
491 135	4916/1350	Katovice	
491 135	4916/1354	Nove Strakonice	
491 135	4916/1354	Strakonice	
491 140	4916/1401	Steken	
491 140	4918/1409	Pisek	
491 141	4912/1415	Krc	
491 141	4912/1413	Protivin	
491 141	4913/1412	Mysenec	
491 142	4912/1421	Temelin	
491 142	4913/1421	Vsemyslice	
491 142	4914/1423	Neznasov	
491 142	4914/1425	Tyn nad Vltavou	
491 142	4915/1425	Kolodeje nad Luznici	
491 142	4918/1429	Bechyne	
491 143	4918/1438	Hlavatce	
491 144	4911/1445	Drahov	
491 144	4911/1442	Mezimosti nad Nezarkou	
491 144	4914/1448	Lzin	
491 144	4916/1443	Sobeslav	
491 144	4918/1445	Myslkovice	
491 144	4918/1440	Radimov	
491 145	4912/1453	Kardasova Recice	
491 145	4913/1458	Lodherov	
491 145	4915/1451	Dirna	
491 145	4916/1456	Destna	
491 150	4910/1500	Radounka	
491 150	4918/1505	Kamenice nad Lipou	
491 151	4910/1512	Strmilov	
491 151	4915/1512	Zirovnice	
491 151	4918/1511	Castrov	
491 152	4911/1528	Telc	
491 152	4918/1529	Trest	
491 152	4919/1524	Batelov	
491 152	4919/1520	Horni Cerekev	
491 155	4918/1553	Trebic	
491 160	4913/1609	Namest nad Oslavou	
491 163	4912/1638	Brno	
491 163	4913/1639	Husovice	
491 164	4912/1642	Lisen	
491 170	4917/1700	Vyskov	
491 170	4919/1706	Ivanovice Na Hane	
491 171	4914/1719	Zdounky	
491 171	4915/1711	Pornice	
491 172	4918/1724	Kromeriz	
491 173	4910/1732	Napajedla	
491 173	4917/1738	Rackova	
491 174	4913/1740	Gottwaldov	
491 175	4913/1751	Vizovice	
491 181	4914/1814	Lazy pod Makytou	
491 183	4910/1830	Drienove	
491 183	4913/1834	Velka Bytca	
491 184	4913/1844	Zilina	
491 184	4918/1847	Kysucke Nove Mesto	
491 185	4911/1852	Strecno	
491 185	4912/1853	Varin	
491 185	4913/1850	Nededza	
491 185	4915/1855	Lysica	
491 191	4910/1913	Zaskov	
491 191	4912/1918	Dolny Kubin	
491 191	4913/1917	Velky Bysterec	
491 193	4910/1933	Kvacany	
491 195	4918/1958	Zakopane	
491 201	4916/2016	Zdiar	
491 202	4911/2028	Spisska Bela	
491 202	4914/2026	Slovenska Ves	
491 203	4916/2032	Podolinec	
491 204	4917/2047	Plavnica	
491 204	4918/2042	Stara Lubovna	
491 205	4911/2053	Olsov	
491 205	4914/2052	Durkov	
491 205	4916/2051	Plavec	
491 205	4917/2055	Circ	
491 210	4917/2109	Krive	
491 210	4918/2105	Lukov	
491 210	4919/2103	Snakov	
491 211	4912/2117	Bartosovce	
491 211	4913/2115	Hertnik	
491 211	4917/2117	Bardejov	
491 211	4919/2111	Rokytov	
491 212	4910/2128	Marhan	
491 212	4911/2125	Harhaj	
491 212	4914/2127	Kurima	
491 212	4916/2123	Hrabovec	
491 213	4912/2139	Stropkov	
491 213	4914/2133	Benadikovce	
491 213	4914/2138	Tisinec	
491 213	4918/2134	Vysnyj Svidnik	
491 214	4917/2140	Vislava	
491 215	4910/2155	Nizne Cabiny	
491 215	4914/2154	Krasny Brod	
491 215	4915/2157	Nagov	
491 215	4916/2155	Medzilaborce	
491 215	4917/2156	Vydran	
491 215	4918/2154	Borov	
491 220	4910/2202	Svetlice	
491 220	4914/2209	Wola Michowa	
491 220	4914/2207	Zubensko	
491 220	4915/2204	Lupkow	
491 220	4915/2205	Nowy Lupkow	

491	220	4916/2208	Smolnik (Baligrod)
491	220	4918/2208	Mikow
491	220	4918/2205	Oslawica
491	220	4918/2204	Radoszyce (Lvov)
491	221	4910/2214	Solinka
491	221	4913/2216	Zubracze
491	221	4916/2216	Kolonice
491	221	4919/2214	Huczwice
491	222	4910/2229	Smerek
491	222	4911/2225	Strubowiska
491	222	4913/2220	Cisna
491	222	4913/2227	Jaworzec
491	222	4913/2225	Kalnica
491	222	4915/2225	Woloska
491	222	4916/2222	Lopienka
491	222	4916/2227	Zawoj
491	222	4917/2227	Studenne
491	222	4917/2229	Tworylne
491	222	4918/2221	Radziejowa
491	222	4918/2226	Terka
491	222	4918/2222	Tyskowa
491	222	4919/2225	Bukowiec
491	222	4919/2229	Rajskie Sakowczyk
491	222	4919/2223	Wola Gorzanska
491	223	4910/2238	Carynskie
491	223	4911/2237	Nasiczne
491	223	4912/2238	Dwernik
491	223	4913/2233	Kalinow
491	223	4913/2236	Ruskie
491	223	4913/2234	Zatwarnica
491	223	4915/2233	Hulskie
491	223	4915/2235	Jureczkowa
491	223	4917/2237	Rosochate
491	223	4917/2239	Skorodne
491	223	4918/2234	Serednie Male
491	224	4911/2242	Stuposiany
491	224	4912/2240	Procisne
491	224	4913/2242	Smolnik
491	224	4914/2244	Zurawin
491	224	4915/2242	Lutowiska
491	224	4915/2242	Posada Dolna
491	224	4916/2247	Khashchuv
491	224	4916/2245	Krywka
491	224	4917/2247	Lopuszanka Lechniowa
491	224	4919/2249	Gronzeva
491	225	4910/2251	Shandrovets
491	225	4913/2253	Volche
491	225	4915/2255	Blozew Gorna
491	225	4918/2253	Golovetskoye
491	230	4912/2303	Yavora
491	230	4913/2307	Isayev
491	230	4915/2309	Svidnik
491	230	4915/2305	Wola Baraniecka
491	230	4919/2301	Topolnitsa
491	231	4912/2310	Yasenitsa
491	231	4914/2312	Lastivka
491	231	4915/2315	Burczyce Stare
491	231	4917/2318	Opaka
491	231	4917/2311	Smolna
491	231	4918/2315	Zalokets
491	232	4910/2321	Dolgoye
491	232	4910/2329	Yamelnitsa
491	232	4911/2324	Urych
491	232	4914/2321	Skhodnitsa
491	232	4915/2325	Bilinka Mala
491	232	4915/2325	Chlopczyce
491	232	4915/2325	Kornalowice
491	232	4915/2323	Mrazhnitsa
491	232	4915/2325	Siekierczyce
491	232	4917/2325	Borislav
491	232	4917/2327	Tustanovitse
491	232	4918/2326	Volanka
491	232	4919/2327	Gubiche
491	232	4919/2329	Modrychi
491	232	4919/2323	Popele
491	233	4914/2339	Gassendorf
491	233	4914/2339	Ulichno
491	233	4917/2330	Truskavets
491	233	4918/2334	Stebnik
491	233	4918/2334	Stebnik (Drogobych)
491	235	4914/2351	Duliby (Stryy)
491	235	4915/2351	Stryy
491	235	4916/2354	Verchany
491	235	4919/2354	Uhersko
491	240	4910/2403	Baliche Podruzhne
491	240	4910/2406	Baliche Zazhechne
491	240	4912/2401	Sekhuv
491	240	4912/2408	Sulyatichi
491	240	4916/2400	Dashava
491	240	4918/2406	Ruda (Zhidachov)
491	241	4910/2415	Cheretezh
491	241	4910/2415	Chertezh
491	241	4911/2412	Lyskuv (Zurawno)
491	241	4913/2412	Lyakhovitse Zazhechke
491	241	4914/2417	Melnich
491	241	4914/2412	Podorozhnoye
491	241	4915/2415	Lanki Male
491	241	4915/2417	Zhuravno
491	241	4916/2411	Yaykovtse
491	241	4919/2416	Goleshuv
491	242	4910/2429	Dolzhka
491	242	4915/2426	Kozari
491	242	4916/2427	Chernev
491	243	4910/2433	Kolodzeyuv
491	243	4910/2438	Ostruv (Kalush)
491	243	4911/2432	Sivka Voynilov
491	243	4912/2434	Martynuv Stary
491	243	4912/2436	Radvanov

491 243	4913/2433	Martynuv Novy	
491 243	4914/2432	Tenetniki	
491 243	4915/2430	Bukachevtsy	
491 243	4916/2438	Burshtyn	
491 243	4918/2432	Chagrov	
491 243	4918/2430	Kolokolin	
491 243	4918/2436	Nastashino	
491 243	4919/2436	Konyushki (Tarnopol)	
491 244	4911/2445	Bolshovtsy	
491 244	4911/2449	Slobudka Konkolnitska	
491 244	4913/2449	Zaguzhe Konkolnitske	
491 244	4916/2444	Sarnki Dolne	
491 244	4918/2444	Sarnki Gurne	
491 244	4918/2448	Svistelniki	
491 245	4910/2454	Podlesnoye	
491 245	4912/2456	Gnilche	
491 245	4912/2451	Yablonov (Turka)	
491 245	4915/2454	Bokov	
491 245	4915/2451	Byblo	
491 245	4917/2453	Shumlyany	
491 245	4918/2452	Slavyatin	
491 250	4912/2502	Zavalov	
491 250	4914/2500	Nosov	
491 250	4916/2508	Podgaytsy	
491 252	4911/2522	Kuydanuv	
491 252	4912/2526	Dobropole Mateuszowka	
491 252	4914/2522	Vishnivchik	
491 252	4917/2523	Burkanuv	
491 252	4917/2523	Zlotniki	
491 253	4913/2535	Mogielnica (Trembovlya)	
491 253	4918/2533	Darakhov	
491 254	4910/2543	Budanov	
491 254	4913/2543	Dolge (Tarnopol)	
491 254	4913/2543	Ivanovka (Terebovlya)	
491 254	4915/2545	Dyczkow	
491 254	4915/2545	Smykowce	
491 254	4918/2543	Terebovlya	
491 255	4914/2555	Khorostkov	
491 255	4915/2555	Romanowe Siolo	
491 260	4915/2605	Holoszynce	
491 260	4917/2609	Sadzhevka	
491 260	4919/2602	Butsyki	
491 260	4919/2604	Lezhanovka	
491 261	4915/2614	Kalagarovka	
491 261	4915/2616	Satanov	
491 261	4916/2615	Bilka	
491 261	4916/2613	Volitsa (Skalat)	
491 261	4918/2610	Krasne (Skalat)	
491 261	4919/2612	Stavki Krasnenske	
491 263	4910/2634	Gorodok (Kamenets Podolskiy)	
491 264	4919/2643	Gvardeyskoye	
491 272	4916/2726	Derazhnya	
491 274	4911/2743	Radovtsy	
491 274	4912/2740	Volkovintsy	
491 282	4914/2829	Vinnitsa	
491 282	4919/2828	Strizhavka	
491 284	4913/2843	Priluki (Berdichev)	
491 285	4919/2851	Vakhnovka	
491 290	4914/2903	Lipovets	
491 291	4918/2917	Kozhanka	
491 293	4914/2932	Zhivotovka	
491 294	4913/2944	Khutor Tarasivka	
491 305	4915/3050	Lysyanka	
491 311	4913/3113	Olshana	
491 312	4917/3127	Gorodishche	
491 315	4914/3153	Smela	
491 315	4919/3155	Belozerye	
491 322	4910/3223	Medvedovka	
491 371	4912/3719	Izyum	
491 385	4916/3856	Starobelsk	
492 063	4922/0639	Siersburg	
492 063	4926/0637	Hilbringen	
492 063	4927/0638	Merzig	
492 064	4920/0646	Fraulautern	
492 064	4921/0644	Dillingen	
492 064	4921/0643	Pachten	
492 064	4921/0649	Saarwellingen	
492 064	4922/0645	Diefflen	
492 064	4923/0647	Nalbach	
492 064	4928/0640	Brotdorf	
492 065	4926/0651	Bettingen	
492 070	4921/0703	Merchweiler	
492 070	4922/0703	Illingen	
492 070	4929/0704	Tholey	
492 071	4921/0716	Mittelbexbach	
492 071	4921/0711	Neunkirchen (Germany)	
492 071	4922/0711	Wiebelskirchen	
492 071	4923/0710	Ottweiler	
492 071	4928/0710	Sankt Wendel	
492 072	4923/0720	Waldmohr	
492 072	4928/0726	Glan Munchweiler	
492 073	4925/0734	Landstuhl	
492 074	4927/0745	Kaiserslautern	
492 075	4927/0754	Hochspeyer	
492 080	4921/0809	Neustadt an der Weinstrasse	
492 081	4922/0816	Hassloch	
492 081	4922/0818	Iggelheim	
492 081	4922/0810	Mussbach	
492 081	4923/0818	Bohl	
492 081	4925/0812	Deidesheim	
492 081	4926/0819	Dannstadt	
492 081	4926/0818	Schauernheim	
492 081	4926/0812	Wachenheim an der Weinstrasse	

492 081	4928/0812	Bad Durkheim
492 081	4928/0816	Ellerstadt
492 081	4928/0818	Fussgonheim
492 081	4929/0818	Maxdorf
492 081	4929/0811	Ungstein
492 082	4922/0827	Otterstadt
492 082	4923/0822	Schifferstadt
492 082	4925/0826	Neuhofen
492 082	4927/0821	Mutterstadt
492 082	4928/0820	Ruchheim
492 082	4929/0827	Feudenheim
492 082	4929/0827	Ludwigshafen
492 082	4929/0828	Mannheim
492 083	4920/0839	Walldorf
492 083	4921/0839	Sandhausen
492 083	4922/0832	Ketsch
492 083	4923/0834	Schwetzingen
492 083	4927/0837	Edingen
492 083	4928/0834	Ilvesheim
492 083	4928/0837	Ladenburg
492 084	4920/0849	Meckesheim
492 084	4920/0842	Nussloch
492 084	4921/0847	Reilsheim
492 084	4923/0848	Neckargemund
492 084	4925/0842	Heidelberg
492 084	4925/0846	Ziegelhausen
492 084	4927/0841	Dossenheim
492 084	4929/0840	Schriesheim
492 085	4920/0855	Epfenbach
492 085	4924/0850	Dilsberg
492 085	4924/0851	Neckarsteinach
492 085	4927/0854	Hirschhorn
492 085	4928/0859	Eberbach
492 090	4921/0909	Mosbach
492 090	4922/0903	Binau
492 090	4925/0901	Lindach
492 090	4928/0905	Strumpfelbrunn
492 091	4921/0915	Billigheim (Baden)
492 091	4924/0913	Auerbach an der Bergstrasse
492 091	4926/0917	Kleineicholzheim
492 091	4927/0917	Grosseicholzheim
492 091	4928/0916	Waldhausen
492 091	4929/0919	Bodigheim
492 092	4920/0929	Berlichingen
492 092	4923/0923	Sennfeld
492 092	4924/0923	Adelsheim
492 092	4926/0925	Osterburken
492 092	4929/0927	Sindolsheim
492 093	4920/0930	Schontal
492 093	4923/0938	Altkrautheim
492 093	4923/0938	Krautheim
492 093	4924/0933	Ballenberg
492 093	4924/0930	Merchingen
492 093	4925/0939	Horrenbach
492 093	4925/0931	Hungheim
492 093	4925/0937	Neunstetten
492 093	4929/0936	Angelturn
492 093	4929/0938	Boxberg
492 094	4920/0948	Mulfingen
492 094	4922/0945	Ailringen
492 094	4922/0944	Hohebach
492 094	4923/0942	Dorzbach
492 094	4927/0947	Wachbach
492 094	4929/0946	Bad Mergentheim
492 095	4921/0953	Bartenstein
492 095	4924/0955	Niederstetten
492 095	4927/0956	Laudenbach
492 095	4928/0950	Markelsheim
492 095	4929/0955	Weikersheim
492 100	4927/1004	Archshofen
492 100	4928/1002	Creglingen
492 101	4921/1014	Kirnberg
492 101	4922/1017	Gunzendorf
492 101	4923/1011	Rothenburg Ob der Tauber
492 101	4926/1014	Endsee
492 101	4927/1019	Burgbernheim
492 102	4922/1025	Colmberg
492 102	4926/1028	Egenhausen
492 102	4927/1028	Obernzenn
492 102	4927/1029	Unternzenn
492 102	4929/1026	Ickelheim
492 103	4920/1031	Lehrberg
492 103	4927/1036	Trautskirchen
492 103	4929/1039	Markt Erlbach
492 104	4920/1048	Heilsbronn
492 104	4924/1041	Dietenhofen
492 104	4929/1043	Wilhermsdorf
492 105	4927/1052	Cadolzburg
492 105	4927/1057	Zirndorf
492 110	4920/1102	Schwabach
492 110	4921/1106	Kornburg
492 110	4925/1101	Stein Bei Nurnberg
492 110	4927/1105	Nurnberg
492 110	4928/1100	Furth
492 111	4921/1114	Schwarzenbruck
492 111	4929/1112	Behringersdorf
492 111	4929/1114	Rothenbach
492 112	4923/1121	Altdorf (Bavaria)
492 112	4929/1122	Sendelbach
492 115	4927/1152	Amberg
492 120	4920/1203	Grain
492 120	4920/1207	Schwandorf in Bayern
492 120	4923/1208	Schwarzenfeld
492 120	4925/1208	Stulln
492 121	4927/1211	Nabburg
492 122	4921/1223	Neunburg Vorm Wald

492	122	4929/1223	Teunz
492	124	4923/1243	Waldmunchen
492	125	4921/1251	Folmava
492	125	4926/1256	Domazlice
492	130	4922/1307	Loucim
492	130	4923/1301	Praporiste
492	130	4924/1302	Kdyne
492	130	4927/1305	Uboc
492	131	4921/1310	Beharov
492	131	4921/1313	Janovice nad Uhlavou
492	131	4922/1310	Dlazov
492	131	4924/1318	Klatovy
492	131	4926/1311	Polen
492	131	4928/1311	Chudenice
492	131	4929/1317	Svihov
492	132	4920/1329	Zavlekov
492	132	4923/1328	Planice
492	132	4924/1322	Bolesiny
492	132	4924/1322	Obytce
492	132	4927/1321	Predslav
492	132	4929/1324	Mecin
492	133	4922/1334	Techonice
492	133	4922/1333	Velenovy
492	133	4925/1338	Kvasnovice
492	133	4926/1337	Nekvasovy
492	133	4929/1336	Nepomuk
492	134	4926/1341	Oselce
492	134	4928/1344	Kasejovice
492	134	4928/1347	Lnare
492	135	4926/1353	Blatna
492	135	4928/1351	Paracov
492	140	4928/1404	Cimelice
492	141	4928/1417	Hrejkovice
492	142	4922/1424	Bernartice
492	142	4922/1427	Srlin
492	142	4924/1429	Oparany
492	142	4925/1425	Lisnice
492	142	4925/1428	Podbori
492	142	4927/1422	Milevsko
492	142	4928/1429	Bozejovice
492	142	4929/1424	Tynice
492	143	4922/1435	Malsice
492	143	4923/1430	Stadlec
492	143	4924/1439	Celkovice
492	143	4927/1438	Svrabov
492	143	4929/1432	Jistebnice
492	144	4921/1442	Plana nad Luznici
492	144	4924/1449	Chynov
492	144	4925/1440	Tabor
492	144	4925/1443	Zaluzi
492	144	4926/1441	Cekanice
492	144	4929/1441	Chotoviny
492	145	4920/1450	Choustnik
492	145	4920/1453	Mlyn Spindleruv
492	145	4920/1458	Vlkosovice
492	145	4921/1454	Vlceves
492	145	4922/1458	Cernovice
492	145	4922/1452	Chrbonin
492	145	4922/1451	Radenin
492	145	4923/1455	Krec
492	145	4925/1453	Porin
492	145	4926/1459	Simpach
492	145	4927/1453	Oblajovice
492	145	4927/1458	Obratan
492	145	4928/1453	Domamysl
492	150	4920/1506	Pravikov
492	150	4925/1507	Nova Cerekev
492	150	4928/1509	Bitetice
492	150	4929/1501	Pacov
492	151	4921/1519	Cernov
492	151	4923/1510	Ustrasin
492	151	4926/1514	Pelhrimov
492	152	4927/1522	Polanky
492	153	4920/1535	Vilanec
492	153	4924/1535	Jihlava
492	153	4926/1534	Hybralec
492	154	4920/1542	Male
492	154	4922/1540	Puklice
492	160	4921/1601	Velke Mezirici
492	160	4927/1609	Moravec
492	161	4927/1613	Bukov
492	162	4925/1625	Lomnice
492	164	4922/1640	Blansko
492	164	4929/1640	Boskovice
492	170	4928/1701	Plumlov
492	170	4928/1707	Prostejov
492	171	4921/1719	Kojetin
492	171	4921/1719	Tovis
492	171	4926/1717	Tovacov
492	172	4920/1723	Plesovec
492	172	4927/1727	Prerov
492	173	4920/1735	Holesov
492	174	4924/1741	Bystrice pod Hostynem
492	174	4929/1749	Kelc
492	175	4928/1758	Valasske Mezirici
492	175	4929/1759	Krasno
492	180	4920/1800	Vsetin
492	181	4921/1813	Novy Hrozenkov
492	183	4924/1838	Turzovka
492	184	4926/1847	Cadca
492	185	4921/1857	Stara Bystrica
492	190	4929/1906	Rycerka Dolna
492	190	4929/1909	Ujsoly
492	191	4923/1911	Oravska Lesna
492	193	4920/1933	Medvedzie
492	193	4922/1937	Trstena
492	193	4924/1930	Namestovo
492	193	4924/1931	Slanica

492	194	4920/1949	Witow
492	194	4922/1949	Chocholow
492	194	4928/1946	Piekielnik
492	194	4929/1942	Jablonka (Krakow)
492	195	4920/1951	Dzianisz
492	195	4921/1957	Zab
492	195	4922/1954	Ratulow
492	195	4924/1953	Mietustwo
492	195	4925/1957	Maruszyna
492	195	4926/1952	Czarny Dunajec
492	195	4926/1955	Stare Bystre
492	195	4928/1959	Ludzimierz
492	195	4928/1953	Wroblowka
492	195	4929/1958	Krauszow
492	200	4920/2001	Poronin
492	200	4922/2001	Bialy Dunajec
492	200	4926/2002	Szaflary
492	200	4927/2009	Nowa Biala
492	200	4929/2008	Lopuszna
492	200	4929/2002	Nowy Targ
492	200	4929/2006	Ostrowsko
492	201	4922/2018	Kacwin
492	201	4924/2015	Lapsze Nizne
492	201	4924/2012	Lapsze Wyzne
492	201	4925/2012	Dursztyn
492	201	4925/2018	Niedzica
492	201	4926/2019	Czorsztyn
492	201	4927/2014	Frydman
492	201	4927/2019	Kluszkowce
492	201	4927/2010	Krempachy
492	201	4927/2016	Maniowy
492	201	4929/2013	Szlembark
492	202	4922/2027	Haligovce
492	202	4923/2022	Spisska Stara Ves
492	202	4925/2021	Sromowce Wyzne
492	202	4926/2025	Kroscienko (Nowy Targ)
492	202	4926/2029	Szczawnica Nizna
492	202	4927/2022	Grywald
492	202	4927/2021	Krosnica
492	202	4929/2025	Tylmanowa
492	203	4925/2034	Jaworki
492	203	4925/2035	Kadcza
492	203	4925/2032	Szlachtowa
492	203	4926/2030	Szczawnica
492	204	4920/2048	Maly Lipnik
492	204	4921/2042	Kremna
492	204	4923/2048	Zegiestow
492	204	4924/2046	Zubrzyk
492	204	4925/2048	Wierchomla Wielka
492	204	4926/2043	Piwniczna
492	204	4927/2045	Lomnica Zdroj
492	204	4928/2044	Kokuszka
492	204	4929/2041	Rytro
492	205	4921/2051	Milik
492	205	4921/2055	Muszyna
492	205	4922/2058	Powroznik
492	205	4923/2052	Szczawnik
492	205	4923/2054	Zlockie
492	205	4924/2055	Jastrzebik
492	205	4924/2058	Krynica Wies
492	205	4926/2058	Krynica Zdroj
492	205	4926/2057	Slotwiny
492	205	4927/2059	Mochnaczka Wyzna
492	205	4929/2057	Krzyzowka
492	210	4921/2100	Wojkowa
492	210	4923/2105	Muszynka
492	210	4924/2102	Tylicz
492	210	4927/2106	Bieliczna
492	210	4927/2104	Izdby
492	210	4928/2108	Ropki
492	210	4929/2105	Czertyzne
492	210	4929/2102	Czyrna
492	210	4929/2100	Piorunka
492	211	4925/2119	Becherov
492	211	4926/2111	Wysowa
492	211	4928/2119	Konieczna
492	211	4929/2110	Hanczowa
492	211	4929/2117	Zdynia
492	212	4921/2124	Sarisske Cierne
492	212	4922/2124	Cigla
492	212	4923/2121	Smilno
492	212	4928/2123	Radocyna
492	212	4928/2129	Zydowskie
492	213	4920/2136	Kapisova
492	213	4920/2138	Ladomirova
492	213	4920/2132	Nizny Orlik
492	213	4921/2130	Vysny Orlik
492	213	4923/2134	Svidnicka
492	213	4925/2138	Sarbov
492	213	4929/2139	Mszana
492	213	4929/2138	Ropianka
492	214	4926/2142	Barwinek
492	214	4927/2148	Daliowa
492	214	4927/2148	Jasliska
492	215	4921/2150	Certizne
492	215	4922/2155	Jasiel
492	215	4924/2159	Wislok Wielki
492	215	4926/2155	Moszczaniec
492	215	4927/2155	Surowica
492	215	4927/2151	Wola Nizna
492	215	4928/2157	Darow
492	215	4928/2153	Polany Surowiczne
492	220	4920/2202	Dolzyca
492	220	4920/2204	Komancza
492	220	4920/2207	Preluki
492	220	4922/2202	Czystohorb
492	220	4922/2206	Rzepedz
492	220	4922/2209	Turzansk

492 220	4924/2208	Szczawne
492 220	4926/2207	Plonna
492 220	4927/2204	Karlikow
492 220	4928/2209	Zawadka Morochowska
492 220	4929/2206	Belchowka
492 220	4929/2204	Bukowsko
492 221	4920/2217	Baligrod
492 221	4921/2212	Sukowate
492 221	4922/2215	Kielczawa
492 221	4922/2216	Mchawa
492 221	4923/2216	Zahoczewie
492 221	4924/2213	Serednie Wielkie
492 221	4924/2219	Zernica Nizna
492 221	4925/2210	Kulaszne
492 221	4925/2214	Lukowe
492 221	4925/2215	Witrynow
492 221	4926/2212	Brzozowiec
492 221	4926/2219	Hoczew
492 221	4927/2219	Lesko
492 221	4927/2210	Mokre
492 221	4927/2210	Wysoczany
492 221	4928/2212	Morochow
492 221	4929/2219	Huzele
492 222	4920/2223	Gorzanka
492 222	4920/2220	Steznica
492 222	4920/2225	Wolkowyja
492 222	4921/2222	Bereznica Wyzna
492 222	4921/2229	Horodek
492 222	4921/2227	Zawoz
492 222	4922/2226	Polanczyk
492 222	4923/2225	Myczkow
492 222	4923/2228	Solina
492 222	4923/2220	Zernica Wyzna
492 222	4924/2223	Bereska
492 222	4925/2225	Bereznica Nizna
492 222	4925/2227	Bobrka (Lesko)
492 222	4925/2228	Nowosiolki (Lisko)
492 222	4925/2222	Srednia Wies (Lwow)
492 222	4926/2221	Bachlowa
492 222	4927/2225	Myczkowce
492 222	4927/2227	Orelec
492 222	4927/2223	Zwierzyn
492 222	4928/2225	Uherce
492 222	4928/2220	Weremien
492 222	4929/2220	Posada Leska
492 223	4920/2232	Chrewt
492 223	4920/2236	Rosolin
492 223	4921/2234	Paniszczow
492 223	4922/2237	Sokolowa Wola
492 223	4922/2231	Telesnica Sanna
492 223	4923/2235	Daszowka
492 223	4923/2233	Telesnica Oszwarowa
492 223	4924/2239	Hoszow (Staryy Sambor)
492 223	4924/2237	Hoszowczyk
492 223	4925/2231	Lobozew
492 223	4925/2236	Rownia
492 223	4926/2238	Berehy Dolne
492 223	4926/2238	Jasien (Staryy Sambor)
492 223	4926/2230	Stetkowa
492 223	4926/2232	Ustianowa
492 223	4926/2235	Ustrzyki Dolne
492 223	4927/2234	Strwiazyk
492 223	4928/2234	Dzwiniacz Dolny
492 223	4929/2236	Lodyna
492 224	4920/2240	Czarna (Lesko)
492 224	4920/2246	Mshanets
492 224	4922/2241	Rabe
492 224	4923/2240	Moczary
492 224	4924/2242	Bandrow Narodowy
492 224	4924/2249	Nanchulka
492 224	4925/2240	Jalowe
492 224	4926/2244	Nanova
492 224	4926/2247	Rosokhi
492 224	4928/2240	Kroscienko
492 224	4928/2243	Smolnitsa
492 224	4928/2246	Terlo
492 225	4920/2259	Strelki
492 225	4922/2252	Lenina Malaya
492 225	4923/2259	Busovisko
492 225	4924/2256	Bolshaya Lenina
492 225	4924/2253	Lavruv
492 225	4924/2258	Spas (Lwow)
492 225	4924/2259	Tershuvo
492 225	4926/2253	Bilichi
492 225	4927/2259	Strilbichi
492 225	4929/2258	Staraya Sol
492 230	4923/2306	Zvur
492 230	4924/2308	Volya Blazhovska
492 230	4925/2305	Buchowice
492 230	4925/2305	Koblo Stare
492 230	4926/2300	Staryy Sambor
492 230	4927/2304	Strashevitse
492 230	4929/2305	Torganovichi
492 230	4929/2307	Vanovitse
492 231	4920/2315	Podbuzh
492 231	4920/2312	Storona
492 231	4922/2319	Ivana Franka
492 231	4922/2315	Podmonasterek
492 231	4922/2315	Urozh
492 231	4924/2314	Lukavytsa
492 231	4924/2316	Vinniki (Drogobych)
492 231	4925/2314	Cherkhava
492 231	4925/2317	Mokryany
492 231	4926/2313	Olshanik
492 231	4927/2318	Selets (Sambor)
492 232	4920/2322	Yasenitsa Solna
492 232	4922/2325	Unyatychi

492	232	4927/2320	Bronitsa
492	232	4927/2329	Glinne
492	232	4927/2323	Luzhek Dolny
492	232	4928/2328	Bykov (Sambor)
492	232	4928/2328	Bykuv
492	232	4928/2320	Gorodishche (Lwow)
492	232	4928/2325	Novoshitse
492	232	4928/2324	Ozimina
492	232	4928/2327	Prusy
492	232	4929/2323	Krantsberg
492	233	4920/2335	Wola Jakubowa
492	233	4921/2330	Dobrovlyany (Drogobych)
492	233	4921/2330	Drogobych
492	233	4922/2336	Mikhaylovichi
492	233	4923/2333	Rykhtsitse
492	233	4923/2331	Stara Wies
492	233	4924/2330	Snyatynka
492	233	4926/2334	Dobrovlyany (Stryy)
492	233	4928/2332	Dorozhev
492	234	4920/2341	Gay Nizhniye
492	234	4921/2348	Kavsko
492	234	4924/2341	Dovge
492	234	4924/2344	Letnya
492	234	4925/2342	Opory
492	234	4925/2345	Zaszkowice
492	234	4926/2345	Medenice
492	234	4926/2345	Medenitsa
492	234	4927/2340	Litynya
492	234	4928/2348	Gorskoye
492	235	4920/2357	Lisyatychi
492	235	4922/2357	Petnichany
492	235	4924/2350	Bilche
492	235	4927/2358	Pyasechna
492	235	4927/2355	Rudniki (Zhidachov)
492	240	4921/2407	Gnizdichev
492	240	4921/2402	Pchany
492	240	4923/2406	Ivanovice
492	240	4923/2408	Zhidachov
492	240	4924/2400	Dezhov
492	240	4926/2404	Bzhezina
492	240	4928/2402	Krupsko
492	240	4928/2404	Rozdol
492	240	4929/2407	Malekhuv
492	241	4921/2418	Bortniki (Chodoruv)
492	241	4921/2417	Molotow
492	241	4922/2415	Demiduv
492	241	4922/2418	Dobrovlyany (Bobrka)
492	241	4924/2419	Khodorov
492	241	4926/2416	Gorodyshche Krulevske
492	241	4926/2419	Ottynovitse
492	241	4927/2414	Ruda (Bobrka)
492	241	4928/2416	Ostruv (Bobrka)
492	241	4929/2411	Dolishnev
492	241	4929/2412	Lyashki Dolne
492	242	4920/2425	Gregorov
492	242	4921/2426	Oskzhesintse
492	242	4923/2428	Knyazhnychi
492	242	4923/2424	Vezhbitsa
492	242	4924/2426	Pomoneta
492	242	4924/2420	Volchatyche
492	242	4925/2425	Dolinyany
492	242	4925/2428	Psary (Stanislawow)
492	242	4925/2425	Rozworzany
492	242	4925/2425	Stanimirz
492	242	4927/2423	Duliby (Bobrka)
492	242	4927/2429	Podkamien (Stanislawow)
492	242	4929/2423	Grusyatychi
492	242	4929/2421	Leshchin
492	243	4921/2431	Yavche
492	243	4923/2439	Putyatintsy
492	243	4924/2436	Zaluzhe
492	243	4925/2437	Rogatin
492	243	4925/2433	Stare Miasto
492	243	4926/2436	Podgrodze
492	243	4928/2435	Ruda (Rogatin)
492	243	4928/2432	Zalanuv
492	243	4929/2436	Klishchevna
492	244	4920/2448	Lipitsa Dolna
492	244	4921/2447	Lipitsa Gurna
492	244	4921/2443	Zholchuv
492	244	4923/2443	Chesniki
492	244	4923/2442	Pukov
492	244	4925/2445	Plenikow
492	244	4926/2448	Kuryany
492	244	4927/2447	Vulka
492	244	4928/2442	Stratin
492	245	4921/2458	Kotuv
492	245	4921/2459	Saranchuki
492	245	4922/2453	Mechishchev
492	245	4924/2450	Gutsisko
492	245	4925/2455	Zazule
492	245	4927/2456	Berezhany
492	245	4929/2455	Lapshin
492	250	4923/2503	Lityatin
492	250	4926/2509	Kozova
492	251	4925/2515	Troscianiec Wielki
492	252	4927/2521	Kupchintsy
492	252	4929/2526	Velikaya Khodachka
492	253	4920/2537	Strusov
492	253	4924/2536	Mikulintsy
492	253	4925/2535	Kurniki Iwanczanskie
492	253	4928/2533	Butsnev
492	253	4929/2535	Ostruv (Tarnopol)
492	254	4922/2544	Loshnev
492	254	4925/2545	Bolizuby
492	254	4925/2545	Zarubince

492	255	4923/2552	Sorotsko
492	255	4926/2559	Skalat
492	255	4928/2555	Kolodeyevka (Skalat)
492	260	4920/2600	Grimaylov
492	260	4923/2602	Ostapovo
492	260	4926/2608	Ivanovka (Skalat)
492	260	4928/2607	Kachanovka
492	261	4922/2614	Malaya Luka
492	261	4923/2614	Fashchevka
492	261	4924/2610	Turovka
492	261	4925/2614	Tarnorudka
492	261	4928/2611	Orekhovets
492	261	4928/2610	Sosnow
492	265	4925/2655	Sharovechka
492	270	4925/2700	Khmelnitskiy
492	272	4923/2721	Goloskov
492	272	4926/2725	Medzhibozh
492	273	4923/2737	Letichev
492	274	4929/2744	Novyy Konstantinov
492	280	4920/2804	Litin
492	282	4923/2828	Medvedka
492	282	4924/2822	Mizyakov
492	283	4928/2832	Kalinovka
492	291	4922/2917	Pliskov
492	291	4929/2916	Pogrebishche
492	293	4928/2930	Knyazha
492	293	4929/2932	Borshchagovka
492	294	4923/2940	Tetiyev
492	295	4921/2956	Pyatigory
492	301	4923/3011	Roskoshnyy
492	301	4923/3012	Stavishche
492	310	4924/3106	Steblev
492	311	4926/3115	Korsun Shevchenkovskiy
492	320	4926/3204	Cherkassy
492	323	4922/3233	Veremiyevka
492	331	4923/3317	Globino
492	340	4922/3405	Bichevaya
492	342	4920/3420	Novyye Sanzhary
492	350	4927/3508	Karlovka
492	352	4922/3527	Krasnograd
492	374	4924/3740	Borovaya
493	062	4933/0629	Kirf
493	063	4933/0632	Freudenburg
493	063	4936/0634	Beurig
493	063	4936/0633	Saarburg
493	064	4933/0649	Weiskirchen
493	064	4936/0641	Zerf
493	065	4939/0657	Hermeskeil
493	070	4934/0703	Bosen
493	070	4935/0709	Nohfelden
493	070	4936/0705	Sotern
493	071	4937/0712	Hoppstadten
493	071	4939/0711	Birkenfeld
493	072	4931/0721	Konken
493	072	4933/0724	Kusel
493	072	4935/0727	Ulmet
493	073	4933/0734	Essweiler
493	073	4937/0733	Offenbach am Glan
493	073	4939/0736	Lauterecken
493	074	4930/0746	Otterberg
493	074	4937/0745	Dorrmoschel
493	074	4938/0744	Teschenmoschel
493	075	4931/0755	Neuhemsbach
493	075	4931/0751	Sembach
493	075	4933/0754	Gonbach
493	075	4933/0751	Lohnsfeld
493	075	4933/0753	Munchweiler an der Alsenz
493	075	4934/0751	Winnweiler
493	075	4935/0757	Borrstadt
493	075	4935/0753	Imsbach
493	075	4936/0757	Steinbach am Donnersberg
493	075	4938/0750	Rockenhausen
493	080	4931/0805	Altleiningen
493	080	4931/0809	Bobenheim am Berg
493	080	4932/0809	Kleinkarlbach
493	080	4933/0806	Eisenberg
493	080	4933/0808	Neuleiningen
493	080	4935/0803	Gollheim
493	080	4935/0804	Kerzenheim
493	080	4936/0801	Dreisen
493	080	4938/0802	Marnheim
493	080	4939/0806	Albisheim
493	081	4931/0811	Herxheim
493	081	4931/0817	Lambsheim
493	081	4931/0815	Weisenheim am Sand
493	081	4932/0811	Kirchheim an der Weinstrasse
493	081	4933/0815	Grosskarlbach
493	081	4933/0818	Hessheim
493	081	4934/0815	Dirmstein
493	081	4934/0810	Grunstadt
493	081	4936/0811	Bockenheim
493	081	4936/0816	Heppenheim an der Wiese
493	081	4936/0812	Obrigheim
493	081	4937/0813	Hohen Sulzen
493	081	4937/0810	Kindenheim
493	081	4938/0818	Pfeddersheim
493	081	4938/0810	Wachenheim
493	081	4939/0810	Molsheim
493	082	4930/0828	Neckarau
493	082	4930/0828	Seckenheim
493	082	4932/0821	Frankenthal
493	082	4935/0822	Roxheim
493	082	4936/0828	Lampertheim
493	082	4938/0827	Burstadt

493 082	4938/0821	Worms
493 083	4932/0835	Viernheim
493 083	4936/0839	Hemsbach
493 083	4938/0839	Heppenheim an der Bergstrasse
493 083	4939/0834	Lorsch
493 084	4930/0840	Leutershausen (Baden)
493 084	4931/0840	Grosssachsen
493 084	4932/0840	Lutzelsachsen
493 084	4933/0840	Weinheim
493 084	4934/0843	Birkenau
493 084	4937/0846	Rimbach
493 085	4934/0859	Beerfelden
493 091	4939/0914	Amorbach
493 092	4931/0920	Buchen
493 092	4932/0920	Hainstadt
493 092	4935/0922	Walldurn
493 092	4937/0929	Hardheim
493 092	4938/0926	Dornberg
493 093	4931/0932	Eubigheim
493 093	4936/0935	Gissigheim
493 093	4936/0937	Konigheim
493 093	4939/0939	Impfingen
493 094	4930/0949	Igersheim
493 094	4931/0945	Edelfingen
493 094	4931/0943	Sachsenflur
493 094	4931/0941	Unterschupf
493 094	4932/0945	Unterbalbach
493 094	4934/0942	Lauda
493 094	4935/0947	Messelhausen
493 094	4936/0945	Grunsfeld
493 094	4937/0940	Tauberbischofsheim
493 095	4930/0956	Tauberrettersheim
493 095	4931/0958	Rottingen
493 095	4936/0953	Butthart
493 095	4938/0954	Allersheim
493 095	4939/0952	Kirchheim (Unterfranken)
493 100	4930/1007	Equarhofen
493 100	4933/1004	Aub
493 100	4938/1000	Gaukonigshofen
493 100	4938/1007	Gnodstadt
493 100	4939/1000	Acholshausen
493 100	4939/1005	Ochsenfurt
493 101	4930/1016	Ermetzhofen
493 101	4932/1015	Uffenheim
493 101	4932/1013	Welbhausen
493 101	4934/1016	Weigenheim
493 101	4938/1014	Bullenheim
493 101	4938/1017	Nenzenheim
493 101	4938/1012	Wasserndorf
493 101	4939/1015	Huttenheim
493 101	4939/1010	Obernbreit
493 102	4930/1029	Lenkersheim
493 102	4930/1025	Windsheim
493 102	4932/1029	Ipsheim
493 102	4932/1028	Kaubenheim
493 102	4935/1025	Deutenheim
493 102	4935/1023	Krautostheim
493 102	4936/1026	Sugenheim
493 102	4937/1029	Ullstadt
493 102	4938/1029	Unterlaimbach
493 103	4930/1035	Linden
493 103	4933/1031	Dottenheim
493 103	4935/1036	Neustadt an der Aisch
493 103	4936/1038	Diespeck
493 103	4937/1039	Pahres
493 104	4930/1048	Langenzenn
493 104	4939/1042	Dachsbach
493 105	4930/1057	Unterfarrnbach
493 105	4931/1059	Stadeln
493 105	4932/1058	Huttendorf
493 105	4932/1058	Vach
493 105	4933/1053	Herzogenaurach
493 105	4935/1058	Buchenbach
493 105	4937/1050	Weisendorf
493 105	4938/1055	Hessdorf
493 105	4938/1051	Kairlindach
493 110	4936/1107	Dormitz
493 110	4936/1101	Erlangen
493 110	4936/1105	Uttenreuth
493 110	4937/1104	Marloffstein
493 111	4930/1115	Ruckersdorf
493 111	4931/1117	Lauf
493 111	4932/1112	Odenberg
493 111	4934/1112	Eschenau
493 111	4936/1114	Forth
493 111	4937/1118	Huttenbach
493 111	4939/1112	Ermreuth
493 111	4939/1115	Grafenberg
493 112	4931/1126	Hersbruck
493 112	4931/1121	Ottensoos
493 112	4934/1121	Schnaittach
493 113	4937/1131	Velden
493 114	4930/1145	Sulzbach Rosenberg
493 114	4935/1144	Weissenberg
493 114	4937/1148	Vilseck
493 120	4935/1209	Luhe
493 120	4938/1206	Etzenricht
493 121	4930/1211	Pfreimd
493 123	4935/1232	Eslarn
493 123	4939/1230	Waidhaus
493 124	4931/1248	Pobezovice
493 124	4933/1240	Mostek
493 124	4933/1245	Mutenin
493 124	4934/1245	Hostoun
493 125	4930/1259	Blizejov
493 125	4930/1253	Meclov

493	125	4932/1257	Horsovsky Tyn
493	125	4936/1255	Semnevice
493	125	4939/1253	Darmysl
493	125	4939/1254	Prostibor
493	130	4931/1303	Osvracin
493	130	4933/1301	Puclice
493	130	4933/1304	Stankov
493	130	4939/1302	Nedrazice
493	131	4932/1315	Roupov
493	131	4932/1316	Vreskovice
493	131	4934/1319	Prestice
493	131	4936/1317	Dnesice
493	131	4938/1310	Stod
493	131	4939/1318	Dobrany
493	131	4939/1312	Mantov
493	132	4931/1326	Skasov
493	132	4932/1323	Horsice
493	132	4932/1327	Letiny
493	132	4936/1321	Dolni Lukavice
493	132	4937/1323	Snopousovy
493	132	4938/1326	Nebilovy
493	132	4939/1329	Chvalenice
493	132	4939/1328	Nezbavetice
493	133	4930/1335	Klaster
493	133	4931/1337	Vrcen
493	133	4934/1335	Smederov
493	133	4935/1333	Blovice
493	133	4937/1337	Spalene Porici
493	133	4939/1337	Mesno
493	133	4939/1331	Nezvestice
493	134	4931/1341	Mercin
493	134	4932/1342	Dozice
493	134	4932/1344	Radosice
493	135	4933/1358	Breznice
493	135	4936/1359	Tochovice
493	140	4930/1409	Probulov
493	140	4934/1402	Nestrasovice
493	140	4935/1406	Zbenice
493	140	4937/1408	Smolotely
493	140	4938/1403	Milin
493	141	4930/1415	Prilepov
493	141	4936/1418	Krasna Hora nad Vltavou
493	142	4930/1429	Nadejkov
493	142	4933/1422	Obdenice
493	142	4936/1422	Pocepice
493	142	4937/1427	Nedrahovice
493	142	4939/1429	Kosova Hora
493	143	4932/1437	Strezimir
493	143	4934/1432	Sedlec
493	143	4934/1430	Susetice
493	143	4935/1431	Mesetice
493	143	4935/1433	Prcice
493	143	4936/1432	Divisovice
493	143	4936/1437	Smilkov
493	143	4937/1436	Arnostovice
493	143	4939/1432	Bezmir
493	143	4939/1431	Vojkov
493	143	4939/1439	Votice
493	144	4930/1445	Hlasivo
493	144	4930/1443	Jedlany
493	144	4931/1446	Remicov
493	144	4932/1449	Mlada Vozice
493	144	4933/1448	Noskov
493	144	4934/1440	Milicin
493	144	4934/1449	Sebirov
493	144	4935/1446	Slapsko
493	144	4936/1445	Vrcholtovice
493	144	4937/1442	Neustupov
493	144	4938/1449	Liboun
493	144	4938/1440	Lysa
493	144	4938/1448	Zvestov
493	145	4930/1454	Pojbuky
493	145	4931/1456	Techobuz
493	145	4934/1452	Vilice
493	145	4935/1453	Damenice
493	145	4936/1450	Zlate Hory (Bohemia)
493	145	4937/1455	Naceradec
493	145	4938/1457	Pravonin
493	150	4933/1504	Burenice
493	150	4934/1500	Lukavec
493	150	4935/1505	Chystovice
493	150	4936/1500	Caslavsko
493	150	4937/1504	Cernici
493	150	4938/1503	Cechtice
493	150	4938/1506	Krivsoudov
493	151	4932/1514	Zeliv
493	151	4937/1519	Rejckov
493	152	4933/1522	Humpolec
493	152	4934/1523	Cejov
493	152	4934/1528	Vez
493	152	4935/1524	Kejzlice
493	152	4938/1521	Meziklasi
493	153	4930/1535	Stoky
493	153	4932/1533	Okrouhlicka
493	153	4934/1531	Kvetinov
493	153	4936/1537	Termesivy
493	153	4937/1535	Havlickuv Brod
493	154	4932/1548	Nizkov
493	155	4934/1557	Mesto Zdar
493	155	4934/1551	Sazava
493	155	4936/1555	Polnicka
493	155	4937/1557	Svetnov
493	160	4934/1605	Nove Mesto Na Morave
493	161	4938/1615	Trhonice
493	162	4937/1625	Predmesti
493	163	4938/1631	Brnenec
493	164	4938/1644	Jevicko

493	165	4935/1653	Konice
493	171	4935/1715	Olomouc
493	172	4931/1729	Radvanice
493	173	4930/1737	Lhota
493	173	4932/1736	Lipnik nad Becou
493	174	4933/1744	Hranice
493	175	4939/1756	Suchdol
493	180	4933/1807	Verovice
493	180	4936/1801	Novy Jicin
493	180	4939/1809	Pribor
493	181	4933/1813	Frenstat pod Radhostem
493	181	4934/1814	Ticha
493	184	4935/1846	Jablunkov
493	185	4931/1859	Zwardon
493	185	4934/1854	Istebna
493	190	4930/1907	Rajcza
493	190	4931/1905	Bystra (Slaskie)
493	190	4933/1905	Nieledwia
493	190	4934/1905	Milowka
493	190	4934/1903	Szare
493	190	4935/1907	Cisiec
493	190	4935/1904	Kamesznica
493	190	4935/1909	Zabnica
493	190	4937/1909	Ciecina
493	190	4939/1908	Radziechowy
493	191	4937/1916	Sopotnia Mala
493	191	4939/1913	Trzebinia Wies
493	192	4937/1920	Krzyzowa
493	192	4937/1922	Przyborow
493	192	4939/1920	Jelesnia
493	192	4939/1925	Koszarowa
493	193	4930/1937	Lipnica Wielka
493	193	4932/1938	Lipnica Mala
493	193	4934/1939	Zubrzyca Gorna
493	194	4931/1943	Orawka
493	194	4932/1941	Zubrzyca Dolna
493	194	4933/1944	Podwilk
493	194	4934/1948	Podsarnie
493	194	4937/1944	Sidzina
493	195	4930/1957	Morawczyna
493	195	4930/1950	Zaluczne
493	195	4933/1951	Harkabuz
493	195	4934/1954	Raba Wyzna
493	195	4935/1959	Rdzawka
493	195	4935/1950	Spytkowice
493	195	4936/1956	Chabowka
493	195	4936/1959	Ponice
493	195	4937/1957	Rabka
493	195	4937/1954	Skawa
493	195	4939/1950	Jordanow
493	200	4937/2008	Konina
493	200	4938/2006	Podobin
493	201	4931/2012	Ustrzyk
493	201	4932/2019	Ochotnica Dolna
493	201	4936/2018	Szczawo
493	201	4937/2012	Lubomierz
493	202	4933/2027	Lacko
493	202	4933/2025	Zarzecze (Nowy Sacz)
493	202	4934/2028	Binczarowa
493	202	4934/2026	Czerniec
493	202	4935/2029	Czarny Potok
493	202	4935/2021	Kamienica (Nowy Sacz)
493	202	4936/2020	Zasadne
493	202	4936/2021	Zbludza
493	202	4937/2029	Lukowica
493	202	4937/2027	Roztoka (Nowy Sacz)
493	202	4937/2021	Zalesie (Nowy Sacz)
493	202	4938/2029	Biczyce
493	203	4932/2039	Barcice
493	203	4932/2030	Brzyna
493	203	4932/2035	Gabon
493	203	4932/2031	Jazowsko
493	203	4933/2038	Moszczenica Nizna
493	203	4934/2031	Olszana
493	203	4934/2039	Stary Sacz
493	203	4935/2036	Podegrodzie
493	203	4936/2037	Brzezna
493	203	4937/2036	Gostwica
493	203	4938/2038	Trzetrzewino
493	203	4939/2030	Przyszowa
493	204	4933/2045	Bacza
493	204	4934/2045	Nawojowa
493	204	4935/2041	Biegonice
493	204	4935/2049	Kamionka Wielka (Nowy Sacz)
493	204	4935/2043	Poreba Mala
493	204	4935/2044	Zawada (Nowy Sacz)
493	204	4937/2040	Dabrowka Niemiecka
493	204	4937/2048	Mystkow
493	204	4938/2041	Chelmiec
493	204	4938/2043	Nowy Sacz
493	204	4938/2047	Paszyn
493	204	4938/2046	Piatkowa (Krakow)
493	205	4931/2059	Berest
493	205	4932/2057	Kamianna
493	205	4932/2052	Maciejowa
493	205	4934/2059	Florynka
493	205	4935/2051	Krolowa Ruska
493	205	4936/2058	Kaclowa
493	205	4937/2058	Biala Wyzna
493	205	4937/2051	Cieniawa
493	205	4937/2053	Ptaszkowa
493	205	4938/2057	Grybow
493	205	4939/2054	Kruzlowa
493	205	4939/2057	Siolkowa
493	210	4930/2105	Stawisza
493	210	4931/2104	Snietnica

493	210	4931/2108	Uscie Ruskie
493	210	4935/2106	Losie
493	210	4936/2103	Ropa
493	210	4938/2106	Szymbark
493	211	4930/2112	Skwirtne
493	211	4931/2119	Krywa
493	211	4931/2114	Smerekowiec
493	211	4932/2116	Gladyszow
493	211	4934/2115	Malastow
493	211	4934/2116	Petna
493	211	4936/2115	Ropica Ruska
493	211	4937/2112	Sekowa
493	211	4938/2116	Mecina Wielka
493	211	4938/2111	Siary
493	211	4938/2117	Wapienne
493	211	4939/2115	Ropica Polska
493	211	4939/2111	Sokol (Krakow)
493	212	4932/2126	Swiatkowa Wielka
493	212	4932/2122	Wolowiec
493	212	4933/2126	Swierzowa Ruska
493	212	4934/2120	Bartne
493	212	4934/2129	Desznica
493	212	4938/2120	Bednarka
493	212	4938/2129	Osiek Grodowski
493	212	4939/2123	Cieklin
493	212	4939/2123	Wola Cieklinska
493	213	4931/2131	Krempna
493	213	4934/2138	Iwla
493	213	4935/2135	Lysa Gora
493	213	4936/2134	Zmigrod Stary
493	213	4937/2131	Mytarz
493	213	4937/2132	Zmigrod Nowy
493	213	4939/2137	Faliszowka
493	214	4930/2149	Krolik Woloski
493	214	4931/2149	Krolik Polski
493	214	4933/2146	Lubatowa
493	214	4934/2141	Dukla
493	214	4935/2143	Rowne (Lwow)
493	214	4935/2142	Zboiska
493	214	4937/2149	Iwonicz
493	214	4938/2142	Bobrka (Krosno)
493	214	4939/2141	Chorkowka
493	214	4939/2148	Lezany
493	215	4931/2153	Wisloczek
493	215	4933/2151	Deszno (Lwow)
493	215	4933/2155	Glebokie (Lwow)
493	215	4933/2159	Odrzechowa
493	215	4933/2156	Sieniawa (Sanok)
493	215	4934/2152	Posada Gorna
493	215	4935/2150	Klimkowka
493	215	4935/2155	Konieczkowa
493	215	4935/2152	Rymanow
493	215	4937/2152	Wroblik Krolewski
493	215	4937/2153	Wroblik Szlachecki
493	215	4938/2150	Targowiska
493	215	4939/2157	Trzezniow
493	215	4939/2159	Wzdow
493	220	4930/2201	Wola Sekowa
493	220	4931/2203	Nagorzany
493	220	4931/2202	Nowotaniec
493	220	4931/2206	Wolica (Sanok)
493	220	4932/2203	Nadolany
493	220	4932/2208	Prusiek
493	220	4933/2204	Pielnia
493	220	4933/2209	Sanoczek
493	220	4934/2204	Nowosielce Gniewosz
493	220	4935/2201	Zarszyn
493	220	4936/2207	Kostarowce
493	220	4937/2201	Jacmierz
493	220	4937/2206	Strachocina
493	220	4938/2206	Pakoszowka
493	220	4939/2202	Gorki (Lwow)
493	220	4939/2205	Grabownica Starzenska
493	221	4931/2210	Niebieszczany
493	221	4931/2216	Zagorz
493	221	4932/2216	Nowy Zagorz
493	221	4932/2215	Zahutyn
493	221	4932/2218	Zaluz
493	221	4933/2213	Posada Olchowska
493	221	4933/2211	Stroze Male
493	221	4933/2218	Wujskie
493	221	4934/2210	Dabrowka Ruska
493	221	4934/2214	Olchowce
493	221	4934/2212	Sanok
493	221	4935/2215	Kosztowa
493	221	4936/2219	Siemuszowa
493	221	4937/2214	Debna
493	221	4937/2217	Tyrawa Solna
493	221	4938/2210	Falejowka
493	221	4938/2217	Hlomcza
493	221	4939/2218	Dobra Szlachecka
493	221	4939/2211	Raczkowa
493	222	4930/2226	Rudenka
493	222	4931/2223	Bezmichowa Dolna
493	222	4931/2224	Bezmichowa Gorna
493	222	4931/2222	Monasterzec
493	222	4931/2229	Wankowa
493	222	4932/2226	Paszowa
493	222	4934/2224	Rakowa
493	222	4934/2227	Stankowa
493	222	4935/2220	Holuczkow
493	222	4935/2222	Tyrawa Woloska
493	222	4936/2225	Rozpucie
493	222	4937/2222	Krecow
493	222	4937/2226	Kuzmina
493	222	4937/2228	Roztoka (Lwow)
493	222	4938/2225	Leszczawka
493	222	4939/2222	Lachawa

493	222	4939/2227	Leszczawa Gorna
493	223	4930/2234	Leszczowate
493	223	4930/2231	Serednica
493	223	4931/2231	Brelikow
493	223	4931/2237	Liskowate
493	223	4932/2231	Ropienka
493	223	4934/2232	Nowosielce Kozickie
493	223	4934/2234	Wojtkowa
493	223	4934/2235	Wojtkowka
493	223	4935/2230	Trzcianiec
493	223	4935/2234	Turze
493	223	4936/2233	Graziowa
493	223	4936/2237	Jamna Gorna
493	223	4937/2236	Reczpol
493	223	4938/2234	Jamna Dolna
493	223	4938/2231	Lomna
493	223	4939/2238	Boryslawka
493	223	4939/2239	Rybotycze
493	224	4930/2244	Lopushnitsa
493	224	4930/2246	Staryava
493	224	4932/2246	Polyana
493	224	4933/2240	Kwaszenina
493	224	4933/2248	Tarnava
493	224	4934/2247	Dobromil
493	224	4934/2247	Guchok
493	224	4934/2245	Knyazhpol
493	224	4935/2245	Dobkowice
493	224	4935/2244	Kropevnik
493	224	4938/2245	Hujsko
493	224	4938/2243	Kalwaria Paclawska
493	224	4938/2241	Makowa Rustykalna
493	224	4938/2244	Nowosiolki (Przemysl)
493	224	4938/2244	Nowosiolki Dydynskie
493	224	4939/2242	Huwniki
493	225	4930/2250	Sushitsa Velikaya
493	225	4932/2259	Glemboka
493	225	4932/2251	Khyrov
493	225	4932/2258	Skelivka
493	225	4934/2258	Konyuv
493	225	4934/2250	Pyatnitsa
493	225	4935/2250	Bonevichi
493	225	4937/2252	Nowe Miasto (Lwow)
493	225	4938/2258	Chishki
493	225	4938/2254	Grushatichi
493	225	4939/2256	Gdeshichi
493	230	4931/2302	Chapli
493	230	4933/2306	Voyutychi
493	230	4935/2300	Bukova
493	230	4938/2304	Rogozno (Sambor)
493	230	4938/2306	Verkhovtsy
493	231	4930/2317	Kulchitsy
493	231	4931/2315	Radlovichi
493	231	4931/2315	Ralevka
493	231	4931/2312	Sambor
493	231	4932/2312	Biskovichi
493	231	4934/2311	Maksimovichi
493	231	4935/2315	Nowosielica
493	231	4935/2312	Pyanovichi
493	231	4938/2314	Kornichi
493	231	4938/2318	Vankovichi
493	232	4930/2324	Dublyany
493	232	4931/2327	Tatary
493	232	4932/2328	Bolshaya Belina
493	232	4932/2323	Gordynya
493	232	4937/2321	Chernikhov
493	232	4937/2323	Luky
493	232	4937/2321	Ostrov (Rudki)
493	232	4937/2322	Zagorye
493	232	4938/2328	Novoselki
493	232	4939/2320	Kupnovichi Staryye
493	232	4939/2329	Rudki
493	232	4939/2325	Shcheptitsy
493	233	4930/2336	Voloshcha
493	233	4931/2333	Maynich
493	233	4935/2337	Malinovka
493	233	4936/2331	Chaykovichi
493	233	4936/2334	Pokhortsy
493	233	4936/2338	Tuligolovy
493	233	4939/2331	Podgaychiki
493	234	4930/2348	Kolodruby
493	234	4932/2342	Monastyrets
493	234	4935/2340	Nowa Wies (Dobromil)
493	234	4935/2340	Nowe Siolo (Stanislawow)
493	234	4936/2346	Grimnoye
493	234	4938/2342	Komarno (Lvov)
493	234	4938/2340	Peremozhnoye
493	234	4938/2344	Yakimchitsy
493	235	4930/2357	Rozvadov
493	235	4931/2359	Nikolayev (Stanislawow)
493	235	4933/2354	Verbizh
493	235	4935/2350	Velikaya Gorozhanka
493	235	4938/2352	Lany (Lvov)
493	235	4938/2357	Ternopolye
493	235	4939/2352	Shchirets
493	240	4932/2405	Stilskoye
493	240	4935/2405	Lesienice
493	240	4935/2405	Podliski Wielkie
493	240	4935/2404	Polyana (Lvov)
493	240	4939/2401	Rakovets (Lwow)
493	241	4930/2413	Boryniche
493	241	4931/2417	Devyatniki
493	241	4933/2413	Vybranovka
493	241	4934/2417	Kologury
493	241	4934/2418	Sokolovka (Lwow)
493	241	4935/2417	Khoderkovtse
493	241	4935/2410	Khuta Sukhodolska
493	241	4936/2418	Lany (Bobrka)

493	241	4937/2410	Sukhodul (Lwow)
493	241	4937/2414	Velikiye Glibovichi
493	241	4937/2414	Voloshchizna
493	241	4938/2418	Bobrka
493	241	4938/2411	Olkhovets (Bobrka)
493	242	4930/2427	Lyubsha
493	242	4931/2422	Kneselo
493	242	4931/2424	Novyye Strelishcha
493	242	4932/2421	Repekhuv
493	242	4932/2425	Stsheliska Stare
493	242	4934/2428	Tuchne
493	242	4935/2425	Ubinie
493	242	4937/2426	Khlebovitse Svizhske
493	242	4939/2426	Svirzh
493	243	4931/2434	Lipovka
493	243	4932/2439	Bachuv
493	243	4932/2436	Dusanov
493	243	4934/2437	Ivanovka (Tarnopol)
493	243	4935/2435	Olszanka Mala
493	243	4936/2432	Ostalovitse
493	243	4937/2436	Volkov
493	243	4938/2438	Ladantsy
493	243	4938/2433	Ushkovitse
493	243	4939/2430	Kimizh
493	244	4931/2442	Podusilna
493	244	4932/2446	Narayev
493	244	4933/2441	Bolotnya
493	244	4935/2441	Podusuv
493	244	4937/2441	Polukhuv Maly
493	244	4939/2441	Pnyatyn
493	245	4933/2454	Bushche
493	245	4934/2450	Rekshin
493	245	4934/2451	Strygantse
493	245	4934/2457	Urman
493	245	4934/2456	Volitsa (Podgaytsy)
493	245	4937/2450	Dunayev
493	245	4938/2458	Kalne
493	245	4938/2456	Pomoryany
493	250	4930/2501	Kuropatniki
493	250	4931/2502	Potok (Buchach)
493	250	4931/2506	Tsenyuv
493	250	4936/2508	Khorostsets
493	250	4937/2501	Goduv
493	250	4938/2509	Szczepanow
493	250	4939/2505	Yezezhanka
493	251	4931/2515	Budylov
493	251	4932/2517	Taurov
493	251	4935/2511	Glinna
493	251	4935/2512	Malaya Plavucha
493	251	4935/2514	Plaucha Velka
493	251	4936/2511	Krasna (Tarnopol)
493	252	4933/2521	Kozlow
493	252	4938/2529	Kurovtsy
493	252	4938/2520	Ozernyany
493	253	4930/2537	Velikaya Berezovitsa
493	253	4933/2535	Ternopol
493	253	4937/2534	Plotych
493	253	4938/2532	Hluboczek Wielki
493	254	4931/2545	Velikiye Borki
493	254	4932/2540	Obodovka
493	254	4938/2544	Chernikhovtsy
493	255	4935/2555	Matwijowce
493	255	4938/2555	Dobromirka
493	255	4938/2555	Obodovka (Tarnopol)
493	260	4930/2601	Chmieliska
493	260	4931/2602	Molchanovka
493	260	4931/2608	Zadnishevka
493	260	4932/2609	Podvolochisk
493	260	4933/2601	Kamenki
493	260	4933/2603	Rosokhovatets
493	260	4933/2605	Supranuvka
493	260	4934/2604	Korshyluvka
493	260	4935/2601	Klebanovka
493	260	4936/2606	Klimkovtse
493	260	4936/2609	Medin
493	260	4936/2608	Skoriki
493	260	4937/2603	Terpilovka
493	260	4939/2604	Nowe Siolo (Tarnopol)
493	261	4932/2610	Volochisk
493	261	4938/2613	Toki
493	261	4939/2610	Golotki
493	263	4936/2631	Kupel
493	264	4930/2645	Chernyy Ostrov
493	265	4935/2651	Nikolayev (Podolia)
493	265	4939/2658	Krasilov
493	272	4936/2727	Pilyava
493	273	4936/2737	Staraya Sinyava
493	275	4933/2758	Khmelnik
493	281	4934/2816	Novyy Pikov
493	285	4932/2851	Samgorodok
493	295	4931/2955	Volodarka
493	303	4934/3030	Tarashcha
493	305	4933/3053	Boguslav
493	311	4935/3117	Tagancha
493	331	4936/3310	Semenovka
493	334	4937/3345	Balakliya
493	340	4934/3404	Reshetilovka
493	343	4935/3434	Poltava
494	063	4941/0633	Konen
494	063	4942/0635	Konz
494	063	4945/0638	Trier
494	063	4949/0637	Butzweiler
494	064	4949/0644	Issel
494	064	4949/0645	Schweich
494	065	4942/0654	Hinzert
494	065	4949/0653	Leiwen
494	065	4949/0654	Trittenheim
494	070	4945/0700	Thalfang

494	071	4942/0718	Idar Oberstein
494	072	4942/0728	Oberreidenbach
494	072	4947/0727	Kirn
494	072	4949/0726	Hennweiler
494	073	4941/0739	Odenbach
494	073	4947/0734	Merxheim
494	073	4948/0739	Sobernheim
494	074	4940/0749	Dielkirchen
494	074	4940/0744	Waldgrehweiler
494	074	4943/0749	Alsenz
494	074	4943/0740	Meisenheim
494	074	4944/0748	Niedermoschel
494	074	4944/0746	Obermoschel
494	074	4946/0742	Odernheim
494	074	4947/0741	Staudernheim
494	075	4940/0752	Gerbach
494	075	4941/0753	Schneebergerhof
494	075	4942/0752	Gaugrehweiler
494	075	4944/0759	Nieder Wiesen
494	075	4946/0750	Hochstatten
494	075	4946/0758	Stein Bockenheim
494	075	4947/0750	Altenbamberg
494	075	4947/0754	Furfeld
494	075	4948/0754	Frei Laubersheim
494	075	4948/0757	Siefersheim
494	075	4949/0750	Ebernburg
494	080	4940/0804	Gauersheim
494	080	4940/0801	Kirchheimbolanden
494	080	4945/0807	Alzey
494	080	4945/0802	Erbes Budesheim
494	080	4946/0800	Wendelsheim
494	080	4947/0802	Flonheim
494	080	4948/0804	Armsheim
494	081	4940/0817	Abenheim
494	081	4942/0810	Eppelsheim
494	081	4942/0815	Westhofen
494	081	4943/0814	Monzernheim
494	081	4944/0815	Hessloch
494	081	4946/0811	Framersheim
494	081	4946/0812	Gau Odernheim
494	081	4948/0812	Bechtolsheim
494	082	4941/0827	Biblis
494	082	4941/0825	Wattenheim
494	082	4942/0820	Osthofen
494	082	4943/0829	Gross Rohrheim
494	082	4945/0824	Eich
494	082	4945/0829	Gernsheim
494	082	4946/0820	Alsheim
494	082	4947/0828	Biebesheim
494	082	4947/0823	Gimbsheim
494	082	4948/0821	Guntersblum
494	083	4941/0837	Bensheim
494	083	4943/0837	Zwingenberg
494	083	4944/0838	Alsbach
494	083	4944/0834	Hahnlein
494	083	4945/0837	Bickenbach
494	083	4945/0838	Jugenheim
494	083	4948/0833	Hahn
494	083	4948/0836	Pfungstadt
494	083	4949/0831	Crumstadt
494	083	4949/0839	Eberstadt
494	083	4949/0834	Eschollbrucken
494	084	4946/0848	Lichtenberg
494	084	4946/0840	Seeheim
494	084	4949/0842	Nieder Ramstadt
494	085	4941/0853	Rohrbach
494	085	4943/0852	Pfaffen Beerfurth
494	085	4943/0851	Reichelsheim
494	085	4945/0852	Frankisch Crumbach
494	085	4948/0850	Gross Bieberau
494	085	4948/0859	Hochst im Odenwald
494	085	4949/0853	Ober Klingen
494	085	4949/0850	Reinheim
494	090	4941/0901	Michelstadt
494	090	4945/0901	Bad Konig
494	090	4946/0900	Mumling Grumbach
494	090	4947/0907	Seckmauern
494	090	4948/0904	Neustadt in Oldenwald
494	091	4940/0913	Weilbach
494	091	4942/0915	Miltenberg
494	091	4943/0913	Kleinheubach
494	091	4944/0913	Grossheubach
494	091	4945/0919	Freudenberg
494	091	4946/0919	Reistenhausen
494	091	4946/0915	Rollbach
494	091	4946/0911	Rollfeld
494	091	4947/0912	Klingenberg am Main
494	091	4947/0911	Trennfurt
494	091	4948/0916	Monchberg
494	091	4948/0910	Worth am Main
494	091	4949/0916	Eschau
494	092	4942/0920	Eichenbuhl
494	092	4946/0920	Fechenbach
494	093	4940/0931	Kulsheim
494	093	4943/0933	Bronnbach
494	093	4945/0931	Wertheim
494	093	4946/0937	Dertingen
494	093	4947/0937	Homburg am Main
494	094	4941/0945	Baierthal
494	094	4942/0942	Wenkheim
494	094	4944/0940	Neubrunn
494	094	4944/0946	Oberaltertheim
494	094	4944/0944	Unteraltertheim
494	094	4948/0949	Hettstadt
494	094	4948/0942	Remlingen
494	094	4949/0946	Greussenheim
494	095	4940/0956	Giebelstadt
494	095	4941/0954	Geroldshausen

494 095	4943/0958	Rottenbauer	
494 095	4944/0955	Reichenberg	
494 095	4946/0958	Heidingsfeld	
494 095	4946/0959	Randersacker	
494 095	4947/0953	Hochberg	
494 095	4948/0956	Wurzburg	
494 100	4940/1008	Segnitz	
494 100	4941/1002	Gossmannsdorf am Main	
494 100	4942/1002	Sommerhausen	
494 100	4942/1001	Winterhausen	
494 100	4944/1000	Eibelstadt	
494 100	4945/1007	Repperndorf	
494 100	4945/1002	Theilheim	
494 100	4947/1009	Mainstockheim	
494 100	4948/1006	Bibergau	
494 100	4948/1002	Rottendorf	
494 100	4949/1009	Bruck	
494 101	4940/1010	Marktsteft	
494 101	4941/1017	Iphofen	
494 101	4941/1014	Willanzheim	
494 101	4942/1015	Mainbernheim	
494 101	4943/1010	Hohenfeld	
494 101	4943/1011	Sickershausen	
494 101	4944/1010	Kitzingen	
494 101	4944/1014	Rodelsee	
494 101	4945/1014	Grosslangheim	
494 101	4945/1018	Wiesenbronn	
494 101	4946/1017	Kleinlangheim	
494 101	4948/1011	Dettelbach	
494 101	4948/1013	Stadtschwarzach	
494 102	4940/1028	Scheinfeld	
494 102	4941/1025	Burgambach	
494 102	4941/1026	Schnodsenbach	
494 102	4946/1028	Geiselwind	
494 102	4946/1026	Rehweiler	
494 102	4949/1024	Altenschonbach	
494 102	4949/1023	Kirchschonbach	
494 102	4949/1021	Prichsenstadt	
494 103	4940/1039	Schornweisach	
494 103	4941/1038	Vestenbergsgreuth	
494 103	4944/1036	Burghaslach	
494 103	4946/1034	Aschbach	
494 103	4946/1038	Schlusselfeld	
494 104	4940/1043	Demantsfurth	
494 104	4940/1044	Uhlfeld	
494 104	4942/1048	Hochstadt an der Aisch	
494 104	4942/1046	Lonnerstadt	
494 104	4945/1047	Thungfeld	
494 104	4946/1048	Steppach	
494 104	4947/1042	Reichmannsdorf	
494 105	4943/1054	Adelsdorf	
494 105	4946/1059	Hallerndorf	
494 105	4948/1059	Sassanfahrt	
494 105	4949/1052	Frensdorf	
494 110	4940/1102	Baiersdorf	
494 110	4940/1108	Gaiganz	
494 110	4941/1109	Kunreuth	
494 110	4942/1106	Pinzberg	
494 110	4943/1104	Forchheim	
494 110	4943/1108	Wiesenthau	
494 110	4945/1108	Oberweilersbach	
494 110	4945/1108	Reifenberg	
494 110	4946/1103	Eggolsheim	
494 110	4948/1102	Buttenheim	
494 110	4949/1100	Hirschaid	
494 111	4941/1110	Mittelehrenbach	
494 111	4941/1112	Oberehrenbach	
494 111	4942/1115	Egloffstein	
494 111	4945/1111	Pretzfeld	
494 111	4946/1110	Russenbach	
494 111	4947/1112	Ebermannstadt	
494 112	4946/1129	Hollenberg	
494 112	4947/1122	Tuchersfeld	
494 113	4945/1133	Pegnitz	
494 113	4946/1139	Thurndorf	
494 115	4943/1154	Grafenwohr	
494 115	4945/1151	Wannbach	
494 115	4946/1156	Pressath	
494 115	4949/1150	Neustadt am Kulm	
494 121	4941/1210	Weiden	
494 121	4944/1217	Floss	
494 121	4944/1210	Neustadt an der Waldnaab	
494 122	4944/1221	Flossenburg	
494 123	4944/1236	Porejov	
494 123	4945/1234	Bazantov	
494 123	4948/1238	Tachov	
494 124	4940/1241	Primda	
494 124	4940/1247	Straz	
494 124	4944/1240	Nove Sedliste	
494 124	4947/1248	Damnov	
494 125	4943/1258	Kladruby	
494 125	4946/1252	Oselin	
494 125	4946/1255	Svojsin	
494 125	4949/1253	Cernosin	
494 125	4949/1257	Tepla Mesto	
494 130	4942/1308	Prehysov	
494 130	4943/1305	Vlkys	
494 130	4944/1309	Rochlov	
494 130	4945/1300	Stribro	
494 130	4945/1305	Sulislav	
494 130	4948/1303	Erpuzice	
494 130	4948/1300	Ksice	
494 130	4949/1304	Trpisty	
494 131	4941/1313	Zbuch	
494 131	4942/1316	Line	
494 131	4943/1312	Nyrany	

494	131	4945/1318	Krimice
494	131	4946/1314	Bdeneves
494	131	4946/1315	Kozolupy
494	131	4946/1318	Malesice
494	131	4946/1311	Plesnice
494	131	4946/1317	Vochov
494	131	4947/1315	Mesto Touskov
494	131	4948/1317	Kusti
494	132	4940/1324	Stenovice
494	132	4945/1322	Plzen
494	132	4946/1322	Bolevec
494	132	4947/1329	Dysina
494	133	4940/1330	Stahlavy
494	133	4944/1336	Rokycany
494	133	4946/1334	Litohlavy
494	133	4947/1338	Volduchy
494	133	4948/1330	Chrast
494	134	4943/1341	Dobriv
494	134	4944/1346	Strasice
494	134	4947/1347	Cheznovice
494	134	4947/1342	Holoubkov
494	134	4948/1342	Teskov
494	134	4949/1347	Karez
494	135	4943/1357	Obecnice
494	135	4944/1358	Drahlin
494	135	4944/1359	Sadek
494	135	4946/1351	Zajecov
494	135	4947/1359	Jince
494	140	4942/1401	Pribram
494	140	4946/1407	Rosovice
494	141	4942/1417	Hrimezdice
494	141	4942/1414	Necin
494	141	4944/1414	Drhovy
494	141	4946/1411	Dobris
494	142	4940/1422	Dublovice
494	142	4940/1423	Pricovy
494	142	4940/1425	Sedlcany
494	142	4942/1422	Nalzovice
494	142	4943/1425	Radic
494	142	4944/1427	Nahoruby
494	142	4946/1428	Belice
494	143	4942/1437	Bozkovice
494	143	4945/1432	Neveklov
494	143	4945/1430	Stranny
494	143	4948/1436	Krusicany
494	143	4949/1432	Netvorice
494	144	4942/1448	Celivo
494	144	4944/1447	Postupice
494	144	4945/1449	Chotysany
494	144	4947/1441	Benesov
494	144	4947/1446	Verice
494	144	4949/1443	Bedrc
494	144	4949/1445	Petroupim
494	144	4949/1444	Sobehrdy
494	145	4942/1454	Vlasim
494	145	4945/1456	Nemiz
494	145	4945/1458	Psare
494	145	4946/1455	Libez
494	145	4946/1450	Takonin
494	145	4947/1453	Divisov
494	145	4947/1458	Zdebuzeves
494	145	4948/1454	Mechnov
494	145	4948/1457	Sobesin
494	145	4949/1456	Cesky Sternberk
494	145	4949/1454	Drahnovice
494	150	4940/1508	Brzotice
494	150	4940/1509	Dolni Kralovice
494	150	4941/1504	Keblov
494	150	4942/1503	Dubejovice
494	150	4942/1504	Sedmpany
494	150	4943/1505	Hulice
494	150	4944/1504	Soutice
494	150	4944/1506	Zruc nad Sazavou
494	150	4945/1503	Holsice
494	150	4946/1505	Rendejov
494	150	4947/1504	Polipsy
494	150	4949/1501	Zbizuby
494	151	4942/1517	Ledec nad Sazavou
494	151	4942/1514	Sechov
494	151	4949/1511	Zbraslavice
494	152	4940/1523	Lipnicka
494	152	4940/1524	Svetla nad Sazavou
494	152	4941/1528	Malcin
494	152	4944/1528	Backov
494	152	4944/1520	Cihost
494	152	4944/1525	Smrdov
494	152	4945/1529	Habry
494	152	4946/1524	Lestina
494	152	4947/1520	Dobrovitov
494	152	4949/1529	Golcuv Jenikov
494	153	4943/1534	Sedletin
494	153	4945/1536	Nejepin
494	153	4948/1538	Chuchel
494	153	4948/1534	Uhrov
494	153	4949/1539	Hojesin
494	154	4942/1541	Dobkov
494	154	4943/1540	Chotebor
494	155	4941/1559	Cesky Heralec
494	155	4946/1559	Dedova
494	155	4946/1554	Hlinsko
494	160	4943/1602	Svratka
494	160	4946/1602	Krouna
494	160	4948/1607	Prosec
494	161	4940/1615	Korouhev
494	161	4943/1616	Policka
494	161	4943/1619	Pomezi
494	162	4940/1628	Banin
494	162	4945/1628	Svitavy

494	162	4948/1625	Mikulec
494	163	4940/1633	Horni Hyncina
494	163	4944/1633	Lechovice
494	164	4945/1640	Moravska Trebova
494	165	4945/1656	Lostice
494	165	4947/1655	Mohelnice
494	170	4943/1705	Litovel
494	170	4946/1708	Unicov
494	170	4948/1701	Usov
494	171	4944/1718	Sternberk
494	173	4943/1731	Mesto Libava
494	175	4943/1755	Fulnek
494	180	4946/1802	Bilovec
494	180	4946/1809	Fonovice
494	180	4948/1808	Klimkovice
494	181	4949/1816	Vitkovice
494	182	4941/1821	Frydek
494	183	4941/1839	Trinec
494	183	4945/1837	Cesky Tesin
494	183	4946/1836	Cieszyn
494	184	4943/1848	Ustron
494	184	4944/1843	Bazanowice
494	184	4944/1845	Goleszow
494	184	4946/1840	Bobrek
494	184	4946/1849	Nierodzim
494	184	4947/1842	Gumna
494	184	4947/1846	Kisielow
494	184	4948/1849	Harbutowice
494	184	4948/1840	Hazlach
494	184	4948/1848	Miedzyswiec
494	184	4948/1848	Skoczow
494	184	4948/1841	Zamarski
494	184	4949/1843	Debowiec
494	184	4949/1845	Iskrzyczyn
494	185	4940/1852	Wisla
494	185	4947/1852	Gorki Wielkie
494	185	4948/1855	Biery
494	185	4949/1859	Wapienica
494	190	4943/1909	Lodygowice
494	190	4943/1905	Slotwina
494	190	4943/1902	Szczyrk
494	190	4944/1904	Buczkowice
494	190	4946/1905	Bystra (Bielsko Biala)
494	190	4946/1907	Wilkowice
494	190	4947/1905	Mikuszowice
494	190	4948/1902	Kamienica
494	190	4948/1903	Olszow Dolny
494	190	4949/1901	Aleksandrowice
494	190	4949/1902	Biala (Krakow)
494	190	4949/1902	Bielsko Biala
494	191	4940/1917	Pewel Mala
494	191	4941/1914	Sporysz
494	191	4941/1913	Zywiec
494	191	4942/1915	Kocurow
494	191	4942/1910	Pietrzykowice
494	191	4944/1915	Oczkow
494	191	4944/1918	Okrajnik
494	191	4944/1912	Zadziele
494	192	4940/1921	Pewel Wielka
494	192	4943/1923	Slemien
494	193	4940/1934	Zawoja
494	193	4941/1938	Skawica
494	193	4943/1931	Stryszawa
494	193	4944/1936	Sucha
494	193	4947/1936	Zembrzyce
494	193	4948/1935	Skawce
494	194	4941/1946	Osielec
494	194	4944/1941	Makow Podhalanski
494	194	4945/1940	Bottingheim
494	195	4940/1953	Malejowa
494	195	4940/1952	Naprawa
494	195	4941/1956	Krzeczow (Nowy Targ)
494	195	4943/1959	Lubien (Nowy Targ)
494	195	4944/1950	Skomielna Czarna
494	195	4945/1958	Pcim
494	195	4945/1952	Wiecierza
494	200	4940/2006	Mszana Gorna
494	200	4941/2009	Lostowka
494	200	4941/2005	Mszana Dolna
494	200	4941/2007	Slomka
494	200	4943/2003	Kasinka
494	200	4944/2009	Kosina Wielka
494	200	4946/2008	Wierzbanowa
494	200	4947/2007	Wisniowa
494	200	4948/2006	Lipnik
494	200	4949/2007	Poznachowice Dolne
494	201	4940/2014	Polrzeczki
494	201	4943/2016	Dobra (Limanowa)
494	201	4944/2018	Jasna Podlopien
494	201	4946/2010	Przenosza
494	201	4946/2011	Skrzydlna
494	201	4946/2016	Wilkowisko
494	201	4947/2014	Jodlownik
494	201	4947/2017	Kostrza Ryje
494	201	4947/2011	Szczyrzyc
494	201	4948/2019	Szyk
494	201	4949/2014	Krasne (Krakow)
494	202	4940/2024	Stara Wies (Grybow)
494	202	4941/2026	Stara Wies (Cimarowa)
494	202	4942/2026	Limanowa
494	202	4942/2021	Slopnice
494	202	4943/2028	Mordarka
494	202	4944/2024	Lososina Gorna
494	202	4944/2025	Sowliny
494	202	4944/2020	Tymbark
494	202	4944/2021	Zamiescie
494	202	4945/2025	Mlynne
494	202	4947/2020	Rybie Nowe

494	202	4948/2026	Zegocina
494	202	4949/2024	Beldno
494	202	4949/2028	Bytomsko
494	202	4949/2023	Kamionna
494	202	4949/2020	Rybie Stare
494	203	4940/2032	Bilsko
494	203	4940/2038	Kleczany
494	203	4940/2035	Krasne Potockie
494	203	4941/2034	Mecina
494	203	4942/2030	Pisarzowa
494	203	4943/2038	Tegoborze
494	203	4945/2034	Kobylczyna
494	203	4945/2037	Lososina Dolna
494	203	4945/2034	Ujanowice
494	203	4945/2036	Zbikowice
494	203	4946/2037	Michalczowa
494	203	4948/2034	Dobrociesz
494	203	4948/2037	Druzkow Pusty
494	203	4949/2031	Iwkowa
494	203	4949/2034	Wojakowa
494	203	4949/2038	Wytrzyszczka
494	204	4940/2048	Koniuszowa
494	204	4940/2046	Librantowa
494	204	4940/2040	Marcinkowice
494	204	4941/2047	Siedlce (Nowy Sacz)
494	204	4942/2044	Slowikowa
494	204	4942/2046	Wilczyska
494	204	4943/2047	Janczowa
494	204	4943/2042	Sienna
494	204	4943/2040	Zbyszyce
494	204	4944/2044	Kobyle
494	204	4944/2044	Lipie
494	204	4945/2042	Tabaszowa
494	204	4946/2045	Bartkowa Posadowa
494	204	4947/2043	Radajowice
494	204	4948/2047	Borowa (Brzesko)
494	204	4948/2046	Dzierzaniny
494	204	4948/2048	Palesnica
494	204	4948/2040	Tropie
494	204	4949/2045	Ruda Kameralna
494	205	4940/2051	Posadowa
494	205	4940/2058	Stroze
494	205	4940/2056	Wojnarowa
494	205	4941/2051	Korzenna
494	205	4942/2056	Bobowa
494	205	4942/2056	Jankowa
494	205	4943/2056	Brzana
494	205	4943/2054	Lipniczka
494	205	4944/2058	Sedziszowa
494	205	4945/2055	Brusnik
494	205	4945/2058	Plawna
494	205	4946/2059	Zborowice
494	205	4947/2058	Ciezkowice (Tarnow)
494	205	4947/2054	Jastrzebia
494	205	4947/2055	Kasna Gorna
494	205	4948/2056	Kasna Dolna
494	205	4949/2059	Bogoniowice
494	210	4940/2106	Bystra
494	210	4941/2108	Strozowka
494	210	4941/2102	Szalowa
494	210	4943/2103	Luzna
494	210	4944/2107	Moszczenica
494	210	4946/2108	Sietnica
494	210	4946/2102	Staszkowka
494	210	4947/2101	Ostrusza
494	210	4948/2105	Rzepiennik Biskupi
494	210	4948/2103	Rzepiennik Strzyzewski
494	210	4949/2109	Olszyny
494	211	4940/2110	Gorlice
494	211	4940/2116	Kryg
494	211	4941/2115	Libusza
494	211	4941/2118	Lipinki
494	211	4942/2119	Wojtowa
494	211	4942/2111	Zagorzany
494	211	4944/2115	Biecz
494	211	4944/2111	Strzeszyn
494	211	4945/2114	Binarowa
494	211	4945/2119	Grudna Kepska
494	211	4946/2110	Rozembark
494	211	4946/2118	Siepietnica
494	211	4946/2117	Swiecany
494	211	4949/2118	Czermna
494	211	4949/2112	Olpiny
494	211	4949/2116	Szerzyny
494	212	4940/2124	Dulabka
494	212	4941/2129	Zarzecze (Jaslo)
494	212	4942/2125	Osobnica
494	212	4942/2121	Pagorzyna
494	212	4943/2129	Zolkow
494	212	4944/2120	Kunowa
494	212	4944/2128	Nieglowice
494	212	4945/2128	Jaslo
494	212	4945/2126	Kaczonowy
494	212	4945/2121	Skolyszyn
494	212	4946/2120	Bielowy
494	212	4946/2127	Jareniowka
494	212	4946/2124	Opacie
494	212	4946/2124	Wola Jasienicka
494	212	4947/2122	Baczal Gorny
494	212	4947/2123	Lipnica Dolna
494	212	4948/2120	Jablonica
494	212	4948/2128	Nawsie Kolaczyckie
494	212	4949/2126	Kolaczyce
494	213	4940/2137	Kopytowa
494	213	4940/2133	Lajsce
494	213	4940/2132	Lezyny
494	213	4940/2135	Lubienko
494	213	4940/2135	Lubno Opace

494	213	4941/2137	Podniebyle
494	213	4942/2139	Zarnowiec (Krosno)
494	213	4943/2138	Chlebna
494	213	4943/2139	Jedlicze
494	213	4943/2133	Umieszcz
494	213	4944/2139	Jaszczew
494	213	4944/2131	Wolica (Jaslo)
494	213	4945/2134	Sadkowa
494	213	4946/2138	Moderowka
494	213	4946/2136	Szebnie
494	213	4946/2133	Warzyce
494	213	4948/2132	Lublica
494	213	4949/2130	Biezdziedza
494	213	4949/2136	Lubla
494	214	4940/2146	Glowienka
494	214	4940/2140	Zeglce
494	214	4940/2142	Zrecin
494	214	4941/2148	Kroscienko Nizne
494	214	4941/2147	Krosno
494	214	4941/2142	Szczepancowa
494	214	4943/2141	Dobieszyn
494	214	4943/2149	Korczyna
494	214	4944/2143	Turaszowka
494	214	4945/2145	Odrzykon
494	214	4945/2142	Ustrobna
494	214	4946/2140	Bajdy
494	214	4946/2143	Bratkowka
494	214	4947/2141	Wojaszowka
494	214	4947/2142	Wojkowka
494	214	4948/2140	Przybowka
494	214	4948/2145	Rzepnik
494	214	4949/2148	Bonarowka
494	214	4949/2141	Leki (Lwow)
494	214	4949/2141	Pietrusza Wola
494	215	4940/2154	Haczow
494	215	4941/2150	Kroscienko Wyzne
494	215	4942/2152	Iskrzynia
494	215	4942/2155	Jablonica Polska
494	215	4942/2158	Zmiennica
494	215	4944/2153	Kombornia
494	215	4945/2159	Blizne
494	215	4945/2157	Jasienica Rosielna
494	215	4947/2157	Domaradz
494	215	4949/2154	Lutcza
494	220	4940/2204	Humniska
494	220	4941/2207	Niebocko
494	220	4942/2201	Brzozow
494	220	4943/2201	Stara Wies (Brzozow)
494	220	4944/2203	Przysietnica
494	220	4945/2208	Izdebki
494	220	4945/2209	Rzeki
494	220	4946/2203	Golcowa
494	220	4947/2209	Hludno
494	220	4948/2206	Wesola
494	221	4940/2218	Dobra (Sanok)
494	221	4940/2212	Krzywe (Brzozow)
494	221	4941/2217	Ulucz
494	221	4942/2216	Hroszowka
494	221	4942/2212	Krzemienna
494	221	4942/2215	Lipnik (Brzozow)
494	221	4942/2214	Temeszow
494	221	4943/2214	Jablonica Ruska
494	221	4943/2211	Obarzym
494	221	4944/2219	Jawornik Ruski
494	221	4944/2214	Niewistka
494	221	4944/2213	Wolodz
494	221	4946/2215	Siedliska (Rzeszow)
494	221	4946/2213	Wara
494	221	4947/2215	Dabrowka Starzenska
494	221	4947/2213	Nozdrzec
494	221	4949/2214	Dynow
494	221	4949/2210	Lubno
494	221	4949/2217	Pawlokoma
494	221	4949/2217	Wielopole (Lwow)
494	222	4940/2224	Dobrzanka
494	222	4940/2227	Leszczawa Dolna
494	222	4941/2228	Bircza
494	222	4941/2222	Brzezawa
494	222	4941/2228	Lomna (Lwow)
494	222	4942/2227	Bircza Stara
494	222	4943/2223	Lipa
494	222	4944/2229	Sufczyna
494	222	4944/2221	Zohatyn
494	222	4946/2229	Brzuska
494	222	4946/2227	Jasienica Sufczynska
494	222	4947/2227	Iskan
494	222	4949/2223	Dubetsko
494	222	4949/2224	Ruska Wies
494	223	4940/2237	Posada Rybotycka
494	223	4941/2232	Lodzinka Gorna
494	223	4942/2233	Huta (Lwow)
494	223	4942/2230	Wola Korzeniecka
494	223	4943/2231	Korzeniec
494	223	4944/2231	Huta Brzuska
494	223	4945/2239	Olszany
494	223	4946/2235	Cholowice
494	223	4946/2237	Mielnow
494	223	4947/2239	Korytniki
494	223	4947/2234	Kupna
494	223	4948/2230	Bachow
494	223	4948/2233	Chyrzyna
494	223	4948/2233	Krzywcza
494	223	4949/2231	Ruszelczyce
494	223	4949/2235	Wola Krzywiecka
494	224	4940/2246	Sierakosce
494	224	4941/2249	Nizhankovichi
494	224	4942/2245	Fredropol
494	224	4943/2240	Brylince

494	224	4943/2245	Kniazyce
494	224	4943/2244	Kormanice
494	224	4944/2249	Hermanovice
494	224	4944/2244	Witoszynce
494	224	4945/2247	Pikulice
494	224	4946/2240	Krasiczyn
494	224	4946/2244	Kruhel Wielki
494	224	4946/2248	Nehrybka
494	224	4946/2249	Sielec (Przemysl)
494	224	4947/2247	Przemysl
494	224	4948/2243	Kunkowce
494	224	4948/2244	Ostrow (Przemysl)
494	224	4948/2249	Wilcza
494	224	4948/2246	Zasanie
494	224	4949/2248	Buszkowice
494	224	4949/2249	Buszkowiczki
494	224	4949/2240	Wapowce
494	224	4949/2248	Zurawica
494	225	4941/2255	Mizhinets
494	225	4944/2259	Boyovichi
494	225	4944/2254	Popovichi
494	225	4945/2251	Rozubowice
494	225	4945/2253	Jaksmanice
494	225	4945/2250	Luczyce
494	225	4946/2256	Bykov (Przemysl)
494	225	4946/2254	Siedliska (Przemysl)
494	225	4947/2250	Krowniki
494	225	4948/2252	Hureczko
494	225	4948/2256	Medyka
494	225	4948/2258	Shegyni
494	225	4949/2252	Bolestraszyce
494	225	4949/2253	Hurko
494	230	4941/2304	Bolyanovichi
494	230	4941/2300	Radokhontsy
494	230	4943/2300	Gusakov
494	230	4943/2303	Zolotkovichi
494	230	4944/2304	Myshlyatichi
494	230	4945/2304	Konyushki (Stanislawow)
494	230	4946/2301	Balichi
494	230	4946/2309	Krysovitse
494	230	4946/2305	Rustvechko
494	230	4948/2309	Mostiska
494	230	4948/2309	Rudniki (Mosciska)
494	230	4948/2309	Tverdza
494	230	4948/2305	Volitsa (Dobromil)
494	231	4940/2312	Khliple
494	231	4940/2315	Nikhovichi
494	231	4941/2310	Krukenitsa
494	231	4942/2314	Vishenka
494	231	4943/2315	Podliski
494	231	4944/2311	Radenitse
494	231	4944/2318	Volchishchovitsa
494	231	4945/2315	Krowica Lasowa
494	231	4945/2315	Krowica Holodowska Wies
494	231	4945/2315	Krowica Sama
494	231	4945/2319	Volostkov
494	231	4946/2317	Stoyantsy
494	231	4947/2314	Voykovitse
494	231	4949/2316	Khorosnitsa
494	232	4940/2324	Rozdilovichi
494	232	4940/2325	Voshchantsy
494	232	4944/2325	Niklovichi
494	232	4946/2324	Milyatyn (Lwow)
494	232	4947/2322	Sudovaya Vishnya
494	232	4949/2324	Bortyatin
494	233	4941/2334	Koropuzh
494	233	4942/2331	Dubanevitse
494	233	4942/2339	Zavidovitse
494	233	4944/2332	Sholomenitse
494	233	4944/2337	Ugry
494	233	4945/2331	Dobzhany
494	233	4947/2339	Gorodok (Lvov)
494	233	4948/2332	Rodatyche
494	234	4940/2344	Chulovichi
494	234	4944/2344	Velikiy Lyuben
494	234	4945/2345	Szabelnia
494	234	4946/2341	Artyshchuv
494	234	4946/2343	Kernitsa
494	235	4940/2352	Ostruv (Lvov)
494	235	4940/2355	Semyanovka
494	235	4942/2350	Malinuvka
494	235	4943/2357	Porshna
494	235	4945/2356	Navariya
494	235	4946/2350	Stavchany
494	235	4947/2359	Sokolniki (Lwow)
494	235	4948/2357	Sknilov
494	235	4949/2359	Kulparkuv
494	235	4949/2357	Sygnyuvka
494	235	4949/2354	Zimna Voda
494	240	4940/2408	Selisko
494	240	4942/2406	Milyatyche
494	240	4942/2407	Tolshchev
494	240	4943/2404	Volkuv (Lwow)
494	240	4945/2408	Davidov
494	240	4947/2404	Sikhov
494	240	4949/2408	Vinniki
494	241	4941/2411	Budkov
494	241	4942/2419	Podgorodishche
494	241	4942/2414	Vodniki
494	241	4944/2415	Dzvinogrud
494	241	4945/2418	Gorodyslavichi
494	241	4945/2415	Zuchorzyce
494	241	4946/2415	Glukhovitse
494	241	4948/2410	Chizhki
494	241	4949/2418	Bilka Shlyakhetska
494	242	4942/2425	Ganachuvka

494	242	4942/2421	Romanuv
494	242	4943/2425	Ganachevka
494	242	4944/2422	Podyarkov
494	242	4944/2429	Pogoreltsy
494	242	4945/2421	Podsosnuv
494	242	4945/2424	Solova
494	242	4946/2426	Kurovichi
494	242	4946/2420	Nikolayev (Tarnopol)
494	242	4948/2420	Germanuv
494	242	4948/2425	Vyzhnyany
494	242	4949/2420	Charnushovitse
494	243	4940/2436	Borshchev (Rogatin)
494	243	4940/2433	Novosyulka (Przemyslany)
494	243	4940/2433	Peremyshlyany
494	243	4940/2439	Vypyski
494	243	4942/2430	Krosenko
494	243	4943/2436	Mlynovtse
494	243	4944/2434	Yaktoruv
494	243	4946/2438	Mitulin
494	243	4947/2439	Novosyulki
494	243	4949/2431	Glinyany
494	244	4940/2447	Chemerintsy
494	244	4941/2448	Kropivna
494	244	4942/2440	Lipovtsy
494	244	4942/2445	Vishnivchik (Peremyshlyany)
494	244	4943/2448	Zhukov (Tarnopol)
494	244	4944/2440	Lone
494	244	4945/2443	Gologory
494	244	4946/2443	Gologurki
494	244	4947/2449	Zalese (Zolochev)
494	244	4948/2440	Olshanitsa (Lisko)
494	245	4940/2457	Bogutyn
494	245	4943/2453	Remizovtsy
494	245	4944/2456	Snovich
494	245	4947/2455	Strutin
494	245	4947/2454	Voronyaki
494	245	4948/2454	Zolochev
494	250	4940/2506	Presovtse
494	250	4940/2509	Zborov
494	250	4943/2502	Slavna
494	250	4945/2502	Plugov
494	250	4946/2503	Podliptse
494	251	4940/2518	Danilovtse
494	251	4940/2513	Volosuvka
494	251	4941/2518	Bogdanuvka (Zboruv)
494	251	4941/2518	Bogdanuvka (Skalat)
494	251	4945/2515	Oleyev
494	252	4942/2523	Nesterovtsy
494	252	4947/2524	Novosyulka (Podgaytsy)
494	252	4947/2522	Zalozhtsy
494	252	4948/2529	Milno
494	253	4943/2531	Igrovitsa
494	253	4945/2535	Jurydyka
494	253	4946/2534	Berezovitsa Mala
494	253	4949/2532	Bashuki
494	254	4940/2547	Zbarazh
494	254	4945/2542	Stryjowka
494	255	4946/2558	Vyshgorodok
494	260	4940/2606	Gnilichki
494	260	4940/2603	Sukhnovtse
494	260	4941/2609	Koshlyaki
494	260	4942/2606	Gnilitsy
494	260	4945/2601	Pecharna
494	260	4946/2603	Buglov
494	260	4948/2608	Ivankovtsy
494	261	4941/2614	Palchintsy
494	261	4946/2611	Belozerka
494	262	4940/2629	Bogdanovka (Wolyn)
494	262	4943/2628	Bazaliya
494	265	4945/2654	Kulchiny
494	265	4948/2652	Antoniny
494	270	4942/2705	Kuzmin
494	271	4945/2713	Starokonstantinov
494	273	4948/2734	Ostropol
494	280	4942/2808	Ulanov
494	285	4943/2850	Kazatin
494	290	4941/2902	Belilovka
494	291	4942/2910	Pustokha
494	291	4943/2914	Ruzhin
494	294	4944/2940	Skvira
494	300	4947/3007	Belaya Tserkov
494	305	4942/3057	Rossava
494	311	4942/3118	Stepantsy
494	312	4945/3128	Kanev
494	312	4949/3121	Gelmyazov
494	320	4940/3202	Zolotonosha
494	331	4947/3317	Khorol
494	340	4945/3409	Peschanoye
494	360	4948/3603	Merefa
494	362	4941/3621	Zmiyev
494	370	4941/3709	Shevchenkovo
494	373	4942/3738	Kupyansk
495	062	4951/0622	Bollendorf
495	062	4951/0628	Irrel
495	063	4958/0632	Bitburg
495	065	4950/0651	Klusserath
495	065	4951/0654	Neumagen
495	065	4953/0655	Niederemmel
495	065	4953/0657	Wintrich
495	065	4955/0659	Brauneberg
495	065	4955/0657	Monzel
495	065	4955/0657	Osann
495	065	4959/0653	Wittlich
495	070	4953/0701	Veldenz
495	070	4955/0704	Bernkastel Kues
495	070	4955/0701	Lieser

495 070	4955/0701	Mulheim am Mosel
495 070	4957/0701	Zeltingen
495 070	4958/0700	Rachtig
495 071	4950/0718	Hottenbach
495 071	4951/0717	Stipshausen
495 071	4954/0718	Laufersweiler
495 071	4955/0716	Buchenbeuren
495 071	4956/0719	Sohren
495 072	4951/0721	Rhaunen
495 072	4954/0728	Gemunden (Rhineland Pfalz)
495 072	4954/0724	Lindenschied
495 072	4957/0724	Kirchberg
495 073	4959/0731	Simmern
495 074	4953/0742	Argenschwang
495 074	4954/0749	Windesheim
495 074	4955/0748	Schweppenhausen
495 074	4958/0743	Seibersbach
495 075	4950/0752	Bad Kreuznach
495 075	4952/0754	Bretzenheim
495 075	4952/0755	Planig
495 075	4952/0752	Winzenheim
495 075	4954/0756	Gensingen
495 075	4954/0754	Langenlonsheim
495 075	4955/0758	Dromersheim
495 075	4956/0758	Ockenheim
495 075	4958/0754	Bingen
495 075	4959/0758	Geisenheim
495 075	4959/0755	Rudesheim
495 080	4950/0803	Wallertheim
495 080	4950/0806	Worrstadt
495 080	4952/0804	Vendersheim
495 080	4952/0802	Wolfsheim
495 080	4953/0809	Nieder Saulheim
495 080	4953/0804	Partenheim
495 080	4955/0808	Stadecken
495 080	4956/0809	Essenheim
495 080	4956/0806	Schwabenheim
495 080	4957/0801	Gau Algesheim
495 080	4958/0803	Ingelheim
495 081	4951/0815	Kongernheim
495 081	4951/0810	Schornsheim
495 081	4952/0814	Hahnheim
495 081	4952/0815	Selzen
495 081	4953/0816	Mommenheim
495 081	4953/0812	Sorgenloch
495 081	4954/0813	Nieder Olm
495 081	4955/0815	Ebersheim
495 081	4956/0818	Bodenheim
495 081	4957/0811	Ober Olm
495 081	4958/0817	Hechtsheim
495 081	4959/0810	Finthen
495 081	4959/0818	Mainz Weisenau
495 082	4950/0821	Dienheim
495 082	4950/0828	Erfelden
495 082	4951/0821	Oppenheim
495 082	4952/0827	Leeheim
495 082	4953/0829	Dornheim
495 082	4953/0824	Geinsheim
495 082	4955/0829	Grossgerau
495 082	4955/0821	Nackenheim
495 082	4955/0824	Trebur
495 083	4950/0830	Goddelau
495 083	4951/0830	Wolfskehlen
495 083	4952/0839	Darmstadt
495 083	4952/0833	Griesheim
495 083	4954/0831	Buttelborn
495 083	4954/0835	Weiterstadt
495 083	4955/0839	Arheilgen
495 083	4956/0836	Grafenhausen
495 083	4956/0839	Wixhausen
495 083	4957/0838	Erzhausen
495 083	4959/0834	Morfelden
495 084	4950/0845	Ober Ramstadt
495 084	4951/0848	Georgenhausen
495 084	4956/0845	Messel
495 084	4958/0840	Egelsbach
495 084	4958/0848	Urberach
495 084	4959/0840	Langen
495 085	4950/0854	Lengfeld
495 085	4951/0853	Habitzheim
495 085	4951/0850	Spachbrucken
495 085	4952/0850	Gross Zimmern
495 085	4952/0856	Gross Umstadt
495 085	4953/0857	Klein Umstadt
495 085	4954/0851	Dieburg
495 085	4957/0851	Eppertshausen
495 085	4958/0857	Babenhausen
495 090	4951/0905	Momlingen
495 090	4954/0909	Sulzbach am Main
495 090	4955/0905	Grossostheim
495 090	4955/0909	Niedernberg
495 090	4955/0904	Pflaumheim
495 090	4955/0901	Schaafheim
495 090	4956/0908	Obernau
495 090	4959/0909	Aschaffenburg
495 091	4950/0915	Sommerau
495 091	4951/0917	Hobbach
495 091	4952/0912	Hofstetten
495 091	4953/0910	Kleinwallstadt
495 091	4953/0915	Rossbach
495 092	4952/0929	Bischbrunn
495 093	4950/0937	Marktheidenfeld
495 093	4952/0938	Karbach
495 093	4953/0936	Rothenfels
495 093	4954/0935	Bergrothenfels
495 093	4959/0935	Lohr
495 094	4952/0949	Unterleinach

495 094	4954/0941	Urspringen	
495 094	4954/0949	Zellingen	
495 094	4956/0948	Himmelstadt	
495 094	4957/0946	Karlstadt	
495 094	4959/0941	Wiesenfeld	
495 095	4950/0952	Veitshochheim	
495 095	4951/0951	Erlabrunn	
495 095	4951/0957	Rimpar	
495 095	4957/0951	Thungen	
495 095	4959/0959	Arnstein	
495 100	4950/1001	Estenfeld	
495 100	4952/1004	Unterpleichfeld	
495 100	4953/1005	Oberpleichfeld	
495 100	4953/1009	Untereisenheim	
495 100	4955/1008	Schwanfeld	
495 100	4959/1006	Werneck	
495 101	4950/1012	Sommerach	
495 101	4952/1014	Volkach	
495 101	4953/1019	Frankenwinheim	
495 101	4953/1014	Gaibach	
495 101	4954/1013	Oettershausen	
495 101	4954/1016	Zeilitzheim	
495 101	4959/1015	Schwebheim	
495 102	4951/1020	Jarkendorf	
495 102	4952/1021	Brunnau	
495 102	4952/1020	Lulsfeld	
495 102	4952/1025	Oberschwarzach	
495 102	4953/1024	Lisberg	
495 102	4954/1021	Gerolzhofen	
495 102	4955/1024	Bischwind	
495 102	4956/1026	Traustadt	
495 103	4950/1030	Ebrach	
495 103	4959/1033	Knetzgau	
495 103	4959/1038	Limbach	
495 103	4959/1030	Westheim Bei Hassfurt	
495 104	4950/1045	Burgebrach	
495 104	4950/1046	Grasmannsdorf	
495 104	4952/1047	Walsdorf	
495 104	4954/1044	Trabelsdorf	
495 104	4956/1045	Trunstadt	
495 104	4956/1047	Viereth	
495 104	4958/1040	Eltmann	
495 104	4959/1041	Ebelsbach	
495 105	4952/1052	Bamberg	
495 105	4955/1050	Bischberg	
495 105	4956/1056	Gugel	
495 105	4956/1053	Hallstadt	
495 105	4956/1057	Memmelsdorf	
495 105	4956/1057	Seehof	
495 105	4959/1051	Baunach	
495 110	4950/1102	Friesen	
495 110	4957/1104	Zeckendorf	
495 110	4958/1103	Demmelsdorf	
495 110	4959/1103	Burgellern	

495 110	4959/1102	Schesslitz	
495 111	4952/1110	Heiligenstadt (Bavaria)	
495 111	4954/1113	Aufsess	
495 111	4956/1118	Hollfeld	
495 111	4957/1110	Konigsfeld	
495 111	4959/1118	Wonsees	
495 112	4951/1121	Waischenfeld	
495 113	4951/1137	Creussen	
495 113	4952/1134	Haag	
495 113	4957/1135	Bayreuth	
495 114	4957/1143	Weidenberg	
495 115	4954/1154	Kulmain	
495 120	4950/1203	Erbendorf	
495 120	4952/1205	Siegritz	
495 121	4957/1215	Mitterteich	
495 122	4953/1221	Tirschenreuth	
495 123	4950/1235	Halze	
495 123	4951/1238	Stokov	
495 124	4952/1245	Plana	
495 124	4953/1244	Chodova Plana	
495 124	4955/1245	Holubin	
495 124	4956/1240	Drmoul	
495 124	4957/1243	Usovice	
495 124	4958/1242	Marianske Lazne	
495 125	4951/1251	Koren	
495 125	4953/1257	Celiv	
495 125	4953/1257	Kokasice	
495 125	4954/1258	Bezdruzice	
495 125	4958/1259	Vidzin	
495 130	4950/1303	Svinomazy	
495 130	4952/1304	Roznevice	
495 130	4952/1307	Skupec	
495 130	4953/1309	Unesov	
495 130	4956/1304	Krsy	
495 130	4956/1300	Utery	
495 130	4958/1308	Brezin	
495 131	4950/1311	Listany	
495 131	4950/1315	Vseruby	
495 131	4951/1310	Chrancovice	
495 131	4954/1317	Loza	
495 131	4955/1316	Lite	
495 131	4958/1310	Nectiny	
495 131	4959/1314	Manetin	
495 132	4953/1324	Kaznejov	
495 132	4953/1325	Obora	
495 132	4955/1322	Rybnice	
495 132	4956/1324	Plasy	
495 133	4950/1333	Krise	
495 133	4951/1336	Radnice	
495 133	4952/1338	Chomle	
495 133	4952/1339	Vejvanov	
495 134	4951/1346	Zbiroh	
495 134	4954/1340	Hlohovicky	
495 134	4954/1342	Teresov	

495	134	4957/1342	Podmokly
495	134	4957/1341	Zvikovec
495	135	4950/1355	Horovice
495	135	4951/1359	Lochovice
495	135	4951/1353	Tlustice
495	135	4952/1350	Drozdov
495	135	4952/1356	Praskolesy
495	135	4954/1359	Chodoun
495	135	4954/1359	Zdice
495	140	4950/1403	Hostomice
495	140	4950/1406	Vizina
495	140	4951/1403	Neumetely
495	140	4951/1401	Radous
495	140	4952/1400	Libomysl
495	140	4953/1404	Bykos
495	140	4953/1407	Vseradice
495	140	4954/1409	Liten
495	140	4954/1401	Lounin
495	140	4954/1404	Suchomasty
495	140	4957/1405	Beroun
495	140	4959/1403	Hyskov
495	141	4951/1413	Kytin
495	141	4952/1419	Cisovice
495	141	4954/1411	Svinare
495	141	4955/1415	Revnice
495	141	4955/1414	Rovina
495	141	4956/1417	Dobrichovice
495	141	4956/1411	Poucnik
495	141	4958/1418	Trebotov
495	141	4959/1410	Lodenice
495	142	4951/1429	Krnany
495	142	4951/1424	Stechovice
495	142	4953/1424	Davle
495	142	4953/1429	Studene
495	142	4954/1420	Klinec
495	142	4956/1428	Liben
495	142	4957/1423	Lipence
495	142	4958/1424	Zbraslav
495	142	4959/1422	Radotin
495	143	4950/1437	Pecerady
495	143	4950/1435	Podelusy
495	143	4950/1436	Tynec nad Sazavou
495	143	4951/1433	Krhanice
495	143	4953/1434	Teptin
495	143	4955/1436	Stirin
495	143	4957/1439	Vsechromy
495	143	4958/1435	Herink
495	143	4958/1438	Jazlovice
495	143	4959/1439	Ricany
495	144	4951/1443	Cercany
495	144	4953/1448	Chocerady
495	144	4953/1441	Pysely
495	144	4954/1443	Senohraby
495	144	4957/1441	Strancice
495	144	4958/1444	Svojetice
495	144	4959/1446	Lounovice
495	144	4959/1445	Srbin
495	144	4959/1444	Tehovec
495	145	4950/1450	Ostredek
495	145	4951/1450	Vodslivy
495	145	4954/1454	Vlkancice
495	145	4956/1452	Oplany
495	145	4957/1458	Barchovice
495	145	4959/1452	Kostelec nad Cernymi Lesy
495	150	4950/1501	Makolusky
495	150	4952/1506	Sudejov
495	150	4953/1504	Uhlirske Janovice
495	150	4954/1500	Skvrnov
495	150	4956/1504	Drahobudice
495	150	4957/1505	Becvary
495	150	4957/1502	Zasmuky
495	150	4958/1500	Doubravcany
495	150	4958/1508	Korenice
495	150	4958/1509	Sedlov
495	151	4951/1513	Cerniny
495	151	4955/1514	Malesov
495	151	4957/1516	Hora Kutna
495	151	4957/1516	Kutna Hora
495	151	4959/1518	Hlizov
495	152	4951/1520	Hrabesin
495	152	4952/1523	Schorov
495	152	4953/1525	Drobovice
495	152	4953/1522	Zaky
495	152	4954/1521	Mocovice
495	152	4955/1524	Caslav
495	152	4958/1528	Zaricany
495	152	4958/1525	Zehusice
495	153	4950/1536	Bestvina
495	153	4951/1531	Zvestovice
495	153	4957/1535	Holotin
495	153	4958/1537	Stojice
495	154	4955/1549	Slatinany
495	154	4956/1545	Stolany
495	154	4957/1548	Chrudim
495	154	4957/1540	Hermanuv Mestec
495	154	4958/1544	Bylany
495	154	4959/1546	Medlesice
495	155	4954/1557	Podlazice
495	155	4956/1559	Bor U Chroustovic
495	155	4956/1556	Zajezdec
495	160	4951/1600	Skutec
495	160	4953/1600	Hroubovice
495	160	4954/1602	Luze
495	160	4955/1607	Brtec
495	160	4955/1608	Lhuta
495	160	4955/1602	Voletice
495	160	4958/1600	Chroustovice

495	161	4952/1619	Litomysl
495	161	4957/1610	Vysoke Myto
495	162	4954/1627	Ceska Trebova
495	162	4955/1626	Parnik
495	162	4957/1623	Hylvaty
495	162	4959/1624	Usti nad Orlici
495	163	4951/1633	Anenska Studanka
495	163	4955/1637	Lanskroun
495	165	4953/1652	Zabreh
495	165	4958/1658	Sumperk
495	172	4959/1728	Bruntal
495	173	4950/1734	Dvorce
495	173	4958/1736	Horni Benesov
495	174	4950/1746	Radkov
495	175	4957/1755	Opava
495	175	4959/1758	Oldrisov
495	181	4950/1817	Ostrava
495	181	4951/1818	Muglinov
495	181	4952/1818	Hrusov
495	181	4954/1811	Hlucin
495	181	4957/1815	Hat
495	181	4959/1816	Krzyzanowice
495	182	4950/1829	Doly
495	182	4950/1821	Michalkovice
495	182	4950/1824	Petrvald
495	182	4951/1826	Orlova
495	182	4952/1829	Doubrava
495	182	4955/1820	Bohumin
495	183	4951/1838	Konczyce Male
495	183	4952/1833	Karvina
495	183	4953/1837	Zebrzydowice
495	184	4952/1841	Pruchna
495	184	4953/1844	Knaj
495	184	4954/1849	Chybie
495	184	4955/1848	Frelichow
495	184	4955/1846	Strumien
495	184	4956/1845	Zbytkow
495	185	4951/1857	Miedzyrzecze Gorne
495	185	4955/1859	Renardowice
495	185	4958/1857	Pszczyna
495	185	4959/1851	Brzezce
495	190	4950/1901	Stare Bielsko
495	190	4951/1906	Halcnow
495	190	4953/1901	Czechowice
495	190	4954/1904	Bestwina
495	190	4955/1901	Dziedzice
495	190	4957/1909	Jawiszowice
495	190	4959/1909	Brzeszcze
495	191	4951/1915	Czaniec
495	191	4953/1914	Kety
495	191	4954/1910	Hecznarowice
495	191	4955/1910	Wilamowice
495	191	4956/1915	Malec
495	191	4957/1913	Leki (Krakow)
495	191	4957/1917	Osiek (Krakow)
495	191	4959/1916	Lazy (Oswiecim)
495	191	4959/1919	Polanka Wielka
495	192	4951/1921	Andrychow
495	192	4952/1924	Inwald
495	192	4953/1928	Chocznia
495	192	4953/1929	Wadowice
495	192	4953/1923	Wieprz
495	192	4955/1926	Frydrychowice
495	192	4955/1920	Nidek
495	192	4957/1924	Gieraltowiczki
495	192	4957/1920	Glebowice
495	192	4957/1927	Graboszyce
495	192	4957/1925	Przybradz
495	192	4959/1922	Piotrowice (Bielsko Biala)
495	192	4959/1927	Zator
495	193	4950/1935	Lekawica
495	193	4950/1937	Stryszow
495	193	4950/1932	Swinna Poreba
495	193	4951/1930	Gorzen Gorny
495	193	4952/1934	Barwald Dolny
495	193	4952/1930	Gorzen Dolny
495	193	4953/1934	Klecza Dolna
495	193	4954/1937	Czerna
495	193	4955/1931	Rokow
495	193	4956/1933	Witanowice
495	193	4958/1939	Brzezinka
495	193	4958/1938	Brzeznica (Bielsko Biala)
495	193	4959/1933	Ryczow
495	194	4950/1940	Stronie
495	194	4951/1943	Lanckorona
495	194	4951/1948	Sulkowice
495	194	4952/1942	Brody (Bielsko Biala)
495	194	4952/1946	Izdebnik
495	194	4952/1941	Kalwaria Zebrzydowska
495	194	4954/1943	Lencze
495	194	4955/1941	Przytkowice
495	194	4955/1947	Wola Radziszowska
495	194	4956/1949	Radziszow
495	194	4957/1945	Krzecin
495	194	4957/1941	Paszkowka
495	194	4957/1947	Polanka Haller
495	194	4957/1949	Rzozow
495	194	4958/1947	Borek Szlachecki
495	194	4958/1943	Facimiech
495	194	4958/1943	Wielkie Drogi
495	194	4958/1945	Zelczyna
495	194	4959/1944	Wolowice
495	195	4950/1956	Myslenice
495	195	4955/1959	Siepraw
495	195	4955/1955	Wlosan
495	195	4957/1958	Rzeszotary

495	195	4958/1953	Libertow
495	195	4958/1957	Zbydniowice
495	195	4959/1959	Rajsko
495	195	4959/1950	Skawina
495	195	4959/1959	Soboniowice
495	195	4959/1956	Swoszowice
495	200	4952/2004	Brzaczowice
495	200	4952/2009	Czaslaw
495	200	4952/2005	Dobczyce
495	200	4952/2002	Droginia
495	200	4954/2003	Stojowice
495	200	4956/2001	Byszyce
495	200	4956/2005	Jankowka
495	200	4956/2004	Kozmice Male
495	200	4956/2007	Zakowa
495	200	4957/2005	Choragwica
495	200	4957/2009	Lazany
495	200	4957/2004	Taszyce
495	200	4958/2007	Biskupice
495	200	4959/2005	Lednica
495	200	4959/2007	Przebieczany
495	200	4959/2003	Siercza
495	200	4959/2004	Wieliczka
495	201	4950/2015	Zeroslawice
495	201	4951/2016	Grabie
495	201	4951/2014	Kawec
495	201	4952/2013	Gruszow
495	201	4952/2018	Lapanow
495	201	4952/2012	Mierzen
495	201	4955/2012	Gdow
495	201	4956/2015	Niegowic
495	201	4956/2016	Nieznanowice
495	201	4956/2019	Stradomka
495	201	4957/2016	Cichawa
495	201	4957/2013	Liplas
495	201	4957/2018	Pierzchow
495	201	4957/2013	Wiatowice
495	201	4958/2011	Zablocie
495	201	4959/2014	Brzezie
495	201	4959/2019	Klaj
495	201	4959/2018	Targowisko
495	202	4950/2025	Lakta Dolna
495	202	4950/2026	Lakta Gorna
495	202	4950/2029	Rajbrot
495	202	4951/2022	Trzciana (Bochnia)
495	202	4954/2028	Leksandrowa
495	202	4954/2023	Wola Nieszkowska
495	202	4955/2021	Sobolow
495	202	4955/2028	Wisnicz Nowy
495	202	4955/2029	Wisnicz Stary
495	202	4957/2020	Nieszkowice Male
495	202	4958/2026	Bochnia
495	202	4958/2022	Lapczyca
495	202	4959/2023	Chodenice
495	202	4959/2024	Damienice
495	202	4959/2026	Proszowki
495	203	4951/2038	Tymowa
495	203	4952/2032	Lipnica Murowana
495	203	4953/2035	Gosprzydowa
495	203	4953/2039	Lewniowa
495	203	4954/2037	Gnojnik
495	203	4955/2037	Uszew
495	203	4957/2037	Okocim
495	203	4957/2034	Poreba Spytkowska
495	203	4958/2037	Brzesko
495	203	4958/2038	Brzezowiec
495	203	4958/2031	Lazy (Bochnia)
495	203	4959/2033	Jodlowka (Bochnia)
495	203	4959/2036	Kopaliny
495	203	4959/2031	Rzezawa
495	204	4950/2041	Czchow
495	204	4951/2044	Filipowice
495	204	4951/2048	Zdonia
495	204	4952/2043	Biskupice Melsztynskie
495	204	4952/2040	Tworkowa
495	204	4952/2047	Wesolow
495	204	4952/2049	Zakliczyn
495	204	4953/2045	Charzewice (Brzesko)
495	204	4955/2046	Jaworsko
495	204	4956/2042	Doly (Poland)
495	204	4957/2049	Wielka Wies
495	204	4958/2040	Jadowniki
495	204	4959/2047	Lopon
495	204	4959/2042	Maszkienice
495	205	4950/2051	Slona
495	205	4951/2051	Fasciszowa
495	205	4951/2058	Gromnik
495	205	4951/2050	Konczyska
495	205	4951/2055	Siemiechow
495	205	4953/2059	Chojnik
495	205	4953/2057	Lichwin
495	205	4953/2051	Luslawice
495	205	4953/2052	Wroblowice
495	205	4954/2053	Janowice
495	205	4954/2054	Lubinka
495	205	4954/2059	Meszna Opacka
495	205	4955/2052	Dabrowka Szczepanowska
495	205	4955/2059	Lowczowek
495	205	4955/2058	Meszna Szlachecka
495	205	4956/2057	Plesna
495	205	4957/2057	Rzuchowa
495	205	4957/2054	Szczepanowice
495	205	4957/2058	Wozniczna
495	205	4958/2053	Lukanowice
495	205	4958/2050	Wojnicz
495	205	4959/2051	Letowice
495	205	4959/2053	Mikolajowice

495	205	4959/2055	Zbylitowska Gora
495	210	4950/2104	Jodlowka Tuchowska
495	210	4952/2103	Lubaszowa
495	210	4953/2105	Bistuszowa
495	210	4953/2108	Ryglice
495	210	4953/2107	Uniszowa
495	210	4954/2103	Dabrowka Tuchowska
495	210	4954/2104	Tuchow
495	210	4955/2100	Lowczow
495	210	4956/2105	Karwodrza
495	210	4956/2101	Piotrkowice (Tuchow)
495	210	4956/2104	Zabledza
495	210	4956/2108	Zalasowa
495	211	4951/2114	Swoszowa
495	211	4952/2118	Jodlowa
495	211	4953/2112	Kowalowy
495	211	4954/2111	Joniny
495	211	4955/2118	Dzwonowa
495	211	4957/2117	Slotowa
495	211	4957/2113	Zwiernik
495	211	4958/2118	Pilzno
495	211	4959/2111	Leki Gorne
495	211	4959/2114	Leki Dolne
495	212	4950/2123	Brzyska
495	212	4951/2123	Blaszkowa
495	212	4951/2120	Debowa
495	212	4952/2128	Januszkowice
495	212	4953/2125	Brzostek
495	212	4953/2128	Nawsie Brzosteckie
495	212	4953/2123	Skurowa
495	212	4954/2122	Przeczyca
495	212	4954/2128	Wola Brzostecka
495	212	4955/2120	Deborzyn
495	212	4955/2122	Kamienica Dolna
495	212	4955/2125	Siedliska Bogusz
495	212	4956/2122	Gorzejowa
495	212	4957/2129	Grudna Gorna
495	212	4957/2122	Jaworze Gorne
495	212	4958/2124	Gebiczyna
495	212	4958/2127	Globikowa
495	212	4958/2121	Goleczyna
495	212	4958/2122	Jaworze Dolne
495	212	4959/2121	Dobrkow
495	213	4950/2137	Frysztak
495	213	4950/2130	Sowina
495	213	4950/2138	Twierdza
495	213	4951/2135	Glinik Gorny
495	213	4951/2136	Glinik Sredni
495	213	4951/2131	Gogolow
495	213	4951/2137	Pulanki
495	213	4952/2137	Cieszyna
495	213	4953/2132	Huta Gogolowska
495	213	4953/2137	Pstragowka
495	213	4953/2134	Stepina
495	213	4955/2138	Szufnarowa
495	213	4957/2137	Wielopole Skrzynskie
495	213	4958/2135	Glinik
495	213	4958/2131	Mala
495	213	4959/2131	Niedzwiada
495	213	4959/2139	Szkodna
495	214	4951/2149	Godowa
495	214	4951/2141	Kozlowek
495	214	4952/2143	Markuszowa
495	214	4952/2148	Strzyzow
495	214	4953/2145	Dobrzechow
495	214	4954/2140	Niewodna
495	214	4955/2143	Grodzisko
495	214	4956/2149	Nowa Wies Czudecka
495	214	4956/2146	Pstragowa
495	214	4959/2144	Bystrzyca
495	215	4951/2159	Gwoznica Dolna
495	215	4952/2154	Niebylec
495	215	4953/2157	Blizianka
495	215	4954/2153	Polomia
495	215	4954/2159	Straszydle
495	215	4955/2150	Glinik Charzewski
495	215	4955/2158	Solonka
495	215	4956/2157	Lubenia
495	215	4956/2153	Wyzne
495	215	4957/2150	Czudec
495	215	4958/2155	Lutoryz
495	215	4959/2157	Boguchwala
495	215	4959/2153	Niechobrz
495	220	4950/2201	Gwoznica Gorna
495	220	4951/2208	Futoma
495	220	4951/2205	Kakolowka
495	220	4952/2201	Lecka
495	220	4953/2203	Bialka
495	220	4953/2206	Blazowa
495	220	4955/2206	Borek Nowy
495	220	4957/2207	Borek Stary
495	220	4957/2201	Hermanowa
495	220	4958/2204	Kielnarowa
495	220	4958/2202	Tyczyn
495	220	4959/2209	Chmielnik (Rzeszow)
495	221	4950/2217	Bachorz
495	221	4951/2211	Ulanica
495	221	4952/2218	Laskowka
495	221	4953/2217	Jawornik Polski
495	221	4953/2210	Piatkowa
495	221	4955/2213	Dylagowka
495	221	4955/2218	Hadle Szklarskie
495	221	4955/2219	Widaczow
495	221	4956/2211	Hyzne
495	221	4957/2217	Tarnawka
495	221	4958/2212	Zabratowka
495	221	4959/2214	Handzlowka
495	221	4959/2217	Husow

495 222	4950/2226	Nienadowa	
495 222	4951/2222	Przedmiescie Dubieckie	
495 222	4952/2221	Drohobyczka	
495 222	4953/2228	Jodlowka (Pruchnik)	
495 222	4954/2221	Hucisko Jawornickie	
495 222	4955/2227	Raczyna	
495 222	4955/2227	Swiebodna	
495 222	4956/2224	Lopuszka Wielka	
495 222	4957/2222	Manasterzh (Lisko)	
495 222	4957/2227	Pantalowice	
495 222	4957/2222	Zagorze (Rudki)	
495 222	4958/2226	Lopuszka Mala	
495 222	4958/2222	Siedleczka	
495 222	4959/2225	Kanczuga	
495 222	4959/2222	Sietesz	
495 223	4950/2230	Skopow	
495 223	4950/2235	Srednia	
495 223	4951/2235	Wola Wegierska	
495 223	4954/2231	Pruchnik Wies	
495 223	4954/2239	Rokietnica	
495 223	4955/2235	Chorzow (Lwow)	
495 223	4955/2237	Czelatyce	
495 223	4955/2231	Pruchnik	
495 223	4956/2235	Bystrowice	
495 223	4956/2232	Hawlowice	
495 223	4956/2230	Rozborz Okragly	
495 223	4956/2234	Tyniowice	
495 223	4957/2234	Czastkowice	
495 223	4957/2231	Rozborz Dlugi	
495 223	4957/2236	Rozwienica	
495 223	4957/2237	Rudolowice	
495 223	4958/2234	Pelnatycze	
495 223	4958/2230	Siennow	
495 223	4958/2234	Wola Rozwieniecka	
495 223	4959/2239	Pawlosiow	
495 223	4959/2233	Zarzecze (Jaroslaw)	
495 224	4951/2242	Mackowice	
495 224	4951/2243	Ujkowice	
495 224	4952/2247	Dunkowiczki	
495 224	4952/2247	Orzechowce	
495 224	4953/2242	Kosienice	
495 224	4953/2246	Trojczyce	
495 224	4954/2244	Ciemierzowice	
495 224	4954/2245	Dmytrowice	
495 224	4954/2248	Drohojow	
495 224	4955/2245	Kaszyce	
495 224	4955/2241	Tapin	
495 224	4956/2240	Boratyn (Jaroslaw)	
495 224	4956/2244	Lowce	
495 224	4956/2249	Skoloszow	
495 224	4956/2245	Zamiechow	
495 224	4956/2249	Zamojsce	
495 224	4958/2241	Chlopice	
495 224	4959/2245	Munina	
495 224	4959/2249	Wysocko	
495 225	4950/2256	Torki (Przemysl)	
495 225	4951/2258	Pozdziacz	
495 225	4951/2253	Wyszatyce	
495 225	4952/2250	Malkowice	
495 225	4953/2253	Dusowce	
495 225	4953/2254	Walawa	
495 225	4954/2258	Stubno	
495 225	4955/2254	Sklad Solny	
495 225	4955/2256	Stubienko	
495 225	4955/2251	Swiete	
495 225	4956/2256	Nienowice	
495 225	4957/2259	Gaje	
495 225	4957/2250	Radymno	
495 225	4958/2254	Dunkowice	
495 225	4959/2259	Dabrowa (Jaroslaw)	
495 225	4959/2252	Lazy (Jaroslaw)	
495 225	4959/2259	Wola Zaleska	
495 230	4951/2302	Staviska	
495 230	4952/2303	Staryava (Mostiska)	
495 230	4955/2302	Kalnikow	
495 230	4956/2307	Volya Gnoynitska	
495 230	4957/2301	Chotyniec	
495 230	4957/2307	Gnoynitse	
495 230	4957/2300	Hruszowice	
495 230	4959/2309	Czaplaki	
495 231	4950/2314	Volya Arlamovskaya	
495 231	4954/2316	Bunov	
495 231	4954/2319	Kalynivka	
495 231	4955/2319	Porudenko	
495 231	4955/2310	Sarny (Lvov)	
495 231	4958/2310	Krakovets	
495 231	4959/2315	Kokhanovka	
495 231	4959/2311	Ruda Krakovetska	
495 232	4951/2326	Malchitse	
495 232	4952/2321	Rogozno (Jaworow)	
495 232	4953/2328	Prilbichi	
495 232	4956/2323	Yavorov	
495 232	4957/2327	Olshanitsa (Yavorov)	
495 232	4958/2325	Zaluzhe (Lwow)	
495 232	4959/2320	Chernilyava	
495 232	4959/2326	Stariy Yarov	
495 233	4950/2335	Tverdopillya	
495 233	4951/2338	Kamenobrod	
495 233	4952/2338	Dobrostany	
495 233	4952/2334	Lesnevichi	
495 233	4957/2330	Krajowice	
495 233	4957/2332	Shklo	
495 234	4952/2349	Vrotsuv	
495 234	4954/2344	Zalese (Gorodok)	
495 234	4955/2344	Ivano Frankovo	
495 234	4957/2341	Lelekhovka	
495 234	4957/2349	Lozina	
495 235	4950/2354	Rudno	

495	235	4951/2356	Bilogorshche
495	235	4951/2359	Kleparov
495	235	4952/2350	Karachinuv
495	235	4953/2351	Domazhir
495	235	4954/2358	Bryukhovichi
495	235	4955/2355	Choronow
495	235	4957/2354	Rokitno (Lvov)
495	235	4957/2359	Zashkov
495	240	4950/2400	Lvov
495	240	4951/2409	Podbortse
495	240	4957/2401	Kalinuvka
495	240	4959/2405	Kulikov
495	241	4951/2417	Nizhnyaya Belka
495	241	4952/2416	Borshchovichi
495	241	4952/2413	Pikulovitse
495	241	4952/2411	Prusy (Lvov)
495	241	4955/2418	Novyy Yarychev
495	241	4955/2410	Podliski Malyye
495	241	4955/2412	Zapytov
495	241	4956/2416	Kukizov
495	241	4957/2412	Remenuv
495	241	4957/2416	Rudantse
495	241	4959/2414	Zhovtantsy
495	242	4952/2422	Polonichi
495	242	4956/2422	Dedilov
495	242	4957/2424	Banunin
495	243	4951/2434	Baluchin
495	243	4951/2438	Bortkov
495	243	4952/2430	Peltev
495	243	4952/2438	Skniluv
495	243	4953/2438	Firleyuvka
495	243	4955/2433	Bezbrudy
495	243	4955/2437	Krasne (Zolochev)
495	243	4956/2436	Ostruv (Kamenka Strumilovska)
495	243	4956/2438	Stronibaby
495	243	4958/2438	Busk
495	243	4958/2432	Kozlov (Tarnopol)
495	243	4959/2430	Zhepnyuv
495	244	4954/2443	Ostrovchik Polny
495	244	4955/2441	Brykon
495	244	4955/2443	Petryche
495	244	4955/2440	Utsishkuv
495	244	4958/2449	Ozhidiv
495	245	4950/2455	Yelekhovichi
495	245	4952/2457	Sasov
495	245	4952/2452	Zhulitse
495	245	4953/2455	Ushnya
495	245	4954/2450	Belyy Kamen
495	245	4957/2459	Podgortse
495	245	4958/2453	Olesko
495	250	4950/2508	Krugov
495	250	4951/2503	Koltov
495	250	4952/2503	Opaki
495	250	4954/2509	Gutsisko Penyatske
495	250	4955/2505	Strzemilcze
495	250	4958/2503	Yasenov
495	251	4951/2517	Markopol
495	251	4953/2515	Shishkovtse
495	251	4954/2511	Penyaki
495	251	4955/2510	Golubitsa
495	251	4956/2519	Podkamen
495	251	4957/2511	Gutsisko Brodzke
495	251	4957/2516	Pankovtse
495	251	4958/2515	Chernitsa
495	251	4958/2519	Nakvasha
495	252	4952/2523	Seretets
495	252	4957/2523	Popovtse
495	253	4950/2530	Novyy Oleksinets
495	253	4950/2533	Staryy Oleksinets
495	254	4954/2545	Vishnevets
495	260	4950/2608	Orishkovtsy
495	260	4951/2608	Grinki
495	260	4952/2605	Lanovtsy
495	260	4954/2604	Krasnoluka
495	260	4959/2608	Radoshevka
495	261	4958/2615	Yampol (Wolyn)
495	262	4950/2625	Teofipol
495	263	4950/2630	Troyanovka
495	271	4958/2713	Gritsev
495	274	4955/2745	Lyubar
495	281	4951/2813	Ivanopol
495	283	4954/2835	Berdichev
495	283	4957/2832	Skraglevka
495	285	4951/2852	Belopolye
495	290	4952/2909	Vcherayshe
495	292	4952/2927	Pavoloch
495	292	4958/2927	Popelnya
495	295	4959/2950	Trilesy
495	301	4957/3012	Grebenki
495	302	4955/3025	Krasnoye (Belaya Tserkov)
495	305	4951/3050	Kagarlyk
495	310	4958/3103	Rzhishchev
495	320	4958/3208	Drabov
495	323	4957/3232	Yablonevo
495	333	4958/3336	Mirgorod
495	335	4955/3350	Gogolevo
495	340	4953/3400	Shishaki
495	340	4957/3406	Karpety
495	343	4958/3437	Oposhnya
495	353	4950/3537	Valki
495	355	4957/3558	Lyubotin
495	360	4953/3602	Budy
495	360	4956/3609	Pokotilovka
495	363	4950/3639	Chuguyev
495	384	4950/3844	Lozno Aleksandrovka
500	062	5007/0629	Wawern

500 063	5002/0635	Kyllburg
500 070	5001/0700	Bausendorf
500 070	5001/0704	Bengel
500 070	5008/0709	Cochem
500 071	5002/0711	Zell
500 071	5005/0713	Senheim
500 071	5006/0710	Ediger
500 071	5008/0714	Bruttig
500 071	5008/0711	Sehl
500 072	5000/0722	Kappel
500 072	5004/0727	Kastellaun
500 074	5001/0740	Rheinbollen
500 074	5004/0746	Bacharach
500 074	5006/0744	Oberwesel
500 074	5008/0746	Bornich
500 074	5009/0743	Sankt Goar
500 074	5009/0744	Sankt Goarshausen
500 080	5000/0807	Heidesheim
500 080	5001/0802	Ostrich
500 080	5002/0807	Eltville
500 080	5008/0804	Bad Schwalbach
500 081	5000/0815	Mainz
500 081	5003/0818	Erbenheim
500 081	5005/0817	Bierstadt
500 081	5005/0819	Igstadt
500 081	5005/0815	Schierstein (Now Wiesbaden)
500 081	5005/0815	Wiesbaden
500 081	5009/0811	Wehen
500 082	5000/0825	Russelsheim
500 082	5001/0826	Florsheim
500 082	5001/0821	Hochheim am Main
500 082	5002/0828	Eddersheim
500 082	5003/0822	Delkenheim
500 082	5004/0825	Diedenbergen
500 082	5004/0821	Nordenstadt
500 082	5005/0822	Breckenheim
500 082	5005/0827	Hofheim am Taunus
500 082	5005/0829	Kriftel
500 082	5008/0824	Eppstein
500 083	5004/0832	Kelsterbach
500 083	5006/0832	Frankfurt am Hochst
500 083	5006/0830	Zeilsheim
500 083	5007/0835	Frankfurt am Rodelheim
500 083	5008/0830	Bad Soden am Taunus
500 084	5001/0847	Dietzenbach
500 084	5001/0842	Sprendlingen
500 084	5003/0842	Neu Isenburg
500 084	5004/0848	Heusenstamm
500 084	5006/0846	Offenbach
500 084	5007/0847	Burgel
500 084	5007/0841	Frankfurt am Main
500 084	5008/0845	Fechenheim
500 084	5009/0845	Bergen Enkheim
500 084	5009/0848	Bischofsheim
500 085	5002/0853	Jugesheim
500 085	5003/0853	Hainhausen
500 085	5003/0859	Seligenstadt
500 085	5004/0851	Obertshausen
500 085	5005/0859	Grosskrotzenburg
500 085	5005/0858	Kleinkrotzenburg
500 085	5007/0850	Muhlheim am Main
500 085	5007/0855	Steinheim am Main
500 085	5008/0850	Dornigheim
500 085	5008/0855	Hanau am Main
500 090	5000/0904	Kleinostheim
500 090	5003/0905	Horstein
500 090	5004/0905	Wasserlos
500 090	5005/0904	Alzenau in Unterfranken
500 090	5009/0902	Niederrodenbach
500 091	5000/0911	Goldbach
500 091	5000/0912	Hosbach
500 091	5004/0910	Mensengesass
500 091	5004/0914	Schollkrippen
500 092	5008/0929	Lohrhaupten
500 093	5001/0936	Steinbach (Bavaria)
500 093	5006/0939	Rieneck
500 093	5009/0939	Burgsinn
500 094	5002/0945	Adelsberg
500 094	5003/0942	Gemunden (Bavaria)
500 094	5004/0948	Hollrich
500 094	5005/0944	Wolfsmunster
500 094	5006/0948	Weickersgruben
500 094	5009/0946	Dittlofsroda
500 095	5003/0952	Bonnland
500 095	5004/0952	Hundsfeld
500 095	5006/0956	Fuchsstadt
500 095	5006/0954	Pfaffenhausen
500 095	5007/0954	Hammelburg
500 095	5007/0956	Westheim Bei Hammelburg
500 095	5009/0953	Untererthal
500 100	5003/1009	Geldersheim
500 100	5004/1008	Euerbach
500 100	5004/1006	Obbach
500 100	5005/1007	Kutzberg
500 101	5001/1017	Gochsheim
500 101	5003/1019	Schonungen
500 101	5003/1014	Schweinfurt
500 101	5004/1011	Niederwerrn
500 101	5008/1010	Pfersdorf
500 102	5000/1022	Obereuerheim
500 102	5001/1028	Wonfurt
500 102	5005/1029	Mechenried
500 102	5007/1027	Kleinsteinach
500 102	5009/1026	Aidhausen

500	103	5001/1036	Zeil
500	103	5002/1030	Hassfurt
500	103	5005/1035	Konigsberg (Bavaria)
500	103	5008/1039	Burgpreppach
500	103	5008/1032	Hofheim (Bavaria)
500	103	5008/1031	Lendershausen
500	104	5000/1045	Rudendorf
500	104	5004/1048	Rentweinsdorf
500	104	5005/1048	Ebern
500	104	5008/1044	Kraisdorf
500	104	5009/1044	Pfarrweisach
500	105	5001/1050	Reckendorf
500	105	5004/1057	Ebensfeld
500	105	5005/1051	Gleusdorf
500	105	5006/1059	Staffelstein
500	105	5008/1051	Untermerzbach
500	110	5000/1105	Burglesau
500	110	5000/1105	Stubig
500	110	5008/1106	Mistelfeld
500	110	5008/1103	Seubelsdorf
500	110	5009/1104	Lichtenfels
500	111	5004/1116	Niesten
500	111	5005/1114	Weismain
500	111	5007/1118	Maineck
500	111	5007/1119	Mainroth
500	111	5008/1115	Burgkunstadt
500	111	5009/1110	Hochstadt am Main
500	111	5009/1114	Weidnitz
500	112	5001/1123	Thurnau
500	112	5002/1121	Kasendorf
500	112	5006/1127	Kulmbach
500	112	5007/1121	Fassoldshof
500	113	5004/1136	Himmelkron
500	113	5006/1136	Neuenmarkt
500	113	5007/1136	Wirsberg
500	114	5003/1140	Bad Berneck im Fichtelgebirge
500	120	5000/1205	Marktredwitz
500	120	5000/1207	Wolsau
500	120	5002/1209	Seussen
500	120	5002/1201	Wunsiedel
500	121	5000/1218	Waldsassen
500	121	5007/1215	Dobrosov
500	121	5009/1216	Hazlov
500	122	5004/1222	Cheb
500	122	5007/1222	Frantiskovy Lazne
500	123	5001/1233	Dolni Zandov
500	123	5001/1238	Lazne Kynzvart
500	123	5006/1233	Stedra
500	123	5007/1237	Kostelni Briza
500	123	5007/1232	Kynsperk nad Ohri
500	123	5007/1234	Libavske Udoli
500	123	5009/1239	Prosau
500	124	5004/1244	Prameny
500	124	5005/1249	Becov nad Teplou
500	125	5008/1257	Rybnicna
500	130	5004/1300	Touzim
500	130	5007/1308	Veselov
500	130	5008/1305	Udrc
500	130	5009/1303	Bochov
500	131	5001/1316	Rutka (Czechoslovakia)
500	131	5003/1314	Mocidlec
500	131	5006/1315	Chyse
500	131	5006/1311	Zlutice
500	131	5009/1319	Lubenec
500	131	5009/1311	Tyniste
500	132	5001/1324	Potvorov
500	132	5003/1323	Zihle
500	132	5006/1329	Jesenice
500	132	5008/1328	Bilenec
500	132	5008/1327	Petrohrad
500	132	5008/1320	Repany
500	132	5009/1322	Vidhostice
500	133	5002/1335	Cista
500	133	5002/1332	Kuzova
500	133	5004/1339	Petrovice
500	133	5004/1337	Zavidovo
500	133	5005/1332	Sosen
500	133	5007/1333	Oracov
500	133	5008/1337	Kolesovice
500	133	5009/1334	Hokov
500	134	5000/1342	Slabce
500	134	5006/1345	Rakovnik
500	135	5002/1353	Krivoklat
500	135	5002/1356	Sykorice
500	135	5008/1355	Rynholec
500	135	5009/1355	Nove Straseci
500	140	5001/1405	Chynava
500	140	5004/1401	Bratronice
500	140	5005/1409	Unhost
500	140	5006/1406	Braskov
500	140	5006/1403	Druzec
500	140	5006/1406	Krocehlavy
500	140	5008/1405	Rozdelov
500	140	5009/1406	Kladno
500	141	5001/1417	Zbuzany
500	141	5002/1414	Dusniky
500	141	5002/1413	Horelice
500	141	5003/1411	Uhonice
500	141	5005/1416	Hostivice
500	141	5005/1414	Litovice
500	141	5008/1414	Beloky
500	141	5008/1412	Lidice
500	141	5009/1411	Bustehrad
500	142	5005/1428	Praha
500	143	5000/1436	Nupaky
500	143	5001/1435	Pitkovice
500	143	5002/1436	Uhrineves

500	143	5004/1439	Kolodeje	500	154	5001/1548	Nemosice
500	143	5005/1437	Bechovice	500	154	5002/1547	Pardubice
500	143	5009/1436	Jenstejn	500	154	5002/1543	Svitkov
500	144	5001/1448	Doubravcice	500	154	5006/1545	Steblova
500	144	5002/1445	Hradesin	500	154	5009/1540	Syrovatka
500	144	5002/1440	Krenice	500	155	5000/1557	Moravany
500	144	5003/1442	Dobrocovice	500	155	5001/1554	Kostenice
500	144	5003/1444	Skvorec	500	155	5002/1555	Dasice
500	144	5004/1440	Sibrina	500	155	5007/1556	Chvojenec
500	144	5004/1449	Tismice	500	155	5008/1555	Byst
500	144	5005/1442	Koumice	500	155	5009/1557	Belecko
500	144	5005/1446	Tlustovousy	500	160	5000/1606	Tynistko
500	144	5006/1440	Klanovice	500	160	5001/1602	Litetiny
500	144	5007/1449	Vykan	500	160	5003/1602	Ostretin
500	144	5007/1447	Vysehorovice	500	160	5005/1600	Holice
500	144	5008/1444	Nehvizdy	500	160	5006/1606	Borohradek
500	145	5000/1459	Kourim	500	161	5000/1618	Brandys nad Orlici
500	145	5001/1454	Chotys	500	161	5000/1614	Chocen
500	145	5002/1458	Trebovle	500	161	5001/1613	Bestovice
500	145	5003/1453	Pristoupim	500	161	5002/1615	Koldin
500	145	5004/1451	Cesky Brod	500	161	5005/1619	Potstejn
500	145	5004/1459	Chotutice	500	161	5007/1616	Doudleby nad Orlici
500	145	5005/1459	Tatce	500	161	5007/1618	Vamberk
500	145	5006/1456	Poricany	500	161	5008/1614	Kostelec nad Orlici
500	145	5008/1459	Sadska	500	162	5001/1626	Hnatnice
500	150	5000/1505	Libodrice	500	162	5004/1627	Dlouhonovice
500	150	5002/1502	Hradenin	500	162	5004/1621	Sopotnice
500	150	5002/1501	Zalesany	500	162	5006/1628	Zamberk
500	150	5003/1502	Planany	500	163	5002/1630	Letohrad
500	150	5004/1506	Velim	500	164	5002/1641	Orlicky
500	150	5005/1505	Cerhenice	500	164	5005/1646	Kraliky
500	150	5005/1509	Pnov	500	165	5005/1657	Hanusovice
500	150	5005/1504	Ratenice	500	170	5004/1706	Loucna nad Desnou
500	150	5006/1501	Pecky	500	173	5004/1733	Cakova
500	150	5009/1508	Podebrady	500	174	5006/1743	Krnov
500	151	5002/1512	Kolin	500	180	5005/1800	Kietrz
500	151	5004/1516	Bychory	500	181	5005/1812	Raciborz
500	151	5005/1511	Veltruby	500	183	5002/1834	Michalkowice
500	151	5006/1518	Ohare	500	183	5007/1832	Ujvasar (Silesia)
500	151	5008/1515	Sany	500	184	5001/1843	Baranowice
500	151	5008/1517	Zehun	500	184	5001/1849	Kryry (Poland)
500	151	5009/1514	Kolaje	500	184	5003/1842	Zory
500	152	5001/1528	Zdechovice	500	184	5009/1845	Jaskowice
500	152	5005/1527	Tetov	500	185	5008/1859	Tychy
500	152	5009/1527	Chlumec nad Cidlinou	500	190	5003/1909	Jedlina
500	153	5002/1534	Prelouc	500	191	5001/1913	Stare Stawy
500	153	5002/1537	Valy	500	191	5002/1918	Monowice
500	153	5003/1532	Semin	500	191	5002/1914	Oswiecim
500	153	5004/1539	Zivanice	500	191	5003/1912	Babice
500	153	5005/1531	Strasov	500	191	5003/1918	Gromiec
500	153	5006/1533	Soprec	500	191	5003/1914	Klucznikowice
500	153	5006/1534	Zaravice	500	191	5004/1914	Gorzow
500	153	5007/1530	Klamos	500	191	5005/1911	Bierun Nowy
500	153	5007/1534	Volec	500	191	5006/1914	Chelmek

500 191	5006/1918	Libiaz	
500 192	5001/1923	Przeciszow	
500 192	5003/1922	Metkow	
500 192	5003/1929	Rozkochow	
500 192	5006/1928	Plaza	
500 192	5008/1924	Chrzanow	
500 193	5001/1931	Miejsce	
500 193	5002/1931	Oklesna	
500 193	5002/1939	Zagorze (Krakow)	
500 193	5003/1936	Brodla	
500 193	5004/1932	Alwernia	
500 193	5004/1930	Kwaczala	
500 193	5004/1934	Poreba Zegoty	
500 193	5004/1939	Sanka	
500 193	5006/1932	Nieporaz	
500 193	5006/1932	Regulice	
500 193	5007/1937	Tenczynek	
500 193	5008/1938	Krzeszowiec	
500 193	5008/1935	Wola Filipowska	
500 193	5009/1931	Dulowa	
500 194	5000/1941	Czernichowek	
500 194	5000/1946	Dabrowa Szlachecka	
500 194	5001/1945	Raczna	
500 194	5002/1946	Liszki	
500 194	5003/1948	Kryspinow	
500 194	5007/1940	Nowojowa Gora	
500 194	5009/1944	Radwanowice	
500 194	5009/1940	Zbik	
500 195	5000/1957	Kurdwanow	
500 195	5001/1954	Kobierzyn	
500 195	5001/1959	Piaski Wielkie	
500 195	5002/1956	Borek Falecki	
500 195	5002/1958	Podgorze	
500 195	5002/1954	Pychowice	
500 195	5002/1959	Wola Duchacka	
500 195	5003/1955	Debniki	
500 195	5003/1959	Plaszow	
500 195	5003/1952	Przegorzaly	
500 195	5004/1953	Wola Justowska	
500 195	5005/1955	Krakow	
500 195	5005/1951	Mydlniki	
500 195	5005/1957	Pradnik Czerwony	
500 195	5005/1959	Rakowice	
500 195	5006/1957	Pradnik	
500 195	5006/1950	Rzaska	
500 195	5007/1952	Modlniczka	
500 195	5007/1955	Tonie	
500 195	5007/1956	Zielonki	
500 195	5008/1957	Bibice	
500 195	5008/1952	Modlnica	
500 195	5009/1953	Giebultow	
500 200	5000/2009	Ochmanow	
500 200	5001/2003	Biezanow	
500 200	5001/2000	Prokocim	
500 200	5001/2007	Wegrzce Wielkie	
500 200	5004/2001	Czyzyny	
500 200	5004/2005	Mogila	
500 200	5005/2007	Pleszow	
500 200	5006/2007	Luczanowice	
500 200	5007/2002	Batowice	
500 200	5007/2007	Dojazdow	
500 200	5008/2009	Gleboka	
500 200	5008/2008	Kocmyrzow	
500 200	5009/2007	Luborzyca	
500 201	5000/2015	Dabrowa (Niepolomice)	
500 201	5001/2015	Grodkowice	
500 201	5001/2012	Staniatki	
500 201	5002/2014	Niepolomice	
500 201	5004/2016	Wola Batorska	
500 201	5004/2010	Wyciaze	
500 201	5005/2015	Igolomia	
500 201	5006/2011	Koscielniki	
500 201	5008/2010	Karniow	
500 201	5008/2018	Stregoborzyce	
500 201	5009/2015	Wierzbno	
500 201	5009/2012	Wronin	
500 202	5001/2029	Ostrow Krolewski	
500 202	5001/2028	Slomka (Bochnia)	
500 202	5002/2028	Gawlow	
500 202	5002/2029	Ostrow Szlachecki	
500 202	5004/2029	Mikluszowice	
500 202	5004/2021	Wola Zabierzowska	
500 202	5004/2020	Zabierzow	
500 202	5005/2028	Dziewin	
500 202	5005/2029	Wyzyce	
500 202	5006/2027	Drwinia	
500 202	5007/2024	Ispina	
500 202	5008/2023	Brzesko Nowe	
500 202	5008/2025	Grobla	
500 202	5008/2020	Rudno Dolne	
500 202	5009/2025	Hebdow	
500 203	5002/2038	Mokrzyska	
500 203	5003/2034	Buczkow	
500 203	5003/2039	Rudy Rysie	
500 203	5005/2033	Wrzepia	
500 203	5007/2030	Niedary	
500 203	5007/2035	Strzelce Wielkie	
500 203	5007/2039	Szczurowa	
500 203	5007/2032	Uscie Solne	
500 203	5008/2033	Barczkow	
500 203	5008/2034	Dabrowka Morska	
500 203	5008/2037	Rzachowa	
500 204	5001/2042	Wokowice	
500 204	5002/2044	Bielcza	
500 204	5005/2042	Borzecin	
500 204	5006/2040	Rylowa	
500 204	5007/2048	Wal Ruda	
500 204	5009/2044	Jadowniki Mokre	

500 204	5009/2040	Kwikow
500 204	5009/2043	Pojawie
500 205	5001/2056	Moscice
500 205	5001/2055	Swierczkow
500 205	5001/2059	Tarnow
500 205	5003/2059	Krzyz
500 205	5004/2055	Bobrowniki Wielkie
500 205	5004/2059	Pawezow
500 205	5005/2051	Radlow
500 205	5005/2050	Wola Radlowska
500 205	5008/2052	Biskupice Radlowskie
500 205	5008/2057	Fiuk
500 205	5008/2054	Zabno
500 205	5008/2050	Zdrochec
500 205	5009/2051	Nieciecza
500 210	5001/2102	Gumniska
500 210	5001/2108	Pogorz
500 210	5001/2109	Poskle
500 210	5001/2103	Rzedzin
500 210	5004/2107	Jodlowka (Tarnow)
500 210	5005/2109	Jastrzabka Nowa
500 210	5005/2103	Lisia Gora
500 210	5005/2100	Smigno
500 210	5005/2107	Zukowice Stare
500 210	5005/2108	Zukowice Nowe
500 210	5006/2100	Bagienica
500 210	5008/2100	Brnik
500 210	5008/2106	Luszowice Gorne
500 210	5008/2104	Szarwark
500 210	5008/2100	Zelazowka
500 210	5009/2107	Podkosciele
500 211	5001/2113	Machowa
500 211	5001/2110	Pogorska Wola
500 211	5003/2119	Glowaczowa
500 211	5004/2116	Czarna (Pilzno)
500 211	5005/2118	Borowa (Pilzno)
500 211	5005/2115	Jazwiny
500 211	5007/2118	Roza
500 211	5008/2115	Jastrzabka Stara
500 212	5000/2120	Parkosz
500 212	5003/2125	Debica
500 212	5003/2125	Gawrzylowa
500 212	5003/2127	Nagawczyna
500 212	5004/2122	Straszecin
500 212	5005/2126	Kedzierz
500 212	5005/2127	Pustynia
500 212	5005/2124	Zyrakow
500 212	5006/2123	Gora Motyczna
500 212	5006/2125	Wola Zyrakowska
500 212	5007/2121	Wiewiorka
500 212	5008/2126	Nagoszyn
500 212	5008/2120	Zassow
500 212	5009/2127	Korzeniow
500 213	5002/2133	Lopuchowa

500 213	5003/2138	Brzyzna
500 213	5003/2135	Chechly
500 213	5003/2137	Ropczyce
500 213	5004/2132	Lubzina
500 213	5004/2138	Pietrzejowa
500 213	5004/2131	Sepnica
500 213	5004/2133	Skrzyszow
500 213	5005/2135	Ostrow (Ropczyce)
500 213	5005/2131	Paszczyna
500 213	5005/2135	Reichsheim
500 213	5006/2137	Kozodrza
500 213	5006/2130	Wola Brzeznicka
500 213	5008/2135	Ocieka
500 213	5009/2130	Pustkow
500 214	5000/2149	Wola Zglobienska
500 214	5001/2147	Nockowa
500 214	5001/2145	Wiercany
500 214	5002/2146	Iwierzyce
500 214	5002/2141	Zagorzyce
500 214	5003/2147	Bedziemysl
500 214	5003/2141	Gora Ropczycka
500 214	5004/2143	Przedmiescie Sedziszowskie
500 214	5004/2142	Sedziszow
500 214	5005/2144	Kaweczyn
500 214	5005/2143	Wolica Lugowa
500 214	5008/2145	Czarna (Ropczyce)
500 214	5008/2142	Ruda (Ropczyce)
500 215	5001/2155	Raclawowka
500 215	5001/2151	Zglobien
500 215	5002/2158	Staroniwa
500 215	5003/2157	Przybyszowka
500 215	5004/2155	Swilcza
500 215	5005/2157	Rudna Wielka
500 215	5006/2156	Mrowla
500 215	5007/2152	Bratkowice
500 215	5008/2158	Wola Cicha
500 215	5009/2158	Glogow
500 215	5009/2157	Zabajka
500 220	5001/2201	Drabinianka
500 220	5001/2204	Matysowka
500 220	5001/2202	Zalesie (Rzeszow)
500 220	5001/2202	Zalesie (Lancut)
500 220	5002/2206	Malawa
500 220	5002/2202	Pobitno
500 220	5002/2203	Slocina
500 220	5003/2206	Krasne (Rzeszow)
500 220	5003/2200	Rzeszow
500 220	5003/2200	Tycha
500 220	5004/2207	Strazow
500 220	5005/2206	Laka
500 220	5006/2205	Terliczka
500 220	5006/2201	Zaczernie
500 220	5007/2204	Jasionka

500 220	5007/2209	Pogwizdow
500 220	5008/2208	Medynia Lancucka
500 220	5009/2205	Stobierna
500 221	5001/2214	Albigowa
500 221	5001/2219	Markowa
500 221	5002/2210	Kraczkowa
500 221	5003/2216	Wysoka (Lancut)
500 221	5004/2214	Lancut
500 221	5004/2213	Przedmiescie
500 221	5004/2217	Sonina
500 221	5006/2218	Debina (Lancut)
500 221	5009/2215	Rakszawa
500 222	5001/2225	Ostrow (Jaroslaw)
500 222	5001/2228	Urzejowice
500 222	5002/2226	Debow
500 222	5004/2229	Gorliczyna
500 222	5004/2228	Grzeska
500 222	5004/2220	Kosina
500 222	5004/2225	Nowosielce
500 222	5004/2223	Rogozno (Lancut)
500 222	5005/2222	Korniaktow
500 222	5006/2221	Bialobrzegi (Lancut)
500 222	5006/2226	Swietoniowa
500 222	5007/2226	Budy Lancuckie
500 222	5007/2229	Gniewczyna Lancucka
500 222	5008/2225	Opaleniska
500 223	5001/2231	Zurawiczki
500 223	5002/2234	Mirocin
500 223	5002/2238	Tywonia
500 223	5002/2236	Wierzbna
500 223	5003/2230	Mokra Strona
500 223	5003/2233	Rozborz
500 223	5004/2238	Pelkinie
500 223	5004/2230	Przeworsk
500 223	5004/2235	Ujezna
500 223	5005/2237	Wolka Pelkinska
500 223	5006/2230	Gniewczyna Tryniecka
500 223	5006/2234	Jagiela
500 223	5006/2236	Wola Buchowska
500 223	5008/2235	Gorzyce (Przeworsk)
500 223	5008/2231	Wolka Malkowa
500 223	5008/2234	Wolka Ogryzkowa
500 223	5009/2231	Chodaczow
500 223	5009/2237	Lezachow
500 224	5001/2241	Jaroslaw
500 224	5001/2245	Sobiecin
500 224	5001/2249	Wietlin
500 224	5002/2244	Koniaczow
500 224	5002/2246	Surochow
500 224	5003/2243	Szowsko
500 224	5005/2242	Wiazownica
500 224	5006/2242	Nielepkowice
500 224	5007/2240	Manasterz
500 224	5008/2246	Radawa
500 224	5009/2243	Czerwona Wola
500 224	5009/2248	Zaradawa
500 225	5001/2254	Laszki
500 225	5002/2252	Bobrowka
500 225	5002/2256	Korzenica
500 225	5002/2258	Miekisz Stary
500 225	5002/2259	Miekisz Nowy
500 225	5004/2252	Ryszkowa Wola
500 225	5005/2257	Onyszki
500 225	5005/2253	Zapalow
500 225	5007/2255	Bachory
500 225	5009/2258	Stare Siolo (Lwow)
500 230	5000/2307	Kobylnica Woloska
500 230	5001/2305	Kobylnica Ruska
500 230	5001/2309	Wielkie Oczy
500 230	5005/2302	Bihale
500 230	5005/2307	Lukawiec (Cieszanow)
500 230	5005/2301	Nowa Grobla
500 230	5006/2308	Szczutkow
500 230	5008/2301	Suchowola (Lwow)
500 230	5009/2309	Ostrowiec (Lvov)
500 231	5000/2310	Skolin
500 231	5001/2318	Nagachev
500 231	5002/2312	Zmijowiska
500 231	5003/2318	Drogomyshl
500 231	5004/2319	Kolonitsa
500 231	5005/2319	Grushev
500 231	5007/2317	Budomierz
500 231	5009/2313	Borowa Gora
500 231	5009/2318	Sieniawka
500 232	5003/2326	Verbyany
500 232	5004/2324	Zalukh
500 232	5004/2323	Zavadov
500 232	5005/2321	Shcheploty
500 232	5007/2327	Nemirov (Lvov)
500 232	5008/2328	Voroblyachin
500 232	5009/2328	Smolin
500 233	5000/2338	Vereshitsa
500 233	5004/2337	Vishenka Mala
500 233	5005/2335	Huta Obedynska
500 233	5007/2334	Shcherets
500 233	5008/2332	Parypsy
500 233	5009/2333	Seredkevychi
500 234	5002/2349	Fuyna
500 234	5004/2349	Ruda Krekhuvska
500 234	5006/2340	Belaya
500 234	5006/2348	Kunin
500 234	5007/2345	Borki (Lvov)
500 234	5007/2343	Magerov
500 234	5007/2346	Shostaki
500 234	5008/2347	Gorodzuv
500 235	5001/2357	Mokrotyn
500 235	5003/2353	Skvazhava Nova
500 235	5004/2354	Glinskoye

500 235	5004/2350	Krekhov
500 235	5004/2358	Nesterov
500 235	5005/2356	Volya Vysotska
500 235	5007/2359	Vionzova
500 235	5008/2351	Dobrosin
500 235	5008/2353	Pily
500 235	5008/2357	Zamochek
500 235	5009/2351	Bobroydy
500 240	5000/2402	Mezhvitsa
500 240	5000/2401	Vesenberg
500 240	5001/2408	Artasuv
500 240	5001/2403	Pshemivulki
500 240	5002/2406	Dernuvka
500 240	5002/2403	Vezhblyany
500 240	5003/2404	Blyshchyvody
500 240	5003/2404	Ehrenfeld
500 240	5005/2405	Wyzlow
500 240	5008/2403	Turinka
500 241	5000/2417	Klodno Velikoye
500 241	5000/2416	Kolodentse
500 241	5000/2418	Pechikhvosty (Lwow)
500 241	5001/2410	Dzibulki
500 241	5004/2416	Dalnich
500 241	5005/2412	Teodorsgof
500 241	5006/2416	Batyatychi
500 241	5006/2410	Zheldets
500 241	5007/2414	Lipnik (Rava Russkaya)
500 241	5009/2419	Zubov Most
500 242	5000/2422	Gorpin
500 242	5000/2423	Nagortse Male
500 242	5000/2426	Velikoselka
500 242	5002/2423	Lodyna Nova
500 242	5002/2427	Streptov
500 242	5003/2429	Spas (Tarnopol)
500 242	5003/2426	Yamne
500 242	5005/2420	Sapezhanka
500 242	5005/2425	Tadany
500 242	5006/2421	Kamenka Bugskaya
500 242	5008/2422	Lany Polske
500 242	5009/2424	Ruda Seletska
500 243	5000/2433	Rakobuty
500 243	5001/2433	Pobuzhany
500 243	5001/2436	Yablonovka
500 243	5002/2431	Volitsa Derevlyanska
500 243	5004/2436	Grabova
500 243	5004/2430	Sokola
500 243	5006/2436	Mazyarnya Vavrshkova
500 243	5007/2439	Guta Polonetska
500 243	5009/2438	Polonichna
500 244	5001/2444	Bolozhinov
500 244	5003/2448	Perevolochna
500 244	5005/2441	Chanyzh
500 244	5007/2443	Toporov
500 245	5002/2452	Labach
500 245	5002/2451	Sokolovka (Tarnopol)
500 245	5002/2458	Zabolottsy
500 245	5004/2457	Razhnyuv
500 245	5005/2456	Ruda Brodska
500 245	5005/2450	Turye
500 250	5000/2507	Sukhodoly
500 250	5003/2504	Ponikovitsa
500 250	5005/2509	Brody
500 251	5000/2515	Sukhovolya (Tarnopol)
500 251	5004/2510	Stare Brody
500 251	5008/2515	Chervonoarmeisk
500 252	5001/2529	Pochayev
500 252	5004/2524	Podzamche
500 252	5005/2525	Rohozne
500 252	5009/2522	Mikhaylovka (Wolyn)
500 253	5000/2531	Novyy Pochayev
500 253	5006/2537	Velikiye Berezhtsy
500 254	5005/2545	Zniesienie
500 254	5006/2543	Kremenets
500 255	5000/2553	Katerinovka
500 255	5003/2554	Viliya (Kremenets)
500 255	5008/2559	Zholobki
500 260	5000/2602	Velikiye Zagaytsy
500 260	5003/2606	Dederkaly Male
500 260	5004/2607	Bykovtsy
500 260	5006/2608	Brykov
500 260	5007/2607	Shumskoye
500 260	5008/2606	Rakhmanov
500 260	5009/2601	Obych
500 261	5003/2617	Stavishchany
500 261	5005/2615	Wierzchow
500 262	5000/2625	Belogorye
500 262	5006/2624	Shimkovtsy
500 264	5005/2646	Klubovka
500 264	5007/2648	Izyaslav
500 272	5001/2721	Novo Labun
500 272	5001/2722	Yurovshchina
500 273	5007/2731	Polonnoye
500 280	5003/2807	Chudnov
500 282	5001/2822	Pyatka
500 283	5007/2833	Troyanov
500 284	5005/2843	Kodnya
500 285	5006/2858	Staraya Kotelnya
500 291	5006/2918	Khodorkov
500 293	5005/2932	Kornin
500 295	5005/2955	Fastov
500 303	5006/3038	Obukhov
500 312	5005/3128	Pereyaslav Khmelnitskiy
500 322	5007/3226	Grebenka
500 330	5001/3300	Lubny
500 332	5000/3320	Romodan
500 350	5004/3509	Krasnokutsk
500 352	5003/3520	Murafa
500 355	5003/3553	Olshany

500 361	5000/3615	Kharkov	
500 363	5007/3632	Petrovka (Kharkov)	
501 061	5010/0611	Auf Dem Bock	
501 063	5013/0633	Budesheim	
501 063	5019/0631	Schonfeld	
501 064	5013/0640	Gerolstein	
501 064	5018/0640	Hillesheim	
501 070	5011/0702	Alflen	
501 070	5014/0709	Kaisersesch	
501 071	5011/0718	Treis	
501 071	5012/0711	Illerich	
501 071	5014/0711	Hambuch	
501 071	5016/0710	Dungenheim	
501 071	5016/0719	Mertloch	
501 071	5018/0719	Polch	
501 072	5014/0727	Brodenbach	
501 072	5014/0725	Hatzenport	
501 072	5014/0726	Lof	
501 072	5015/0722	Munstermaifeld	
501 072	5016/0721	Gappenach	
501 072	5019/0728	Kobern	
501 073	5014/0736	Boppard	
501 073	5018/0736	Niederlahnstein	
501 073	5018/0737	Oberlahnstein	
501 074	5010/0743	Nochern	
501 074	5010/0742	Wellmich	
501 074	5011/0748	Bogel	
501 074	5011/0743	Weyer	
501 074	5014/0745	Gemmerich	
501 074	5015/0748	Geisig	
501 074	5017/0740	Braubach	
501 074	5019/0748	Nassau	
501 075	5012/0752	Nastatten	
501 075	5013/0755	Holzhausen (Koblenz)	
501 075	5013/0750	Miehlen	
501 075	5017/0755	Kordorf	
501 075	5017/0750	Singhofen	
501 075	5019/0757	Biebrich	
501 080	5013/0800	Laufenselden	
501 080	5015/0804	Kettenbach	
501 081	5014/0816	Idstein	
501 081	5017/0811	Bechtheim	
501 081	5018/0816	Camberg	
501 082	5011/0828	Konigstein im Taunus	
501 082	5019/0828	Merzhausen	
501 083	5011/0830	Kronberg	
501 083	5012/0835	Oberursel	
501 083	5013/0837	Bad Homburg vor der Hohe	
501 083	5018/0834	Wehrheim	
501 084	5011/0845	Bad Vilbel	
501 084	5011/0841	Harheim	
501 084	5012/0840	Nieder Eschbach	
501 084	5014/0848	Grosskarben	
501 084	5014/0845	Kloppenheim	
501 084	5014/0841	Obererlenbach	
501 084	5015/0840	Burgholzhausen	
501 084	5016/0848	Burg Grafenrode	
501 084	5017/0846	Niederwollstadt	
501 084	5018/0849	Assenheim	
501 084	5018/0845	Oberwollstadt	
501 085	5010/0859	Langendiebach	
501 085	5010/0852	Wachenbuchen	
501 085	5013/0859	Markobel	
501 085	5014/0852	Heldenbergen	
501 085	5014/0853	Windecken	
501 085	5016/0852	Erbstadt	
501 085	5016/0858	Rommelhausen	
501 085	5017/0857	Altenstadt (Hessen)	
501 085	5017/0851	Bonstadt	
501 085	5018/0858	Heegheim	
501 085	5018/0859	Lindheim	
501 085	5019/0852	Niederflorstadt	
501 085	5019/0855	Stammheim	
501 090	5010/0908	Niedermittlau	
501 090	5010/0900	Ruckingen	
501 090	5011/0902	Langenselbold	
501 090	5011/0908	Meerholz	
501 090	5012/0908	Lieblos	
501 090	5013/0903	Huttengesass	
501 090	5014/0903	Altwiedermus	
501 090	5014/0900	Langen Bergheim	
501 090	5015/0909	Hain Grundau	
501 090	5016/0900	Hainchen	
501 090	5016/0900	Himbach	
501 090	5018/0907	Budingen	
501 090	5018/0902	Dudelsheim	
501 090	5019/0900	Glauberg	
501 091	5011/0912	Altenhasslau	
501 091	5012/0911	Gelnhausen	
501 091	5016/0918	Wachtersbach	
501 091	5019/0918	Hellstein	
501 092	5013/0921	Bad Orb	
501 092	5017/0922	Salmunster	
501 092	5019/0922	Romsthal	
501 093	5012/0937	Mittelsinn	
501 093	5015/0937	Altengronau	
501 093	5019/0937	Sterbfritz	
501 094	5011/0947	Volkersleier	
501 094	5014/0946	Detter	
501 094	5016/0943	Eckarts Rupboden	
501 094	5016/0949	Unterleichtersbach	
501 094	5016/0940	Zeitlofs	
501 094	5017/0945	Wernarz	
501 094	5018/0948	Bruckenau	
501 094	5019/0944	Zuntersbach	
501 095	5012/0958	Oberthulba	
501 095	5016/0955	Platz	

501 095	5016/0952	Schondra
501 095	5017/0954	Geroda
501 095	5019/0952	Unterriedenberg
501 100	5012/1005	Bad Kissingen
501 100	5017/1006	Steinach an der Saale
501 101	5011/1017	Massbach
501 101	5012/1019	Thundorf in Unterfranken
501 101	5013/1014	Poppenlauer
501 101	5015/1011	Munnerstadt
501 101	5019/1018	Eichenhausen
501 101	5019/1017	Rodelmaier
501 102	5010/1029	Friesenhausen
501 102	5011/1022	Stadtlauringen
501 102	5013/1023	Oberlauringen
501 102	5016/1024	Kleinbardorf
501 102	5018/1029	Ipthausen
501 102	5018/1022	Kleineibstadt
501 102	5018/1029	Konigshofen
501 103	5010/1038	Ditterswind
501 103	5011/1034	Schweinshaupten
501 103	5013/1031	Bundorf
501 103	5013/1037	Ermershausen
501 103	5014/1034	Sulzdorf an der Lederhecke
501 103	5016/1033	Oberessfeld
501 103	5019/1035	Trappstadt
501 104	5010/1044	Altenstein
501 104	5012/1040	Maroldsweisach
501 105	5011/1051	Sesslach
501 105	5015/1058	Coburg
501 110	5013/1108	Sonnefeld
501 110	5016/1107	Fechheim
501 110	5019/1107	Neustadt Bei Coburg
501 111	5010/1115	Ebneth
501 111	5010/1112	Redwitz an der Rodach
501 111	5011/1115	Oberlangenstadt
501 111	5012/1117	Kups
501 111	5014/1119	Kronach
501 111	5015/1113	Mitwitz
501 114	5012/1147	Munchberg
501 114	5019/1142	Naila
501 115	5016/1156	Oberkotzau
501 115	5019/1155	Hof
501 115	5019/1151	Wolbattendorf
501 120	5010/1208	Selb
501 120	5010/1203	Spielberg
501 120	5015/1202	Rehau
501 121	5013/1211	As
501 121	5019/1219	Markneukirchen
501 122	5010/1222	Skalna
501 123	5011/1238	Sokolov (Czechoslovakia)
501 123	5012/1233	Habartov
501 123	5015/1233	Olovi
501 123	5018/1230	Snezna
501 124	5011/1241	Kralovske Porici
501 124	5011/1245	Loket
501 124	5013/1244	Nove Sedlo
501 124	5015/1245	Chodov
501 124	5016/1247	Bozicany
501 125	5013/1254	Karlovy Vary
501 125	5014/1252	Rybare
501 125	5014/1255	Tuhnice
501 125	5018/1252	Hroznetin
501 125	5019/1254	Dlouha
501 130	5011/1300	Struzna
501 130	5014/1301	Hartmanov
501 130	5015/1309	Doupov
501 131	5010/1310	Luka
501 131	5010/1318	Skytaly
501 131	5011/1310	Lochotin
501 131	5013/1319	Nepomysl
501 131	5013/1316	Podboransky Rohozec
501 131	5015/1312	Turec
501 131	5016/1317	Mastov
501 131	5016/1310	Trmova
501 131	5018/1317	Radonice
501 132	5011/1326	Kryry
501 132	5011/1323	Vroutek
501 132	5013/1328	Blsany
501 132	5013/1322	Buskovice
501 132	5014/1327	Letov
501 132	5014/1325	Podborany
501 132	5017/1328	Klicin
501 132	5017/1327	Oploty
501 132	5017/1323	Siroke Trebcice
501 132	5019/1323	Libedice
501 132	5019/1321	Petipsy
501 132	5019/1328	Zabokliky
501 133	5010/1337	Horesedly
501 133	5011/1331	Besno
501 133	5011/1337	Svojetin
501 133	5014/1337	Destnice
501 133	5014/1338	Necemice
501 133	5014/1330	Sirem
501 133	5015/1330	Libesovice
501 133	5015/1331	Liborice
501 133	5016/1333	Mecholupy
501 133	5016/1339	Treskonice
501 133	5017/1336	Klucek
501 133	5017/1338	Lickov
501 133	5018/1337	Dobricany
501 133	5018/1335	Veletice
501 133	5019/1330	Ceradice
501 133	5019/1339	Drahomysl
501 134	5011/1348	Revnicov
501 134	5012/1340	Milostin

501 134	5012/1342	Mutejovice	
501 134	5013/1345	Treboc	
501 134	5014/1344	Domousice	
501 134	5016/1340	Tuchorice	
501 134	5018/1344	Touchovice	
501 134	5019/1345	Jimlin	
501 135	5013/1358	Hlina	
501 135	5014/1357	Pozden	
501 135	5016/1355	Bilichov	
501 135	5017/1358	Horesovicky	
501 135	5018/1352	Hriskov	
501 135	5018/1359	Klobuky	
501 140	5010/1408	Hnidousy	
501 140	5010/1403	Libusin	
501 140	5011/1405	Trebichovice	
501 140	5012/1403	Prelic	
501 140	5013/1408	Knoviz	
501 140	5014/1402	Bysen	
501 140	5014/1406	Slany	
501 140	5015/1407	Dolin	
501 140	5017/1408	Tman	
501 140	5017/1406	Zlonice	
501 140	5019/1405	Jarpice	
501 140	5019/1408	Postovice	
501 141	5010/1412	Stehelceves	
501 141	5011/1411	Brandysek	
501 141	5013/1416	Otvovice	
501 141	5014/1419	Kralupy nad Vltavou	
501 141	5014/1413	Neumerice	
501 141	5016/1412	Jesin	
501 141	5016/1418	Nelahozeves	
501 141	5017/1417	Uhy	
501 141	5017/1415	Velvary	
501 142	5011/1425	Klecany	
501 142	5011/1423	Letky	
501 142	5012/1426	Klicany	
501 142	5012/1423	Maslovice	
501 142	5014/1421	Chvateruby	
501 142	5014/1423	Kozomin	
501 142	5014/1423	Postrizin	
501 142	5014/1429	Predboj	
501 142	5016/1420	Veltrusy	
501 142	5017/1422	Zlosyn	
501 142	5018/1429	Obristvi	
501 142	5019/1420	Mlcechvosty	
501 142	5019/1422	Vranany	
501 143	5011/1434	Sluhy	
501 143	5012/1433	Mratin	
501 143	5013/1431	Zlonin	
501 143	5014/1436	Kostelec nad Labem	
501 143	5015/1439	Drisy	
501 143	5016/1437	Nedomice	
501 143	5016/1431	Neratovice	
501 143	5016/1433	Tisice	
501 143	5018/1437	Cecelice	
501 143	5019/1437	Bysice	
501 144	5010/1446	Celakovice	
501 144	5010/1447	Sedlcanky	
501 144	5010/1443	Tousen	
501 144	5011/1440	Brandys nad Labem	
501 144	5011/1440	Vrabi	
501 144	5014/1442	Hlavenec	
501 144	5017/1449	Obodr	
501 144	5019/1446	Hrivno	
501 145	5011/1451	Litol	
501 145	5015/1457	Vsejany	
501 145	5017/1450	Benatky nad Jizerou	
501 150	5011/1503	Nymburk	
501 150	5016/1509	Krinec	
501 150	5017/1502	Loucen	
501 150	5018/1505	Mcely	
501 151	5011/1515	Opocnice	
501 151	5012/1518	Mestec Kralove	
501 151	5014/1513	Cineves	
501 151	5015/1512	Dymokury	
501 151	5017/1514	Bristev	
501 151	5017/1516	Chotesice	
501 151	5018/1511	Rozdalovice	
501 151	5019/1519	Vrsce	
501 152	5014/1520	Slovec	
501 152	5016/1528	Kricov	
501 152	5018/1529	Smidary	
501 153	5010/1536	Kratonohy	
501 153	5012/1530	Mlekosrby	
501 153	5015/1535	Kobylice	
501 153	5015/1530	Novy Bydzov	
501 154	5013/1545	Stezery	
501 154	5016/1545	Rozberice	
501 155	5013/1550	Hradec Kralove	
501 155	5014/1551	Pouchov	
501 155	5018/1553	Smirice	
501 160	5012/1600	Trebechovice pod Orebem	
501 160	5018/1609	Pulice	
501 161	5010/1617	Rychnov nad Kneznou	
501 161	5012/1615	Solnice	
501 161	5013/1616	Kvasiny	
501 161	5016/1613	Podbrezi	
501 161	5018/1610	Dobruska	
501 162	5013/1628	Ricky	
501 165	5013/1656	Urlich	
501 171	5013/1714	Sec	
501 171	5014/1712	Jesenik	
501 172	5016/1724	Zlate Hory (Moravia)	
501 173	5019/1735	Prudnik	
501 174	5012/1749	Glubczyce	
501 174	5015/1743	Bohusov	
501 174	5017/1743	Osoblaha	

501	180	5010/1800	Bauerwitz
501	183	5017/1832	Sosnicowice
501	184	5011/1849	Bujakow
501	184	5011/1846	Ornontowice
501	184	5013/1840	Knurow
501	184	5017/1840	Gliwice
501	184	5019/1847	Zabrze
501	185	5010/1854	Mikolow
501	185	5011/1858	Zarzecze (Slaskie)
501	185	5014/1852	Stara Kuznica
501	185	5015/1855	Kochlowice
501	185	5016/1850	Bielszowice
501	185	5016/1852	Nowa Wies (Katowice)
501	185	5017/1853	Nowy Bytom
501	185	5017/1855	Swietochlowice
501	185	5018/1858	Chorzow
501	185	5019/1855	Lipiny
501	190	5014/1909	Myslowice
501	190	5015/1909	Modrzejow
501	190	5016/1901	Katowice
501	190	5016/1907	Szopienice
501	190	5018/1902	Siemianowice Slaskie
501	190	5019/1906	Czeladz
501	191	5010/1919	Byczyna
501	191	5010/1915	Jelen
501	191	5013/1917	Jaworzno
501	191	5014/1912	Jezor
501	191	5014/1917	Szczakowa
501	191	5016/1911	Dandowka
501	191	5017/1912	Klimontow (Bedzin)
501	191	5017/1915	Niemce
501	191	5017/1914	Pekin
501	191	5018/1915	Grabocin
501	191	5018/1910	Sosnowiec
501	191	5019/1910	Jozefow (Bedzin)
501	191	5019/1917	Strzemieszyce Wielkie
501	192	5010/1929	Trzebinia
501	192	5010/1927	Trzebionka
501	192	5010/1926	Wodna
501	192	5011/1925	Gory Luszowskie
501	192	5011/1929	Myslachowice
501	192	5013/1922	Ciezkowice
501	192	5013/1928	Czyzowka
501	192	5016/1928	Starczynow
501	192	5018/1929	Boleslaw (Katowice)
501	192	5018/1924	Slawkow
501	192	5019/1925	Krzykawka
501	193	5010/1936	Miekinia
501	193	5011/1936	Nowa Gora
501	193	5011/1934	Ostreznica
501	193	5012/1931	Ploki
501	193	5017/1934	Olkusz
501	194	5010/1945	Bedkowice
501	194	5013/1941	Czubrowice
501	195	5010/1956	Gorna Wies
501	195	5010/1953	Korzkiew
501	195	5010/1959	Michalowice
501	195	5011/1959	Zerwana
501	195	5013/1959	Iwanowice (Krakow)
501	195	5013/1950	Ojcow
501	195	5015/1955	Minoga
501	195	5015/1959	Sieciechowice
501	195	5018/1959	Czaple Wielkie
501	195	5018/1957	Czaple Male
501	195	5019/1954	Ulina Wielka
501	200	5010/2000	Maslomiaca
501	200	5012/2007	Tratnowice
501	200	5012/2001	Widoma
501	200	5014/2007	Bronczyce
501	200	5014/2006	Niedzwiedz
501	200	5014/2008	Waganowice
501	200	5015/2006	Slomniki
501	201	5011/2012	Machory
501	201	5012/2018	Proszowice
501	201	5013/2016	Makocice
501	201	5015/2019	Nadzow
501	201	5015/2010	Wierzbica (Miechow)
501	201	5017/2010	Janikowice
501	201	5017/2015	Lelowice
501	201	5018/2011	Dziewiecioly
501	201	5019/2016	Gorka Kosciejowska
501	202	5011/2029	Koczanow
501	202	5011/2025	Plawowice
501	202	5012/2027	Dalechowice
501	202	5014/2020	Klimontow (Jedrzejow)
501	202	5014/2022	Ostrow (Miechow)
501	202	5015/2022	Kadzice
501	202	5015/2028	Odonow
501	202	5015/2027	Skorczow
501	202	5016/2029	Kazimierza Wielka
501	202	5018/2029	Cudzynowice
501	202	5019/2021	Tempoczow
501	203	5010/2034	Koszyce
501	203	5010/2035	Sokolowice
501	203	5010/2039	Wola Przemykowska
501	203	5011/2032	Ksiaznice Male
501	203	5011/2033	Lapszow
501	203	5012/2034	Prokocice
501	203	5013/2035	Dobieslawice
501	203	5013/2038	Morawianki
501	203	5013/2037	Morawiany
501	203	5015/2037	Bejsce
501	203	5015/2032	Stradlice
501	203	5016/2037	Czyzowice
501	203	5016/2037	Grodowice
501	203	5016/2032	Kazimierza Mala
501	203	5017/2037	Charbinowice
501	203	5017/2033	Gabultow

501 204	5010/2046	Miechowice Male
501 204	5010/2049	Pasieka Otfinowska
501 204	5011/2045	Miechowice Wielkie
501 204	5011/2049	Otfinow
501 204	5011/2048	Pierszyce
501 204	5011/2046	Siedliszowice
501 204	5011/2047	Sikorzyce
501 204	5012/2045	Wietrzychowice
501 204	5013/2046	Bieniaszowice
501 204	5013/2044	Deblin
501 204	5013/2045	Paluszyce
501 204	5014/2047	Lubiczko
501 204	5014/2043	Podskale
501 204	5015/2047	Greboszow
501 204	5015/2044	Opatowiec
501 204	5015/2045	Ujscie Jezuickie
501 204	5015/2048	Wola Greboszowska
501 204	5017/2048	Borusowa
501 204	5018/2049	Nowy Korczyn
501 204	5019/2046	Sepichow
501 205	5010/2051	Czyzow
501 205	5010/2059	Dabrowa Tarnowska
501 205	5012/2050	Klyz
501 205	5012/2056	Olesno
501 205	5012/2057	Swarzow
501 205	5013/2052	Pilcza
501 205	5014/2051	Zalipie
501 205	5014/2050	Zelichow
501 205	5015/2057	Dabrowki Brenskie
501 205	5015/2056	Grady
501 205	5015/2055	Skadle
501 205	5016/2050	Hubienice
501 205	5016/2053	Samocice
501 205	5017/2055	Boleslaw (Tarnow)
501 205	5018/2057	Medrzechow
501 205	5018/2059	Wojcina
501 205	5019/2050	Grotniki Duze
501 210	5010/2104	Nieczajna
501 210	5012/2103	Gruszow Wielki
501 210	5012/2107	Radgoszcz
501 210	5012/2100	Zagrody Skalbmierskie
501 210	5015/2103	Radwan
501 210	5016/2106	Brzezowka
501 210	5016/2103	Skrzynka
501 210	5016/2108	Suchy Grunt
501 210	5016/2102	Wolka Medrzechowska
501 210	5018/2104	Szczucin
501 210	5019/2101	Oblekon
501 210	5019/2103	Rataje Slupskie
501 211	5010/2114	Zarowka
501 211	5010/2116	Zdziarzec
501 211	5011/2114	Dulcza Wielka
501 211	5012/2116	Radomysl Wielki
501 211	5012/2116	Wolka Dulecka

501 211	5013/2113	Dulcza Mala
501 211	5013/2117	Partynia
501 211	5014/2117	Zgorsko
501 211	5016/2117	Wadowice Gorne
501 211	5016/2111	Wola Wadowska
501 211	5017/2115	Wadowice Dolne
501 211	5018/2116	Wampierzow
501 211	5019/2116	Bren Osuchowski
501 212	5010/2129	Meciszow
501 212	5011/2123	Laczki Brzeskie
501 212	5012/2128	Przeclaw
501 212	5013/2123	Kadziolki
501 212	5013/2124	Wylow
501 212	5014/2127	Goleszow (Tarnow)
501 212	5014/2128	Kielkow
501 212	5014/2123	Rydzow
501 212	5015/2129	Rzochow
501 212	5016/2125	Podleszany
501 212	5016/2127	Wojslaw
501 212	5017/2125	Mielec
501 212	5017/2125	Ruda (Mielec)
501 212	5017/2122	Wola Mielecka
501 212	5018/2126	Cyranka
501 212	5019/2124	Rzedzianowice
501 212	5019/2121	Trzciana (Mielec)
501 212	5019/2125	Zlotniki (Mielec)
501 213	5012/2132	Dobrynin
501 213	5012/2131	Tuszyma
501 213	5013/2131	Rzemien
501 213	5014/2137	Niwiska
501 213	5016/2134	Biesiadka
501 213	5016/2137	Przylek
501 213	5017/2139	Kosowy
501 213	5018/2139	Ostrowy Tuszowskie
501 213	5019/2139	Ostrowy Baranowskie
501 214	5012/2146	Domatkow
501 214	5012/2143	Wola Domatkowska
501 214	5014/2148	Kolbuszowa Gorna
501 214	5014/2144	Nowa Wies (Kolbuszowa)
501 214	5015/2146	Kolbuszowa
501 214	5016/2145	Dubas
501 214	5017/2141	Trzesowka
501 214	5018/2145	Cmolas
501 215	5012/2153	Widelka
501 215	5013/2152	Klapowka
501 215	5013/2157	Przewrotne
501 215	5015/2150	Werynia
501 215	5016/2159	Ranizow
501 215	5017/2151	Dzikowiec
501 215	5018/2158	Wola Ranizowska
501 215	5019/2150	Poreby Dymarskie
501 220	5010/2208	Medynia Glogowska
501 220	5012/2206	Nienadowka

501	220	5012/2209	Trzebos
501	220	5013/2204	Trzebuska
501	220	5014/2207	Sokolow
501	220	5015/2200	Staniszewskie
501	220	5016/2207	Lukawiec (Rzeszow)
501	220	5016/2205	Mazury
501	220	5016/2203	Zielonka
501	220	5018/2209	Gorno
501	221	5010/2212	Wegliska
501	221	5010/2219	Zolynia
501	221	5012/2217	Brzoza Stadnicka
501	221	5015/2212	Wolka Sokolowska
501	221	5018/2211	Lowisko
501	221	5018/2215	Wola Zarczycka
501	221	5018/2212	Wolka Letowska
501	222	5010/2228	Grodzisko Dolne
501	222	5010/2222	Zmyslowka
501	222	5013/2224	Giedlarowa
501	222	5015/2220	Brzoza Krolewska
501	222	5015/2228	Wierzawice
501	222	5016/2228	Dornbach
501	222	5016/2225	Lezajsk
501	222	5016/2226	Siedlanka
501	222	5017/2226	Stare Miasto (Lwow)
501	222	5018/2222	Jelna
501	222	5018/2228	Kurylowka
501	222	5018/2224	Przychojec
501	222	5019/2221	Ruda (Lancut)
501	223	5010/2237	Dybkow
501	223	5010/2234	Tryncza
501	223	5010/2235	Ubieszyn
501	223	5012/2231	Debno (Przemysl)
501	223	5012/2238	Sieniawa
501	223	5012/2238	Wylewa
501	223	5014/2231	Piskorowice
501	223	5014/2238	Rudka (Jaroslaw)
501	223	5015/2238	Cieplice
501	223	5017/2232	Ozenna
501	223	5019/2238	Luchow Dolny
501	224	5014/2245	Dobcza
501	224	5017/2245	Majdan Sieniawski
501	225	5010/2250	Molodycz
501	225	5012/2253	Milkow
501	225	5014/2258	Dzikow Nowy
501	225	5015/2252	Cewkow
501	225	5015/2256	Dzikow Stary
501	225	5018/2254	Moszczanica
501	225	5019/2258	Obsza
501	225	5019/2255	Wola Obszanska
501	230	5010/2308	Lubaczow
501	230	5010/2300	Oleszyce Stare
501	230	5010/2302	Oleszyce
501	230	5012/2307	Dachnow
501	230	5014/2308	Cieszanow
501	230	5016/2304	Niemstow
501	230	5017/2306	Lubliniec Nowy
501	230	5017/2305	Lubliniec Stary
501	230	5017/2300	Ulazow
501	230	5019/2302	Zamch
501	231	5010/2315	Basnia Gorna
501	231	5011/2314	Basnia Dolna
501	231	5011/2319	Wolka Horyniecka
501	231	5013/2319	Krzywe (Rava Russkaya)
501	231	5013/2318	Podemszczyzna
501	231	5014/2310	Nowe Siolo (Lwow)
501	231	5015/2315	Chotylub
501	231	5017/2310	Zukow
501	231	5018/2319	Lowcza
501	231	5019/2315	Plazow
501	231	5019/2311	Ruda Rozaniecka
501	232	5010/2325	Radruz
501	232	5011/2322	Horyniec
501	232	5013/2329	Aynzingen
501	232	5013/2329	Dziewiecierz
501	232	5014/2320	Brusno Nowe
501	232	5014/2323	Nowiny Horynieckie
501	232	5015/2322	Brusno Stare
501	232	5015/2329	Werchrata
501	232	5017/2328	Mrzyglody
501	232	5018/2324	Wola Wielka
501	233	5010/2337	Monasterek
501	233	5010/2339	Zamek (Lwow)
501	233	5014/2334	Guta Zelena
501	233	5014/2334	Potylich
501	233	5015/2332	Prusie
501	233	5015/2337	Rava Russkaya
501	233	5016/2334	Siedliska (Jaworow)
501	233	5017/2339	Rechki
501	233	5019/2336	Kornie
501	233	5019/2333	Mosty Male
501	234	5011/2340	Staraya Ves Gorby
501	234	5012/2348	Kamennyye Budy
501	234	5014/2342	Hole Rawskie
501	234	5015/2346	Geyche
501	234	5015/2343	Senkovitse
501	234	5016/2348	Gzhenda
501	234	5017/2345	Zaborye
501	235	5011/2352	Bishkiv
501	235	5012/2357	Lyubelya
501	235	5014/2359	Butyny
501	235	5014/2357	Pshistan
501	235	5015/2352	Vulka Mazovetskaya
501	235	5017/2351	Salashe
501	235	5019/2358	Khlevchany
501	240	5010/2406	Boyanets
501	240	5010/2400	Kulyava
501	240	5014/2409	Velikiye Mosty

501	240	5014/2406	Volitsa (Nesterov)	501	261	5014/2616 Novorodchitsy
501	240	5017/2404	Vechorki	501	261	5015/2615 Nieswicz
501	240	5018/2405	Kulichkov	501	261	5015/2612 Peremorovka
501	241	5010/2411	Kupichvolya	501	262	5015/2622 Kunev
501	241	5012/2418	Konstantinuvka (Sarny)	501	262	5018/2629 Mezherichi
501	241	5013/2415	Reklinets	501	262	5018/2622 Novo Malin
501	241	5016/2412	Borove	501	265	5016/2657 Lencin
501	241	5019/2412	Selets (Sokal)	501	265	5018/2652 Slavuta
501	242	5010/2429	Budki Neznanovske	501	270	5010/2708 Sudilkov
501	242	5011/2425	Selets (Radekhov)	501	270	5011/2704 Shepetovka
501	242	5014/2422	Dobrotvor	501	273	5011/2732 Poninka
501	242	5014/2429	Nestanitse	501	274	5018/2740 Baranovka
501	242	5018/2426	Radvantse	501	275	5017/2759 Bykovka
501	242	5019/2429	Novyy Vitkov	501	284	5015/2840 Zhitomir
501	242	5019/2421	Yastshembitsa	501	285	5015/2850 Levkov
501	243	5010/2433	Neznanuv	501	290	5019/2904 Korostyshev
501	243	5012/2437	Dmitrov	501	293	5017/2932 Brusilov
501	243	5013/2432	Babiche	501	301	5011/3019 Vasilkov
501	243	5014/2439	Krzywe (Tarnopol)	501	301	5019/3019 Boyarka
501	243	5014/2433	Uzlovoye	501	302	5015/3026 Roslavichi
501	243	5015/2435	Strzelcza	501	305	5013/3054 Voronkov
501	243	5016/2436	Ganunin	501	312	5019/3128 Berezan
501	243	5017/2439	Radekhov	501	314	5016/3148 Lisnyaki
501	244	5010/2446	Maydan Stary	501	314	5017/3146 Yagotin
501	244	5010/2446	Nivitse	501	323	5015/3231 Piryatin
501	244	5012/2442	Oglyadov	501	324	5015/3246 Makeyevka
501	244	5012/2445	Oplutsko	501	325	5016/3257 Chernukhi
501	244	5014/2445	Mukane	501	330	5011/3304 Gorodishche (Lubny)
501	244	5016/2446	Nemiluv	501	342	5012/3422 Zenkov
501	244	5017/2449	Rudenko Ruske	501	345	5018/3454 Akhtyrka
501	244	5018/2446	Senkuv	501	353	5010/3532 Bogodukhov
501	244	5019/2443	Peratin	501	353	5015/3531 Okhrimovka
501	245	5010/2454	Stanislavchik	501	365	5018/3657 Volchansk
501	245	5011/2457	Bordulyaki	501	380	5014/3808 Valuyki
501	245	5012/2456	Podmanastyrek	501	393	5012/3935 Rossosh
501	245	5013/2451	Lopatin	502	062	5029/0626 Hellenthal
501	245	5015/2450	Khmelno	502	070	5023/0706 Langenfeld (Rhineland)
501	245	5015/2455	Lashkuv	502	071	5020/0713 Mayen
501	245	5017/2452	Batyyuv	502	071	5021/0717 Thur
501	245	5018/2456	Zavidche	502	071	5022/0717 Niedermendig
501	250	5014/2508	Korsov	502	071	5027/0717 Burgbrohl
501	250	5014/2505	Leshnev	502	071	5027/0712 Oberzissen
501	250	5016/2502	Shchurovichi	502	071	5028/0714 Niederzissen
501	252	5015/2529	Tarnavka	502	072	5021/0723 Ochtendung
501	252	5016/2528	Kozin (Kiev)	502	072	5022/0728 Bassenheim
501	252	5016/2528	Kozin	502	072	5023/0729 Karlich
501	254	5012/2540	Bereg (Wolyn)	502	072	5023/0725 Saffig
501	254	5013/2549	Martynovka	502	072	5024/0725 Miesenheim
501	255	5013/2556	Antonovtsy	502	072	5026/0724 Andernach
501	261	5011/2617	Zagreblye	502	072	5026/0728 Neuwied
501	261	5012/2617	Viliya	502	072	5029/0728 Altwied
501	261	5012/2617	Viliya (Ostrog)	502	072	5029/0729 Niederbieber
501	261	5013/2614	Teremno	502	073	5020/0733 Guls
501	261	5014/2610	Andrushovka	502	073	5021/0738 Arzheim

502 073	5021/0736	Koblenz
502 073	5022/0739	Arenberg
502 073	5023/0730	Mulheim (Koblenz)
502 073	5024/0738	Vallendar
502 073	5025/0731	Urmitz
502 073	5026/0735	Bendorf Sayn
502 073	5026/0734	Bendorf
502 073	5028/0739	Sessenbach
502 073	5029/0730	Oberbieber
502 074	5020/0743	Bad Ems
502 074	5020/0746	Dausenau
502 074	5020/0741	Fachbach
502 074	5020/0741	Nievern
502 074	5026/0740	Hohr Grenzhausen
502 074	5028/0748	Wirges
502 075	5021/0754	Holzappel
502 075	5021/0757	Langenscheid
502 075	5024/0754	Isselbach
502 075	5026/0750	Montabaur
502 075	5027/0753	Ruppach
502 080	5021/0803	Flacht
502 080	5022/0801	Diez
502 080	5023/0803	Limburg an der Lahn
502 080	5025/0807	Dehrn
502 080	5027/0803	Hadamar
502 081	5020/0811	Dauborn
502 081	5021/0812	Oberbrechen
502 081	5021/0810	Werschau
502 081	5023/0812	Villmar
502 081	5024/0810	Runkel
502 081	5024/0810	Schadeck
502 081	5027/0810	Schupbach
502 081	5029/0815	Weilburg
502 082	5024/0827	Gravenwiesbach
502 083	5020/0832	Usingen
502 083	5028/0839	Pohl Gons
502 084	5021/0846	Friedberg
502 084	5022/0845	Bad Nauheim
502 084	5022/0849	Beienheim
502 084	5023/0849	Melbach
502 084	5024/0848	Sodel
502 084	5024/0845	Steinfurth
502 084	5025/0841	Nieder Weisel
502 084	5026/0841	Butzbach
502 084	5026/0842	Griedel
502 084	5027/0847	Munzenberg
502 084	5028/0844	Gambach
502 084	5029/0848	Muschenheim
502 085	5020/0857	Nieder Mockstadt
502 085	5020/0855	Staden
502 085	5021/0858	Ober Mockstadt
502 085	5021/0859	Ranstadt
502 085	5022/0851	Weckesheim
502 085	5024/0854	Bisses
502 085	5024/0854	Echzell
502 085	5024/0858	Geiss Nidda
502 085	5026/0852	Berstadt
502 085	5026/0853	Utphe
502 085	5026/0850	Wohnbach
502 085	5027/0850	Bellersheim
502 085	5027/0854	Inheiden
502 085	5027/0850	Obbornhofen
502 085	5028/0854	Hungen
502 090	5020/0901	Stockheim
502 090	5021/0903	Ortenberg
502 090	5022/0907	Usenborn
502 090	5024/0904	Fauerbach Bei Nidda
502 090	5025/0900	Nidda
502 091	5021/0918	Birstein
502 091	5023/0918	Fischborn
502 091	5023/0912	Wenings
502 091	5025/0914	Oberseemen
502 091	5026/0912	Gedern
502 091	5028/0919	Bermuthshain
502 092	5022/0925	Ulmbach
502 092	5025/0928	Hintersteinau
502 092	5026/0920	Lichenroth
502 092	5029/0921	Crainfeld
502 092	5029/0921	Grebenhain
502 092	5029/0923	Nieder Moos
502 093	5020/0935	Vollmerz
502 093	5021/0931	Schluchtern
502 093	5025/0934	Flieden
502 093	5026/0937	Neuhof
502 094	5022/0943	Heubach
502 094	5025/0944	Uttrichshausen
502 094	5027/0947	Schmalnau
502 095	5020/0952	Oberriedenberg
502 095	5027/0957	Gersfeld
502 100	5020/1000	Waldberg
502 100	5023/1000	Haselbach
502 100	5025/1005	Weisbach
502 100	5026/1008	Oberelsbach
502 101	5020/1013	Bad Neustadt an der Saale
502 101	5020/1014	Herschfeld
502 101	5021/1018	Hollstadt
502 101	5022/1011	Lebenhan
502 101	5023/1016	Mittelstreu
502 101	5023/1016	Unsleben
502 101	5023/1013	Wechterswinkel
502 101	5024/1012	Bastheim
502 101	5024/1019	Oberstreu
502 101	5024/1010	Reyersbach
502 101	5025/1011	Unterwaldbehrungen
502 101	5026/1019	Mellrichstadt
502 101	5026/1011	Oberwaldbehrungen
502 101	5028/1013	Ostheim vor der Rhon

502	101	5029/1011	Nordheim vor der Rhon
502	101	5029/1017	Volkershausen
502	102	5020/1026	Aubstadt
502	102	5021/1024	Waltershausen
502	102	5022/1027	Hochheim
502	102	5026/1024	Berkach
502	102	5027/1021	Muhlfeld
502	102	5028/1026	Bibra
502	103	5022/1038	Gleicherwiesen
502	104	5020/1047	Rodach
502	104	5025/1045	Hildburghausen
502	105	5025/1055	Eisfeld
502	111	5021/1119	Rothenkirchen
502	111	5021/1110	Sonneberg
502	111	5024/1113	Judenbach
502	122	5022/1228	Klingenthal
502	122	5029/1222	Falkenstein
502	123	5020/1231	Kraslice
502	123	5022/1238	Prebuz
502	123	5023/1233	Nancy
502	124	5020/1245	Nejdek
502	124	5022/1249	Abertamy
502	124	5022/1247	Pernink
502	124	5024/1249	Bludna
502	125	5022/1255	Jachymov
502	130	5020/1301	Damice
502	130	5022/1305	Boc
502	130	5028/1308	Prisecnice
502	131	5020/1315	Zvonickov
502	131	5023/1316	Kadan
502	131	5025/1316	Prunerov
502	131	5028/1314	Vysluni
502	132	5020/1321	Polaky
502	132	5026/1328	Udlice
502	132	5027/1326	Chomutov
502	132	5027/1323	Sporice
502	133	5020/1331	Libocany
502	133	5020/1339	Strkovice
502	133	5020/1333	Zatec
502	133	5021/1337	Selibice
502	133	5025/1337	Moraveves
502	133	5026/1330	Bilence
502	133	5028/1332	Strupcice
502	133	5029/1338	Velebudice
502	133	5029/1330	Vrskman
502	134	5020/1348	Citoliby
502	134	5020/1341	Mradice
502	134	5021/1348	Louny
502	134	5022/1346	Lenesice
502	134	5022/1342	Postoloprty
502	134	5024/1344	Brvany
502	134	5029/1343	Korozluky
502	134	5029/1349	Merunice
502	134	5029/1340	Vtelno
502	135	5020/1355	Hrivcice
502	135	5020/1358	Peruc
502	135	5027/1350	Libceves
502	135	5027/1355	Solany
502	135	5027/1354	Trebivlice
502	135	5028/1358	Dlazkovice
502	135	5028/1355	Dremcice
502	140	5020/1401	Vrany
502	140	5024/1409	Budyne nad Ohri
502	140	5024/1402	Libochovice
502	140	5026/1401	Klapy
502	140	5027/1407	Rochov
502	140	5029/1402	Cizkovice
502	141	5022/1417	Mnetes
502	141	5024/1415	Klenec
502	141	5025/1415	Roudnice nad Labem
502	141	5027/1410	Doksany
502	141	5028/1414	Hrobce
502	142	5021/1425	Bykev
502	142	5021/1420	Jevineves
502	142	5025/1427	Libechov
502	142	5025/1428	Zelizy
502	142	5027/1423	Steti
502	142	5029/1426	Chcebuz
502	143	5025/1433	Bosyne
502	143	5026/1434	Kokorin
502	143	5027/1438	Mseno
502	143	5029/1433	Strezivojice
502	144	5020/1441	Krpy
502	144	5024/1449	Nimerice
502	144	5025/1449	Petikozly
502	145	5020/1458	Kosorice
502	145	5020/1456	Lustenice
502	145	5022/1457	Dobrovice
502	145	5022/1456	Sycina
502	145	5023/1451	Krnsko
502	145	5024/1450	Strenice
502	145	5025/1454	Mlada Boleslav
502	145	5026/1456	Kosmonosy
502	150	5020/1506	Seletice
502	150	5022/1500	Semcice
502	150	5024/1500	Brezno
502	150	5025/1500	Zidneves
502	150	5026/1508	Dolni Bousov
502	150	5028/1509	Osek
502	150	5029/1508	Podkost
502	151	5020/1516	Kopidlno
502	151	5021/1518	Pseves
502	151	5027/1515	Oharice
502	152	5026/1522	Jicin
502	153	5020/1536	Basnice
502	153	5022/1530	Chomutice
502	153	5022/1538	Horice
502	153	5022/1532	Ostromer

502	153	5022/1531	Sobcice
502	153	5025/1538	Tetin
502	154	5021/1541	Jerice
502	154	5026/1549	Dvur Kralove
502	154	5029/1547	Koclerov
502	154	5029/1543	Souvrat
502	155	5020/1555	Josefov
502	155	5021/1551	Velichovky
502	155	5022/1555	Jaromer
502	160	5021/1607	Krcin
502	160	5024/1603	Ceska Skalice
502	160	5027/1607	Zabrodi
502	160	5029/1606	Cerveny Kostelec
502	161	5020/1610	Nove Mesto nad Metuji
502	161	5020/1619	Sedlonov
502	161	5025/1610	Nachod
502	161	5029/1611	Hronov
502	163	5026/1639	Klodzko
502	165	5021/1653	Ladek Zdroj
502	171	5022/1711	Vidnava
502	173	5023/1739	Biala (Prudnik)
502	173	5029/1736	Korfantow
502	175	5022/1752	Glogowek
502	175	5029/1758	Krapkowice
502	175	5029/1758	Otmet
502	180	5029/1802	Gogolin
502	181	5020/1810	Kozle
502	181	5022/1817	Blachownia Slaska
502	181	5026/1811	Lesnica
502	181	5028/1814	Dolna
502	182	5023/1821	Ujazd
502	183	5025/1834	Paczyna
502	183	5027/1831	Toczek
502	184	5020/1847	Mikulczyce
502	184	5027/1849	Opatowice
502	185	5021/1858	Bytom
502	185	5021/1852	Karb
502	185	5022/1852	Miechowice
502	185	5026/1850	Tarnowice
502	185	5027/1853	Lasowice
502	185	5027/1859	Niezdara
502	185	5027/1852	Tarnowskie Gory
502	190	5020/1909	Bedzin
502	190	5021/1906	Grodziec (Kielce)
502	190	5021/1908	Lagisza
502	190	5021/1906	Nowa Wies (Bedzin)
502	190	5022/1904	Wojkowice Komorne
502	190	5024/1900	Dobieszowice
502	190	5024/1905	Gora Siewierska
502	190	5026/1902	Saczow
502	191	5020/1912	Dabrowa Gornicza
502	191	5021/1914	Golonog
502	191	5023/1915	Bielowizna
502	191	5023/1917	Zabkowice
502	191	5024/1915	Ujejsce
502	191	5025/1919	Chruszczobrod
502	191	5028/1914	Siewierz
502	192	5021/1925	Lazy
502	192	5023/1926	Niegowoniczki
502	192	5026/1927	Rokitno Szlacheckie
502	192	5026/1922	Wysoka
502	192	5028/1923	Turza
502	193	5026/1939	Zlozeniec
502	193	5027/1931	Ogrodzieniec
502	193	5028/1939	Pilica
502	193	5029/1931	Kromolow
502	194	5020/1949	Porabka
502	194	5024/1946	Wolbrom
502	195	5020/1954	Chobedza
502	195	5020/1956	Golcza
502	195	5023/1956	Witowice Gorne
502	195	5023/1956	Witowice
502	195	5024/1957	Miechow Charsznica
502	195	5025/1956	Charsznica
502	195	5027/1950	Chlina
502	195	5027/1953	Jelcza
502	195	5029/1952	Zarnowiec
502	200	5022/2002	Miechow
502	200	5023/2009	Kalina Wielka
502	200	5024/2006	Antolka
502	200	5026/2008	Ksiaz Wielki
502	200	5027/2004	Przybyslawice
502	200	5027/2004	Rogow (Miechow)
502	200	5029/2002	Kozlow (Miechow)
502	200	5029/2000	Przysieka (Krakow)
502	201	5020/2016	Kosciejow
502	201	5020/2019	Rosiejow
502	201	5021/2013	Dale
502	201	5022/2019	Slupow
502	201	5023/2018	Buszkow
502	201	5023/2017	Nieszkow
502	201	5023/2014	Redziny Zabigalskie
502	201	5023/2017	Slaboszow
502	201	5024/2019	Biedrzykowice
502	201	5027/2012	Krzeszowka
502	201	5027/2015	Zaryszyn
502	202	5020/2021	Bronocice
502	202	5020/2029	Ciuslice
502	202	5020/2027	Krepice
502	202	5020/2025	Skalbmierz
502	202	5021/2028	Milawczyce
502	202	5021/2020	Szczotkowice
502	202	5022/2021	Dzialoszyce
502	202	5023/2020	Niewiatrowice
502	202	5025/2022	Dziewieczyce
502	202	5026/2020	Stepocice
502	202	5027/2023	Tomaszow
502	202	5028/2021	Lubcza

502 202	5028/2021	Wechadlow
502 202	5029/2025	Gory (Kielce)
502 203	5020/2032	Cieszkowy
502 203	5020/2038	Miernow
502 203	5022/2032	Kostrzeszyn
502 203	5022/2034	Pelczyska
502 203	5023/2036	Zlota
502 203	5024/2039	Skorocice
502 203	5024/2030	Zawarza
502 203	5025/2030	Byczow
502 203	5026/2034	Chroberz
502 203	5026/2031	Mlodzawy Duze
502 203	5026/2031	Mozgawa
502 203	5028/2037	Marzecin
502 203	5029/2036	Bogucice
502 204	5020/2040	Koniecmosty
502 204	5020/2048	Uciskow
502 204	5021/2047	Badrzychowice
502 204	5021/2042	Goryslawice
502 204	5021/2041	Wislica
502 204	5022/2045	Gorki (Stopnica)
502 204	5022/2047	Piasek Wielki
502 204	5023/2043	Chotel Czerwony
502 204	5024/2046	Bilczow
502 204	5024/2046	Dobrowoda
502 204	5024/2043	Gluzy
502 204	5024/2043	Holudza
502 204	5025/2046	Olganow
502 204	5026/2045	Kawczyce
502 204	5026/2045	Zbludowice
502 204	5027/2047	Peczelice
502 204	5027/2040	Welecz
502 204	5028/2043	Busko Zdroj
502 204	5029/2046	Zbrodzice
502 205	5020/2059	Trzebica
502 205	5023/2059	Biechow
502 205	5023/2050	Piasek Maly
502 205	5023/2057	Piestrzec
502 205	5023/2054	Zborow
502 205	5024/2059	Wojcza
502 205	5026/2057	Stopnica
502 205	5027/2058	Katy Nowe
502 205	5027/2054	Skrobaczow
502 205	5028/2050	Ruczynow
502 210	5020/2103	Kepa Lubawska
502 210	5020/2108	Leka Szczucinska
502 210	5021/2105	Zabiec
502 210	5023/2104	Karsy
502 210	5024/2103	Pacanow
502 210	5025/2107	Beszowa
502 210	5026/2101	Klepie Gorne
502 210	5027/2104	Olesnica (Staszow)
502 210	5028/2105	Sufczyce
502 211	5020/2112	Slupiec
502 211	5020/2114	Ziempniow
502 211	5021/2114	Otalez
502 211	5023/2119	Lysakowek
502 211	5024/2119	Gliny Wielkie
502 211	5025/2119	Gliny Male
502 211	5025/2111	Grabowa
502 211	5025/2112	Przeczow
502 211	5025/2113	Zdzieci
502 211	5026/2117	Polaniec
502 211	5027/2110	Wilkowa
502 212	5021/2127	Chorzelow
502 212	5021/2121	Czermin
502 212	5021/2124	Wola Plawska
502 212	5022/2128	Tuszow Narodowy
502 212	5023/2126	Borki Nizinskie
502 212	5023/2122	Borowa (Mielec)
502 212	5024/2129	Jaslany
502 212	5025/2123	Gawluszowice
502 212	5025/2124	Kliszow
502 212	5025/2126	Mlodochow
502 212	5025/2125	Wola Zdakowska
502 212	5026/2125	Krzemienica (Mielec)
502 212	5027/2125	Niekurza
502 212	5028/2129	Domacyny
502 212	5029/2124	Niekrasow
502 212	5029/2122	Osowek
502 212	5029/2122	Ossala
502 213	5023/2131	Czajkowa
502 213	5024/2132	Babule
502 213	5024/2134	Piechoty
502 213	5025/2136	Durdy
502 213	5025/2132	Zarownie
502 213	5026/2130	Padew
502 213	5027/2130	Wojkow
502 213	5028/2131	Dymitrow Duzy
502 213	5028/2134	Skopanie
502 213	5029/2132	Baranow Sandomierski
502 213	5029/2137	Dabrowica
502 213	5029/2130	Dymitrow Maly
502 213	5029/2132	Osiek
502 214	5023/2147	Brzostowa Gora
502 214	5023/2145	Majdan Krolewski
502 214	5024/2143	Huta Komorowska
502 214	5026/2146	Deba
502 215	5021/2156	Wilcza Wola
502 215	5022/2150	Wola Rusinowska
502 215	5023/2159	Gwozdziec
502 215	5024/2158	Korabina
502 215	5024/2151	Krzatka
502 215	5026/2157	Bojanow
502 215	5027/2159	Stany (Lwow)
502 220	5020/2208	Kamen (Rudnik)
502 220	5020/2201	Nart Nowy
502 220	5021/2204	Cholewiana Gora

502 220 5021/2200 Nart Stary
502 220 5022/2209 Jezowe
502 220 5023/2204 Jata
502 220 5024/2203 Sojkowa
502 220 5024/2204 Zalesie (Nisko)
502 221 5020/2215 Letownia
502 221 5025/2219 Kopki
502 221 5026/2219 Bukowina
502 221 5026/2215 Rudnik
502 221 5027/2218 Bieliny
502 221 5027/2210 Nowosielec
502 221 5028/2216 Bieliniec
502 221 5028/2217 Wolka Bielinska
502 221 5029/2214 Przedzel
502 221 5029/2216 Ulanow
502 222 5020/2229 Kulno
502 222 5021/2225 Lazow (Bilgoraj)
502 222 5021/2221 Sarzyna
502 222 5022/2225 Sigelki
502 222 5023/2220 Koziarnia
502 222 5023/2228 Naklik
502 222 5024/2221 Krzeszow
502 222 5024/2223 Kustrawa
502 222 5025/2226 Jasiennik Stary
502 222 5025/2223 Krzeszow Gorny
502 222 5025/2229 Lipiny Dolne
502 222 5026/2229 Lipiny Gorne
502 222 5028/2226 Kusze
502 222 5029/2228 Derylaki
502 223 5020/2235 Brzyska Wola
502 223 5021/2233 Zagrodki
502 223 5023/2234 Potok Gorny
502 223 5025/2239 Biszcza
502 223 5025/2233 Jedlinki
502 223 5026/2235 Wolka Biska
502 223 5027/2234 Gozd Lipinski
502 223 5029/2239 Ruda Solska
502 224 5020/2242 Luchow Gorny
502 224 5020/2249 Rozaniec
502 224 5021/2240 Jastrzebiec
502 224 5022/2245 Tarnogrod
502 224 5025/2245 Ksiezpol
502 224 5026/2246 Krole Stare
502 224 5026/2244 Markowice
502 224 5029/2240 Wola Dereznianska
502 225 5021/2257 Dorbozy
502 225 5022/2257 Lukowa
502 225 5023/2253 Chmielek
502 225 5023/2252 Szarajowka
502 230 5021/2303 Borowiec
502 230 5027/2308 Nowiny
502 230 5028/2302 Jozefow
502 231 5021/2319 Narol
502 231 5023/2319 Narol Wies

502 231 5025/2312 Susiec
502 231 5026/2310 Oseredek
502 231 5028/2312 Ciotusza
502 231 5028/2310 Majdan Sopocki
502 232 5021/2320 Lipsko (Zamosc)
502 232 5022/2321 Kadlubiska (Lwow)
502 232 5023/2326 Belzec
502 232 5025/2329 Ruda Zelazna
502 232 5026/2329 Ruda Wolowska
502 232 5027/2326 Laszczowka
502 232 5027/2325 Tomaszow Lubelski
502 233 5020/2331 Lubycza Kam
502 233 5020/2331 Lubycza Kniazie
502 233 5020/2332 Lubycza Krolewska
502 233 5020/2334 Teniatyska
502 233 5021/2337 Machnow
502 233 5023/2334 Zurawce
502 233 5025/2338 Chodywance
502 233 5025/2336 Jarczow
502 233 5025/2332 Korchynie
502 233 5028/2333 Klekacze
502 233 5028/2335 Nedezow
502 233 5029/2332 Podhorce (Tomaszow
Lubelski)
502 233 5029/2335 Typin
502 234 5020/2344 Yuzefuvka
502 234 5021/2348 Karuv
502 234 5021/2343 Poddembtse
502 234 5021/2341 Wierzbica (Rava
Ruskayya)
502 234 5022/2345 Ugnev
502 234 5023/2340 Nowosiolki Przednie
502 234 5023/2345 Zastave
502 234 5025/2343 Dyniska
502 234 5025/2348 Tarnoszyn
502 234 5026/2341 Szlatyn
502 234 5027/2348 Ulhowek
502 234 5029/2341 Pieniany
502 234 5029/2341 Podlodow
502 234 5029/2345 Zerniki
502 235 5020/2351 Domashov
502 235 5022/2353 Ostobuzh
502 235 5023/2353 Staye
502 235 5024/2359 Tushkuv
502 235 5026/2357 Budzynin
502 235 5026/2352 Krzewica
502 235 5026/2355 Machnowek
502 235 5026/2359 Oserdow
502 235 5026/2350 Szczepiatyn
502 235 5027/2359 Chlopiatyn
502 235 5028/2356 Przewodow
502 235 5028/2352 Rzeplin
502 235 5029/2359 Zniatyn
502 240 5021/2402 Prusinuv

502 240	5022/2406	Vanyuv	
502 240	5023/2401	Belz	
502 240	5024/2403	Zhuzhel	
502 240	5025/2403	Tsebluv	
502 240	5025/2406	Zhabche Murovane	
502 240	5026/2408	Krasnoselye	
502 240	5026/2404	Vezhbenzh	
502 240	5027/2400	Mycow	
502 240	5028/2406	Leshchkuv	
502 240	5029/2409	Moshkuv	
502 241	5020/2413	Parkhach	
502 241	5020/2418	Volsvin	
502 241	5021/2419	Pozdzimezh	
502 241	5023/2414	Chervonograd	
502 241	5025/2412	Boratyn (Sokal)	
502 241	5025/2414	Dobrochin	
502 241	5028/2410	Savchin	
502 241	5029/2417	Ostrow (Sokal)	
502 241	5029/2417	Sokal	
502 242	5023/2421	Volytsya	
502 242	5024/2424	Zubkuv	
502 242	5028/2424	Tartakov	
502 242	5029/2422	Gorbkuv	
502 243	5020/2433	Sushno	
502 243	5021/2439	Sabinuvka	
502 243	5022/2431	Orduv	
502 243	5022/2439	Stoyanov	
502 243	5023/2433	Zabava	
502 243	5025/2435	Torki (Tartakow)	
502 243	5027/2439	Kvasuv	
502 243	5027/2431	Shpikolosy	
502 243	5028/2434	Bodzyachuv	
502 243	5028/2439	Okhlopov	
502 243	5029/2430	Leshchatuv	
502 244	5020/2442	Tetevchitse	
502 244	5021/2447	Rzhishchev (Wolyn)	
502 244	5026/2441	Druzhkopol	
502 244	5028/2447	Tsekhuv	
502 245	5021/2453	Baryluv	
502 245	5021/2459	Nikolayev (Lwow)	
502 245	5022/2450	Buzhany	
502 245	5023/2453	Pulgany	
502 245	5025/2459	Lobachevka	
502 245	5027/2450	Borochiche	
502 245	5028/2459	Novosyulki Ruske	
502 245	5029/2458	Mysliny	
502 245	5029/2454	Yelizarov	
502 250	5021/2507	Berestechko	
502 251	5020/2513	Ostrow (Dubno)	
502 251	5020/2513	Ostrow (Tarnopol)	
502 251	5024/2510	Peremyl	
502 251	5028/2512	Baremel	
502 252	5022/2523	Volkovyye	
502 252	5025/2520	Demidovka	
502 252	5026/2521	Lishnya (Wolyn)	
502 253	5022/2531	Povcha	
502 253	5029/2532	Smordva	
502 254	5021/2549	Semiduby	
502 254	5025/2545	Dubno	
502 255	5020/2553	Trostyanets (Wolyn)	
502 255	5028/2558	Varkovichi	
502 260	5020/2608	Buderazh	
502 260	5024/2600	Listvin	
502 260	5024/2609	Mizoch	
502 260	5025/2605	Karajewicze	
502 260	5028/2602	Ozeryany (Wolyn Ii)	
502 261	5022/2614	Ustenskoye Pervoye	
502 261	5026/2617	Gulcha Pervaya	
502 261	5026/2619	Mirotyn	
502 263	5020/2631	Ostrog	
502 263	5024/2630	Khorov (Ostrog)	
502 263	5026/2634	Mogilyany	
502 263	5027/2637	Milyatin	
502 263	5027/2639	Pochapka	
502 264	5025/2645	Myczow	
502 264	5029/2641	Sadki (Ostrog)	
502 265	5027/2654	Annopol (Ukraine)	
502 270	5028/2707	Berezdov	
502 271	5024/2711	Krasnostav	
502 281	5028/2816	Chervonoarmeysk	
502 284	5027/2840	Chernyakhov	
502 285	5028/2857	Kamennyy Brod	
502 293	5027/2933	Borovka	
502 294	5028/2949	Makarov	
502 301	5023/3013	Belogorodka	
502 303	5026/3033	Babi Yar	
502 303	5026/3038	Darnitsa	
502 303	5026/3031	Kiyev	
502 303	5027/3035	Nikolskaya	
502 305	5021/3057	Borispol	
502 331	5022/3316	Lokhvitsa	
502 340	5022/3400	Gadyach	
503 063	5033/0633	Kall	
503 063	5034/0630	Gemund	
503 063	5036/0639	Mechernich	
503 063	5037/0639	Kommern	
503 063	5038/0637	Floisdorf	
503 064	5033/0646	Munstereifel	
503 064	5036/0647	Arloff	
503 065	5036/0656	Merzbach	
503 065	5037/0651	Flamersheim	
503 065	5038/0657	Rheinbach	
503 065	5039/0650	Kuchenheim	
503 070	5031/0700	Altenahr	
503 070	5032/0703	Dernau	
503 070	5033/0705	Ahrweiler	
503 070	5033/0708	Bad Neuenahr	
503 070	5035/0702	Gelsdorf	

503 070	5038/0701	Meckenheim
503 071	5033/0718	Leubsdorf
503 071	5033/0715	Sinzig
503 071	5034/0717	Linz am Rhein
503 071	5034/0714	Remagen
503 071	5036/0713	Unkel
503 071	5038/0714	Bad Honnef
503 071	5038/0714	Honnef
503 072	5030/0720	Rheinbrohl
503 072	5033/0725	Waldbreitbach
503 073	5036/0737	Puderbach
503 073	5037/0738	Steimel
503 073	5038/0733	Flammersfeld
503 074	5030/0746	Mogendorf
503 074	5032/0740	Giershofen
503 074	5032/0746	Selters
503 074	5033/0740	Dierdorf
503 074	5033/0747	Maxsain
503 074	5034/0745	Ruckeroth
503 075	5030/0754	Meudt
503 075	5033/0758	Willmenrod
503 075	5034/0759	Westerburg
503 075	5038/0752	Alpenrod
503 075	5039/0750	Hachenburg
503 080	5030/0801	Frickhofen
503 080	5031/0806	Ellar
503 081	5031/0816	Lohnberg
503 081	5031/0811	Merenberg
503 081	5032/0811	Reichenborn
503 082	5030/0825	Bonbaden
503 082	5031/0824	Braunfels
503 082	5036/0828	Asslar
503 083	5031/0837	Hochelheim
503 083	5032/0839	Grossenlinden
503 083	5033/0830	Wetzlar
503 083	5035/0839	Giessen
503 083	5037/0836	Rodheim
503 083	5039/0831	Hohensolms
503 084	5030/0849	Birklar
503 084	5030/0840	Lang Gons
503 084	5031/0840	Leihgestern
503 084	5032/0845	Garbenteich
503 084	5032/0842	Steinberg
503 084	5032/0843	Watzenborn
503 084	5033/0847	Steinbach (Hessen)
503 084	5035/0849	Burkhardsfelden
503 084	5036/0847	Grossen Buseck
503 084	5036/0845	Rodgen
503 084	5036/0842	Wieseck
503 084	5037/0845	Alten Buseck
503 084	5038/0849	Beuern
503 084	5039/0844	Daubringen
503 084	5039/0842	Lollar
503 085	5030/0851	Langsdorf

503 085	5031/0850	Lich
503 085	5033/0859	Laubach
503 085	5036/0850	Reiskirchen
503 085	5039/0854	Geilshausen
503 090	5030/0904	Einartshausen
503 090	5030/0908	Schotten
503 090	5035/0908	Bobenhausen Zwei
503 090	5037/0902	Merlau
503 090	5039/0902	Nieder Ohmen
503 091	5035/0912	Ulrichstein
503 091	5039/0911	Kestrich
503 091	5039/0916	Storndorf
503 092	5033/0921	Herbstein
503 092	5036/0923	Eisenbach
503 092	5038/0924	Lauterbach
503 093	5037/0930	Bad Salzschlirf
503 094	5033/0940	Fulda
503 100	5030/1001	Wustensachsen
503 100	5031/1001	Melperts
503 100	5039/1001	Tann Bei Fulda
503 101	5030/1013	Neustadtles
503 101	5030/1015	Willmars
503 101	5031/1010	Fladungen
503 101	5033/1017	Bettenhausen
503 101	5033/1012	Weimarschmieden
503 101	5036/1012	Aschenhausen
503 101	5037/1010	Kaltensundheim
503 101	5038/1010	Kaltennordheim
503 101	5039/1015	Oepfershausen
503 102	5031/1027	Ritschenhausen
503 102	5033/1025	Meiningen
503 102	5034/1023	Dreissigacker
503 102	5037/1023	Walldorf an der Werra
503 103	5030/1038	Themar
503 103	5033/1034	Marisfeld
503 103	5036/1039	Heinrichs
503 103	5038/1032	Schwarza
503 104	5031/1045	Schleusingen
503 104	5036/1042	Suhl
503 111	5032/1112	Wallendorf
503 115	5039/1159	Zeulenroda
503 120	5030/1208	Plauen
503 121	5037/1218	Reichenbach (Im Saale)
503 121	5039/1212	Greiz
503 122	5032/1225	Rodewisch
503 124	5033/1247	Schwarzenberg
503 130	5030/1302	Vejprty
503 130	5034/1300	Annaberg
503 132	5030/1327	Jirkov
503 133	5031/1332	Ervenice
503 133	5032/1339	Most
503 133	5033/1338	Kopisty
503 133	5036/1337	Horni Litvinov
503 134	5030/1341	Chanov

503 134	5030/1342	Patokryje	
503 134	5032/1348	Bilina	
503 134	5035/1347	Ledvice	
503 134	5036/1345	Duchcov	
503 134	5036/1349	Kremyz	
503 134	5036/1340	Lom U Mostu	
503 134	5038/1347	Hudcov	
503 134	5039/1349	Novosedlice	
503 135	5032/1359	Velemin	
503 135	5035/1358	Zim	
503 135	5036/1357	Rehlovice	
503 135	5037/1358	Stadice	
503 135	5038/1350	Teplice	
503 135	5038/1350	Turn	
503 135	5039/1354	Modlany	
503 135	5039/1357	Vyklice	
503 140	5030/1403	Sulejovice	
503 140	5031/1404	Lovosice	
503 140	5031/1404	Pistany	
503 140	5031/1406	Prosmyky	
503 140	5031/1409	Terezin	
503 140	5031/1405	Zalhostice	
503 140	5032/1408	Litomerice	
503 140	5033/1405	Malic	
503 140	5034/1402	Libochovany	
503 140	5035/1404	Sebuzin	
503 140	5039/1400	Trmice	
503 141	5030/1417	Vrutice	
503 141	5032/1419	Drahobuz	
503 141	5032/1415	Encovany	
503 141	5032/1417	Jisterpy	
503 141	5032/1417	Libinky	
503 141	5033/1411	Trnovany	
503 141	5033/1410	Zitenice	
503 141	5034/1418	Libesice	
503 141	5035/1419	Zimor	
503 141	5036/1419	Habrina	
503 141	5037/1418	Bukovina	
503 142	5030/1420	Hostka	
503 142	5033/1425	Robec	
503 142	5035/1421	Ustek	
503 143	5031/1433	Duba	
503 144	5030/1448	Bela pod Bezdezem	
503 144	5035/1449	Kurivody	
503 144	5039/1444	Mimon	
503 145	5032/1459	Mnichovo Hradiste	
503 145	5035/1456	Rostkov	
503 150	5036/1509	Dalimerice	
503 151	5035/1510	Turnov	
503 151	5038/1515	Zelezny Brod	
503 152	5036/1529	Mricna	
503 152	5036/1520	Podmoklice	
503 153	5031/1530	Stara Paka	
503 153	5031/1534	Vidochov	
503 153	5036/1531	Jilemnice	
503 153	5038/1536	Vrchlabi	
503 154	5031/1549	Pilnikov	
503 154	5033/1544	Hostinne	
503 155	5034/1554	Trutnov	
503 155	5035/1557	Voletiny	
503 155	5039/1554	Zacler	
503 160	5031/1601	Upice	
503 160	5035/1602	Chvalec	
503 160	5039/1608	Libna	
503 161	5032/1614	Police nad Metuji	
503 161	5032/1610	Starkov	
503 161	5034/1611	Javor	
503 161	5037/1615	Mezimesti	
503 161	5038/1616	Ruprechtice	
503 162	5035/1620	Broumov	
503 172	5030/1720	Nysa	
503 181	5031/1818	Strzelce Opolskie	
503 183	5031/1838	Langendorf	
503 183	5031/1838	Wielowies (Katowice)	
503 184	5032/1842	Tworog	
503 185	5035/1851	Drutarnia	
503 185	5038/1853	Prady	
503 190	5030/1906	Zendek	
503 191	5035/1919	Mijaczow	
503 191	5036/1910	Kozieglowy	
503 192	5030/1924	Marciszow	
503 192	5030/1926	Zawiercie	
503 192	5031/1928	Blanowice	
503 192	5033/1922	Mrzyglod	
503 192	5033/1927	Wlodowice	
503 192	5035/1921	Myszkow	
503 192	5037/1925	Jaworznik	
503 192	5038/1923	Przewodziszowice	
503 192	5038/1920	Wysoka Lelowska	
503 192	5038/1923	Zarki	
503 193	5034/1935	Kroczyce Stare	
503 193	5034/1939	Pradla	
503 193	5036/1935	Dzibice	
503 193	5036/1932	Zdow	
503 193	5037/1937	Bodziejowice	
503 194	5032/1949	Brzeziny (Krakow)	
503 194	5037/1945	Grabiec	
503 194	5038/1941	Irzadze	
503 195	5030/1958	Karczowice	
503 195	5031/1951	Lany Wielkie	
503 195	5032/1959	Mstyczow	
503 195	5034/1952	Obiechow	
503 195	5036/1954	Sprowa	
503 195	5038/1950	Szczekociny	
503 195	5039/1958	Lubachowy	
503 195	5039/1956	Moskorzew	
503 200	5030/2000	Marcinowice	
503 200	5030/2005	Norta	

503 200	5031/2008	Brzescie (Miechow)	
503 200	5031/2003	Klimontow (Miechow)	
503 200	5031/2005	Pekoslaw	
503 200	5032/2004	Gniewiecin	
503 200	5034/2003	Podsedziszow	
503 200	5035/2004	Sedziszow (Jedrzejow)	
503 200	5036/2007	Lowinia	
503 200	5037/2009	Deszno (Kielce)	
503 200	5037/2002	Roznica	
503 200	5038/2006	Trzcieniec	
503 200	5039/2002	Jaronowice	
503 200	5039/2008	Nowa Wies (Sedziszow)	
503 200	5039/2006	Rakoszyn	
503 201	5030/2018	Nowa Wies (Jedrzejow)	
503 201	5030/2019	Przyrab	
503 201	5031/2017	Nawarzyce	
503 201	5032/2014	Pokrzywnica	
503 201	5032/2012	Wodzislaw	
503 201	5034/2015	Przyleczek	
503 201	5035/2011	Krzciecice	
503 201	5035/2012	Slaboszowice	
503 201	5036/2014	Potok Maly	
503 201	5036/2014	Potok Wielki (Kielce)	
503 201	5038/2018	Jedrzejow	
503 201	5038/2011	Warzyn	
503 202	5030/2023	Wrocieryz	
503 202	5032/2025	Tur Dolny	
503 202	5032/2025	Tur Piaski	
503 202	5033/2022	Opatkowice Pojalowskie	
503 202	5033/2022	Opatkowice Drewniane	
503 202	5033/2024	Zegartowice	
503 202	5036/2023	Dalechowy	
503 202	5036/2025	Jakubow	
503 202	5038/2024	Lscin	
503 202	5039/2023	Rakow (Jedrzejow)	
503 203	5030/2034	Pasturka	
503 203	5032/2032	Pinczow	
503 203	5033/2039	Szarbkow	
503 203	5034/2031	Umianowice	
503 203	5035/2036	Czechow	
503 203	5035/2038	Samostrzalow	
503 203	5036/2033	Kokot	
503 203	5036/2039	Wola Zydowska	
503 203	5037/2035	Kije	
503 203	5038/2035	Wierzbica (Pinczow)	
503 203	5038/2037	Wloszczowice	
503 204	5031/2046	Slabkowice	
503 204	5031/2041	Szaniec	
503 204	5032/2045	Skorzow	
503 204	5033/2040	Chomentowek	
503 204	5033/2048	Kostera	
503 204	5033/2048	Suskrajowice	
503 204	5034/2044	Mlyny	
503 204	5035/2045	Sladkow Maly	
503 204	5038/2045	Chmielnik	
503 205	5030/2052	Kolaczkowice	
503 205	5032/2059	Grzymala	
503 205	5033/2055	Ruda (Stopnica)	
503 205	5034/2058	Wolica (Stopnica)	
503 205	5035/2057	Grabki Duze	
503 205	5036/2053	Gorzakiew	
503 205	5036/2054	Wola Bokrzycka	
503 205	5037/2051	Gnojno	
503 205	5037/2052	Poreba	
503 210	5030/2102	Niecieslawice	
503 210	5032/2102	Wierzbica (Stopnica)	
503 210	5033/2107	Ziemblice	
503 210	5035/2106	Kurozweki	
503 210	5036/2100	Osowka	
503 210	5036/2100	Szydlow	
503 210	5037/2104	Korytnica (Kielce)	
503 210	5039/2105	Chancza	
503 211	5032/2112	Rytwiany	
503 211	5033/2110	Staszow	
503 211	5034/2112	Golejow	
503 211	5037/2114	Mostki	
503 211	5037/2119	Peclawice	
503 212	5035/2127	Wojcieszyce	
503 212	5036/2127	Bazow	
503 212	5036/2127	Gieraszowice	
503 212	5036/2126	Krolewice	
503 212	5036/2120	Smerdyna	
503 212	5037/2127	Nawodzice	
503 212	5038/2123	Samotnia	
503 213	5030/2135	Suchorzow	
503 213	5031/2137	Nagnajow	
503 213	5032/2136	Chodkow Nowy	
503 213	5032/2130	Zawidza	
503 213	5033/2134	Jasienica (Kielce)	
503 213	5034/2136	Krzcin	
503 213	5034/2133	Skrzypaczowice	
503 213	5035/2135	Koprzywnica	
503 213	5036/2131	Beszyce	
503 213	5036/2130	Skwirzowa	
503 213	5037/2131	Niedrzwice	
503 213	5037/2139	Skotniki (Sandomierz)	
503 213	5037/2136	Sosniczany	
503 213	5037/2130	Zbigniewice	
503 213	5038/2136	Gorzyczany	
503 213	5038/2132	Postronna	
503 213	5039/2139	Samborzec	
503 214	5034/2149	Jeziorko	
503 214	5034/2140	Miechocin	
503 214	5034/2143	Mokrzyszow	
503 214	5034/2140	Radowaz	
503 214	5034/2145	Stale	
503 214	5035/2141	Tarnobrzeg	
503 214	5035/2147	Zupawa	

503 214 5037/2148 Furmany
503 214 5038/2144 Sielec (Tarnobrzeg)
503 214 5038/2145 Wielowies
503 215 5034/2152 Grebow
503 215 5037/2156 Kotowa Wola
503 215 5038/2159 Turbia
503 215 5038/2157 Zbydniow
503 220 5032/2209 Nisko
503 220 5034/2204 Plawo
503 220 5034/2208 Pysznica
503 220 5034/2203 Stalowa Wola
503 220 5035/2203 Rozwadow
503 220 5036/2203 Charzewice
                      (Tarnobrzeg)
503 220 5037/2204 Brandwica
503 220 5037/2206 Jastkowice
503 220 5037/2203 Pilchow
503 220 5039/2202 Kepa Rzeczycka
503 221 5030/2212 Wolina
503 221 5030/2216 Wolka Tanewska
503 221 5031/2210 Raclawice (Lwow)
503 221 5032/2212 Zarzecze (Nisko)
503 221 5033/2215 Huta Deregowska
503 221 5033/2210 Klyzow
503 221 5034/2218 Szyperki
503 221 5037/2217 Domostawa
503 222 5030/2222 Kurzyna
503 222 5030/2222 Rauchersdorf
503 222 5031/2227 Huta Plebanska
503 222 5034/2220 Jarocin (Tarnobrzeg)
503 223 5035/2234 Bukowa (Zamosc)
503 224 5030/2242 Dereznia Solska
503 224 5030/2244 Korczow
503 224 5032/2245 Roznowka
503 224 5032/2242 Rzeczyca
503 224 5033/2242 Bilgoraj
503 224 5036/2248 Dyle
503 224 5036/2245 Rapy Dylanskie
503 224 5039/2243 Katy
503 225 5034/2256 Tereszpol
503 225 5036/2258 Zwierzyniec
503 225 5037/2259 Rudka
503 225 5039/2259 Zurawnica
503 230 5032/2300 Gorecko Stare
503 230 5033/2305 Potok Senderski
503 230 5033/2308 Stanislawow (Bilgoraj)
503 230 5034/2306 Bondyrz
503 230 5036/2307 Blizow
503 230 5037/2302 Obrocz
503 230 5038/2305 Kosobudy
503 231 5032/2318 Majdan Maly
503 231 5033/2312 Krasnobrod
503 231 5034/2316 Hutkow
503 231 5035/2310 Jacnia

503 231 5038/2317 Rachodoszcze
503 231 5038/2310 Szewnia
503 231 5039/2310 Zarzecze (Zamosc)
503 232 5030/2322 Szara Wola
503 232 5031/2325 Skrzypny Ostrow
503 232 5032/2323 Tarnawatka
503 232 5036/2324 Huta Komarowska
503 232 5037/2328 Komarow
503 232 5037/2325 Ksiezostany
503 232 5038/2323 Wolka Labunska
503 232 5039/2322 Labunie
503 233 5032/2337 Grodyslawice
503 233 5032/2333 Rachanie
503 233 5032/2331 Werachanie
503 233 5033/2338 Siemnice
503 233 5034/2334 Wozuczyn
503 233 5034/2330 Zwiartow
503 233 5035/2336 Czartowczyk
503 233 5035/2331 Siemierz
503 233 5036/2334 Kraczew
503 233 5037/2334 Zubowice
503 233 5039/2332 Sniatycze
503 234 5030/2349 Posadow
503 234 5031/2340 Hopkie
503 234 5031/2347 Steniatyn
503 234 5031/2344 Zimno
503 234 5032/2343 Laszczow
503 234 5033/2347 Kmiczyn
503 234 5034/2345 Dobuzek
503 234 5035/2347 Nabroz
503 234 5037/2349 Molozow
503 234 5037/2346 Tuczapy
503 234 5037/2342 Tyszowce
503 235 5030/2352 Lachowce
503 235 5031/2358 Liski (Rava Russkaya)
503 235 5032/2355 Nowosiolki (Tomaszow
Lubelski)
503 235 5032/2351 Telatyn
503 235 5033/2352 Franusin
503 235 5033/2357 Suszow
503 235 5033/2354 Wasylow
503 235 5034/2350 Lykoszyn
503 235 5034/2357 Poturzyn
503 235 5035/2354 Wiszniow
503 235 5035/2359 Witkow
503 235 5035/2355 Wreby
503 235 5036/2351 Stara Wies (Tomaszow
Lubelski)
503 235 5036/2356 Wereszyn
503 235 5039/2355 Mircze
503 240 5030/2401 Hulcze
503 240 5030/2402 Liwcze
503 240 5031/2406 Novo Ukrainka (Lwow)
503 240 5031/2406 Novoukrainka

503	240	5033/2404	Oszczow
503	240	5033/2400	Zabcze
503	240	5034/2406	Dubrovka (Lwow)
503	240	5034/2400	Horoszczyce
503	240	5035/2402	Dolhobyczow
503	240	5038/2405	Holubie
503	240	5038/2406	Pyasechno
503	240	5039/2401	Malkow (Hrubieszow)
503	241	5031/2416	Tselenzh
503	241	5032/2410	Pravda
503	241	5033/2418	Ulvuvek
503	241	5034/2416	Gorodlovitse
503	241	5034/2412	Voyslavitse
503	241	5035/2410	Tudorkovitse
503	241	5035/2416	Zastavne
503	241	5038/2411	Litovizh
503	241	5038/2416	Zabolottsi
503	242	5030/2426	Bobyatyn
503	242	5032/2422	Stenyatin
503	242	5039/2421	Ivanichi
503	243	5030/2437	Pechikhvosty (Wolyn)
503	243	5032/2439	Podberezye
503	243	5033/2432	Sharpantsa
503	243	5034/2434	Milyatyn
503	243	5035/2430	Trubki
503	243	5036/2438	Derechin (Wolyn)
503	243	5038/2433	Rykoviche
503	244	5030/2446	Gorokhov
503	244	5030/2447	Skobelka
503	244	5032/2445	Markoviche
503	244	5036/2446	Kolpytov
503	244	5038/2448	Korytnitsa
503	244	5038/2445	Svinyukhi
503	245	5030/2452	Kholonev
503	245	5030/2454	Zvinyacheye
503	245	5031/2451	Bozhuv
503	245	5032/2453	Tereshkovtsy
503	245	5033/2455	Yadvinuvka
503	245	5037/2455	Bludov
503	245	5037/2453	Umantse
503	245	5039/2459	Skurche
503	250	5032/2502	Senkevichevka
503	250	5034/2500	Shklin
503	250	5037/2506	Charukuv
503	250	5039/2500	Voyutin
503	251	5033/2516	Radomysl (Wolyn)
503	251	5035/2515	Bryszcze
503	251	5035/2515	Wolnianka Mala
503	251	5037/2515	Lavrov
503	252	5032/2521	Krasne (Wolyn)
503	252	5033/2524	Torgovitsa
503	253	5030/2536	Mlinov
503	253	5035/2535	Chopniow
503	255	5031/2557	Zhornuv
503	255	5035/2555	Eleonorowka
503	255	5035/2556	Yanevichi
503	260	5033/2602	Grushvitsy Pervyye
503	260	5036/2604	Dyadkovichi
503	261	5030/2615	Zdolbitsa
503	261	5031/2615	Zdolbunov
503	261	5037/2615	Rovno
503	262	5035/2625	Glinki
503	262	5036/2626	Antopol (Wolyn)
503	262	5038/2622	Gorodishche (Kustyn)
503	263	5030/2638	Tesov
503	263	5033/2632	Bugryn
503	263	5035/2638	Simonov
503	263	5036/2639	Gorbakov
503	263	5039/2631	Goryngrad
503	264	5031/2647	Maykov
503	264	5033/2649	Sennoye
503	264	5034/2644	Kurozvany
503	264	5036/2640	Goshcha
503	265	5030/2654	Dolzhki
503	265	5039/2652	Mezhirichi
503	270	5036/2700	Koryst
503	271	5037/2710	Korets
503	272	5031/2728	Gorki (Wolyn)
503	273	5036/2737	Novograd Volynskiy
503	282	5036/2827	Volodarsk Volynskiy
503	284	5030/2841	Jedrezejow
503	291	5030/2914	Radomyshl
503	295	5039/2956	Borodyanka
503	300	5033/3009	Vorzel
503	300	5035/3001	Klavdiyevo Tarasovo
503	301	5031/3015	Irpen
503	301	5035/3016	Gostomel
503	304	5030/3046	Brovary
503	313	5034/3131	Novaya Basan
503	314	5030/3147	Zgurovka
503	322	5036/3224	Priluki
503	342	5035/3429	Lebedin
503	363	5036/3634	Belgorod
504	060	5046/0606	Aachen
504	060	5049/0608	Wurselen
504	061	5044/0611	Kornelimunster
504	061	5046/0618	Gressenich
504	061	5047/0610	Eilendorf
504	061	5049/0617	Eschweiler
504	061	5049/0619	Weisweiler
504	062	5042/0629	Nideggen
504	062	5044/0629	Udingen
504	062	5044/0627	Untermaubach
504	062	5045/0625	Gey
504	062	5045/0629	Kreuzau
504	062	5046/0629	Lendersdorf
504	062	5047/0627	Gurzenich
504	062	5048/0629	Duren

504 062	5049/0628	Birkesdorf
504 062	5049/0621	Langerwehe
504 063	5040/0639	Sinzenich
504 063	5041/0634	Embken
504 063	5042/0631	Thum
504 063	5042/0639	Zulpich
504 063	5044/0631	Drove
504 063	5044/0636	Vettweiss
504 063	5046/0638	Luxheim
504 063	5048/0639	Norvenich
504 064	5040/0647	Euskirchen
504 064	5043/0648	Lommersum
504 064	5045/0646	Friesheim
504 064	5045/0640	Muddersheim
504 064	5046/0644	Erp
504 064	5048/0647	Lechenich
504 064	5049/0648	Liblar
504 065	5040/0654	Ludendorf
504 065	5043/0655	Heimerzheim
504 065	5046/0657	Waldorf
504 065	5046/0650	Weilerswist
504 065	5047/0657	Sechtem
504 065	5048/0655	Walberberg
504 070	5041/0709	Bad Godesberg
504 070	5044/0701	Alfter
504 070	5044/0708	Beuel
504 070	5044/0706	Bonn
504 070	5045/0700	Roisdorf
504 070	5045/0708	Vilich Rheindorf
504 070	5046/0706	Bergheim (Bonn)
504 070	5046/0700	Bornheim
504 070	5046/0707	Geislar
504 070	5046/0702	Hersel
504 070	5047/0704	Mondorf
504 070	5047/0701	Widdig
504 070	5048/0708	Sieglar
504 071	5040/0718	Agidienberg
504 071	5041/0711	Konigswinter
504 071	5042/0711	Oberdollendorf
504 071	5045/0716	Rott
504 071	5047/0717	Hennef
504 071	5048/0712	Siegburg
504 071	5049/0710	Troisdorf
504 072	5046/0727	Eitorf
504 073	5041/0734	Neitersen
504 073	5042/0739	Altenkirchen
504 073	5043/0738	Busenhausen
504 073	5048/0734	Dattenfeld
504 073	5048/0737	Rosbach
504 074	5041/0743	Oberingelbach
504 074	5046/0740	Hamm
504 074	5047/0745	Wissen
504 075	5047/0753	Betzdorf
504 081	5041/0819	Herborn
504 081	5045/0813	Haiger
504 082	5042/0829	Niederweidbach
504 083	5043/0836	Rollshausen
504 083	5044/0838	Lohra
504 083	5046/0834	Gladenbach
504 083	5047/0837	Frohnhausen
504 084	5040/0844	Mainzlar
504 084	5040/0842	Ruttershausen
504 084	5040/0843	Staufenberg
504 084	5040/0847	Treis an der Lumda
504 084	5044/0849	Ebsdorf
504 084	5044/0849	Leidenhofen
504 084	5048/0841	Elnhausen
504 084	5048/0845	Ockershausen
504 084	5049/0846	Marburg an der Lahn
504 085	5040/0852	Kesselbach
504 085	5040/0852	Londorf
504 085	5041/0850	Allendorf an der Lumda
504 085	5041/0850	Nordeck
504 085	5041/0855	Ruddingshausen
504 085	5045/0853	Rauischholzhausen
504 085	5045/0851	Wittelsberg
504 085	5046/0855	Mardorf
504 085	5046/0858	Schweinsberg
504 085	5047/0859	Niederklein
504 085	5048/0854	Amoneburg
504 085	5049/0858	Kirchhain
504 090	5044/0900	Homberg Kassel
504 090	5044/0900	Homberg
504 090	5045/0908	Obergleen
504 090	5046/0907	Kirtorf
504 091	5043/0913	Romrod
504 091	5045/0916	Alsfeld
504 091	5046/0912	Angenrod
504 092	5045/0928	Grebenau
504 092	5046/0921	Berfa
504 092	5048/0923	Ottrau
504 093	5040/0934	Schlitz
504 093	5043/0938	Langenschwarz
504 093	5046/0931	Breitenbach am Herzberg
504 093	5048/0936	Niederaula
504 094	5040/0946	Hunfeld
504 094	5040/0948	Mackenzell
504 094	5042/0943	Burghaun
504 094	5045/0941	Rhina
504 094	5046/0948	Eiterfeld
504 094	5047/0940	Holzheim
504 094	5048/0947	Erdmannrode
504 095	5043/0958	Geisa
504 095	5047/0955	Mansbach
504 095	5049/0951	Schenklengsfeld
504 100	5043/1007	Unteralba
504 100	5045/1005	Gehaus

504	100	5047/1008	Stadtlengsfeld
504	101	5042/1013	Rossdorf
504	101	5048/1018	Barchfeld
504	101	5049/1014	Bad Salzungen
504	102	5043/1027	Schmalkalden
504	104	5046/1044	Schwarzwald
504	104	5049/1044	Ohrdruf
504	105	5041/1054	Ilmenau
504	105	5042/1051	Elgersburg
504	105	5047/1054	Plaue
504	112	5043/1120	Rudolstadt
504	113	5042/1136	Possneck
504	114	5041/1149	Mossbach
504	122	5049/1223	Crimmitschau
504	123	5044/1230	Zwickau
504	123	5049/1232	Glauchau
504	125	5049/1251	Siegmarschonau
504	130	5049/1304	Erdmannsdorf
504	132	5040/1320	Olbernhau
504	133	5043/1339	Moldava nad Bodvou
504	134	5040/1343	Hrob
504	134	5040/1346	Mstisov
504	134	5041/1349	Behanky
504	134	5041/1347	Dubi
504	135	5040/1359	Predlice
504	135	5040/1352	Sobedruhy
504	135	5041/1356	Chabarovice
504	135	5041/1350	Pritkov
504	140	5040/1409	Nestedice
504	140	5040/1406	Nestemice
504	140	5040/1403	Stribrniky
504	140	5040/1402	Usti nad Labem
504	140	5042/1404	Libov
504	140	5046/1402	Libouchec
504	141	5040/1410	Povrly
504	141	5044/1419	Benesov nad Ploucnici
504	141	5047/1413	Decin
504	143	5041/1433	Ceska Lipa
504	143	5041/1439	Zakupy
504	143	5047/1438	Cvikov
504	144	5040/1440	Bohatice
504	144	5043/1443	Hlemyzdi
504	144	5046/1447	Jablonne v Podjestedi
504	144	5047/1445	Lada
504	144	5048/1449	Rynoltice
504	145	5042/1455	Osecna
504	145	5048/1459	Machnin
504	145	5049/1459	Chrastava
504	150	5042/1507	Radlo
504	150	5044/1509	Rynovice
504	150	5046/1502	Ruzodol
504	150	5046/1506	Stary Harcov
504	150	5047/1503	Liberec
504	151	5043/1511	Jablonec nad Nisou
504	151	5044/1514	Smrzovka
504	151	5044/1518	Tanvald
504	152	5046/1520	Polubny
504	153	5044/1537	Spindleruv Mlyn
504	155	5040/1557	Lampertice
504	160	5047/1602	Kamienna Gora
504	161	5040/1611	Mieroszow
504	161	5046/1617	Walbrzych
504	161	5047/1615	Weisstein
504	163	5043/1639	Dzierzoniow
504	165	5041/1651	Niemcza
504	170	5047/1704	Strzelin
504	171	5046/1717	Bakow
504	171	5049/1712	Wiazow
504	172	5042/1723	Grodkow
504	173	5045/1737	Lewin Brzeski
504	175	5040/1757	Opole
504	182	5044/1827	Dobrodzien
504	184	5040/1842	Biala Opolskie
504	184	5040/1841	Lubliniec
504	184	5048/1844	Kamiensko
504	185	5040/1856	Boronow
504	185	5040/1850	Cieszowa
504	185	5049/1851	Weglowice
504	190	5041/1909	Kamienica Polska
504	190	5044/1901	Konopiska
504	190	5046/1905	Dzbow
504	190	5048/1907	Czestochowa
504	190	5048/1903	Gnaszyn Dolny
504	191	5040/1913	Poraj
504	191	5044/1910	Nowa Wies (Czestochowa)
504	191	5045/1916	Olsztyn (Kielce)
504	192	5040/1929	Postaszowice
504	192	5043/1927	Zloty Potok
504	192	5044/1927	Janow (Czestochowa)
504	192	5044/1920	Zrebice
504	192	5048/1920	Malusy Wielkie
504	192	5049/1924	Mokrzesz
504	193	5040/1930	Mzurow
504	193	5041/1937	Lelow
504	193	5044/1938	Drochlin
504	193	5045/1939	Przysieka
504	193	5048/1931	Przyrow
504	194	5042/1940	Biala Wielka
504	194	5043/1942	Grodek (Kielce)
504	194	5044/1948	Kluczyce
504	194	5047/1941	Koniecpol
504	194	5048/1943	Teresow
504	195	5041/1958	Chlewska Wola
504	195	5041/1951	Druzykowa
504	195	5043/1954	Czaryz
504	195	5043/1958	Dzierzgow
504	195	5045/1957	Krzepin

504	195	5046/1950	Secemin
504	195	5049/1956	Czarnca
504	200	5040/2001	Chlewice
504	200	5040/2005	Slecin
504	200	5040/2009	Zdanowice
504	200	5041/2001	Kwilina
504	200	5041/2007	Naglowice
504	200	5043/2002	Kossow (Kielce)
504	200	5044/2007	Oksa
504	200	5044/2002	Podlazie
504	200	5045/2004	Rzeszowek
504	200	5047/2004	Ogarka
504	200	5047/2008	Zalesie (Jedrzejow)
504	200	5048/2003	Konieczno
504	201	5041/2014	Chorzewa
504	201	5045/2013	Kanice Stare
504	201	5045/2017	Lipnica (Kielce)
504	201	5046/2018	Rembieszyce
504	201	5046/2011	Wegleszyn
504	201	5048/2011	Lasochow
504	201	5049/2017	Malogoszcz
504	202	5042/2022	Mnichow
504	202	5042/2028	Sobkow
504	202	5043/2022	Miasowa
504	202	5046/2029	Wolica
504	202	5048/2027	Checiny
504	203	5040/2035	Obice
504	203	5042/2033	Chmielowice
504	203	5042/2035	Drochow Dolny
504	203	5044/2036	Debska Wola
504	203	5044/2038	Wola Morawicka
504	203	5045/2038	Morawica
504	203	5049/2034	Sitkowka
504	204	5040/2041	Piotrkowice
504	204	5041/2040	Lisow
504	204	5041/2044	Maleszowa
504	204	5042/2047	Pierzchnianka
504	204	5043/2043	Gorki (Kielce)
504	204	5046/2043	Marzysz
504	204	5049/2048	Daleszyce
504	205	5040/2051	Drugnia
504	205	5041/2059	Drogowle
504	205	5044/2056	Korzenno
504	205	5045/2059	Ocieseki
504	205	5046/2056	Widelki
504	205	5049/2058	Makoszyn
504	205	5049/2054	Napekow
504	210	5041/2103	Rakow
504	210	5042/2108	Pulaczow
504	210	5042/2106	Szumsko
504	210	5044/2102	Kolonia Bardo Dolne
504	210	5044/2109	Melonek
504	210	5044/2107	Zbelutka
504	210	5047/2105	Lagow
504	210	5048/2101	Lechowek
504	210	5049/2101	Lechow
504	210	5049/2105	Wola Zamkowa
504	211	5040/2116	Bogoria
504	211	5041/2115	Gorzkow (Kielce)
504	211	5041/2119	Szczeglice
504	211	5042/2110	Lagowica Nowa
504	211	5042/2116	Lopatno
504	211	5044/2117	Iwaniska
504	211	5044/2111	Jastrzebska Wola
504	211	5048/2114	Backowice
504	211	5048/2110	Piorkow
504	211	5048/2116	Stanislawow (Opatow)
504	211	5049/2112	Nieskurzow Stary
504	211	5049/2115	Olszownica
504	212	5040/2126	Gorki (Sandomierz)
504	212	5040/2127	Klimontow
504	212	5040/2128	Pechow
504	212	5040/2123	Ulanowice
504	212	5043/2121	Boduszow
504	212	5043/2123	Mydlow
504	212	5044/2123	Mydlowiec
504	212	5047/2126	Oficjalow
504	212	5048/2126	Opatow
504	213	5040/2138	Smiechowice
504	213	5041/2132	Jugoszow
504	213	5041/2132	Naslawice
504	213	5042/2139	Obrazow
504	213	5042/2136	Wegrce
504	213	5043/2135	Swiecica
504	213	5044/2134	Miedzygorz
504	213	5045/2132	Slaboszewice
504	213	5045/2138	Tulkowice
504	213	5046/2131	Malice Koscielne
504	213	5047/2130	Nikisialka Duza
504	213	5047/2130	Nikisialka Mala
504	213	5049/2135	Stodoly
504	214	5040/2142	Andruszkowice
504	214	5040/2146	Nadbrzezie
504	214	5040/2147	Trzesn
504	214	5040/2144	Zawiselcze
504	214	5041/2145	Nowa Wies (Sandomierz)
504	214	5041/2145	Sandomierz
504	214	5042/2140	Lenarczyce
504	214	5043/2149	Msciow
504	214	5043/2140	Wieprzki
504	214	5044/2147	Dwikozy
504	214	5044/2145	Kichary
504	214	5046/2149	Slupcza
504	215	5040/2156	Berdechow
504	215	5040/2151	Gorzyce (Tarnobrzeg)
504	215	5040/2151	Motycze Poduchowne
504	215	5041/2157	Radomysl (Nad Sanem)

504 215	5041/2155	Skowierzyn
504 215	5043/2151	Wrzawy
504 215	5045/2154	Antoniow
504 215	5045/2153	Orzechow
504 215	5046/2154	Chwalowice
504 215	5048/2151	Zawichost
504 220	5046/2207	Zaklikow
504 220	5047/2207	Zdziechowice
504 220	5048/2203	Baraki
504 220	5049/2207	Weglin
504 221	5046/2211	Lysakow
504 221	5046/2217	Stojeszyn
504 221	5047/2213	Potok Wielki (Lublin)
504 221	5048/2211	Osinki
504 221	5048/2213	Radwanowka
504 221	5048/2218	Zarajec
504 221	5049/2218	Huta Jozefow
504 222	5043/2223	Borownica
504 222	5043/2225	Janow Lubelski
504 222	5045/2220	Modliborzyce
504 222	5046/2226	Andrzejow (Lublin)
504 222	5048/2225	Wierzchowiska
504 223	5041/2237	Kocudza Dolna
504 223	5043/2233	Branewka
504 223	5047/2237	Chrzanow (Janow Lubelski)
504 223	5049/2235	Otrocz
504 223	5049/2232	Zdzilowice
504 224	5040/2247	Smoryn
504 224	5041/2240	Frampol
504 224	5042/2241	Radziecin
504 224	5043/2240	Goraj Lubelski
504 224	5046/2249	Zaporze
504 224	5048/2249	Czerniecin
504 225	5042/2258	Szczebrzeszyn
504 225	5044/2250	Latyczyn
504 225	5045/2252	Mokrelipie
504 225	5045/2250	Radecznica
504 225	5045/2253	Sasiadka
504 225	5046/2258	Sulow
504 225	5046/2251	Zaklodzie
504 225	5047/2254	Sulowiec
504 225	5047/2256	Tworyczow
504 225	5048/2256	Kitow
504 230	5044/2302	Klemensow
504 230	5046/2301	Deszkowice
504 230	5048/2306	Krzak
504 230	5048/2303	Nielisz
504 230	5049/2309	Nowa Wies (Krasnystaw)
504 230	5049/2307	Ruskie Piaski
504 230	5049/2301	Staw Noakowski
504 230	5049/2306	Wolka Nieliska
504 231	5042/2319	Wolka Panienska
504 231	5043/2315	Zamosc
504 231	5044/2314	Hyza
504 231	5044/2311	Ploskie
504 231	5045/2312	Wysokie (Zamosc)
504 231	5046/2315	Sitaniec
504 231	5048/2310	Chomeciska Duze
504 231	5048/2317	Udrycze
504 231	5049/2316	Wislowiec
504 232	5040/2320	Ruszow
504 232	5041/2322	Barchaczow
504 232	5041/2321	Labunki
504 232	5044/2325	Wolka Horyszowska
504 232	5045/2325	Horyszow Polski
504 232	5045/2323	Sitno
504 232	5049/2326	Szorcowka
504 233	5040/2331	Kadlubiska (Lublin)
504 233	5041/2339	Kazimierowka
504 233	5042/2331	Niewirkow
504 233	5043/2335	Kotlice
504 233	5044/2337	Koniuchy
504 233	5045/2337	Horyszow Ruski
504 233	5045/2330	Miaczyn
504 233	5045/2333	Zawalow
504 233	5047/2339	Gdeszyn
504 233	5049/2335	Danczypol
504 233	5049/2330	Szczelatyn
504 234	5040/2342	Czermno
504 234	5040/2344	Turkowice
504 234	5041/2348	Sahryn
504 234	5041/2342	Wakijow
504 234	5041/2345	Wronowice
504 234	5044/2340	Lotow
504 234	5044/2349	Terebin
504 234	5045/2342	Hostynne
504 234	5045/2342	Konopne
504 234	5045/2346	Werbkowice
504 234	5048/2344	Bohutycze
504 234	5049/2342	Molodziatycze
504 235	5041/2354	Modryn
504 235	5041/2359	Szychowice
504 235	5043/2359	Cichoburz
504 235	5044/2357	Mieniany
504 235	5046/2355	Czerniczyn
504 235	5048/2355	Hrubieszow
504 235	5048/2350	Obrowiec
504 240	5041/2404	Krylow
504 240	5041/2404	Prehoryle
504 240	5045/2405	Poromuv
504 240	5046/2400	Ambukuv
504 240	5046/2401	Slipcze
504 240	5047/2406	Bortnuv
504 240	5047/2404	Tsutsnyuv
504 240	5048/2403	Ludin
504 241	5041/2415	Grybovitsa

504	241	5041/2411	Lishnya
504	241	5045/2412	Niskenichi
504	241	5046/2410	Verkhnov
504	241	5048/2411	Laskuv
504	242	5041/2420	Myshev
504	242	5041/2427	Orishche
504	242	5043/2423	Markostav
504	242	5046/2423	Selets (Wolyn)
504	242	5048/2428	Khmelyuv
504	242	5049/2427	Khobultova
504	243	5042/2439	Goruv
504	243	5044/2439	Lokachi
504	243	5044/2433	Zamliche
504	243	5047/2434	Yakoviche
504	243	5049/2439	Gubin
504	244	5042/2443	Zayenchitse
504	244	5043/2441	Kozluv
504	244	5043/2447	Shelvov
504	244	5045/2440	Krukhinichi
504	244	5047/2440	Voynitsa
504	245	5040/2453	Vatyn
504	245	5042/2459	Belostok
504	245	5042/2456	Sadov
504	245	5045/2456	Okorsk
504	250	5040/2507	Korshev (Wolyn)
504	250	5041/2506	Oderady
504	250	5046/2500	Torchin
504	250	5046/2505	Usichi
504	250	5047/2507	Shepel
504	251	5042/2516	Gorodishche (Charukuv)
504	252	5045/2520	Lutsk
504	253	5040/2533	Ostrozhets
504	253	5046/2531	Poddubtsy
504	254	5043/2549	Olyka
504	255	5045/2559	Klevan
504	260	5042/2601	Shubkov
504	261	5040/2616	Shpanov
504	261	5041/2611	Gorodok (Rovno)
504	262	5043/2626	Kozlin
504	262	5045/2625	Wolosza
504	263	5042/2634	Tuchin
504	263	5048/2630	Antonuvka
504	263	5049/2638	Male Sedlishche
504	264	5049/2649	Grushevka
504	265	5041/2657	Koloverti
504	265	5045/2653	Solpa Mala
504	270	5040/2700	Danichuv
504	270	5047/2709	Dermanka
504	271	5041/2719	Sukhovolya (Wolyn)
504	271	5044/2716	Storozhov
504	271	5048/2719	Gorodnitsa
504	280	5043/2801	Barashi
504	291	5046/2914	Malin
504	293	5041/2939	Peskovka
504	301	5047/3018	Dymer
504	332	5045/3328	Romny
504	341	5042/3416	Grun
504	390	5049/3900	Ostrogorsk
505	060	5050/0603	Bank
505	060	5050/0606	Kohlscheid
505	060	5051/0607	Bardenberg
505	060	5052/0606	Herzogenrath
505	060	5058/0609	Geilenkirchen
505	060	5059/0600	Gangelt
505	061	5052/0614	Langweiler
505	061	5053/0610	Alsdorf
505	061	5054/0615	Durboslar
505	061	5055/0619	Koslar
505	061	5057/0618	Barmen
505	061	5057/0610	Immendorf
505	061	5059/0616	Linnich
505	062	5051/0625	Merken
505	062	5056/0622	Julich
505	062	5058/0620	Boslar
505	062	5058/0627	Rodingen
505	062	5059/0621	Hompesch
505	062	5059/0622	Muntz
505	063	5050/0630	Arnoldsweiler
505	063	5051/0638	Blatzheim
505	063	5055/0635	Berrendorf
505	063	5056/0633	Angelsdorf
505	063	5057/0637	Zieverich
505	063	5058/0639	Bergheim
505	063	5058/0635	Glesch
505	064	5050/0644	Gymnich
505	064	5052/0641	Kerpen
505	064	5055/0649	Frechen
505	064	5055/0642	Horrem
505	064	5056/0642	Quadrath Ichendorf
505	064	5057/0640	Kenten
505	064	5059/0644	Fliesteden
505	065	5050/0654	Bruhl
505	065	5050/0659	Wesseling
505	065	5052/0652	Hurth
505	065	5052/0658	Rondorf
505	065	5053/0656	Hochkirchen
505	065	5056/0657	Koln Deutz
505	065	5056/0657	Koln Mulheim
505	065	5056/0657	Koln
505	070	5052/0703	Zundorf
505	070	5053/0703	Porz
505	070	5053/0705	Urbach
505	070	5059/0708	Bergisch Gladbach
505	071	5058/0710	Bensberg
505	072	5051/0729	Ruppichteroth
505	072	5055/0724	Much
505	073	5051/0731	Benroth

505 073	5052/0735	Hoff	
505 073	5054/0733	Numbrecht	
505 074	5059/0745	Husten	
505 075	5050/0759	Eiserfeld	
505 080	5052/0802	Siegen	
505 080	5055/0802	Geisweid	
505 080	5055/0806	Netphen	
505 080	5058/0800	Ferndorf	
505 080	5059/0806	Hilchenbach	
505 081	5059/0816	Erndtebruck	
505 082	5053/0828	Breidenbach	
505 082	5056/0824	Laasphe	
505 082	5056/0828	Wallau	
505 083	5053/0836	Buchenau	
505 083	5057/0839	Oberasphe	
505 083	5059/0837	Laisa	
505 084	5050/0845	Wehrda	
505 084	5051/0849	Burgeln	
505 084	5051/0840	Caldern	
505 084	5051/0842	Sterzhausen	
505 084	5052/0844	Gossfelden	
505 084	5054/0843	Wetter	
505 084	5059/0844	Ernsthausen	
505 085	5051/0850	Betziesdorf	
505 085	5053/0855	Rauschenberg	
505 085	5053/0850	Schonstadt	
505 085	5053/0859	Wolferode	
505 085	5054/0851	Banfe	
505 085	5055/0857	Halsdorf	
505 085	5056/0857	Wohra	
505 085	5057/0859	Schiffelbach	
505 085	5058/0858	Gemunden an der Wohra	
505 085	5058/0853	Rosenthal	
505 090	5051/0901	Erksdorf	
505 090	5051/0907	Neustadt in Hessen	
505 090	5052/0906	Momberg	
505 090	5052/0903	Speckswinkel	
505 090	5053/0901	Hatzbach	
505 090	5054/0900	Josbach	
505 090	5057/0904	Gilserberg	
505 091	5050/0917	Schrecksbach	
505 091	5051/0912	Willingshausen	
505 091	5055/0912	Treysa	
505 091	5055/0915	Ziegenhain	
505 091	5056/0911	Rommershausen	
505 091	5059/0912	Waltersbruck	
505 092	5051/0928	Oberaula	
505 092	5052/0920	Neukirchen	
505 092	5055/0927	Schwarzenborn	
505 092	5056/0922	Grossropperhausen	
505 092	5059/0920	Frielendorf	
505 093	5056/0933	Muhlbach	
505 094	5052/0942	Bad Hersfeld	

505 094	5058/0948	Bebra	
505 094	5059/0943	Rotenburg	
505 095	5050/0955	Ausbach	
505 095	5058/0952	Iba	
505 100	5050/1001	Vacha	
505 100	5059/1001	Richelsdorf	
505 101	5059/1019	Eisenach	
505 103	5053/1031	Tabarz	
505 104	5057/1043	Gotha	
505 105	5050/1057	Arnstadt	
505 110	5059/1102	Erfurt	
505 111	5059/1119	Weimar	
505 113	5056/1135	Jena	
505 113	5057/1139	Laasan	
505 120	5052/1205	Gera	
505 120	5058/1204	Lessen	
505 122	5051/1228	Meerane	
505 122	5059/1227	Altenburg	
505 125	5050/1255	Karlmarxstadt	
505 125	5059/1259	Mittweida	
505 133	5057/1337	Lubau	
505 134	5051/1341	Schmiedeberg	
505 134	5057/1347	Saida	
505 135	5052/1352	Liebstadt	
505 135	5058/1356	Pirna	
505 141	5058/1417	Sebnitz	
505 142	5052/1429	Chribska	
505 142	5057/1422	Mikulasovice	
505 143	5052/1430	Rybniste	
505 143	5054/1431	Krasna Lipa	
505 143	5055/1437	Varnsdorf	
505 143	5057/1434	Rumburk	
505 143	5059/1435	Jirikov	
505 144	5050/1442	Krompach	
505 144	5053/1446	Olbersdorf	
505 145	5054/1450	Zittau	
505 150	5054/1508	Raspenava	
505 150	5055/1505	Frydlant	
505 154	5054/1544	Jelenia Gora	
505 160	5055/1606	Bolkenhain	
505 162	5052/1620	Swiebodzice	
505 162	5055/1628	Jaworzyna Slaska	
505 162	5058/1621	Strzegom	
505 163	5051/1630	Swidnica	
505 164	5053/1645	Sobotka	
505 171	5058/1718	Olawa	
505 172	5052/1727	Brzeg	
505 175	5055/1750	Pokoj	
505 181	5059/1813	Kluczbork	
505 183	5051/1839	Wezina	
505 183	5052/1838	Stany (Kielce)	
505 184	5051/1842	Kostrzyna	
505 184	5051/1848	Kuleje	
505 184	5053/1843	Bagna	

505	184	5053/1845	Panki
505	184	5053/1842	Przystajn
505	184	5055/1845	Osiakow
505	184	5058/1844	Krzepice
505	185	5050/1851	Bor Zapilski
505	185	5051/1856	Wreczyca Wielka
505	185	5052/1850	Truskolasy
505	185	5053/1859	Libidza
505	185	5053/1852	Puszczew
505	185	5054/1856	Klobuck
505	185	5057/1852	Wilkowiecko
505	185	5059/1859	Miedzno
505	190	5055/1902	Kamyk
505	190	5055/1909	Radostkow
505	190	5056/1906	Kocin Nowy
505	190	5056/1900	Lobodno
505	190	5057/1907	Kocin Stary
505	190	5058/1901	Debnik
505	190	5059/1904	Ostrowy
505	191	5050/1918	Mstow
505	191	5051/1911	Wyczerpy Dolne
505	191	5053/1915	Rudniki (Czestochowa)
505	192	5050/1920	Klobukowice
505	192	5053/1928	Garnek
505	192	5053/1925	Rzeki Male
505	192	5053/1925	Rzeki Wielkie
505	192	5054/1924	Pacierzow
505	192	5054/1920	Rzerzeczyce
505	192	5055/1921	Aurelow
505	192	5055/1923	Bartkowice
505	192	5056/1922	Klomnice
505	192	5058/1929	Gidle
505	192	5059/1928	Plawno
505	193	5050/1939	Labedz
505	193	5053/1937	Sekursko
505	193	5054/1935	Cieletniki
505	193	5055/1938	Bugaj
505	194	5055/1948	Maluszyn
505	194	5056/1947	Barycz
505	194	5056/1942	Silnica Wielka
505	194	5056/1946	Silniczka
505	194	5057/1949	Wola Zycinska
505	195	5052/1958	Wloszczowa
505	195	5053/1953	Kurzelow
505	195	5057/1952	Ciemietniki
505	195	5059/1958	Zalesie (Wloszczowa)
505	200	5050/2004	Rzabiec
505	200	5050/2000	Wola Wisniowa
505	200	5051/2007	Ludynia
505	200	5054/2007	Krasocin
505	200	5055/2008	Podlesko
505	200	5056/2002	Kozia Wies
505	200	5057/2003	Oleszno
505	201	5052/2016	Gniezdziska
505	201	5052/2013	Skorkow
505	201	5052/2012	Wystepy
505	201	5055/2012	Mieczyn
505	201	5056/2016	Eustachow
505	201	5056/2014	Jedle
505	201	5057/2015	Lopuszno
505	201	5057/2019	Snochowice
505	201	5059/2012	Mnin
505	202	5050/2022	Miedzianka
505	202	5052/2025	Rykoszyn
505	202	5053/2028	Piekoszow
505	202	5056/2021	Korczyn
505	202	5057/2025	Strawczyn
505	202	5058/2026	Niedzwiedz (Kielce)
505	202	5059/2020	Dobrzeszow
505	202	5059/2021	Kuzniaki
505	202	5059/2022	Wolka Klucka
505	203	5051/2034	Bialogon
505	203	5053/2032	Gorki Szczukowskie
505	203	5053/2039	Szydlowek
505	203	5054/2031	Szczukowice
505	203	5056/2030	Chelmce
505	203	5058/2035	Tumlin
505	203	5059/2037	Samsonow
505	203	5059/2034	Umer
505	204	5050/2047	Brzechow
505	204	5050/2040	Kielce
505	204	5050/2040	Piotrowice (Kielce)
505	204	5052/2048	Beczkow
505	204	5052/2044	Cedzyna
505	204	5052/2046	Radlin
505	204	5054/2043	Maslow
505	204	5055/2041	Dabrowa (Kielce)
505	204	5059/2047	Laczna
505	204	5059/2041	Zagnansk
505	205	5050/2053	Skorzeszyce
505	205	5051/2055	Bieliny Kapitulne
505	205	5051/2052	Wola Jachowa
505	205	5052/2054	Porabki
505	205	5053/2051	Krajno
505	205	5054/2058	Wola Szczygielkowa
505	205	5056/2053	Psary (Kielce)
505	205	5057/2058	Bodzentyn
505	205	5058/2053	Wzdol
505	210	5052/2106	Slupia Nowa
505	210	5052/2103	Swiety Krzyz
505	210	5053/2102	Mirocice
505	210	5054/2100	Debno (Kielce)
505	210	5056/2107	Chybice
505	210	5057/2102	Sierzawy
505	211	5053/2110	Grzegorzewice (Kielce)
505	211	5054/2115	Strupice
505	211	5054/2113	Wasniow
505	211	5055/2117	Mychow

505	211	5055/2110	Skaly
505	211	5056/2115	Chocimow
505	211	5057/2117	Kunow
505	211	5059/2113	Doly Biskupie
505	212	5051/2120	Czerwona Gora
505	212	5051/2124	Szczucice
505	212	5054/2129	Brzostowa
505	212	5054/2126	Gozdzielin
505	212	5054/2121	Olszowka
505	212	5055/2124	Denkowek
505	212	5055/2128	Kraskow
505	212	5056/2122	Czestocice
505	212	5056/2126	Denkow
505	212	5056/2124	Ostrowiec Swietokrzyski
505	212	5056/2127	Wolka Bodzechowska
505	213	5052/2139	Wyszmontow
505	213	5053/2131	Cmielow
505	213	5053/2134	Wolka Wojnowska
505	213	5054/2133	Skala
505	213	5057/2133	Ruda Koscielna
505	213	5058/2133	Stoki Stare
505	213	5058/2133	Stoki Male
505	213	5059/2133	Boria
505	214	5052/2149	Linow
505	214	5053/2140	Ozarow
505	214	5054/2145	Krukow
505	214	5054/2145	Lasocin
505	214	5057/2148	Slupia Nadbrzezna
505	214	5058/2143	Cegielnia
505	215	5050/2155	Kosin
505	215	5050/2157	Mniszek
505	215	5053/2151	Annopol (Lublin)
505	215	5053/2151	Opoczka Mala
505	215	5054/2153	Rachow
505	215	5055/2159	Ksiezomierz
505	215	5055/2155	Sucha Wolka
505	215	5056/2158	Grabowka
505	215	5057/2150	Bliskowice
505	215	5057/2152	Swieciechow
505	215	5059/2158	Boiska Stare
505	220	5052/2201	Goscieradow
505	220	5052/2208	Trzydnik
505	220	5052/2202	Wolka Goscieradowska
505	220	5053/2205	Lisnik Duzy
505	220	5053/2207	Olbiecin
505	220	5053/2203	Rownianki
505	220	5056/2201	Ludmilowka
505	220	5056/2209	Wyznianka
505	220	5056/2209	Wyznica
505	220	5058/2205	Dzierzkowice
505	220	5059/2200	Sosnowa Wola
505	220	5059/2209	Urzedow
505	221	5051/2211	Rzeczyca Ziemianska
505	221	5054/2216	Stroza

505	221	5055/2214	Krasnik
505	221	5057/2212	Budzyn (Lublin)
505	221	5058/2219	Pulankowice
505	221	5059/2214	Popkowice
505	222	5051/2229	Batorz
505	222	5051/2226	Blazek
505	222	5051/2225	Moczydla Nowe
505	222	5052/2224	Blinow
505	222	5054/2225	Studzianki
505	222	5056/2228	Debina (Janow Lubelski)
505	222	5057/2229	Majdan Starowiejski
505	222	5057/2224	Zakrzowek
505	223	5052/2231	Wolka Batorska
505	223	5053/2238	Bockow
505	223	5053/2232	Stawce
505	224	5050/2244	Turobin
505	224	5051/2247	Zabno (Lublin)
505	224	5054/2240	Dragany
505	224	5054/2244	Maciejow Stary
505	224	5055/2244	Slupeczno
505	224	5055/2240	Wysokie
505	224	5058/2246	Sobieska Wola
505	224	5058/2247	Zakrzyze
505	224	5059/2243	Borzecinek
505	225	5050/2256	Bzowiec
505	225	5050/2253	Chlaniow
505	225	5050/2259	Plonka
505	225	5051/2251	Wierzchowina
505	225	5052/2251	Majdan Wierzchowinski
505	225	5052/2256	Wierzbica (Janow Lubelski)
505	225	5054/2257	Joanin
505	225	5054/2250	Srednia Wies (Lublin)
505	225	5054/2257	Suchelipie
505	225	5054/2251	Zolkiew
505	225	5054/2250	Zolkiewka
505	225	5055/2254	Poperczyn
505	225	5056/2257	Borow
505	225	5057/2257	Czystadebina
505	225	5059/2259	Bobrowe
505	225	5059/2251	Pilaszkowice
505	230	5050/2302	Srednie Male
505	230	5051/2301	Srednie Duze
505	230	5052/2309	Szajowka
505	230	5052/2306	Wirkowice
505	230	5053/2308	Tarnogora
505	230	5056/2309	Dworzyska
505	230	5056/2304	Piaski Szlacheckie
505	230	5057/2301	Gorzkow
505	230	5058/2308	Zazolkiew
505	230	5059/2306	Niemienice
505	231	5053/2310	Izbica
505	231	5053/2310	Izbica (Lubelska)

505 231	5053/2319	Sulmice	505 241	5059/2411	Zablotse (Wolyn)
505 231	5054/2313	Orlow Drewniany	505 242	5051/2420	Vladimir Volynskiy
505 231	5056/2316	Surchow	505 242	5052/2425	Kogilno
505 231	5059/2311	Krasnystaw	505 242	5053/2427	Kamelyuvka
505 231	5059/2317	Siennica Krolewska	505 242	5054/2429	Gnoyno
505 232	5050/2326	Hajowniki	505 242	5055/2426	Mogilno
505 232	5051/2324	Lipina Nowa	505 242	5055/2424	Ovadno
505 232	5051/2322	Skierbieszow	505 242	5056/2420	Werba
505 232	5053/2323	Majdan Skierbieszowski	505 242	5058/2426	Luchine
505 232	5054/2329	Majdan Kukawiecki	505 242	5059/2420	Stanislavuvka
505 232	5055/2320	Stara Wies (Zamosc)	505 243	5051/2436	Tumin
505 232	5056/2320	Brzeziny (Lublin)	505 243	5053/2432	Svoychuv
505 232	5056/2322	Krasniczyn	505 243	5059/2437	Vezhbichno
505 232	5057/2329	Majdan Ostrowski	505 244	5051/2443	Ozyutichi
505 232	5057/2323	Sady	505 244	5052/2449	Kiselin
505 232	5057/2329	Wilhelmow	505 244	5053/2445	Tverdyn
505 232	5058/2327	Rakolupy	505 244	5054/2441	Mochulki
505 233	5050/2334	Grabowiec	505 244	5055/2441	Osekruv
505 233	5051/2331	Skomorochy Duze	505 244	5057/2440	Svinarin
505 233	5054/2335	Roziecin	505 244	5058/2441	Cherniyuv
505 233	5054/2338	Uchanie	505 245	5050/2458	Khorokhorin
505 233	5055/2335	Chromowka	505 245	5053/2454	Beresk
505 233	5055/2333	Wojslawice	505 245	5054/2451	Studiny
505 233	5056/2330	Czarnolozy	505 245	5055/2458	Vichyne
505 233	5059/2330	Lesniowice	505 245	5055/2453	Voronchin
505 234	5050/2345	Trzeszczany	505 245	5056/2456	Trysten
505 234	5051/2346	Zadubce	505 245	5059/2459	Nemir
505 234	5053/2347	Mojslawice	505 245	5059/2457	Yasinuvka
505 234	5054/2346	Teratyn	505 250	5050/2507	Ulyaniki
505 234	5055/2342	Jaroslawiec	505 250	5055/2505	Krovatka
505 234	5056/2341	Aurelin	505 250	5057/2501	Novyye Dorosini
505 234	5056/2342	Putnowice Gorne	505 251	5053/2511	Bashova
505 234	5057/2346	Raciborowice	505 251	5053/2513	Kopachovka
505 234	5057/2340	Wolka Putnowiecka	505 251	5055/2516	Rozhishche
505 234	5058/2345	Busno	505 251	5056/2517	Topulno
505 234	5058/2341	Putnowice Dolne	505 251	5059/2517	Staraya Yelenovka
505 235	5050/2355	Dziekanow	505 252	5050/2528	Kivertsy
505 235	5050/2359	Husynne (Hrubieszow)	505 252	5057/2526	Susk
505 235	5050/2356	Moroczyn	505 252	5059/2521	Wiszenki
505 235	5052/2352	Moniatycze	505 253	5059/2533	Ostruv (Lutsk)
505 235	5052/2356	Szpikolosy	505 254	5055/2542	Zofyuvka
505 235	5053/2358	Koblo	505 255	5050/2553	Tsuman
505 235	5054/2358	Kopylow	505 260	5050/2606	Dyuksin
505 235	5055/2351	Stefankowice	505 260	5052/2603	Derazhno
505 235	5055/2352	Ubrodowice	505 260	5055/2605	Haly
505 235	5057/2359	Matcze	505 260	5055/2607	Postoyno
505 235	5059/2356	Skryhiczyn	505 261	5052/2618	Berestovets
505 240	5050/2406	Izuv	505 261	5054/2611	Zvizhdzhe
505 240	5051/2402	Strzyzow (Lublin)	505 261	5055/2612	Stavok
505 240	5052/2409	Ustilug	505 261	5056/2613	Zlazno
505 240	5053/2402	Horodlo	505 261	5059/2616	Yapolots
505 240	5057/2404	Nikityche	505 262	5053/2627	Kostopol
505 241	5052/2414	Khrypaliche	505 263	5056/2633	Pechalovka
505 241	5055/2413	Vorchin	505 264	5051/2649	Pogorelovka (Wolyn)

505 264	5052/2641	Borek Kuty	
505 264	5054/2648	Drukhov	
505 264	5057/2648	Pershotravnevoye	
505 265	5053/2655	Bystrichi	
505 270	5050/2700	Sosnovoye	
505 270	5052/2709	Glushkovo	
505 270	5055/2705	Kreta Sloboda	
505 271	5052/2712	Myshakuvka	
505 274	5052/2748	Yemilchino	
505 282	5051/2828	Ushomir	
505 283	5057/2839	Korosten	
505 285	5050/2857	Chopovichi	
505 290	5055/2902	Vladovka	
505 304	5055/3045	Desna	
505 305	5057/3053	Oster	
505 310	5055/3107	Kozelets	
505 313	5050/3130	Kobyzhcha	
505 313	5056/3135	Nosovka	
505 321	5050/3210	Monastyrishche	
505 322	5052/3224	Ichnya	
505 344	5054/3448	Sumy	
510 060	5104/0605	Heinsberg	
510 060	5106/0609	Wassenberg	
510 061	5100/0616	Korrenzig	
510 061	5103/0613	Huckelhoven	
510 061	5105/0619	Erkelenz	
510 062	5100/0629	Kirchherten	
510 062	5106/0627	Hochneukirch	
510 062	5108/0627	Odenkirchen	
510 062	5108/0625	Wickrath	
510 062	5109/0622	Rheindahlen	
510 063	5100/0635	Bedburg	
510 063	5103/0635	Frimmersdorf	
510 063	5103/0633	Gindorf	
510 063	5104/0630	Garzweiler	
510 063	5104/0634	Gustorf	
510 063	5105/0635	Grevenbroich	
510 063	5106/0630	Juchen	
510 063	5106/0637	Wevelinghoven	
510 063	5107/0634	Bedburdyck	
510 063	5107/0636	Hemmerden	
510 063	5109/0630	Giesenkirchen	
510 064	5101/0646	Stommeln	
510 064	5108/0649	Sturzelberg	
510 065	5101/0659	Leverkusen	
510 065	5104/0656	Hitdorf	
510 065	5106/0650	Dormagen	
510 065	5107/0651	Zons	
510 065	5108/0656	Richrath	
510 070	5104/0701	Opladen	
510 071	5104/0711	Bomberg	
510 071	5109/0713	Wermelskirchen	
510 072	5109/0720	Waag	
510 073	5102/0733	Gummersbach	
510 073	5107/0739	Meinerzhagen	
510 075	5100/0757	Krombach	
510 075	5100/0759	Littfeld	
510 075	5102/0751	Olpe	
510 075	5107/0754	Attendorn	
510 081	5109/0818	Schmallenberg	
510 082	5103/0824	Berleburg	
510 083	5100/0830	Beddelhausen	
510 083	5101/0839	Battenberg	
510 083	5103/0839	Osterfeld	
510 083	5105/0837	Bromskirchen	
510 083	5107/0838	Hallenberg	
510 084	5101/0841	Rennertehausen	
510 084	5102/0840	Battenfeld	
510 084	5103/0845	Roddenau	
510 084	5104/0848	Frankenberg	
510 085	5100/0857	Grusen	
510 085	5104/0851	Geismar	
510 085	5106/0856	Frankenau	
510 085	5107/0855	Altenlotheim	
510 090	5100/0909	Jesberg	
510 090	5107/0907	Bad Wildungen	
510 091	5100/0917	Dillich	
510 091	5100/0914	Zimmersrode	
510 091	5101/0911	Gilsa	
510 091	5103/0917	Borken	
510 091	5103/0911	Zwesten	
510 091	5104/0916	Grossenenglis	
510 091	5107/0913	Ungedanken	
510 091	5108/0917	Fritzlar	
510 092	5104/0923	Falkenberg	
510 092	5108/0925	Felsberg	
510 092	5108/0926	Gensungen	
510 092	5109/0926	Gelsungen	
510 092	5109/0921	Obervorschutz	
510 093	5101/0932	Rengshausen	
510 093	5104/0935	Binsforth	
510 093	5104/0936	Neumorschen	
510 093	5105/0933	Beiseforth	
510 093	5105/0932	Malsfeld	
510 093	5108/0933	Melsungen	
510 093	5109/0933	Rohrenfurth	
510 094	5101/0941	Hergershausen	
510 094	5102/0940	Baumbach	
510 094	5103/0940	Heinebach	
510 094	5107/0940	Spangenberg	
510 095	5101/0956	Nentershausen	
510 095	5104/0951	Diemerode	
510 095	5104/0956	Sontra	
510 095	5108/0956	Bischhausen	
510 095	5109/0951	Harmuthsachsen	
510 100	5101/1006	Nesselroden	
510 100	5106/1006	Netra	
510 100	5107/1001	Datterode	

510 100	5109/1000	Reichensachsen	
510 101	5101/1010	Herleshausen	
510 105	5109/1050	Bad Tennstedt	
510 113	5101/1130	Apolda	
510 120	5101/1205	Raba	
510 120	5103/1209	Zeitz	
510 121	5103/1211	Gleina	
510 121	5103/1218	Meuselwitz	
510 122	5106/1221	Lucka	
510 130	5104/1301	Waldheim	
510 132	5109/1329	Meissen	
510 133	5101/1339	Freital	
510 133	5106/1337	Kotzschenbroda	
510 133	5106/1339	Radebeul	
510 134	5103/1345	Dresden	
510 135	5100/1351	Zschachwitz	
510 135	5107/1355	Radeberg	
510 142	5101/1421	Lipova	
510 142	5101/1428	Sluknov	
510 142	5106/1428	Carlsberg	
510 144	5106/1440	Lobau	
510 150	5100/1502	Boleslav	
510 153	5107/1535	Lwowek Slaski	
510 155	5107/1554	Zlotoryja	
510 161	5101/1618	Rogoznica	
510 161	5103/1611	Jawor	
510 164	5102/1646	Katy Wroclawskie	
510 170	5105/1700	Wroclaw	
510 172	5102/1721	Laskowice Olawskie	
510 173	5107/1732	Bernstadt in Schlesien	
510 174	5105/1743	Namyslow	
510 175	5107/1754	Sadogora	
510 175	5109/1751	Rychtal	
510 180	5101/1803	Wolczyn	
510 181	5102/1817	Maciejow	
510 182	5102/1826	Gorzow Slaski	
510 182	5103/1828	Praszka	
510 182	5106/1826	Przedmoscie	
510 183	5101/1837	Cieciulow	
510 183	5101/1834	Zytniow Rzedowy	
510 183	5102/1839	Jaworzno (Czestochowa)	
510 183	5102/1836	Rudniki (Wielun)	
510 183	5105/1836	Dalachow	
510 183	5105/1839	Kaluze	
510 183	5106/1832	Soltysy	
510 183	5107/1839	Bieniec	
510 183	5107/1837	Dzietrzniki	
510 183	5109/1835	Grebien	
510 183	5109/1834	Jozefow (Wielun)	
510 183	5109/1839	Laszow	
510 184	5103/1844	Parzymiechy	
510 184	5105/1843	Zalecze Male	
510 184	5105/1841	Zalecze Wielkie	
510 184	5109/1843	Przywoz	

510 185	5101/1851	Rebielice Szlacheckie	
510 185	5102/1851	Stanislawow (Czestochowa)	
510 185	5103/1856	Debie	
510 185	5106/1852	Raciszyn	
510 185	5107/1852	Dzialoszyn	
510 190	5104/1901	Wasosz Poduchowny	
510 190	5105/1908	Dworszowice Koscielne	
510 190	5105/1903	Gajecice	
510 190	5106/1907	Wola Jajkowska	
510 190	5108/1902	Lezce	
510 190	5109/1900	Pajeczno	
510 191	5100/1918	Wiklow	
510 191	5102/1912	Prusicko	
510 191	5103/1916	Jankowice	
510 191	5103/1913	Zakrzowek Szlachecki	
510 191	5105/1915	Jedlno	
510 191	5108/1914	Wiewiec	
510 191	5108/1918	Wola Blakowa	
510 192	5103/1929	Strzalkow	
510 192	5104/1927	Radomsko	
510 192	5105/1928	Bartodzieje Podlesne	
510 192	5105/1923	Stobiecko Miejskie	
510 192	5106/1926	Bogwidzowy	
510 192	5106/1926	Mlodzowy	
510 192	5108/1929	Fryszerka	
510 193	5101/1933	Cadow	
510 193	5101/1938	Kobiele Male	
510 193	5102/1938	Kobiele Wielkie	
510 193	5103/1939	Ujazdowek	
510 193	5104/1934	Dmenin	
510 193	5104/1932	Dziepulc	
510 193	5104/1938	Wola Malowana	
510 193	5106/1938	Kodrab	
510 193	5106/1932	Konradow	
510 193	5107/1936	Widawka	
510 193	5109/1939	Lipowczyce	
510 194	5101/1947	Wielgomlyny Poduchowne	
510 194	5102/1948	Kruszyna	
510 194	5103/1949	Trzebce	
510 194	5103/1945	Zagorze	
510 194	5104/1945	Chelmo	
510 194	5104/1947	Koconia	
510 194	5105/1941	Biestrzykow Wielki	
510 194	5106/1944	Granice	
510 194	5106/1948	Maslowice	
510 194	5106/1944	Tworowice	
510 194	5109/1943	Przerab	
510 195	5100/1951	Krzetow	
510 195	5101/1954	Raczki (Lodz)	
510 195	5104/1959	Wojciechow (Przedborz)	
510 195	5105/1953	Przedborz	
510 195	5107/1957	Nosalewice	

510 195	5109/1952	Bakowa Gorna
510 200	5101/2000	Mojzeszow
510 200	5101/2002	Zagacie
510 200	5102/2006	Pilczyca
510 200	5102/2006	Rytlow
510 200	5107/2007	Wola Szkucka
510 200	5109/2005	Skornice
510 201	5102/2010	Pianow
510 201	5102/2019	Wegrzyn
510 201	5105/2015	Kamien Wielki
510 201	5105/2014	Radoszyce
510 201	5109/2013	Ruda Maleniecka
510 202	5101/2024	Grzymalkow
510 202	5101/2029	Mniow
510 202	5101/2028	Wegrzynow
510 202	5102/2022	Klucko
510 202	5103/2021	Wyrebow
510 202	5103/2029	Zaborowice
510 202	5105/2024	Miedzierza
510 202	5105/2027	Przylogi
510 202	5107/2021	Sielpia Duza
510 203	5101/2036	Koloman
510 203	5103/2035	Rogowice
510 203	5103/2033	Serbinow
510 203	5106/2031	Duraczow
510 203	5106/2035	Gosan
510 203	5106/2039	Odrowazek
510 203	5107/2037	Pardolow
510 203	5108/2032	Czarna (Konskie)
510 203	5108/2032	Czarniecka Gora
510 203	5108/2034	Koprusa
510 203	5108/2039	Odrowaz
510 203	5108/2036	Wolow
510 203	5109/2033	Staporkow
510 204	5101/2049	Ostojow
510 204	5106/2044	Wojtyniow
510 204	5107/2045	Blizyn
510 204	5107/2042	Sorbin
510 204	5108/2043	Gorki (Konskie)
510 204	5108/2046	Gostkow
510 204	5108/2043	Placzkow
510 204	5109/2043	Mroczkow
510 204	5109/2042	Soltykow
510 205	5102/2051	Berezow
510 205	5104/2050	Suchedniow
510 205	5106/2051	Bzinek
510 205	5106/2050	Rejow
510 205	5107/2051	Bzin
510 205	5107/2054	Skarzysko Kamienna
510 205	5108/2051	Milica
510 205	5109/2051	Skarzysko Ksiazece
510 205	5109/2056	Skarzysko Koscielne
510 210	5100/2109	Stykow
510 210	5103/2105	Wierzbnik
510 210	5104/2101	Wachock
510 210	5108/2104	Mirzec
510 211	5100/2119	Siennica Rozana
510 211	5101/2111	Ruda (Ilza)
510 211	5102/2114	Brody (Radom)
510 211	5104/2111	Lubienia
510 211	5107/2116	Koszary
510 211	5108/2113	Jasieniec Nowy
510 211	5109/2111	Seredzice
510 212	5101/2127	Sarnowek
510 212	5105/2128	Sienno
510 212	5106/2124	Grabowiec (Radom)
510 212	5108/2123	Rzechow
510 212	5109/2129	Jawor Solecki
510 212	5109/2120	Predocin
510 212	5109/2121	Wiewiorow
510 213	5101/2133	Baltow
510 213	5101/2138	Wolka Petkowska
510 213	5102/2137	Petkowice
510 213	5102/2132	Wolka Baltowska
510 213	5106/2133	Nowa Wies (Ilza)
510 213	5108/2138	Gruszczyn
510 213	5109/2134	Krepa Koscielna
510 214	5100/2143	Tarlow
510 214	5102/2141	Czekarzewice
510 214	5104/2147	Wola Pawlowska
510 214	5108/2146	Solec
510 214	5109/2143	Przedmiescie (Zelechow)
510 215	5101/2155	Mazanow
510 215	5102/2158	Chruslanki Mazanowskie
510 215	5105/2156	Kluczkowice
510 215	5107/2154	Socha
510 215	5109/2158	Opole Lubelskie
510 220	5100/2201	Chruslanki Jozefowskie
510 220	5101/2200	Idalin
510 220	5102/2206	Moniaki
510 220	5103/2200	Chruslina
510 220	5107/2208	Chodel
510 220	5107/2200	Leonin
510 221	5100/2215	Ostrow (Janow Lubelski)
510 221	5101/2212	Skorczyce
510 221	5103/2218	Dobrowola
510 221	5103/2214	Majdan Radlinski
510 221	5104/2216	Kepa
510 221	5104/2214	Lopiennik
510 221	5105/2214	Zosinek
510 221	5106/2217	Borzechow
510 221	5109/2213	Dylazki
510 222	5101/2225	Borkowizna
510 222	5101/2226	Kielczewice
510 222	5101/2220	Wilkolaz

510 222	5103/2226	Rechta	
510 222	5105/2222	Niedrzwica Koscielna	
510 222	5107/2224	Niedrzwica Duza	
510 222	5109/2229	Kreznica Jara	
510 222	5109/2226	Strzeszkowice Male	
510 223	5101/2232	Bychawa	
510 223	5105/2232	Tuszow	
510 223	5107/2230	Osmolice	
510 223	5107/2231	Zabia Wola	
510 224	5100/2243	Krzczonow	
510 224	5103/2248	Policzyzna	
510 224	5107/2248	Kozice Dolne	
510 224	5107/2246	Kozice Gorne	
510 224	5107/2242	Majdan Kozic Dolnych	
510 224	5109/2246	Bystrzejowice	
510 225	5101/2252	Czestoborowice	
510 225	5102/2252	Rybczewice	
510 225	5105/2258	Suchodoly	
510 225	5106/2258	Fajslawice	
510 225	5106/2251	Gardzienice	
510 225	5106/2259	Wola Idzikowska	
510 225	5108/2257	Biskupice Lubelskie	
510 225	5108/2252	Piaski Luterskie	
510 225	5109/2255	Struza	
510 230	5100/2304	Jaslikow	
510 230	5100/2300	Majdan Krzywski	
510 230	5103/2302	Lopiennik Gorny	
510 230	5104/2307	Borowica	
510 230	5104/2300	Dziecinin	
510 230	5107/2307	Liszno	
510 230	5107/2302	Olesniki	
510 230	5108/2300	Trawniki	
510 230	5108/2305	Wolka Kanska	
510 230	5109/2300	Czemierniki (Krasnystaw)	
510 230	5109/2307	Kanie	
510 231	5101/2312	Siennica Nadolna	
510 231	5102/2315	Krupe	
510 231	5103/2311	Bzite	
510 231	5104/2311	Jozefow (Krasnystaw)	
510 231	5105/2317	Rejowiec	
510 231	5107/2311	Zalesie Kraszenskie	
510 231	5108/2311	Krasne (Wlodawa)	
510 231	5109/2313	Pawlowka	
510 232	5100/2320	Wola Siennicka	
510 232	5101/2322	Zagroda	
510 232	5101/2323	Zdzanne	
510 232	5103/2329	Kasilan	
510 232	5104/2329	Krzywiczki	
510 232	5105/2327	Depultycze Krolewskie	
510 233	5100/2332	Majdan Lesniowski	
510 233	5101/2338	Wolka Leszczanska	
510 233	5102/2335	Koczow	
510 233	5102/2333	Kumow Majoracki	

510 233	5102/2331	Sielec	
510 233	5104/2330	Rozdzalow	
510 233	5104/2335	Wolawce	
510 233	5105/2338	Czerniejow	
510 233	5105/2335	Kossyn	
510 233	5106/2336	Kamien (Chelm)	
510 233	5107/2339	Plawanice	
510 233	5107/2337	Rudolfin	
510 233	5108/2330	Chelm	
510 233	5108/2335	Ignatow	
510 233	5108/2337	Olenowka	
510 234	5101/2349	Siedliszcze (Hrubieszow)	
510 234	5101/2345	Syczow	
510 234	5101/2340	Zmudz	
510 234	5102/2346	Radziejow (Lublin)	
510 234	5102/2348	Tuchanie	
510 234	5102/2340	Wolkowiany	
510 234	5103/2346	Bielin	
510 234	5103/2345	Rostoka	
510 234	5106/2342	Pogranicze	
510 234	5106/2344	Skordiow	
510 234	5107/2340	Kroczyn	
510 234	5107/2345	Majdan Skordiow	
510 234	5107/2347	Ostrow (Chelm)	
510 234	5108/2348	Turka (Chelm)	
510 234	5109/2345	Teosin	
510 234	5109/2347	Zalisocze	
510 235	5101/2356	Kladnev	
510 235	5102/2350	Holendry	
510 235	5103/2355	Bystraki	
510 235	5103/2353	Dubienka	
510 235	5104/2359	Murava	
510 235	5105/2352	Uchanka	
510 235	5108/2351	Husynne (Chelm)	
510 235	5108/2358	Zamlynye	
510 241	5104/2411	Stavki	
510 241	5105/2415	Ovlochin	
510 241	5105/2410	Stavochki	
510 241	5107/2411	Olesk	
510 241	5108/2412	Glinyanka	
510 242	5100/2429	Bobly	
510 242	5101/2424	Mokrets	
510 242	5107/2423	Dolsk	
510 242	5107/2426	Rastov	
510 242	5108/2420	Pshovaly	
510 243	5100/2439	Tulichev	
510 243	5104/2436	Klyusk	
510 243	5106/2432	Turiysk	
510 243	5108/2438	Zadibi	
510 244	5100/2443	Kupichov	
510 244	5101/2448	Ozeryany (Wolyn)	
510 245	5104/2453	Gonchiy Brod	
510 245	5106/2452	Drozdni	

510 245	5108/2458	Byten (Kovel)
510 245	5109/2450	Lyubitov
510 245	5109/2459	Radoshin
510 250	5105/2501	Goloby
510 250	5109/2506	Melnitsa
510 251	5103/2511	Borshchevka
510 251	5105/2516	Ivanovka
510 252	5103/2528	Chetvertnya
510 252	5103/2525	Nezvir
510 252	5103/2520	Sokol
510 254	5106/2540	Kolki
510 255	5105/2555	Olizarka
510 255	5105/2558	Osova
510 260	5101/2602	Lipno (Wolyn)
510 261	5101/2610	Stydyn Maly
510 261	5102/2616	Trostenets
510 261	5103/2610	Bolshoy Stydin
510 261	5103/2618	Zolotolin
510 261	5105/2611	Mydzk Maly
510 261	5108/2618	Stepan
510 262	5102/2625	Maryanuvka (Kolki)
510 262	5103/2628	Yablonka (Wolyn)
510 262	5105/2625	Cepcewicze Wielkie Smolki
510 262	5105/2625	Cepcewicze Wielkie Obolonie
510 262	5107/2628	Kazimirka
510 262	5109/2623	Zulnya
510 263	5103/2639	Polyany
510 263	5105/2635	Bielatycze
510 263	5106/2633	Malynsk
510 264	5100/2645	Berezno
510 264	5101/2645	Gorodishche (Berezno)
510 264	5101/2640	Ilniki
510 264	5103/2643	Orluvka
510 264	5106/2645	Bogushi
510 265	5102/2656	Mikhalin
510 270	5103/2704	Rudnya Bobrovska
510 271	5106/2713	Borovoye
510 271	5109/2712	Karpilovka (Kisorichi)
510 272	5106/2720	Netreba
510 280	5107/2802	Belokorovichi
510 281	5103/2814	Kremno
510 282	5105/2824	Luginy
510 301	5104/3015	Gornostaypol
510 315	5103/3153	Nezhin
510 322	5107/3226	Pliski
510 355	5101/3551	Penskiy
511 061	5112/0613	Niederkruchten
511 061	5114/0616	Waldniel
511 061	5119/0613	Kaldenkirchen
511 062	5110/0627	Rheydt
511 062	5112/0626	Monchen Gladbach
511 062	5115/0621	Dulken
511 062	5115/0623	Viersen
511 062	5117/0623	Suchteln
511 063	5110/0635	Glehn
511 063	5111/0631	Korschenbroich
511 063	5114/0632	Schiefbahn
511 063	5119/0630	Sankt Tonis
511 064	5112/0642	Neuss
511 064	5113/0646	Dusseldorf
511 064	5115/0640	Hulchrath
511 065	5110/0656	Hilden
511 065	5113/0654	Erkrath
511 065	5115/0658	Mettmann
511 065	5118/0651	Ratingen
511 070	5111/0705	Solingen
511 070	5112/0700	Haan
511 070	5117/0703	Wulfrath
511 070	5119/0705	Hardenberg
511 070	5119/0705	Neviges
511 071	5111/0712	Remscheid
511 071	5116/0711	Wuppertal Barmen
511 071	5116/0711	Wuppertal
511 071	5117/0717	Schwelm
511 072	5110/0724	Egen
511 072	5119/0720	Gevelsberg
511 073	5113/0737	Ludenscheid
511 074	5116/0746	Werdohl
511 074	5118/0740	Altena
511 075	5113/0753	Plettenberg
511 080	5111/0801	Schonholthausen
511 082	5119/0824	Ramsbeck
511 083	5118/0830	Assinghausen
511 084	5112/0843	Medebach
511 084	5118/0842	Eimelrod
511 085	5112/0856	Vohl
511 085	5116/0859	Horinghausen
511 085	5117/0852	Korbach
511 090	5114/0901	Sachsenhausen
511 091	5114/0912	Elben
511 091	5114/0919	Niedenstein
511 091	5115/0910	Naumburg
511 091	5116/0919	Elmshagen
511 091	5119/0910	Wolfhagen
511 092	5110/0926	Neuenbrunslar
511 092	5111/0922	Gudensberg
511 092	5112/0929	Guxhagen
511 092	5117/0922	Elgershausen
511 092	5117/0921	Hoof
511 093	5116/0938	Oberkaufungen
511 093	5119/0930	Kassel
511 094	5112/0943	Hessisch Lichtenau
511 095	5112/0956	Abterode
511 095	5114/0955	Frankershausen
511 095	5117/0959	Allendorf an der Werra
511 100	5111/1004	Eschwege

511	101	5111/1010	Wanfried
511	102	5113/1027	Muhlhausen
511	111	5111/1114	Kolleda
511	111	5117/1110	Sachsenburg
511	115	5112/1158	Weissenfels
511	115	5116/1152	Leiha
511	120	5118/1202	Spergau
511	122	5117/1224	Markkleeberg
511	122	5118/1220	Leipzig
511	124	5114/1243	Grimma
511	130	5118/1307	Oschatz
511	131	5118/1318	Riesa
511	141	5113/1412	Neustadtel
511	141	5117/1412	Piskowitz
511	142	5111/1426	Bautzen
511	150	5110/1500	Gorlitz
511	150	5115/1503	Piensk
511	150	5118/1502	Bielawa Dolna
511	155	5116/1556	Chojnow
511	161	5110/1611	Legnica
511	163	5110/1636	Sroda Slaska
511	164	5111/1641	Brzeg Dolny
511	170	5113/1700	Trzebnica
511	172	5112/1723	Olesnica
511	172	5116/1720	Dobroszyce
511	174	5118/1743	Sycow
511	175	5117/1754	Bralin
511	175	5117/1759	Kepno
511	180	5118/1808	Podzamcze
511	181	5110/1819	Dzietrzkowice
511	181	5112/1812	Boleslawiec
511	181	5113/1812	Chotynin
511	181	5114/1819	Parcice
511	181	5116/1819	Czastary
511	181	5117/1810	Wieruszow
511	181	5118/1816	Ochedzyn
511	181	5118/1818	Tyble
511	182	5111/1829	Mokrsko
511	182	5111/1823	Skomlin
511	182	5113/1826	Piaski (Wielun)
511	182	5116/1824	Lyskornia
511	182	5116/1826	Mirkow
511	182	5118/1826	Naramice
511	182	5118/1823	Walichnowy
511	182	5119/1825	Smiechen
511	182	5119/1820	Sokolniki
511	183	5110/1839	Jajczaki
511	183	5113/1833	Wielun
511	183	5114/1838	Starzenice
511	183	5119/1838	Bolkow
511	184	5110/1842	Mierzyce
511	184	5111/1846	Krzeczow (Sieradz)
511	184	5112/1846	Kochlew
511	184	5112/1843	Kraszkowice
511	184	5113/1846	Folwark Raducki
511	184	5113/1841	Wierzchlas
511	184	5115/1841	Sieniec
511	184	5117/1845	Jasien (Wielun)
511	184	5117/1848	Osjakow
511	185	5111/1853	Ozegow
511	185	5113/1854	Siemkowice
511	185	5113/1857	Tuchan
511	185	5114/1859	Kielczyglow
511	185	5114/1853	Lipnik (Lodz)
511	185	5117/1855	Kielczyglowek
511	185	5117/1857	Pierzyny
511	185	5118/1851	Chorzyna
511	185	5119/1856	Deby Wolskie
511	190	5110/1906	Dworszowice Pakoszowe
511	190	5112/1904	Suchowola (Lodz)
511	190	5112/1909	Wola Wydrzyna
511	190	5114/1903	Rzasnia
511	190	5116/1907	Chabielice
511	190	5117/1905	Broszecin
511	190	5117/1900	Obrow
511	190	5118/1900	Jastrzebice
511	191	5111/1912	Sulmierzyce
511	191	5114/1918	Kleszczow
511	191	5114/1918	Kucow
511	191	5114/1917	Trzas
511	191	5114/1915	Zlobnica
511	191	5117/1919	Janow Nowy
511	191	5118/1916	Zarzecze (Kielce)
511	192	5110/1920	Brudzice
511	192	5110/1929	Gomunice
511	192	5112/1927	Pytowice
511	192	5113/1921	Lekinsko
511	192	5114/1928	Ozga
511	192	5115/1929	Danielow
511	192	5116/1925	Kalisko
511	192	5117/1924	Lekawa
511	192	5119/1928	Bukowa (Piotrkow Trybunalski)
511	193	5110/1937	Wola Kotkowska
511	193	5113/1938	Bujniczki
511	193	5113/1933	Gorzedow
511	193	5113/1936	Gorzkowice
511	193	5113/1930	Kamiensk
511	193	5115/1939	Wilkoszewice
511	193	5116/1935	Wola Niechcicka Nowa
511	193	5117/1935	Niechcice
511	193	5118/1931	Parzniewice
511	193	5118/1938	Rozprza
511	194	5111/1948	Ignacow Szlachecki
511	194	5111/1948	Leki Szlacheckie
511	194	5113/1946	Piwaki
511	194	5113/1944	Trzepnica
511	194	5114/1940	Daniszewice

511	194	5114/1945	Zerechowa
511	194	5115/1947	Tomawa
511	194	5117/1941	Rajsko Duze
511	194	5118/1941	Lochynsko
511	194	5118/1944	Zmozna Wola
511	195	5110/1955	Faliszew
511	195	5111/1958	Jozefow Stary (Kielce)
511	195	5111/1951	Leki Krolewskie
511	195	5111/1952	Reczno
511	195	5112/1956	Skotniki
511	195	5113/1957	Wolka Skotnicka
511	195	5114/1950	Dorszyn
511	195	5114/1953	Paskrzyn
511	195	5114/1958	Stara
511	195	5115/1956	Szarbsko
511	200	5110/2004	Plaskowice
511	200	5111/2009	Koloniec
511	200	5111/2005	Starzechowice
511	200	5112/2000	Sosnowice
511	200	5112/2002	Sulborowice
511	200	5113/2003	Klew
511	200	5114/2003	Skorkowice
511	200	5115/2007	Dluzniewice
511	200	5115/2002	Siucice
511	200	5116/2002	Ciechomin
511	200	5118/2009	Daleszewice
511	200	5118/2008	Paradyz
511	201	5111/2014	Koliszowy
511	201	5111/2011	Maleniec
511	201	5112/2019	Bedlenko
511	201	5112/2018	Przybyszowy
511	201	5114/2012	Paszkowice
511	201	5115/2011	Zarnow
511	201	5118/2018	Bialaczow
511	201	5118/2014	Miedzna Murowana
511	201	5119/2012	Stawowiczki
511	202	5112/2025	Konskie
511	202	5113/2022	Modliszewice
511	202	5114/2028	Nieswin
511	202	5115/2027	Morzywol
511	202	5116/2023	Ruda Bialaczowska
511	202	5117/2026	Gowarczow
511	202	5117/2023	Skronina
511	202	5119/2026	Bernow
511	203	5111/2037	Nieklan Wielki
511	203	5112/2037	Furmanow
511	203	5112/2033	Smarkow
511	203	5113/2030	Chelb
511	203	5114/2034	Paruchy
511	203	5115/2030	Jozefow (Konskie)
511	203	5115/2035	Kolonia Szczerbacka
511	203	5118/2035	Wawrzynow
511	204	5110/2047	Ciechostowice
511	204	5113/2044	Huta (Kielce)
511	204	5115/2046	Chlewiska
511	204	5115/2042	Skloby
511	204	5115/2048	Stanislawow (Konskie)
511	204	5117/2048	Broniow
511	204	5117/2045	Rzucow
511	205	5111/2059	Zbijow
511	205	5112/2059	Rogow Komorniki
511	205	5114/2051	Szydlowiec
511	205	5115/2057	Jastrzab
511	205	5117/2050	Krawara
511	210	5110/2104	Trebowiec
511	210	5111/2104	Mirow Stary
511	210	5112/2101	Rogow (Radom)
511	210	5115/2105	Wierzbica
511	210	5117/2105	Bledow
511	210	5118/2108	Maliszow
511	210	5118/2104	Ruda Wielka
511	210	5118/2105	Stanislawow (Tczow)
511	211	5110/2115	Ilza
511	211	5113/2113	Gaworzyna
511	211	5115/2117	Zalesie (Radom)
511	211	5118/2118	Brzescie (Zwolen)
511	211	5119/2115	Skaryszew
511	212	5110/2121	Pasztowa Wola
511	212	5110/2126	Pawliczka
511	212	5112/2126	Czerwona
511	212	5112/2121	Malomierzyce
511	212	5112/2127	Pasieki
511	212	5115/2124	Kowalkow
511	212	5117/2128	Kazanow
511	212	5117/2121	Niedarczow Gorny
511	212	5119/2120	Odechowiec
511	213	5110/2137	Lipa Miklas
511	213	5110/2137	Lipa Krepa
511	213	5110/2139	Lipsko
511	213	5114/2138	Swiesielice
511	213	5115/2134	Ciepielow
511	213	5116/2133	Gardzienice Stare
511	214	5110/2141	Nowe Pole
511	214	5110/2147	Przedmiescie Kludzie
511	214	5112/2143	Wola Solecka
511	214	5113/2147	Jaretowskie Pole
511	214	5113/2149	Las Debowy
511	214	5114/2148	Chotcza Dolna
511	214	5115/2147	Chotcza Gorna
511	214	5116/2148	Gniazdkow
511	214	5116/2143	Niemiryczow
511	214	5117/2141	Tymienica Stara
511	214	5119/2146	Szlachecki Las
511	214	5119/2141	Wysocin
511	215	5114/2151	Lubomirka
511	215	5115/2159	Karczmiska
511	215	5115/2150	Kepa Chotecka
511	215	5119/2157	Kazimierz Dolny

511 220	5110/2205	Sewerynowka
511 220	5111/2208	Poniatowa
511 220	5113/2200	Glusko Duze
511 220	5113/2207	Kraczewice
511 220	5115/2208	Niezabitow
511 221	5110/2212	Cuple
511 221	5111/2217	Belzyce
511 221	5114/2219	Palikije
511 221	5114/2211	Szczuczki
511 221	5115/2216	Maszki
511 221	5117/2214	Charz
511 221	5117/2213	Chruszczow
511 221	5117/2213	Naleczow
511 221	5117/2217	Sadurki
511 221	5117/2210	Wawolnica
511 222	5112/2224	Radawiec Duzy
511 222	5112/2225	Tereszyn
511 222	5114/2228	Konopnica
511 222	5115/2224	Motycz
511 222	5115/2227	Uniszowice
511 222	5116/2225	Plonszowice
511 222	5117/2223	Tomaszowice
511 222	5118/2224	Sieprawice
511 222	5119/2228	Jastkow
511 222	5119/2224	Jozefow (Lublin)
511 222	5119/2229	Snopkow
511 223	5110/2239	Wilczopole
511 223	5111/2236	Glusk
511 223	5114/2236	Majdanek
511 223	5115/2234	Lublin
511 223	5116/2235	Czechowka Dolna
511 224	5114/2247	Melgiew
511 224	5115/2248	Trzeszkowice
511 224	5118/2241	Sobianowice
511 225	5110/2259	Pelczyn
511 225	5111/2259	Siostrzytow
511 225	5116/2254	Wolka Lancuchowska
511 225	5117/2252	Ciechanki Krzesimowskie
511 225	5118/2253	Leczna
511 225	5118/2259	Stara Wies (Krasne)
511 225	5119/2258	Puchaczow
511 230	5110/2301	Dorohucza
511 230	5111/2306	Chojno Stare
511 230	5111/2304	Chojno Nowe
511 230	5111/2304	Wojciechow
511 230	5114/2303	Kamionka (Chelm)
511 230	5114/2305	Wola Korybutowa
511 230	5115/2308	Streczyn
511 230	5118/2309	Cycow
511 230	5118/2306	Glebokie (Chelm)
511 230	5119/2309	Abramowka
511 230	5119/2307	Wolka Cycowska
511 231	5112/2310	Siedliszcze
511 231	5114/2317	Olchowiec
511 231	5116/2318	Busowno
511 231	5117/2315	Syczyn
511 231	5118/2313	Bekiesza
511 231	5119/2314	Malkow (Chelm)
511 232	5111/2327	Horodyszcze
511 232	5113/2327	Czulczyce
511 232	5113/2323	Krobonosz
511 232	5113/2321	Ochoza
511 232	5115/2321	Pniowno
511 232	5115/2327	Sajczyce
511 232	5116/2326	Sawin
511 232	5116/2320	Wierzbica (Krasnystaw)
511 232	5117/2320	Chylin
511 232	5119/2327	Malinowka
511 233	5113/2338	Zalin
511 233	5114/2335	Zarudnia
511 233	5115/2336	Ruda Huta
511 233	5116/2333	Ilowa
511 233	5117/2339	Siedliszcze (Wlodawa)
511 233	5118/2331	Bukowa Mala
511 233	5118/2333	Lukowek
511 233	5118/2338	Uhrusk
511 233	5118/2339	Vulka Ugruska
511 233	5119/2336	Stanislawow (Chelm)
511 233	5119/2338	Wola Uhruska
511 234	5110/2349	Dorohusk
511 234	5111/2340	Okopy (Chelm)
511 234	5111/2347	Volchkov Perevoz
511 234	5113/2341	Dobrylow
511 234	5113/2344	Swierze
511 234	5114/2348	Rovno (Ii)
511 234	5116/2344	Gushcha
511 234	5117/2342	Opalin
511 235	5111/2354	Rymachi
511 235	5112/2355	Yagodin
511 235	5119/2357	Palany
511 240	5110/2405	Radzikhuv
511 240	5111/2407	Mashev
511 240	5112/2402	Vishnyuv
511 240	5114/2402	Lyuboml
511 240	5114/2407	Skiby
511 240	5116/2408	Gorodno (Lyubomyl)
511 241	5112/2414	Khvorostov
511 241	5115/2415	Jarewiszcze
511 241	5115/2412	Podgorodno
511 242	5110/2424	Turovichi
511 242	5111/2427	Milyanovichi
511 242	5112/2420	Somin
511 242	5113/2420	Matsiov
511 242	5118/2426	Smidyn
511 243	5115/2431	Krugel
511 244	5113/2443	Kovel
511 245	5112/2458	Maryanuvka

511 250	5112/2508	Miryn	
511 250	5115/2501	Gryvyatki	
511 250	5116/2508	Povorsk	
511 250	5119/2501	Cheremoshno	
511 251	5115/2513	Gulevichi	
511 252	5110/2521	Kashivka	
511 253	5117/2532	Manevichi (Polesie)	
511 254	5110/2545	Komarov	
511 255	5111/2557	Velikaya Osnitsa	
511 255	5113/2553	Staryy Chartoriysk	
511 255	5116/2556	Kozlinichi	
511 260	5116/2603	Politsy	
511 260	5119/2607	Bolshoy Zhelutsk	
511 261	5112/2616	Bolshaya Verbcha	
511 261	5113/2618	Verbche Male	
511 261	5116/2613	Romeyki	
511 261	5117/2619	Gorodets	
511 262	5112/2620	Korost	
511 262	5114/2622	Krichilsk	
511 262	5115/2625	Moczuliszcze	
511 262	5119/2620	Antonowka (Polesie)	
511 263	5116/2638	Nemovichi	
511 263	5119/2631	Kolets	
511 264	5110/2647	Tynnoye	
511 264	5113/2642	Znosichi	
511 264	5115/2644	Chudel	
511 265	5112/2654	Selishche	
511 265	5112/2657	Yasnogorka	
511 270	5114/2706	Stariki	
511 270	5117/2709	Osnitsk	
511 271	5111/2716	Kisorichi	
511 271	5117/2713	Rokitnoye	
511 272	5112/2720	Dert	
511 272	5117/2724	Snovidovichi	
511 273	5113/2739	Olevsk	
511 282	5112/2822	Malakhovka	
511 282	5119/2828	Novyye Veledniki	
511 283	5116/2836	Norinsk	
511 284	5119/2848	Ovruch	
511 290	5112/2905	Narodichi	
511 292	5114/2923	Polesskoye	
511 301	5116/3014	Chernobyl	
511 320	5114/3209	Komarovka	
511 322	5115/3226	Borzna	
511 324	5111/3247	Bakhmach	
511 331	5114/3312	Konotop	
511 334	5112/3349	Buryn	
511 342	5114/3424	Podobriyevka	
511 351	5112/3515	Sudzha	
511 361	5112/3616	Oboyan	
511 375	5117/3751	Staryy Oskol	
512 061	5127/0616	Straelen	
512 062	5126/0626	Aldekerk	
512 062	5128/0628	Rheurdt	

512 063	5120/0634	Krefeld	
512 063	5122/0631	Huls	
512 063	5127/0639	Moers	
512 064	5125/0645	Rheinhausen	
512 064	5126/0645	Duisburg	
512 064	5126/0645	Duisburg Ruhrort	
512 064	5126/0645	Ruhrort	
512 065	5122/0657	Kettwig	
512 065	5126/0653	Mulheim an der Ruhr	
512 065	5128/0651	Oberhausen	
512 065	5128/0652	Sterkrade	
512 070	5120/0703	Velbert	
512 070	5121/0708	Langenberg	
512 070	5125/0704	Essen Heisingen	
512 070	5126/0705	Essen Steele	
512 070	5127/0701	Essen	
512 070	5129/0708	Wattenscheid	
512 071	5124/0710	Hattingen	
512 071	5125/0716	Herbede	
512 071	5129/0713	Bochum	
512 072	5121/0728	Hagen	
512 072	5124/0726	Herdecke	
512 072	5126/0720	Witten	
512 073	5121/0736	Hohenlimburg	
512 073	5122/0737	Letmathe	
512 073	5127/0734	Schwerte	
512 073	5129/0730	Horde	
512 074	5122/0742	Iserlohn	
512 074	5122/0742	Langenfeld	
512 074	5123/0746	Hemer	
512 074	5126/0748	Menden	
512 074	5128/0746	Frondenberg	
512 075	5127/0759	Neheim Husten	
512 075	5129/0752	Wickede	
512 080	5123/0805	Arnsberg	
512 080	5124/0808	Oeventrop	
512 081	5120/0813	Calle	
512 081	5121/0817	Meschede	
512 081	5122/0810	Freienohl	
512 082	5121/0828	Bigge	
512 082	5122/0826	Nuttlar	
512 082	5127/0822	Warstein	
512 082	5129/0820	Belecke	
512 083	5121/0830	Olsberg	
512 083	5124/0835	Brilon	
512 084	5123/0840	Messinghausen	
512 084	5124/0849	Giershagen	
512 084	5124/0846	Padberg	
512 084	5125/0846	Bredelar	
512 084	5126/0844	Madfeld	
512 085	5121/0859	Mengeringhausen	
512 085	5127/0851	Niedermarsberg	
512 090	5122/0901	Arolsen	
512 090	5124/0907	Volkmarsen	

512 090	5127/0901	Rhoden
512 091	5122/0919	Zierenberg
512 091	5124/0912	Niederelsungen
512 091	5127/0914	Oberlistingen
512 091	5127/0911	Wettesingen
512 091	5128/0912	Herlinghausen
512 091	5128/0918	Niedermeiser
512 091	5129/0917	Liebenau
512 092	5124/0921	Meimbressen
512 092	5127/0925	Grebenstein
512 092	5129/0924	Hofgeismar
512 093	5125/0930	Immenhausen
512 094	5125/0941	Munden
512 095	5120/0952	Witzenhausen
512 095	5123/0955	Hebenshausen
512 100	5123/1008	Heiligenstadt
512 100	5129/1005	Wollmarshausen
512 102	5121/1026	Rudigershagen
512 103	5126/1035	Bleicherode
512 105	5122/1052	Sondershausen
512 111	5128/1118	Sangerhausen
512 114	5129/1142	Seeburg
512 115	5123/1151	Bad Lauchstadt
512 115	5126/1159	Ammendorf
512 120	5122/1200	Merseburg
512 121	5122/1210	Horburg
512 121	5124/1213	Schkeuditz
512 135	5129/1352	Schwarzheide
512 141	5121/1417	Rachlau
512 141	5126/1415	Hoyerswerda
512 144	5124/1448	Neuhammer
512 162	5125/1625	Scinawa
512 163	5128/1638	Winsko
512 165	5122/1658	Prusice
512 165	5128/1655	Zmigrod
512 172	5122/1728	Twardogora
512 174	5124/1740	Miedzyborz (Kalisz)
512 174	5127/1749	Szklarka Myslniewska
512 174	5128/1748	Jesiona
512 175	5125/1757	Ostrzeszow
512 181	5121/1815	Galewice
512 181	5122/1812	Osiek (Kalisz)
512 181	5124/1816	Biedaszki
512 181	5128/1811	Debicze
512 181	5128/1819	Mielcuchy
512 182	5122/1826	Lututow
512 182	5125/1826	Klonowa
512 182	5125/1822	Leliwa
512 182	5127/1823	Czekaje
512 182	5128/1825	Kuznica Blonska
512 182	5129/1820	Czajkow
512 183	5120/1836	Gwizdalki
512 183	5121/1837	Ostrowek (Wielun)
512 183	5122/1836	Janow (Sieradzkie)
512 183	5125/1837	Zloczew
512 184	5120/1849	Strobin
512 184	5120/1843	Wielgie
512 184	5122/1845	Wolnica Niechmirowska
512 184	5123/1846	Niechmirow
512 184	5123/1849	Rychlocice
512 184	5125/1844	Gronow
512 184	5125/1847	Waszkowskie
512 184	5126/1843	Brzeznica
512 184	5126/1849	Majaczewice
512 184	5128/1849	Samborz
512 185	5120/1857	Dabrowa Rusiecka
512 185	5122/1856	Grabowie
512 185	5126/1858	Rogozno (Kielce)
512 185	5126/1858	Rogozno (Sieradz)
512 185	5126/1857	Widawa
512 185	5128/1850	Burzenin
512 185	5128/1857	Gorki Grabienskie
512 190	5120/1907	Szczercow
512 190	5121/1902	Korablew Zagrodniki
512 190	5122/1901	Klecz
512 190	5122/1901	Sarnow (Kielce)
512 190	5127/1904	Korczyska
512 190	5128/1901	Wola Wezykowa
512 191	5123/1915	Parzno
512 191	5124/1914	Rozdzin
512 191	5127/1911	Pozdzienice
512 191	5128/1914	Zelow
512 191	5129/1915	Zelowek
512 192	5120/1922	Grocholice
512 192	5122/1923	Belchatow
512 192	5122/1926	Dobiecin
512 192	5122/1927	Zwierzchow
512 192	5123/1922	Belchatowek
512 192	5123/1924	Dobrzelow
512 192	5124/1925	Paulinow
512 192	5129/1928	Dziewuliny
512 193	5121/1935	Wola Krzysztoporska
512 193	5128/1935	Kamocin
512 194	5121/1947	Klodzice
512 194	5121/1947	Kludzice
512 194	5121/1943	Milejow
512 194	5124/1941	Piotrkow Trybunalski
512 194	5124/1946	Poniatow
512 194	5124/1947	Uszczyn
512 195	5120/1951	Wojtostwo
512 195	5122/1953	Podklasztorze
512 195	5122/1953	Sulejow
512 195	5122/1950	Wlodzimierzow
512 195	5123/1950	Przyglow
512 195	5124/1950	Nowa Wies
512 200	5120/2008	Dabrowa (Opoczno)
512 200	5122/2002	Mniszkow
512 200	5123/2008	Owadow

512	200	5125/2005	Potok B
512	200	5126/2005	Celestynow
512	200	5127/2009	Lokietka
512	200	5127/2008	Tomaszowek
512	200	5127/2005	Unewel
512	200	5128/2001	Tresta Rzadowa
512	201	5121/2019	Ogonowice
512	201	5121/2011	Zachorzow
512	201	5122/2017	Opoczno
512	201	5124/2012	Gawrony
512	201	5125/2011	Kuniczki
512	201	5127/2015	Krasnica
512	202	5120/2025	Kuraszkow
512	202	5121/2025	Stuzno
512	202	5123/2027	Rozwady
512	202	5124/2023	Bielowice
512	202	5124/2029	Gielniow
512	202	5125/2025	Wolka Karwicka
512	202	5126/2027	Jelnia
512	202	5126/2020	Libiszow
512	202	5126/2022	Trzebina
512	202	5127/2029	Drzewica
512	202	5128/2023	Gielzow
512	202	5128/2025	Radzice
512	203	5122/2037	Przysucha
512	203	5124/2038	Smogorzow
512	203	5124/2030	Wywoz
512	203	5127/2032	Zychorzyn
512	204	5120/2045	Politow
512	204	5120/2047	Rykow
512	204	5122/2043	Skrzynno
512	204	5122/2048	Wieniawa
512	204	5123/2047	Sokolniki Suche
512	204	5123/2042	Zbozenna
512	204	5125/2048	Plec
512	205	5123/2055	Wawrzyszow
512	205	5123/2058	Wolanow
512	205	5125/2059	Chruslice
512	205	5125/2052	Glogow (Kielce)
512	205	5126/2052	Mlodnice
512	205	5128/2054	Przytyk
512	205	5129/2055	Podgajek
512	210	5123/2108	Zakowice
512	210	5125/2109	Piotrowice (Radom)
512	210	5125/2109	Radom
512	210	5128/2102	Taczow
512	210	5129/2105	Kaminsk
512	211	5121/2111	Zenonow
512	211	5122/2111	Malczow
512	211	5124/2119	Klwatka
512	211	5126/2111	Firlej (Radom)
512	211	5126/2118	Groszowice
512	211	5126/2119	Piotrowice (Lublin)
512	211	5128/2117	Dabrowa Kozlowska
512	212	5123/2120	Niemianowice
512	212	5125/2124	Slupica
512	212	5126/2127	Czarna (Radom)
512	212	5126/2120	Jedlnia Letnisko
512	212	5128/2122	Jedlnia
512	212	5128/2129	Suskowola
512	212	5129/2127	Pionki
512	212	5129/2122	Poswietne
512	213	5121/2136	Zwolen
512	213	5125/2139	Jozefow (Nad Wisla)
512	213	5126/2131	Sucha (Radom)
512	213	5127/2135	Patkow
512	213	5129/2138	Garbatka
512	213	5129/2136	Ponikwa
512	213	5129/2138	Wygwizdow
512	214	5120/2147	Mszadla Nowa
512	214	5121/2147	Mszadla Stara
512	214	5122/2147	Laguszow
512	214	5123/2148	Pajakow
512	214	5123/2144	Zalazy
512	214	5125/2143	Jablonow
512	214	5125/2141	Jadwinow
512	214	5125/2148	Polesie Duze
512	214	5126/2143	Czarnolas
512	214	5127/2144	Piatkow
512	214	5128/2148	Gniewoszow
512	214	5128/2146	Sarnow (Lublin)
512	215	5120/2159	Bochotnica
512	215	5120/2153	Janowiec
512	215	5121/2157	Wojszyn
512	215	5124/2154	Stanislawow (Gora Pulawska)
512	215	5125/2157	Gora Pulawska
512	215	5125/2154	Pachnowola
512	215	5125/2158	Pulawy
512	215	5125/2151	Zarzecze (Radom)
512	215	5126/2157	Jaroszyn
512	220	5121/2207	Karmanowice
512	220	5121/2209	Klementowice
512	220	5125/2204	Konskowola
512	220	5128/2203	Wronow
512	221	5120/2219	Ozarow Przy Lugowie
512	221	5122/2216	Markuszow
512	221	5123/2212	Kurow
512	221	5126/2217	Wolka Katna
512	221	5128/2212	Choszczow
512	222	5121/2221	Garbow
512	222	5122/2228	Krasienin
512	222	5124/2225	Staroscin
512	222	5124/2220	Wola Przybyslawska
512	222	5128/2229	Siedliska
512	222	5128/2223	Stanislawow Duzy
512	223	5121/2230	Majdan Krasieninski
512	223	5122/2238	Zalesie (Lublin)

512 223	5128/2238	Lubartow	
512 224	5120/2248	Ziolkow	
512 224	5121/2248	Kijany Blizsze	
512 224	5121/2246	Spiczyn	
512 225	5120/2250	Karolin	
512 225	5121/2257	Dratow	
512 225	5121/2255	Ludwin	
512 225	5121/2251	Zezulin	
512 225	5123/2259	Rogozno (Lublin)	
512 225	5125/2252	Rozkopaczow	
512 225	5126/2252	Rudka Kijanska	
512 225	5128/2251	Kolechowice	
512 225	5128/2257	Masluchy	
512 225	5129/2256	Glebokie (Wlodawa)	
512 225	5129/2251	Ostrow Lubelski	
512 230	5121/2302	Nadrybie	
512 230	5122/2307	Garbatowka	
512 230	5124/2307	Zalucze	
512 230	5125/2301	Rozplucie	
512 230	5126/2308	Wola Wereszczynska	
512 230	5128/2306	Jamniki	
512 230	5128/2301	Orzechow Nowy	
512 230	5129/2303	Komarowka	
512 231	5120/2311	Swierszczow	
512 231	5122/2315	Sekow	
512 231	5122/2313	Wereszczyn	
512 231	5123/2311	Kozubata	
512 231	5123/2319	Kulczyn	
512 231	5124/2312	Urszulin	
512 231	5126/2316	Wytyczno	
512 231	5128/2319	Kolacze	
512 231	5129/2318	Brus	
512 232	5120/2328	Lowcza (Chelm)	
512 232	5121/2322	Serniawy	
512 232	5121/2325	Wolka Petrylowska	
512 232	5122/2327	Bukowski Las	
512 232	5123/2323	Ujazdow	
512 232	5124/2325	Hansk	
512 232	5125/2324	Kratie	
512 232	5126/2326	Dubeczno	
512 232	5126/2325	Glinianki	
512 232	5127/2328	Gorki (Wlodawa)	
512 232	5128/2329	Luta	
512 233	5120/2332	Mszanna	
512 233	5121/2330	Tomaszowka	
512 233	5123/2337	Stulno	
512 233	5125/2331	Osowa	
512 233	5126/2339	Wolczyny	
512 233	5129/2339	Sobibor	
512 234	5124/2342	Zbereze	
512 235	5121/2359	Zgorany	
512 235	5129/2351	Svityaz	
512 240	5120/2405	Golovno	
512 240	5120/2404	Kuchany	

512 240	5123/2407	Nudyzhi Peski	
512 240	5129/2403	Vilitsa	
512 241	5120/2410	Byk	
512 241	5125/2410	Sukach	
512 241	5128/2413	Lyubokhiny	
512 242	5124/2425	Novaya Vyzhva	
512 242	5125/2420	Galinovolya	
512 243	5121/2437	Shushki	
512 243	5125/2436	Butsyn	
512 243	5125/2432	Sedlishche	
512 244	5123/2449	Nesukhoyezhe	
512 244	5125/2440	Serekhovichi	
512 244	5127/2445	Meltsy	
512 244	5129/2448	Kachin	
512 245	5128/2453	Soshichno	
512 250	5127/2506	Verkhi	
512 251	5124/2511	Stobykhva	
512 252	5123/2520	Gradysk	
512 252	5129/2524	Lishnevka	
512 253	5122/2532	Manevichi	
512 254	5122/2548	Kolodya	
512 254	5127/2549	Belskaya Volya	
512 255	5120/2558	Sukhovolya (Polesie)	
512 255	5122/2552	Rafalovka	
512 255	5125/2553	Sopachiv	
512 260	5124/2602	Lupisuki	
512 260	5125/2604	Dolgovolya	
512 260	5125/2605	Murowin	
512 260	5125/2608	Vladimirets	
512 260	5129/2605	Pechenki	
512 261	5126/2613	Kanonichi	
512 262	5121/2622	Tutovichi	
512 262	5122/2624	Tseptsevichi	
512 262	5123/2627	Tryskine	
512 262	5125/2629	Remchitsy	
512 262	5127/2620	Kidry	
512 262	5127/2625	Rudnya (Sarny)	
512 262	5128/2622	Osowa (Sarny)	
512 263	5120/2636	Sarny	
512 263	5123/2638	Lyukhcha	
512 263	5124/2639	Glushitsa	
512 263	5126/2639	Strelsk	
512 263	5127/2632	Kurash	
512 263	5129/2637	Lyubikovichi	
512 264	5125/2645	Buchlicze	
512 264	5125/2642	Karpilovka (Sarny)	
512 264	5126/2647	Folvark Karasin	
512 265	5120/2656	Klesov	
512 265	5129/2651	Karasin	
512 270	5122/2705	Tomashgorod	
512 272	5123/2728	Belovizh	
512 272	5123/2720	Zalavye	
512 272	5126/2721	Blezhovo	
512 285	5128/2852	Priluki (Ovruch)	

512	313	5122/3139	Kulikovka	513	090	5131/0900	Wrexen
512	321	5122/3214	Kholmy	513	090	5132/0903	Rimbeck
512	325	5121/3253	Baturin	513	090	5132/0902	Scherfede
512	335	5120/3352	Putivl	513	090	5133/0903	Bonenburg
512	375	5120/3750	Stary Oskol	513	090	5136/0908	Peckelsheim
513	061	5138/0614	Weeze	513	090	5137/0905	Helmern
513	062	5131/0620	Geldern	513	091	5130/0910	Warburg
513	062	5132/0626	Issum	513	091	5131/0914	Daseburg
513	062	5134/0622	Kapellen	513	091	5131/0915	Rosebeck
513	062	5137/0622	Sonsbeck	513	091	5134/0915	Borgentreich
513	063	5133/0636	Rheinberg	513	091	5137/0916	Borgholz
513	063	5135/0631	Alpen	513	092	5132/0924	Humme
513	063	5138/0635	Buderich	513	092	5133/0922	Eberschutz
513	064	5132/0648	Holten	513	092	5133/0923	Sielen
513	064	5132/0642	Orsoy	513	092	5135/0925	Trendelburg
513	064	5132/0642	Walsum	513	092	5136/0925	Deisel
513	064	5134/0644	Dinslaken	513	092	5138/0927	Karlshafen
513	065	5131/0655	Bottrop	513	092	5139/0925	Herstelle
513	065	5134/0659	Gladbeck	513	093	5138/0934	Bodenfelde
513	070	5131/0706	Gelsenkirchen	513	094	5130/0946	Dransfeld
513	070	5136/0708	Herten	513	094	5135/0945	Adelebsen
513	070	5139/0705	Marl	513	095	5130/0954	Rosdorf
513	071	5132/0717	Kray	513	095	5132/0956	Gottingen
513	071	5132/0710	Wanne Eickel	513	095	5135/0956	Bovenden
513	071	5133/0719	Castrop Rauxel	513	095	5138/0956	Norten Hardenberg
513	071	5133/0713	Herne	513	101	5131/1016	Duderstadt
513	071	5137/0712	Recklinghausen	513	101	5133/1010	Grosseneder
513	072	5130/0721	Somborn	513	103	5130/1038	Immenrode
513	072	5131/0725	Dorstfeld	513	103	5135/1039	Ellrich
513	072	5131/0727	Dortmund	513	104	5131/1048	Nordhausen
513	072	5138/0724	Waltrop	513	105	5134/1057	Harz
513	073	5134/0736	Kolonie Kaiserau	513	110	5138/1109	Harzgerode
513	073	5137/0731	Lunen	513	113	5132/1133	Eisleben
513	073	5138/0738	Bergkamen	513	113	5138/1137	Gerbstedt
513	074	5132/0741	Unna	513	120	5130/1200	Halle
513	074	5136/0745	Altenbogge	513	121	5131/1210	Landsberg
513	074	5136/0740	Kamen (Westfalen)	513	121	5137/1219	Bitterfeld
513	074	5137/0743	Lerche	513	122	5132/1221	Delitzsch
513	075	5133/0755	Werl	513	130	5131/1306	Camitz
513	080	5130/0807	Korbecke	513	130	5134/1300	Torgau
513	080	5135/0807	Soest	513	132	5136/1326	Trobitz
513	080	5138/0806	Oestinghausen	513	140	5131/1401	Senftenberg
513	081	5138/0812	Ostinghausen	513	150	5138/1509	Zary
513	082	5134/0820	Anrochte	513	151	5137/1519	Zagan
513	082	5134/0826	Ostereiden	513	154	5131/1548	Przemkow
513	082	5137/0821	Erwitte	513	165	5133/1659	Lakta
513	082	5138/0822	Westernkotten	513	165	5134/1659	Kubeczki
513	083	5133/0834	Buren	513	165	5137/1652	Rawicz
513	083	5135/0836	Brenken	513	165	5138/1652	Laszczyn
513	083	5139/0831	Geseke	513	165	5138/1654	Sarnowa
513	084	5134/0844	Haaren	513	170	5134/1709	Ostoje
513	084	5138/0841	Niederntudorf	513	170	5134/1704	Zaorle
513	085	5137/0854	Lichtenau (Westphalia)	513	170	5137/1708	Dubin
513	090	5131/0905	Ossendorf	513	171	5132/1716	Milicz

513	171	5138/1711	Nadstawem
513	171	5139/1710	Jutrosin
513	172	5139/1723	Zduny
513	173	5131/1732	Zabnik
513	173	5132/1734	Bogdaj
513	173	5132/1739	Garki
513	174	5131/1740	Granowiec
513	174	5134/1742	Odolanow
513	174	5139/1749	Ostrow Wielkopolski
513	175	5132/1759	Mikstat
513	180	5131/1807	Grabow
513	180	5131/1807	Grabow (Poznan)
513	180	5137/1808	Kakawa
513	180	5137/1808	Kolano Swierczyno
513	181	5130/1817	Kuznica Grabowska
513	181	5130/1811	Nieszkodna
513	181	5131/1814	Kraszewice
513	181	5131/1810	Raclawice (Lodz)
513	181	5133/1813	Ostrow Kaliski
513	181	5135/1817	Czempisz
513	181	5135/1813	Moczalec
513	181	5135/1811	Przystajnia
513	181	5136/1814	Jagodziniec
513	181	5139/1811	Godziesze Wielkie
513	182	5130/1827	Braszewice
513	182	5130/1822	Salamony Grabowskie
513	182	5137/1820	Sobieseki
513	182	5139/1820	Iwanowice (Kalisz)
513	183	5132/1834	Kliczkow Wielki
513	183	5134/1838	Charlupia Wielka
513	183	5134/1839	Drzazna
513	183	5136/1833	Waglczew
513	184	5136/1845	Sieradz
513	184	5137/1843	Dzigorzew
513	185	5136/1856	Zdunska Wola
513	190	5131/1902	Sedziejowice
513	190	5132/1909	Buczkowska Wola
513	190	5134/1907	Lopatki
513	190	5135/1908	Lask
513	190	5136/1900	Krobanow
513	191	5135/1912	Teodory
513	191	5137/1911	Kolumna
513	191	5138/1915	Dobron
513	192	5131/1920	Chynow
513	192	5131/1925	Wadlew
513	192	5134/1924	Dlutow
513	192	5139/1929	Babichy
513	193	5130/1933	Lubanow
513	193	5130/1930	Rusociny
513	193	5131/1939	Rekoraj
513	193	5132/1938	Srock
513	193	5136/1938	Rzepki
513	193	5136/1933	Tuszyn
513	194	5130/1941	Gajkowice
513	194	5130/1943	Moszczenica (Lodz)
513	194	5135/1945	Bedkow
513	194	5137/1943	Zamosc (Piotrkow Trybunalski)
513	194	5139/1945	Laznowska Wola
513	195	5130/1950	Wolborz
513	195	5133/1958	Niebrow
513	195	5134/1953	Wolka Krzykowska
513	200	5132/2004	Ludwikow
513	200	5132/2003	Niwka
513	200	5132/2008	Spala
513	200	5132/2001	Tomaszow Mazowiecki
513	201	5132/2013	Inowlodz
513	201	5134/2013	Poswietne (Skierniewice)
513	201	5136/2018	Rzeczyca (Tomaszow Mazowiecki)
513	201	5138/2011	Wielka Wola
513	202	5132/2023	Poswietne (Opoczno)
513	202	5134/2029	Stanislawow (Opoczno)
513	202	5136/2022	Grotowice
513	202	5137/2023	Lubocz
513	202	5137/2029	Myslakowice
513	203	5130/2031	Domaszno
513	203	5131/2038	Sulgostow
513	203	5132/2038	Klwow
513	203	5132/2033	Odrzywol
513	203	5137/2032	Legonice
513	203	5138/2035	Nowe Miasto nad Pilica
513	204	5132/2042	Kozieniec
513	204	5132/2048	Ociesc
513	204	5137/2047	Grzmiaca
513	204	5138/2047	Gorki (Mogielnica)
513	205	5130/2052	Glinice
513	205	5134/2052	Radzanow
513	205	5134/2054	Rogolin
513	205	5137/2050	Wysmierzyce
513	205	5138/2053	Witaszyn
513	205	5139/2057	Bialobrzegi
513	210	5131/2107	Jedlinsk
513	210	5132/2103	Mokrosek
513	210	5134/2103	Gozd Stary
513	210	5134/2101	Kielbow
513	210	5136/2105	Kadlubek
513	210	5138/2105	Pirog
513	210	5139/2106	Stromiec
513	211	5133/2115	Gorynska Wola
513	211	5134/2110	Bierwce
513	211	5138/2119	Glowaczow
513	211	5139/2114	Lipskie Budy
513	212	5134/2122	Cecylowka
513	212	5139/2124	Laszowka
513	213	5130/2131	Januszno
513	213	5135/2134	Kozienice

513 214	5132/2149	Wolka Wojcieszkowska	
513 214	5133/2145	Sieciechow	
513 214	5135/2147	Stezyca	
513 214	5137/2140	Pawlowice	
513 215	5134/2156	Bobrowniki	
513 215	5134/2152	Irena	
513 215	5134/2159	Sedowice	
513 215	5137/2159	Chrustne	
513 215	5138/2150	Brzeziny (Garwolin)	
513 215	5138/2156	Ryki	
513 220	5130/2206	Zyrzyn	
513 220	5133/2202	Parafianka	
513 220	5134/2209	Baranow	
513 220	5134/2203	Skrudki	
513 220	5134/2204	Wilczanka	
513 220	5135/2208	Drazgow	
513 220	5136/2204	Bialki Dolne	
513 220	5136/2205	Bialki Gorne	
513 220	5138/2207	Grabowce	
513 220	5138/2200	Janisze	
513 221	5131/2211	Sniadowka	
513 221	5132/2218	Michow Lubartowski	
513 221	5133/2211	Wola Czolnowska	
513 221	5135/2212	Skladow	
513 221	5136/2213	Blizocin	
513 221	5136/2217	Drewnik	
513 221	5136/2210	Sobieszyn	
513 221	5137/2217	Lysobyki	
513 221	5137/2216	Przytoczno	
513 221	5137/2215	Wola Blizocka	
513 221	5139/2211	Podlodowka	
513 222	5130/2223	Golab	
513 222	5131/2229	Sobolew (Lublin)	
513 222	5133/2229	Firlej	
513 222	5134/2225	Antonin Nowy	
513 222	5135/2227	Antonin Stary	
513 222	5136/2220	Ostrow (Lubartow)	
513 222	5138/2227	Kock	
513 223	5131/2239	Gorka Lubartowska	
513 223	5133/2237	Leszkowice	
513 223	5134/2232	Stalnia	
513 223	5135/2238	Kamiennowola	
513 223	5135/2234	Luszawa	
513 223	5135/2235	Szaniawy Matysy	
513 223	5136/2231	Suloszyn	
513 223	5136/2233	Zurawieniec	
513 223	5138/2235	Zawada (Piotrkowskie)	
513 224	5130/2246	Kaznow	
513 224	5131/2245	Berejow	
513 224	5131/2242	Tarlo	
513 224	5132/2245	Brzeznica Bychawska	
513 224	5133/2245	Brzeznica Ksiazeca	
513 224	5135/2245	Jurki	
513 224	5136/2242	Dzialyn	

513 224	5138/2246	Siemien	
513 225	5134/2251	Tysmienica (Lublin)	
513 225	5135/2256	Makoszka	
513 225	5137/2255	Sowin	
513 225	5137/2257	Stepkow	
513 225	5138/2254	Parczew	
513 230	5131/2305	Sosnowica	
513 230	5134/2300	Mosciska (Wlodawa)	
513 230	5135/2304	Nietiahy	
513 230	5135/2302	Uhnin	
513 230	5136/2308	Kodeniec	
513 230	5136/2301	Zmiarki	
513 230	5137/2305	Lubiczyn	
513 230	5139/2309	Zaliszcze	
513 231	5132/2316	Kamien (Wlodawa)	
513 231	5132/2318	Skorodnica	
513 231	5133/2311	Hola	
513 231	5133/2319	Lubien (Chelm)	
513 231	5133/2310	Turno	
513 231	5134/2313	Zamolodycze	
513 231	5136/2315	Horostyta	
513 231	5137/2310	Wyhalew	
513 232	5130/2326	Suchawa	
513 232	5134/2323	Wyryki	
513 232	5136/2321	Kaplonosy	
513 233	5130/2331	Okuninka	
513 233	5131/2334	Orchowek	
513 233	5132/2334	Vlodavka	
513 233	5133/2336	Tomashevka	
513 233	5134/2333	Wlodawa	
513 234	5131/2347	Pulmo	
513 234	5132/2343	Pulemets	
513 235	5130/2357	Shatsk	
513 235	5136/2350	Pishcha	
513 240	5130/2407	Pripyat	
513 242	5134/2422	Rakita	
513 243	5134/2434	Zamshany	
513 243	5137/2433	Vydranitsa	
513 244	5131/2446	Datyn	
513 244	5136/2441	Ternets	
513 244	5138/2449	Buzaki	
513 245	5133/2454	Nuyno	
513 245	5133/2457	Zalese (Kamen Kashirskiy)	
513 245	5138/2458	Kamen Kashirskiy	
513 246	5130/2460	Aleksandriya	
513 250	5134/2507	Politsy (Kamen Kashirskiy)	
513 252	5131/2525	Griva (Polesie)	
513 255	5132/2553	Mulchitsy	
513 255	5135/2557	Tselkoviche Velikoye	
513 260	5130/2606	Zeleno	
513 260	5133/2606	Voronki	
513 260	5135/2608	Khinoch	

513 261	5130/2613	Ozero (Wolyn)	
513 261	5133/2619	Tryputna	
513 261	5138/2611	Stepangorod	
513 262	5131/2626	Nivetsk	
513 262	5132/2621	Gran	
513 262	5134/2629	Krupove	
513 263	5130/2633	Orvanitsa	
513 263	5131/2637	Berezhki	
513 263	5132/2633	Berestye	
513 263	5134/2634	Dubrovitsa	
513 263	5135/2637	Kolki (Polesie)	
513 263	5139/2637	Lyutynsk	
513 264	5130/2646	Gradki	
513 264	5139/2640	Velyun	
513 265	5134/2655	Ozero (Polesie)	
513 265	5137/2653	Shakhi	
513 270	5137/2708	Stare Siolo (Polesie)	
513 271	5139/2714	Drozdin	
513 272	5131/2725	Glinne (Polesie)	
513 272	5133/2723	Yuzefin	
513 272	5135/2721	Berezovo	
513 285	5138/2850	Skorodnoye	
513 290	5138/2904	Slovechno	
513 311	5130/3118	Chernigov	
513 311	5133/3119	Khutor Shevchenko	
513 312	5131/3122	Bobrovitsa	
513 314	5134/3147	Berezna	
513 321	5131/3213	Mena	
513 323	5132/3230	Sosnitsa	
513 325	5134/3258	Korop	
513 332	5133/3323	Krolevets	
513 344	5134/3440	Rylsk	
513 455	5130/4555	Saratov	
513 455	5130/4555	Saratova	
514 060	5147/0609	Kleve	
514 061	5140/0610	Goch	
514 061	5140/0618	Udem	
514 061	5144/0618	Kalkar	
514 062	5140/0627	Xanten	
514 062	5144/0629	Mehr	
514 062	5146/0628	Haldern	
514 062	5146/0624	Rees	
514 063	5140/0637	Wesel	
514 063	5144/0635	Hamminkeln	
514 063	5149/0630	Werth	
514 064	5143/0641	Brunen	
514 065	5140/0658	Dorsten	
514 065	5146/0651	Raesfeld	
514 070	5140/0701	Hervest	
514 070	5146/0700	Lembeck	
514 070	5147/0702	Klein Reken	
514 071	5144/0711	Haltern	
514 072	5140/0723	Datteln	
514 072	5142/0728	Selm	
514 072	5146/0728	Ludinghausen	
514 073	5140/0730	Bork	
514 073	5140/0738	Werne an der Lippe	
514 074	5142/0742	Horst Emscher	
514 074	5145/0741	Herbern	
514 074	5148/0745	Drensteinfurt	
514 075	5145/0755	Ahlen	
514 080	5140/0809	Hovestadt	
514 080	5145/0802	Beckum	
514 080	5149/0809	Oelde	
514 082	5140/0821	Lippstadt	
514 082	5142/0823	Lipperode	
514 082	5148/0826	Rietberg	
514 083	5140/0836	Salzkotten	
514 083	5141/0834	Verne	
514 084	5140/0846	Hamborn	
514 084	5143/0846	Paderborn	
514 084	5147/0849	Bad Lippspringe	
514 085	5149/0850	Schlangen	
514 090	5147/0904	Pombsen	
514 090	5148/0907	Nieheim	
514 091	5141/0914	Erkeln	
514 091	5143/0911	Brakel	
514 091	5147/0918	Ovenhausen	
514 092	5140/0922	Beverungen	
514 092	5145/0923	Boffzen	
514 092	5146/0923	Hoxter	
514 092	5149/0927	Holzminden	
514 093	5140/0939	Uslar	
514 094	5148/0941	Dassel	
514 094	5149/0947	Markoldendorf	
514 095	5140/0959	Sudheim	
514 095	5142/0952	Moringen	
514 095	5149/0952	Einbeck	
514 100	5142/1000	Northeim	
514 100	5145/1003	Imbshausen	
514 101	5144/1011	Osterode am Harz	
514 102	5149/1021	Clausthal Zellerfeld	
514 103	5144/1037	Braunlage	
514 110	5144/1108	Gernrode	
514 110	5145/1103	Thale	
514 110	5147/1109	Quedlinburg	
514 111	5143/1114	Ballenstedt	
514 111	5147/1118	Hoym	
514 112	5142/1128	Quenstedt	
514 112	5145/1128	Aschersleben	
514 113	5141/1134	Sandersleben	
514 113	5147/1136	Gusten	
514 114	5145/1149	Plomnitz	
514 114	5148/1144	Bernburg	
514 115	5141/1152	Grobzig	
514 115	5145/1158	Kothen	
514 121	5141/1218	Jessnitz	
514 124	5149/1247	Wartenburg	

514	140	5141/1408	Casel
514	142	5146/1420	Cottbus
514	143	5144/1438	Forst
514	151	5147/1515	Krzystkowice
514	153	5145/1536	Kozuchow (Nowa Sol)
514	154	5148/1543	Nowa Sol
514	155	5144/1550	Bytom Odrzanski
514	161	5148/1619	Wschowa
514	163	5140/1632	Gora
514	163	5147/1639	Rydzyna
514	164	5142/1647	Golina Wielka
514	164	5142/1649	Golinka
514	164	5146/1648	Poniec
514	165	5146/1651	Dzieczyna
514	165	5147/1653	Rokosowo
514	170	5141/1700	Woszczkowo
514	170	5146/1700	Krobia
514	171	5140/1712	Pawlowo (Leszno)
514	171	5149/1713	Pogorzela
514	172	5142/1727	Krotoszyn
514	172	5149/1727	Kozmin
514	173	5140/1730	Smoszew
514	174	5143/1744	Raszkow
514	175	5142/1752	Lewkow
514	175	5143/1759	Skalmierzyce Nowe
514	180	5144/1806	Piwonice
514	180	5144/1802	Szczypiorno
514	180	5145/1805	Kalisz
514	180	5145/1806	Zagorzynek
514	180	5147/1806	Chmielnik (Lodz)
514	181	5140/1816	Kuczewola
514	181	5144/1814	Opatowek
514	182	5140/1827	Blaszki
514	182	5140/1826	Boryslawice
514	182	5142/1823	Staw
514	182	5148/1820	Kozminek
514	183	5141/1833	Raczkow
514	183	5142/1838	Warta
514	183	5142/1835	Zagajew
514	183	5149/1833	Chocim (Lodz)
514	183	5149/1833	Kaszew
514	183	5149/1838	Maszew
514	183	5149/1830	Podkowa
514	184	5142/1847	Rossoszyca
514	184	5146/1843	Lubola
514	184	5148/1844	Peczniew
514	185	5140/1859	Szadkowice
514	185	5141/1859	Szadek
514	185	5143/1850	Lipiny Nowe
514	185	5144/1859	Krokocka Wola
514	185	5144/1851	Rzeczyca (Lodz)
514	185	5149/1854	Bratkow Gorny
514	190	5143/1909	Wodzierady
514	190	5144/1906	Dobruchow
514	190	5146/1904	Przyrownica
514	190	5147/1902	Malyn
514	191	5140/1916	Wincentow
514	191	5141/1918	Piatkowisko
514	191	5142/1919	Swiatniki
514	191	5145/1913	Lutomiersk
514	191	5146/1910	Czolczyn
514	191	5149/1918	Aleksandrow Lodzki
514	191	5149/1919	Bruzyca
514	192	5140/1920	Karniszewice
514	192	5140/1922	Pabianice
514	192	5142/1927	Ruda Pabianicka
514	192	5143/1925	Chocianowice
514	192	5143/1929	Chojny Stare
514	192	5143/1929	Chojny
514	192	5145/1920	Konstantynow Lodzki
514	192	5145/1928	Lodz
514	192	5148/1928	Baluty
514	192	5148/1921	Kochanowka
514	192	5149/1922	Kaly
514	192	5149/1927	Radogoszcz
514	193	5140/1938	Brojce
514	193	5140/1930	Rzgow
514	193	5142/1936	Giemzow
514	193	5142/1931	Konstantyna
514	193	5143/1938	Wisniowa Gora
514	193	5144/1939	Andrespol
514	193	5144/1938	Andrzejow (Lodz)
514	193	5146/1935	Mileszki
514	194	5140/1949	Rokiciny
514	194	5142/1948	Chrusty Nowe
514	194	5143/1947	Kaletnik
514	194	5144/1947	Rozyca
514	194	5145/1944	Galkowek
514	194	5146/1948	Koluszki
514	194	5147/1943	Malczew
514	194	5148/1945	Brzeziny
514	195	5140/1957	Subina
514	195	5141/1958	Jozefow Stary (Warszawa)
514	195	5143/1952	Redzen Nowy
514	195	5144/1950	Katarzynow
514	195	5145/1950	Felicjanow Nowy
514	195	5146/1950	Felicjanow
514	195	5149/1958	Jezow
514	195	5149/1953	Jozefow (Brzeziny)
514	195	5149/1954	Marianow Rogowski
514	195	5149/1951	Rogow
514	200	5140/2004	Walentynow
514	200	5141/2001	Janinow (Rava Russkaya)
514	200	5144/2009	Byliny Stare
514	200	5147/2006	Milochniewice
514	201	5142/2012	Zubki Duze

514 201	5146/2015	Rawa Mazowiecka
514 201	5146/2011	Soszyce
514 202	5140/2021	Mroczkowice
514 202	5140/2023	Stolniki
514 202	5145/2023	Regnow
514 202	5145/2029	Turobowice
514 202	5148/2029	Biala Rawska
514 202	5148/2020	Zagorze (Warszawa)
514 204	5142/2044	Mogielnica
514 205	5140/2051	Przybyszew
514 205	5141/2057	Falecice
514 205	5141/2057	Promna
514 205	5142/2050	Piotrowka
514 205	5144/2051	Goszczyn
514 205	5146/2053	Dlugowola
514 205	5149/2059	Boglewice
514 210	5140/2109	Ksawerow Stary
514 210	5140/2105	Niedabyl
514 210	5142/2101	Biejkow
514 210	5142/2108	Boze
514 210	5142/2107	Ducka Wola
514 210	5143/2102	Brankow
514 210	5144/2104	Boncza
514 210	5146/2108	Grzegorzewice (Warszawa)
514 210	5147/2106	Opozdzew
514 210	5148/2106	Brzezinki
514 210	5149/2105	Nowa Wies (Grojec)
514 211	5141/2112	Budy Augustowskie
514 211	5143/2110	Boska Wola
514 211	5147/2112	Warka
514 211	5148/2118	Rozniszew
514 212	5140/2129	Swierze Gorne
514 212	5141/2126	Ryczywol
514 212	5145/2129	Podlez
514 212	5146/2124	Magnuszew
514 212	5146/2122	Wola Magnuszewska
514 212	5148/2127	Tarnow (Siedlce)
514 213	5142/2133	Maciejowice
514 213	5146/2134	Budy Krepskie
514 213	5148/2136	Laskarzew
514 213	5149/2132	Krzywda
514 214	5141/2144	Wola Zycka
514 214	5143/2146	Damianow
514 214	5143/2140	Godzisz
514 214	5144/2147	Korytnica (Lublin)
514 214	5144/2140	Sobolew
514 214	5144/2145	Wola Korycka
514 214	5147/2144	Gonczyce
514 214	5148/2145	Ostrozen
514 215	5142/2155	Ownia
514 215	5142/2151	Zabianka
514 215	5143/2154	Kurzelaty
514 215	5143/2155	Wylezin
514 215	5144/2158	Kloczew
514 215	5146/2152	Ostrowek (Wegrow)
514 215	5149/2158	Jarczew
514 215	5149/2152	Wola Zelechowska
514 215	5149/2154	Zelechow
514 220	5141/2206	Grabow Rycki
514 220	5141/2208	Zawitala
514 220	5144/2205	Wojciechowka
514 220	5145/2206	Okrzeja
514 220	5146/2209	Wola Okrzejska
514 220	5147/2200	Gesia Wolka
514 220	5148/2202	Koryczany
514 220	5149/2203	Huta Dabrowa
514 220	5149/2203	Nowiny Pokarczmiska
514 221	5140/2217	Charlejow
514 221	5143/2216	Czarna (Lublin)
514 221	5143/2215	Sobiska
514 221	5143/2214	Wola Gulowska
514 221	5144/2216	Adamow
514 221	5146/2219	Wojcieszkow
514 221	5148/2216	Burzec
514 222	5142/2220	Serokomla
514 222	5146/2228	Krasew
514 222	5146/2220	Wola Bystrzycka
514 222	5147/2228	Wola Chomejowa
514 222	5148/2228	Zarzyc Ulanski
514 222	5149/2229	Ulan
514 223	5141/2237	Czemierniki
514 223	5143/2231	Borki (Lublin)
514 223	5143/2238	Lichty
514 223	5144/2239	Nieweglosz
514 223	5144/2236	Paszki Duze
514 223	5145/2235	Paszki Male
514 223	5147/2237	Radzyn Podlaski
514 223	5149/2233	Bedlno
514 224	5140/2247	Zminne
514 224	5141/2249	Cichostow
514 224	5142/2244	Suchowola (Parczew)
514 224	5143/2240	Skoki (Kock)
514 224	5145/2247	Wohyn
514 224	5146/2248	Bezwola
514 224	5147/2245	Bojanowka
514 225	5142/2255	Kostry
514 225	5142/2253	Milanow
514 225	5146/2259	Radcze
514 225	5149/2251	Ossowa
514 225	5149/2252	Przegaliny Male
514 230	5141/2304	Kolano
514 230	5143/2308	Paszenki
514 230	5144/2306	Jablon
514 230	5147/2305	Polubicze Wiejskie
514 230	5149/2302	Woroniec
514 231	5141/2312	Podedworze
514 231	5144/2315	Lyniew

514 231	5145/2318	Rozwadowka		514 293	5148/2930	Narovlya
514 231	5148/2313	Wisznice		514 301	5147/3016	Bragin
514 232	5141/2324	Holeszow		514 303	5142/3039	Lyubech
514 232	5143/2320	Motwica		514 315	5149/3156	Shchors
514 233	5141/2331	Dolhobrody		514 321	5146/3216	Koryukovka
514 233	5143/2330	Hanna		514 332	5146/3328	Voronezh
514 233	5145/2336	Domachevo		514 335	5141/3355	Glukhov
514 233	5145/2333	Slawatycze		514 351	5141/3516	Lgov
514 233	5147/2334	Liszna		515 061	5150/0615	Emmerich
514 233	5149/2331	Krzywowolka		515 062	5150/0628	Isselburg
514 234	5146/2340	Leplevka		515 062	5151/0626	Anholt
514 235	5146/2359	Zburazh		515 063	5150/0636	Bocholt
514 240	5147/2405	Malorita		515 064	5150/0642	Rhede
514 241	5140/2417	Tur		515 065	5151/0652	Borken (Essen)
514 242	5143/2429	Gorniki		515 065	5151/0652	Gemen
514 243	5140/2431	Ratno		515 065	5154/0659	Velen
514 244	5143/2448	Khoteshov		515 065	5155/0651	Weseke
514 244	5148/2447	Shchedrogir		515 065	5156/0652	Sudlohn
514 245	5144/2452	Cherche		515 065	5159/0656	Stadtlohn
514 245	5147/2452	Shchityn		515 070	5156/0709	Coesfeld
514 245	5148/2459	Malaya Glusha		515 070	5157/0701	Gescher
514 250	5142/2504	Vorokomle		515 071	5150/0718	Dulmen
514 250	5144/2501	Vyderta		515 071	5156/0714	Gerleve
514 250	5149/2503	Velikaya Glusha		515 071	5158/0718	Billerbeck
514 251	5140/2516	Farynki		515 072	5156/0721	Nottuln
514 251	5140/2510	Krymno		515 073	5158/0738	Munster
514 251	5140/2516	Pnevno		515 074	5155/0744	Wolbeck
514 251	5145/2516	Bykhov (Polesie)		515 075	5150/0757	Enniger
514 251	5149/2517	Tsyr		515 075	5155/0758	Freckenhorst
514 252	5145/2521	Derevok		515 075	5155/0754	Mehringen
514 253	5144/2535	Sudche		515 075	5157/0759	Warendorf
514 253	5146/2531	Lyubeshov		515 080	5156/0808	Beelen
514 254	5140/2542	Kukhotskaya Volya		515 081	5150/0819	Wiedenbruck
514 254	5149/2546	Kutyn		515 081	5151/0818	Rheda
514 255	5149/2550	Loknitsa		515 081	5158/0814	Harsewinkel
514 260	5141/2609	Dubrovsk		515 082	5154/0823	Gutersloh
514 260	5149/2608	Zarechnoye		515 083	5151/0834	Kaunitz
514 261	5143/2616	Svaritsevichi		515 083	5159/0831	Brackwede
514 261	5149/2614	Serniki Pervyye		515 084	5150/0846	Haustenbeck
514 262	5140/2629	Zolotoye		515 084	5158/0840	Oerlinghausen
514 263	5141/2634	Lyudyn		515 084	5158/0843	Wahrentrup
514 263	5144/2639	Vysotsk		515 085	5156/0853	Detmold
514 263	5146/2633	Rechitsa (Sarny)		515 090	5151/0906	Steinheim
514 264	5140/2644	Byala (Sarny)		515 090	5155/0909	Schieder
514 264	5147/2644	Smorodek		515 090	5156/0905	Blomberg
514 264	5149/2643	Terebezhov		515 090	5159/0907	Barntrup
514 265	5140/2659	Budymlya		515 091	5152/0912	Schwalenberg
514 265	5143/2650	Zhaden		515 091	5157/0915	Lugde
514 265	5144/2659	Perebrodye		515 091	5159/0915	Bad Pyrmont
514 270	5148/2704	Olmany		515 092	5157/0928	Hohe
514 272	5142/2729	Khrapun		515 092	5157/0924	Ottenstein
514 273	5140/2733	Radzilovichi		515 092	5158/0928	Brokeln
514 282	5147/2820	Lelchitsy		515 092	5159/0929	Hehlen
514 290	5148/2909	Yelsk		515 093	5154/0939	Stadtoldendorf

515 093	5155/0939	Eschershausen	
515 093	5158/0937	Dielmissen	
515 093	5159/0931	Kemnade	
515 094	5151/0943	Luthorst	
515 094	5152/0949	Wenzen	
515 095	5151/0956	Greene	
515 100	5152/1002	Bad Gandersheim	
515 100	5157/1007	Gross Rhuden	
515 100	5158/1001	Lamspringe	
515 101	5154/1011	Seesen	
515 102	5154/1026	Goslar	
515 103	5153/1034	Bad Harzburg	
515 104	5150/1047	Wernigerode	
515 105	5152/1054	Derenburg	
515 110	5154/1103	Halberstadt	
515 111	5153/1110	Wegeleben	
515 111	5156/1113	Groningen	
515 111	5156/1118	Kroppenstedt	
515 111	5159/1117	Alikendorf	
515 111	5159/1114	Grossalsleben	
515 111	5159/1118	Hadmersleben	
515 111	5159/1116	Kleinalsleben	
515 112	5157/1126	Egeln	
515 112	5158/1124	Westeregeln	
515 113	5151/1135	Leopoldshall	
515 113	5152/1135	Stassfurt	
515 114	5154/1146	Calbe	
515 114	5157/1142	Grossmuhlingen	
515 115	5158/1153	Barby	
515 120	5151/1203	Aken	
515 120	5158/1205	Zerbst	
515 121	5150/1215	Dessau	
515 121	5153/1215	Rosslau	
515 122	5150/1225	Worlitz	
515 122	5153/1227	Coswig	
515 123	5152/1239	Lutherstadt Wittenberg	
515 124	5152/1242	Labetz	
515 124	5158/1244	Kropstadt	
515 130	5159/1305	Juterbog	
515 131	5153/1313	Lichterfelde	
515 132	5156/1320	Heinsdorf	
515 133	5152/1335	Pitschen	
515 135	5157/1354	Lubben	
515 141	5159/1418	Lieberose	
515 142	5152/1425	Peitz	
515 144	5157/1443	Wilhelmpieckstadt Guben	
515 144	5159/1442	Gross Breesen	
515 153	5156/1530	Zielona Gora	
515 154	5151/1543	Otyn	
515 154	5157/1543	Zabor	
515 155	5158/1556	Lasko (Poland)	
515 160	5153/1604	Slawa	
515 162	5150/1629	Ogrody	

515 163	5151/1635	Leszno
515 164	5154/1641	Osieczna
515 164	5157/1649	Krzywin
515 170	5153/1702	Gostyn
515 171	5155/1715	Borek
515 171	5158/1718	Jaraczew
515 172	5155/1725	Potarzyca
515 173	5152/1736	Dobrzyca
515 173	5158/1731	Jarocin
515 173	5159/1732	Annapol
515 174	5154/1748	Pleszew
515 175	5157/1755	Kuznia
515 175	5158/1752	Chocz
515 180	5154/1809	Ostrowek (Kalisz)
515 180	5155/1809	Stawiszyn
515 180	5156/1805	Dluga Wies
515 180	5159/1804	Wiory
515 181	5150/1814	Kamien (Kalisz)
515 181	5153/1819	Plewnia Nowa
515 181	5154/1818	Cekow
515 181	5155/1817	Gostynie
515 181	5157/1813	Korzeniew
515 181	5159/1816	Danowice
515 181	5159/1811	Zamety
515 182	5153/1827	Bedziechow
515 182	5153/1825	Madalin
515 182	5153/1820	Prazuchy
515 182	5154/1825	Swidle
515 182	5156/1825	Milaczew
515 182	5156/1823	Poroze Stare
515 183	5155/1837	Dobra
515 183	5155/1831	Dzierzbotki
515 183	5156/1833	Kowale Panskie
515 184	5150/1849	Druzbin
515 184	5154/1849	Gibaszewo
515 184	5158/1848	Uniejow
515 185	5153/1857	Poddebice
515 185	5156/1857	Chrapy
515 190	5151/1909	Sarnow
515 190	5151/1904	Wilczyca
515 190	5151/1906	Zdrzychow
515 190	5159/1904	Biala Gora
515 190	5159/1907	Sucha Gorna
515 191	5150/1912	Beldow
515 191	5152/1916	Nakielnica
515 191	5157/1913	Parzeczew
515 191	5158/1917	Ozorkow
515 191	5159/1911	Borszyn
515 192	5151/1925	Zgierz
515 192	5152/1922	Lucmierz
515 192	5155/1922	Emilia
515 192	5156/1927	Biala (Lodz)
515 192	5156/1928	Wola Branicka
515 193	5150/1939	Glogowice

515	193	5154/1936	Strykow
515	193	5155/1933	Swedow
515	193	5156/1938	Wola Bledowa
515	194	5153/1940	Niesulkow
515	194	5158/1944	Glowno
515	194	5158/1945	Paleniec
515	194	5158/1943	Warchalow Nowy
515	195	5152/1956	Krosnowa
515	195	5159/1955	Lyszkowice
515	200	5150/2006	Michowice
515	200	5156/2006	Dabrowice
515	200	5158/2009	Skierniewice
515	201	5155/2010	Strobow
515	201	5158/2019	Karolinow Stary
515	202	5154/2027	Chojnata
515	202	5159/2021	Puszcza Marianska
515	203	5150/2031	Dankow
515	203	5154/2034	Bialogorne
515	203	5155/2037	Lutkowka
515	203	5159/2031	Mszczonow
515	204	5150/2048	Mala Wies (Radom)
515	204	5151/2046	Rozce
515	204	5152/2041	Ciechlin
515	204	5154/2040	Cychry
515	204	5158/2048	Swietochow
515	205	5151/2055	Pabierowice
515	205	5152/2058	Czestoniew
515	205	5152/2052	Grojec
515	205	5154/2050	Bikowek
515	205	5155/2053	Duzy Dol
515	205	5155/2057	Goscienczyce
515	205	5158/2050	Tarczyn
515	205	5159/2056	Prace Duze
515	205	5159/2054	Prace Male
515	210	5150/2102	Miedzechow
515	210	5152/2104	Budziszynek
515	210	5152/2109	Watraszew
515	210	5153/2104	Budziszyn
515	210	5153/2101	Kukaly
515	210	5156/2103	Wola Pieczyska
515	211	5151/2111	Gaski
515	211	5151/2110	Hornigi
515	211	5151/2117	Mniszow
515	211	5152/2119	Podole Nowe
515	211	5153/2114	Konary
515	211	5155/2114	Potycz
515	211	5156/2119	Sobienie Jeziory
515	211	5157/2114	Czersk
515	211	5159/2114	Gora Kalwaria
515	212	5151/2121	Wolka Gruszczynska
515	212	5152/2120	Kepa Celejowska
515	212	5152/2123	Wilga
515	212	5155/2128	Budy Usniackie
515	212	5155/2128	Koscieliska
515	212	5156/2126	Czarnowiec
515	212	5157/2120	Sobienie Szlacheckie
515	212	5158/2125	Osieck
515	212	5159/2129	Grabianka
515	213	5152/2135	Gorki (Garwolin)
515	213	5152/2135	Ruda Talubska
515	213	5152/2135	Ruda (Garwolin)
515	213	5152/2139	Sulbiny
515	213	5153/2134	Rebkow
515	213	5153/2131	Stoczek
515	213	5154/2132	Ewelin
515	213	5154/2138	Garwolin
515	213	5157/2132	Pilawa
515	213	5159/2135	Puznowka
515	214	5150/2146	Samorzadki
515	214	5151/2143	Gorzno
515	214	5151/2140	Kobyla Wola
515	214	5155/2144	Gozdzik
515	214	5155/2148	Miastkow Stary
515	214	5156/2148	Filipowka
515	214	5158/2141	Parysow
515	215	5151/2159	Myslow
515	215	5152/2151	Ryczyska
515	215	5153/2153	Zwola
515	215	5157/2158	Stoczek Lukowski
515	215	5159/2153	Iwowe
515	220	5150/2208	Wola Trzydnicka
515	220	5154/2205	Wnetrzne
515	220	5155/2207	Niedzwiadka
515	220	5156/2207	Zagozdzie
515	220	5157/2202	Kobialki Nowe
515	220	5159/2202	Toczyska
515	221	5151/2215	Jonik
515	221	5152/2216	Jeleniec
515	221	5153/2212	Stanin
515	221	5154/2218	Czersl
515	221	5154/2214	Tuchowicz
515	221	5157/2219	Zalesie (Lukow)
515	221	5157/2210	Zastawie
515	221	5159/2218	Grezowka
515	221	5159/2211	Jagodne
515	221	5159/2210	Warkocz
515	222	5150/2221	Wolka Domaszewska
515	222	5151/2223	Domaszewnica
515	222	5151/2229	Skrzyszew
515	222	5152/2227	Dminin
515	222	5152/2229	Kepki
515	222	5152/2229	Rzymki
515	222	5152/2220	Szczygly Gorne
515	222	5155/2223	Lukow
515	222	5156/2221	Lapiguz
515	222	5157/2228	Debowica
515	222	5158/2228	Nurzyna
515	222	5158/2226	Suleje

515	222	5159/2228	Celiny
515	222	5159/2225	Role
515	223	5151/2233	Paskudy
515	223	5152/2233	Zakrzew
515	223	5154/2236	Lipniaki
515	223	5155/2235	Olszewnica
515	223	5156/2238	Olszewnica Mala
515	223	5157/2239	Brzozowica Mala
515	223	5157/2237	Mosciska (Radzyn)
515	223	5157/2232	Szaniawy
515	223	5158/2237	Brzozowica Duza
515	223	5159/2235	Obelniki
515	224	5152/2242	Zakowola
515	224	5154/2242	Kakolewnica
515	224	5159/2247	Miedzyrzec Podlaski
515	225	5150/2253	Przegaliny Duze
515	225	5150/2259	Walinna
515	225	5152/2257	Zelizna
515	225	5155/2253	Drelow
515	225	5157/2250	Zahajki
515	225	5157/2255	Zerocin
515	230	5150/2303	Romaszki
515	230	5151/2308	Rossosz
515	230	5156/2304	Burwin
515	230	5156/2302	Leszczanka
515	231	5154/2317	Koszoly
515	231	5154/2310	Lomazy
515	231	5154/2314	Lubienka
515	231	5156/2313	Studzianka
515	231	5157/2313	Dokudow
515	231	5157/2316	Ortel Krolewski
515	231	5159/2315	Ortel Ksiazecy
515	232	5154/2322	Bokinka Krolewska
515	232	5158/2323	Piszczac
515	233	5154/2336	Koden
515	234	5152/2345	Medna
515	234	5158/2340	Kostomloty
515	240	5156/2404	Gusak
515	241	5151/2416	Mokrany
515	241	5154/2414	Lukovo
515	241	5159/2412	Chernyany
515	242	5152/2426	Kortilisy
515	242	5155/2427	Borysuvka
515	243	5152/2437	Samary
515	243	5158/2435	Divin
515	244	5155/2442	Lelikov
515	244	5159/2446	Povitye
515	245	5150/2452	Zalukhuv
515	245	5152/2459	Nevir
515	250	5153/2507	Vetly
515	250	5158/2502	Svaryn
515	252	5150/2528	Lyubyaz
515	252	5152/2528	Shlapan
515	252	5158/2528	Odrizhin
515	252	5159/2528	Vlasovtse
515	254	5152/2546	Nebel
515	255	5150/2554	Morochno
515	260	5151/2600	Mutvitsa
515	261	5150/2618	Vitchevka
515	261	5155/2613	Ostrow (Luninets)
515	261	5156/2617	Lasitsk
515	262	5154/2620	Zholkin
515	262	5155/2625	Boryczewicze
515	263	5152/2630	Gorodno
515	263	5157/2634	Radchisk
515	263	5158/2637	Tsmen Pervsha
515	264	5151/2648	Rechitsa (Luninets)
515	264	5156/2640	Glinka
515	265	5153/2651	Stolin
515	265	5156/2655	Belogusha
515	270	5158/2704	Rubel
515	293	5157/2932	Yurevichi
515	295	5154/2958	Khoyniki
515	304	5150/3042	Radul
515	304	5156/3048	Loyev
515	313	5153/3136	Gorodnya
515	322	5155/3227	Rybinsk
515	324	5155/3244	Bobrik Pervyy
515	332	5152/3329	Shostka
515	335	5157/3357	Svessa
520	065	5202/0650	Vreden
520	070	5202/0706	Legden
520	070	5204/0700	Ahaus
520	070	5208/0706	Nienborg
520	071	5205/0719	Horstmar
520	072	5208/0725	Borghorst
520	072	5209/0720	Burgsteinfurt
520	080	5203/0809	Versmold
520	080	5209/0803	Iburg
520	081	5205/0818	Cleve
520	081	5206/0818	Borgholzhausen
520	082	5204/0825	Werther
520	083	5202/0832	Bielefeld
520	083	5202/0837	Heepen
520	084	5204/0846	Schotmar
520	084	5205/0846	Bad Salzuflen
520	084	5208/0841	Herford
520	085	5202/0854	Lemgo
520	085	5202/0856	Sternberg Barntrup
520	085	5207/0857	Hohenhausen
520	090	5204/0907	Bosingfeld
520	090	5208/0904	Silixen
520	091	5202/0916	Arzen
520	091	5208/0911	Friedrichsburg
520	092	5203/0923	Kirchohsen
520	092	5204/0922	Tundern
520	092	5206/0921	Hameln
520	093	5201/0937	Wallensen

520 093	5202/0933	Bremke
520 093	5203/0933	Harderode
520 093	5204/0937	Salzhemmendorf
520 093	5206/0930	Bessingen
520 093	5207/0933	Coppenbrugge
520 094	5200/0948	Limmer
520 094	5205/0947	Gronau
520 095	5209/0958	Hildesheim
520 102	5208/1020	Salder
520 103	5201/1037	Hornburg
520 103	5205/1039	Kalme
520 104	5201/1047	Hessen
520 104	5208/1047	Schoppenstedt
520 105	5208/1057	Schoningen
520 111	5202/1115	Oschersleben
520 113	5206/1135	Ottersleben
520 113	5206/1136	Sudenburg
520 114	5201/1145	Schonebeck
520 122	5207/1227	Wiesenburg
520 123	5208/1236	Belzig
520 125	5206/1252	Treuenbrietzen
520 131	5205/1310	Luckenwalde
520 133	5203/1330	Baruth
520 134	5201/1340	Rietzneuendorf
520 140	5200/1404	Gross Leine
520 143	5209/1439	Eisenhuttenstadt
520 150	5203/1505	Krosno Odrzanskie
520 153	5205/1537	Sulechow
520 155	5204/1551	Kargowa
520 160	5205/1603	Obra
520 160	5207/1608	Wolsztyn
520 161	5200/1611	Mochy
520 161	5201/1618	Przemet
520 161	5208/1618	Rakoniewice
520 162	5207/1622	Wielichowo
520 163	5201/1635	Bruszczewo
520 163	5201/1632	Smigiel
520 163	5202/1633	Koszanowo
520 163	5206/1638	Koscian
520 163	5208/1631	Leki Wielkie
520 164	5209/1646	Czempin
520 164	5209/1644	Piotrkowice (Poznan)
520 165	5209/1653	Brodnica (Poznan)
520 170	5204/1704	Pyszaca
520 170	5205/1701	Srem
520 172	5201/1729	Cielcza
520 172	5202/1728	Mieszkow
520 172	5206/1725	Nowe Miasto nad Warta
520 173	5204/1734	Zerkow
520 180	5200/1807	Grady Nowe
520 180	5201/1807	Grady Stare
520 180	5202/1804	Grodziec (Konin)
520 180	5202/1801	Ladek
520 180	5203/1801	Krolikow

520 181	5200/1815	Dzierzbin
520 181	5204/1810	Rychwal
520 181	5204/1811	Stara Wies Rychwalska
520 181	5205/1818	Tuliszkow
520 182	5201/1826	Slodkow
520 182	5201/1825	Wrzaca
520 182	5206/1829	Russocice
520 183	5202/1830	Turek
520 183	5207/1836	Brudzew
520 184	5203/1847	Czepow Dolny
520 184	5207/1840	Janow (Koninske)
520 185	5205/1850	Dabie
520 185	5209/1858	Besiekiery
520 190	5205/1906	Siemszyce
520 190	5206/1904	Chorki
520 190	5206/1906	Golbice
520 191	5201/1915	Sierpow
520 191	5204/1913	Leczyca
520 191	5205/1912	Topola Krolewska
520 192	5200/1922	Malachowice
520 192	5204/1929	Piatek
520 192	5207/1926	Siemieniczki
520 193	5204/1939	Bielawy
520 193	5204/1937	Janinow (Blonie)
520 194	5207/1941	Sobota
520 195	5207/1956	Lowicz
520 200	5203/2002	Lubno (Warszawa)
520 200	5206/2002	Myslakow
520 201	5200/2019	Budy Zaklasztorne
520 201	5205/2010	Bolimow
520 201	5206/2018	Wola Miedniewska
520 202	5204/2026	Zyrardow
520 202	5205/2024	Wiskitki
520 202	5207/2023	Oryszew Nowy
520 203	5200/2033	Radziejowice
520 203	5207/2038	Grodzisk Mazowiecki
520 204	5202/2049	Parole
520 204	5203/2046	Rozalin
520 204	5206/2048	Nadarzyn
520 204	5208/2041	Milanowek
520 204	5209/2043	Brwinow
520 205	5203/2059	Golkow
520 205	5207/2055	Laszczki
520 205	5209/2055	Raszyn
520 210	5205/2103	Chyliczki
520 210	5205/2106	Jeziorna Krolewska
520 210	5205/2107	Jeziorna Oborska
520 210	5205/2107	Konstancin
520 210	5205/2102	Piaseczno
520 210	5205/2107	Skolimow
520 210	5206/2107	Klarysew
520 210	5207/2108	Bielawa
520 210	5208/2109	Kepa Falenicka
520 210	5209/2106	Powsinek

520 211	5203/2111	Cieciszew	520 222	5208/2229	Rzazew
520 211	5205/2115	Karczew	520 222	5208/2225	Tarcze
520 211	5206/2119	Srodborow	520 223	5200/2233	Trzebieszow
520 211	5207/2115	Swider	520 223	5201/2230	Golowierzchy
520 211	5208/2119	Otwock	520 223	5202/2237	Teczki
520 212	5204/2129	Kolbiel	520 223	5202/2234	Wierzejki
520 212	5208/2126	Glinianka	520 223	5203/2239	Grochowka
520 212	5208/2123	Wola Karczewska	520 223	5203/2230	Miklusy
520 212	5209/2120	Jozefow (Otwock)	520 223	5204/2237	Krzesk Krolowa Niwa
520 213	5206/2137	Siennica	520 223	5205/2239	Wesolka
520 213	5209/2130	Zamienie	520 223	5206/2234	Izdebki Wasy
520 214	5201/2144	Chyzyny	520 223	5207/2235	Izdebki Blazeje
520 214	5201/2142	Transbor	520 223	5207/2236	Izdebki Kosmy
520 214	5202/2142	Budy Wielgoleskie	520 224	5201/2244	Zabce
520 214	5202/2148	Latowicz	520 224	5206/2245	Mostow
520 214	5204/2142	Huta Zakowska	520 224	5208/2248	Liwki Szlacheckie
520 214	5204/2149	Wezyczyn	520 225	5202/2253	Rogozniczka
520 214	5204/2140	Zakow	520 225	5202/2257	Sycyna
520 214	5205/2144	Kiczki	520 225	5203/2253	Krzymowskie
520 214	5205/2142	Siodlo	520 225	5205/2256	Swory
520 214	5206/2149	Kuflew	520 225	5207/2253	Makarowka
520 214	5206/2140	Zglechow	520 225	5208/2250	Huszlew
520 214	5209/2144	Ceglow	520 230	5201/2304	Porosiuki
520 214	5209/2142	Mienia	520 230	5202/2308	Biala Podlaska
520 215	5200/2151	Oleksianka	520 230	5206/2307	Hrud
520 215	5201/2156	Seroczyn	520 230	5208/2302	Lesna Podlaska
520 215	5203/2158	Wodynie	520 230	5209/2300	Bukowice
520 215	5204/2156	Debowce	520 230	5209/2307	Komarno (Chelm)
520 215	5204/2151	Jeruzal	520 231	5203/2316	Woskorzenice Duze
520 215	5204/2152	Plomieniec	520 231	5204/2318	Husinka
520 215	5207/2157	Leki (Siedlce)	520 231	5209/2310	Polinow
520 215	5208/2156	Topor	520 232	5200/2322	Chotylow
520 215	5208/2159	Zeliszew	520 232	5200/2329	Dobrynka
520 215	5209/2157	Sosnowe	520 232	5202/2322	Zalesie (Brest)
520 220	5200/2204	Rosy	520 232	5205/2325	Dereczanka
520 220	5202/2207	Olszyc	520 232	5206/2329	Malowa Gora
520 220	5202/2201	Wola Wodynska	520 232	5208/2323	Olszyn
520 220	5203/2200	Olesnica (Garwolin)	520 233	5202/2331	Malaszewicze
520 220	5204/2205	Zebrak	520 233	5203/2336	Polatycze
520 220	5205/2206	Grala Dabrowizna	520 233	5205/2337	Terespol
520 220	5207/2209	Dabrowka Lug	520 233	5209/2336	Kleyniki
520 220	5207/2206	Dabrowka Stany	520 234	5206/2342	Brest
520 220	5207/2202	Ozorow	520 234	5208/2349	Kosiche Velke
520 221	5203/2215	Jastrzebie	520 235	5203/2351	Zabolotye (Polesie)
520 221	5204/2210	Drupia	520 235	5207/2356	Bulkovo
520 221	5208/2217	Grabianow	520 235	5208/2359	Rokitnitsa
520 221	5209/2210	Dabrowka Wylazy	520 240	5202/2400	Radvanichi
520 222	5201/2224	Krynka	520 240	5206/2409	Ozyaty
520 222	5202/2228	Wolka Konopna	520 240	5209/2403	Khvedkovichi
520 222	5203/2224	Dziewule	520 241	5205/2418	Verkholesye
520 222	5203/2228	Lecznowola	520 242	5204/2429	Khabovichi
520 222	5205/2226	Zbuczyn	520 242	5207/2422	Velikiye Korchitsy
520 222	5207/2221	Borki Wyrki	520 243	5205/2435	Kamien Szlachecki
520 222	5207/2223	Lugi Wielkie	520 243	5205/2436	Moczulniki

520 245	5208/2458	Volovel	
520 250	5203/2507	Zarechka	
520 250	5206/2502	Sulichevo	
520 250	5206/2509	Vulka Popinskaya	
520 251	5205/2515	Osovtsy Pervyye	
520 251	5207/2513	Yaloch	
520 252	5206/2522	Gorbakha	
520 252	5206/2523	Vorotsevichi	
520 252	5208/2527	Snitovo	
520 253	5209/2532	Ivanovo	
520 254	5205/2540	Yayechkovichi	
520 254	5207/2543	Yukhnovichi	
520 254	5209/2542	Brodnitsa	
520 255	5204/2559	Zhitnovichi	
520 260	5202/2605	Meskoviche	
520 260	5203/2603	Zavidchitsy	
520 260	5207/2608	Karlin	
520 260	5207/2607	Pinsk	
520 261	5204/2615	Sernichki	
520 261	5205/2619	Lemeshevichi	
520 262	5200/2629	Ovsemerov	
520 262	5201/2628	Gzhivkoviche	
520 262	5202/2622	Kolby	
520 262	5203/2627	Bizherevichi	
520 262	5207/2626	Kochanovichi	
520 262	5207/2625	Ploshchevo	
520 263	5203/2639	Plotnitsa	
520 263	5203/2630	Vuyvichi	
520 264	5205/2643	Stakhovo	
520 265	5202/2652	Duboy	
520 270	5201/2704	Ugolets	
520 270	5202/2707	Khoromsk	
520 270	5202/2702	Malyye Orly	
520 270	5203/2704	Bolshiye Orly	
520 271	5201/2714	Velemichi	
520 271	5203/2713	David Gorodok	
520 272	5201/2721	Mochula	
520 272	5201/2726	Tereblichi	
520 272	5203/2729	Olgomel	
520 272	5203/2720	Remel	
520 272	5206/2725	Semigostichi	
520 273	5201/2733	Korotichi	
520 273	5202/2736	Lutki	
520 273	5202/2732	Tolmachevo	
520 273	5205/2732	Malyy Malyshev	
520 274	5204/2744	Turov	
520 284	5206/2849	Skrygalovo	
520 291	5203/2916	Mozyr	
520 291	5208/2919	Kalinkovichi	
520 303	5209/3037	Kholmech	
520 311	5205/3111	Poddobryanka	
520 331	5200/3316	Novgorod Severskiy	
520 343	5209/3430	Sevsk	
520 355	5205/3552	Fatezh	
521 070	5211/0702	Epe	
521 070	5218/0707	Gildehaus	
521 071	5213/0711	Ochtrup	
521 071	5219/0710	Bentheim	
521 071	5219/0714	Schuttorf	
521 072	5215/0722	Neuenkirchen	
521 072	5217/0727	Rheine	
521 074	5216/0744	Ibbenburen	
521 075	5211/0752	Lengerich	
521 080	5213/0800	Holzhausen	
521 080	5216/0803	Osnabruck	
521 082	5212/0821	Melle	
521 082	5215/0824	Buer	
521 082	5219/0824	Rabber	
521 083	5212/0835	Bunde	
521 083	5217/0839	Lage	
521 083	5218/0837	Lubbecke	
521 083	5218/0830	Preussisch Oldendorf	
521 084	5211/0840	Lohne	
521 084	5212/0848	Bad Oeynhausen	
521 085	5210/0859	Varenholz	
521 085	5210/0851	Vlotho	
521 085	5214/0855	Hausberge an der Porta	
521 085	5214/0852	Kostedt	
521 085	5216/0859	Clus	
521 085	5217/0855	Minden	
521 090	5211/0905	Rinteln	
521 090	5212/0901	Eisbergen	
521 090	5213/0907	Steinbergen	
521 090	5214/0906	Heessen	
521 090	5216/0903	Buckeburg	
521 090	5216/0908	Obernkirchen	
521 091	5210/0915	Hessisch Oldendorf	
521 091	5219/0912	Stadthagen	
521 092	5215/0922	Hulsede	
521 092	5215/0921	Meinsen	
521 092	5215/0923	Messenkamp	
521 092	5216/0922	Lauenau	
521 092	5216/0920	Pohle	
521 092	5218/0927	Barsinghausen	
521 092	5219/0921	Rodenberg	
521 093	5210/0939	Eldagsen	
521 093	5219/0936	Gehrden	
521 094	5210/0947	Nordstemmen	
521 094	5211/0949	Rossing	
521 094	5212/0947	Schulenburg	
521 094	5214/0940	Bennigsen	
521 094	5214/0942	Gestorf	
521 094	5216/0946	Pattensen	
521 095	5214/0951	Sarstedt	
521 095	5217/0950	Gleidingen	
521 095	5219/0957	Sehnde	
521 100	5216/1004	Hohenhameln	
521 101	5219/1014	Peine	

521 102	5216/1023	Vechelde
521 103	5210/1033	Wolfenbuttel
521 103	5216/1032	Braunschweig
521 104	5215/1049	Konigslutter
521 105	5215/1058	Emmerstedt
521 110	5214/1100	Helmstedt
521 112	5217/1120	Suplingen
521 112	5218/1125	Haldensleben
521 114	5210/1140	Magdeburg
521 115	5216/1151	Burg
521 122	5218/1227	Gruningen
521 122	5219/1223	Rogozno Wielkopolskie
521 124	5215/1240	Cammer
521 125	5214/1258	Beelitz
521 130	5213/1306	Stangenhagen
521 130	5218/1301	Michendorf
521 131	5213/1312	Trebbin
521 132	5213/1327	Zossen
521 134	5218/1342	Zernsdorf
521 135	5215/1356	Storkow
521 141	5210/1415	Beeskow
521 142	5215/1425	Mullrose
521 142	5219/1427	Lichtenberg (Brandenburg)
521 145	5219/1456	Bottschow
521 152	5218/1526	Lubrza
521 153	5215/1532	Swiebodzin
521 154	5210/1549	Babimost
521 155	5215/1556	Zbaszyn
521 160	5216/1608	Boruja Koscielna
521 160	5218/1604	Jastrzebsko Stare
521 160	5219/1609	Nowy Tomysl
521 162	5211/1621	Ruchocice
521 162	5214/1622	Grodzisk Wielkopolski
521 162	5218/1626	Opalenica
521 162	5219/1621	Porazyn
521 165	5215/1651	Mosina
521 165	5219/1651	Wiry
521 170	5211/1704	Czmon
521 170	5215/1706	Kornik
521 171	5210/1712	Zaniemysl
521 171	5214/1717	Sroda Wielkopolska
521 171	5218/1717	Plawce
521 172	5210/1723	Miaskowo
521 172	5212/1729	Miloslaw
521 173	5219/1735	Wrzesnia
521 174	5210/1742	Pyzdry
521 174	5211/1747	Bialobrzeg
521 174	5213/1749	Ciazen
521 175	5210/1759	Kopojno
521 175	5210/1752	Kosciolkow
521 175	5210/1754	Zagorow
521 175	5212/1752	Policko
521 175	5213/1754	Lad
521 175	5217/1753	Slupca
521 180	5211/1807	Osiecza
521 180	5215/1806	Golina
521 181	5211/1813	Stare Miasto (Lodz)
521 181	5213/1816	Konin
521 181	5214/1814	Chorzen
521 181	5214/1815	Czarkow
521 181	5219/1810	Kazimierz Biskupi
521 182	5211/1827	Drozen
521 182	5212/1826	Krzymow
521 182	5213/1826	Piersk
521 182	5216/1826	Kramsk
521 182	5218/1828	Pachow
521 183	5211/1837	Kolo
521 184	5212/1844	Grzegorzew
521 184	5212/1849	Ponetow Gorny
521 184	5212/1846	Ponetow Dolny
521 184	5214/1844	Kielczewek
521 185	5215/1855	Klodawa
521 190	5216/1904	Koserz
521 190	5218/1903	Liliopol
521 191	5212/1919	Grabkow
521 191	5213/1911	Milosna
521 191	5213/1916	Wroczyny
521 191	5215/1911	Krosniewice
521 192	5214/1925	Bielawki
521 192	5214/1922	Kutno
521 193	5210/1932	Waliszew
521 193	5213/1937	Grabow (Dabie)
521 193	5213/1937	Pniewo
521 193	5213/1932	Wojszyce
521 193	5215/1937	Zychlin
521 193	5219/1938	Helenow
521 194	5212/1944	Wiskienice
521 194	5213/1945	Grzybow
521 195	5215/1955	Juliszew
521 195	5216/1952	Kiernozia
521 195	5218/1950	Osmolin
521 200	5210/2009	Kozlow Szlachecki
521 200	5215/2003	Rybionek
521 200	5218/2003	Brzozow Stary
521 201	5214/2015	Sochaczew
521 201	5215/2016	Nowa Wies (Sochaczew)
521 201	5219/2011	Radziwilka
521 202	5215/2021	Szczytno (Sochaczew)
521 202	5216/2028	Kampinos
521 202	5216/2024	Lazy (Warszawa)
521 203	5212/2037	Blonie
521 203	5216/2036	Leszno (Blonie)
521 203	5219/2037	Roztoka
521 204	5210/2040	Czubin
521 204	5212/2048	Duchnice
521 204	5212/2042	Jozefow (Swidry Male)
521 204	5213/2047	Oltarzew

521 204	5213/2049	Ozarow (Warszawa)	
521 204	5215/2048	Koczargi Nowe	
521 204	5216/2049	Lipkow	
521 205	5210/2050	Pruszkow	
521 205	5210/2050	Tworki	
521 205	5210/2056	Zaluski	
521 205	5212/2051	Piastow	
521 205	5212/2057	Szczesliwice	
521 205	5212/2055	Wlochy	
521 205	5213/2059	Ochota	
521 205	5214/2051	Latchorzew	
521 205	5218/2059	Zeran	
521 205	5219/2058	Swidry Stare	
521 210	5210/2109	Miedzeszyn	
521 210	5210/2106	Wilanow	
521 210	5211/2108	Zerzen	
521 210	5212/2101	Mokotow	
521 210	5214/2108	Goclawek	
521 210	5214/2109	Wawer	
521 210	5215/2100	Warszawa	
521 210	5216/2105	Praga	
521 210	5216/2103	Targowek	
521 210	5217/2107	Zabki	
521 210	5219/2102	Bialoleka	
521 210	5219/2107	Drewnica	
521 210	5219/2108	Marki	
521 211	5210/2114	Falenica	
521 211	5210/2118	Wiazowka	
521 211	5210/2118	Wiazowna	
521 211	5213/2118	Krolewskie Bagno	
521 211	5213/2116	Zakret	
521 211	5213/2115	Zwir	
521 211	5214/2110	Anin	
521 211	5215/2119	Cechowka	
521 211	5215/2119	Dluga Szlachecka	
521 211	5215/2110	Rembertow	
521 211	5215/2117	Sulejowek	
521 211	5215/2115	Wioska Radzyminska	
521 211	5216/2118	Okuniew	
521 212	5211/2128	Chrosla	
521 212	5211/2121	Duchnow	
521 212	5211/2125	Gorki (Grubaki)	
521 212	5211/2128	Ruda (Minsk Mazowiecki)	
521 212	5212/2127	Debe Wielkie	
521 212	5217/2128	Pustelnik	
521 212	5219/2124	Wola Reczajska	
521 213	5210/2138	Barczaca	
521 213	5210/2138	Budy Barczackie	
521 213	5211/2134	Minsk Mazowiecki	
521 213	5211/2132	Stojadla	
521 213	5214/2137	Mistow	
521 213	5218/2133	Stanislawow (Warszawa)	
521 214	5210/2148	Mrozy	
521 214	5210/2140	Tyborow	
521 214	5210/2147	Wola Kaluska	
521 214	5213/2149	Kaluszyn	
521 214	5213/2148	Zawoda	
521 214	5215/2148	Chroscice	
521 214	5217/2147	Zimnowoda	
521 214	5218/2146	Czarnoglow	
521 215	5211/2155	Ryczyca	
521 215	5211/2150	Szymony	
521 215	5212/2158	Bojmie	
521 215	5212/2157	Zdzar	
521 215	5214/2158	Sluchocin	
521 215	5214/2154	Trzebucza	
521 215	5215/2150	Wasy	
521 215	5216/2155	Grebkow	
521 215	5216/2153	Zarnowka	
521 215	5217/2157	Podsusze	
521 215	5217/2156	Polkow Sagaly	
521 220	5211/2208	Grezow	
521 220	5211/2204	Kotun	
521 220	5213/2204	Czarnowaz	
521 220	5217/2207	Mokobody	
521 220	5217/2204	Wolka Proszewska	
521 220	5218/2200	Oszczerze	
521 220	5219/2205	Ksiezopole Smolaki	
521 220	5219/2201	Wyszkow (Lublin)	
521 221	5210/2218	Siedlce	
521 221	5210/2218	Ulica Starowiejska	
521 221	5211/2211	Sabinka	
521 221	5215/2216	Przygody	
521 221	5215/2214	Wola Suchozebrska	
521 221	5216/2215	Suchozebry	
521 221	5218/2214	Podniesno	
521 221	5218/2216	Stany Male	
521 222	5210/2228	Krzymosze	
521 222	5210/2221	Stok Lacki	
521 222	5210/2229	Wielgorz	
521 222	5213/2227	Stok Ruski	
521 222	5215/2225	Jablonna Ruska	
521 222	5215/2225	Jablonna Lacka	
521 222	5215/2220	Kownaciska	
521 222	5215/2221	Krzeslin	
521 222	5216/2223	Strusy	
521 222	5217/2226	Holubla	
521 222	5217/2220	Nakory	
521 222	5217/2223	Rzeszotkow	
521 222	5219/2225	Ostrowek	
521 222	5219/2220	Patrykozy	
521 223	5210/2236	Bejdy	
521 223	5210/2234	Skolimow Ptaszki	
521 223	5211/2231	Klimonty	
521 223	5211/2234	Sosenki Jajki	
521 223	5211/2236	Suchodol Wypychy	
521 223	5213/2231	Mordy	

521 223	5213/2235	Wojnow	
521 223	5214/2234	Stara Wies (Siedlce)	
521 223	5216/2235	Przesmyki	
521 223	5216/2237	Rzewuski Stare	
521 223	5216/2231	Tarkow	
521 223	5219/2232	Trebice Gorne	
521 223	5219/2230	Trebice Dolne	
521 224	5210/2241	Hadynow	
521 224	5210/2241	Pietrusy	
521 224	5210/2242	Szawly	
521 224	5212/2247	Chotycze	
521 224	5213/2243	Losice	
521 224	5214/2241	Biernaty Stare	
521 224	5216/2242	Niemojki	
521 224	5216/2248	Puczyce	
521 224	5217/2247	Czuchow Pienki	
521 224	5218/2242	Lysow	
521 224	5219/2243	Hruszew	
521 224	5219/2248	Kisielew	
521 224	5219/2244	Ruskow	
521 225	5210/2254	Kobylany	
521 225	5211/2256	Kornica	
521 225	5213/2250	Falatycze	
521 225	5216/2252	Chlopkow	
521 225	5216/2250	Ostromeczyn	
521 225	5219/2253	Sarnaki	
521 230	5212/2308	Jakowki	
521 230	5212/2306	Zakanale	
521 230	5213/2305	Konstantynow	
521 230	5213/2307	Witoldow	
521 230	5214/2302	Horoszki Male	
521 230	5215/2302	Bonin	
521 230	5217/2303	Serpelice	
521 230	5218/2309	Niemirow (Bialystok)	
521 230	5219/2303	Zabuze	
521 231	5210/2317	Kajetanka	
521 231	5212/2313	Janow Podlaski	
521 231	5213/2310	Pawlow Nowy	
521 231	5213/2312	Pawlow Stary	
521 231	5214/2312	Bubel Lukowisko	
521 231	5216/2312	Bubel Stary	
521 231	5217/2319	Volchin	
521 232	5210/2323	Derlo	
521 232	5210/2326	Pratulin	
521 232	5210/2325	Zaczopki	
521 232	5211/2320	Ostrow (Konstantynow)	
521 232	5213/2328	Sychi	
521 234	5213/2344	Chernavchitsy	
521 234	5219/2347	Vidomlya	
521 240	5212/2401	Zhabinka	
521 241	5211/2419	Patryki	
521 241	5214/2411	Litvinki	
521 241	5218/2417	Strigovo	
521 242	5213/2421	Kobrin	

521 242	5213/2429	Zalese (Kobrin)	
521 242	5214/2429	Selets (Pruzhany)	
521 242	5216/2424	Bosyach	
521 242	5217/2428	Ostromichi	
521 244	5212/2447	Antopol	
521 244	5212/2440	Merkulovichi	
521 244	5212/2449	Pervoye Maya	
521 244	5215/2449	Zelovo	
521 244	5216/2441	Demidovshchina	
521 245	5214/2451	Zanivye	
521 250	5211/2509	Drogichin	
521 250	5215/2506	Belinek	
521 250	5217/2507	Simonovichi	
521 251	5214/2513	Roviny	
521 251	5218/2514	Goshevo	
521 251	5218/2519	Zastavye	
521 252	5211/2524	Kleshchi	
521 252	5215/2528	Krivitsa	
521 252	5217/2527	Varatytsk	
521 252	5219/2524	Lyadovichi	
521 253	5210/2534	Lyaskovichi	
521 253	5211/2536	Lyakhoviche (Polesie)	
521 253	5214/2533	Druzhilovichi	
521 253	5215/2532	Tryliski	
521 253	5219/2536	Motol	
521 254	5214/2546	Krotovo	
521 254	5217/2541	Molodovo (Polesie)	
521 254	5217/2549	Porechye (Polesie)	
521 255	5211/2551	Vyzhlovichi	
521 255	5215/2558	Masevichi	
521 260	5211/2605	Ivaniki	
521 260	5219/2608	Stoshany	
521 261	5210/2616	Gorodishche (Polesie)	
521 262	5212/2626	Sieliszcze	
521 262	5214/2627	Parokhonsk	
521 262	5215/2621	Soshno	
521 262	5217/2624	Bokinichi	
521 262	5219/2621	Pogost Zagorodskiy	
521 263	5218/2638	Lunin	
521 264	5215/2648	Luninets	
521 265	5213/2656	Rokitno (Luninets)	
521 265	5215/2655	Yazvinki	
521 265	5216/2657	Vichin	
521 270	5213/2701	Kozhan Gorodok	
521 270	5213/2706	Lakhva	
521 270	5214/2701	Drebsk	
521 270	5215/2700	Tsna	
521 270	5216/2704	Lyubachin	
521 270	5217/2701	Ozernitsa	
521 271	5213/2714	Mokrovo	
521 271	5213/2715	Sinkevichi	
521 272	5212/2722	Sitnitsa	
521 272	5213/2728	Mikashevichi	
521 272	5218/2725	Yelno	

521 274	5213/2742	Lyudenevichi	
521 275	5214/2752	Zhitkovichi	
521 283	5214/2836	Krasnyy Oktyabr	
521 284	5219/2849	Kopatkevichi	
521 294	5213/2946	Amur	
521 313	5215/3136	Byki	
521 320	5210/3200	Churovichi	
521 340	5211/3403	Seredina Buda	
522 070	5226/0705	Nordhorn	
522 073	5229/0733	Freren	
522 080	5229/0806	Vorden	
522 081	5221/0814	Ostercappeln	
522 082	5228/0823	Lemforde	
522 083	5226/0837	Rahden	
522 083	5227/0837	Ortlingerhausen	
522 084	5225/0843	Diepenau	
522 085	5223/0858	Petershagen	
522 085	5225/0858	Ovenstadt	
522 085	5228/0851	Warmsen	
522 090	5220/0900	Frille	
522 090	5220/0909	Meerbeck	
522 090	5221/0902	Quetzen	
522 091	5222/0917	Lindhorst	
522 091	5224/0916	Sachsenhagen	
522 091	5228/0914	Rehburg	
522 092	5226/0920	Hagenburg	
522 092	5226/0925	Wunstorf	
522 092	5227/0921	Steinhude	
522 093	5224/0936	Seelze	
522 093	5227/0937	Berenbostel	
522 094	5222/0943	Hannover	
522 094	5222/0941	Linden Bei Hannover	
522 094	5223/0940	Ahlem	
522 095	5223/0958	Lehrte	
522 095	5223/0951	Misburg	
522 100	5221/1007	Hamelerwald	
522 100	5227/1001	Burgdorf	
522 111	5223/1110	Etingen	
522 111	5224/1118	Calvorde	
522 121	5224/1210	Genthin	
522 121	5226/1219	Vehlen	
522 122	5223/1224	Wusterwitz	
522 123	5225/1233	Brandenburg	
522 130	5221/1300	Caputh	
522 130	5224/1306	Babelsberg	
522 130	5224/1304	Potsdam	
522 134	5225/1345	Erkner	
522 134	5227/1347	Rudersdorf	
522 140	5222/1404	Furstenwalde	
522 143	5221/1433	Frankfurt an der Oder	
522 144	5221/1449	Rzepin	
522 145	5227/1452	Osno	
522 150	5225/1505	Brzezin	
522 150	5226/1506	Sulecin	
522 151	5226/1515	Trzemeszno Lubuskie	
522 153	5226/1535	Miedzyrzecz (Poznan)	
522 154	5228/1546	Pszczew	
522 155	5222/1552	Trzciel	
522 160	5224/1608	Bolewice	
522 161	5222/1615	Wasowo	
522 161	5227/1611	Lwowek	
522 162	5224/1626	Turkowo	
522 163	5222/1637	Ciesle	
522 164	5220/1643	Konarzewo	
522 164	5228/1640	Tarnowo Podgorne	
522 165	5221/1659	Krzesiny	
522 165	5223/1653	Gorczyn	
522 165	5225/1658	Poznan	
522 165	5226/1652	Golecin	
522 170	5220/1700	Krzesinki	
522 170	5223/1701	Kobyle Pole	
522 170	5225/1705	Swarzedz	
522 170	5227/1706	Kobylnica	
522 170	5228/1701	Kicin	
522 171	5226/1710	Sarbinowo	
522 171	5228/1718	Pobiedziska	
522 173	5226/1730	Czerniejewo	
522 173	5226/1731	Kapiel	
522 174	5220/1742	Otoczna	
522 174	5227/1748	Witkowo	
522 175	5227/1755	Sloszewo	
522 180	5225/1801	Siernicze Wielkie	
522 181	5222/1815	Goranin	
522 181	5222/1810	Kleczew	
522 181	5229/1810	Wilczyn	
522 182	5229/1820	Skulsk	
522 183	5223/1831	Sompolno	
522 183	5226/1831	Wierzbinek	
522 184	5220/1845	Nowiny Brdowskie	
522 184	5221/1840	Babiak	
522 184	5221/1843	Brdow	
522 184	5222/1847	Smielnik	
522 184	5224/1849	Kazanki	
522 184	5225/1847	Izbica Kujawska	
522 185	5220/1854	Przedecz	
522 185	5222/1851	Ciepliny	
522 185	5225/1856	Lania	
522 190	5223/1903	Kromszewice	
522 190	5224/1902	Chodecz	
522 191	5222/1917	Lanieta	
522 191	5224/1911	Lubien Kujawski	
522 192	5223/1920	Sokolow (Plock)	
522 192	5226/1929	Gostynin	
522 193	5220/1931	Wola Trebska	
522 194	5224/1944	Gabin	
522 194	5228/1945	Dobrzykow	
522 194	5229/1942	Ciechomice	
522 195	5220/1952	Sanniki	

522 195 5223/1954 Studzieniec
522 195 5225/1956 Zyck Polski
522 195 5225/1955 Zyck Niemiecki
522 195 5226/1955 Nowosiadlo
522 195 5226/1951 Wymysle Niemieckie
522 195 5227/1951 Troszyn Niemiecki
522 200 5220/2002 Ilow
522 200 5222/2001 Gilowka Dolna
522 200 5222/2009 Januszew
522 200 5227/2002 Chylin Stary
522 200 5228/2006 Mala Wies (Plock)
522 201 5223/2018 Sladow
522 201 5223/2012 Wyszogrod
522 201 5224/2018 Czerwinsk nad Wisla
522 201 5228/2014 Kobylniki
522 202 5220/2020 Miszory
522 202 5223/2026 Secymin Polski
522 202 5224/2026 Secymin Niemiecki
522 202 5224/2025 Wychodzc
522 203 5220/2032 Gorki (Sochaczew)
522 203 5223/2038 Cybulice
522 203 5224/2033 Leoncin
522 203 5226/2038 Zakroczym
522 204 5220/2040 Wiersze
522 204 5222/2042 Malocice
522 204 5222/2047 Palmiry
522 204 5223/2044 Czosnow
522 204 5225/2047 Suchocin
522 204 5226/2041 Modlin
522 204 5226/2043 Nowy Dwor Mazowiecki
522 204 5228/2042 Nowy Modlin
522 204 5228/2044 Pomiechowek
522 205 5220/2058 Henrykow
522 205 5221/2057 Dabrowka Szlachecka
522 205 5221/2052 Dziekanow Niemiecki
522 205 5221/2054 Lomianki
522 205 5221/2050 Sadowa
522 205 5222/2050 Dziekanow Polski
522 205 5222/2056 Jablonna
522 205 5223/2051 Rajszew
522 205 5224/2056 Jablonna Legionowo
522 205 5225/2053 Chotomow
522 205 5227/2052 Kaluszyn (Nowy Dwor
 Mazowiecki
522 205 5227/2058 Wieliszew
522 210 5220/2104 Grodzisk
522 210 5222/2106 Czarna Struga
522 210 5224/2109 Slupno
522 210 5225/2106 Wolka Radzyminska
522 210 5226/2103 Nieporet
522 210 5228/2109 Ruda (Grojec)
522 211 5221/2115 Wolomin
522 211 5222/2111 Nadma
522 211 5225/2111 Radzymin

522 211 5227/2119 Roszczep
522 211 5227/2118 Wola Rasztowska
522 211 5228/2116 Chajety
522 211 5229/2118 Malopole
522 212 5222/2120 Grabie Stare
522 212 5223/2126 Szczepanek
522 212 5224/2129 Jazwie
522 212 5224/2127 Miase
522 212 5225/2124 Jasienica (Warszawa)
522 212 5225/2120 Klembow Koscielny
522 212 5225/2127 Tluszcz
522 212 5227/2128 Postoliska
522 213 5225/2138 Czernik
522 213 5226/2139 Strachowka
522 213 5227/2134 Sulejow (Warszawa)
522 213 5227/2135 Wujowka
522 213 5228/2138 Jadow
522 213 5228/2130 Mokra Wies
522 214 5220/2141 Dobre
522 214 5221/2144 Makowiec Duzy
522 214 5222/2149 Nojszew
522 214 5223/2149 Pniewnik
522 214 5223/2143 Radoszyna
522 214 5223/2145 Swietochow Stary
522 214 5224/2146 Polazie
522 214 5225/2147 Rabiany
522 214 5225/2144 Trawy
522 214 5225/2149 Wola Korytnicka
522 214 5226/2142 Annopol (Bialystok)
522 214 5227/2145 Kupce
522 215 5220/2155 Strupiechow
522 215 5221/2150 Skarzyn
522 215 5222/2159 Jarnice
522 215 5223/2158 Liw
522 215 5223/2151 Roguszyn
522 215 5224/2150 Wieladki
522 215 5225/2153 Zalesie (Wegrow)
522 215 5226/2150 Komory
522 215 5227/2151 Gorki Borze
522 215 5227/2152 Gorki Srednie
522 215 5228/2155 Borzychy
522 215 5228/2150 Jaczew
522 215 5229/2150 Kalinowiec
522 215 5229/2153 Paplin
522 220 5221/2203 Szaruty
522 220 5221/2209 Weze
522 220 5224/2201 Wegrow
522 220 5225/2208 Grochow
522 220 5225/2206 Jartypory
522 220 5228/2206 Miedzna
522 220 5228/2208 Orzeszkowka
522 220 5228/2204 Zelezniki
522 221 5220/2211 Rozbity Kamien
522 221 5222/2214 Wojewodki Dolne

522 221	5222/2215	Wojewodki Gorne	522 244	5229/2442	Malech

522 221	5222/2215	Wojewodki Gorne
522 221	5224/2215	Sokolow Podlaski
522 221	5226/2210	Zabkow
522 221	5228/2219	Nieciecz
522 222	5220/2222	Kobylany Gorne
522 222	5221/2220	Kozuchow
522 222	5221/2221	Kozuchowek
522 222	5222/2227	Baczki
522 222	5222/2222	Zawady
522 222	5226/2229	Nowomodna
522 222	5228/2221	Bujaly Gniewosze
522 222	5228/2222	Bujaly Mikosze
522 222	5228/2225	Morszkow
522 222	5228/2228	Niemirki
522 223	5221/2237	Korczew
522 223	5221/2230	Sawice
522 223	5222/2236	Szczeglacin
522 223	5223/2230	Liszki (Siedlce)
522 223	5224/2239	Drohiczyn
522 223	5224/2237	Starczewice
522 223	5226/2234	Chrolowice
522 223	5226/2231	Wirow
522 223	5227/2231	Molozew
522 223	5228/2238	Lisowo
522 223	5228/2236	Putkowice Nagorne
522 224	5220/2242	Tokary
522 224	5222/2242	Drazniew
522 224	5226/2240	Sieniewice
522 225	5222/2253	Turna Mala
522 225	5224/2258	Homoty
522 225	5225/2257	Boratyniec Lacki
522 225	5225/2259	Oksiutycze
522 225	5227/2253	Siemiatycze
522 230	5220/2303	Mielnik
522 230	5223/2302	Radziwillowka
522 230	5226/2306	Borysowszczyzna
522 230	5227/2301	Moszczona Panska
522 230	5229/2305	Zerczyce
522 231	5229/2310	Nurzec
522 232	5222/2322	Vysokoye
522 232	5223/2325	Ryasno
522 232	5228/2327	Kopyly
522 233	5224/2338	Voyskaya
522 233	5229/2331	Verkhovichi
522 234	5224/2349	Kamenets
522 234	5224/2348	Zamosty
522 240	5225/2409	Shcherchevo
522 241	5220/2415	Tevli
522 242	5221/2427	Zasimy
522 243	5220/2434	Zaprudy
522 243	5228/2433	Oranchitsy
522 243	5229/2430	Linevo
522 244	5224/2444	Gorsk
522 244	5228/2446	Zhychin
522 244	5229/2442	Malech
522 245	5220/2455	Leskovichi
522 250	5224/2506	Vysokaya
522 250	5226/2502	Shilin
522 251	5220/2514	Khomsk
522 251	5225/2515	Zditovo
522 251	5226/2516	Gorbovo
522 251	5228/2510	Nivki (Polesie)
522 251	5228/2510	Nivy
522 251	5228/2512	Olshevo
522 252	5225/2520	Sporovo
522 253	5225/2535	Hac Wielka
522 254	5225/2544	Kletnaya
522 254	5228/2547	Kolonsk
522 255	5224/2551	Ozarichi (Polesie)
522 260	5220/2603	Kovnyatin
522 260	5224/2607	Zaborovtsy
522 260	5226/2609	Puchiny
522 261	5220/2615	Chukhovo
522 261	5228/2616	Ploskin
522 262	5222/2627	Bogdanovka (Polesie)
522 262	5227/2620	Tereben
522 264	5223/2645	Bostyn
522 264	5223/2643	Zamoshye (Polesie)
522 264	5228/2648	Voluta
522 265	5220/2650	Dyatlovichi
522 265	5221/2659	Wolka
522 270	5223/2704	Krasnaya Volya
522 271	5225/2715	Czolowiec
522 271	5225/2715	Czuczewicze Wielkie
522 271	5225/2715	Czuczewicze Male
522 272	5220/2729	Lenin
522 272	5222/2726	Polustseviche
522 272	5223/2721	Grichinovichi
522 273	5224/2732	Zalyutichi
522 273	5228/2736	Milevichi
522 291	5228/2916	Ozarichi
522 302	5222/3023	Rechitsa
522 310	5225/3100	Gomel
522 311	5225/3119	Dobrush
522 313	5220/3133	Ogorodnya Gomelskaya
522 314	5224/3145	Zlynka
522 320	5225/3209	Mitkovka
522 321	5224/3213	Klimovo
522 323	5221/3234	Voronok
522 331	5220/3317	Gremyach
522 345	5224/3450	Komarichi
522 362	5220/3627	Rakitina
522 363	5224/3630	Maloarkhangelsk
522 373	5225/3737	Livny
523 065	5230/0658	Neuenhaus
523 065	5230/0653	Uelsen
523 065	5237/0651	Emlichheim
523 070	5231/0700	Veldhausen

523 071	5231/0719	Lingen
523 074	5231/0743	Furstenau
523 074	5237/0743	Berge
523 075	5238/0759	Badbergen
523 082	5236/0822	Diepholz
523 082	5237/0829	Rehden
523 085	5230/0855	Uchte
523 090	5231/0904	Stolzenau
523 091	5238/0913	Nienburg
523 092	5230/0928	Neustadt am Rubenberge
523 100	5237/1005	Celle
523 110	5231/1101	Belfort
523 112	5232/1122	Gardelegen
523 115	5233/1157	Tangermunde
523 115	5236/1151	Stendal
523 121	5236/1217	Steckelsdorf
523 122	5236/1220	Rathenow
523 125	5230/1252	Knoblauch
523 125	5236/1253	Nauen
523 130	5234/1305	Falkensee
523 130	5238/1305	Wansdorf
523 131	5231/1318	Charlottenburg
523 131	5233/1312	Spandau
523 132	5231/1324	Berlin
523 135	5235/1353	Strausberg
523 140	5230/1408	Muncheberg
523 142	5231/1423	Seelow
523 142	5238/1422	Letschin
523 143	5235/1439	Kustrin
523 152	5231/1524	Bledzew
523 153	5236/1530	Skwierzyna
523 155	5236/1554	Miedzychod
523 160	5239/1606	Sierakow
523 161	5231/1616	Pniewy
523 162	5237/1620	Orliczko
523 162	5238/1628	Ostrorog
523 163	5231/1635	Kazmierz
523 163	5236/1631	Jastrowo
523 163	5237/1635	Szamotuly
523 164	5233/1641	Pamiatkowo
523 164	5239/1649	Oborniki
523 165	5231/1650	Zlotkowo
523 165	5233/1657	Biedrusko
523 165	5238/1653	Lukowo
523 170	5233/1705	Huciska
523 170	5234/1701	Murowana Goslina
523 171	5235/1715	Kiszkowo
523 172	5238/1726	Klecko
523 173	5233/1736	Gniezno
523 175	5232/1755	Milawa
523 175	5234/1750	Trzemeszno
523 175	5237/1756	Wylatowo
523 180	5234/1800	Kamionek
523 180	5235/1802	Gebice
523 180	5237/1803	Kwieciszewo
523 181	5238/1812	Strzelno
523 182	5230/1821	Mniszki
523 182	5234/1825	Brzesc
523 182	5234/1827	Jerzyce
523 183	5232/1838	Gluszyn
523 183	5234/1836	Byton
523 183	5234/1830	Piotrkow Kujawski
523 183	5237/1832	Radziejow
523 184	5238/1843	Osieciny
523 185	5233/1851	Lubraniec
523 185	5236/1854	Brzesc Kujawski
523 190	5235/1905	Walewskie
523 190	5239/1905	Wloclawek
523 191	5232/1910	Kowal
523 192	5232/1926	Duninow Duzy
523 192	5235/1929	Duninow Nowy
523 192	5236/1925	Skoki Male
523 192	5237/1921	Dab Wielki
523 192	5239/1920	Dobrzyn nad Wisla
523 193	5232/1933	Emilin
523 193	5232/1934	Soczewka
523 193	5233/1935	Mozdzierz
523 193	5234/1939	Maszewo Male
523 193	5234/1938	Maszewo Duze
523 193	5235/1937	Ludwikowo
523 193	5237/1933	Lasotki
523 193	5239/1939	Milodroz
523 194	5231/1946	Imielnica
523 194	5232/1942	Radziwie
523 194	5233/1942	Plock
523 194	5239/1946	Niszczyce
523 195	5237/1955	Smardzewo
523 195	5238/1959	Starozreby
523 200	5230/2001	Bodzanow
523 200	5230/2002	Chodkowo
523 200	5236/2009	Wloki
523 200	5237/2005	Rogowo Falecin
523 200	5238/2009	Karwowo Krzywanice
523 200	5238/2003	Zdziar Wielki
523 201	5230/2015	Nacpolsk
523 202	5231/2026	Rabiez
523 202	5232/2025	Krysk
523 202	5235/2021	Radzyminek
523 202	5238/2023	Plonsk
523 203	5233/2031	Przyborowice Gorne
523 203	5236/2035	Joniec
523 203	5238/2036	Florentynowo
523 203	5239/2032	Idzikowice
523 203	5239/2037	Miszewo
523 203	5239/2038	Nowe Miasto
523 204	5234/2042	Lelewo
523 204	5235/2043	Malczyn

523	204	5235/2048	Nasielsk
523	204	5236/2046	Kosewo (Warszawa)
523	205	5235/2056	Bledostowo
523	210	5231/2104	Serock
523	210	5233/2106	Gasiorowo
523	210	5237/2108	Kruczy Borek
523	211	5231/2118	Dreszew
523	211	5231/2111	Kuligow
523	211	5233/2115	Jackowo Gorne
523	211	5234/2118	Somianka
523	211	5235/2115	Suwin
523	211	5236/2111	Zatory
523	211	5238/2116	Mystkowiec Stary
523	211	5238/2119	Wielatki Rosochate
523	212	5234/2121	Kregi
523	212	5235/2129	Skuszew
523	212	5236/2128	Wyszkow
523	212	5238/2120	Wola Mystkowska
523	213	5231/2139	Barchow
523	213	5233/2138	Gwizdaly
523	213	5236/2133	Kamienczyk
523	213	5238/2136	Branszczyk
523	214	5231/2143	Lochow
523	214	5232/2140	Budziska
523	214	5233/2143	Jasiorowka
523	214	5233/2144	Lopianka
523	214	5233/2147	Ostrowek (Sokolow)
523	214	5233/2149	Wieliczna
523	214	5237/2145	Szynkarzyzna
523	214	5238/2147	Grabiny
523	214	5238/2148	Ociete
523	215	5231/2150	Zambrzeniec Nowy
523	215	5233/2154	Stoczek (Lochow)
523	215	5233/2154	Stok
523	215	5234/2157	Lipki
523	215	5235/2152	Mrozowa Wola
523	215	5239/2151	Sadoles
523	215	5239/2151	Sadowne
523	220	5232/2208	Kutyski
523	220	5236/2209	Kosow Lacki
523	220	5238/2209	Tosie
523	220	5239/2201	Kutaski Grady
523	220	5239/2202	Kutaski Stare
523	221	5230/2217	Holowienki
523	221	5230/2211	Skibniew Podawce
523	221	5231/2218	Sabnie
523	221	5234/2210	Telaki
523	221	5235/2218	Sterdyn
523	221	5238/2214	Ceranow
523	221	5239/2218	Adolfow
523	222	5230/2222	Tchorznica
523	222	5232/2226	Dzierzby
523	222	5233/2220	Paderewek
523	222	5233/2229	Wieska
523	222	5234/2223	Lazow
523	222	5237/2221	Kielpiniec
523	222	5238/2223	Murawskie Nadbuzne
523	223	5230/2236	Obnize
523	223	5231/2235	Chechlowo
523	223	5232/2231	Granne
523	223	5234/2235	Pieczyski
523	223	5235/2238	Twarogi Mazury
523	223	5238/2239	Pobikry
523	223	5238/2233	Przybyszyn
523	224	5232/2247	Krynki Sobole
523	224	5234/2246	Makarki
523	224	5235/2244	Grodzisk (Bialystok)
523	224	5236/2249	Czarna Srednia
523	224	5236/2240	Zery Czubiki
523	224	5237/2247	Siemiony
523	224	5239/2244	Koryciny
523	225	5232/2256	Zurobice
523	225	5233/2259	Hornowo
523	225	5234/2250	Czarna Wielkie
523	225	5234/2258	Osmola
523	225	5237/2255	Smolugi
523	230	5231/2308	Milejczyce
523	230	5234/2305	Kosciukowicze
523	230	5234/2307	Sobiatyn
523	230	5237/2300	Andryjanki
523	230	5239/2303	Bocki
523	231	5231/2314	Rogacze
523	231	5233/2311	Nowosiolki (Konstantynow)
523	231	5234/2316	Kosna
523	231	5235/2319	Kleszczele
523	231	5239/2310	Krasna Wies
523	232	5231/2321	Czeremcha
523	240	5232/2403	Khidry
523	240	5239/2408	Khvalovo Pervoye
523	241	5233/2413	Shereshevo
523	241	5238/2413	Murava (Bialystok)
523	241	5238/2419	Velikoye Selo
523	241	5239/2410	Sukhopol
523	242	5233/2428	Pruzhany
523	243	5230/2434	Olshany (Polesie)
523	243	5238/2435	Khorevo
523	245	5232/2459	Bereza
523	245	5232/2454	Bluden
523	245	5235/2453	Selets
523	251	5230/2513	Staryye Peski
523	251	5239/2513	Nekhachevo
523	254	5232/2541	Svyataya Volya
523	254	5237/2547	Bobrovichi (Polesie)
523	255	5231/2551	Telekhany
523	261	5238/2618	Khotynichi
523	262	5232/2627	Zadubye
523	263	5238/2631	Lyusino

523	270	5231/2709	Gotsk
523	270	5238/2706	Gavrilchitsy
523	271	5230/2717	Khorostov
523	271	5232/2715	Puzichi
523	273	5230/2730	Bereznyaki
523	273	5231/2737	Grabov (Polesie)
523	273	5234/2731	Yaskovichi
523	275	5232/2750	Skavshin
523	285	5238/2853	Oktyabrskiy
523	301	5234/3011	Gorval
523	304	5236/3044	Uvarovichi
523	311	5233/3110	Vetka
523	315	5232/3156	Novozybkov
523	324	5235/3242	Starodub
523	331	5233/3316	Pogar
523	334	5236/3346	Trubchevsk
523	350	5230/3509	Dmitrovsk Orlovskiy
523	383	5237/3830	Yelets
524	071	5241/0719	Meppen
524	071	5247/0714	Haren
524	073	5249/0737	Lahn
524	074	5241/0749	Menslage
524	074	5244/0746	Loningen
524	075	5241/0757	Quakenbruck
524	075	5241/0750	Schandorf
524	081	5243/0817	Vechta
524	083	5245/0834	Rustingen
524	083	5248/0839	Twistringen
524	084	5241/0848	Sulingen
524	090	5248/0909	Hoya
524	093	5246/0933	Ahlden
524	095	5249/0958	Bergen
524	100	5246/1002	Sulze
524	115	5247/1151	Uchtenhagen
524	120	5240/1200	Arneburg
524	120	5247/1203	Sandau
524	120	5249/1205	Havelberg
524	124	5248/1246	Fehrbellin
524	130	5246/1302	Kremmen
524	131	5241/1317	Birkenwerder
524	131	5245/1314	Oranienburg
524	133	5240/1335	Bernau
524	133	5243/1337	Rudnitz
524	140	5243/1408	Wriezen
524	140	5247/1402	Bad Freienwalde
524	140	5247/1402	Freienwalde
524	144	5244/1441	Debno (Gorzow Wielkopolskie)
524	145	5240/1454	Witnica
524	151	5244/1514	Gorzow Wielkopolski
524	161	5243/1618	Wartoslaw
524	162	5243/1624	Wronki
524	163	5242/1632	Obrzycko
524	163	5243/1630	Piotrowo
524	163	5247/1636	Tarnowko
524	164	5248/1640	Krosin
524	164	5249/1641	Krosinek
524	165	5249/1650	Ryczywol (Poznan)
524	170	5245/1701	Rogozno
524	171	5240/1710	Skoki
524	171	5243/1716	Popowo Koscielne
524	171	5247/1715	Laziska
524	171	5248/1712	Wagrowiec
524	172	5244/1720	Miescisko
524	173	5245/1730	Janowiec Wielkopolski
524	173	5245/1737	Szkolki
524	174	5243/1740	Rogowo
524	174	5246/1746	Gasawa
524	175	5240/1758	Mogilno (Poznan)
524	180	5245/1807	Janikowo
524	180	5248/1806	Pakosc
524	181	5241/1818	Kruszwica
524	181	5248/1816	Inowroclaw
524	182	5245/1825	Radojewice
524	183	5240/1831	Broniewo
524	185	5247/1852	Zbrachlin
524	185	5249/1854	Przypust
524	190	5240/1909	Orszulewo
524	190	5240/1905	Szpetal Dolny
524	190	5240/1902	Zazamcze
524	190	5244/1907	Fabianki
524	190	5245/1906	Lochocin
524	191	5240/1919	Plomiany
524	191	5240/1917	Zbyszewo
524	191	5242/1919	Plonczyn
524	192	5242/1920	Kochon
524	192	5244/1925	Turza Wilcza
524	192	5245/1928	Tluchowo
524	193	5240/1931	Brudzen Duzy
524	193	5241/1935	Lukoszyn
524	193	5245/1936	Zalszyn
524	193	5246/1934	Mochowo
524	193	5247/1931	Malanowo Stare
524	194	5240/1948	Bielsk
524	194	5245/1945	Zbojno
524	194	5247/1945	Bialyszewo
524	195	5245/1959	Drobin
524	195	5246/1958	Nowa Wies (Pultusk)
524	195	5247/1955	Chabowo Swiniary
524	200	5243/2007	Gralewo
524	200	5246/2006	Lempino
524	200	5247/2007	Raciaz
524	200	5249/2003	Kraszewo Czubaki
524	201	5240/2010	Starczewo Duze
524	201	5246/2014	Dramin
524	201	5246/2010	Kiniki
524	201	5248/2016	Kondrajec Szlachecki
524	201	5249/2018	Glinojeck

524 202	5241/2028	Sochocin	
524 202	5245/2025	Maluzyn	
524 202	5246/2023	Placiszewo	
524 202	5247/2025	Wola Mlocka	
524 203	5240/2030	Kuchary (Plonsk)	
524 204	5244/2043	Gasocin	
524 204	5247/2042	Golotczyzna	
524 204	5247/2043	Sonsk	
524 205	5241/2055	Budy Bielanskie	
524 205	5244/2053	Zebry Falbogi	
524 205	5245/2050	Begno	
524 205	5247/2056	Grochy Stare	
524 205	5248/2053	Golymin Polnoc	
524 210	5240/2105	Kacice	
524 210	5242/2106	Poplawy	
524 210	5243/2106	Pultusk	
524 210	5245/2106	Kleszewo	
524 211	5240/2119	Wolka Przekory	
524 211	5243/2119	Grodek (Warszawa)	
524 211	5243/2116	Obryte	
524 211	5245/2114	Zambski Stare	
524 211	5246/2117	Rozdzialy	
524 211	5246/2114	Zambski Koscielne	
524 211	5247/2113	Przeradowo	
524 212	5244/2121	Golystok	
524 212	5244/2126	Grady Polewne	
524 212	5244/2123	Wincentowo	
524 212	5245/2128	Marianowo	
524 212	5246/2124	Wolka Lubielska	
524 213	5243/2131	Jaszczulty	
524 213	5244/2136	Blochy	
524 213	5244/2138	Debienica	
524 213	5244/2130	Sieczychy	
524 213	5245/2137	Laczka	
524 213	5246/2136	Dlugosiodlo	
524 213	5247/2130	Chrzczanka	
524 214	5240/2144	Udrzyn	
524 214	5242/2141	Poreba Koceby	
524 214	5244/2143	Dybki	
524 214	5248/2145	Koziki Majdan	
524 215	5240/2159	Prostyn	
524 215	5241/2154	Morzyczyn	
524 215	5242/2151	Brok (Warszawa)	
524 215	5248/2154	Ostrow Mazowiecka	
524 220	5240/2202	Treblinka	
524 220	5241/2201	Malkinia Gorna	
524 220	5241/2207	Rytele	
524 220	5241/2204	Zawisty Dzikie	
524 220	5242/2208	Podgorze Gazdy	
524 220	5243/2200	Malkinia Dolna	
524 220	5244/2202	Danilowka	
524 220	5245/2208	Zareby Koscielne	
524 220	5248/2203	Jasienica (Bialystok)	
524 220	5248/2201	Smolechy	
524 221	5240/2216	Dlugie Kamienskie	
524 221	5240/2219	Nur	
524 221	5243/2218	Godlewo Mierniki	
524 221	5243/2211	Petkowo Wielkie	
524 221	5244/2219	Godlewo Wielkie	
524 221	5244/2212	Petkowo Wymiarowo	
524 221	5244/2215	Smolewo	
524 221	5246/2213	Szulborze	
524 221	5248/2219	Czyzew	
524 222	5242/2221	Zebry Laskowiec	
524 222	5245/2228	Luniewo Wielkie	
524 222	5245/2226	Zlotki	
524 222	5246/2226	Kutylowo Perysie	
524 222	5248/2225	Godlewo Backi	
524 222	5249/2229	Dabrowa Tworki	
524 223	5240/2231	Ciechanowiec	
524 223	5241/2236	Winna Chroly	
524 223	5242/2239	Koce Schaby	
524 223	5245/2233	Lubowicz Wielki	
524 223	5245/2237	Wyszonki	
524 223	5247/2230	Klukowo	
524 223	5247/2236	Warele Stare	
524 224	5240/2249	Spieszyn	
524 224	5241/2242	Czaje Wolka	
524 224	5241/2249	Plonowo	
524 224	5244/2244	Rudka (Bransk)	
524 224	5247/2245	Domanowo Stare	
524 224	5247/2242	Mien	
524 224	5249/2243	Markowo Wolka	
524 225	5240/2252	Golonki	
524 225	5240/2255	Klichy	
524 225	5240/2250	Puchaly	
524 225	5243/2258	Chojewo	
524 225	5244/2251	Bransk	
524 225	5248/2258	Malesze	
524 225	5248/2253	Oledzkie	
524 225	5248/2252	Swirydy	
524 231	5242/2316	Topczykaly	
524 231	5246/2312	Bielsk Podlaski	
524 231	5248/2312	Proniewicze	
524 232	5242/2320	Orla	
524 232	5242/2327	Stary Kornin	
524 232	5247/2325	Czyze	
524 232	5247/2329	Kojly	
524 233	5244/2335	Hajnowka	
524 233	5246/2336	Dubiny	
524 233	5247/2332	Czyzyki	
524 233	5249/2332	Trywieza	
524 234	5241/2349	Bialowieza	
524 235	5242/2352	Stoczek (Bialystok)	
524 235	5242/2350	Zastawa	
524 235	5249/2355	Masiewo	
524 240	5240/2405	Rovbitskaya	
524 241	5242/2411	Galeny	

524	241	5242/2419	Kotra
524	243	5242/2438	Smolyanitsa
524	245	5242/2456	Guta Mikhalin
524	250	5245/2509	Kossovo
524	250	5249/2500	Kolozuby
524	251	5242/2513	Goshchevo
524	252	5240/2526	Gichitsy
524	252	5242/2523	Yaglevichi
524	252	5243/2521	Ivatsevichi
524	255	5249/2558	Tukhovichi
524	260	5249/2603	Zaluze
524	262	5245/2626	Gantsevichi
524	262	5247/2626	Lyubashevo
524	262	5247/2623	Sukach (Polesie)
524	263	5245/2635	Karack Maly
524	264	5242/2640	Yaskovichi (Luninets)
524	264	5244/2641	Deniskovichi
524	265	5245/2650	Budcha
524	270	5247/2707	Novyy Rozhan
524	271	5245/2717	Zalazye
524	272	5244/2728	Starobin
524	280	5248/2800	Lyuban
524	284	5242/2847	Byelov
524	292	5248/2925	Parichi
524	300	5243/3007	Streshin
524	300	5246/3005	Zaton
524	303	5243/3034	Buda Koshelevo
524	313	5240/3133	Svyatsk
524	321	5245/3215	Klintsy
524	354	5240/3546	Kromy
525	071	5252/0719	Lathen
525	071	5257/0719	Dorpen
525	073	5251/0731	Sogel
525	073	5259/0737	Esterwegen
525	074	5251/0741	Werlte
525	080	5251/0802	Cloppenburg
525	081	5257/0816	Grossenkneten
525	082	5254/0826	Wildeshausen
525	083	5254/0835	Harpstedt
525	084	5250/0846	Eschenhausen
525	084	5251/0844	Bassum
525	085	5254/0850	Syke
525	090	5250/0901	Bruchhausen
525	091	5255/0914	Verden
525	093	5252/0935	Walsrode
525	095	5259/0950	Soltau
525	103	5258/1034	Uelzen
525	110	5251/1109	Salzwedel
525	113	5252/1134	Neulingen
525	122	5253/1228	Wusterhausen
525	122	5257/1224	Kyritz
525	124	5256/1248	Neuruppin
525	132	5252/1324	Liebenwalde
525	132	5259/1320	Zehdenick
525	135	5250/1350	Eberswalde
525	140	5259/1407	Stolpe
525	142	5251/1423	Moryn
525	142	5258/1426	Chojna
525	145	5255/1452	Mysliborz
525	151	5259/1512	Barlinek
525	152	5251/1521	Santoczno
525	153	5252/1532	Strzelce Krajenskie
525	154	5250/1549	Drezdenko
525	154	5258/1545	Dobiegniew
525	155	5253/1559	Lukatz Kreuz
525	160	5251/1602	Drawsko
525	161	5254/1611	Wielen
525	163	5251/1637	Jedrzejewo
525	163	5252/1631	Lubasz
525	163	5254/1634	Czarnkow
525	165	5253/1659	Budzyn (Poznan)
525	165	5259/1655	Chodziez
525	170	5258/1706	Margonin
525	171	5257/1718	Golancz
525	173	5257/1732	Zarczyn
525	173	5259/1730	Kcynia
525	174	5251/1744	Znin
525	174	5252/1747	Murczyn
525	174	5259/1744	Nowy Swiat
525	175	5250/1758	Wapienno
525	175	5252/1758	Barcin
525	175	5254/1753	Lubostron
525	175	5257/1756	Labiszyn
525	175	5258/1755	Arnoldowo
525	180	5258/1805	Dziemionna
525	181	5252/1812	Jaksice
525	181	5258/1817	Zawiszyn
525	182	5253/1826	Gniewkowo
525	182	5258/1821	Glinno Wielkie
525	183	5251/1839	Sluzewo
525	184	5252/1842	Aleksandrow Kujawski
525	184	5252/1848	Ciechocinek
525	184	5252/1849	Raciazek
525	184	5254/1845	Woluszewo
525	185	5250/1854	Nieszawa
525	185	5257/1856	Czernikowo
525	190	5253/1907	Konotopie
525	190	5254/1907	Kikol
525	190	5258/1900	Steklinek
525	191	5250/1912	Lipno
525	191	5257/1915	Chrostkowo
525	191	5258/1919	Kobrzyniec Nowy
525	192	5252/1921	Skepe
525	192	5252/1920	Wymyslin
525	192	5254/1924	Szczekarzewo
525	192	5259/1920	Kobrzyniec Stary
525	193	5254/1937	Szczechowo
525	193	5258/1930	Czumsk Duzy

525	194	5252/1949	Rzeszotary Gortaty
525	194	5252/1945	Sniedzanowo
525	194	5253/1940	Sierpc
525	195	5251/1950	Skoczkowo
525	195	5252/1954	Kosemin
525	195	5253/1950	Rzeszotary Chwaly
525	195	5258/1955	Biezun
525	200	5251/2006	Krzeczanowo
525	201	5251/2018	Unierzyz
525	201	5252/2012	Unieck
525	201	5254/2017	Strzegowo
525	201	5257/2018	Mdzewo
525	201	5258/2011	Bonkowo Podlesne
525	202	5250/2029	Gumowo Szlacheckie
525	202	5250/2027	Oscislowo
525	202	5253/2023	Wola Kanigowska
525	202	5258/2029	Krosnice
525	203	5251/2035	Niechodzin
525	203	5253/2037	Ciechanow
525	205	5250/2059	Karniewo
525	205	5251/2059	Malechy
525	205	5252/2053	Milewo Brzegedy
525	205	5252/2056	Wolka Lukowska
525	205	5257/2059	Bogate
525	205	5258/2051	Bartoldy
525	205	5259/2058	Dobrzankowo
525	210	5250/2108	Ciepielewo
525	210	5251/2107	Zakliczewo
525	210	5252/2106	Makow Mazowiecki
525	210	5255/2104	Mlodzianowo
525	210	5256/2105	Krzyzewo Nadrzeczne
525	210	5256/2101	Szlasy Lozino
525	210	5257/2100	Wielodroz
525	210	5258/2105	Jaciazek
525	211	5250/2111	Smrock
525	211	5250/2113	Szelkow Stary
525	211	5251/2114	Rostki Strozne
525	211	5254/2114	Czerwonka
525	211	5259/2113	Gasewo
525	211	5259/2115	Zamosc Mierzejewo
525	212	5250/2121	Rzewnie
525	212	5253/2125	Rozan
525	212	5255/2124	Dyszobaba
525	212	5257/2126	Ogony
525	212	5258/2126	Mlynarze
525	213	5251/2135	Kaczka
525	213	5254/2134	Goworowo Probostwo
525	213	5254/2134	Goworowo
525	213	5256/2139	Suchcice
525	213	5259/2136	Borowe
525	214	5250/2142	Rzasnik
525	214	5253/2148	Jelonki
525	214	5253/2146	Trynosy
525	214	5253/2140	Wasewo
525	214	5253/2142	Wysocze
525	214	5257/2145	Czerwin
525	214	5258/2143	Dzwonek
525	214	5259/2140	Janki Mlode
525	215	5250/2151	Komorowo
525	215	5250/2152	Legionowo
525	215	5255/2154	Kosewo
525	215	5255/2159	Podbielsko
525	215	5256/2156	Lubotyn
525	215	5259/2152	Piski
525	220	5250/2204	Krole Duze
525	220	5251/2202	Guty Bujno
525	220	5252/2206	Paproc Mala
525	220	5253/2202	Prosienica
525	220	5253/2204	Wyszomierz
525	220	5256/2205	Szumowo
525	221	5251/2212	Andrzejewo
525	221	5252/2215	Przezdziecko
525	221	5257/2215	Dlugoborz
525	221	5258/2216	Wola Zambrowska
525	221	5259/2215	Zambrow
525	222	5250/2221	Dmochy Glinki
525	222	5251/2227	Dabrowa Lazy
525	222	5251/2224	Dabrowa Wielka
525	222	5251/2220	Krzeczkowo Mianowskie
525	222	5252/2221	Rosochate Koscielne
525	222	5254/2227	Dabrowa Dzieciel
525	222	5255/2225	Kolaki Koscielne
525	222	5257/2222	Jablonka
525	223	5251/2234	Dabrowka Koscielna
525	223	5251/2237	Pulazie Swierze
525	223	5253/2234	Srednica
525	223	5255/2239	Jablon Koscielna
525	223	5255/2231	Wysokie Mazowieckie
525	223	5256/2235	Brok
525	224	5250/2247	Hodyszewo
525	224	5250/2249	Sciony
525	224	5251/2241	Krasowo Czestki
525	224	5251/2242	Krasowo Wielkie
525	224	5251/2243	Piekuty
525	224	5252/2248	Liza Stara
525	224	5255/2242	Jablon Dabrowa
525	224	5257/2245	Dworaki
525	224	5257/2247	Zdrody
525	224	5258/2242	Noski Snietne
525	224	5259/2248	Gasowka Skwarki
525	224	5259/2242	Sokoly
525	225	5250/2252	Wolka Zaleska
525	225	5252/2257	Wypychy
525	225	5254/2253	Pietkowo
525	225	5257/2253	Gasowka Oleksin
525	225	5257/2257	Suraz
525	225	5258/2254	Lapy Debowizna
525	225	5259/2252	Lapy

525	230	5250/2304	Stacewicze
525	230	5251/2309	Rajsk
525	230	5252/2305	Mulawicze
525	230	5252/2301	Warpechy Stare
525	230	5254/2307	Strabla
525	230	5257/2305	Zimnochy Swiechy
525	231	5250/2311	Hacki
525	231	5256/2316	Ryboly
525	231	5256/2313	Wojszki
525	231	5259/2311	Klewinowo
525	232	5251/2328	Tyniewicze Male
525	232	5252/2329	Tyniewicze Wielkie
525	233	5255/2331	Narew
525	234	5250/2345	Narewka Mala
525	234	5250/2342	Skupowo
525	234	5251/2341	Bernadzki Most
525	235	5254/2350	Siemionowka
525	242	5256/2422	Porozovo
525	243	5250/2432	Kuklichi
525	243	5251/2437	Lyskovo
525	243	5252/2439	Osochniki
525	243	5257/2432	Dashkevichi
525	245	5250/2455	Berezhnitsa
525	245	5250/2455	Pawlowo
525	245	5252/2453	Ruzhany
525	250	5257/2509	Nowosiolki (Slonim)
525	252	5255/2525	Choroszewicze
525	252	5257/2526	Mironim
525	253	5252/2530	Zarechye (Slonim)
525	253	5253/2530	Byten
525	253	5257/2536	Kolbovichi
525	255	5253/2559	Ostrow (Nowogrodek)
525	255	5253/2552	Skorynki
525	260	5252/2608	Krivoshin
525	260	5255/2605	Benkovtse
525	260	5255/2607	Shcherbinovo
525	260	5259/2609	Olkhovtsy
525	261	5255/2615	Lotwa Mala
525	261	5256/2618	Medvedichi
525	261	5259/2615	Mysloboye
525	262	5254/2625	Lopatyche
525	262	5255/2623	Gaynin
525	262	5257/2622	Talminovichi
525	262	5258/2628	Sinyavka
525	264	5250/2643	Loktyshi
525	264	5254/2642	Drabovshchyzna
525	264	5255/2646	Logvinoviche
525	264	5255/2640	Voronino
525	264	5256/2649	Komlevshchyzna
525	264	5256/2646	Rubezh
525	264	5258/2647	Nagornoye
525	265	5254/2650	Uznoga
525	265	5256/2652	Mokrany Nove
525	271	5251/2710	Krasnaya Sloboda
525	275	5257/2754	Urechye
525	275	5259/2758	Yazyl
525	284	5254/2841	Glussk
525	291	5250/2911	Kovchitsy Vtoryye
525	293	5253/2933	Shchedrin
525	295	5254/2950	Kazimirovo
525	300	5254/3003	Zhlobin
525	301	5250/3017	Staraya Rudnya
525	305	5255/3055	Chechersk
525	324	5252/3242	Unecha
525	332	5255/3329	Pochepy
525	360	5258/3604	Orel
525	494	5258/4941	Chapayevsk
530	072	5304/0722	Aschendorf
530	072	5304/0724	Papenburg
530	075	5301/0751	Friesoythe
530	081	5304/0812	Wardenburg
530	082	5303/0823	Hatten
530	083	5303/0837	Delmenhorst
530	084	5305/0848	Bremen
530	090	5302/0901	Achim
530	111	5308/1115	Domitz
530	114	5300/1145	Wittenberge
530	115	5304/1152	Perleberg
530	121	5309/1211	Pritzwalk
530	123	5303/1234	Rossow
530	123	5309/1230	Wittstock
530	125	5306/1253	Rheinsberg
530	130	5306/1301	Ludwigshorst
530	133	5307/1332	Ahrensdorf
530	133	5307/1330	Templin
530	135	5307/1355	Wilmersdorf
530	140	5302/1400	Angermunde
530	141	5304/1418	Schwedt
530	142	5307/1423	Widuchowa
530	143	5306/1439	Bahn
530	145	5308/1453	Pyrzyce
530	151	5302/1518	Pelczyce
530	160	5305/1607	Czlopa
530	162	5302/1627	Trzcianka
530	164	5303/1645	Ujscie
530	164	5309/1645	Pila
530	165	5302/1657	Strzelecin
530	165	5305/1650	Dziembowo
530	170	5302/1708	Szamocin
530	171	5308/1716	Wyrzysk
530	173	5309/1736	Naklo
530	174	5301/1745	Szubin
530	174	5304/1749	Rynarzewo
530	174	5304/1743	Samokleski Male
530	180	5309/1800	Bydgoszcz
530	181	5304/1818	Przylubie
530	181	5305/1815	Solec Kujawski
530	181	5309/1811	Fordon

530	183	5302/1836	Torun
530	184	5302/1845	Osada Lubicz
530	184	5303/1848	Krobia (Wloclawek)
530	184	5305/1849	Mlyniec
530	185	5300/1859	Swietoslaw
530	190	5303/1900	Rudaw
530	190	5307/1903	Golub Dobrzyn
530	191	5302/1917	Radzynek
530	191	5302/1919	Zale
530	191	5307/1919	Gulbiny
530	192	5302/1928	Zakrocz
530	192	5304/1927	Rypin
530	192	5308/1929	Klosno
530	193	5301/1936	Skrwilno
530	193	5303/1934	Przywitowo
530	193	5304/1937	Okalewo
530	193	5306/1934	Kotowy
530	193	5309/1933	Swiedziebnia
530	194	5300/1943	Chrapon
530	194	5302/1948	Przeradz Maly
530	194	5306/1947	Sinogora
530	194	5307/1942	Plociczno
530	195	5304/1955	Zuromin
530	195	5305/1953	Brudnice
530	200	5301/2007	Szrensk
530	200	5305/2003	Kuczbork
530	200	5307/2004	Chojnowo
530	200	5307/2001	Gosciszka
530	202	5307/2023	Mlawa
530	202	5307/2024	Zabrody
530	203	5308/2036	Kitki
530	205	5302/2053	Przasnysz
530	210	5303/2104	Bobino Wielkie
530	210	5305/2107	Drazdzewo
530	210	5309/2109	Nakiel
530	211	5302/2119	Jarzyly
530	211	5302/2110	Krasnosielc
530	211	5302/2116	Rawy
530	211	5303/2119	Mamino
530	211	5304/2116	Niesulowo
530	211	5304/2110	Przytuly
530	212	5300/2128	Kolaki
530	212	5303/2123	Zebry Wierzchlas
530	212	5305/2122	Zabiele Wielkie
530	212	5306/2125	Nowa Wies (Ostroleka)
530	212	5306/2125	Nowa Wies (Turobin)
530	213	5302/2130	Zeran Duzy
530	213	5303/2138	Rzekun
530	213	5305/2134	Ostroleka
530	214	5302/2146	Chrzczony
530	214	5302/2145	Troszyn
530	214	5304/2143	Janochy
530	214	5304/2148	Opechowo
530	214	5306/2148	Latczyn
530	214	5306/2145	Rozwory
530	214	5309/2146	Drogoszewo
530	214	5309/2149	Zaruzie
530	215	5301/2157	Jakac Stara
530	215	5304/2151	Kleczkowo
530	215	5305/2155	Usnik
530	215	5307/2159	Czaplice
530	215	5307/2156	Wszerzecz
530	215	5308/2157	Szczepankowo
530	215	5309/2154	Leopoldowo
530	215	5309/2152	Luby Kurki
530	220	5302/2200	Sniadowo
530	220	5304/2200	Ratowo Piotrowo
530	220	5309/2201	Jarnuty
530	220	5309/2201	Lochtynowo
530	221	5302/2216	Cieciorki
530	221	5305/2215	Gac Sokola
530	221	5306/2219	Pruszki Wielkie
530	222	5306/2226	Rutki
530	222	5307/2221	Kossaki
530	223	5302/2231	Kulesze Koscielne
530	223	5303/2232	Grodzkie Nowe
530	223	5303/2237	Kloski Mlynowieta
530	224	5303/2249	Jenki
530	224	5304/2248	Waniewo
530	224	5307/2241	Kobylin
530	224	5307/2241	Kobylino
530	225	5303/2255	Bokiny
530	225	5303/2252	Lupianka Stara
530	225	5309/2259	Choroszcz
530	230	5304/2304	Zalesiany
530	230	5308/2309	Bialystok
530	230	5308/2309	Grodek
530	230	5308/2305	Starosielce
530	230	5309/2306	Bacieczki
530	231	5304/2314	Skrybicze
530	231	5309/2316	Grabowka (Bialystok)
530	232	5301/2321	Zabludow
530	232	5302/2328	Tylwica
530	232	5305/2320	Kamionka (Bialystok)
530	233	5302/2336	Michalowo
530	234	5304/2342	Mieleszki
530	235	5301/2354	Jalowka
530	235	5305/2353	Mostowlany
530	235	5305/2352	Swisloczany
530	240	5302/2406	Svisloch
530	241	5300/2413	Golobudy
530	241	5307/2415	Mstibovo
530	243	5300/2439	Konyukhi
530	243	5302/2430	Malaya Lopenitsa
530	243	5306/2433	Izabelin
530	244	5304/2446	Mezhrechye
530	244	5305/2444	Tulovo
530	244	5309/2449	Zelwa

530	251	5301/2511	Orlovichi
530	251	5306/2519	Slonim
530	252	5301/2521	Zhirovitsy
530	254	5309/2543	Polonka
530	255	5305/2550	Darevnaya
530	255	5308/2554	Novaya Mysh
530	260	5300/2603	Bolshiye Luki
530	260	5308/2602	Baranovichi
530	261	5302/2616	Lyakhovichi
530	261	5305/2615	Zarowie
530	262	5307/2629	Orda
530	262	5309/2621	Svoyatichi
530	263	5300/2639	Yanoviche
530	263	5301/2633	Liskovo
530	263	5304/2638	Kletsk
530	264	5300/2640	Kaplanoviche
530	264	5309/2641	Lan
530	265	5304/2659	Timkovichi
530	270	5300/2700	Leshnya
530	270	5309/2705	Kopyl
530	273	5301/2733	Slutsk
530	281	5302/2816	Staryye Dorogi
530	284	5303/2846	Gorodok (Bobruysk)
530	285	5305/2852	Glusha
530	291	5309/2914	Bobruysk
530	294	5301/2947	Pobolovo
530	294	5306/2941	Pereseka
530	300	5305/3003	Rogachev
530	302	5309/3028	Dovsk
530	304	5308/3048	Korma
530	325	5304/3251	Mglin
530	345	5307/3459	Karachev
530	380	5309/3807	Yefremov
531	071	5311/0716	Bunde (Emden)
531	072	5310/0727	Ihrhove
531	072	5310/0721	Weener
531	072	5314/0726	Leer
531	072	5316/0723	Jemgum
531	075	5315/0756	Westerstede
531	081	5310/0812	Oldenburg
531	081	5315/0812	Rastede
531	083	5310/0837	Vegesack
531	083	5311/0835	Blumenthal
531	083	5311/0832	Warfleth
531	083	5315/0834	Reitberg
531	084	5311/0845	Ritterhude
531	084	5314/0848	Osterholz Scharmbeck
531	085	5313/0856	Worpswede
531	091	5318/0917	Zeven
531	092	5314/0921	Elsdorf
531	094	5317/0943	Tostedt
531	100	5318/1002	Brackel
531	102	5311/1024	Melbeck
531	102	5315/1024	Luneburg
531	110	5318/1105	Lubtheen
531	113	5317/1134	Grabow (Schwerin)
531	113	5319/1130	Ludwigslust
531	120	5312/1207	Steffenshagen
531	130	5311/1309	Furstenberg
531	130	5312/1309	Ravensbruck
531	135	5319/1352	Prenzlau
531	142	5312/1423	Gartz
531	142	5315/1429	Gryfino
531	144	5313/1443	Parsow
531	152	5310/1525	Choszczno
531	154	5313/1545	Drawno
531	160	5311/1609	Tuczno
531	162	5311/1626	Gostomia
531	162	5316/1628	Walcz
531	165	5318/1659	Krajenka
531	171	5316/1716	Lobzenica
531	172	5312/1724	Radzicz
531	173	5315/1737	Mrocza
531	175	5319/1757	Koronowo
531	180	5316/1809	Dobrcz
531	180	5317/1806	Karczemka
531	181	5318/1814	Niewiescin
531	183	5311/1837	Chelmza
531	183	5313/1837	Skape
531	183	5319/1831	Stolno
531	184	5313/1840	Dziemiany
531	185	5317/1857	Wabrzezno
531	190	5318/1902	Jaworze
531	191	5310/1917	Radziki Duze
531	191	5313/1913	Cieszyny
531	191	5314/1915	Malki
531	192	5310/1921	Wrzeszczewo
531	192	5311/1926	Kretki Duze
531	192	5311/1922	Lapinoz
531	192	5313/1923	Gorczenica
531	194	5316/1949	Lidzbark
531	195	5310/1951	Zielun
531	200	5317/2001	Plosnica
531	201	5311/2012	Bursz
531	201	5314/2011	Dzialdowo
531	204	5310/2040	Dzierzgowo
531	204	5310/2048	Krzynowloga Mala
531	204	5311/2045	Chmielen Wielki
531	204	5317/2040	Zembrzus Mokry Grunt
531	204	5319/2040	Janowo
531	205	5310/2053	Bronowo Plewnik
531	205	5311/2057	Ulatowo
531	205	5313/2051	Krzynowloga Wielka
531	205	5316/2054	Chorzele
531	210	5318/2102	Zareby
531	211	5311/2118	Baranowo
531	212	5310/2126	Oberwia
531	212	5314/2128	Kadzidlo

531 214 5315/2148 Zbojna
531 214 5318/2140 Kuzie
531 215 5311/2151 Korytki Lesne
531 215 5313/2155 Matwica
531 215 5314/2152 Nowogrod
531 215 5318/2154 Rudka Skroda
531 220 5311/2205 Lomza
531 220 5311/2203 Lomzyca
531 220 5312/2206 Piatnica
531 220 5314/2204 Peza
531 220 5316/2204 Nagorki
531 220 5317/2206 Rogienice Wypychy
531 220 5317/2205 Rogienice Wielkie
531 220 5319/2202 Maly Plock
531 221 5313/2217 Taraskowo
531 221 5314/2216 Wyludzin
531 221 5317/2218 Jedwabne
531 222 5312/2223 Wizna
531 222 5314/2229 Gielczyn
531 223 5310/2239 Targonie Wity
531 223 5311/2237 Targonie Wielkie
531 223 5313/2233 Gora Strykowa
531 223 5313/2237 Las Toczylowo
531 223 5314/2234 Laskowiec
531 224 5312/2247 Tykocin
531 224 5318/2241 Szorce
531 224 5319/2249 Penskie
531 225 5315/2256 Kobuzie
531 225 5316/2258 Chraboly
531 225 5319/2255 Knyszyn
531 231 5312/2316 Ogrodniczki
531 231 5312/2313 Wasilkow
531 231 5318/2317 Wodokaczka
531 231 5319/2319 Buksztel
531 232 5313/2321 Suprasl
531 232 5318/2325 Dworzysk
531 233 5319/2333 Wierzchlesie
531 234 5311/2349 Kruszyniany
531 234 5315/2342 Ostrow Poludniowy
531 234 5316/2347 Krynki
531 234 5316/2341 Ostrow Polnocny
531 235 5311/2355 Holynka (Grodno)
531 240 5311/2401 Bolshaya Berestovitsa
531 240 5311/2401 Brzostowica
531 240 5318/2401 Golne
531 241 5315/2412 Vereyki
531 242 5310/2428 Volkovysk
531 242 5316/2426 Podros
531 242 5317/2424 Ross
531 243 5313/2436 Staneleviche
531 243 5319/2437 Kopachi
531 244 5312/2445 Samarovichi
531 244 5313/2441 Kremyanitsa
531 245 5315/2455 Derechin

531 251 5319/2518 Kozlovshchina
531 252 5312/2529 Derevna (Slonim)
531 253 5314/2532 Vishev
531 253 5315/2539 Perkhovichi
531 254 5313/2541 Ivankovichi
531 254 5314/2542 Lyushnevo
531 254 5319/2542 Molchad
531 255 5311/2550 Zabolotye
              (Nowogrodek)
531 260 5313/2602 Stolovichi
531 260 5317/2603 Koldychevo
531 260 5319/2600 Gorodishche
              (Nowogrodek)
531 261 5318/2614 Volna
531 262 5311/2620 Syche
531 262 5313/2624 Snov
531 263 5319/2632 Gorodeya
531 264 5313/2640 Nesvizh
531 265 5315/2657 Bobovnya
531 272 5310/2729 Gresk
531 272 5310/2720 Grozovo
531 283 5318/2838 Osipovichi
531 285 5311/2851 Demenka
531 285 5313/2856 Yasen
531 285 5315/2850 Tatarka
531 291 5317/2914 Lyubonichi
531 295 5310/2952 Tikhinichi
531 303 5315/3033 Zhuravichi
531 304 5318/3048 Slavnya
531 310 5312/3100 Volyntsy
531 312 5315/3129 Sbornyy
531 315 5313/3150 Samotevichi
531 320 5315/3208 Belynkovichi
531 341 5319/3418 Bezhitsa
531 342 5314/3421 Bryansk
531 363 5317/3635 Mtsensk
532 070 5326/0706 Woquard
532 071 5322/0713 Emden
532 071 5329/0712 Wirdum
532 072 5320/0720 Oldersum
532 072 5328/0729 Aurich
532 073 5329/0730 Sandhorst
532 075 5329/0759 Neustadtgodens
532 080 5324/0808 Varel
532 082 5320/0829 Brake
532 083 5327/0831 Dedesdorf
532 090 5329/0908 Bremervorde
532 093 5329/0934 Bliedersdorf
532 094 5327/0942 Buxtehude
532 095 5320/0952 Buchholz
532 095 5328/0959 Harburg Wilhelmsburg
532 100 5321/1009 Scharmbeck
532 104 5323/1043 Boizenburg
532 111 5326/1111 Hagenow

532	113	5328/1131	Goldenstadt
532	114	5320/1146	Herzfeld
532	115	5326/1151	Parchim
532	120	5327/1202	Lubz
532	120	5329/1202	Ruthen
532	121	5327/1216	Plau
532	122	5329/1226	Malchow
532	123	5323/1236	Robel
532	130	5320/1306	Strelitz
532	130	5322/1305	Neustrelitz
532	140	5326/1404	Fahrenwalde
532	141	5327/1413	Locknitz
532	143	5327/1431	Szczecin
532	150	5320/1503	Stargard Szczecinski
532	150	5329/1503	Maszewo
532	152	5322/1525	Dobrzany
532	153	5325/1532	Insko
532	160	5320/1606	Miroslawiec
532	160	5327/1606	Wierzchowo
532	170	5321/1703	Zlotow
532	172	5327/1726	Lutowo
532	173	5321/1730	Wiecbork
532	173	5327/1732	Sepolno
532	181	5321/1819	Gruczno
532	181	5321/1816	Malociechowo
532	181	5326/1818	Przysiersk
532	182	5321/1826	Chelmno
532	182	5324/1825	Przechowo
532	182	5325/1827	Swiecie
532	183	5323/1836	Male Lunawy
532	183	5323/1837	Wielkie Lunawy
532	184	5329/1846	Grudziadz
532	185	5321/1852	Pienki
532	185	5328/1858	Gruta
532	191	5328/1910	Lisnowo
532	193	5325/1936	Nowe Miasto Lubawskie
532	193	5328/1937	Bratian
532	195	5320/1958	Koszelewy
532	200	5326/2003	Dabrowno
532	202	5322/2026	Nidzica
532	203	5323/2035	Wilczki
532	211	5321/2117	Charciabalda
532	211	5322/2112	Czarnia
532	211	5329/2112	Kielbasy
532	212	5323/2121	Myszyniec
532	213	5322/2134	Lyse
532	213	5326/2134	Zalas
532	213	5327/2138	Ksebki
532	214	5323/2142	Cieloszka
532	215	5321/2153	Niksowizna
532	215	5325/2156	Kolno
532	215	5326/2151	Koziol
532	220	5322/2201	Korzeniste
532	220	5322/2205	Poryte
532	220	5322/2209	Stawiski
532	220	5324/2201	Zaskrodzie
532	220	5326/2206	Skroda Wielka
532	220	5329/2205	Kumelsk
532	221	5329/2214	Lubiane
532	222	5324/2224	Radzilow
532	222	5325/2229	Ostrowik
532	222	5326/2220	Slucz
532	222	5328/2223	Rydzewo Pieniazek
532	224	5320/2241	Trzcianne
532	224	5321/2240	Zubole
532	224	5326/2242	Kramkowka Duza
532	224	5327/2248	Hornostaje
532	224	5329/2245	Goniadz
532	225	5328/2256	Jaswily
532	230	5323/2302	Jasionowka
532	230	5326/2306	Krukowszczyzna
532	230	5327/2306	Korycin
532	231	5320/2311	Oleszkowo
532	231	5328/2314	Janow Sokolski
532	232	5322/2324	Podkamionka
532	232	5328/2322	Troscianka
532	233	5325/2330	Sokolka
532	233	5328/2335	Poplawce
532	234	5320/2340	Knyszewicze
532	234	5323/2344	Zubrzyca Wielka
532	234	5324/2346	Odelsk
532	234	5327/2340	Czepiele
532	235	5320/2357	Olekshitsa
532	235	5327/2353	Indura
532	241	5327/2416	Lunna
532	242	5322/2422	Volpa
532	242	5325/2425	Dziembrow
532	243	5321/2438	Piaski
532	243	5324/2432	Zelvyany
532	243	5325/2432	Mosty
532	244	5324/2448	Malkevichi
532	244	5328/2449	Perekop
532	250	5324/2507	Ruda Yavorskaya
532	251	5323/2518	Medvinovtsy
532	252	5328/2524	Dyatlovo
532	253	5320/2538	Khoroshovchitsy
532	253	5324/2534	Dvorets
532	253	5324/2539	Ozerany (Nowogrodek)
532	253	5328/2535	Novoyelnya
532	254	5322/2547	Svorotva
532	254	5325/2548	Yatra
532	255	5321/2552	Burdykovshchina
532	255	5325/2555	Brolniki
532	255	5328/2554	Valevka
532	260	5324/2609	Tsirin
532	261	5321/2615	Polonechka
532	261	5325/2619	Bolshiye Zhukhovichi
532	261	5326/2614	Dolmatovshchina

532	262	5320/2621	Ishkold
532	262	5327/2628	Mir
532	262	5327/2622	Radun
532	264	5327/2644	Novyy Sverzhen
532	264	5329/2644	Stolbtsy
532	265	5325/2659	Mogilno (Stolbtsy)
532	271	5327/2713	Uzda
532	272	5325/2724	Losha
532	274	5325/2741	Shatsk (Byelorussia)
532	282	5322/2821	Talka
532	283	5326/2833	Lapichi
532	284	5325/2849	Lipen
532	285	5326/2859	Svisloch (Bobruysk)
532	292	5329/2921	Klichev
532	305	5321/3059	Gayshin
532	310	5327/3100	Slavgorod
532	312	5320/3124	Krasnopolye
532	320	5320/3203	Kostyukovichi
532	323	5324/3235	Khotimsk
532	360	5327/3601	Bolkhov
532	384	5325/3843	Kulikovo Pole
533	070	5330/0706	Greetsiel
533	071	5332/0716	Marienhafe
533	071	5336/0712	Norden
533	071	5337/0716	Hage
533	072	5339/0725	Dornum
533	073	5339/0736	Esens
533	074	5334/0747	Wittmund
533	075	5335/0754	Jever
533	080	5331/0808	Wilhelmshaven
533	080	5338/0800	Pakens
533	082	5330/0829	Nordenham
533	082	5335/0822	Burhave
533	083	5332/0832	Blexen
533	083	5333/0835	Bremerhaven
533	095	5336/0959	Lokstedt
533	100	5333/1000	Altona
533	100	5333/1008	Billstedt
533	100	5333/1000	Hamburg
533	100	5334/1001	Wandsbek
533	101	5336/1010	Rahlstedt
533	110	5331/1104	Wittenburg
533	113	5335/1139	Crivitz
533	124	5331/1241	Waren
533	130	5330/1305	Penzlin
533	131	5334/1316	Neubrandenburg
533	135	5331/1359	Pasewalk
533	143	5339/1431	Trzebiez
533	144	5334/1449	Goleniow
533	150	5339/1507	Nowogard
533	151	5335/1518	Dobra (Szczecin)
533	153	5332/1533	Wegorzyno
533	154	5332/1548	Drawsko Pomorskie
533	160	5332/1600	Zlocieniec
533	161	5333/1614	Czaplinek
533	165	5332/1657	Ledyczek
533	171	5332/1714	Debrzno
533	173	5331/1735	Mala Cerkwica
533	173	5336/1734	Ogorzeliny
533	175	5335/1751	Tuchola
533	181	5332/1813	Lniano
533	181	5338/1811	Trzebciny
533	182	5330/1827	Laskowice
533	182	5336/1821	Osie
533	183	5335/1835	Bakowski Mlyn
533	183	5335/1838	Warlubie
533	184	5331/1848	Male Tarpno
533	184	5339/1845	Nowe
533	185	5337/1857	Gardeja
533	190	5332/1906	Lasin
533	191	5336/1916	Kisielice
533	193	5336/1934	Ilawa
533	194	5330/1945	Lubawa
533	194	5338/1940	Rudzienice
533	201	5335/2018	Olsztynek
533	202	5335/2029	Rybaki
533	210	5334/2100	Szczytno
533	213	5331/2136	Turosl
533	214	5338/2148	Pisz
533	220	5332/2202	Jakuby
533	221	5331/2219	Wasosz
533	221	5333/2210	Kurki
533	221	5334/2218	Szczuczyn (Bialystok)
533	222	5336/2223	Boczki Swidrowo
533	222	5339/2227	Grajewo
533	223	5333/2231	Pieniazki
533	223	5338/2237	Pienczykowo
533	223	5339/2237	Pienczykowek
533	225	5332/2251	Wrocien
533	230	5335/2306	Suchowola
533	232	5334/2327	Sidra
533	232	5337/2327	Grzebienie
533	232	5337/2322	Kruhle
533	233	5330/2338	Kruhlany
533	233	5331/2339	Kuznica
533	233	5333/2331	Bieniasze
533	233	5338/2333	Nowy Dwor
533	240	5335/2405	Kamczatka
533	241	5335/2415	Skidel
533	244	5332/2444	Rozhanka
533	244	5336/2445	Shchuchin
533	244	5336/2445	Szczuczyn (Novogrudok)
533	245	5330/2456	Golynka
533	245	5330/2459	Orlya
533	245	5336/2459	Zheludok
533	251	5334/2510	Peskovtsy
533	251	5339/2519	Belitsa
533	255	5336/2550	Novogrudok

533	260	5334/2608	Korelichi
533	260	5339/2605	Negnevichi
533	261	5331/2619	Turets
533	262	5333/2620	Obryn
533	262	5334/2620	Yeremichi
533	262	5337/2622	Antonovo
533	265	5334/2650	Zasulye
533	265	5335/2651	Zarechye (Stolbtsy)
533	274	5337/2743	Uzlyany
533	275	5331/2750	Rusakovichi
533	275	5336/2755	Ostrov (Minsk)
533	280	5331/2809	Marina Gorka
533	281	5332/2815	Pukhovichi
533	285	5337/2858	Seliba
533	301	5331/3015	Bykhov
533	312	5334/3123	Cherikov
533	312	5334/3128	Gronov
533	315	5337/3158	Klimovichi
533	320	5333/3201	Shumovka
533	334	5332/3345	Zhukovka
533	342	5336/3420	Dyatkovo
534	075	5348/0754	Wangerooge
534	092	5347/0925	Gluckstadt
534	093	5345/0939	Elmshorn
534	101	5341/1015	Ahrensburg
534	104	5342/1046	Ratzeburg
534	110	5342/1107	Gadebusch
534	110	5347/1103	Rehna
534	114	5342/1149	Sternberg
534	114	5344/1143	Bruel
534	114	5348/1142	Warin
534	121	5348/1210	Gustrow
534	123	5347/1234	Teterow
534	124	5344/1247	Malchin
534	124	5349/1247	Neukalen
534	125	5342/1254	Reuterstadt Stavenhagen
534	134	5346/1347	Ducherow
534	140	5341/1405	Eggesin
534	141	5344/1418	Nowe Warpno
534	152	5346/1524	Resko
534	154	5346/1547	Swidwin
534	160	5345/1605	Polczyn Zdroj
534	162	5344/1621	Barwice
534	164	5343/1642	Szczecinek
534	165	5341/1656	Czarne
534	173	5342/1734	Chojnice
534	175	5348/1759	Czersk Pomorski
534	180	5343/1808	Rosochatka
534	181	5343/1811	Sliwice
534	183	5348/1832	Skorcz
534	185	5344/1855	Kwidzyn
534	191	5344/1911	Kleczewo
534	191	5346/1913	Prabuty
534	192	5343/1921	Susz
534	195	5340/1957	Ornowo
534	195	5342/1959	Ostroda
534	202	5347/2029	Olsztyn
534	213	5348/2135	Mikolajki
534	214	5344/2140	Glodowo
534	214	5349/2148	Tuchlin
534	215	5349/2157	Orzysz
534	222	5340/2222	Cyprki
534	222	5342/2225	Prostki
534	222	5344/2226	Ostrykol
534	223	5341/2237	Belda
534	224	5344/2242	Rajgrod
534	225	5347/2252	Barglow Dworny
534	230	5341/2306	Sztabin
534	230	5347/2303	Kolnica
534	231	5341/2319	Starokamienna
534	232	5340/2321	Dabrowa
534	232	5344/2324	Lipsk
534	233	5344/2333	Rygalowka
534	233	5347/2332	Kopczany
534	233	5348/2333	Bohatery Lesne
534	234	5340/2347	Lososno
534	235	5341/2350	Grodno
534	235	5347/2355	Holynka (Augustow)
534	235	5349/2352	Gozha
534	241	5343/2411	Ozery
534	242	5342/2425	Shchenets
534	243	5344/2432	Ostryna
534	243	5348/2434	Novyy Dvor
534	245	5340/2454	Ishcholnyany
534	245	5347/2451	Vasilishki
534	252	5340/2525	Selets (Nowogrodek)
534	253	5349/2535	Burnosy
534	254	5342/2542	Naliboki
534	254	5343/2548	Vselyub
534	255	5347/2559	Delyatichi
534	260	5341/2601	Ostashin
534	260	5345/2604	Lyubcha
534	263	5342/2634	Derevna (Volozhin)
534	264	5343/2646	Tonovo
534	265	5341/2652	Rubezhevichi
534	270	5341/2708	Dzerzhinsk
534	271	5343/2718	Antosino
534	271	5348/2710	Novosady
534	273	5344/2730	Samokhvalovichi
534	275	5340/2757	Dukora
534	280	5345/2801	Smilovichi
534	280	5347/2805	Lyady
534	282	5342/2826	Cherven
534	284	5342/2849	Bogushevichi
534	294	5344/2948	Gorodishche (Bobruysk)
534	301	5344/3016	Dashkovka
534	302	5340/3026	Stuzica

534	305	5348/3058	Chausy
534	311	5340/3113	Shchetinka
534	314	5342/3143	Krichev
534	315	5342/3154	Krasnopole Malastowki
534	321	5341/3215	Miloslavichi
534	322	5347/3224	Shumiachi
534	341	5340/3413	Ivot
534	344	5341/3440	Zhizdra
534	380	5346/3808	Bogoroditsk
535	084	5353/0842	Cuxhaven
535	090	5357/0909	Eddelak
535	101	5356/1019	Bad Segeberg
535	103	5351/1039	Genin
535	103	5351/1039	Moisling
535	104	5352/1042	Lubeck
535	104	5358/1049	Warnsdorf
535	110	5357/1104	Borkenhagen
535	112	5351/1128	Mecklenburg
535	112	5354/1128	Wismar
535	115	5351/1159	Butzow
535	120	5357/1207	Schwaan
535	122	5356/1221	Laage
535	124	5351/1246	Schorrentin
535	124	5353/1246	Kammerich
535	124	5358/1243	Gnoien
535	125	5354/1251	Dargun
535	130	5354/1302	Demmin
535	133	5358/1337	Karlsburg
535	134	5352/1342	Anklam
535	134	5357/1349	Papendorf
535	141	5355/1415	Swinoujscie
535	141	5358/1410	Seebad Heringsdorf
535	142	5356/1427	Miedzyzdroje
535	143	5350/1436	Wolin
535	144	5358/1447	Kamien Pomorski
535	152	5355/1521	Gryfice
535	165	5353/1650	Baldenburg
535	165	5353/1650	Bialy Bor
535	174	5353/1743	Brusy
535	175	5355/1756	Karsin
535	183	5353/1834	Bobowo
535	183	5358/1833	Starogard
535	183	5359/1831	Kocborowo
535	184	5354/1848	Szprudowo
535	185	5350/1850	Gniew
535	190	5352/1904	Postolin
535	190	5356/1902	Sztum
535	191	5356/1911	Stary Targ
535	192	5356/1921	Dzierzgon
535	193	5350/1936	Zalewo
535	195	5355/1956	Morag
535	202	5355/2024	Cerkiewnik
535	202	5359/2024	Dobre Miasto
535	204	5350/2042	Barczewo
535	204	5359/2045	Jeziorany
535	205	5350/2054	Nowe Marcinkowo
535	205	5352/2058	Biskupiec
535	211	5352/2118	Mragowo
535	213	5354/2139	Szymonka
535	220	5359/2202	Wydminy
535	222	5350/2221	Elk
535	224	5358/2241	Cimochy
535	224	5358/2245	Moczydly
535	224	5359/2247	Raczki
535	225	5350/2253	Zarnowo
535	225	5356/2257	Szczeberka
535	230	5351/2300	Augustow
535	231	5354/2315	Plaska
535	233	5350/2339	Sopotskin
535	234	5352/2346	Nemnovo
535	235	5357/2355	Privalki
535	240	5353/2408	Porechye
535	241	5357/2418	Kabeliai
535	242	5352/2424	Bershty
535	243	5354/2439	Pervomayskaya
535	243	5356/2438	Motyli
535	244	5357/2440	Skarby
535	245	5350/2458	Vaverka
535	250	5355/2508	Yantsevichi
535	251	5353/2518	Kolesniki
535	251	5353/2518	Lida
535	252	5357/2520	Sporkovshchizna
535	254	5351/2542	Krivichi (Nowogrodek)
535	254	5356/2546	Ivye
535	255	5350/2550	Nikolayev (Nowogrodek)
535	255	5355/2559	Lazduny
535	260	5353/2604	Pesevichi
535	261	5356/2611	Bakshty
535	263	5352/2639	Kamen (Nowogrodek)
535	264	5352/2646	Starinki
535	264	5353/2645	Ivenets
535	265	5352/2657	Volma
535	265	5358/2659	Perezhiri
535	270	5358/2703	Rakow (Volozhin)
535	273	5354/2734	Minsk
535	273	5356/2733	Khutor Novinki
535	274	5350/2743	Malyy Trostenets
535	274	5356/2746	Kolodishchi
535	284	5357/2842	Krupa
535	300	5358/3009	Knyazhitsy
535	301	5357/3015	Novo Pashkovo
535	302	5353/3020	Lupolovo
535	302	5354/3021	Mogilev
535	310	5352/3105	Barishevka
535	313	5351/3132	Molyatichi
535	325	5357/3252	Roslavl
535	360	5350/3608	Belev

540	095	5404/0959	Neumunster	540	240	5400/2401	Ratnycia
540	100	5405/1001	Aufeld	540	240	5406/2403	Liskiava
540	103	5408/1037	Eutin	540	242	5404/2423	Marcinkonys
540	113	5404/1139	Russow	540	244	5401/2444	Dubiciai
540	114	5402/1140	Neubukow	540	244	5404/2441	Rudnya (Lida)
540	114	5404/1148	Kropelin	540	245	5404/2450	Nacha
540	120	5405/1208	Rostock	540	251	5401/2513	Zhirmuny
540	122	5402/1228	Tessin	540	251	5405/2513	Bolshoye Osovo
540	123	5409/1235	Marlow	540	251	5409/2519	Voronovo
540	124	5406/1246	Tribsees	540	251	5409/2519	Voronuv
540	130	5402/1307	Gulzow	540	252	5402/2525	Trokeli
540	130	5406/1303	Grimmen	540	253	5400/2537	Lipnishki
540	132	5406/1323	Greifswald	540	253	5407/2535	Geranony
540	134	5403/1346	Wolgast	540	254	5406/2545	Subbotniki
540	134	5409/1342	Spandowerhagen	540	255	5402/2556	Yuratishki
540	144	5402/1448	Dziwnowek	540	255	5409/2555	Traby
540	151	5404/1516	Trzebiatow	540	261	5408/2614	Vishnevo
540	153	5405/1534	Charzyno	540	262	5407/2622	Sakovshchina
540	154	5403/1540	Goscino	540	263	5401/2631	Belokorets
540	155	5402/1552	Karlino	540	263	5403/2634	Bobrovichi
540	160	5400/1600	Bialogard				(Nowogrodek)
540	164	5407/1641	Polanow	540	263	5405/2632	Volozhin
540	165	5400/1659	Miastko	540	263	5406/2639	Mezheyki
540	174	5403/1748	Kalisz Pomorski	540	263	5407/2634	Bril
540	175	5407/1759	Koscierzyna	540	264	5402/2641	Pershay
540	180	5402/1808	Nowe Polaszki	540	265	5405/2655	Buchowszczyzna Nowa
540	182	5404/1827	Skarszewy	540	265	5409/2655	Gorodok (Molodechno)
540	184	5406/1848	Tczew	540	270	5406/2706	Dubrovo
540	190	5402/1903	Malbork	540	271	5400/2717	Zaslavl
540	190	5408/1901	Nowy Staw	540	271	5409/2714	Radoshkovichi
540	194	5404/1940	Paslek	540	272	5404/2724	Vyshkovo
540	195	5408/1956	Dobry	540	274	5404/2742	Ostroshitskiy Gorodok
540	200	5401/2004	Milakowo	540	280	5402/2805	Smolevichi
540	200	5407/2008	Orneta	540	294	5400/2942	Belynichi
540	203	5408/2035	Lidzbark Warminski	540	304	5405/3046	Chernevka
540	210	5403/2109	Reszel	540	310	5408/3106	Dribin
540	212	5405/2123	Ketrzyn	540	311	5401/3112	Ryasna
540	214	5402/2146	Gizycko	540	314	5402/3144	Mstislavl
540	222	5409/2225	Borysowo	540	352	5407/3521	Sukhinichi
540	223	5402/2231	Olecko	540	354	5402/3548	Kozelsk
540	223	5406/2239	Bakalarzewo	541	094	5418/0940	Rendsburg
540	225	5401/2250	Koniecbor	541	120	5410/1205	Warnemunde
540	225	5406/2256	Suwalki	541	123	5415/1230	Ribnitzdamgarten
540	230	5401/2307	Krusznik	541	125	5411/1253	Franzburg
540	231	5407/2312	Krasnopol	541	130	5418/1306	Stralsund
540	232	5402/2322	Giby	541	153	5411/1535	Kolobrzeg
540	232	5405/2328	Berzniki	541	161	5413/1617	Sianow
540	232	5406/2322	Posejny	541	170	5412/1705	Trzebielino
540	232	5406/2321	Sejny	541	171	5415/1714	Alt Kolziglow
540	233	5400/2339	Kapciamiestis	541	173	5410/1730	Butow
540	233	5408/2331	Kuciunai	541	180	5413/1802	Golubie
540	234	5406/2342	Veisiejai	541	180	5414/1808	Wiezyca
540	235	5401/2358	Druskininkai	541	180	5416/1805	Brodnica
540	235	5405/2351	Leipalingis	541	181	5414/1811	Kaplica

541	183	5410/1830	Czerniewo
541	185	5419/1855	Przegalina
541	190	5415/1905	Lesnowo
541	192	5410/1923	Elblag
541	192	5414/1928	Prochnik
541	194	5412/1943	Mlynary
541	195	5411/1959	Wolki
541	200	5414/2008	Pieniezno
541	203	5417/2030	Gorowo Ilaweckie
541	204	5415/2048	Bartoszyce
541	210	5416/2101	Sepopol
541	212	5413/2121	Barciany
541	213	5413/2131	Srokowo
541	214	5413/2144	Wegorzewo
541	221	5419/2218	Goldap
541	223	5411/2237	Filipow
541	223	5415/2239	Przerosl
541	223	5419/2231	Budwiecie
541	224	5413/2244	Lanowicze
541	224	5417/2245	Bucki
541	224	5418/2249	Klejpeda
541	225	5412/2255	Jeleniewo
541	225	5416/2258	Podsumowo
541	225	5417/2253	Smolniki
541	230	5413/2301	Szury
541	230	5414/2309	Szlinokiemie
541	230	5415/2304	Szypliszki
541	230	5418/2303	Biale Blota
541	230	5419/2301	Trzcianka (Bialystok)
541	231	5410/2316	Romanowce
541	231	5411/2313	Smolany
541	231	5415/2319	Polunce
541	231	5415/2311	Punsk
541	232	5416/2320	Strumbagalve
541	232	5418/2320	Budvietis
541	233	5414/2331	Lazdijai
541	233	5414/2339	Sventezeris
541	234	5410/2340	Slavantai
541	234	5414/2349	Seirijai
541	234	5418/2345	Meteliai
541	240	5418/2402	Nemunaitis
541	241	5410/2410	Merkine
541	242	5415/2420	Nedinge
541	243	5413/2434	Varena
541	244	5411/2441	Barciai
541	244	5417/2441	Matuizai
541	250	5410/2500	Eisiskes
541	250	5415/2508	Reziai
541	252	5415/2522	Benyakoni
541	252	5418/2523	Salcininkai
541	253	5412/2537	Dieveniskes
541	253	5417/2536	Dailydai
541	260	5415/2601	Golshany
541	260	5415/2601	Olshany (Vilnius)
541	261	5419/2617	Krevo
541	262	5411/2628	Zabrezhye
541	262	5416/2626	Losk
541	263	5410/2639	Dvozhyshche
541	263	5411/2632	Uzbolot
541	263	5414/2637	Gorodilovo
541	263	5414/2637	Zhurevichi
541	264	5413/2643	Polochany
541	264	5419/2645	Domashe
541	264	5419/2642	Lebedevo
541	265	5419/2651	Molodechno
541	270	5413/2704	Ivantseviche
541	270	5413/2700	Ulanovshchina
541	270	5414/2705	Krasne (Molodechno)
541	271	5413/2714	Sychevichi
541	272	5415/2725	Baturyn
541	272	5417/2720	Karpovichi
541	272	5417/2723	Pleshchany
541	272	5419/2723	Khotenchitsy
541	274	5414/2743	Gayna
541	275	5412/2751	Logoysk
541	280	5411/2804	Antonopol
541	283	5415/2830	Borisov
541	290	5419/2908	Krupki
541	293	5415/2932	Krucha
541	294	5415/2948	Krugloye
541	301	5413/3018	Shklov
541	301	5419/3018	Kopys
541	305	5417/3059	Gorki
541	312	5412/3122	Shamovo
541	313	5415/3134	Tatarsk
541	314	5411/3143	Lubavichi
541	321	5411/3210	Khislavichi
541	323	5410/3238	Stodolichi
541	351	5419/3517	Meshchovsk
542	090	5422/0905	Friedrichstadt
542	094	5429/0946	Kochendorf
542	100	5420/1008	Kiel
542	124	5422/1244	Barth
542	131	5429/1316	Grosow
542	162	5426/1623	Darlowo
542	164	5421/1641	Slawno
542	170	5427/1702	Slupsk
542	171	5427/1713	Mianowice
542	180	5424/1805	Staniszewo
542	181	5420/1812	Kartuzy
542	181	5422/1810	Prokowo
542	182	5427/1821	Kielno
542	183	5427/1834	Sopot
542	184	5421/1840	Gdansk
542	191	5420/1911	Sztutowo
542	194	5422/1941	Frombork
542	195	5423/1950	Braniewo
542	201	5427/2018	Kornevo

542 203	5423/2039	Bagrationovsk	
542 203	5426/2031	Dolgorukovo	
542 205	5425/2050	Domnovo	
542 210	5420/2106	Lipica	
542 210	5427/2101	Pravdinsk	
542 211	5422/2119	Zheleznodorozhnyy	
542 213	5420/2134	Krylovo	
542 220	5425/2201	Ozersk	
542 224	5427/2243	Vistytis	
542 225	5421/2259	Wingrany	
542 225	5422/2251	Wizajny	
542 225	5423/2251	Burniszki	
542 230	5422/2303	Liubavas	
542 231	5424/2314	Kalvarija	
542 231	5424/2314	Kalwarja	
542 232	5429/2321	Liudvinavas	
542 233	5423/2333	Krosna	
542 233	5424/2339	Simnas	
542 235	5420/2354	Miroslavas	
542 235	5423/2353	Balkunai	
542 240	5424/2403	Alytus	
542 241	5421/2412	Alove	
542 242	5422/2420	Daugai	
542 242	5428/2422	Pivasiunai	
542 243	5429/2436	Onuskis	
542 245	5421/2450	Valkininkas	
542 251	5426/2510	Rudninkai	
542 252	5423/2523	Salcininkeliai	
542 252	5427/2520	Jasiunai	
542 255	5425/2555	Karolinka	
542 255	5425/2556	Oshmyany	
542 260	5423/2607	Kutsevichi	
542 260	5428/2605	Zhuprany	
542 262	5422/2623	Sakovichi	
542 262	5425/2620	Oleshonki	
542 262	5426/2622	Vasilevichi	
542 262	5429/2624	Smorgon	
542 263	5424/2637	Zaskevichi	
542 264	5420/2642	Moroski	
542 264	5426/2649	Kopishche	
542 271	5425/2718	Ilya	
542 271	5425/2710	Vyazyn	
542 273	5428/2735	Vrublevshchina	
542 275	5425/2750	Pleshchenitsy	
542 275	5428/2755	Zamoshye (Wilen)	
542 281	5422/2813	Zembin	
542 291	5420/2916	Bobr	
542 294	5425/2942	Tolochin	
542 295	5428/2959	Kokhanovo	
542 301	5429/3018	Baran	
542 315	5422/3151	Monastyrshchina	
542 340	5424/3401	Spas Demensk	
542 381	5422/3815	Venev	
543 093	5431/0933	Schleswig	
543 133	5434/1332	Bobbin	
543 174	5433/1746	Lebork	
543 181	5436/1814	Wejherowo	
543 182	5432/1829	Chylonia	
543 183	5430/1833	Gdynia	
543 183	5430/1830	Witomino	
543 184	5437/1847	Hel	
543 195	5439/1955	Baltiysk	
543 200	5430/2006	Pyatidorozhnoye	
543 204	5433/2043	Chekhovo	
543 210	5439/2105	Gvardeysk	
543 211	5437/2113	Znamensk	
543 213	5439/2133	Kamensk	
543 214	5438/2149	Chernyakhovsk	
543 221	5436/2212	Gusev	
543 223	5438/2234	Nesterov (RFSR)	
543 223	5438/2234	Turyn	
543 224	5438/2249	Virbalis	
543 224	5439/2244	Chernyshevskoye	
543 224	5439/2245	Kybartai	
543 225	5438/2255	Alvitas	
543 230	5430/2302	Bartininkai	
543 230	5433/2309	Keturvalakiai	
543 230	5439/2302	Vilkaviskis	
543 232	5434/2321	Marijampole	
543 232	5439/2328	Sasnava	
543 235	5432/2353	Balbieriskis	
543 235	5438/2357	Prienai	
543 240	5431/2406	Punia	
543 240	5434/2405	Nemajunai	
543 240	5437/2402	Birstonas	
543 241	5436/2410	Jieznas	
543 241	5436/2419	Stakliskes	
543 243	5435/2432	Aukstadvaris	
543 244	5431/2448	Markauciskes	
543 244	5431/2444	Panoskiu Zydkaimis	
543 245	5438/2456	Trakai	
543 250	5438/2505	Voke	
543 250	5439/2503	Liutavariskes	
543 251	5430/2518	Galiniai	
543 251	5434/2510	Keturiasdesimt Totoriu	
543 251	5436/2512	Baltoja Voke	
543 251	5436/2512	Baltoji Voke	
543 252	5435/2524	Rudamina	
543 253	5437/2530	Rukainiai	
543 253	5439/2538	Kine	
543 255	5437/2557	Ostrovets	
543 261	5430/2610	Ivashkovtsy	
543 261	5431/2615	Vasyuki	
543 265	5430/2655	Vileyka	
543 265	5433/2657	Kurenets	
543 265	5435/2652	Lyuban (Volozhin)	
543 265	5436/2655	Sukhari	
543 265	5437/2657	Kuzmichi	

543	270	5439/2707	Nivki
543	271	5431/2714	Sosenka
543	271	5434/2713	Yerkhi
543	271	5435/2712	Kostenevichi
543	272	5430/2726	Olkovichi
543	272	5439/2729	Dolginovo
543	273	5431/2735	Derevno
543	273	5437/2734	Pogost
543	285	5431/2858	Kholopenichi
543	285	5437/2850	Krasnoluki
543	291	5433/2912	Kolodnitsa
543	291	5437/2917	Chereya
543	295	5436/2950	Oboltsy
543	300	5436/3004	Smolyany
543	302	5431/3026	Orsha
543	304	5435/3041	Dubrovno
543	311	5431/3117	Zverovichi
543	312	5435/3128	Krasny
543	331	5436/3313	Yelnya
543	361	5431/3616	Kaluga
543	370	5431/3707	Aleksin
544	092	5447/0926	Flensburg
544	173	5445/1733	Leba
544	182	5442/1825	Puck
544	182	5448/1825	Wladyslawowo
544	203	5443/2030	Kaliningrad
544	213	5448/2136	Vysokoye (Kaliningrad)
544	221	5444/2214	Mayskoye
544	223	5446/2231	Dobrovolsk
544	225	5446/2253	Kudirkos Naumiestis
544	225	5447/2251	Kutuzovo
544	231	5443/2313	Pilviskiai
544	232	5446/2329	Jure
544	232	5448/2326	Visakio Ruda
544	233	5446/2330	Kazlu Ruda
544	234	5446/2343	Veiveriai
544	234	5447/2345	Mauruciai
544	235	5449/2352	Garliava
544	240	5441/2400	Asminta
544	240	5443/2403	Pakuonis
544	240	5444/2407	Darsuniskis
544	241	5446/2414	Kruonis
544	242	5448/2427	Ziezmariai
544	244	5440/2440	Semeliskes
544	244	5446/2448	Vievis
544	245	5441/2457	Drasne (Molodechno)
544	245	5441/2457	Krasne (Vilnius)
544	245	5447/2455	Paneriai
544	250	5444/2505	Cekoniskes
544	251	5441/2519	Vilnius
544	251	5442/2519	Antakalnis
544	251	5449/2517	Riese
544	252	5442/2525	Naujoji Vilnia
544	253	5448/2532	Bezdonys
544	261	5445/2619	Nestanishki
544	261	5449/2610	Mikhalishki
544	262	5444/2629	Slavchynenta
544	263	5445/2632	Gorane
544	265	5445/2655	Miadziol Nowy
544	265	5445/2655	Miadziol Stary
544	270	5441/2707	Vygolovichi
544	270	5444/2708	Gorodishche (Wilen)
544	270	5445/2705	Svatki
544	271	5443/2717	Krivichi
544	272	5446/2723	Komarovo
544	272	5446/2726	Kurchino
544	272	5447/2727	Budslav
544	273	5441/2737	Milcha
544	273	5447/2738	Kripuli
544	274	5443/2741	Vardomichi
544	274	5447/2740	Berezovka (Lida)
544	280	5444/2804	Begoml
544	294	5449/2943	Senno
544	304	5448/3041	Rudnya
544	312	5444/3122	Gusino
544	320	5449/3204	Smolensk
544	351	5445/3514	Yukhnov
545	195	5452/1957	Yantarnyy
545	210	5452/2107	Polessk
545	211	5459/2116	Golovkino
545	212	5452/2127	Zelenyy
545	212	5457/2121	Naberezhnoye
545	212	5458/2125	Gromovo
545	213	5451/2132	Zalesye
545	214	5453/2140	Bolshakovo
545	225	5450/2256	Bubleliai
545	230	5453/2300	Sintautai
545	230	5457/2303	Sakiai
545	231	5451/2310	Griskabudis
545	232	5451/2320	Jankai
545	233	5458/2330	Lekeciai
545	234	5455/2340	Zapyskis
545	234	5456/2348	Raudondvaris
545	235	5451/2358	Aukstoji Panemune
545	235	5453/2354	Aleksotas
545	235	5454/2354	Kaunas
545	235	5454/2352	Marwianka
545	235	5455/2353	Vilijampole
545	235	5455/2355	Vilyampolskaya Sloboda
545	241	5451/2412	Rumsiskes
545	241	5455/2414	Pravieniskes
545	242	5452/2427	Kaisiadorys
545	243	5452/2436	Zasliai
545	245	5450/2458	Dukstos
545	245	5457/2451	Musninkai
545	250	5452/2504	Maisiagala
545	251	5456/2514	Paberze
545	252	5451/2529	Nemencine

545	254	5458/2544	Karkaziskes
545	255	5451/2553	Kamelishki
545	261	5453/2616	Kostevichi
545	261	5457/2613	Mostsyany
545	262	5451/2624	Svir
545	264	5453/2647	Podrezy
545	264	5454/2643	Narocz
545	264	5456/2641	Kobylnik
545	264	5456/2641	Kobylniki (Minsk)
545	265	5453/2657	Myadel
545	265	5456/2657	Yushkevichi
545	270	5451/2701	Lukyanovichi
545	272	5456/2722	Volkolata
545	273	5450/2735	Voznovshchina
545	273	5453/2736	Parafyanovo
545	273	5456/2732	Bolshiye Sittsy
545	273	5458/2739	Porplishche
545	274	5453/2741	Azartsy
545	274	5454/2746	Dokshitsy
545	275	5453/2754	Komaysk
545	275	5456/2757	Tumilovichi
545	281	5454/2812	Berezino
545	282	5458/2829	Pyshno
545	284	5453/2842	Lepel
545	291	5452/2910	Chashniki
545	301	5451/3013	Bogushevsk
545	303	5450/3035	Babinovichi
545	304	5455/3048	Selo
545	304	5456/3040	Dobromysl
545	331	5454/3318	Dorogobuzh
550	212	5504/2124	Zapovednoye
550	215	5505/2153	Sovetsk
550	215	5506/2154	Panemune
550	223	5503/2238	Sudargas
550	223	5505/2235	Smalininkai
550	224	5504/2246	Jurbarkas
550	224	5504/2247	Kiduliai
550	230	5506/2308	Raudone
550	231	5505/2311	Ploksciai
550	231	5505/2317	Veliuona
550	232	5504/2322	Paezereliai
550	232	5505/2325	Seredzius
550	233	5503/2335	Vilkija
550	234	5506/2348	Babtai
550	235	5507/2358	Vandziogala
550	241	5505/2417	Jonava
550	243	5509/2434	Vepriai
550	244	5504/2442	Gelvonai
550	244	5505/2446	Bagaslaviskis
550	245	5503/2457	Sirvintos
550	245	5506/2459	Matukai
550	251	5505/2515	Giedraiciai
550	252	5504/2527	Dubingiai
550	254	5500/2547	Pabrade

550	255	5505/2559	Grybai
550	261	5503/2619	Lyntupy
550	261	5509/2610	Svencionys
550	263	5509/2636	Adutiskis
550	265	5502/2654	Mankoviche
550	265	5507/2650	Postavy
550	270	5505/2705	Siemionowicze
550	271	5504/2714	Dunilovichi
550	271	5509/2713	Voropayevo
550	272	5502/2723	Darevo
550	272	5509/2720	Ruda (Vilnius)
550	274	5502/2745	Krulevshchina
550	274	5508/2741	Glebokie
550	275	5505/2752	Yasevichi
550	275	5507/2758	Golubichi
550	275	5509/2758	Podsvilye
550	280	5505/2805	Chyste
550	281	5504/2810	Potok (Byelorussia)
550	283	5504/2833	Zvon
550	285	5501/2853	Kamen
550	290	5501/2909	Bocheykovo
550	292	5503/2927	Beshenkovichi
550	292	5505/2920	Pyatigorsk
550	293	5500/2935	Budniki
550	295	5508/2953	Ostrovno
550	304	5502/3048	Liozno
550	310	5502/3105	Mikulino
550	333	5509/3337	Izdeshkovo
550	362	5501/3628	Maloyaroslavets
551	212	5518/2122	Rusne
551	213	5511/2133	Yasnoye
551	214	5517/2149	Katyciai
551	221	5515/2217	Taurage
551	222	5512/2221	Meskai
551	222	5515/2228	Gaure
551	224	5516/2243	Erzvilkas
551	224	5519/2248	Pikeliai
551	225	5513/2259	Simkaiciai
551	231	5519/2313	Girkalnis
551	232	5516/2328	Ariogala
551	233	5510/2331	Cekiske
551	233	5516/2339	Pernarava
551	234	5517/2345	Paupis
551	235	5515/2350	Josvainiai
551	235	5517/2358	Kedainiai
551	241	5517/2415	Seta
551	242	5511/2426	Panoteriai
551	243	5518/2430	Siesikai
551	244	5510/2446	Pabaiskas
551	244	5515/2445	Ukmerge
551	245	5511/2457	Sasuoliai
551	245	5518/2454	Siesartis
551	245	5518/2452	Vidiskiai
551	245	5518/2458	Zemaitkiemis

551	250	5513/2506	Zelva
551	250	5518/2508	Balninkai
551	251	5511/2512	Bastunai
551	252	5514/2525	Moletai
551	253	5510/2533	Anturke
551	255	5518/2557	Linkmenys
551	260	5510/2600	Svencioneliai
551	260	5516/2600	Kaltanenai
551	263	5519/2636	Tverecius
551	265	5513/2652	Kuropolye
551	265	5518/2652	Kozyany
551	271	5518/2716	Rymki
551	272	5511/2722	Kozlovshchyzna
551	273	5512/2738	Meretske
551	274	5513/2742	Ginki
551	274	5514/2740	Zaprudze
551	274	5516/2741	Bushyki
551	275	5513/2757	Plissa
551	281	5511/2814	Sho
551	281	5516/2810	Zyabki
551	281	5518/2813	Prozoroki
551	281	5519/2817	Kulgai
551	282	5510/2820	Kublichi
551	283	5511/2837	Ushachi
551	291	5514/2915	Ulla
551	293	5518/2937	Shumilino
551	295	5518/2952	Zaronovo
551	301	5512/3011	Vitebsk
551	301	5513/3018	Tulovo (Vitebsk)
551	304	5517/3042	Yanovichi
551	305	5510/3058	Kolyshki
551	313	5516/3131	Demidov
551	341	5512/3417	Vyazma
551	363	5512/3630	Borovsk
552	212	5521/2129	Silute
552	214	5522/2142	Zemaiciu Naumiestis
552	215	5522/2150	Vainutas
552	221	5528/2212	Silale
552	222	5527/2227	Upyna
552	223	5521/2231	Batakiai
552	223	5525/2237	Skaudvile
552	224	5526/2246	Nemaksciai
552	225	5524/2254	Vidukle
552	230	5522/2307	Raseiniai
552	232	5522/2322	Betygala
552	233	5529/2332	Meiliskiai
552	234	5524/2344	Krakes
552	235	5521/2354	Dotnuva
552	240	5527/2402	Surviliskis
552	240	5529/2408	Butrimoniai
552	241	5522/2417	Paezeriai
552	241	5526/2414	Truskava
552	242	5521/2424	Pagiriai
552	244	5522/2443	Salnos
552	244	5524/2445	Taujenai
552	244	5526/2443	Baleliai Antrieji
552	245	5526/2455	Kavarskas
552	250	5525/2503	Kurkliai
552	251	5521/2518	Alanta
552	251	5525/2516	Skiemonys
552	252	5523/2527	Skudutiskis
552	252	5528/2524	Leliunai
552	254	5524/2540	Kuktiskes
552	254	5527/2549	Tauragnai
552	255	5526/2553	Sela
552	261	5521/2610	Ignalina
552	261	5522/2618	Naujasis Daugeliskis
552	263	5524/2638	Vidzy
552	265	5529/2656	Eyvidovichi
552	270	5525/2705	Jejse
552	271	5527/2714	Iody
552	271	5527/2719	Snegi
552	272	5522/2728	Sharkovshchina
552	272	5526/2727	Borsuchizna
552	272	5529/2723	Bildyugi
552	274	5522/2741	Shkuntiki
552	274	5524/2748	Germanovichi
552	275	5521/2752	Luzhki
552	281	5521/2813	Bloshniki
552	281	5525/2814	Pligavki
552	282	5522/2823	Orekhovno
552	282	5522/2823	Oriechowno
552	284	5529/2847	Polotsk
552	291	5523/2914	Golovatchino
552	293	5523/2937	Sirotino
552	295	5528/2959	Gorodok (Vitebsk)
552	304	5525/3044	Surazh (Vitebsk)
553	213	5531/2137	Sveksna
553	213	5536/2136	Veivirzenai
553	213	5537/2133	Juodupis
553	220	5533/2200	Kvedarna
553	221	5537/2214	Laukuva
553	222	5534/2227	Kaltinenai
553	224	5536/2242	Kraziai
553	225	5538/2256	Kelme
553	230	5530/2306	Lyduvenai
553	231	5532/2314	Siluva
553	231	5536/2312	Tytuvenai
553	232	5534/2321	Miskiniai
553	232	5537/2321	Debeikiai
553	233	5534/2338	Grinkiskis
553	233	5535/2336	Pasusvys
553	234	5531/2348	Gudziunai
553	234	5538/2343	Baisogala
553	235	5534/2352	Pociuneliai
553	240	5533/2406	Krekenava
553	241	5531/2418	Ramygala
553	243	5530/2430	Vadokliai

553	243	5534/2436	Raguva
553	244	5531/2445	Traupis
553	245	5536/2451	Troskunai
553	250	5532/2506	Anyksciai
553	250	5536/2503	Andrioniskis
553	253	5530/2536	Utena
553	253	5536/2530	Vyzuonos
553	253	5539/2535	Uzpaliai
553	254	5533/2545	Radeikiai
553	255	5536/2550	Daugailiai
553	260	5535/2608	Salakas
553	262	5532/2620	Dukstas
553	262	5532/2626	Rimse
553	262	5538/2622	Smalvos
553	264	5535/2640	Drisvyaty
553	265	5532/2650	Opsa
553	270	5535/2707	Akhremovtsy
553	270	5538/2702	Braslav
553	271	5537/2716	Ikazn
553	272	5530/2729	Novyy Pogost
553	272	5537/2724	Perebrodye (Wilen)
553	273	5537/2738	Miory
553	274	5538/2743	Cheres
553	281	5534/2813	Disna
553	290	5531/2900	Orlovo
553	292	5538/2922	Trudy
553	304	5537/3040	Ponizovye
553	311	5536/3112	Velizh
553	350	5533/3500	Gagarin
554	210	5543/2107	Klaipeda
554	210	5546/2105	Giruliai
554	212	5543/2124	Gargzdai
554	212	5543/2129	Vezaiciai
554	212	5546/2128	Lapiai
554	213	5548/2139	Kuliai
554	215	5541/2156	Pajuris
554	215	5544/2156	Rietavas
554	220	5544/2209	Tverai
554	220	5549/2205	Medingenai
554	222	5542/2222	Godeliai
554	222	5545/2222	Varniai
554	223	5547/2239	Uzventis
554	224	5542/2240	Meskuiciai
554	224	5542/2245	Vaiguva
554	225	5548/2253	Saukenai
554	230	5548/2308	Padubysys
554	231	5541/2317	Simaniskiai
554	231	5546/2311	Bagdoniske
554	232	5541/2324	Siaulenai
554	233	5549/2332	Radviliskis
554	234	5542/2347	Kauleliskiai
554	234	5546/2346	Seduva
554	240	5541/2409	Naujamiestis
554	240	5548/2401	Smilgiai

554	242	5542/2426	Velzys
554	242	5544/2421	Panevezys
554	242	5547/2422	Piniava
554	243	5548/2436	Karsakiskis
554	244	5544/2447	Subacius
554	245	5542/2459	Viesintos
554	252	5541/2522	Svedasai
554	252	5549/2522	Salos
554	253	5549/2530	Kamajai
554	254	5547/2541	Juzintai
554	255	5540/2551	Antaliepte
554	255	5545/2551	Dusetos
554	260	5547/2606	Imbradas
554	261	5544/2615	Zarasai
554	262	5542/2627	Turmantas
554	262	5543/2628	Zemgale
554	263	5544/2632	Demene
554	264	5544/2649	Bobri
554	264	5545/2647	Silene
554	264	5549/2643	Skrudaliena
554	265	5546/2657	Dubinovo
554	265	5547/2656	Vanagishki
554	270	5542/2700	Okmyanitsa
554	270	5549/2702	Plyussy
554	271	5544/2717	Druysk
554	271	5546/2710	Kovalishki
554	272	5547/2727	Druya
554	272	5548/2727	Piedruja
554	273	5545/2738	Stashule
554	274	5548/2747	Leonpol
554	275	5547/2756	Verkhnedvinsk
554	373	5545/3735	Moskva
554	490	5545/4908	Kazan
555	210	5555/2103	Palanga
555	211	5553/2115	Kretinga
555	211	5558/2114	Tarvydai
555	212	5555/2128	Kartena
555	214	5559/2147	Godeliai (Ii)
555	215	5555/2151	Plunge
555	221	5550/2213	Zarenai
555	221	5558/2218	Rainiai
555	221	5559/2215	Telsiai
555	223	5553/2231	Luoke
555	225	5555/2253	Kruopine
555	230	5550/2303	Kurtuvenai
555	230	5559/2308	Kuziai
555	231	5556/2319	Siauliai
555	231	5557/2313	Luksiai
555	232	5558/2325	Zeimiai
555	233	5555/2330	Siubaiciai
555	235	5553/2353	Rozalimas
555	235	5556/2356	Klovainiai
555	235	5558/2352	Pakruojis
555	241	5554/2414	Mikaliskis

555	241	5555/2415	Pusalotas
555	242	5556/2421	Pampenai
555	243	5558/2431	Daujenai
555	244	5550/2442	Geleziai
555	244	5558/2445	Vabalninkas
555	245	5550/2458	Kupiskis
555	251	5553/2512	Skapiskis
555	253	5558/2535	Rokiskis
555	254	5551/2548	Kriaunos
555	254	5556/2548	Obeliai
555	260	5551/2603	Popiszki
555	260	5557/2608	Eglaine
555	260	5557/2608	Lasi
555	261	5551/2612	Paupyne
555	261	5558/2618	Ilukste
555	262	5555/2627	Mezciems
555	262	5559/2623	Liksna
555	263	5550/2632	Peski
555	263	5551/2630	Griva
555	263	5551/2634	Judovka
555	263	5553/2632	Daugavpils
555	270	5552/2700	Kaplava
555	270	5557/2702	Izvalta
555	271	5554/2710	Kraslava
555	271	5557/2719	Skaista
555	273	5552/2732	Indra
555	273	5558/2736	Pustina
555	274	5555/2745	Rositsa
555	280	5552/2808	Kokhanovichi
555	280	5559/2808	Galkovshchina
555	314	5557/3140	Ilino
560	211	5601/2115	Darbenai
560	213	5602/2133	Kalnalis
560	213	5604/2134	Salantai
560	214	5603/2149	Plateliai
560	220	5602/2203	Alsedziai
560	220	5607/2201	Zemaiciu Kalvarija
560	221	5606/2217	Nevarenai
560	223	5604/2235	Tryskiai
560	224	5601/2243	Raudenai
560	224	5609/2248	Papile
560	225	5600/2256	Kursenai
560	230	5606/2306	Mazeikiai
560	231	5606/2316	Gruzdziai
560	233	5600/2339	Lygumai
560	234	5605/2340	Pamusis
560	234	5609/2349	Pasvitinys
560	235	5605/2359	Linkuva
560	241	5602/2410	Joniskelis
560	241	5604/2419	Simoniai
560	242	5604/2424	Pasvalys
560	243	5605/2432	Krincinas
560	250	5607/2500	Papilys
560	251	5601/2513	Pandelys
560	251	5603/2517	Panemunis
560	255	5601/2554	Subata
560	255	5604/2557	Varkava
560	255	5606/2550	Garsene
560	255	5607/2554	Asare
560	260	5604/2607	Bebrene
560	260	5608/2600	Rubene
560	264	5603/2647	Viski
560	270	5608/2706	Kapini
560	270	5608/2701	Somerseta
560	271	5603/2717	Auleja
560	273	5602/2737	Asune
560	273	5606/2732	Dagda
560	280	5601/2806	Osveya
560	280	5608/2800	Skaune
560	283	5602/2839	Yukhovichi
560	295	5600/2959	Nevel
561	210	5610/2109	Rucava
561	212	5617/2120	Dunika
561	213	5610/2135	Mosedis
561	213	5616/2132	Skuodas
561	215	5610/2152	Barstyciai
561	215	5617/2151	Ylakiai
561	220	5610/2206	Seda
561	220	5619/2201	Zidikai
561	221	5616/2219	Tirksliai
561	222	5617/2224	Krakiai
561	223	5614/2231	Vieksniai
561	224	5615/2245	Akmene
561	233	5614/2337	Joniskis
561	235	5618/2350	Kriukai
561	240	5617/2400	Zeimys
561	241	5610/2412	Vaskai
561	242	5613/2424	Salociai
561	243	5611/2439	Pabirze
561	243	5619/2430	Krastini
561	244	5612/2445	Birzai
561	244	5614/2442	Kirkilai
561	245	5613/2454	Vinksniniai
561	250	5610/2509	Kvetkai
561	250	5616/2503	Vecmemele
561	251	5610/2518	Nereta
561	251	5610/2517	Suvainiskis
561	252	5611/2527	Rite
561	252	5617/2529	Sauka
561	253	5613/2536	Elksni
561	254	5610/2545	Akniste
561	261	5618/2610	Dignaja
561	264	5612/2647	Aizkalni
561	264	5618/2643	Preili
561	272	5611/2723	Andrupene
561	273	5611/2739	Bukmuiza
561	273	5614/2739	Mortini
561	275	5615/2758	Istra

561	275	5616/2750	Rundeni
561	280	5615/2802	Borovaja
561	281	5617/2810	Pasiene
561	300	5619/3009	Novosokolniki
561	303	5619/3031	Velikye Luki
561	320	5616/3204	Zapadnaya Dvina
561	342	5615/3420	Rzhev
562	210	5621/2104	Nica
562	212	5626/2127	Paplaka
562	212	5629/2125	Virga
562	213	5622/2137	Diz Gramzda
562	213	5624/2131	Purmsati
562	213	5626/2135	Priekule
562	214	5628/2140	Asite
562	215	5624/2157	Streliske
562	215	5626/2152	Vainode
562	221	5623/2215	Leckava
562	223	5623/2234	Laizuva
562	223	5624/2233	Rubas
562	224	5627/2242	Jaunauce
562	225	5622/2250	Klykoliai
562	225	5624/2257	Vegeriai
562	225	5628/2253	Auce
562	230	5623/2306	Snikere
562	231	5621/2315	Zagare
562	231	5629/2312	Penkule
562	232	5629/2328	Gaurini
562	232	5629/2324	Tervete
562	233	5625/2333	Vilce
562	234	5624/2341	Eleja
562	240	5625/2407	Jumpravmuiza
562	241	5624/2411	Bauska
562	242	5620/2426	Kukuci
562	242	5621/2426	Vecamuiza
562	242	5622/2424	Brunava
562	242	5626/2420	Vecsaule
562	243	5623/2439	Skaistkalne
562	243	5627/2436	Barbele
562	244	5624/2446	Nemunelio Radviliskis
562	251	5628/2514	Daudzese
562	253	5621/2533	Viesite
562	254	5624/2547	Birzi
562	255	5629/2551	Jekabpils
562	261	5622/2611	Livani
562	262	5625/2628	Rudzeti
562	264	5620/2648	Riebini
562	264	5621/2648	Ribene
562	265	5621/2656	Silajani
562	265	5629/2650	Vidsmuiza
562	270	5624/2706	Silmala
562	273	5620/2732	Kaunata
562	273	5626/2730	Rozenmuiza
562	274	5627/2744	Pilda
562	275	5624/2756	Nirza
562	280	5623/2807	Zilupe
562	364	5620/3645	Klin
563	210	5631/2101	Liepaja
563	210	5639/2108	Medze
563	211	5630/2115	Gavieze
563	211	5633/2110	Grobina
563	212	5631/2126	Tadaiki
563	212	5635/2128	Bunkas
563	212	5635/2121	Durbe
563	212	5635/2120	Liegi
563	212	5638/2129	Vecpils
563	214	5637/2142	Kalvene
563	215	5632/2156	Nikrace
563	221	5632/2213	Pampali
563	223	5634/2238	Veczvarde
563	225	5631/2254	Lielauce
563	231	5633/2316	Sakukrogs
563	231	5637/2316	Dobele
563	233	5632/2331	Zalenieki
563	233	5633/2332	Vitrupes
563	234	5635/2340	Svete
563	234	5639/2342	Jelgava
563	235	5630/2356	Jaunsvirlauka
563	240	5639/2405	Zalite
563	241	5636/2412	Iecava
563	244	5638/2446	Birzgale
563	250	5637/2505	Jaunjelgava
563	250	5639/2508	Skriveri
563	251	5634/2513	Serenes
563	251	5635/2515	Samani
563	251	5636/2511	Aizkraukle
563	252	5633/2523	Sece
563	252	5639/2526	Koknese
563	253	5635/2539	Selpils
563	253	5635/2536	Tirumbaltgalvji
563	254	5637/2547	Gostini
563	254	5637/2543	Plavinas
563	255	5630/2551	Krustpils
563	260	5637/2605	Medni
563	260	5639/2605	Zilini
563	262	5632/2624	Atasiene
563	264	5637/2644	Varaklani
563	265	5633/2657	Vilani
563	271	5630/2719	Rezekne
563	271	5635/2719	Makaseni
563	271	5639/2711	Driceni
563	273	5638/2730	Berzgale
563	274	5633/2743	Ludza
563	274	5634/2740	Zvirgzdene
563	275	5633/2753	Eversmuiza
563	283	5639/2838	Opochka
563	313	5630/3139	Toropets
563	321	5639/3215	Andreapol
564	211	5642/2112	Vergali

564	212	5641/2120	Dunalka
564	212	5644/2123	Cirava
564	213	5643/2136	Aizpute
564	214	5642/2148	Valtaiki
564	214	5648/2147	Turlava
564	215	5643/2154	Sieksate
564	220	5641/2201	Skrunda
564	221	5642/2211	Dzerves
564	222	5644/2224	Lutrini
564	223	5640/2230	Saldus
564	223	5642/2232	Broceni
564	223	5647/2235	Gaiki
564	224	5645/2242	Remte
564	225	5642/2258	Biksti
564	231	5647/2315	Dzukste
564	233	5643/2330	Livberze
564	235	5646/2357	Peternieki
564	235	5648/2359	Olaine
564	242	5645/2424	Baldone
564	243	5645/2438	Tome
564	243	5649/2430	Ikskile
564	243	5649/2436	Ogre
564	244	5643/2448	Lielvarde
564	250	5644/2507	Krape
564	250	5648/2503	Laubere
564	252	5641/2524	Ratniceni
564	252	5649/2524	Mengele
564	253	5647/2536	Irsi
564	253	5649/2537	Liepkalns
564	254	5640/2542	Kurmeni
564	254	5644/2546	Vietalva
564	254	5648/2542	Sausneja
564	255	5645/2554	Kalsnava
564	260	5640/2606	Saviena
564	260	5646/2606	Marciena
564	260	5648/2602	Berzaune
564	261	5640/2619	Metriena
564	261	5642/2611	Laudona
564	262	5646/2624	Saikava
564	263	5643/2636	Barkava
564	274	5641/2745	Merdzene
564	274	5647/2740	Karsava
564	402	5645/4028	Ludinka
565	211	5653/2111	Pavilosta
565	213	5654/2138	Gudenieki
565	215	5650/2157	Snepele
565	215	5657/2157	Taurkalni
565	215	5658/2159	Kuldiga
565	221	5650/2211	Spares
565	221	5652/2214	Varme
565	223	5658/2236	Matkule
565	224	5656/2248	Zemite
565	225	5654/2253	Grenci
565	230	5657/2309	Tukums
565	230	5658/2303	Tume
565	231	5651/2317	Slampe
565	231	5656/2316	Ruzas
565	231	5659/2314	Milzkalne
565	233	5657/2336	Sloka
565	233	5658/2334	Jurmala
565	240	5657/2406	Riga
565	241	5652/2411	Katlakalns
565	241	5659/2414	Strazdumuiza
565	242	5651/2421	Salaspils
565	242	5656/2423	Stopini
565	245	5655/2457	Suntazi
565	251	5650/2513	Platere
565	251	5651/2510	Madliena
565	251	5653/2511	Keipene
565	253	5654/2538	Ergli
565	255	5652/2553	Vestiena
565	255	5655/2553	Vejava
565	261	5650/2615	Lazdona
565	261	5650/2618	Prauliena
565	261	5651/2613	Madona
565	261	5654/2618	Patkule
565	261	5658/2619	Cesvaine
565	261	5659/2613	Karzdaba
565	263	5650/2637	Meirani
565	264	5654/2643	Lubana
565	270	5651/2705	Berzpils
565	272	5654/2722	Tilza
565	273	5657/2739	Baltinava
565	273	5658/2737	Abrini
565	355	5652/3555	Kalinin
570	212	5700/2123	Jurkalne
570	214	5701/2142	Edole
570	221	5701/2219	Strojno
570	223	5703/2235	Sabile
570	224	5702/2246	Kandava
570	224	5708/2244	Strazde
570	225	5702/2254	Pure
570	225	5707/2252	Cere
570	225	5708/2259	Zentene
570	233	5700/2330	Valdai
570	240	5703/2409	Mangali
570	241	5700/2410	Mezaparks
570	245	5709/2451	Sigulda
570	251	5700/2516	Zaube
570	251	5704/2512	Nitaure
570	251	5706/2519	Keci
570	255	5701/2557	Medzula
570	255	5701/2550	Vecpiebalga
570	255	5704/2550	Velki
570	260	5701/2604	Liezere
570	262	5700/2626	Dzelzava
570	262	5708/2626	Tirza
570	263	5704/2636	Jaungulbene

570	270	5700/2708	Rugaji
570	270	5706/2704	Sebeza
570	271	5708/2715	Balvi
571	212	5714/2127	Uzava
571	213	5711/2134	Ziras
571	214	5713/2140	Piltene
571	215	5710/2152	Laidzesciems
571	220	5713/2209	Usma
571	220	5716/2202	Ugale
571	223	5711/2233	Stende
571	223	5713/2231	Pastende
571	223	5715/2236	Talsi
571	224	5714/2246	Nurmuiza
571	225	5718/2250	Igene
571	231	5710/2313	Engure
571	242	5714/2424	Pabazi
571	243	5714/2439	Birini
571	244	5716/2445	Lode
571	244	5719/2445	Ledurga
571	245	5710/2450	Krimulda
571	250	5711/2502	Ligatne
571	251	5710/2517	Vecdoles
571	251	5714/2517	Drabesi
571	251	5718/2515	Cesis
571	252	5713/2522	Ramuli
571	254	5712/2540	Dzerbene
571	255	5713/2554	Gatarta
571	255	5714/2552	Drusti
571	260	5711/2603	Jaunpiebalga
571	260	5714/2603	Viesites
571	261	5713/2611	Ranka
571	263	5711/2634	Galgauska
571	263	5715/2630	Sinole
571	263	5717/2635	Lejasciems
571	264	5711/2645	Gulbene
571	270	5711/2702	Litene
571	274	5711/2741	Vilaka
572	213	5724/2131	Ventspils
572	220	5720/2201	Puze
572	223	5722/2235	Valdemarpils
572	223	5724/2236	Arlava
572	223	5725/2238	Lubezere
572	224	5720/2248	Vandzene
572	230	5723/2301	Upesgriva
572	243	5726/2432	Stiene
572	243	5729/2436	Jumprava
572	245	5721/2457	Lielstraupe
572	245	5724/2458	Rozbeki
572	251	5723/2512	Lenci
572	252	5723/2526	Liepas
572	253	5720/2537	Rauna
572	253	5726/2537	Marsneni
572	255	5726/2554	Smiltene
572	260	5724/2606	Rauza
572	261	5723/2611	Palsmane
572	261	5728/2613	Grundzales
572	265	5724/2653	Alsviki
572	270	5725/2703	Aluksne
572	272	5721/2728	Liepna
572	303	5726/3034	Komarin
572	435	5723/4354	Vysokovskaya
573	220	5731/2201	Ance
573	222	5731/2221	Dundaga
573	243	5737/2434	Vilkene
573	244	5731/2442	Limbazi
573	244	5731/2448	Umurga
573	252	5733/2524	Valmiera
573	254	5733/2542	Trikata
573	254	5737/2541	Strenci
573	261	5731/2612	Aumeisteri
573	262	5731/2624	Gaujiena
573	264	5732/2640	Ape
573	265	5732/2652	Jaunlaicene
573	322	5738/3228	Demyansk
574	245	5741/2453	Puikule
574	245	5746/2453	Aloja
574	251	5745/2511	Bauni
574	252	5744/2526	Renceni
574	255	5746/2557	Lugazi
574	260	5746/2600	Valka
574	260	5747/2602	Valga
574	273	5749/2736	Petseri
574	293	5746/2932	Porkhov
575	242	5752/2421	Ainazi
575	243	5753/2438	Rozeni
575	251	5754/2519	Rujiena
575	252	5753/2527	Naukseni
575	254	5755/2545	Omuli
575	264	5751/2648	Somerpalu
575	270	5750/2703	Voru
575	282	5750/2820	Pskov
575	295	5750/2959	Dno
580	245	5809/2458	Kilingi Nomme
580	312	5800/3123	Staraya Russa
581	222	5815/2228	Kuressaare
581	262	5813/2625	Elva
581	271	5812/2715	Rasina
581	303	5812/3030	Soltsy
582	224	5821/2248	Kalevi
582	235	5827/2353	Tammistu
582	243	5821/2434	Raekula
582	243	5824/2432	Parnu
582	253	5824/2536	Viljandi
582	264	5823/2643	Tartu
582	340	5822/3400	Borovichi
583	231	5838/2314	Kapi
583	311	5831/3117	Novogorod
584	255	5841/2558	Poltsamaa

584 262 5845/2624 Jogeva
584 274 5846/2748 Gdov
584 295 5844/2952 Luga
585 233 5856/2333 Haapsalu
585 253 5854/2533 Paide
585 254 5856/2544 Jumurda
585 265 5851/2656 Mustvee
585 320 5853/3208 Malaya Vishera
585 510 5852/5109 Klimovka
590 244 5901/2447 Rapla
590 261 5908/2615 Vaike Maarja
591 241 5919/2416 Klooga
591 242 5916/2428 Tuula
591 261 5916/2618 Tamna
591 290 5913/2900 Pustoshka
591 290 5919/2908 Kursk
591 300 5917/3008 Druzhnaya Gorka
591 314 5910/3141 Chudovo
591 335 5919/3357 Yartsevo
592 240 5920/2406 Paldiski
592 244 5923/2440 Nomme
592 244 5925/2445 Tallinn
592 245 5924/2456 Lagedi
592 262 5922/2620 Rakvere
592 272 5922/2727 Johvi
592 280 5927/2803 Narva Joesuu
592 281 5923/2812 Narva
592 283 5922/2836 Kingisepp
592 302 5925/3021 Vyritsa
593 251 5931/2516 Kaberneeme
593 300 5934/3008 Gatchina
593 305 5933/3053 Tosno
593 322 5936/3224 Zadnevo
593 333 5939/3331 Tikhvin
594 302 5941/3027 Pavlovsk
594 302 5941/3027 Slutsk (Leningrad)
594 302 5943/3025 Pushkin
594 303 5945/3036 Kolpino
594 335 5940/3355 Dukhovshchina
594 342 5946/3425 Kholm
595 295 5953/2954 Petrodvorets
595 300 5951/3002 Strelna
595 301 5955/3015 Leningrad
595 310 5957/3102 Petrokrepost
595 322 5955/3220 Volkhov
600 301 6002/3018 Shuvalovo Ozerki
600 341 6002/3413 Petrova Gora
604 284 6042/2845 Vyborg
605 301 6058/3011 Pochinok
614 342 6149/3420 Petrozavodsk